COMMERCIAL PROPERTY

COMMERCIAL PROPERTY

Paul Butt LLB (Manchester), Solicitor

Published by

College of Law Publishing,
Braboeuf Manor, Portsmouth Road, St Catherines, Guildford GU3 1HA

© The College of Law 2010

British Library Cataloguing-in-Publication Data

A catalogue record for this book is available from the British Library.

ISBN 978 1 905391 85 1

Typeset by Style Photosetting Ltd, Mayfield, East Sussex

Printed in Great Britain by Ashford Colour Press Ltd, Gosport, Hampshire

Preface

The aim of this book is to provide law students with a comprehensive introduction to three important areas of property law:

(a)   town and country planning;

(b)   commercial leases; and

(c)   residential tenancies.

At first sight, the inclusion of residential tenancies in a book on Commercial Property might seem a little unusual. However, many sites bought for commercial development are subject to existing residential tenancies and it is thus important for all commercial property lawyers to know the protection they may enjoy and the chances of securing vacant possession.

Although it is hoped that the book will provide a useful guide to trainee solicitors and others involved in this type of work, it is primarily intended to complement the Advanced Property Elective on the Legal Practice Course. This elective is only undertaken once the compulsory Conveyancing and Property course has been completed and this book, therefore, contains a few references to the book accompanying that course.

The author would like to acknowledge the many valuable contributions made by Alan Riley of Hill Dickinson to previous editions of this book.

In the interests of brevity, the masculine pronoun has been used throughout to include the feminine. The law is stated as at 1 September 2009.

PAUL BUTT

The College of Law
Chester

Table of Statutes

1.3.4 The position in Wales

The legislative powers of the DCLG are exercised in Wales by the Welsh Assembly Government. Although the basics of planning law are the same in the two countries, the Welsh Assembly Government will exercise its legislative powers in the best interests of the people of Wales, and this may sometimes mean that there are differences between the positions of the two countries.

1.4 Local planning authorities (ss 1–9 and Sch 1)

1.4.1 The general rule (s 1)

Subject to any express provision to the contrary (see **1.4.2**), all references in the Planning Acts to an LPA should be construed as a reference to both the relevant county planning authority and district planning authority. The county council is the county planning authority and the district council is the district planning authority.

1.4.1.1 The county planning authority

The county planning authority normally has exclusive jurisdiction over preparing the structure plan (see **1.5.1.1**), mineral planning, and development control and enforcement which relate to 'county matters'. 'County matters' are defined in Sch 1, para 1, as being concerned with minerals and operational development falling partly within and partly outside a national park.

1.4.1.2 The district planning authority

Subject to the exceptions mentioned below, the district planning authority has exclusive jurisdiction over preparation of the local plan, development control and enforcement which does not concern a county matter and hazardous substances.

1.4.2 Exceptions to the general rule

1.4.2.1 Unitary councils

Where unitary councils have been established, those councils will normally be the LPAs for all purposes.

1.4.2.2 Greater London and the metropolitan areas (s 1(2))

In these areas there is only one planning authority, namely the appropriate London borough council (the Common Council in the City of London) or metropolitan district council.

1.5 Development plans (ss 10–54 and Sch 2)

1.5.1 What are they?

1.5.1.1 Outside Greater London and the metropolitan areas

In the majority of the country the development plan consists of the structure plan and any local plan(s) in force.

Structure plan (ss 31–35C)

The structure plan is prepared normally by the county planning authority for the whole of their area. It basically consists of a broad statement of the county planning authority's strategic planning policies for the area illustrated by such diagrams and other illustrations as are necessary to explain the proposals. It must deal in particular with conservation of beauty and amenity, improvement of the physical environment, management of traffic, and social and economic conditions. It must also take into account regional planning guidance from the

DCLG, national policies, resources and any other matters which the DCLG may prescribe (by regulations) or direct.

Local plan (ss 36–45)

The local plan is prepared normally by the district planning authority in general conformity with the structure plan. Each district planning authority was due to prepare a local plan for the whole of their area within five years from 10 February 1992. Although the date for implementation has now passed, many LPAs have not yet completed the adoption of their area-wide local plan. Until the new local plans have been made and adopted, the local plans which were in force on that date will remain in force.

Local plans are much more detailed. They must deal with the same type of matters as structure plans and take into account the same guidance, but in greater depth. In addition, they must contain a reasoned justification of the policies formulated by the plan.

1.5.1.2 In Greater London and the metropolitan areas

In these areas the development plan consists of a 'unitary development plan' (ss 12–16).

The responsibility for making and altering a unitary development plan is that of the relevant London borough or metropolitan district council. Despite its name, a unitary development plan is in two parts where Part I is the broad equivalent of a structure plan, and Part II is the equivalent of a local plan. These two parts have to deal with and take into account very similar matters to their ordinary development plan counterparts and must be illustrated and justified in a similar way.

1.5.2 The importance of the development plan

In various parts of the Planning Acts, the development plan and any other material considerations are required to be taken into account. By s 54A (introduced by the PCA 1991):

> where, in making any determination under the Planning Acts, regard is to be had to the development plan, the determination shall be made in accordance with the plan unless material considerations indicate otherwise.

The House of Lords confirmed in *City of Edinburgh Council v Secretary of State for Scotland and Others* [1997] 3 PLR 71 that there is now a statutory presumption that the development plan is to govern the decision on an application for planning permission.

The practical consequences of s 54A are that because there is now, in effect, largely a plan-led development system, developers will need to look very carefully at the development plan to see if it contains any policy on the development proposed; if it does so and the proposal is not in accordance with the plan, any planning application is unlikely to succeed in most cases.

1.5.3 Planning and Compulsory Purchase Act 2004

The Planning and Compulsory Purchase Act 2004 (PCPA 2004) received the Royal Assent on 13 May 2004 and will be brought into force gradually over the next few years. It seeks to improve the existing planning system by making it speedier and more predictable.

1.5.3.1 Regional planning

A new system of regional planning is to be established. New regional planning bodies (RPBs) will be established for each region. At least 60% of the members of each RPB has to consist of elected members of county councils or local planning authorities.

Each RPB will have to prepare a regional spatial strategy (RSS) for its region. This will involve a broader based approach than purely looking at land use planning.

There will be a separate system for Wales. The National Assembly must produce a Wales Spatial Plan setting out policies for use and development of land in Wales.

The RSS and the Wales Spatial Plan will form part of the statutory development plan for the purposes of s 54A of the TCPA 1990; see **1.5.2**.

1.5.3.2 The new local development plan system

The PCPA 2004 marks a departure from the single local or unitary development plan document, and introduces a new 'folder' approach to policy making. A portfolio of documents, collectively known as the local development framework (LDF), will contain the authority's policies for meeting the community's economic, environmental and social aims where these affect the development and the use of land.

The new system of local planning will entail the following:

(a) The preparation by each local planning authority of a local development scheme (LDS). This will specify which documents are to be local development documents (LDDs), their subject matter and area, those LDDs that are to be 'development plan' documents for the purposes of s 54A and the timetable for their preparation and revision. The LDS will require the Secretary of State's approval, following a public examination before an inspector appointed by the Secretary of State.

(b) The independent examination of the above statement together with those LDDs that constitute 'development plan' documents. Those making representations will have a right to be heard at the examination in public of the plan.

(c) Following an inquiry inspector's report, finalisation of the LDDs. An authority's final discretion over the content of its development plan policies therefore disappears. It is anticipated that an authority will have a number of development plan documents, comprising a core strategy, site allocations, area action plans, a proposals map and policies for the control of development.

The Act sets out transitional provisions for the changeover to the new system. An existing development plan will retain its status for three years. During that time, authorities will move towards the LDD system

1.5.3.3 Statutory duty to enable sustainable development

The PCPA 2004 imposes a statutory duty on every authority that exercises a plan-making function to exercise that function with the objective of contributing to the achievement of sustainable development. It does not provide a definition of 'sustainable development', but guidance on that issue is contained in Planning Policy Statement 1 (PPS 1), due to be published in the autumn of 2004. PPS 7, relating to rural areas, was published in August 2004 and emphasises the need to discourage the use of previously undeveloped 'green field' land.

1.5.3.4 Development control

The PCPA 2004 contains a series of provisions that affect control over development and the system of applying for planning permission. Authorities will be able to make local development orders (LDOs) to provide local permitted development rights.

It had originally been intended that the system of applying for outline planning permission would be abolished. However, it is to be retained and a proposal to introduce statements of development principles has been dropped. Regulations may be introduced requiring certain types of planning application to include a design statement, an access statement, or both, and these are likely to be used to increase the level of detail required at the outline stage.

The standard life of a planning permission, listed building consent and conservation area consent is to be reduced from five to three years, with an extension to four years where legal proceedings are issued challenging the validity of the permission or consent. It will be possible, when permission is granted, to negotiate more than three years for commencement of appropriate schemes. Further, the s 73 procedure for subsequently varying time limits contained in conditions is no longer available. These new time limits and the s 73 restriction affect only those applications received by authorities after the new provisions come into effect.

Crown immunity will end, although special provisions will relate to matters of national security and developments of national importance.

Chapter 2

What is Development?

2.1 The basic rule

The basic rule is to be found in s 57(1) which states that planning permission is required for the carrying out of any development of land. The term 'development' is defined in s 55(1) as: 'the carrying out of building, engineering, mining or other operations in, on, over or under land, or the making of any material change in the use of any buildings or other land'. It is important to realise at the outset that the term 'development' thus has two mutually exclusive parts to it, namely the carrying out of operations and the making of a material change of use.

2.1.1 Operations

2.1.1.1 Relevant definitions (ss 55(1A) and 336(1))

'Building operations' include demolition of buildings (see **2.1.1.3**), rebuilding, structural alterations of, or additions to buildings, and other operations normally undertaken by a person carrying on business as a builder.

'Engineering operations' includes the formation or laying out of means of access to highways.

'Mining operations' and 'other operations' are not defined in the Act.

2.1.1.2 Operations not constituting development (s 55(2))

Works for the maintenance, improvement or other alteration of a building which affect only the interior of the building or which do not materially affect its external appearance and which do not provide additional space underground do not constitute development (s 55(2)(a)). However, increasing retail floor space by internal works (eg, the construction of a mezzanine floor) will require planning permission in England if the increase is more than 200m^2.

2.1.1.3 Demolition

The position as regards demolition is governed by the provisions of s 55(1A) and (2)(g) which state that the demolition of any description of building specified in a direction given by the DCLG does not constitute development. The direction exempts demolition of the following:

(a)   listed buildings;

(b)   buildings in a conservation area;

(c)   scheduled monuments;

(d)   buildings other than dwelling houses or buildings adjoining dwelling houses;

(e)   buildings not exceeding 50m^3 in volume.

(Note as regards the first three categories in the above list that, although planning permission is not required for demolition, consents under the legislation dealing with these types of buildings and structures will be needed, eg, listed buildings consent.)

Thus, the control of demolition will apply mainly to that of dwelling houses and buildings adjoining dwelling houses. However, demolition of these buildings may be permitted development under the GPDO, Sch 2, Pt 31 (see **2.2.2**).

2.1.2 Change of use

In order to constitute development, a change of use must be material. The Act does not define what is meant by 'material'.

2.1.2.1 Case law

Case law makes it clear that the question as to whether a change of use is material is one of fact and degree in each case. It follows, therefore, that the courts will not normally interfere with a planning decision on the question of the materiality of a particular change of use unless the decision is totally unreasonable on the facts, or the deciding body has misdirected itself as to the relevant law.

Note, however, the following general points decided by case law.

(a)   It is necessary to look at the change in the use of the relevant 'planning unit'. In many cases this will be the whole of the land concerned, ie, the land in the same ownership and occupation. Occasionally, particularly with larger sites, a single unit of occupation may comprise two or more physically distinct and separate areas which are occupied for substantially different and unrelated purposes, in which case each area (with its own main or primary use) should be considered as a separate planning unit (see *Burdle and Another v Secretary of State for the Environment and Another* [1972] 3 All ER 240 and *Thames Heliport plc v Tower Hamlets LBC* [1997] 2 PLR 72). In a mall-type development, it now seems that each shop unit will be a separate planning unit (*Church Commissioners for England v Secretary of State for the Environment* (1995) 7 P & CR 73).

(b)   The use of a planning unit may involve various (and possibly fluctuating) ancillary uses which do not need planning permission provided that they remain ancillary to, and retain their connection with, the primary use. For instance, where produce grown on an agricultural unit is sold on a limited scale from the farmhouse, this retail use is ancillary to the primary agricultural use; however, the ancillary status is lost if, for example, produce is subsequently bought in for the purposes of resale (see *Wood v Secretary of State for the Environment* [1973] 1 WLR 707, HL).

2.1.2.2 Non-statutory guidance

As the courts will not normally interfere with decisions on questions of fact and degree, it will therefore be the DCLG or one of his inspectors who will generally be the final arbiter of the question as to whether a particular change of use is material. Thus, their views in similar cases will be important and guidance can be found, in particular, in relevant DCLG circulars, PPGs and in Ministerial Decisions such as those reported in the JPL.

2.1.2.3 Statutory provisions

Changes of use declared to be material

For the avoidance of doubt, s 55(3) and (5) declare the following to be material changes of use:

(a)   the use as two or more separate dwelling houses of any building previously used as a single dwelling house;

(b)   (generally) the deposit of refuse or waste materials.

Changes of use not constituting development

These are set out in s 55(2) and include the following:

(a)   The use of any building or other land within the curtilage of a dwelling house for any purpose incidental to the enjoyment of the dwelling house as such (s 55(2)(d)).

Factors to be considered in deciding whether the use is 'incidental to the enjoyment of the dwelling house as such' include the nature and scale of the use and whether it is one which could reasonably be expected to be carried out in or around the house for domestic needs or incidental to the personal enjoyment of the house by its occupants: see *Ministerial Decision* [1977] JPL 116. Thus, for example, in *Wallington v Secretary of State for the Environment* [1991] JPL 942, CA, the keeping of 44 dogs as pets was held not to be an incidental use. Note that enjoyment of the dwelling house must be distinguished from the enjoyment of the occupier (ie, the test for enjoyment is objective, not subjective).

(b)   The use of any land or buildings occupied with it for the purposes of agriculture or forestry (s 55(2)(e)).

(c)   In the case of buildings or other land which are used for a purpose of any class specified in the Town and Country Planning (Use Classes) Order 1987, the use of the buildings or other land for any other purpose of the same class (s 55(2)(f)). This very important exemption is dealt with in more detail at **2.1.3**.

2.1.3   The Town and Country Planning (Use Classes) Order 1987

The Use Classes Order specifies 13 use classes for the purposes of s 55(2)(f). Thus, a change of use within any such class does not, prima facie, amount to development (but see UCO checklist at **2.1.3.3**).

The classes are divided into four main groups as follows:

(a)   Group A: shopping area uses;

(b)   Group B: other business and industrial uses;

(c)   Group C: residential uses;

(d)   Group D: non-residential uses.

Note in particular the following seven use classes.

Class A1: shops

Use for all or any of the following purposes: retail sale of goods other than hot food; post office; ticket or travel agency; sale of cold food for consumption off the premises; hairdressing; direction of funerals; display of goods for sale; hiring out of domestic or personal goods; washing or cleaning of clothes on the premises; internet cafe. In all cases, however, the sale, display or service must be to visiting members of the public.

Class A2: financial and professional services

Use for the provision of financial services, professional services (other than health or medical services) or any other services (including use as a betting office) which it is appropriate to provide in a shopping area, where the services are provided principally to visiting members of the public.

Class A3: restaurants and cafes

Use for the sale of food and drink for consumption on the premises.

Class A4: drinking establishments

Use as a public house, wine bar or other drinking establishment.

Class A5: hot food takeaways

Use for the sale of hot food for consumption off the premises.

Class B1: business

Use for all or any of the following purposes, namely as an office other than a use within Class A2, for research and development of products or processes, or for any industrial process, being a use which can be carried out in any residential area without detriment to the amenity of that area.

Class B2: general industrial

Use for the carrying out of an industrial process other than one falling within Class B1.

Class B8: storage or distribution

Use for storage or as a distribution centre.

Class C3: dwelling houses

Use as a dwelling house by a single person or by people living together as a family or by not more than six residents living together as a single household (including a household where care is provided for residents).

Wales

Note that, in Wales, Class A3 covers use for the sale of food and drink for consumption on the premises or of hot food for consumption off the premises. Classes A4 and A5 do not exist. Class B8 in Wales does not include use of a building or land for the storage of, or as a distribution centre for, radioactive material or radioactive waste.

2.1.3.1 Exclusions

Nothing in the Use Classes Order permits use as a theatre, amusement arcade, launderette, garage or motor showroom, taxi or hire-car business, hostel, or scrapyard, waste disposal installation, retail warehouse club, night club or casino (Use Classes Order, art 3(6)).

Note also that not all uses come within the Use Classes Order. The courts have consistently held that there is no justification for stretching the meaning of the wording of the classes and that other uses will therefore be outside the terms of the Order.

2.1.3.2 Problems

Many of the above use classes are not without their problems. For example, is a sandwich bar which sells tea and coffee and a few hot pies, within Class A1 or Class A5?

Is a high street solicitor's office within Class A2 or Class B1? The crucial question here is whether the firm principally serves visiting members of the public. (In *Kalra v Secretary of State for the Environment* [1996] JPL 850, CA, the Court of Appeal held that the introduction of an appointment system did not of itself prevent a solicitor's office falling within Class A2.)

2.1.3.3 UCO checklist

Although a change of use within a class does not amount to development, it does not necessarily follow that a change of use from one class to another will constitute development. Whether it will depends on the basic rule, ie is that change of use 'material'? However, *Palisade Investments Ltd v Secretary of State for the Environment* [1995] 69 P & CR 638, CA, suggests that it will be extremely rare for this not to be the case.

A change of use within a class may be accompanied by building operations which could amount to development in their own right (remember that development has two parts to it).

A change of use within a class may have been validly restricted by a condition attached to a previous planning permission, in which case permission will be needed to change to a use restricted by that condition.

2.2 Permitted development

Once it has been established that development is involved, then the basic rule is that planning permission will be required. However, it is not always necessary to make an express application for planning permission for the reasons given below.

2.2.1 Resumption of previous use

By s 57(2)–(6), certain changes of use do not require planning permission even though they may amount to development, for example, the resumption of a previous lawful use after service of an enforcement notice.

2.2.2 The Town and Country Planning (General Permitted Development) Order 1995 (as amended)

By ss 59–61, the DCLG may provide by statutory instrument for the automatic grant of planning permission by means of development orders. The most important of these orders is the GPDO. This lists, in Sch 2, 31 broad categories of development for which planning permission is automatically granted, ie, there is not normally any need to make an application for planning permission in these cases (but see GPDO checklist at **2.2.2.1**).

Note in particular the following six categories.

Part 1: development within the curtilage of a dwelling house

Part 1 is divided into classes as follows:

(a)   Class A: the enlargement, improvement or other alteration of the dwelling house;

(b)   Classes B and C: additions or alterations to its roof; Class D: the erection of a porch;

(c)   Class E: the provision within the curtilage of the dwelling house of any building, enclosure or pool for a purpose incidental to the enjoyment of the dwelling house as such, or the maintenance, improvement or alteration of such a building or enclosure;

(d)   Classes F and G: the provision of a hard surface or a container for the storage of domestic heating oil;

(e)   Class H: the installation, alteration or replacement of a satellite antenna.

All of these classes of permitted development (except for Class F) are, however, subject to certain restrictions, limitations or conditions (see below).

There may occasionally be problems in determining the extent of the curtilage of the dwelling house. It is the small area of land forming part of the land on which the house stands and used for the purposes of the enjoyment of the house. Its extent is a question of fact and degree in each case. It is not necessarily synonymous with 'garden'.

Restrictions on Class A development (enlargement, improvement, etc) include:

(a)   a limit on the increase in the cubic content of the dwelling house;

(b)   height;

(c)   distance from highway;

(d)   the area covered by all the buildings (other than the original dwelling house) within the curtilage must not exceed one half of the area of the curtilage excluding the area of the original dwelling house.

Restrictions on Class E development (the provision of buildings within the curtilage, etc) include the latter two restrictions above (ie, distance from highway and area covered by buildings within the curtilage). Additional restrictions include:

(a)   a height limit; and

(b)   a volume and nearness to house restriction.

Note that for a dwelling house on 'article 1(5) land' (ie, within a National Park, an area of outstanding natural beauty or conservation area) there are further restrictions.

Restrictions on Class H development (satellite antennae) include dish size, height and siting.

Part 2: minor operations

Part 2 permits:

(a)   the erection, construction, maintenance, improvement or alteration of a gate, fence, wall or other means of enclosure (Class A);

(b)   the construction of a means of access to a highway which is not a trunk or classified road (Class B);

(c)   the painting of the exterior of a building (Class C).

In Class A, any gates, fences, etc must be for the purpose of enclosure. They must not exceed 1 metre in height if they adjoin a highway, or 2 metres in any other case.

In Class C, painting of the exterior is not permitted if it is for the purpose of advertisement, announcement or direction.

Part 3: changes of use

Part 3 permits certain changes of use within Classes A and B of the Use Classes Order as follows:

(a)   from A3, A4 and A5 (food and drink) to A2 (financial and professional services);

(b)   from A2 to A1 (shops) provided the premises have a display window at ground level;

(c)   from A3, A4 and A5 directly to A1;

(d)   from B8 (storage and distribution) to B1 (business) and vice versa;

(e)   from B2 (general industrial) to B8 or B1;

(f)   from A4 (drinking establishment) and A5 (hot food takeaways) to A3 (restaurants and cafes).

Part 4: temporary buildings and uses

Part 4 permits:

(a)   the provision of buildings, structures, plant, etc required temporarily in connection with authorised operations (Class A);

(b)   the use of open land for any purpose for not more than 28 days in any calendar year of which not more than 14 days may be used for holding a market or motor racing/trials (Class B).

Class A rights are subject to conditions requiring removal of the buildings, etc or reinstatement of land at the end of the operations.

The right to revert to the previous use of the land after the expiry of the temporary use is permitted by s 57(2) (see **2.2.1**).

Part 6: agricultural buildings and operations

Part 6 permits, inter alia, the carrying out on agricultural land of certain operations (in particular the erection, extension or alteration of buildings or excavation or engineering operations) which are reasonably necessary for the purposes of agriculture on that unit. These are subject to many exceptions and conditions.

Part 31: demolition of buildings

Part 31 permits any building operation consisting of the demolition of a building except where the building has been made unsafe or uninhabitable by the fault of anyone who owns the relevant land or where it is practicable to secure health or safety by works of repair or temporary support. Because of the provisions of s 55(2)(g) (see **2.1.1.3**), this provision will need to be applied only in the case of demolition of a dwelling house or a building (exceeding $50m^3$) adjoining a dwelling house.

2.2.2.1 GPDO checklist

If the proposed development is permitted by the GPDO there should, prima facie, be no need to make an application for planning permission. However, before deciding, the following other matters should also be checked.

Limitations, etc

Confirm that all the limitations, restrictions and conditions imposed by the GPDO will be complied with. There are two categories of these. First, there is a general one in art 3(5) which applies to all the Parts in Sch 2 and which states that (subject to limited exceptions) the making or altering of an access to a trunk or classified road, or any development which obstructs the view of road users so as to cause them danger, is not permitted. Secondly, there are specific limitations, conditions, etc in almost all of the Parts of Sch 2 which must be observed (see above).

If the limitations, etc are not complied with then, as a general rule, the whole development will be unauthorised and not merely the excess. This, though, is subject to the LPA's power to under-enforce if they think fit (see **5.8.7** for details of this). If the excess is *de minimis* it can be ignored.

Conditions on existing planning permission

Check any existing planning permission to see whether it contains a condition excluding or restricting relevant permitted development rights. Such conditions can be imposed in appropriate cases (see further **3.6**).

Article 4 direction

Ascertain by means of an appropriate inquiry of the local authority whether an art 4 direction is in force which may affect the proposed development.

GPDO, art 4, empowers the DCLG or an LPA (usually with the DCLG's approval) to make a direction removing from the classes of permitted development under the GPDO any development specified in the direction as regards the area of land specified in it.

The making of an art 4 direction will not affect the lawfulness of any permitted development commenced before the direction was made.

Special development orders

Check whether the land is in an area covered by a special development order (SDO).

Some SDOs restrict the provisions of the GPDO which would otherwise apply in the relevant area; others (especially those made for urban development areas) confer wider permitted development rights. It is therefore important to be aware of what SDOs exist and, where relevant, their provisions.

2.3 Problem cases

2.3.1 General considerations

It will be seen from the above that there are many matters to be considered before it can properly be decided whether a particular proposal amounts to development and, if so, whether it is permitted development or whether it needs an express grant of planning permission. Although, in practice, it will be obvious in many cases whether or not planning permission will be needed, in quite a few cases (especially those involving small-scale development proposals) there may be some considerable uncertainty as to whether a particular proposal amounts to development or whether it is permitted development. In such a case there are two main options, namely either to go ahead without permission (thereby risking enforcement action if it did need an express grant of permission) or to apply under s 192 to the LPA for a determination of the question.

2.3.2 Certificate of lawful use or development

Under s 192, any person who wishes to ascertain the lawfulness of any proposed use or development can apply to an LPA for a Certificate of Lawful Use or Development (see **5.3**).

If a certificate is granted, it will be conclusive as to the lawfulness of the use or operations described in it unless there was a material change, before the use was instituted or the operations were begun, in any of the matters relevant to the determination.

Chapter 3
Applying for Planning Permission

3.1 Introduction

Solicitors are not often involved in the completing and submission of an application for planning permission as this is usually done by the client's architect or planning consultant. However, it is very important to know what the statutory requirements are as this may be crucial in later negotiations with the LPA or on an appeal in case the action previously taken was flawed.

3.2 Preliminary steps

(a) Consider whether planning permission is required at all: ie, do the proposals amount to development and, if so, are they permitted development (see **2.1** and **2.2**)?

(b) Assuming planning permission is needed, the next step is to visit the site if possible. A site visit can be very valuable as it may:

    (i)   clarify the client's maps, diagrams and plans;

    (ii)   provide information about the immediate environment;

    (iii) alert the solicitor to potential problems with the application.

(c) Obtain copies of the relevant parts of the development plan and any non-statutory plans which may affect the proposed development. This could be vital in many cases as, for the application to stand a chance of succeeding, the development proposed will usually have to be in accordance with the development plan (see s 54A at **3.5.1**).

(d) Investigate the title to the land concerned. This is necessary for two main reasons, namely to check whether the proposed development is in breach of an enforceable covenant affecting the land concerned and to identify any other 'owners' who will need to be given notice of the application (see further **3.4.4**).

(e) Obtain the relevant application form from the LPA. Note that each LPA produces its own form which can be obtained free of charge.

(f) Consider whether a pre-application discussion with the appropriate case officer might be beneficial. This is encouraged by the DCLG in order to reduce uncertainty and delay in processing applications. Such discussions can be particularly helpful in the case of large-scale or potentially controversial development proposals to enable the developer to find out in what respects the proposals may not be acceptable and in what ways chances of success can be improved; it also enables the LPA to advise the developer of probable objections to the development which, if remedied, should lead to a quicker determination. Note that LPAs have no statutory duty to enter into such discussions (although recent research has shown that 93% of LPAs do so regularly). It follows therefore that any advice, etc given in such discussions is merely informal and advisory and cannot bind the LPA ultimately. Note also that LPAs may not charge a fee for the time taken in such pre-application discussions.

3.3   Full or outline permission?

One final matter to consider before completing and submitting the application form is whether to apply in full for planning permission or whether to apply for outline permission.

3.3.1   General

By the GDPO, arts 3 and 4, where the application is for permission to erect a building, the applicant may, if he wishes, apply for outline permission. In such a case, the application merely has to contain a description of the proposed development sufficient to indicate its major features (eg, for residential developments, the number and type of dwellings). A plan is also required of sufficient detail to identify the boundaries of the site and the nearest classified public highway. However, the application need not contain the considerable amount of detail that is required for a full application for permission.

3.3.2   The 'reserved matters'

If outline planning permission is granted, it will be subject to a condition setting out certain matters for which the subsequent approval of the LPA is required. The only matters which can be so specified ('reserved matters') are defined in the GDPO, art 1(2), and the Town and Country Planning (Applications) Regulations 1988 (SI 1988/1812) as those concerned with siting, design, external appearance, means of access and landscaping of the development.

3.3.3   The effect of outline permission

The effect of outline planning permission is that the LPA are committed to allowing the development in principle subject to approval of any reserved matters. This is because it is the grant of the outline permission which constitutes the grant of planning permission for the proposed development, ie, no further planning permission is required.

Accordingly, the LPA cannot revoke the outline permission except on payment of compensation (see revocation of planning permissions at **3.5.2.1**) nor can they impose additional conditions subsequently except as regards the reserved matters.

3.3.4   Approval of reserved matters

When an applicant comes to apply for approval of the reserved matters he is equally bound by the outline permission. If the application for approval of reserved matters includes additional development, it will normally be invalid.

3.3.5   The Planning and Compulsory Purchase Act 2004

The Act contains proposals which may see the replacement of outline planning consent with 'statements of development principles', which will not amount to planning permission but would be a material consideration in determining any future planning application.

3.4   The procedure

Procedure is governed mainly by ss 62 to 69, the GDPO and the Town and Country Planning (Applications) Regulations 1988.

3.4.1   What is submitted to whom?

The application form and such other documents, plans, drawings, etc as are needed to describe the proposed development should be submitted (usually in triplicate) to the district planning authority, London borough or metropolitan district council or unitary council (as the case may be).

The application must be accompanied by the appropriate fee and a GDPO article 7 Certificate (see **3.4.2** and **3.4.3**).

3.4.2 The fee

The fees vary according to the type of application and the scale of development involved.

3.4.3 Article 7 certificate

The application must be accompanied by an article 7 Certificate and an Agricultural Holdings Certificate.

The certificates have to be given to certify compliance with the GDPO, art 6, which requires the applicant, where he is not the sole owner of the land concerned, to notify or try to notify the owners of the land and any relevant agricultural tenant of the fact of the application for planning permission (see **3.4.4**).

3.4.4 Notification of persons by the applicant

By the GDPO, art 6, where the applicant is not the sole owner of the application site, he must give notice (in the form prescribed in the GDPO, Sch 2, Pt I) to all persons who are 'owners' or 'tenants' of the land.

'Owner' is defined by s 65(8) as meaning any person who owns the fee simple or a tenancy granted or extended for a term certain of which not less than seven years remain unexpired.

'Tenant' is defined by the GDPO, art 6(6), as meaning the tenant of an agricultural holding any part of which is comprised in the application site.

3.4.5 Action by the LPA

3.4.5.1 Entry in the planning register

By s 69, the LPA must enter certain particulars of the application in the register that they are required to keep by that section. The register is open to public inspection.

3.4.5.2 Notification

By the GDPO, art 8, the LPA must publicise the application. This publicity may consist of a site notice, notifying neighbours, or a local advertisement, depending upon the type of development proposed.

3.4.5.3 Power to decline to determine applications

Section 43 of the PCPA 2004 (in force 24 August 2005) gives local planning authorities the power to decline to determine:

(a)   repeat planning applications;

(b)   overlapping planning applications.

Repeat planning applications are applications that are submitted repeatedly with the intention that, over time, opposition to a controversial proposed development is reduced, and permission granted. This process may result in undesirable developments being built.

The new powers are not intended to prevent similar applications from being submitted, such as when a new application is submitted that is similar to an earlier one but altered to address objections raised in relation to the earlier application.

Section 43 allows the LPA to decline to determine an application which is similar to one refused by the authority within the preceding two years.

3.4.5.4   Major infrastructure projects

Section 44 of the PCPA 2004 (in force 24 August 2005) adds ss 76A and 76B to the TCPA 1990. These provisions:

(a)   allow the Secretary of State to direct that an application for a major infrastructure project be referred to the Secretary of State instead of being dealt with by the local planning authority. If a direction is made requiring the application to be referred to the Secretary of State, the applicant must prepare an economic impact report (EIR). The EIR must be in the prescribed form;

(b)   allow the Secretary of State to appoint a lead inspector to consider applications for major infrastructure projects and to make recommendations to the Secretary of State, including a recommendation that an inquiry is conducted in concurrent sessions by a number of inspectors.

3.5   The decision

3.5.1   General points

By s 70(1), the LPA may grant planning permission either unconditionally or subject to such conditions as they think fit or they may refuse planning permission.

In reaching their decision they must have regard to the provisions of the development plan if it is relevant to the application and to any other material considerations (see further, below). They must also take into account any representations received in response to the publicity of the application (see **3.4.5**) and certain other matters if the development affects a listed building or a conservation area.

'... have regard to ... the development plan ...'

This must be read in conjunction with s 54A which states that where regard is to be had to the development plan, any determination must be made in accordance with the plan unless material considerations indicate otherwise. Thus, if the proposed development is covered by the plan, the LPA's decision should be made in accordance with the plan unless there are material considerations to the contrary.

Policy guidance on s 54A can be found in PPG 1 where, in para 40, the DCLG advises that:

> Applications which are not in accordance with relevant policies in the plan should not be allowed unless material considerations justify granting planning permission ... In all cases where the plan is relevant, it will be necessary to decide if the proposal is in accordance with the plan and then to take into account other material considerations.

The section does not, however, create a legitimate expectation that a particular application will or must be determined solely by reference to the development plan (see *Trustees of the Viscount Folkestone 1963 Settlement and Camden Homes Ltd v Secretary of State for the Environment and Salisbury District Council* [1995] JPL 502).

Recently, however, there has been a spate of cases (see, eg, *St Albans District Council v Secretary of State for the Environment and Allied Breweries Ltd* [1993] JPL 374; *R v Canterbury City Council, Robert Brett & Sons, ex p Springimage Ltd* [1994] JPL 427; and *Bylander Waddell Partnership v Secretary of State for the Environment and Harrow London Borough Council* [1994] JPL 440) which have suggested that 'material considerations to the contrary' can include advice in DCLG circulars and PPGs.

The LPA, or the inspector or DCLG on an appeal, do not have to refer expressly to s 54A in their decision. It is sufficient that the decision was reached in accordance with the section: see, for example, *Newham London Borough Council v Secretary of State for the Environment* [1995] EGCS 6; *Spelthorne Borough Council v Secretary of State for the Environment and Lawlor Land plc* [1995] JPL 412; and *North Yorkshire County Council v Secretary of State for the Environment and Griffin* [1996] JPL 32, CA.

Note that it seems that s 54A applies also to the determination of an application for approval of reserved matters pursuant to an outline planning permission (see *St George Developments Ltd and Kew Riverside Developments v Secretary of State for the Environment and Richmond upon Thames London Borough Council* [1996] JPL 35).

'... other material considerations'

For other considerations to be 'material', they must be relevant to the application and be planning considerations, ie, relate to the use and development of land: see *Stringer v Minister of Housing and Local Government* [1971] 1 All ER 65. Note the following examples (which are not exhaustive) of matters which the courts have held to be capable of being 'material considerations':

(a)   a development plan which is in the course of preparation (see, eg, *Allen v Corporation of the City of London* [1981] JPL 685 and *Kissel v Secretary of State for the Environment and Another* [1994] JPL 819). The closer the new plan gets to adoption, the greater the weight that should be given to it;

(b)   the protection of private interests in a proper case and, in exceptional circumstances, personal hardship (see, eg, *Great Portland Estates plc v Westminster City Council* [1985] AC 661, HL);

(c)   financial considerations involved in the proposed development (see, eg, *Sovmots v Secretary of State for the Environment; Brompton Securities Ltd v Secretary of State for the Environment* [1977] 1 QB 411);

(d)   planning obligations (as to which, see **4.2**);

(e)   retention of an existing use (see, eg, *London Residuary Body v Lambeth Borough Council* [1990] 2 All ER 309, HL);

(f)   the previous planning history of the site;

(g)   a real danger of setting an undesirable precedent (see, eg, *Anglia Building Society v Secretary of State for the Environment and Another* [1984] JPL 175);

(h)   planning policies of the DCLG (as evidenced in circulars and PPGs), of other government departments where relevant (eg, transport, energy, etc) and the LPA concerned (as evidenced in their own policy statements and non-statutory plans);

(i)   racial discrimination (by s 19A of the Race Relations Act 1976 it is unlawful for an LPA to discriminate on racial grounds when exercising any of their planning functions);

(j)   environmental considerations: likely environmental pollution from a proposed development is a material consideration. However, it is not the function of the planning system to duplicate statutory pollution controls (see *Gateshead Metropolitan Borough Council v Secretary of State for the Environment* [1995] JPL 432, CA; and *Envirocor Waste Holdings v Secretary of State for the Environment* [1995] EGCS 60, QB).

3.5.1.1   The making of the decision

The decision should be made within eight weeks of the submission of the application or such longer period as may have been agreed in writing with the applicant (GDPO, art 20). However, in the case of major developments, the time limit is 13 weeks, and if an environmental assessment accompanies the application then the period is 16 weeks. If no decision has been made in time the applicant can appeal to the DCLG.

3.5.1.2   Procedure after the decision

After making the decision, the LPA must register it in their planning register (which they are required to keep by virtue of s 69: see **3.4.5.1** and also the GDPO, art 25(2)). In addition, the applicant must be given written notification of the decision and, where the decision is a planning permission subject to conditions or a refusal, written reasons (see the GDPO, art 22, and **3.5.4**).

It is the written notification which constitutes the grant of planning permission (see *R v West Oxfordshire District Council, ex p CH Pearce Homes* [1986] JPL 523).

3.5.2   Effect of planning permission

By s 75(1), without prejudice to the provisions of the Act on duration, revocation or modification (for all of which, see below), planning permission shall (except in so far as the permission otherwise provides) enure for the benefit of the land and of all persons for the time being interested in it.

Therefore, the benefit of planning permission runs with the land concerned and, prima facie, lasts forever, but see **3.5.3.1**. Note, however, that any conditions attached to the planning permission will also run, ie, will burden the relevant land.

A grant of planning permission is effective for planning purposes only; it does not confer, for example, listed building consent, building regulation consent or any consent required under any other enactment, nor does it confer the right to break any enforceable covenant affecting the land.

Note also that planning permission is merely permissive; it does not have to be implemented and the LPA cannot compel implementation, but see **3.5.3.4** as to the service of a completion notice.

'... the permission otherwise provides'

Planning permission may be expressly granted for a limited period or be made personal to the applicant.

Once such a permission lapses, the right to revert to the previous use of the land is permitted by s 57(2) (see **2.2.1**).

3.5.2.1   Revocation and modification of planning permissions

By s 97, the LPA may, if they think it expedient to do so, revoke or modify (to the extent they consider necessary) any planning permission provided they do so before the development authorised by the permission is completed.

3.5.2.2   Abandonment of planning permission

It follows from the provisions in s 75(1) that the doctrine of abandonment cannot apply to planning permissions. Note, however, that once a permission has been fully implemented its effect is spent, ie, it does not authorise the re-carrying out of that development.

3.5.3   Duration

3.5.3.1   General

Although, prima facie, the benefit of a planning permission lasts forever, there are some important statutory time limits governing the implementation of the permission which, if not observed, may terminate it. For permissions granted before 24 August 2005, this is five years. For permissions granted on or after 24 August 2005, the PCPA 2004 has reduced the period to three years.

Note also that the LPA may substitute longer or shorter time limits if they think it appropriate on planning grounds; if they do this, however, they must give their reasons for doing so in case the applicant should wish to appeal against this.

3.5.3.2   The start and end of the period

If the time limit expires without the development having been started, then the permission effectively lapses. Any further development will be unauthorised and subject to possible enforcement proceedings. Because of this, it is important to know two things, namely what is the effective date of the permission and when does development commence?

As regards the effective date of the permission, the Act provides no guidance; however the case of *R v West Oxfordshire District Council, ex p CH Pearce Homes* [1986] JPL 523 established that this is the date which appears on the written notification to the applicant (ie it is not the date on which the decision was made by the LPA). This is, therefore, the starting date for the time limit.

As regards the date when development commences, the Act defines this very carefully in s 56 which provides that development is taken to be begun on the earliest date on which any of the following operations begin to be carried out:

(a)   any work of construction in the course of erection of a building;

(b)   any work of demolition of a building;

(c)   the digging of a trench for the foundations of a building;

(d)   the laying of an underground main or pipe to the foundations;

(e)   any operation in the course of laying out or constructing a road;

(f)   any material change in the use of any land.

3.5.3.3   Renewal of a planning permission

What if a developer cannot start the development within the time limit because of, for instance, financial problems? In such a case, the developer can apply for a renewal of the permission using a simplified procedure, but should do so before the original permission expires, otherwise the whole permission will lapse and a fresh application for planning permission will therefore have to be made.

3.5.3.4   Completion notice (ss 94–95)

What happens if a developer starts the development within the time limit but the time limit subsequently expires without the development having been completed? In such a case, if the LPA is of the opinion that the development will not be completed within a reasonable period, it may serve a completion notice on the owner and any occupier of the land stating that the permission will cease to have effect at the expiration of a further period specified in the notice (being not less than 12 months after the notice takes effect). The notice is subject to confirmation by the DCLG. Any part of the development carried out before a confirmed completion notice takes effect is not affected.

3.5.4   Refusals and planning permissions subject to conditions

As stated at **3.5.1**, by s 70(1), an LPA may grant planning permission unconditionally or subject to such conditions as they think fit or they may refuse permission (permissions subject to conditions are dealt with in detail at **3.6**). In the latter two cases, the written notification of the decision must state clearly and precisely the full reasons for the conditions imposed or the refusal as the case may be. If full reasons are not given this will probably not invalidate the decision itself although the decision could be challenged by judicial review or dealt with by way of appeal.

There is also a general right of appeal to the DCLG against a permission subject to conditions, a refusal and a 'deemed refusal' (ie, where no decision is reached within the relevant period, as to which see **3.5.1**).

3.6 Planning permissions subject to conditions

3.6.1 General points

The power in s 70(1) for an LPA to impose such conditions as they think fit (see **3.5.1**) is supplemented by s 72(1) which provides that, without prejudice to the generality of s 70(1), conditions may be imposed on the grant of planning permission for the purpose of:

(a) regulating the development or use of any land under the control of the applicant (whether or not it is land in respect of which the application was made) or requiring the carrying out of works on any such land, so far as appears to the LPA to be expedient for the purposes of or in connection with the development authorised by the permission; or

(b) requiring the removal of any buildings or works authorised by the permission, or the discontinuance of any use of land so authorised, at the end of a specified period, and the carrying out of any works required for the reinstatement of land at the end of that period.

Whether an applicant has 'control' of the relevant land is a question of fact and degree in each case.

3.6.2 Judicial restrictions on the power

The general power to impose conditions in s 70(1) is not as wide or unfettered as it appears because over the years the courts have imposed restraints on it.

The leading case on the judicial control of the power is *Newbury District Council v Secretary of State for the Environment; Newbury District Council v International Synthetic Rubber Co* [1981] AC 578, where Viscount Dilhorne (at p 599) said:

> The conditions imposed must be for a planning purpose and not for any ulterior one and … they must fairly and reasonably relate to the development permitted. Also they must not be so unreasonable that no reasonable planning authority could have imposed them.

3.6.2.1 'Planning purpose'

There are many cases illustrating the first element of the above test (ie, that conditions must be imposed for a planning purpose). For example, in *R v Hillingdon London Borough Council, ex p Royco Homes Ltd* [1974] 1 QB 720, outline permission for a residential development was granted subject to a condition that the dwellings should first be occupied by persons on the local authority's housing waiting list with security of tenure for 10 years. The court held that the principal purpose of the condition was to require the applicants to assume at their expense a significant part of the authority's statutory duties as a housing authority. The condition was therefore ultra vires.

3.6.2.2 'Fairly and reasonably related to the development permitted'

The second part of the test in *Newbury* is probably the most difficult one to understand and apply. In *Newbury* the facts were that planning permission was granted for a change of use of aircraft hangers to warehouses subject to a condition requiring removal of the hangers at the end of 10 years. The House of Lords held that, although this condition satisfied the first test in that the removal of unsightly old buildings was a proper planning purpose, the condition was not sufficiently related to the change of use permitted by the permission and was therefore void.

3.6.2.3 'Manifestly unreasonable'

The final part of the test in *Newbury* is that the condition must not be manifestly unreasonable in the sense that no reasonable LPA would have imposed the condition in question.

Under this element, a condition may not require the applicant to pay money or provide other consideration for the granting of planning permission (but see **Chapter 4** where a similar practical result can be achieved by means of a planning obligation). Nor may a condition require the ceding of land owned by the applicant for public purposes (eg, a highway) even if the applicant consents.

3.6.2.4 General note on *Newbury*

It is important to bear in mind that the majority of conditions imposed by LPAs on planning permissions do not fall foul of the test in *Newbury*.

In the very few cases where a condition does fail, it will normally breach more than one of the elements in the test. This is because there are potentially considerable areas of overlap between the three elements in the test. This is illustrated by the *Ministerial Decision* noted at [1991] JPL 184 where a condition attached to a planning permission restricting car parking spaces on the land to residents of a specified London borough was held to be void on the grounds that it did not fulfil a proper planning purpose and that it was manifestly unreasonable. In reality, despite the three elements, there is just one basic test.

3.6.2.5 Severability of void conditions

If the condition in question is fundamental to the permission (ie, if the permission would not have been granted without the condition) the court will not sever the offending condition. (Most conditions are considered to be fundamental to their permissions.) Thus, if the condition is quashed, the whole permission will fail, ie, the applicant will be left with no permission at all. This is, therefore, an important point to bear in mind in deciding how to challenge a particular condition's validity (ie, by way of application to the High Court for judicial review, or by appeal to the DCLG). In most cases, it will be better to appeal to the DCLG as, unlike the courts, he has power to grant the permission free from the offending condition or conditions if he thinks fit (see **3.6.3**). In addition, an application for judicial review must be made promptly, and in any event within three months of the decision, whereas an appeal to the DCLG must be made within six months (see **3.7**).

3.6.3 The Secretary of State's guidance

The Annex to DCLG Circular 11/95 gives detailed guidance to planning authorities on the imposition of conditions. It is, therefore, essential reading when considering whether or not to appeal against a permission subject to conditions.

The main starting point is para 14 of the Annex to the Circular, which sets out six criteria that conditions must satisfy, namely that they should be imposed only where they are:

(a)   necessary (see further paras 15–17 of the Annex);

(b)   relevant to planning (see paras 20–23);

(c)   relevant to the development to be permitted (see paras 24 and 25);

(d)   enforceable (see paras 26–29);

(e)   precise (see paras 30–33); and

(f)   reasonable in all other respects (see paras 34–42).

These basic principles (which are clearly based on the courts' criteria, see **3.6.2**) are expanded in paras 15 to 42, following which there are a further 78 paragraphs dealing with particular problem areas.

3.6.4   Section 73 and section 73A applications

3.6.4.1   Section 73

Section 73 entitles a person to apply for planning permission to develop land without complying with conditions subject to which a previous planning permission was granted. Such an application must, though, be made before the previous permission expires.

The application merely has to be made in writing and give sufficient information to enable the LPA to identify the previous grant of planning permission and the condition or conditions in question (Town and Country Planning (Applications) Regulations 1988 (SI 1988/1812), reg 3).

The important feature of a s 73 application is that in determining the application, the planning authority may consider only the question of the conditions subject to which the permission should be granted and thus may only:

(a)   grant unconditional permission;

(b)   grant permission subject to different conditions; or

(c)   refuse the application.

In the first two cases above, the applicant will then have the benefit of two permissions (ie, the original one and the one obtained on the s 73 application). In cases (b) and (c), the applicant can appeal to the DCLG in the usual way. Thus, whatever happens on the s 73 application, the applicant will retain the benefit of the original planning permission.

This procedure may be particularly useful in securing the removal of a condition restricting freedom of change of use within a class of the Use Classes Order 1987 or a condition restricting permitted development rights under the GPDO. Further, this is the only procedure available for challenging a condition where the time limit for appealing has passed.

In *Allied London Property Investment Ltd v Secretary of State for the Environment* (1996) 72 P & CR 327, it was held that there is no distinction to be drawn between time and other conditions. Therefore, s 73 could be used to apply for, for example, an extension of time for applying for approval of reserved matters under an outline permission (instead of applying for a renewal of the outline permission – see **3.5.3.3**).

3.6.4.2   Section 73A

Section 73 applies only to applications for the removal, etc of a condition before it is breached. However, under s 73A an application may be made for planning permission for, inter alia, development carried out before the date of the application in breach of a condition subject to which planning permission was previously granted.

Permission for such development may be granted to have effect from the date on which the development was carried out thereby rendering it retrospectively lawful.

3.7   Appeals against adverse planning determinations

Where an LPA has:

(a)   refused to grant planning permission, or

(b)   granted planning permission subject to conditions to which the applicant objects, or

(c)   refused approval of reserved matters on an outline permission, or

(d)   refused an application or granted a permission subject to conditions under s 73 or s 73A, or

(e)   failed to notify their decision within the prescribed period (normally eight weeks),

the applicant may appeal to the DCLG within six months of the notice of the decision or failure to determine as the case may be (s 78, and the GDPO, arts 20 and 23).

3.7.1 Who may appeal?

Only the applicant may appeal; this is so even though the applicant may not be the owner of an interest in the land. Third parties have no right of appeal and neither does the owner of the freehold have an independent right of appeal.

3.7.2 Initial procedure (GDPO, art 23)

An appeal must be made on the form supplied by the DCLG.

As well as setting out the grounds of appeal, the appellant must also indicate whether he would like the appeal to be determined by the written representations procedure, whether he wishes it to be heard by an inspector, or whether he wishes the appeal to be heard at a public inquiry (see **3.8**). Note, however, that it is the Planning Inspectorate that will choose the procedure; it will not necessarily adopt the method desired by the appellant. The LPA's views as to the choice of procedure will also be taken into account. The Planning Inspectorate's decision will be made in the light of published criteria approved by Ministers. These are as follows:

Criteria for Determining the Procedure for Planning Appeals

Written representations

If your appeal meets the following criteria, the most appropriate procedure would be written representations:

1. the grounds of appeal and issues raised can be clearly understood from the appeal documents plus a site inspection; and/or

2. the Inspector should not need to test the evidence by questioning or to clarify any other matters; and/or

3. an environmental impact assessment (EIA) is either not required or the EIA is not in dispute.

Hearing

If the criteria for written representations are not met because questions need to be asked, for example where any of the following apply:

- the status of the appellant is at issue, eg Gypsy/Traveller;

- the need for the proposal is at issue, eg agricultural worker's dwelling; Gypsy/Traveller site;

- the personal circumstances of the appellant are at issue, eg people with disabilities or other special needs;

the most appropriate procedure would be a hearing if:

1. there is no need for evidence to be tested by formal cross-examination; and

2. the issues are straightforward (and do not require legal or other submissions to be made) and you should be able to present your own case (although you can choose to be represented if you wish); and

3. your case and that of the LPA and interested persons is unlikely to take more than one day to be heard.

Inquiry

If the criteria for written representations and hearings are not met because the evidence needs to be tested and/or questions need to be asked, as above, the most appropriate procedure would be a local inquiry if:

1. the issues are complex and likely to need evidence to be given by expert witnesses; and/or

2. you are likely to need to be represented by an advocate, such as a lawyer or other professional expert because material facts and/or matters of expert opinion are in dispute and formal cross-examination of witnesses is required; and/or

3. legal submissions may need to be made.

NOTE: Where proposals are controversial and have generated significant local interest, they may not be suitable for the written representation procedure. We consider that the LPA is in the best position to indicate that a hearing or inquiry may be required in such circumstances.

There is also an expedited process based on written representations where a householder is appealing through the Householder Appeals Service. This is dealt with on an electronic basis and covers appeals in relation to minor developments affecting existing dwellings, eg extensions, garages, etc.

The completed form together with all relevant documents must be sent to the Planning Inspectorate to reach them within the time limit. Copies of the form must also be sent to the LPA together with copies of any documents sent to the Inspectorate which the LPA have not yet seen (GDPO, art 23(1)(b)).

3.8   Types of appeal

3.8.1   Written representations

Under the written representations procedure the appeal is decided, as its name suggests, almost entirely on the basis of written representations submitted to the Inspectorate by the appellant, the LPA and any other interested parties. No oral evidence is permitted and that includes evidence by way of video or audio tape; maps, plans and photographs are, however, acceptable and in many cases will be necessary. At some point before a decision is made, the inspector will visit the site either unaccompanied, if the site can be seen sufficiently well from a public road or place, or accompanied by the appellant or his representative and a representative from the LPA.

The procedure is governed by the Town and Country Planning (Appeals) (Written Representations Procedure) Regulations 2009 (SI 2009/452). It is speedy and cost-effective and is recommended by the DCLG for the simpler or non-controversial cases. It is by far the most common appeal procedure accounting for about 80% of current appeals. Because of its nature, it also offers less scope for third parties to influence the eventual decision.

3.8.1.1   Statement of case

The appellant's statement of case must be set out in the appeal form. As a general guide, the statement should:

(a)   Start with quotations from planning policy guidance notes and DCLG circulars which support the appellant's case.

(b)   Consider each of the reasons given (where relevant) for the refusal, etc and analyse and refute them, by logical argument. In this part, any precedent (ie, showing that the LPA have granted a similar application) should be mentioned as should any policies of the LPA which contradict the LPA's reasons.

(c)   Justify the appellant's case. Here there should be a brief description of the development proposed together with additional plans, photographs, etc if desired. The local environment may be described (although the inspector will visit the site). Any policies from the structure or local plans which support the appellant's case should be quoted. Any special circumstances should be set out and any objections from third parties should be addressed.

(d)   Conclude (optional) with a general policy statement in support of the appellant's case.

3.8.2   Inquiry

This is the most formal of the appeal procedures and is reserved for larger and more controversial developments. Inquiries are usually held in LPA offices, village halls or community centres. The procedure is governed by the Town and Country Planning (Inquiries Procedure) (England) Rules 2000 (SI 2000/1624) and the Town and Country Planning (Determination by Inspectors) (Inquiries Procedure) (England) Rules 2000 (SI 2000/1625) as amended by the Town and Country Planning (Hearings and Inquiries Procedure) (Amendment) (England) Rules 2009 (SI 2009/455). Guidance as to the procedure to be followed can be found on the Planning Inspectorate website or on the Government Planning Portal (www.planningportal.gov.uk).

These are often cases where expert evidence is presented, and witnesses are cross-examined. An inquiry may last for several days, or even weeks. It is not a court of law, but the proceedings will often seem to be quite similar, and the appellant and the LPA usually have legal representatives. It is thus a much slower and more costly procedure.

The Planning Inspectorate sets out the following guidance in its 'Guide to taking part in enforcement appeals proceeding by an inquiry' (July 2009):

> Inquiries are open to members of the public, and although there is no legal right to speak the Inspector will normally allow [local people to take part in the inquiry process]. Local knowledge and opinion can often be a valuable addition to the more formal evidence given by the appellant and the LPA.
>
> …
>
> At the inquiry opening, the Inspector will go through some routine matters, including asking who will be taking part in the inquiry. This is often called 'taking the appearances'. When the appellant and the LPA have given their details, the Inspector will ask if anyone else wants to speak. …
>
> …
>
> The appellant will usually be asked to make a brief opening statement first, to set the scene [and describe the nature of the proposal]. The LPA will then make their opening statement. Their witnesses will then give their evidence and the appellant can cross-examine them. After that the Inspector will normally ask if anyone who supports the proposal has any questions to put to the witnesses.
>
> The appellant will then call their witnesses, and the LPA can cross-examine them. After that the Inspector will normally ask if anyone who objects to the proposal has any questions to put to the witnesses.
>
> …
>
> The inquiry ends with closing speeches by those who have spoken at the inquiry, followed by the LPA and finally the appellant. This is normally followed by the Inspector visiting the appeal site. Because the inquiry is over, there can be no further discussion about the case during that visit.
>
> At the discretion of the Inspector, video, audio cassette, CD/DVD or electronic media files may be played at the inquiry. … The recording will become part of the inquiry evidence and will be retained.

3.8.2.1 The appeal form

In the appeal form, it is not necessary or desirable to give a full statement of case. Full grounds of appeal must, however, be included. Thus, the appellant must, as before, consider each of the LPA's reasons and analyse and refute them briefly. The entire case should be summarised by describing the development proposed, the environment and any special needs or circumstances, and by referring to any appropriate parts of the structure and local plans and government policies. Any relevant previous decisions (whether by the LPA or on appeal) should be set out as being 'material considerations' and potential planning gain to the LPA should also be outlined.

It is important that the full grounds of appeal are stated and that nothing is omitted, as the appellant or his representative at the appeal will largely be bound by the grounds, and any omissions may cause adjournments and may have financial consequences (see **3.9**).

3.8.3 Hearing

This is less formal than a public inquiry. The hearing is an inquisitorial process led by the Inspector who identifies the issues for discussion based on the evidence submitted and any representations made. The hearing may include a discussion at the site, or the site may be inspected, without discussion, on an accompanied or unaccompanied basis.

The procedure is governed by the Town and Country Planning (Hearings Procedure) (England) Rules 2000 (SI 2000/1626) as amended by the Town and Country Planning (Hearings and Inquiries Procedure) (Amendment) Rules 2009 (SI 2009/455). The procedure is intended to save time and money for the parties. In essence, it will be an informal hearing before an inspector who will try to stimulate a discussion on the main issues between the parties. It is not appropriate for complex or controversial appeals but where it is appropriate it is quicker and more cost-effective than an inquiry.

3.9 Costs in appeals

By ss 320(2) and 322, the DCLG is given the powers of s 250(5) of the Local Government Act 1972 to award costs in planning appeals. Inspectors may now exercise the DCLG's powers. There is power to make an award in all cases irrespective of the procedure for deciding the appeal.

Detailed guidance on the exercise of power to award costs is contained in Circular 03/09. The basic principle is that, unlike in civil cases, costs do not 'follow the event', ie, normally, each party will bear their own costs. Costs may, however, be awarded against one party in favour of another where:

(a)   a party has sought an award at the appropriate stage of the proceedings; and

(b)   the party against whom costs are sought has behaved unreasonably; and

(c)   this has caused the party seeking costs to incur or waste expense unnecessarily.

3.10 Challenging the appeal decision

By s 284, the validity of an appeal decision may not be challenged in any legal proceedings. However, by s 288, a 'person aggrieved' may question the decision by appeal to the High Court if the decision was not within the powers of the Act or if any relevant procedural requirements have not been complied with.

In certain limited cases, a challenge may alternatively be mounted by way of judicial review.

Chapter 4

Planning Obligations

4.1 Introduction

A planning obligation (formerly a planning agreement) is a negotiating tool available to an LPA and a developer who is seeking planning permission. It is a legal instrument which offers a degree of flexibility to both parties which might not otherwise be available through the medium of a planning permission subject to conditions (see **3.6**).

Planning obligations have often been criticised for bringing uncertainty into the planning process: uncertainty, for example, as to what kind of obligations a particular local authority might require. They have also been the cause of delays in the ultimate granting of permission. For many years local authorities were required to comply with the guidance in Circular 1/97, but this has now been replaced by Circular 5/05 which places emphasis on the need for sustainable development and affordable housing. To deal with the certainty issue, it also puts more emphasis on the use of standard forms of agreement and the need to follow planning policies published in local and other plans. In 2006 the DCLG published further practice guidance for local authorities and a model form of s 106 agreement drafted by the Law Society's Planning and Environmental Law Committee (available at www.communities.gov.uk).

The Planning Act 2008 will introduce powers to enable local authorities to charge developers a Community Infrastructure Levy to fund improvements in local infrastructure for the benefit of the community at large. This will be introduced alongside the s 106 provisions (see **4.7**)

4.2 Planning obligations (s 106)

4.2.1 The basic provision

Any person interested in land in the area of an LPA may, by agreement or otherwise, enter into a planning obligation which may:

(a) restrict the development or use of the land in a specified way; or

(b) may require specified operations or activities to be carried out in, on, over or under the land; or

(c) require the land to be used in a specified way; or

(d) require money to be paid to the LPA on a specified date or dates, or periodically (s 106(1)).

Note the following points:

(a) 'Person interested in land' means a person with a legal estate or interest in the land concerned and not, for example, a developer who merely has an option to purchase the land at the time the obligation is entered into.

(b) 'Agreement or otherwise' indicates that a planning obligation may be created either by agreement between the LPA and the developer or by means of a unilateral undertaking offered by the developer or a combination of both (as to the potential use of unilateral undertakings, see **4.6**).

(c) A planning obligation may impose both restrictive covenants (eg, restricting the development or use of the land) and positive ones (eg, requiring works to be done or money to be paid). These covenants will then be enforceable against successors in title of the developer (see **4.2.3**).

(d) A planning obligation may be unconditional or subject to conditions and may impose its restrictions and requirements either indefinitely or for a specified period. It may also provide that a person will only be bound by the obligation while he has an interest in the land (s 106(2) and (4)).

4.2.2 Formalities

A planning obligation must be made by a deed which states that it is a planning obligation for the purposes of s 106 and identifies the land and the parties concerned (including the interest of the developer). It is registrable by the LPA as a local land charge.

4.2.3 Enforceability

By s 106(3) and (4), a planning obligation is enforceable by the LPA against the original person interested (the 'developer') and any person deriving title from him but subject to the terms of the obligation (see **4.2.1**).

Note the following points:

(a) The obligation will bind only the interest or estate of the developer and those deriving title from him. It cannot bind a superior title. Thus, for example, if a tenant enters into a planning obligation, it cannot bind the landlord of that tenant.

(b) A planning obligation cannot bind parties who have rights in the land existing at the time the obligation is entered into unless they consent to be bound by it. Thus, for example, existing mortgagees of the land will not be bound (unless they consent) so that if they subsequently sell under their statutory power, the purchaser will take the land free from the obligation which will only be enforceable against the original covenantor.

4.2.4 Enforcement by the LPA

Section 106 provides three main methods of enforcement as follows:

(a) Injunction to restrain a breach of any restrictive covenant in the obligation (s 106(5)).

(b) By s 106(6), where there is a failure to carry out any operations required by a planning obligation, the LPA may enter upon the land, carry out the operations and recover their expenses from the person or persons against whom the obligation is enforceable (see **4.2.3**).

(c) Any sums due under the planning obligation (including any expenses recoverable under s 106(6) above) may be charged on the land in accordance with regulations yet to be made (s 106(12)). Until regulations have been made, it is unclear whether such a charge will be registrable as a local land charge or as a private charge (and therefore registrable as a land charge or by notice, etc on the register of title).

4.3 'Planning gain'

4.3.1 Introduction

The main function of planning obligations is to allow the LPA and the developer to deal with issues that are necessary to be dealt with in order for a proposal to be acceptable, but which cannot be dealt with by condition, given the limitations (imposed by case law etc) on the purposes for which conditions can be used. Planning obligations are not subject to such strict limitations and so can be used as a flexible means of solving any problems that a development proposal may cause.

The danger with this flexibility is that the use of planning obligations could be open to abuse. The fear was that developers would be tempted to offer inappropriate inducements to LPAs in order to obtain, or effectively 'buy', planning permission, and equally that LPAs would be tempted to draw up 'shopping lists', which they would expect developers to agree to pay for, in return for planning permission. This is sometimes referred to as planning gain and is clearly not in the public interest.

It is not surprising, therefore, that there is detailed policy and case law guidance setting out what it is legitimate to include in a planning obligation. What follows is a summary of the key policy and case law principles that govern this area.

4.3.2   DCLG advice – Circular 5/05

4.3.2.1   General policy

As a matter of policy, Circular 5/05 states that the use of planning obligations will be acceptable if they are:

    (i)   necessary to make a proposal acceptable in planning terms;

    (ii)   relevant to planning;

    (iii) directly related to the proposed development;

    (iv) fairly and reasonably related in scale and kind to the proposed development;

    (v)   reasonable in all other respects.

4.3.2.2   Specific guidance

Circular 5/05 includes the following guidance:

B2. In dealing with planning applications, local planning authorities consider each on its merits and reach a decision based on whether the application accords with the relevant development plan, unless material considerations indicate otherwise. Where applications do not meet these requirements, they may be refused. However, in some instances, it may be possible to make acceptable development proposals which might otherwise be unacceptable, through the use of planning conditions ... or, where this is not possible, through planning obligations. (Where there is a choice between imposing conditions and entering into a planning obligation, the imposition of a condition is preferable ...)

B3. Planning obligations (or 's106 agreements') are ... intended to make acceptable development which would otherwise be unacceptable in planning terms. Obligations can also be secured through unilateral undertakings by developers. For example, planning obligations might be used to prescribe the nature of a development (eg by requiring that a given proportion of housing is affordable); or to secure a contribution from a developer to compensate for loss or damage created by a development (eg loss of open space); or to mitigate a development's impact (eg through increased public transport provision). The outcome of all three of these uses of planning obligations should be that the proposed development concerned is made to accord with published local, regional or national planning policies.

B4. Planning obligations are unlikely to be required for all developments but should be used whenever appropriate according to the Secretary of State's policy set out in this Circular ...

B6. The use of planning obligations must be governed by the fundamental principle that planning permission may not be bought or sold. It is therefore not legitimate for unacceptable development to be permitted because of benefits or inducements offered by a developer which are not necessary to make the development acceptable in planning terms ...

B7. Similarly, planning obligations should never be used purely as a means of securing for the local community a share in the profits of development, ie as a means of securing a 'betterment levy'.

B8. As summarised above, it will in general be reasonable to seek, or take account of, a planning obligation if what is sought or offered is necessary from a planning point of view, ie in order to bring a development in line with the objectives of sustainable development as articulated through the relevant local, regional or national planning policies .... Obligations must also be so directly related to proposed developments that the development ought not to be permitted without them – for example, there should be a functional or geographical link between the development and the item being provided as part of the developer's contribution.

B9. Within these categories of acceptable obligations, what is sought must also be fairly and reasonably related in scale and kind to the proposed development and reasonable in all other respects. For example, developers may reasonably be expected to pay for or contribute to the cost of all, or that part of, additional infrastructure provision which would not have been necessary but for their development. The effect of the infrastructure investment may be to confer some wider benefit on the community but payments should be directly related in scale to the impact which the proposed development will make. Planning obligations should not be used solely to resolve existing deficiencies in infrastructure provision or to secure contributions to the achievement of wider planning objectives that are not necessary to allow consent to be given for a particular development.

B12. Planning obligations can be used to secure the implementation of a planning policy in order to make acceptable a development proposal that would otherwise be unacceptable in planning terms. For example, where not possible through a planning condition, planning obligations can be used to secure the inclusion of an element of affordable housing in a residential or mixed-use development where there is a residential component.

B15. Where a proposed development would, if implemented, create a need for a particular facility that is relevant to planning but cannot be required through the use of planning conditions, it will usually be reasonable for planning obligations to be secured to meet this need. For example, where a proposed development is not acceptable in planning terms due to inadequate access or public transport provision, planning obligations might be used to secure contributions towards a new access road or provision of a bus service, perhaps co-ordinated through a Travel Plan. Similarly, if a proposed development would give rise to the need for additional or expanded community infrastructure, for example, a new school classroom, which is necessary in planning terms and not provided for in an application, it might be acceptable for contributions to be sought towards this additional provision through a planning obligation.

B16. Planning obligations might be used, when appropriate, to offset through substitution, replacement or regeneration the loss of, or damage to, a feature or resource present or nearby, for example, a landscape feature of biodiversity value, open space or right of way. It may not be necessary to provide an exact substitute of the item lost, but there should be some relationship between what is lost and what is to be offered. A reasonable obligation will seek to restore facilities, resources and amenities to a quality equivalent to that existing before the development.

B17. Contributions may either be in kind or in the form of a financial contribution. In the case of financial contributions, payments can be made in the form of a lump sum or an endowment, or, if beneficial to all parties and not unduly complex, as phased payments over a period of time, related to defined dates, events and triggers. Policies on types of payment, including pooling and maintenance payments, should be set out in Local Development Frameworks. The local authority's generic policies on payment types should be contained in Development Plan Documents, and the details of their application in Supplementary Planning Documents.

B18. Where contributions are secured through planning obligations towards the provision of facilities which are predominantly for the benefit of the users of the associated development, it may be appropriate for the developer to make provision for subsequent maintenance (ie physical upkeep). Such provision may be required in perpetuity.

B19. As a general rule, however, where an asset is intended for wider public use, the costs of subsequent maintenance and other recurrent expenditure associated with the developer's contributions should normally be borne by the body or authority in which the asset is to be vested. Where contributions to the initial support ('pump priming') of new facilities are necessary, these should reflect the time lag between the provision of the new facility and its inclusion in public sector funding streams, or its ability to recover its own costs in the case of privately-run bus services, for example. Pump priming maintenance payments should be time limited and not be required in perpetuity by planning obligations.

B25. In order to allow developers to predict as accurately as possible the likely contributions they will be asked to make through planning obligations and therefore anticipate the financial implications for development projects, local authorities should seek to include as much information as possible in their published documents in the Local Development Framework. In line with previous advice in Circular 1/97, local planning authorities should include in their new-style Development Plan Documents general policies about the principles and use of planning obligations …

B31. It is important that the negotiation of planning obligations does not unnecessarily delay the planning process, thereby holding up development. It is therefore essential that all parties proceed as quickly as possible towards the resolution of obligations in parallel to planning applications (including through pre-application discussions where appropriate) and in a spirit of early warning and co-operation, with deadlines and working practices agreed in advance as far as possible.

B51. It is important to recognise that, if there is a choice between imposing conditions and entering into a planning obligation, the imposition of a condition which satisfies the policy tests of Department of the Environment Circular 11/95 is preferable because it enables a developer to appeal to the Secretary of State regarding the imposition of the condition … The terms of conditions imposed on a planning permission should not be re-stated in a planning obligation; that is to say, an obligation should not be entered into which requires compliance with the conditions imposed on a planning permission. Such obligations entail unnecessary duplication and could frustrate a developer's right of appeal. Further, as per the guidance in Department of the Environment Circular 11/95, permission cannot be granted subject to a condition that the developer enters into a planning obligation under section 106 of the Act or an agreement under other powers.

4.3.3 Case law

There have recently been several cases concerned with the reasonableness of benefits contained in planning obligations and what weight should be given to them in deciding whether planning permission should be granted. The principal cases are *R v Plymouth City Council and Others, ex p Plymouth and South Devon Co-operative Society Ltd* [1993] JPL B81, CA; *Tesco Stores Ltd v Secretary of State for the Environment and Others* [1995] 2 All ER 636, HL; and *Good and Another v Epping Forest District Council* [1994] 1 WLR 376, CA. These cases are authority for the following propositions.

(a)   The tests in *Newbury District Council v Secretary of State for the Environment; Newbury District Council v International Synthetic Rubber Co* [1981] AC 578 (see **3.6.2**) apply in determining whether the benefits offered in a planning obligation are material considerations to be taken into account when the LPA are deciding whether to grant planning permission. There is no requirement that the benefits offered also have to be necessary in the sense that they overcome what would otherwise be a planning objection to the development.

(b)   If a benefit is a material consideration because it passes the tests in *Newbury*, the weight to be given to it is a matter of discretion (governed by policy considerations) for the LPA or DCLG.

(c)   The powers of LPAs under s 106 are not controlled by the nature and extent of the power to impose conditions under s 70(1). Thus, provided a benefit in a planning obligation satisfies s 106(1) (see above) and is not manifestly unreasonable, it is valid.

4.4 Practical points

In view of the law and guidance above, the following points should be borne in mind when drafting and negotiating a planning obligation.

4.4.1 By the LPA

(a)   It is important that the title to the land is thoroughly investigated before the LPA enters into the planning obligation. All parties with a legal interest in the land should be made parties to it including any persons with existing interests (such as a prior mortgagee); otherwise the obligation may not be enforceable against a successor in title to that interest.

(b)   The future exercise of any of the LPA's statutory powers should not be fettered by the obligation. If this does occur and the obligation is later challenged in court, it could invalidate the planning obligation (see *Royal Borough of Windsor and Maidenhead v Brandrose Investments* [1983] 1 WLR 509, CA).

(c)   The planning obligation should be executed either before, or simultaneously with, the grant of the planning permission otherwise the developer may have the benefit of the permission without being bound by the obligation.

(d)   The timing of related infrastructure agreements should be carefully considered. It will normally be preferable, where possible, to have all related agreements (eg, agreements under the Highways Act 1980) executed at the same time as the planning obligation.

(e)   Consideration should be given as to whether the obligation ought, in the circumstances of the case, to provide that liability under the obligation will cease once the owner of the interest parts with it. In the absence of such a provision, liability will continue against not only the original covenantor(s) but also against all subsequent successors in title to him (them).

(f)   If there is a disagreement about the inclusion of a particular term in the planning obligation, the LPA should consider whether it is within the guidance contained in Circular 5/05. If it is doubtful, or may be considered excessive, the LPA may find that the developer will appeal and offer a unilateral undertaking on the appeal (see further **4.6**).

(g)   Consideration should also be given as to whether a clause should be included providing for payment of the LPA's costs in connection with the negotiation, drafting and execution of the planning obligation. If there is no such clause the LPA will have to bear their own costs.

4.4.2   By the developer

(a)   The draft planning permission should be included in one of the schedules to the obligation so that it is clear from the terms of the obligation what conditions, etc will be attached to the planning permission.

(b)   The developer should try to ensure that the terms of the obligation do not continue to bind after he has sold his interest to a successor. This is particularly important where positive covenants in the obligation are likely to continue well into the future.

(c)   For the same reasons as for the LPA, it is important for the developer that the LPA do not fetter their statutory powers in the obligation. If there is such a fetter, the planning obligation may be challenged later by a third party.

(d)   The developer should attempt to have a clause inserted to the effect that the planning obligation will be discharged or cease to have effect if the planning permission expires or is revoked or if planning permission is later granted for some other development which is incompatible with that originally granted.

(e)   The obligation should not contain a covenant to comply with the conditions attached to the related planning permission (see para B51 of Circular 5/05 quoted at **4.3.2.2**). If there is such a covenant and the conditions on the planning permission are subsequently varied (under s 73 or s 73A, see **3.6.4**) or the permission lapses or is revoked, the conditions will continue to bind the land by virtue of the covenant in the planning obligation. (As an alternative, the obligation could contain a covenant to comply with the conditions originally imposed or as subsequently varied or removed and only in so far as the planning permission remains in effect.)

(f)   Covenants should be avoided which impose obligations (in particular, positive ones) which take effect as soon as the planning obligation is executed (as opposed to when the planning permission is implemented). There may be a gap of quite a few months, if not a few years, between the developer obtaining the permission and being in a position to implement it.

4.5 Modification and discharge of planning obligations (s 106A)

4.5.1 The power to modify or discharge

A planning obligation may be modified or discharged by either agreement between the LPA and the person(s) against whom it is then enforceable, or by application by such person to the LPA, or by appeal to the DCLG.

4.5.2 Application for modification or discharge

A person against whom a planning obligation is enforceable may, at any time after the expiry of five years from the date of the planning obligation, apply to the LPA for the obligation to have effect, subject to such modifications as may be specified in the application, or to be discharged (s 106A(3)–(4)).

4.5.3 Determination of application by the LPA

The LPA must notify the applicant of their decision within eight weeks or such longer period as may be agreed in writing between the parties. Where the application is refused, the notification must state clearly and precisely the LPA's full reasons for their decision and tell the applicant of his rights of appeal (see below).

4.5.4 Appeal against determination (s 106B)

Where the LPA fails to reach a decision in the eight-week period or determine that the planning obligation shall continue to have effect without modification, the applicant may appeal to the DCLG within six months of the date of the notice or deemed refusal, or such longer period as the DCLG may allow.

The appeal procedure is closely modelled on that for ordinary planning appeals (see **Chapter 3**).

4.6 Unilateral undertakings

4.6.1 Introduction

By s 106(1), planning obligations may be entered into 'by agreement or otherwise'; 'or otherwise' indicates that a fully enforceable obligation may be offered unilaterally by the developer. The rules as to the contents and formalities of unilateral undertakings are the same as those that apply to ordinary planning obligations entered into by agreement except that the agreement of the LPA is not needed.

The reason for the introduction of the unilateral undertaking was 'to enable developers to break the stalemate when local planning authorities play for time or hold out for excessive gain … They should be particularly useful in clarifying the position at appeal' (Baroness Blatch quoted in *Hansard*, House of Lords, 27 November 1990, col 907).

4.6.2 DCLG guidance

The DCLG's guidance to LPAs on the use of unilateral undertakings is contained in paras B46 to B49 of Circular 5/05, which state:

B46. In most cases, it is expected that local planning authorities and developers will finalise planning obligations by *agreement*. However, where there is difficulty reaching a negotiated agreement, a developer may offer unilaterally to enter into a planning obligation.

B47. Further, there may be circumstances where local planning authorities may wish to encourage developers to submit unilateral undertakings with their planning application (if possible based on a standard document) in the interest of speed. These circumstances may arise where: a) only the developer needs to be bound by the agreement with no reciprocal commitments by the local planning authority (so long as the authority by whom the obligation is enforceable is identified within the deed); and b) it is possible to ascertain the likely requirements in advance, due to the presence of detailed policies, particularly those based on formulae and standard charges or following pre-application discussions.

B48. Unilateral undertakings, like other planning obligations, are usually drafted so that they come into effect at a time when planning permission is granted and provide that, unless the developer implements the permission (by carrying out a material operation as defined in section 56(4) of the 1990 Act), he is under no obligation to comply with the relevant obligations.

B49. Unilateral undertakings are commonly used at planning appeals or call-ins where there are planning objections that only a planning obligation can resolve. Where a unilateral undertaking is offered, it will be referred to the local planning authority to seek their views. Undertakings should be consistent with the policies set out in this Circular and when completed should be submitted with the appeal or call-in.

4.6.3 Practical effect

Thus, the normal course of events will be to attempt to reach an agreement first. If there is deadlock on this, the developer will then appeal to the DCLG against the refusal or deemed refusal of planning permission. At the appeal the developer will offer a unilateral undertaking which, if it is considered appropriate by the inspector, may result in the developer obtaining planning permission. The unilateral undertaking will then become enforceable by the LPA.

4.7 Community Infrastructure Levy

The Planning Act 2008 will allow local authorities to charge developers a Community Infrastructure Levy (CIL) to fund the cost of improvements to local infrastructure. It will operate alongside the s 106 procedure and its use by local authorities will be voluntary. Where a CIL is imposed, local authorities will still be able to use the s 106 procedure as well in order to fund non-infrastructure matters, such as sustainable housing. The Crossrail scheme in London is an example of a major infrastructure project that is likely to be funded by CIL.

One of the benefits of CIL will be certainty in costs for developers, rather than the vagueness of the s 106 scheme. At the time of writing, detailed proposals and draft regulations are out for consultation until October 2009. Developers have, however, criticised anything that might result in increased costs in the current economic climate.

Chapter 5

Enforcement of Planning Law

5.1 Introduction

In order to ensure that the planning controls set out in Pt III of the Act (ss 55–106) are observed, LPAs are given wide powers of enforcement in Pt VII (ss 171A– 196). These powers are:

(a)   a right of entry for certain enforcement purposes;

(b)   service of a planning contravention notice to obtain information about a breach or suspected breach;

(c)   service of a breach of condition notice to require compliance with a condition or limitation attached to a planning permission;

(d)   the right to apply for an injunction to restrain any breach or threatened breach of planning control;

(e)   service of an enforcement notice (sometimes followed by a stop notice) to secure compliance with planning controls.

Before looking at these powers in more detail, though, it is necessary to set out some basic definitions and time limits which apply to enforcement generally and to consider certificates of lawful use or development which can provide immunity from enforcement action.

5.2 Definitions and time limits

5.2.1 Definitions (s 171A)

For the purposes of the Act:

(a)   A 'breach of planning control' occurs when development is carried out without the requisite planning permission or when any condition or limitation attached to a permission is not complied with.

(b)   'Taking enforcement action' means the issue of an enforcement notice or the service of a breach of condition notice.

5.2.2 Time limits (s 171B)

The LPA can take enforcement action only if they do so within the appropriate time limits. There are two of these:

(a)   Where the breach of planning control consists of:

    (i)   operational development carried out without planning permission; or

(ii)   a change of use of any building to use as a single dwelling house;

the LPA must take enforcement action within four years from the date on which the operations were substantially completed or the change of use occurred (as the case may be).

(b)   With all other breaches (ie, any material change of use other than to use as a single dwelling house and any breach of condition or limitation attached to a planning permission) no enforcement action may be brought after the expiry of 10 years from the date of the breach.

As regards both of the above time limits, see the provisions of s 171B(4)(b) at **5.8.3**.

Once the relevant time limit has passed, immunity is in effect given to the breach. It is therefore vital to check whether the relevant time limit has passed and this in turn depends on the nature of the breach committed.

5.3   Certificates of lawful use or development (CLEUD) (ss 191–192)

5.3.1   Preliminary definitions (s 191(2) and (3))

Uses and operations are 'lawful' if no enforcement action can be taken for any reason, including the expiry of the relevant time limit (see **5.2.2**), and they are not in contravention of a current enforcement notice.

Breach of a condition or limitation attached to a permission is 'lawful' if the 10-year time limit for taking enforcement action has expired and the breach is not in contravention of a current enforcement notice.

5.3.2   Existing development (s 191)

Any person who wishes to ascertain the lawfulness of any existing use or any operations which have been carried out or any other matter constituting a breach of condition or limitation may apply to the LPA specifying the land and describing the use, operations or other matter (s 191(1)). The certificate is often referred to as a CLEUD. (Note that 'any person' may apply; so, for instance, a prospective purchaser of land could apply for such a certificate.)

5.3.2.1   Onus of proof

The onus of proof is on the applicant who must prove the lawfulness on a balance of probabilities. The planning merits of the case (ie, whether or not the development is desirable) are irrelevant; the sole question in issue is whether or not the matters described in the application are lawful.

5.3.2.2   Issue of CLEUD (s 191(4))

If the LPA is satisfied of the lawfulness at the time of the application of the use, etc, they must issue a certificate. In any other case they must refuse one; note, though, that a refusal merely indicates that the matter has not been proved on a balance of probabilities.

5.3.2.3   Effect of CLEUD (s 191(6) and (7))

The lawfulness of any use, operations, etc for which a certificate is in force shall be conclusively presumed. Thus, no enforcement action may be brought in respect of the matters stated as lawful in the certificate.

5.3.3   Proposed development (s 192)

Any person who wishes to ascertain the lawfulness of any proposed use or operational development of land can apply to the LPA specifying the land and describing the use or operations in question.

5.3.3.1   Effect of certificate (s 192(4))

The lawfulness of any use or operations stated in the certificate shall be conclusively presumed unless there is a material change, before the proposed use or operations are started, in any of the matters relevant to the determination.

5.3.4   General provisions applying to certificates of lawful use or development

A certificate may be issued in respect of part only of the land or just some of the matters specified in the application (s 193(4)) or, with existing development, may be issued in terms which differ from those specified in the application (s 191(4)).

The LPA must enter prescribed details of any applications and decisions in its s 69 register (s 193(6)) and must notify the applicant of its decision within eight weeks or such longer period as may be agreed in writing between the parties (GDPO, art 24).

5.3.4.1   Appeals (ss 195, 196 and 288)

The applicant can appeal to the DCLG against a refusal, a refusal in part or a deemed refusal (ie, where the LPA fails to determine the application within the relevant time). The time limit is six months from the date of notification of the decision or the deemed refusal.

Further appeal lies to the High Court within six weeks of the decision of the DCLG.

5.3.4.2   Offences (s 194)

It is an offence for any person to procure a particular decision on an application by knowingly or recklessly making a statement which is misleading or false in a material particular, or (with intent to deceive) using a document which is false or misleading in a material particular or withholding any material information.

If a statement was made or a document was used which was false or misleading in a material particular, or if any material information was withheld (whether or not this was done knowingly or recklessly or with intent to deceive), the LPA may revoke the certificate.

5.4   Right of entry for enforcement purposes (ss 196A–196C)

5.4.1   Right of entry without a warrant (s 196A)

Any person duly authorised in writing by the LPA may enter any land at any reasonable hour without a warrant to:

(a)   ascertain whether there is or has been any breach of planning control on that or any other land; or

(b)   determine whether any enforcement power should be exercised and, if so, how; or

(c)   ascertain whether there has been compliance with any enforcement power that has been exercised.

There must, however, be 'reasonable grounds' for doing so, ie, entry must be the logical means of obtaining the information in question.

In the case of a dwelling house (which includes any residential accommodation in, eg, a commercial building), 24 hours' notice of the intended entry must be given to the occupier. This requirement does not apply, however, to land or outbuildings in the curtilage of the house.

5.4.2   Power to enter under a warrant (s 196B)

A justice of the peace may issue a warrant to any person duly authorised as above for any of the purposes listed above if he is satisfied on sworn information in writing that:

(a)   there are reasonable grounds for entering for the purpose in question; and

(b)   admission has been refused, or it is reasonably apprehended that it will be refused, or it is an urgent case.

Entry is deemed to be refused if no reply is received within a reasonable time to a request for admission.

Entry under a warrant must be at a reasonable hour (except in cases of urgency) and must be within one month from the date of issue of the warrant. Each warrant authorises one entry only.

5.4.3   Restrictions and offences (s 196C)

The person entering the land must produce his authority and state the purpose of his entry, if requested, and may take with him such other persons as may be necessary (eg, policeman, expert, etc). On leaving the land, if the owner or occupier is not then present, he must ensure that the land is as secured against trespassers as when he entered.

Anyone who wilfully obstructs a person exercising a lawful right of entry is guilty of an offence.

5.5   Planning contravention notice (ss 171C–171D)

A planning contravention notice (PCN) (rather than the power of entry) is the principal power available to an LPA for obtaining information needed for enforcement purposes.

5.5.1   Contents of a PCN

There is no prescribed form of PCN although a model is suggested in the Appendix to Annex 1 of DCLG Circular 21/91.

Section 171C states that a PCN may require the person on whom it is served to give any information specified in the notice in respect of any operations, use or activities being carried out on the land and any matter relating to conditions or limitations attached to an existing permission. In particular, it may require the person served, so far as he is able, to:

(a)   state whether the land is being used as alleged in the notice or whether alleged operations or activities are or have been carried out;

(b)   state when any use, operation or activity began;

(c)   give particulars of any person known to use or have used the land for any purpose or to be carrying out or have carried out any operations or activities;

(d)   give any information he holds about any relevant planning permission or to state why planning permission is not required;

(e)   state his interest (if any) in the land and the name and address of any person he knows to have an interest in the land.

A PCN may also give notice of a time and place at which the LPA will consider:

(a)   any offer from the person served to apply for planning permission or to refrain from operations or activities or to undertake remedial work; and

(b)   any representations he may wish to make about the notice.

If the notice states this, the LPA must give him the opportunity to make the offer or representations at that time and place.

By s 171C(5), a PCN must warn the person served that if he fails to reply enforcement action may be taken and he may be deprived of compensation if a stop notice is served (see **5.10**).

5.5.2 The person served

A PCN may be served on anyone who is the owner or occupier of the land to which the notice relates or who has any other interest in it, or on anyone who is carrying out operations on the land or using it for any purpose (s 171C(1)).

It is an offence for any person served with a PCN to fail to reply to it within 21 days unless he has a reasonable excuse. The offence is a continuing one, even after conviction (s 171D(2)–(4)).

It is also an offence knowingly or recklessly to make a statement in a purported reply which is false or misleading in a material particular (s 171D(5)–(6)).

5.5.3 Effect of a PCN

Apart from the consequences mentioned above, service of a PCN does not affect the exercise of any other enforcement power available to the LPA.

5.6 Breach of condition notice (s 187A)

A breach of condition notice (BCN) is primarily intended as an alternative remedy to an enforcement notice where the LPA desires to secure compliance with conditions or limitations attached to an existing planning permission.

5.6.1 When and on whom a BCN may be served

Where there has been a breach of condition or limitation attached to an existing permission, the LPA may serve a BCN on any person who is carrying out or has carried out the development or on any person having control of the land.

5.6.2 Contents of a BCN

The notice must specify the steps which the LPA considers ought to be taken or the activities which ought to cease in order to secure compliance with the conditions, etc specified in the notice. Where, however, a notice is served on a person who has control of the land but who is not carrying (or has not carried) out the development, it can only require compliance with any conditions regulating the use of the land.

The notice must also specify a period for compliance which must not be less than 28 days from the date of service of the notice.

5.6.3 Effect of a BCN

If the person served has not remedied the breach by the time specified in the notice (or by the time specified in any further notice served by the LPA), he is guilty of an offence: the offence is a continuing one. It is a defence, however, for the person served to prove that he took all reasonable measures to ensure compliance with the notice or, if he was served as the person having control of the land, that he did not have control at the time he was served.

5.7 Injunctions (s 187B)

An LPA may apply to the High Court or county court for an injunction if it considers it necessary or expedient to restrain an actual or apprehended breach of planning control. It may do this whether or not it has used, or proposes to use, any of its other enforcement powers under the Act.

Whether an injunction is granted and, if so, its terms, are entirely a matter for the discretion of the court as the remedy is an equitable one. Thus, an LPA will need to show not only that the remedy is expedient and necessary but also that it has taken into account all relevant considerations in coming to that decision, that there is a clear breach or a clear likelihood of a breach, and that the remedy is the most appropriate one in the circumstances of the case. (For good illustrations, see *Croydon London Borough Council v Gladden* [1994] JPL 723, CA, at p 729ff; *Harborough District Council v Wheatcroft & Son Ltd* [1996] JPL B128; and *Hambleton District Council v Bird* [1995] 3 PLR 8.)

5.8   Enforcement notice (ss 172–182)

5.8.1   Introduction

As a general rule, there is no criminal liability for breaches of planning control. There are exceptions to this rule, for instance, where unauthorised works are done to a listed building, or where there is a breach of a tree preservation order or the display of an advertisement without consent. Subject to this, however, there is no criminal liability for a breach until a valid enforcement notice has been served, become effective and not complied with.

5.8.2   Issue of enforcement notice

By s 172(1), an LPA may issue an enforcement notice where it appears to the LPA that there has been a breach of planning control and that it is expedient to issue the notice having regard to the provisions of their development plan and any other material considerations. Issue of an enforcement notice is the most commonly used method of enforcement.

5.8.2.1   Pre-requisites to issue

There must be an apparent breach of planning control and it must be expedient to issue an enforcement notice.

Apparent breach of planning control

There is no duty on the LPA to satisfy themselves that there is a breach (see, eg, *Tidswell v Secretary of State for the Environment* [1977] JPL 104) although with the powers now available to them, in particular the right to serve a PCN, it may be required to do some preliminary research before issuing an enforcement notice.

It must be expedient to issue an enforcement notice

The LPA should not automatically issue an enforcement notice whenever there appears to be a breach of planning control. They must consider their development plan and any other material considerations (which will include advice in circulars and PPGs).

In PPG 18 the DCLG gives detailed guidance on this matter to LPAs. For example, in para 5 it states that enforcement action should always be commensurate with the breach to which it relates; thus, it will usually be inappropriate to take enforcement action against a trivial or technical breach which causes no harm to amenity in the locality. Another factor to consider is whether planning permission, if applied for, would be granted for the unauthorised development in question.

The decisive issue, therefore, is whether the breach would unacceptably affect public amenity or the existing use of the land which merits protection in the public interest.

5.8.2.2   Challenging the issue or failure to issue

A decision to issue an enforcement notice cannot be challenged unless the decision was arbitrary or capricious (see, eg, *Donovan v Secretary of State for the Environment* [1988] JPL 118).

Equally, a decision not to issue an enforcement notice is not challengeable unless the decision is arbitrary or capricious (see *Perry v Stanborough (Developments) Ltd* [1978] JPL 36).

5.8.3   Time limits

An enforcement notice must be issued (though not necessarily served) within the relevant time limit as defined in s 171B (see **5.2.2**). Failure to do so will render the breach lawful.

However, by s 171B(4)(b), an LPA is not prevented from taking further enforcement action in respect of a breach of planning control if, during the four years prior to the new action being taken, the LPA has taken or purported to take enforcement action in respect of that breach. This would enable an LPA, for example, to serve another enforcement notice within four years of one which had been set aside on an appeal or one which had been withdrawn (see **5.8.8** and **5.10**).

5.8.4   Contents of an enforcement notice (s 173)

No statutory form is prescribed but the notice must comply with the following.

(a)   It must state the matters alleged to constitute the breach of planning control in such a way as to enable the person served to know what those matters are, and must state the paragraph of s 171A(1) (development without permission or breach of condition/limitation: see **5.2.1**) within which, in the opinion of the LPA, the breach falls (s 173(1) and (2)).

(b)   It must specify the steps to be taken or the activities to be discontinued in order to achieve wholly or partly the remedying of the breach or of any injury to amenity caused by the breach (s 173(3) and (4)). Examples of requirements that may be included are given in s 173(5)–(7) and include:

   (i)   alteration or removal of buildings or works;

   (ii)   carrying out of any building or other operations;

   (iii)   cessation of any activity except to the extent permitted by the notice;

   (iv)   modification of the contour of any deposit of refuse or waste;

   (v)   construction of a replacement building after unauthorised demolition.

(c)   It must state the calendar date on which the notice is to take effect which must be at least 28 days from service of the notice (s 173(8)).

(d)   It must state the period within which any steps specified in the notice are to be taken and may specify different periods for different steps (s 173(9)).

(e)   It must state such additional matters as may be prescribed. These are set out in the Town and Country Planning (Enforcement Notices and Appeals) Regulations 1991 (SI 1991/2804), regs 3 and 4, which require that the notice:

   (i)   states the reasons why the LPA considered it expedient to issue the enforcement notice. This is intended to enable appellants to direct their minds to relevant issues (see Circular 21/91, Annex 2, para 12);

   (ii)   defines the precise boundaries of the site by reference to a plan or otherwise (ibid, para 13);

   (iii)   is accompanied by a copy or summary of ss 172–177, the booklet *Enforcement Notice Appeals – A Guide to Procedure* and a copy of the recommended appeal form.

5.8.5   Service (s 172(2) and (3))

5.8.5.1   Persons to be served

The enforcement notice must be served on:

(a)   the owner: this term is defined in s 336(1) as being the person (other than a mortgagee not in possession) who is entitled to receive a rack (ie, full) rent or who would be so entitled if the land were let; and

(b)   the occupier: this includes any person occupying by virtue of a lease or tenancy but may also extend to licensees if their occupation resembles that of a tenant (see *Stevens v Bromley London Borough Council* [1972] 2 WLR 605, CA); and

(c)   any other person having an interest in the land, being an interest which, in the opinion of the LPA, is likely to be materially affected by the notice; this would include, in particular, known mortgagees.

5.8.5.2   Time for service

The notice must be served not more than 28 days after its issue and not less than 28 days before the date specified in the notice as the date on which it is to take effect. Failure to comply with these provisions is a ground for appeal to the DCLG and, in general, is only challengeable in that way (s 285(1) and see *R v Greenwich London Borough Council, ex p Patel* [1985] JPL 851, CA; see also **5.10**).

5.8.6   Validity of notice

An error or defect in an enforcement notice may render it either a nullity or invalid.

5.8.6.1   Nullity

The notice will only be a nullity where there is a major defect on the face of it, for example, where it does not state what the alleged breach is, what must be done to put it right or on what date the notice takes effect. The notice will also be a nullity if it does not fairly and reasonably tell the recipient what he must do to remedy the breach.

If the notice is a nullity it is of no effect. This is therefore a complete defence to any prosecution brought for non-compliance with it. In addition, there is technically no right of appeal to the DCLG under s 174 although, in practice, an appeal will normally be made at which the DCLG may find as a preliminary issue that the notice is a nullity and that he therefore has no jurisdiction to hear the appeal. Any such finding may be challenged by the LPA by way of judicial review.

5.8.6.2   Invalidity

Other defects, errors or misdescriptions in an enforcement notice do not render it a nullity. In such a case, it can only be challenged by way of appeal under s 174 (see s 285 and **5.10**).

On a s 174 appeal, the DCLG may correct such defects, etc, or vary the terms of the notice if he is satisfied that this will not cause injustice to either the appellant or the LPA (s 176(2)).

5.8.7   Effect of enforcement notice

An enforcement notice does not have to require restoration of the status quo, ie, under-enforcement is possible. Where a notice could have required buildings or works to be removed or an activity to cease but does not do so and the notice is complied with, then planning permission is deemed to have been given under s 73A (see **3.6.4**) for those buildings, works or activities (s 173(11)).

Similarly, where an enforcement notice requires construction of a replacement building and is complied with, planning permission is deemed to have been given (s 173(12)).

Where a notice has become effective and has not been complied with, the then owner is guilty of an offence. In addition, the LPA may enter the land and take the steps required by the notice and recover their expenses of so doing (see **5.8.9**).

5.8.8 Variation and withdrawal (s 173A)

The LPA may withdraw or waive or relax any requirement of an enforcement notice whether or not it has become effective. If they do so they must immediately notify everyone who was served with the enforcement notice or who would have been served if it had been re-issued.

Note that the withdrawal of the notice (but not the waiver or relaxation of any requirement in it) does not affect the power of the LPA to issue a further enforcement notice in respect of the same breach.

5.8.9 Non-compliance with notice (ss 178–179)

5.8.9.1 Offences

Where the notice has become effective and any step required by the notice has not been taken or any activity required to cease is being carried on, the then owner is in breach and is liable on summary conviction to a fine of up to £20,000 or, on indictment, an unlimited amount. The court in assessing any fine must take into account any financial benefit or potential benefit accruing or likely to accrue as a result of the offence (s 179(1), (2), (8) and (9)). Note that the burden of proving ownership is on the prosecutor.

Any person (other than the owner) who has control of, or an interest in, the land must not carry on, or permit to be carried on, any activity required by the notice to cease. If he does so, he is guilty of an offence (s 179(4) and (5)).

5.8.9.2 Defences

It is a defence for the owner to show that he did everything he could be expected to do to secure compliance (s 179(3)).

It is also a defence for the person charged to show that he was not served with the enforcement notice, and that it was not entered in the s 188 register (in which LPAs are required to note all enforcement and stop notices), and that he did not know of the existence of the notice (s 179(7)).

It is no defence to show that the notice was defective because it failed to comply with s 173(2) (see **5.8.4**), although it would be a defence to show that the notice was a nullity (see **5.8.6.1**) or that the LPA exceeded their powers.

5.8.9.3 Action by the LPA

After any period for compliance with an enforcement notice has passed and the notice has not been fully complied with, the LPA, in addition to prosecuting, may enter the land and take any steps required by the notice. They may then recover any reasonable expenses incurred from the owner of the land at that time (s 178(1)).

Where the breach is a continuing one, the LPA may seek an injunction whether or not after any conviction (s 187B, see **5.7**).

5.9 Stop notice (ss 183–187)

5.9.1 Introduction

As an enforcement notice cannot become effective earlier than 28 days after service and as its effect is suspended until final determination of any appeal (but subject to any court order to the contrary), it may be many months before the LPA can take steps to enforce it other than by way of an injunction. In the meantime, local amenity may suffer detriment because of the continuing breach. Accordingly, the Act provides for the possibility of a stop notice to be served to bring activities in breach of planning control to an end before the enforcement notice takes effect.

5.9.2 Procedure

5.9.2.1 General

Where an LPA consider it expedient to prevent, before the expiry of the period for compliance, any activity specified in the enforcement notice they may serve a stop notice (s 183(1) and (2)). Details of this should be entered in the register of enforcement and stop notices kept under s 188.

5.9.2.2 Contents of the notice

The stop notice must refer to the enforcement notice and must have a copy of it annexed. It must also state the date on which it will take effect being at least three days and not more than 28 days after service of the notice. An earlier date may be specified if the LPA consider that there are special reasons and a statement of those reasons is served with the notice (s 184(1)–(3)).

5.9.2.3 Service

A stop notice may be served with the enforcement notice or subsequently but must be served before the enforcement notice takes effect (s 183(1) and (3)).

It must be served on any person who appears to have an interest in the land or to be engaged in any activity prohibited by the enforcement notice (s 183(6)).

Where a stop notice has been served, the LPA may also display a 'site notice' on the land concerned stating that a stop notice has been served, giving its details, and stating that any person contravening it may be prosecuted (see **5.9.4**).

5.9.3 Restrictions

A stop notice cannot prohibit the use of any building as a dwelling house or the carrying out of any activity which has been carried on for more than four years (whether continuously or not) unless, in the latter case, the activities consist of, or are incidental to, building, etc operations or the deposit of waste or refuse.

There is no appeal against the service of a stop notice.

5.9.4 Offences (s 187)

Any person who contravenes a stop notice (or causes or permits its contravention) after a site notice has been displayed or after he has been served with the stop notice is guilty of an offence which is punishable in the same way as for enforcement notices (including the taking into account of any financial benefit, see **5.8.9.1**).

It is a defence to prove that the stop notice was not served on him and that he did not know, and could not reasonably be expected to know, of its existence.

5.9.5 Withdrawal

By ss 183(7) and 184(7), the LPA may at any time withdraw a stop notice without prejudice to their power to serve another one. If they do withdraw a stop notice they must serve notice of this on everyone who was served with the original stop notice and, if a site notice was displayed, display a notice of withdrawal in place of the site notice. Compensation may then become payable (see **5.9.6**).

5.9.6 Compensation (s 186)

5.9.6.1 When payable

The LPA is liable to pay compensation in respect of any prohibition in a stop notice if:

(a)   the enforcement notice is quashed on any ground other than that in s 174(2)(a) (see **5.10.1**); or

(b)   the enforcement notice is varied other than under s 174(2)(a) so that the activity would no longer have fallen within the stop notice; or

(c)   the enforcement notice is withdrawn otherwise than in consequence of a grant of planning permission or of permission to retain or continue the development without complying with a condition or limitation attached to a previous permission; or

(d)   the stop notice is withdrawn.

No compensation is payable:

(a)   if the enforcement notice is quashed or varied on the ground in s 174(2)(a); or

(b)   in respect of any activity which, when the stop notice was in effect, constituted or contributed to a breach of planning control; or

(c)   in respect of any loss or damage which could have been avoided if the claimant had provided the information when required to do so under s 171C (ie, a PCN, see **5.5**).

5.9.6.2   Amount and to whom payable

Compensation is payable to the person who, when the stop notice was first served, had an interest in or occupied the relevant land. The amount payable is that loss or damage which is directly attributable to the prohibition in the notice and can include any sum payable for breach of contract caused by compliance with the stop notice.

Any claim must be made within 12 months of the date compensation became payable (ie, the date on which the enforcement notice was quashed, varied, etc). In the event of a dispute as to the amount, the matter must be referred to the Lands Tribunal.

5.10   Appeals against enforcement notices (ss 174–177)

5.10.1   Grounds of appeal

Section 174(2) lists seven grounds of appeal as follows:

(a)   Planning permission ought to be granted or any condition or limitation attached to an existing permission ought to be discharged (as the case may be) in respect of the matters alleged to be a breach of planning control in the enforcement notice.

(b)   The matters alleged have not occurred.

(c)   The matters, if they occurred, do not amount to a breach of planning control.

(d)   No enforcement action could be taken at the date the notice was issued as regards the matters alleged in it (ie, the LPA were out of time, see **5.2.2**).

(e)   Copies of the enforcement notice were not served as required by s 172 (see **5.8.5**).

(f)   The steps required by the notice or the activities required to cease exceed what is necessary to remedy any breach of planning control or injury to amenity (as the case may be).

(g)   The period specified in the notice for the taking of steps, etc falls short of what should reasonably be allowed.

Note also the following points:

(a)   Whether or not ground (a) is expressly made a ground of appeal, there is a deemed application for planning permission when a notice of appeal is lodged (s 177(5)).

(b)   As regards ground (e), the DCLG may disregard failure to serve any person if that failure has not caused substantial prejudice to that person or to the appellant (s 175(5)).

(c)   Grounds (f) and (g) do not go to the validity of the enforcement notice and the DCLG may vary the requirements of the original notice (s 176(1)).

5.10.2   Time limit (s 174(3))

Written notice of appeal (which can be by letter, although the standard form supplied by the DCLG is normally used) must be given to the DCLG before the date on which the enforcement notice takes effect.

There is no power for the DCLG or the court to extend the time limit for appealing.

Note that if the notice is sent to the proper address by pre-paid post at such time that, in the ordinary course of post (two working days in the case of first-class post), it would have been delivered before the enforcement notice takes effect, the appeal will be in time even if it is delayed in the post (s 174(3)(b)).

5.10.3   Who may appeal? (s 174(1) and (6))

Any person having an interest in the land (whether served with the enforcement notice or not) may appeal as may any person who was occupying the land under a licence at the time the notice was issued and continues to occupy the land when the appeal is brought.

5.10.4   Procedure

5.10.4.1   Documentation and fees to be submitted

By s 174(4), and reg 5 of the Town and Country Planning (Enforcement Notices and Appeals) Regulations 1991 (SI 1991/2804), the applicant may submit with the notice of appeal a statement in writing specifying the grounds on which he is appealing and stating briefly the facts in support of those grounds. If he does not submit this with the appeal he must do so within 14 days of being required to do so by notice from the DCLG. It is important for the appellant to specify all the grounds on which he wishes to rely as amendments adding additional grounds are unlikely to be allowed subsequently.

As there is a deemed application for planning permission, whether or not the applicant also specifies ground (a), a fee is payable.

The fee is refundable in certain circumstances (eg, if the appeal is allowed on grounds (b) to (e) or the enforcement notice is quashed or found to be invalid).

5.10.4.2   Appeal forum

There are three possible procedures for the determination of an appeal: written representations, hearings and inquiries. The Planning Inspectorate will decide which procedure an appeal should follow but will take into account the views of the appellant and the LPA. Its decision will be based on published indicative criteria which have been approved by the Minister (reproduced at **3.7.2**).

5.10.4.3   Effect of appeal

Until the final determination or withdrawal of the appeal, the enforcement notice is of no effect. According to the Court of Appeal in *R v Kuxhaus* [1988] 2 WLR 1005, [1988] 2 All ER 705, CA, 'final determination' means when all rights of appeal have been exhausted, including appeals to the High Court under s 289. However, under s 289(4A) the High Court or Court of Appeal have power to order, if they think fit, that the notice shall have effect in whole or in part pending the final determination. Such an order may also require the LPA to give an undertaking as to damages.

5.10.4.4   Written representations and informal hearings

As mentioned above, the DCLG may suggest these alternatives in appropriate cases but they can be used only with the consent of both parties.

5.10.5 Costs

The DCLG or its inspector has power to award costs in all cases, even where the appeal was by way of written representations or even where the inquiry was not held (ss 320 and 322).

5.10.6 Further appeals (s 289)

Further appeal to the High Court, but on a point of law only, lies against any decision made by the DCLG in proceedings on an enforcement appeal. No such appeal lies, though, under s 289 if the DCLG declined to entertain the appeal or set the enforcement notice aside as being a nullity; in these cases the appropriate way to proceed is by way of judicial review.

Chapter 6

Environmental Issues

6.1 Introduction – the problem of contaminated land

The definition of 'contaminated land' found in the Environment Act 1995 (EA 1995) is:

> Any land which appears to [a] local authority to be in such a condition by reason of substances in, on or under the land that:
>
> (a) significant harm is being caused or there is a significant possibility of such harm being caused; or
>
> (b) pollution of controlled waters is being, or is likely to be caused ...

'Harm' is defined as 'harm to the health of living organisms or other interference with the ecological systems of which they form part and, in the case of man, includes harm to his property'.

In determining whether any land is contaminated the local authority must act in accordance with guidance issued by the Government.

Most contaminated land is located in industrialised urban areas and conurbations.

The Law Society has issued a 'Warning Card' in relation to contaminated land, setting out what it regards as 'best practice' for solicitors in conveyancing transactions. The Card advises that, in relation to purchases, mortgages and leases, solicitors should advise the client of:

(a) the potential liabilities associated with contaminated land;

(b) the possibility and consequences of acquiring an interest in contaminated land; and

(c) the steps that can be taken to assess the risk.

Solicitors should also make specific enquiries of the seller/landlord/mortgagor in relation to contamination. In particular, in commercial cases, solicitors should make enquiries of statutory and regulatory bodies and undertake independent site history investigation, for example, by obtaining a site report. Where there is a likelihood that the site is contaminated, solicitors should advise clients that a full site investigation should be carried out. (See **6.3**.)

6.2 The consequences of contamination

6.2.1 The problem of contaminated land

The presence of contaminants in land can have very serious consequences; the site may be 'blighted', making it difficult to sell or mortgage; the use of the land for certain purposes may be impossible, or only possible if extensive (and expensive) clean-up works are undertaken. Potential buyers and lenders should be aware of the legal and financial consequences of buying land which is already contaminated or of contaminating land which they already own.

6.2.2   The legal risks

The legal risks associated with contaminated land are as follows:

(a)   Potential civil liability for damage caused by migrating pollution. In *Cambridge Water Co v Eastern Counties Leather Ltd* [1994] 2 WLR 53, the House of Lords decided that a defendant can be liable in nuisance if he brings onto his land any substance which may cause damage if it escaped. He will be liable for any damage caused without proof of fault or negligence, the only precondition to liability being that he must have been able reasonably to foresee the consequences of any escape, when he brought the substance onto his land. This means that a landowner could be liable for pollution damage following an escape even where he uses state-of-the art technology, and was not negligent in causing the escape.

(b)   Potential criminal liability for offences resulting from migrating pollution. For example, s 34 of the Environmental Protection Act 1990 (EPA 1990) imposes a duty of care to prevent the escape of waste from your control. Accordingly, any waste must be stored safely and securely.

(c)   Statutory liability for clean-up costs (see **6.2.3**).

(d)   After-care and restoration provisions imposed by LPAs. PPG 23, issued in 1994, sets out guidance to LPAs in relation to contaminated land. As well as encouraging the recycling of 'brownfield sites', it also states that 'such recycling can also provide an opportunity to deal with the threats posed by contamination'. So, a grant of planning permission in relation to contaminated land is likely to include conditions requiring the remediation of the contamination. Indeed, the Government expects that most contaminated land will be remedied via the planning process rather than under the statutory clean-up regime (see **6.2.3**).

(e)   Planning constraints restricting the scope of development of contaminated land. For example, the GPDO requires the LPA to consult with the relevant waste disposal authority in respect of any application for planning permission within 250 metres of existing or past waste disposal sites.

(f)   Section 157 of the EPA 1990 provides that where an offence is committed by a company and it can be proved that a director, manager, secretary or similar officer of the company either consented, connived or was negligent, he as well as the company is guilty of an offence (see also s 158 of the EPA 1990).

These risks may mean heavy financial liabilities on the owner or occupier of the land. In one case, a developer bought a site for residential development only to discover that the site had at one time been used as a gas mantle factory and was mildly radioactive; the clean-up costs exceeded £11 million.

6.2.3   Statutory liability for clean-up costs

The Environment Act 1995 (EA 1995) inserted new provisions into the Environmental Protection Act 1990 (EPA 1990) by introducing a regime to secure the remediation (clean-up) of sites which had been seriously contaminated by historic activities. The statutory provisions are supplemented by a series of Guidance Notes issued by the Government. The primary responsibility for securing clean-up is placed on local authorities. Having identified a site as contaminated, the local authority must then serve a remediation notice on the 'appropriate person' requiring specified clean up works to be carried out. In Wales, responsibility for implementing the clean-up regime rests with the Welsh Assembly Government.

6.2.4   Objectives of the regime

The purpose of the regime is to provide a system for the remediation of land which has been contaminated by historic activities. The principal objectives and features are as follows:

(a)   The regime should be fair and balanced, both for those who are held responsible and also for national and local taxpayers. Therefore, remediation will only be required if it is reasonable, having regard to the cost of effecting it and the seriousness of the harm which the contamination is causing.

(b)   The regime only applies to remediation of historic contamination which is not covered by other existing pollution controls. Current and future pollution will be dealt with under existing controls. Therefore, for example, the regime will not apply when the contamination can be dealt with through the planning permission system.

(c)   The 'polluter pays' principle will apply. This means that the primary responsibility for the remediation will rest with the actual polluter. However, if the polluter cannot be found, then 'innocent' owners or occupiers may be held liable.

(d)   The regime is designed to address only the most heavily contaminated sites which are causing an unacceptable level of harm or a significant possibility of harm to the environment.

(e)   Whether or not a certain degree of harm is considered to be unacceptable will be assessed in light of current uses of the land in question and the level of clean-up required will be gauged according to such use. Therefore, a lower level of clean-up may be required of a site in an industrial area than of a site which is being used for residential purposes. Contamination which might cause problems for a more sensitive future use of land is irrelevant, since this will be addressed as part of the planning permission process at the relevant time.

(f)   Liability is strict, retrospective and is not dependent on culpability. Therefore it is irrelevant if a polluter, at the time of carrying out his polluting activity, was not acting unlawfully in any way.

(g)   Liability is limitless in time. It is irrelevant how long ago the polluting act may have occurred.

6.2.5   What is contaminated land?

Contaminated land is any land which appears to the local authority to be in such a condition, by reason of substances in, on or under the land that:

(a)   significant harm is being caused or there is a significant possibility of such harm being caused;

(b)   pollution of controlled waters is being, or is likely to be, caused. (EPA 1990, s 78A)

For land to be designated as contaminated land, the following must also be present:

(a)   a contaminant. A substance in, on or under the land with the potential to cause harm;

(b)   a receptor. Someone or something which is being harmed by, or potentially could be harmed by, the contamination, for example, human beings, property, flora or fauna;

(c)   a pathway. A route through which the contamination is travelling to the receptor. For example, if contamination from one site is travelling to a neighbouring site through an underground stream, the stream would be the pathway in this case.

6.2.6   How is remediation effected?

There are a number of different stages in the remediation process.

6.2.6.1   Site identification

Local authorities are under an obligation to take active steps to identify contaminated land falling within their respective boundaries. They have specific powers to enter premises and to take samples in order to be able to determine whether or not land is contaminated (EA 1995, s 108).

6.2.6.2   Site designation

A local authority can only determine that a site is contaminated if the authority is satisfied that significant harm is being caused or there is a significant possibility of such harm.

The extent to which the possibility of contamination is considered to be significant will be determined by:

(a)   the nature and degree of harm;

(b)   the susceptibility of the receptors to which the harm might be caused;

(c)   the timescale within which the harm might occur.

6.2.6.3   Interested persons

The local authority is required to notify 'interested persons' once the site has been designated as contaminated land under the regime. This will include the existing site owner and occupier or other potential appropriate persons.

6.2.6.4   The 'appropriate person'

The appropriate person is the person who 'caused or knowingly permitted' the contamination in question. This is the actual polluter (who caused it) or anyone else (probably a subsequent owner or occupier) who knew about the contamination, was in a position to prevent the harm which it was causing, but failed to do so and thus 'knowingly permitted' it (EPA 1990, s 78F(2)).

Persons with this primary responsibility are known as Class A persons. If a Class A appropriate person cannot be found then the responsibility for the contamination will fall on the current owner or occupier of the land (EPA 1990, s 78F(5)). Innocent owners or occupiers are categorised as Class B persons. Thus, if no Class A person can be found then the current owner can be liable as a Class B person. Further, a buyer of land, who discovers that it is contaminated, but does nothing to remedy the situation, could eventually be seen as having 'knowingly permitted' the contamination and thus be a Class A person. Where there are two or more persons within a particular class, there are complex rules (see **6.2.6.6**) for deciding which of those persons is primarily liable.

6.2.6.5   Remediation actions

Subject to any remediation required as a matter of urgency, the local authority is obliged to consult with the interested persons on the remediation requirements before serving the remediation notice. The consultation process cannot be less than three months.

6.2.6.6   Agreements on liability

In relation to both Classes A and B, where two or more persons who are liable agree how the liability should be shared between them, the local authority should honour this agreement providing that the effect would not be to transfer the liability to a party who would ultimately be relieved from paying on the grounds of hardship.

6.2.6.7   Exclusions from liability

Where any liability group has two or more members, the local authority must consider whether any of its members should be excluded from liability. Different exclusion tests apply to Class A and Class B persons, although the Class B exclusion test will only become relevant if a Class A person cannot be found.

The application of the exclusion tests will result in the identification of the people or class amongst whom the remediation liability is to be shared. They will form the liability group for a particular pollutant linkage.

Class A exclusion test

There are six tests which may apply to Class A appropriate persons. These are:

Test 1: Excluded activities. This test excludes certain activities if they are so limited that their causal effect was minimal. This would include, for example, the provision of financial assistance, the providing of insurance, the providing of professional advice, and the grant of a lease.

Test 2: Payments made for remediation. This is where one member of the liability group has paid another member of the same liability group to carry out identified remediation, but the remediation has not been done. If the payment was adequate to cover the cost of the proposed remediation which, if effected, should have dealt with the problem, the first member's share of liability will transfer to the person who received the payment. This will mean that the latter will bear two sets of liabilities: his own and the share which has been transferred to him. This payment can take the form of a reduction in the purchase price, specifically stated to be for the purpose of remediation. In such a case, the seller's liability will thus transfer to the buyer.

Test 3: Sold with information. This test applies when one Class A person has sold the contaminated land to another Class A person and, in the course of the sale, the seller gave the buyer sufficient information which would allow him to be aware of the contamination. The assumption is that the buyer would have had an opportunity to adjust the price to take the contamination into account. The seller is therefore released from his liability and his liability is transferred to the buyer. The test provides that in transactions since the beginning of 1990 where the buyer is a large commercial organisation or a public body, permission from the seller to the buyer to carry out his own investigation of the land should normally be taken as sufficient indication that the buyer had information about the presence of the pollutant.

Test 4: Changes to substances. This test applies where the harm has been caused by the interaction of two substances. If the first person's substance was not harmful in itself and that person could not have foreseen the likelihood of the interaction, the first person is relieved from liability.

Test 5: Escaped substances. This is where a person's land is contaminated by an escape of contamination from another site. The person is excluded from liability if another member or members of the group both caused or knowingly permitted the contamination and its escape.

Test 6: Introduction of pathways or receptors. The original polluter is excluded if there would not have been a pollutant linkage but for the introduction of the receptor or pathway by someone else who is in the same liability group. For example, drilling during the course of building works could introduce a pathway and the change of use of a site (such as from a derelict plot to a housing estate) could result in the introduction of receptors.

The exclusion tests for Class A persons are to be applied in the order in which they appear. In all but tests 2 and 3, the application of a particular test has the effect of releasing the person who falls within that test from his share of liability. As a result, his portion of the liability will be shared by all the remaining members of the class who are not themselves subsequently excluded. In tests 2 and 3, the liability of the person being released is transferred solely to the other party to the transaction.

Class B exclusion test

This test excludes from liability those Class B persons who do not have an interest in the capital value of the land in question. Therefore, Class B persons who are mere licensees, or who pay a full rack rent, are excluded from liability. This means that tenants under a normal commercial lease who are paying the full rack rent for the property will normally be excluded from statutory remediation. However, there may be some provision under the lease which would require them to clean up the site (see **6.2.8**). Freeholders and persons who pay a nominal rent (usually long leaseholders) will not be excluded.

6.2.6.8   Apportionment of liability

It is not possible, in respect of one pollutant linkage, for there to be both a Class A liability group and a Class B liability group. This is because an owner or occupier (Class B liability) will only be liable if the person who caused or knowingly permitted the contamination (Class A liability) cannot be found. However, where the same land has been contaminated by two or more different pollutant linkages and the remediation will address both of them, it may be possible to have two different categories of class members which will share in the remediation.

Class A

Liability is shared in this group according to:

(a)   the proportion of contamination caused by each member of the group (if this can be identified);

(b)   their respective activities and site areas;

(c)   their relative periods of control and the means and opportunities to carry out action.

If none of these factors apply, the costs of remediation are to be apportioned in equal shares.

Class B

Liability is apportioned in this group:

(a)   where the whole or part of the remediation action clearly relates to a particular area of land owned or occupied by a Class B member, then to that member;

(b)   according to the capital values of the respective Class B members, if a single Class B member cannot be identified;

(c)   equally, if the capital values of the Class B members cannot be ascertained.

6.2.6.9   Service of remediation notice

A remediation notice cannot be served in a number of circumstances, including the following:

(a)   the contamination is being or will be remediated voluntarily and the enforcing authority is satisfied that this approach will adequately deal with the problem;

(b)   the act causing the contamination is licensed under another regime;

(c)   regulatory authority has power to deal with the contamination under other controls;

(d)   if the enforcing authority were to do the works itself, it would not recover the costs from the person concerned on grounds of hardship;

(e)   the enforcing authority itself is the appropriate person.

If these provisions do not apply then the enforcing authority must serve a remediation notice on the apropriate persons.

A remediation notice must specify what the recipient must do to remediate and the periods in which the work must be carried out.

6.2.6.10   Sanctions

Section 78M of the EPA 1990 lays down the offences for the failure to comply with a remediation notice. The level of fine depends on whether an offender is an individual or a corporate entity. In the case of a company, the offender is liable in the magistrates' court to a fine not exceeding £20,000 and a further sum equal to one-tenth of the fine for each day after conviction.

More importantly, the enforcing authority may seek an injunction in the High Court to secure compliance (EPA 1990, s 78M(5)). If an order is obtained and breached, the company and its officers may be held personally liable for this (EPA 1990, s 157).

6.2.6.11 Appeals

A person who has been served with a remediation notice may appeal to the magistrates' court (if the local authority is the enforcing authority) or to the Secretary of State (if the Environment Agency is the enforcing authority). The Contaminated Land (England) Regulations 2006 (SI 2006/1380) identify the grounds for appeal, which, along with other matters, include:

(a)   the enforcing authority failed to comply with the Guidance Notes;

(b)   the enforcing authority acted unreasonably in determining that the appellant was an appropriate person;

(c)   disagreement with the requirements of what is to be done by way of remediation.

6.2.7 Impact of the regime

It could be said that the regime set up under the EPA 1990 has not been a great success. One estimate early in 2006 was that only 89 sites had been identified as contaminated since the regime came into force and only four remediation notices actually served. For further information see the Environmental Data Services Ltd website at www.endsreport.com.

Further, the limited case law in this area does nothing to encourage local authorities to enforce the legislation. In the first case to reach the High Court, *Circular Facilities (London) Ltd v Sevenoaks District Council* [2005] EWHC 865, the High Court set aside a magistrates' court ruling finding a developer liable for clean-up costs. The local authority then, for 'financial reasons' – ie costs, came to an undisclosed out-of-court settlement rather than pursue the action further through the courts. A spokesperson for Sevenoaks District Council is reported to have said that the council would not be serving any further remediation notices in future, but that it expected that most contaminated sites would be dealt with via the planning regime. This is the bottom line for a developer. There may be little risk in being served with a remediation notice, but the land will still need cleaning up if development is to take place. This has been the real success of the legislation – it put contamination in the forefront of developers' minds and has ensured that it is considered in full prior to any development or transaction relating to the land taking place.

6.2.8 Landlord and tenant issues

Failure to comply with a remediation notice, without reasonable excuse, is a criminal offence. Moreover, in default of compliance with a remediation notice, the local authority have power to carry out the required works at the expense of the 'appropriate person'.

From a landlord's point of view, he will be anxious to ensure that if pollution is discovered during the term of the lease, he can require the tenant to carry out any necessary clean-up works under the provisions of the lease. Most modern commercial leases deal with environmental issues expressly but in the absence of express provisions are there any other lease terms upon which the landlord could rely to require the tenant to clean-up the site? It is doubtful whether clean-up works would fall within the tenant's repairing covenant unless the pollution caused some physical damage to the building. However, the tenant's covenant to comply with the requirements of all statutory obligations may, depending on the exact form of wording used, be broad enough to extend to requirements under environmental law. Furthermore, if there is a service charge in the lease one of the items of expenditure recoverable from the tenant may include sums spent by the landlord on any necessary clean-up works. Even if this is not expressly mentioned in the list of services to be provided, the 'sweeping up' clause may be wide enough to embrace such work. It will be seen why such matters should be dealt with expressly in the lease.

6.3 Steps to take to reduce the risks

There is no public list or register of sites which may be contaminated. However, s 78R of the EPA 1990 requires local authorities to maintain a register containing particulars of remediation notices served by them. The standard form, Enquiries of the Local Authority (Con 29), has been amended to include questions with regard to the service of remediation notices. Furthermore, from time to time, the Environment Agency, on the basis of the information provided by the authorities, is required to publish a report on the state of contaminated land in an area. Notwithstanding these provisions, there is a very real danger of buying, in ignorance, a contaminated site at a price which does not reflect the cost of necessary clean-up works. Those involved in commercial property, therefore, must make their own careful inquiries to discover whether contamination may be a problem on the site they are buying, leasing or accepting as security for a loan. This may be done in a number of ways:

(a)   A desk-top (or documentary) study. This involves:

    (i)   making specific inquiries of the various regulatory bodies such as local authorities and the Environment Agency to see if any pollution incidents have occurred on the site;

    (ii)   making specific inquiries of the occupier;

    (iii) researching the previous planning history of the site;

    (iv)   checking through the title deeds, including pre-registration documents. Such a check might indicate high risk property. For example, there may be information in old deeds and search certificates relating to previous uses of the land. While a long history of agricultural use may not raise much concern, a history of heavy industrial use will give greater cause for concern. Also, old plans attached to deeds can prove a useful source of information. For example, an old plan may indicate that the land has previously been used as (or is close to) an old quarry. In the same way old Ordnance Survey Maps may reveal useful information.

There are now several commercial organisations specialising in providing environmental searches in relation to both residential and commercial properties.

(b)   Undertaking a detailed physical survey of potentially contaminated sites. The desk-top study should establish the likelihood of contamination being present in which case a physical survey should be considered. This will be very expensive but the risks involved are great and the cost may, therefore, be justified.

6.4 Contractual terms

In some cases, it may be possible to make the contract conditional on, for example, satisfactory site investigations; or on clean-up by the seller prior to completion; or on the buyer securing insurance cover against the risks of liability resulting from past contamination or pollution. Insurance will usually only be granted following an environmental risk assessment by consultants appointed by the insurer and may only cover third-party damage or injury rather than clean-up costs.

It may be possible to negotiate an indemnity from the seller against any future clean-up costs incurred or against damages which become payable as a result of past contamination or pollution. However, a seller will be unwilling to give such an indemnity unless he is convinced that the possibility of contamination is remote and the state of the market requires such an indemnity to be given. As an alternative, the buyer may seek a warranty from the seller that he has no knowledge of any pollution being present on site and that he has made full disclosure to the buyer of all relevant information. Alternatively, the buyer could seek a reduction in the purchase price to cover the likely clean-up costs. As always, much will depend on the relative bargaining power of the parties.

If the buyer considers the risk too high, he should withdraw from the transaction.

6.5 Impact of the Control of Asbestos Regulations 2006, reg 4

6.5.1 Introduction

The Control of Asbestos Regulations 2006 (SI 2006/2739) (replacing the Control of Asbestos at Work Regulations 2002) are mainly concerned with duties of employers to employees, but reg 4 has an important bearing on people who have obligations under tenancies to maintain or repair non-domestic property, or who have control over non-domestic premises or over the access to and from non-domestic property.

Regulation 4 thus affects freehold owners, landlords and tenants.

6.5.2 Duty to manage asbestos in non-domestic premises

Regulation 4 creates a new duty to manage asbestos risk in 'non-domestic premises'.

Regulation 4 imposes an obligation on the 'dutyholder' (who may or may not be an employer) to:

(a)   determine whether asbestos is present in a building or is likely to be present; and

(b)   manage any asbestos that is or is likely to be present.

6.5.2.1 Definition of dutyholder

The duties created by reg 4 are imposed on the 'dutyholder', defined in reg 4(1) as:

(a)   every person who has, by virtue of a contract or tenancy, an obligation of any extent in relation to the maintenance or repair of non-domestic premises or any means of access thereto or egress therefrom; or

(b)   in relation to any part of non-domestic premises where there is no such contract or tenancy, every person who has, to any extent, control of that part of those non-domestic premises or any means of access thereto or egress therefrom.

The broad definition of 'dutyholder' (particularly in para (b)) means that liability under reg 4 will affect a wide range of people, including all owners of non-domestic property, landlords, tenants and, possibly, licensees.

6.5.2.2 Where there is more than one dutyholder in relation to premises

In relation to a particular property, there may be more than one dutyholder, for example, the freehold owner and the tenant. A landlord may still be a dutyholder even where the lease imposes an obligation on the tenant to maintain and repair in relation to the whole premises.

Where there is more than one dutyholder, the relative contributions to be made by each in complying with the reg 4 duties are determined by the 'nature and extent of the maintenance and repair obligations' owed by each dutyholder

6.5.3 Duty to assess whether asbestos is present in the premises

To be able to manage the risks from asbestos in non-domestic premises, the dutyholder is required to carry out a 'suitable and sufficient' assessment to determine whether asbestos or asbestos-containing material (ACM) is, or is liable to be, present in the premises.

The advice from the HSE is to assume that asbestos is present and that products contain asbestos unless there is strong evidence to the contrary. Therefore, in relation to pipe-lagging, insulation, air-handling systems and wall panels, it is to be assumed that asbestos will be present.

6.5.4 Where asbestos is present or liable to be present

Where an assessment shows that asbestos is, or is liable to be, present on the premises, the dutyholder must ensure that:

(a)   determination of the risk from that asbestos is made;

(b)   a written plan is prepared to identify those parts of the premises affected; and

(c)   the measures to be taken for managing the risk are specified in the written plan.

6.5.5 Impact on property lawyers

6.5.5.1 What information should a seller give or be asked to give in relation to asbestos?

A purchaser will want as much information as possible about the presence and condition of asbestos, and the intending purchaser should ask the seller for a copy of the record of the assessment carried out and any revisions of the initial assessment.

Even if the purchaser does obtain a copy of the seller's assessment record, the buyer will probably wish to commission his own survey, in order to obtain more detailed and more up-to-date information which he can rely on directly.

The purchaser may ask the seller to supply a copy of the written plan. The seller's written plan will be determined in part by the seller's use of the property, proposals for alterations, finances and current condition.

6.5.5.2 Acting for landlord or tenant

The lease will set out repairing liabilities, and will usually impose an obligation on the tenant to comply with his statutory liabilities. The landlord and the tenant will each want a copy of each other's record of assessment and written plan and will be under a duty to cooperate to share this information

The landlord will be concerned to establish that the tenant has complied with his statutory obligations. The tenant will be concerned that the landlord has complied with his statutory obligations, and the written plan will give an indication of what work is planned and might be charged for under the service charge provisions. It may also indicate any problems that the tenant may face in carrying out his own alterations.

In multi-let premises, the responsibility for maintenance of the common parts, services, external fabric and main structure of the building will generally lie with the landlord. The landlord will be a dutyholder and will be required under reg 4 to arrange asbestos surveys to be carried out and for copies of asbestos registers to be produced to each tenant.

Where a lease imposes repairing obligations on a tenant, the landlord should ensure that the tenant is aware of his obligations under reg 4 and be satisfied that the tenant has complied with those obligations.

Where the landlord has repairing obligations, he will probably need to gain access to demised parts of the building to carry out the necessary surveys. The lease will set out the terms of entry and whether survey costs and costs of compliance with the Control of Asbestos Regulations 2006 can be recovered from the tenants under the service charge.

Even where the landlord has passed the responsibility for repairs and maintenance for the whole property to the tenant, the landlord will continue to be a dutyholder: the landlord may have to step in and carry out work in the event of the tenant's default. The landlord will become the primary dutyholder on a forfeiture or surrender, and on the expiry of the term of the lease, however determined.

6.5.5.3   What information should a prospective landlord be asked to give in relation to asbestos?

As with the sale and purchase of leasehold property, the intending tenant will be interested in seeing the landlord's record of assessment in respect of the building as a whole, and in relation to the premises to be demised. The whole building assessment will be relevant in terms of assessing potential liabilities under the service charge. The intending tenant will also wish to see the landlord's written plan as this will give a further indication of service charge liability.

6.6   Energy performance

6.6.1   Global warming and carbon emissions

There has been increased awareness in recent years about the threat of 'global warming' and the impact on this of carbon emissions. Some 39% of carbon emissions in England and Wales come from buildings – 25% from residential and 14% from commercial premises. The Energy Performance of Buildings (Certificates and Inspections) (England and Wales) Regulations 2007 (SI 2007/991) will implement Directive 2002/91/EC on the energy performance of buildings ([2003] OJ L1/65), the object of which is to reduce carbon emissions from buildings throughout Europe.

Although there has been much publicity with regard to the need for an Energy Performance Certificate (EPC) to be included as part of the Government's controversial Home Information Pack on the sale of residential properties, from 1 October 2008 EPCs will be required in most commercial transactions as well. The Government estimates a reduction of around 4 million tonnes of carbon emissions from non-domestic buildings (excluding public buildings).

These savings will be brought about by the following provisions:

(a)   the assessment and certification of energy performance;

(b)   the display of energy certificates in public buildings; and

(c)   air conditioning assessments.

These will be produced by certified energy assessors.

6.6.2   Energy Performance Certificates

Energy Performance Certificates (EPCs) will be required for new buildings or when an existing building is sold or let. The responsibility for the provision of an EPC will rest with:

(a)   the contractor, which must provide it to the owner of a new-build property;

(b)   the seller, by making it available to any prospective purchaser; and

(c)   the prospective landlord, by making it available to a prospective occupier.

On a sale or letting, the EPC must be given free of charge to the prospective buyer or tenant at the earliest possible opportunity, but no later than the earlier of the following occasions:

(a)   when written information concerning the building has been provided in response to a request for information from a prospective buyer or tenant; or

(b)   when the property is being viewed; or, in any event,

(c)   before entering into a contract to sell or let.

An EPC must also be obtained if a building has been modified such that it has more or fewer parts designed to be used separately than it had before the modification (for example, where two units in a shopping centre have been combined or separated) and it provides (whether for the first time or by way of replacement) or extends any existing fixed services for heating, hot water, air-conditioning or mechanical ventilation.

It will not be required for existing tenancies, but will be required on a sub-letting out of an existing lease and on lease renewal. Once obtained, it will remain valid for up to 10 years.

Landlords will not have to provide a new EPC on a change of tenant, eg on an assignment of an existing lease.

The EPC will contain an asset rating and will measure and report on the building's intrinsic performance potential by using a standardised energy performance computer model based upon a national calculation methodology. This will produce a grading (based upon CO_2 emissions per square metre of floor area) on an A–G scale relating to the energy performance standards of the building. (Similar gradings have been in use on certain domestic appliances – eg washing machines – for some years.) There will also be suggestions as to how the performance could be improved, eg by better insulation or the installation of double glazing.

6.6.3 Display Energy Certificates

Display Energy Certificates (DECs) will apply only to large buildings (those with a total useful floor area exceeding 1,000m^2) occupied by public authorities or institutions providing public services to a large number of persons. The DEC will contain both the asset rating of the building (as in the EPC), but will also show the actual energy usage of the building as recorded by gas, electricity and other meters. This can then be used to compare the energy usage of different buildings.

6.6.4 Air conditioning assessments

Air conditioning systems with an effective rated output of more than 12Kw must be inspected by an energy assessor on a regular basis and at least once every five years. The energy assessor must then produce a report commenting on the efficiency of the system and any possible improvements to it.

All air conditioning systems with a rated cooling output over 250Kw must have had their first inspection by 4 January 2009. Systems between 12 and 250Kw must have their first inspection by 4 January 2011.

6.6.5 Exemptions

The exemptions from these requirements are narrow. They relate to:

(a)   small non-residential buildings of less than 50m^2 floor area. The term 'stand-alone' is not defined, but it is assumed that it means what one would expect in normal English – namely, unconnected to any other building. So, a kiosk will fall within the exception, but an equally small shop within a parade of shops, or within a shopping centre, will not;

(b)   buildings used primarily or solely as places of worship;

(c)   temporary buildings with a planned time of use of two years or less, industrial sites, workshops and non-residential agricultural buildings with low energy demand.

6.6.6 Effect of energy efficiency on rental value

What remains to be seen is whether the information disclosed by an EPC, or the absence of an EPC, will affect the market rent or sale price of the property in question. The only way the whole EPC system can actually reduce carbon emissions is if landlords/sellers take steps to make their premises more energy efficient. And it is likely that this will only happen if the market recognises that premises that are more energy efficient should command a higher price or rent.

Occupiers usually look at the overall costs of occupation (rent, rates and running costs/service charge). In theory, a building that is more expensive to run would command a lower market value – other things being equal – when compared with a more energy-efficient building.

Prospective tenants with a strong corporate social responsibility (CSR) may wish to enforce this view more forcefully than other occupiers. Many FTSE 100 companies and government departments publish data each year on their carbon emissions/carbon footprint and set themselves targets in respect of these.

Most FTSE 100 companies now publish a separate annual report on CSR that is avidly read by shareholders and pressure groups. Note also s 172 of the Companies Act 2006, whereby directors of a company are required to promote the success of the company. In doing so, however, they must 'have regard to the impact of the company's operations on the community and the environment'. Such tenants may put pressure on landlords to improve the energy efficiency of their buildings. When negotiating lease renewals or new lettings, some tenants may discount the rent they are prepared to pay to reflect the fact that the building is not as energy efficient as other comparables in the local market.

If it is not possible to improve a poor energy rating without undertaking expensive works, it may detrimentally affect the rental values (and corresponding capital values) of buildings that might otherwise be suitable for letting to that class of occupier.

Even in cases where, in the real world, prospective tenants might not be sufficiently interested in energy efficiency to modify their rental bids, there may be a rental effect in the Alice in Wonderland world of rent valuation at a rent review or lease renewal (see **Chapter 16** as to rent review in general).

In such instances, valuers normally consider comparables and make adjustments for differential factors; even slightly narrow permitted uses or unusual restrictions may be said to justify rental discounts that would never be sought at an actual letting. Comparables are usually actual lettings, and an EPC will exist for lettings negotiated following application of the Regulations.

If there is evidence that the energy efficiency of the subject premises is lower than that of comparables, an expert or arbitrator at a rent review, or a judge at a lease renewal, may well adjust the rent to reflect that difference.

Landlords are not statutorily obliged to improve the energy efficiency of existing buildings (except as a building regulations requirement in the course of a major refurbishment) and premises are generally valued in the condition in which they are found. It is not normally possible, therefore, to assume that the landlord has improved the energy efficiency of its premises.

6.6.7   Other practical issues

Other issues may include the following:

(a)   How much will it cost? It is estimated that the cost of an EPC for a large building such as an office block could run to tens of thousands of pounds.

(b)   Who will pay? On a freehold sale, the seller will have to bear this, as will the landlord on the grant of a lease of the whole of a building.

(c)   But in the case of a multi-tenanted building, will landlords be able to recover the cost via the service charge? This will depend upon the terms of the lease. Existing leases will not make any express provision with regard to EPCs as they did not exist when the lease was originally granted. But should new ones make provision for it?

(d)   When will the EPC requirement be triggered?

The Energy Performance of Buildings (Certificates and Inspections) (England and Wales) Regulations 2007 (SI 2007/991) are potentially wide enough to catch an ordinary sale or grant of a lease but also the following transactions:

(a)   sales and leasebacks;

(b)   intra-group transfers (including large property portfolios, where time is usually of the essence in a transaction);

(c)   transfers of engagements;

(d)   lease renewals and surrenders; and

(e)   right-to-buy transactions.

The requirements for EPCs will also apply where:

(a)   a building has been modified, so that it has fewer or greater parts designed or altered for separate use; and

(b)   the modification includes the provision or extension of any fixed services for heating, hot water, air conditioning or mechanical ventilation.

There are special problems with buildings in multiple occupation

'Building' encompasses buildings as a whole 'or a part of a building which has been designed or altered to be used separately'.

As a result, the duty to obtain an EPC in respect of an entire multi-let building or shopping centre may be triggered by a single letting, or even (it appears) by the decision of a single tenant to underlet an individual unit. Since the duty to procure the EPC would seem to fall on the landlord, a single tenant may trigger the landlord's obligation at a much earlier date than the landlord might have anticipated.

Paragraph 1.2 of the Government's guidance states that where a building is being sold or let as a whole, an EPC can be prepared for the entire building, even if that building is divided into parts that have been designed or altered to be used separately and they have separate heating systems.

6.6.8 Sanctions

Trading standards officers are responsible for enforcing the requirement to provide an EPC. The maximum sanction under the legislation is a civil penalty that is equal to 12.5% of the rateable value of the property (with a minimum of £500 and a maximum of £5,000). If the building has no rateable value, the fine will be £750.

Against this, it is estimated that an EPC will cost a minimum of several thousand pounds for a mid-sized commercial building, and perhaps tens of thousands of pounds for a large office building or shopping centre. This assumes that there are accurate floor plans of the building. If these need to be drawn up, the cost will be higher because the process will take longer.

6.6.9 Green leases

6.6.9.1 What is a green lease?

It may well be that, with the ever-increasing awareness of environmental matters, some landlords and tenants will be looking to enter into leases with a leasehold regime that actively promotes a reduction in the building's impact on the environment. Or to put it another way, that encourages a reduction in the building's carbon footprint.

6.6.9.2 How can this be achieved?

Both landlord and tenant will enter into obligations to achieve this. For example, the landlord will covenant to:

(a)   achieve a specific energy rating throughout the term, with the tenant perhaps paying a reduced rent if that rating is not met;

(b)   for multi-let buildings, separately meter the water and electricity consumption of each tenant;

(c)   repair/modify buildings, plant and equipment so as to improve energy efficiency and to produce lower operating costs;

(d)   instigate a green management plan; this should not be too prescriptive, and should set targets rather than set out specific obligations;

(e)   ensure that all plant and equipment, particularly air-conditioning systems, operate to maximum efficiency; and

(f)   obtain an annual independent audit of the building's performance level.

Similarly, the tenant will be required to:

(a)   fit out or alter using recycled materials, or those that can be recycled (if practicable);

(b)   make all alterations energy neutral or provide energy savings;

(c)   not partition in such a way as to make the air-conditioning system less efficient or that leads to a greater use of energy;

(d)   observe and perform the landlord's green management plan; and

(e)   yield up the premises with at least the same energy rating as applied at the beginning of the lease.

6.7 Japanese knotweed

Japanese knotweed is a highly invasive weed, introduced into the UK from its native habitats of Japan and China for use as an ornamental plant and to help stabilise embankments in the 1800s. It subsequently became naturalised. It can grow in almost any habitat and is now found in almost every county in the UK, particulary along rivers and railways and on brownfield sites.

The plant is an increasing problem for many developers. Japanese knotweed shoots can push through tarmac and damage pavements and building foundations. The presence of the plant on a development site can lead to significant delays and huge costs. For example, effective control of the plant using herbicides takes at least three years. Excavation offers rapid removal, but the costs are substantial and the disposal at a licensed landfill site of a stand of Japanese knotweed measuring $1m^2$ will cost in the region of £27,000. Recent reports have indicated that the cost of dealing with Japanese knotweed on the Olympic site in east London could be around £70 million.

A developer that has Japanese knotweed on its site also faces the risk of criminal and civil liability. Under the Wildlife and Countryside Act 1981, for example, it is an offence to plant or otherwise cause the species to grow in the wild. Japanese knotweed is also classed as controlled waste under the Environmental Protection Act 1990 and must therefore be disposed of safely at a licensed landfill site, according to the Environmental Protection Act (Duty of Care) Regulations 1991.

The Knotweed Code of Practice: Managing Japanese Knotweed on Development Sites was produced by the Environment Agency towards the end of 2006, and provides advice and guidance in dealing with knotweed.

Chapter 7
Matters of Contract

7.1 Joint ventures

It is sometimes the case that a developer will purchase a piece of land and then develop that land itself. But this normally only occurs in the case of small-scale developments. In larger developments it is usual to find that the development will be a joint venture between two or more parties.

Joint ventures enable the cost and potential risks, and profits (if any), of a development scheme to be shared. So a developer might find it easier to obtain funding, and those wishing to invest funds (eg banks, pension funds, etc) can share in the profits of a development rather than just obtaining a fixed return. They may also have more control over the nature of the development.

Joint ventures also enable landowners and those without particular skills in a particular aspect of property development to undertake them competently. So, for example, the cleaning up of a seriously contaminated site would need the involvement of specialists. This service could always be purchased, ie a contractor is employed to clean up the site, but if the landowner/developer does not understand the issues involved it can be very difficult to properly manage such outside contractors. If the contractor is involved as a party to the venture, such problems should be avoided.

A joint venture might involve, for example, the landowner (for example a local authority), the developer, the funder and the ultimate occupier of the completed development.

Before entering into a joint venture, various matters need careful consideration. A detailed business plan will need to be agreed, along with possible exit strategies. The duration of the venture will need to be agreed, along with terms of dissolution. The arrangements for the management of the venture will also need to be agreed.

The financial credentials of the proposed partners will need to be confirmed. The profit share (or share of the loss) and financial contributions of each partner will have to be agreed, along with each party's involvement in the development works themselves. And the form which the joint venture will take will also need to be agreed.

There are various ways in which a joint venture can be structured, and the legal documentation setting up the scheme should be in place before the development site is acquired. No one scheme is always appropriate and the advantages and disadvantages of each option should be considered carefully. Often taxation will be of prime consideration and specialist advice should be obtained with regard to the tax implications of the chosen scheme.

7.1.1 Contractual joint venture

This, in essence, involves the parties entering into a contract which sets out the terms of their agreement. These will include each party's financial commitment and duties in relation to the development. As there is no setting up of a separate legal entity, there is no need to transfer the ownership of the land itself, and each party will be responsible for its own taxation position. Equally, as there is no new legal entity, it is less likely that one party would be liable for the actions of another, subject to the terms of the agreement. But as there is no separate legal entity, there will be unlimited liability in relation to any losses. Thus the failure of the venture could result in threats to the continued existence of the contracting parties.

7.1.2   Joint venture partnership

In a joint venture partnership, the joint venture partners will enter into a partnership agreement to purchase the property. This agreement will again regulate the way in which risk and profits are shared and the roles and responsibilities of each partner. It will usually be far more detailed than a joint venture contract.

The property will be held in the name of the partnership. However, as the legal interest in property can only be held by up to four people, if there are more than four partners the legal interest will be held in the names of some of those partners, with the beneficial interest vesting in all of the partners, in specified shares.

A joint venture partnership, like the joint venture contract, is very flexible and can be tailored to suit the needs of the partners. However, unlike a joint venture contract, a partnership is a legally recognised structure, governed by a statutory code in the Partnership Act 1890. As far as tax is concerned, each partner is taxed on its own share of the profits separately, so each partner is able to chose how best to use its tax deductions and reliefs.

As a partnership, there is no requirement to file an annual return, and the accounts will remain private.

The main disadvantage is that in the traditional unlimited liability partnership, each partner will be wholly liable for the debts and obligations of the partnership, so the partners have to know and trust each other to a very high degree. Moreover, each partner will have the authority to bind the partnership and its co-partners when dealing with third parties.

However, parties can now choose to use a limited liability partnership (LLP). An LLP shares many of the features of a normal partnership, but it also offers reduced personal responsibility for business debts. Unlike members of ordinary partnerships, the LLP itself, not the individual partners, is responsible for any debts that it incurs.

Another disadvantage of any form of partnership is the fact that the property is likely to be transferred to the partnership at the outset and out of it on dissolution. This will give rise to expense and a tax charge on each occasion.

However, joint venture partnerships have been commonly used to acquire property and are preferable to a simple contractual relationship where a long-term, complex project is contemplated.

7.1.3   Special purpose vehicle companies

This is a limited company set up for a particular purpose, eg to develop a particular site.

The special purpose vehicle company (SPV) may be a subsidiary of just one company, but it can also be a jointly owned subsidiary of several companies.

The companies that set up the SPV are shareholders in it and have all of the usual rights of a shareholder. Different companies can invest different amounts in the property that the SPV purchases and receive differing profit shares.

A key advantage of using an SPV is that the SPV will have limited liability. This means that the risk of a particular business venture can be isolated from the other businesses of the companies involved. If the property investment turns out to be a very bad one and the SPV becomes insolvent, the other interests of the shareholding companies are protected.

Another reason for choosing an SPV is that it is possible to transfer ownership of the property by selling the shares in the SPV company, rather than by transferring the property itself. The benefit of this comes from the way stamp duty is charged. Stamp duty land tax (SDLT) is paid at the rate of 4% of the purchase price for all property costing more than £500,000. However, if you sell shares in a company, stamp duty is paid at the rate of 0.55% on the consideration. There are, however, special anti-avoidance SDLT rules which need to be considered in this context. As always, specialist taxation advice will be needed. Note also that although it is the buyer, rather than the seller, who pays the SDLT and who therefore benefits from the saving, as the buyer will be making an SDLT saving, it may be prepared to pay a higher purchase price for the SPV than for the property, so the seller benefits too.

However, as a limited company governed by the Companies Acts, annual returns must be filed, which will result in a lack of privacy as to the company's structure and finances. There are also taxation issues other than SDLT to consider. The SPV itself will be assessed to corporation tax on the rental income and on capital gains from the property held as an investment, and the shareholder companies will pay tax on the dividends issued by the SPV.

An SPV is perhaps more suited to a project which involves the carrying out of a development which is then to be disposed of within a short period of its completion, rather than a long-term investment.

7.2 The contract of sale

As in residential conveyancing, it is the seller's solicitor who will draft the contract of sale, in duplicate, for submission to the buyer's solicitor for approval. The seller's solicitor may use the Standard Commercial Property Conditions form of contract and will draft the contract adopting the same drafting principles applicable in residential conveyancing. Further, on the sale of a green field site, where the seller's main interest is in the receipt of money, and the buyer's in obtaining vacant possession, he will include clauses similar to those used in residential conveyancing. It is only where matters are complicated (eg, by the need to obtain planning permission before completion) that drafting techniques will differ from residential conveyancing. Many solicitors will use their own word-processed form of contract which will incorporate the Standard Commercial Property Conditions (or some other comparable conditions of sale).

The following points may be noted in connection with a contract to sell a commercial site.

(a)   The seller will insist upon the payment of a full 10% deposit on exchange of contracts and is very unlikely to agree to accept a reduced deposit. The buyer, being in business, should be able to meet the demand of the usual contractual deposit. However, he is likely to insist that the deposit is to be held by the seller's solicitor as stakeholder and he may insist that the interest on the deposit (which may itself amount to a sizeable sum) is to be paid to the buyer at completion. Some larger organisations may try to dispense with the payment of a deposit when buying a commercial site on the basis that the size and reputation of the organisation is a sufficient guarantee that completion will take place.

(b)   It will be very important to the commercial buyer to ensure that the contract provides for vacant possession of the whole of the site at completion so that the buyer's development plans are not frustrated. In most cases there is an implied term for vacant possession, but for the avoidance of doubt an express term should be included.

(c)   VAT must be clearly dealt with in the agreement. The danger for the buyer is that if the contract is silent as to VAT, and after exchange of contracts, the seller (being a person registered for VAT) elects to charge VAT on the purchase price, the buyer will have to add 17.5% VAT to the purchase price. The buyer may want to ensure that the contract contains an express warranty by the seller that he has not, before exchange, elected to charge VAT on the purchase price, and that he will not do so thereafter, or that the purchase price is paid inclusive of VAT. In any case, the buyer will want to make inquiries of the seller to ascertain his intentions regarding VAT on the purchase price. VAT on property is dealt with more fully at **10.1**.

(d)   The seller, having entered into a bargain with a chosen buyer, will usually want to deal with the chosen buyer alone and will, therefore, want to ensure there is a clause in the contract which prevents the buyer from assigning the benefit of the contract to a third party. Further, the seller will often attempt to prevent the buyer from entering into a sub-sale of the property by stipulating that the seller cannot be required by the buyer to execute a conveyance or transfer of the property to anyone other than the buyer. (This latter clause does not prevent a sub-sale but makes it less attractive to the buyers since stamp duty land tax will be payable both on the conveyance to the buyer, and on the buyer's conveyance to the sub-buyer.)

(e)   Frequently, the seller will deal with the possibility of the buyer becoming bankrupt, or going into liquidation, or becoming subject to other insolvency proceedings before completion of the sale by giving himself the right to rescind the contract upon any such event. This frees the seller to arrange a sale to another buyer without the delay of having to await completion and the expiry of a notice to complete.

(f)   If the buyer has agreed to pay all or part of the seller's legal and other expenses in connection with the sale, the contract should so provide.

(g)   Express provision should be made, where appropriate, for the grant and reservation of easements and the imposition of covenants. If the seller is retaining some adjoining or neighbouring land, he will be anxious to retain some control over the future development of the property.

(h)   Where the property already has the benefit of planning permission obtained by the seller, the benefit of that permission will automatically pass to the buyer, since planning permission enures for the benefit of the land concerned (unless it states otherwise). The buyer will no doubt want to develop in accordance with the plans and specifications upon which the application for permission was based, but copyright in those plans and specifications will be retained by the architect who drew them up in the first place. The buyer should, therefore, ensure that the contract provides for the seller to assign to him, or procure the grant to him, of a valid licence to use the plans and specifications.

(i)   If the land is sold without the benefit of planning permission, the seller may wish to make provision for the payment of 'overage' should planning permission for development be granted in the future. Where land is sold without planning permission for development, the price would have been fixed on the basis of its current use, eg agricultural. If planning permission for development is granted, its value will increase considerably. The seller may wish to share in that increase and so the contract may provide for the buyer to make an additional payment (the overage payment) should planning permission be granted. The circumstances in which such a payment falls due and its amount will require detailed provisions in a separate overage agreement and are outside the scope of this book.

7.3   Different types of contract

Sometimes the sale will be by simple private treaty; sometimes it will be by way of auction or tender; and sometimes the nature of the transaction may justify a departure altogether from the straightforward kind of sale and purchase contract. There are many types of commercial contracts which can be entered into by a seller and buyer of a commercial site, catering for widely different circumstances, and the agreement between the seller and buyer will need to reflect the bargain they have struck. This part of the book considers two alternative forms of agreement, although in practice, the reader will meet many other forms drafted for use in the particular circumstances of the case at hand.

7.3.1 Conditional agreements

There will be occasions when one of the parties to the contract will be either unable, or unwilling immediately to enter into an unconditional agreement for the sale or purchase of the property, and so arrangements may be made to effect a conditional exchange of contracts. The seller is usually reluctant to agree to a conditional exchange, since what the seller ordinarily seeks is the security of knowing that his buyer is firmly committed to paying over money on a specified date for completion.

A conditional contract rarely serves a useful purpose for the seller. It is normally the buyer who suggests a conditional exchange of contracts, in a situation where the buyer is anxious to avoid losing the property to another buyer, but is not yet in a position to commit himself irrevocably to the purchase.

7.3.1.1 Types of conditional agreements

A conditional agreement may be contemplated in the following situations:

(a)   where planning permission in respect of the development of the site has not yet been obtained;

(b)   where the results of the buyer's local search and enquiries of the local authority have not yet been received;

(c)   where vacant possession of the site is not yet available owing to the existence of a tenancy agreement in respect of all or part of the site, which the buyer requires to be terminated;

(d)   where the property is leasehold, and the consent of the landlord is required (and has not yet been obtained) in respect of the proposed assignment to the buyer (see also Standard Commercial Property Condition 10.3), or in respect of alterations to the property, or a change in the use of the property proposed by the buyer.

Great care must be taken to distinguish between a contract which contains a condition precedent to the formation of the contract itself (in which case no contract exists unless and until the condition is performed), and a contract which contains a condition precedent to performance (in which case a binding contract is immediately created, but if the condition is not fulfilled, the contract becomes unenforceable). In drafting the contract, the seller's solicitor should make it expressly clear which type of agreement is intended.

If the former type of contract is used, then, despite the fact that the parties have entered into a written agreement, effectively they will still be in the same position as if negotiations were continuing since, until the condition has been satisfied, no binding contract exists, and either party is free to back out. The condition must be fulfilled if the contract is to come into effect. If the latter type of contract is used (and in order to obtain a degree of certainty and commitment, both of the parties are likely to favour this type), a binding contract immediately comes into effect so that neither party can back out without the other's consent while the condition still remains to be performed. If the condition is not fulfilled, the contract becomes unenforceable, unless the party for whose sole benefit the condition was inserted, waives the benefit of the condition and elects to proceed.

7.3.1.2 The condition

Certainty is required with conditional agreements. If the court cannot judge with certainty whether the conditionality of the contract has been removed, the court will reluctantly declare the entire contract void. Hence, in *Lee-Parker and Another v Izzet and Others (No 2)* [1972] 2 All ER 800, a contract which was stated to be conditional upon the buyer obtaining a satisfactory mortgage was held to be void since the concept of a satisfactory mortgage was too vague and indefinite. By way of contrast, in *Janmohamed v Hassam* (1976) 241 EG 609, a contract which was conditional upon the receipt of a mortgage offer satisfactory to the buyer was held to be valid, since the court was prepared to imply an obligation upon the buyer to act reasonably in deciding whether the mortgage offer was satisfactory to him.

In drafting the conditional clause, the seller's solicitor should clearly set out what is required to be done, by whom, and by when, in order for the contract to become unconditional. Consider the following situations by way of example.

(a)   If the buyer has not yet received the results of his local search and replies to enquiries of the local authority, the contract can be made conditional upon the buyer receiving what he considers to be satisfactory results and replies, by a stipulated date. The contract should contain an obligation upon the buyer to submit the correct forms to the local authority and to pay the fees (in case he has not already done so). Upon receipt of the search certificate and replies, the buyer should be obliged to notify the seller of receipt, indicating one of three things:

(i)   that the buyer considers the results and replies to be satisfactory, in which case the contract proceeds to completion; or

(ii)   that the buyer considers them to be unsatisfactory, in which case the contract becomes unenforceable, and the contract should provide for the return of the deposit to the buyer, and of the evidence of title to the seller; or

(iii)   that the buyer is prepared to waive the benefit of the condition.

Such a contract is heavily weighted in favour of the buyer, since it is up to him to determine whether or not the condition has been satisfied. A more neutral and objectively based conditional clause could make the contract conditional upon the receipt by the buyer of a set of results and replies to the local search and enquiries which disclose no adverse matters of a kind which would materially affect the value or beneficial use or occupation of the property by the buyer. This type of clause may not be favoured by the buyer since it leaves some scope for argument.

(b)   If the buyer is not prepared to complete without the benefit of planning permission for the type of development he proposes to carry out on the property, the contract could be made conditional upon the receipt of an 'acceptable' planning permission by a stipulated date. Again, the buyer should be obliged by the contract to submit a valid planning application without delay, to serve the correct statutory notices, and to pay the fees for the application. Consideration ought to be given as to whether provision should be made so that, upon refusal of permission (which ordinarily would render the contract unenforceable), the buyer may be allowed or, perhaps, obliged to pursue an appeal. Particular consideration must be given to the definition of an 'acceptable' planning permission. It ought to be one which is granted pursuant to an application, precise details of which are set out in the contract, and which is subject only to the usual planning conditions imposed by statute (eg, conditions imposing time limits for the commencement of development), or which relate simply to the materials to be used or the provision of works of landscaping, or which are conditions which the buyer should reasonably accept. If this clause appears to be too objectively based for a developer's liking, he can be given control over the conditionality of the contract (in the same way as above) by having a clause which allows him to accept or reject the suitability of the permission, or to waive the benefit of the clause.

7.3.1.3   Time for performance

The condition must be satisfied either by a stipulated date, or if none is stated, by the contractual completion date, or if neither, within a reasonable time. It is good practice to stipulate in the contract a long-stop date by which the condition must be satisfied. The contract can then provide that if the condition is fulfilled by that date, completion is to take place within 14 or 21 days of the contract becoming unconditional. The contract should be drafted to oblige one party to notify the other that the contract has become unconditional (eg, if the buyer receives the outstanding local search, then unless the seller is notified, the seller will not know that the contract has become unconditional, and that a completion date has been triggered).

If fulfilment of the condition depends upon action by one of the parties (eg, the submission of a local search, or the making of an application for planning permission by the buyer) that party will not be able to rely upon his own inaction to argue that the contract has become unenforceable due to the non-fulfilment of the condition. To avoid this situation arising, the contract should place a contractual obligation upon the party of whom action is required to act with all reasonable speed and endeavour, and to pay the costs of the action required (eg, search fees, planning application fees).

However, in *Jolley v Carmel* [2000] 43 EG 185, the Court of Appeal was prepared to adopt a construction of a conditional contract that was commercially realistic and practical, and to imply terms into it to that end. In particular, terms were implied that the buyer would use reasonable efforts to obtain planning permission within a reasonable time. What was reasonable would depend upon the circumstances that actually existed and would not be judged by an objective test. It was also implied that the seller would do nothing to hinder the grant of the planning permission. It was held that the buyer would not be in breach of the implied term to obtain planning permission so long as any delay in obtaining the permission was attributable to causes beyond the buyer's control and so long as the buyer had not acted negligently or unreasonably.

7.3.2 Option agreements

Whilst a conditional agreement is useful to a developer who is trying to commit a landowner to a sale of land at a time when the developer is not able unconditionally to commit himself, option agreements have many more varying uses for the developer, and are particularly useful in his attempts to piece together a development site. The usual form of option agreement entered into with a landowner gives the grantee of the option the right, within a specified time, to serve notice upon the grantor requiring the latter to convey the property either at an agreed price, or at the market value of the property at the time the option notice is served. Under a conditional contract, unless the contract is drafted in a manner which favours the developer, the developer is usually obliged to complete the purchase at the contract price once the condition has been fulfilled, even though in the meantime market conditions have caused him to rethink the development. With option agreements, the buyer can exercise the option if he wants to, or he can let it lapse if market conditions are no longer in his favour.

7.3.2.1 Nature of an option

At one time, there was considerable academic debate (for good practical reasons) as to whether an option agreement was in the nature of a conditional contract, containing a condition precedent to performance which needed to be satisfied by the grantee by his serving a notice to exercise the option, or whether the agreement was simply an irrevocable offer (ie, one not capable of being withdrawn), which the grantee could accept by service of an option notice, but until such time, no binding contract for the sale of the property had been entered into. The importance of the debate was that, if the latter view prevailed, the contract created by the service of the option notice would fall foul of the strict requirements of s 2 of the Law of Property (Miscellaneous Provisions) Act 1989, since, although the option notice might well incorporate, by reference to the option agreement, all of the agreed terms, it would not be signed by or on behalf of both parties.

These problems appear to have been resolved by the case of *Spiro v Glencrown Properties Ltd* [1991] Ch 537 where Hoffmann J conveniently described an option contract as a relationship '*sui generis* ... not strictly speaking either an offer or a conditional contract' which had some of the characteristics of each, but not all of either. Whilst not declaring an option to be a conditional contract for every purpose, he was content to view an option for the purposes of s 2 in the light of its characteristics as a conditional contract, which therefore meant that the provisions of s 2 were satisfied.

Once the option agreement has been entered into, the grantee acquires an immediate equitable interest in the land which the grantee must protect by registration of a C(iv) land charge, in the case of unregistered land, or by a notice, in the case of registered land.

7.3.2.2 Put and call options

The classic option whereby a potential buyer has the right (but not the obligation) to compel a property owner to sell that property is sometimes referred to as a 'call' option. This is to distinguish it from a 'put' option, which is also sometimes used in commercial property transactions. This is a contract that enables a property owner to require the potential buyer to go ahead and buy the property, subject to the terms of the contract as to price, time limits etc. There is no obligation on the seller to sell.

Option contracts will normally only be entered into on the payment of consideration, ie 'buying' an option. With a call option, the consideration will be paid by the buyer. The buyer is purchasing the right to require the seller to sell and compensating the seller for the uncertainty as to whether the sale will actually proceed and the inconvenience of not being able to dispose of the property elsewhere in the meantime. In the case of a put option, it will be the seller who pays the buyer to take the risk that he may be required to purchase the property.

Put options do not create an interest in land and so cannot be protected by registration at Land Registry.

7.3.2.3 Uses of options

An option agreement may be contemplated in the following situations.

(a)   Where planning permission for development proposed by the developer has not yet been applied for, the developer may consider securing an option over the land before investing resources into making an application for permission. Once the application succeeds, the option can be exercised by the developer. This is very similar to a conditional agreement, but with an option, the developer may be able to delay the exercise of the option until he is prepared to part with his money and commence development, whereas under a conditional agreement, as soon as the condition has been satisfied, the developer will have to complete.

(2)   Where the land proposed as the site for development is sub-divided amongst landowners and there is no guarantee that all of them will sell. The developer can assemble the development site gradually, by acquiring options over each parcel of land. Once the entire site is under option, the developer can then apply for planning permission (it would not make financial sense to do so beforehand), and then once permission has been obtained, he could exercise each option.

(c)   Where a developer developing a site feels that there is some prospect of his being able to expand the development at some future date, he may attempt to acquire an option over adjacent land which can be exercised when the prospect becomes a reality.

(d)   Where a speculator attempts to acquire options over land where there is little immediate prospect of obtaining planning permission (eg, because the land forms part of the green belt, or is land not allocated for any particular purpose in the local planning authority development plan). The developer may either adopt a wait-and-see approach in the hope that planning policy in the area changes, or (as is more likely to be the case) he may invest time and resources in seeking to influence planning policy to get the land released for development purposes when the next draft development plan is being prepared. In this way, developers build up considerable land banks to be drawn upon when conditions are right.

7.3.2.4 Terms of an option

The option will grant the developer the right to acquire the property by serving a written notice on the grantor within a specified period. In an option agreement, time limits are construed by the courts to be of the essence of the agreement. The option agreement should set out the correct method of serving the option notice, or alternatively incorporate the provisions of s 196 of the Law of Property Act 1925 (LPA 1925) into the agreement. In specifying a time for the service of the notice, care should be taken to ensure that the rule against perpetuities is not infringed, and that the grantor has sufficient powers vested in him to grant an option capable of being exercised within the time period proposed.

The option will be granted in consideration of an option fee, which can be nominal, but is more likely to be a considerable sum, depending upon the development potential of the land. A landowner, realising the intentions of the grantee, is not likely to grant a valuable interest to him except for adequate consideration. When the option is exercised, the agreement will usually require the land to be conveyed to the grantee for a further consideration (credit usually being given for the option fee already paid) which may be fixed by the agreement at the outset, or may be determined at the time of the exercise of the option either by reference to the market value of the land at that time or by reference to the development value of the land as ascertained by a valuation formula set out in the agreement. It should be noted that both the option agreement, and the subsequent conveyance of the land are subject to ad valorem stamp duty (at the normal rate, with appropriate certificates of value). Further, because of the VAT implications of the transaction, the developer should ensure that the agreement clearly states that the option fee and purchase price is inclusive of VAT. There are also capital gains tax (CGT) implications for the landowner, since an option is treated as an asset for CGT purposes, separate from the land itself, which is disposed of in consideration of the option fee.

Provision should be made in the agreement for the deduction of title and the raising of requisitions on title after the option notice is served, and for the other usual conveyancing steps which need to be taken before completion. It is usual for the option agreement to incorporate a set of conditions of sale (eg, the Standard Commercial Property Conditions current at the time of the option agreement).

In many cases, the developer will want title to be deduced before the option agreement is entered into (requisitions on title then being barred), and he will require the seller to enter into a condition in the agreement not to incumber the land any further without the developer's consent.

7.4 Searches and enquiries

A buyer of development land (or other commercial property) will make the same pre-contract searches, and raise broadly similar pre-contract enquiries as a buyer of residential property. This part of the book does not intend to repeat sections of the Legal Practice Guide, *Property Law and Practice*, rather it focuses upon the particular concerns of a buyer of a development site at the pre-contract stage.

7.4.1 Local search and enquiries

The usual form of application for a search and enquiries should be submitted to the local authority in duplicate together with the fee. A plan should be attached so that the local authority can identify the land concerned.

In commercial transactions, consideration ought to be given to the possibility of raising the optional enquiries which are set out in Part II of the local authority enquiry form, in addition to the usual Part I enquiries. An additional fee is payable in respect of each optional enquiry. These enquiries are designed to cover matters which are only relevant in particular kinds of transactions. By way of example, on the acquisition of a development site, the buyer's solicitor ought to consider raising the optional enquiry relating to the location of public footpaths or bridleways which may cross the development site (since consent of the local authority would be required in order to divert them), and the optional enquiry relating to the location of gas pipelines, to see if any run under or near the property (since this may affect development of the land). Prudent purchasers will opt for safety by paying for replies to all of the optional enquiries.

In perusing replies to Part I enquiries, particular attention should be given to information relating to planning matters affecting the property, the location of foul and surface water main drains, and access to the site over adopted highways.

7.4.1.1 Planning matters

The developer will want to know whether planning permission currently exists in respect of all or part of the site, or whether there have been any past applications for permission which have been unsuccessful. (The fact that an application for development was recently refused will be an important consideration for a developer.) He will also need to know what type of land use is currently indicated by the local planning authority in the development plans for the area in which the site is situated. Any existing or proposed tree preservation orders must be clearly pointed out to the developer.

7.4.1.2 Drainage

It will be important for the developer to establish how foul and surface water currently drains away from the property to the public sewers (ie, through main drains, private drains, or watercourses) so that he can estimate whether the current drainage system will be able to cope with foul and surface drainage from the developed site, or whether new drains will have to be constructed. If the site is vacant land, there are unlikely to be any drains serving it and, therefore, he will need to know the location of the nearest public sewer where connection of newly constructed drains may be made.

7.4.1.3 Highways

The developer will need to know that immediate access to the site can be obtained from a public highway, and that there are no new highways proposed in the vicinity of the site which would adversely affect his development.

Some of the information to be gleaned from the enquiries may simply confirm matters already known to the developer through site inspections, surveys, and through discussions between the developer and the local authority regarding the possibility of obtaining planning permission to develop the site.

7.4.1.4 Contaminated land

There is a danger that a buyer of land will become liable to pay excessive clean-up costs in relation to contaminated land. See **Chapter 6** on regarding contaminated land and the suggested ways of reducing the risk.

7.4.2 Enquiries of the seller

Pre-contract enquiries of the seller will be raised on one of the standard printed forms of enquiry or on the buyer's solicitors' own word-processed form of enquiry. Additional enquiries may be raised as the buyer's solicitor considers appropriate. These may focus upon discovering further information about the planning status of the site, the location of public drains and highways, the suitability of the land for building purposes, and possible past contamination of the land. Again, information regarding these matters is often discoverable from other sources, but that alone should not be a sufficient reason for the seller to refuse to provide answers.

7.4.3 Survey and inspection

Even though the land may be vacant, the developer-client should be advised to commission a survey of the land. Primarily, his surveyor will be checking on the suitability of the land for building purposes, both in terms of land stability, and means of access and drainage. However, regard must also be had to the provisions of the EA 1995, and a thorough environmental survey of the land should be conducted to ensure that the developer does not acquire land which could have a potential clean-up liability under that Act.

For a number of reasons, an inspection of the property must always be conducted before exchange of contracts in order to:

(a) Assist in establishing ownership of, or responsibility for boundary walls, hedges and fences.

(b) Discover the existence of public or private rights of way which may be evidenced by worn footpaths, stiles, or breaks in the hedgerows.

(c) Spot the presence of overhead electricity power lines which would prevent or impede development. If there are power lines, the land is likely to be subject to a written wayleave agreement between the landowner and the electricity company giving the company the right to maintain its supply across the land. A copy of the agreement should be requested from the seller.

(d) Discover the rights of persons in occupation of the land. Solicitors are accustomed to thinking only in terms of a contributing spouse as the type of person who has occupiers' rights. However, with a development site, it is not unknown for a solicitor to overlook the presence of several cows in the corner of a field, which is unremarkable if the seller is a farmer, but could be serious if the cows are grazing by virtue of rights of common, or under an agricultural or farm business tenancy.

(e) Ensure that adjoining landowners do not enjoy the benefit of easements of light or air which would impede the buyer's proposed development.

7.4.4 Special searches

The need to make a search of the commons register maintained by the county council will depend upon the type and location of the land being acquired, but the case of *G & K Ladenbau (UK) Ltd v Crawley and de Reya* [1978] 1 All ER 682 serves as a warning to all solicitors of the dangers of overlooking the necessity for conducting such a search in appropriate cases. In that case, solicitors were held to be negligent for not having carried out a search in respect of a site being acquired for a new factory development. If a rural site is being acquired, a search of the commons register should always be made. If an inner city industrial site is being acquired for redevelopment, such a search would appear to be inappropriate. However, between these two extremes there will be other cases where the buyer's solicitor is unsure as to whether or not such a search is necessary, and in those cases it would, therefore, be prudent to conduct a search.

Other special searches may be appropriate depending on the circumstances of the acquisition.

7.4.5 Investigation of title

Title is almost invariably deduced and investigated at pre-contract stage of the transaction.

A thorough investigation of title is required in the same way as in the case of residential property. The developer-client will be particularly concerned to ensure that the property enjoys the benefit of all necessary easements and rights of access (both for the purpose of developing, and for future occupiers of the completed development) and drainage (for foul and surface water). He will also need to be satisfied that there are no covenants restricting the proposed development or use of the land, or if there are, that they will be released, removed or modified, or that appropriate insurance will be available, and that any easements which burden the property will not prevent or restrict the proposed development or use.

7.5   Overage

The College of Law would like to thank the Practical Law Company for authorising the adaptation in this publication of the following section on 'Overage' (http://uk.practicallaw.com/4-200-2514). For further information about the Practical Law Company, visit http://uk.practicallaw.com/ or call 020 7202 1200. © Legal & Commercial Publishing Limited 2009.

Many contracts for the sale of development land will include some provision with regard to the possible payment by the buyer of 'overage'. The terms of any such provision will need very careful consideration by both the buyer's and seller's solicitor. But what is an 'overage' payment?

7.5.1   Setting the scene

Your client wants to sell some land. The price is agreed. But what if, in a few years' time, planning consent for development is granted (or for a different type of development from that contemplated) and so it becomes worth a lot more? Or the sale is on the basis that planning permission has already been granted for (say) 100 houses on the land, but, in fact, further planning consent is granted after the sale for 150 houses to be built? Or, due to rising house prices (well, they might be on the up again sometime . . .), the developer is able to sell the houses for much more than anticipated at the time of the sale? In all of these cases, had the future changes been known at the time of the sale, the seller would have been able to obtain a higher sale price for the land.

But in all cases, it is necessary for the sale to take place now. So how can your client secure his share of that extra development value, should that increase in value actually occur. This is often referred to as being able to recover 'overage'.

But it is not just enough to have an agreement in place which provides for the payment of overage; it is also necessary for the seller's solicitor to ensure that the payment will actually be made – to secure the payment of the amount due.

7.5.2   Overage – what is it?

So, overage provisions are generally used where a seller wishes to be able to share in any potential development value in a property that might be realised after completion of a sale. A seller is thus likely to require an overage obligation from the buyer where there is a reasonable belief that the land may be redeveloped, or that permission for change of use may be granted in the future, or that a proposed development may produce more profit than expected due to changes in sale prices or planning consents.

Overage may also be relevant where the land is sold on the basis that a particular type of development is contemplated, but there is a possibility that a different, more profitable development might actually take place, and the seller wishes to share in the extra profit thus accruing.

An overage obligation requires the buyer to make a further payment to the seller, representing a share of the increased market value of the property after the occurrence of an agreed event.

The seller can therefore maximise its return from the sale by realising the current market value of the property immediately, without losing out on future increases in value by having sold the property before the full development potential is actually realised.

Or, if you prefer, the seller can both have his cake, by retaining the chance of future development value, and eat it, by selling the land now.

It is sometimes said that the existence of overage should not affect the initial sale price, but this is not always true. The insistence on overage provisions in a deal may well affect the initial purchase price that the buyer is willing to pay for the land. It will certainly involve more legal work, and the greater costs and potential delays associated with it. It will thus always be a question of judgement of the commercial issues involved as to whether the provision is justified.

7.5.3 Options and conditional contracts

The traditional overage arrangement was intended to cover development occurring maybe 10 or more years after the original disposition. In the property boom of recent years, the need for overage has often arisen over a shorter period.

But where a buyer is purchasing property with an immediate view to redevelopment, it might be thought preferable for the seller to grant the buyer an option or enter into a conditional contract for the sale of the property instead of insisting on a potential overage payment. Completion would not then occur until after planning permission has been obtained, and the purchase price could then be calculated on the basis of the market value using the actual planning permission that had been obtained.

But, until recently, house prices have risen so quickly that, by the time a development is complete, the sale prices actually achieved may be completely out of line with what was anticipated – so again overage agreements might be more beneficial to the seller.

7.5.4 What's in a name – 'overage' or 'clawback'?

The terms 'overage' and 'clawback' are often used interchangeably, and there is no generally accepted definition of either term – although everybody knows vaguely what they mean!

The term 'clawback' is generally used in the public sector where land is sold at a discount which the seller is entitled to recover on particular events occurring in the future. For example, if a buyer acquires property at a discount and resells within a stated period (eg a local authority house under the 'right to buy' legislation), the discount might be 'clawed back'.

Also, additional payments that become due on the grant of planning permission may be described as 'clawback' in the public sector, rather than 'overage', presumably on the basis that the extra value in some way really belonged to the public purse all along and it is being 'clawed back' to where it belongs.

The public sector also sometimes draws a distinction between payments representing part of the increase in value of a property due to an event such as the grant of planning permission (which it calls clawback), and payments representing a share in the sale proceeds following completion of the development (which is referred to as overage).

However, in the private sector, both of these types of payment are normally described as overage.

7.5.5 'Positive' or 'negative' overage

Overage provisions are sometimes described as being either positive or negative in character.

'Positive overage' methods involve the seller extracting an express promise from the buyer to make a further payment if a particular specified event (such as redevelopment) should occur in the future. The way in which the payment will be calculated and the trigger event for payment must be carefully defined in advance.

'Negative overage' methods, however, are where the seller imposes a restrictive covenant, or another mechanism such as a ransom strip (see **7.5.8.11**), that *prevents* a particular development or change of use from taking place. In such a case there is no need for a specific promise to pay overage, as the seller has control over the situation. The development cannot take place without the seller's consent and the seller can then require payment of an additional sum in return for the release of the covenant or the sale of the ransom strip.

7.5.6   Drafting considerations

As overage provisions usually reflect complex arrangements, the parties and their solicitors must take particular care to ensure that the documentation precisely reflects what has been agreed. This is obvious, but the problem with overage is that this can be very difficult to achieve.

7.5.6.1   The trigger event

The first thing that will need to be agreed between the parties – and clearly stated in the contract – is precisely when the overage payment will become payable.

This 'trigger' event could be, for example:

(a)   the grant of planning permission for specified development or change of use;

(b)   the implementation of such planning permission;

(c)   the practical completion of a development;

(d)   the disposal of the property with the benefit of planning permission;

(e)   the disposal of the completed development;

(f)   the disposal of individual units (eg houses) at more than a stated price;

(g)   the amount of profit on the completion of a development exceeding a stated amount.

Ideally, a seller would like the payment to be triggered, ie made when the increase in value actually occurs – for example the grant of planning permission. Equally, a buyer would prefer to have to make such a payment only when it has actually realised that increase in value – for example on the sale of the completed development. And often, the buyer will wish to impose a time limit on the period during which it is at risk of having to pay overage – five years, 10 years or whatever.

7.5.6.2   The amount of the overage payment

Of equal importance to both seller and buyer is the amount of the payment to be made. This could be, for example:

(a)   a percentage of the increase in value of the land;

(b)   a percentage of the profit made on the development;

(c)   a percentage of the profit made on the development if it exceeds a specified amount;

(d)   a percentage of the sale price of units if that exceeds a specified amount.

The amount of negotiation that might be necessary before agreement is reached on precise figures in relation to any of these can well be imagined.

7.5.6.3   Drafting problems

It will be the solicitors' responsibility to ensure that the commercial terms agreed upon are accurately reflected in the contract. But as well as setting out how the overage payment is to be calculated and when it is to be payable, both parties' solicitors need to consider carefully all the various combinations of events which might happen over the period of the overage being potentially payable.

The solicitors thus need to consider all reasonably foreseeable circumstances in order to ensure that the overage provisions remain effective for the whole of the overage period. This can be problematic given the difficulty in predicting future events – and, as recent events have shown, the state of the property market – over what may be many years.

Obviously, issues such as the possible liquidation or insolvency of the buyer must be considered. What if the liquidator then exercises his right to disclaim onerous contracts? How might all these events impact on the payment of the overage?

And the more complex the provisions, the greater the risk that mistakes, oversights and omissions will occur.

In recent years, a slow trickle of cases involving overage has come before the courts and is now developing into a deluge; a selection will make the point as to the need for care.

Examples

In *Ministry of Defence v County and Metropolitan Homes (Rissington) Limited* [2002] EWHC 2113 (Ch), the parties had not considered the possibility of the developer demolishing only 35 out of 37 houses conveyed and whether this was sufficient for the land to be released from the overage payment. The High Court held that all the houses had to be demolished for the land to be released from the overage payment. The developer's decision to convert the remaining two houses into a shop, rather than demolish them, led to an obligation to pay nearly £1 million in overage.

In *Bride Hall Estates Ltd v St George North London Ltd* [2004] EWCA 141, the dispute was over whether the value of car parking spaces was to be taken into account in calculating the overage payments. The overage agreement was unclear on this and this led to a difference of nearly £300,000 in the potential overage payment. The Court of Appeal held that the car parking spaces did form part of the residential units and so their value was to be included in the calculation for the payment of overage.

In *FairBriar Projects Ltd v Chaingold Ltd and Another*, Chancery Division, Claim Number HC05C00199 (noted in the Estates Gazette, 12 May 2005) overage was payable if the developer received more than £27.5 million for the 89 flats in a nine-storey block near Fenchurch Street station. One of the issues was whether the developers were entitled to deduct £500,000 for cash-back incentives given to purchasers, £637,500 for furniture pack incentives and £600,000 for agents' fees. This should be stated clearly.

In *George Wimpey UK Limited v VI Components Ltd* [2005] EWCA Civ 77, the formula for calculating the overage payment was so complex that one party did not notice that a crucial part of the formula had been omitted from the final contract. (The contract had gone through 10 sets of amendments.) The Court of Appeal refused rectification for unilateral mistake.

In *Groveholt Limited v Hughes* [2005] EWHC 48 (Ch), the High Court considered the effect of a liquidator's disclaimer of an overage agreement on the claimant's right to exercise a power of sale under the charge that secured the overage payments. The court held that, on the construction of the agreement, the right to the overage payments was still dependent on a contingent event that had not yet occurred and the claimant could not exercise the power.

In *Chartbrook Ltd v Persimmon Homes Ltd* [2008] EWCA Civ 183, there was a fundamental difference over the meaning of the overage agreement. The seller was claiming that it was entitled to 23.4% of the net proceeds of sale of each residential unit in excess of a minimum guaranteed amount. The developer argued that the seller was entitled to an additional payment only if 23.4% of the net sale price *exceeded* the minimum guaranteed amount. The Court of Appeal agreed with the seller's interpretation – resulting in an overage payment some £4 million more than under the buyer's interpretation.

In *Walker v Kenley* [2008] EWHC 370, overage was payable if planning permission was to be granted for 'residential flats'; planning permission was granted for flats, but subject to a condition that they were to be used for 'holiday accommodation only'. Was overage payable? No, said the court: flats that could only be used for holiday purposes were not 'residential' flats.

7.5.7 Solicitor's duty to ensure that payment is secured

Although it is the responsibility of the parties' solicitors to ensure that the documentation correctly reflects the precise terms agreed, it is also the seller's solicitor's responsibility to ensure that adequate security is given to the seller to protect the future payment and ensure that it will be made if the appropriate trigger event occurs. Without adequate security, overage provisions may be virtually worthless.

In *Akasuc Enterprise Ltd v Farmar & Shirreff* [2003] EWHC 1275 (Ch), the defendant firm failed to incorporate appropriate provisions in an agreement to protect an overage payment. As a result, the claimant lost an opportunity to obtain a further £250,000. The court considered that it was the firm's responsibility to ensure that the documentation contained an appropriate mechanism to secure the overage payment and that it had been negligent.

Normally, the seller will need recourse in some form or other against either the land itself or the buyer's successors in title.

7.5.8   Methods of securing overage

There are various ways in which overage obligations can be drafted and secured, and the most appropriate method should be chosen to suit the particular circumstances. The methods differ according to whether a negative or positive overage provision has been agreed. Each method has its own advantages and disadvantages and will not always be suitable.

The methods listed below are not necessarily exhaustive as overage is a developing area.

7.5.8.1   Personal obligation

With this positive overage method, the buyer gives a contractual commitment to make a further payment to the seller should a specified event, such as the grant of planning permission or redevelopment, occur within an agreed period after completion (the 'overage period'). This overage method is the most basic and simplest in practice.

However, a covenant that requires expenditure of money is a positive covenant, and the burden of positive covenants does not generally run with the land and bind successors in title. Thus, on its own, a personal contractual commitment is generally inadequate from the seller's point of view. The obligation is personal to the original parties, and the seller has no recourse to the land or the buyer's successors in title. The contractual obligation is also dependent on the continuing financial standing and existence of the buyer and provides no real security for the payment.

It is, therefore, only suitable where the buyer is a substantial body, its assets have been investigated, and the seller is satisfied that it is likely to remain financially strong for the length of the overage period. Obviously, the longer the overage period, the greater the risk of something going wrong.

A personal obligation may, however, be supported by a guarantee or bond which may give the desired security

Advantages

- simple;
- straightforward;
- few legal costs;
- method for calculating overage payment is clearly set out.

Disadvantages

- personal to buyer;
- does not bind land or buyer's successors in title;
- dependent on continuing financial strength of buyer and/or guarantor.

7.5.8.2   Positive covenant and restriction

This positive overage method, like the previous, involves the buyer agreeing to make a further payment to the seller should a specified event occur within the overage period, such as the grant of planning permission or redevelopment. However, in contrast to a purely personal obligation, the buyer also covenants to ensure that its successors in title will enter into a similar commitment to the seller.

A chain of deeds of covenant will thus be created, meaning that the seller can enforce the overage provisions against the buyer's successors in title.

But, of course, the covenant to ensure that the successors enter into the similar obligation is itself a positive covenant and, if not complied with, the only remedy is the personal one against the original party. Again, it is thus dependent upon that party's financial status.

However, to remedy this, on completion of the sale of the property to the buyer, a restriction is placed against the buyer's title at Land Registry. It should be an express term of the contract that the buyer will request such a restriction being entered in the transfer of the land.

This restriction provides that no disposition is to be registered without the seller's consent. The seller will give consent provided that the buyer's successor has entered into a direct covenant with the seller to comply with the overage provisions. The restriction is released when the overage payment is made or the agreed overage period expires. This method may also be supported by the buyer giving a legal or equitable charge over the land to secure the future payment.

A variation might be that individual houses, etc on a development can only be sold with consent. The owner of the overage will consent only if it receives its agreed proportion of the sale price.

Advantages

- commonly used in practice;
- binds buyer's successors in title;
- method for calculating overage payment is clearly set out.

Disadvantages

- preparation of deeds of covenant can be costly and cumbersome for buyer.

7.5.8.3 Mortgage or charge

A buyer's obligation to make an overage payment can be secured by the seller taking a legal charge over the property following completion. Once the legal redemption date occurs (for example, when planning permission is granted or the land is redeveloped), the overage payment is secured by the legal charge. If the overage payment is not made as agreed, the seller can sell the land and recover the overage payment from the sale proceeds.

Remember, however, that in *Groveholt Limited v Hughes* [2005] EWHC 48 (Ch), a legal charge was used to secure overage payments. However, the court found that, on the construction of the overage agreement, the right to the overage payments was still dependent on a contingent event that had not yet occurred and so the power of sale under the charge was not exercisable.

A legal charge can be the most effective form of security and is generally the preferred option where the buyer has no lender. However, where there is a lender, it may be unacceptable – most lenders will require a first charge on the property and the whole point of the charge securing the overage payment is that it will be the first charge. It might be acceptable to a buyer's lender if a deed of priorities could be negotiated to restrict the amount secured by the first charge and so protect the security afforded by the second charge.

Advantages

- well understood;
- seller can have recourse to land;

- method for calculating overage payment is clearly set out.

Disadvantages

- buyer's lender may not accept it;
- deed of priorities may be required.

7.5.8.4   Guarantee or bond

A third party guarantee may be provided by the buyer as security for the overage payment. If the buyer does not comply with its contractual commitment to make the overage payment, the seller can have recourse to the guarantor. However, like a buyer's personal obligation (see above), a guarantee is dependent on the continuing financial standing and existence of the guarantor over what may be many years. It may not, therefore, constitute sufficient security for the seller.

Advantages

- method for calculating overage payment is clearly set out;
- provides additional security over and above the buyer's financial standing.

Disadvantages

- dependent on continuing financial strength of guarantor;
- not easy to supply;
- costly.

7.5.8.5   Seller's lien

If the overage payment is expressed in the contract to be part of the purchase price, the seller may acquire an equitable, or seller's, lien over the property. This arises because the buyer will not have paid the full purchase price on completion. An equitable lien arises on exchange of contracts and it is not dependent on the seller retaining possession of the property. The seller can apply to court for a declaration as to the existence of the lien and for an order for sale of the property (*Hewett v Court* (1983) 149 CLR 639). The overage payment would be payable out of the sale proceeds.

The lien is binding upon the buyer but in order to secure the payment and ensure that it is binding upon a subsequent purchaser, the seller must register a notice of the lien against the buyer's title to protect it (LRA 2002, s 29 and Sch 3). Note that as the lien affects the property before the transfer is made, it must be protected before registration of the buyer's transfer occurs. Either an agreed notice or a unilateral notice can be used.

The main problem with a seller's lien is that, like any form of charge, it is likely to prejudice the buyer's position in seeking funding from a lender. It is also unattractive to a seller as the court may grant equitable relief to the buyer where it believes that the existence of a lien is inconsistent with what was intended by the parties.

Advantages

- simple;
- method for calculating overage payment is clearly set out;
- seller can have recourse to land.

Disadvantages

- unacceptable to lenders;
- uncertain enforceability;
- legal costs involved in obtaining order for sale;

- registration issues.

7.5.8.6   Solicitor's undertaking

In limited circumstances, the buyer's solicitor could give an undertaking to deduct the overage payment from the future sale proceeds following the redevelopment of the property and to transmit the money direct to the seller's solicitor. This method will be unacceptable to most solicitors and few firms would be likely to authorise such an undertaking. It could only be used in a very short-term arrangement where it is clear that the proceeds of sale will be passing through the buyer's solicitor's hands. The buyer's solicitor would need to ensure that the buyer has given irrevocable authority for the monies to pass through the solicitor's hands and for such an undertaking to be given.

Advantages

- simple;
- straightforward;
- easy to administer;
- precise amount of overage payment is clearly set out.

Disadvantages

- suitable for use in limited circumstances;
- risks for buyer's solicitor.

7.5.8.7   Freehold right of re-entry

With this method, the seller transfers the property to the buyer but retains an express right of re-entry. Under the right of re-entry, the property will revert to the seller if the overage payment is not made in accordance with the terms agreed. The right of re-entry must comply with the rule against perpetuities. It must also be protected by a notice registered against the buyer's title to the property (LRA 2002, s 64).

There are problems with this method. The rules on equitable relief against forfeiture in relation to freehold land are less certain than in relation to leasehold land. Section 146 of the Law of Property Act 1925 only applies to leasehold land. The courts may grant equitable relief in favour of the buyer so the seller may be unable to enforce the right of re-entry and it may provide inadequate security for the overage payment. Lenders are also unlikely to be familiar with freeholds subject to rights of re-entry, and borrowing against the land may prove problematic.

Advantages

- simple – method for calculating overage is payment clearly set out;
- seller can have recourse to land.

Disadvantages

- uncertain enforceability;
- unacceptable to lenders.

7.5.8.8   Grant of lease – positive overage covenant

The seller can grant the buyer a lease that includes provision for the rent to take account of any increased value due to future development or change of use. Alternatively, the lease may provide for the tenant to make a lump sum payment. Provided that it is a tenant covenant, rather than a covenant 'expressed to be personal', under the Landlord and Tenant (Covenants) Act 1995 the obligation will be enforceable against the tenant's successor in title in the usual way. If the tenant defaults, the landlord can forfeit the lease.

The buyer may in addition be given an option to purchase the freehold that becomes exercisable on the overage payment being made.

Advantages

- commonly used;
- well understood;
- binds buyer's successors in title;
- flexible;
- method for calculating overage payment is clearly set out.

Disadvantages

- legal costs;
- leasehold structure may not suit all situations;
- tenant's statutory rights.

7.5.8.9 Reverse option

Reverse options are occasionally used to secure an overage payment. Here, the buyer purchases the property and grants a call option back in favour of the seller. The seller can thus require the developer to re-sell the property to it once the agreed trigger event has occurred. The resale price will reflect the fact that the seller is to share in the increased development value due to the planning permission having been obtained or the redevelopment having occurred. However, the option is used purely as a vehicle for securing payment with no real intention of it being exercised. Instead, the option is released by the seller in return for a payment from the developer.

The call option will need to be protected by registration of an agreed notice or a unilateral notice against the buyer's title.

Advantages

- method for calculating overage payment is clearly set out;
- option can be registered at Land Registry;
- binds buyer's successors in title.

Disadvantages

- uncommon;
- terms for exercising option must be strictly observed;
- legal costs;
- rule against perpetuities;
- unattractive to lenders.

7.5.8.10 Restrictive covenant

With this negative overage method, the buyer covenants with the seller that it will not build on the land or use it for specified activities, ie the activities that it is anticipated may occur to trigger the overage payment. The land can then only be redeveloped or used for the prohibited activity if the covenant is released. In return for entering into a deed of release, the seller can demand a payment. Once the overage payment has been made, the covenant is released.

This method is likely to be used where there is no immediate prospect of development. As long as the covenant is restrictive in nature, it will run with the land and bind the buyer's successors in title provided it is protected by a notice against the title at Land Registry.

There are, however, several issues with this method. The seller must retain some land that genuinely benefits from the restrictive covenant and a ransom strip is insufficient for this purpose (*Re Withenlee*, Lands Tribunal, 3 April 2003). As the seller must retain some land of substance, issues will arise throughout the overage period in relation to occupier's liability, insurance, trespassers and other property maintenance matters in relation to that retained land. The overage payment may also not be enforceable as courts will not generally enforce restrictive covenants where the principal aim is to obtain payment in return for consent or a release of the covenant, as opposed to genuinely preserving amenity of land.

If the covenant prohibits development unless the buyer obtains the seller's prior consent to the proposed works, it is likely that the courts will imply a term that the seller cannot unreasonably withhold consent to the proposals.

The amount that the seller can obtain from the buyer will be unknown until an attempt is made to enforce the covenant. In *Harris v Williams-Wynne* [2005] EWHC 151 (Ch), the defendant claimed damages for breach of a covenant against building, representing half of the development profit of £62,000. The High Court awarded damages, but these were only a small proportion of the claimed development value.

Further, the Lands Tribunal has the power to discharge or modify a restrictive covenant if it is obsolete, impedes a reasonable use of the land, or the discharge or modification would cause no injury.

Advantages

- commonly used in practice;
- binds buyer's successors in title;
- few legal costs.

Disadvantages

- seller must retain benefiting land;
- amount of overage payment is unknown;
- payment may be unenforceable;
- Land Registry may not remove notice.

7.5.8.11 Ransom strips

Another negative overage method is for the seller to retain ownership of a strip of land adjacent to, or across, the property being sold which effectively prevents the buyer developing the land.

If, for example, the development would require access over the ransom strip to the public highway, the buyer will not be able to proceed unless the seller sells the ransom strip or grants a right of way over it for the purposes of the development in return for payment. If the buyer needs access over the ransom strip pending any future development, for example, for agricultural purposes, care must be taken in drafting of the right of way to ensure that it cannot be used for any other purpose.

One hazard with a ransom strip is that the buyer might be able to negotiate access over neighbouring land, rendering the ransom strip worthless. Its existence may also have an effect on the property's market value and the amount that the seller realises on the actual sale to the buyer. It may also cause difficulties for the buyer in raising finance on the property.

As the seller will continue to own the ransom strip, issues will arise throughout the overage period in relation to occupier's liability, insurance, trespassers and other property maintenance matters. Care must also be taken that the buyer does not acquire title to the ransom strip by adverse possession or acquire rights over it by way of prescription. However, the provisions of the LRA 2002 in relation to obtaining adverse possession to registered land as from 13 October 2003 will reduce the risk of the buyer acquiring title by adverse possession.

Even when this overage method is successful in securing overage, the amount achieved by the ransom strip owner may be less than the seller anticipated.

In *Freeguard v Royal Bank of Scotland* [2005] EWHC 978 (Ch), the High Court held that the overage value was determined by the price that could be obtained from the person with the special interest in buying the strip, ie the owner of the ransomed land. This was substantially less than the 33% to 50% share of the ransomed land's development value which the owner of the strip wanted.

Advantages

- may be effective to prevent development;
- few legal costs.

Disadvantages

- buyer may negotiate alternative access;
- effect on sale price;
- continuing ownership issues;
- value of overage may be less than expected.

7.5.8.12 Reservation of rights

Instead of a ransom strip, the seller might retain certain rights over the property in favour of the seller's retained land which would prevent development of the property unless they are released. The buyer would then be forced to make an overage payment to the seller in order to develop the property. Rights that might be reserved in or over the property to secure an overage payment include a right of way, rights to air space, sporting rights or rights to light.

The effectiveness of these methods depends on the extent to which the development would interfere with the rights, the willingness or otherwise of the courts to grant an injunction, or the amount of damages that might be awarded instead for interference with the rights.

Enforceability depends on the discretion of the courts, and the payment actually received may be substantially less than the desired overage payment.

Alternatively, on the sale to the buyer, the seller could refuse to grant rights over its retained land that would be necessary for any development. If the buyer wishes to develop the property in the future, it would need to seek the grant of the required rights from the seller in return for money. It may, however, be able to negotiate the grant of alternative rights over neighbouring land from a third party. Examples of rights that might be necessary over the seller's retained land for future development include rights to passage of services (although statutory undertakers may have compulsory powers), oversailing rights for cranes or rights of way.

Advantages

- may effectively prevent development;
- flexible;
- few legal costs.

Disadvantages

- uncertain enforceability;
- amount of overage payment unknown;
- damages awarded by courts may be less than desired overage payment.

7.5.8.13   Grant of lease – restricting development

A seller can impose a negative overage obligation on a buyer by granting a long lease of the property and including a user clause that absolutely prohibits a particular use or alterations. If the buyer wishes to redevelop, it would need the seller's consent as landlord, and the seller could impose a payment as a condition of its consent.

This method is similar to imposing a freehold restrictive covenant, but the seller need not retain any other land. However, as with freehold covenants, the Lands Tribunal has the power to modify or release restrictive leasehold covenants if the term is for more than 40 years and at least 25 years have expired. The method is unlikely to be suitable, therefore, if the overage period exceeds 25 years.

Although the landlord will have a right of re-entry if the buyer should breach the terms of the lease, the courts might grant relief against forfeiture under s 146 of the Law of Property Act 1925. The seller's ability to have recourse to the property will, therefore, be dependent on the courts' discretion. The existence of the covenant may have an effect on the price paid by the buyer and the value of the lease on future assignment.

Advantages

- seller does not need any retained land;
- binds buyer's successors in title;
- well understood.

Disadvantages

- uncertain enforceability;
- Lands Tribunal has power to modify;
- legal costs;
- method for calculating overage payment is not specified;
- tenant's statutory rights.

Chapter 8
Construction Projects

8.1 Introduction

Having completed the acquisition of a site which is physically capable of being developed, and which is not incumbered in a way which would impede development, and having obtained satisfactory planning permission and sufficient funds, the client will now want to obtain a building which will be completed within a satisfactory time scale, within budget, and in accordance with his specified requirements.

8.2 Who will be involved? The design and construction team

8.2.1 The employer

The employer is the owner of the site who will employ various professionals to design and construct a building upon his land. For the purposes of this book, the employer is a client who has acquired a site with the aim of developing it, and who will grant leases of the completed development. This part of the book assumes that the client, whilst involved in commercial property, is not a member of the construction industry, and will, therefore, need to employ other persons in connection with design and construction.

8.2.2 The building contractor

In a traditional building contract the building contractor is engaged by the employer to construct a building in accordance with plans and specifications prepared by the employer's architect. The contractor (sometimes called the 'main contractor') will enter into a building contract with the employer, although he may not necessarily carry out all, or indeed any, of the building works. Instead, the contractor may enter into sub-contracts with other builders who will carry out the work. The sub-contractors are likely to be specialists in particular areas of the construction industry, so that, in a large project, there may be several different sub-contractors who execute works on different parts of the development. In some building contracts, the employer chooses who will be the sub-contractors, in which case they are called 'nominated sub-contractors'. In other building contracts, it will be the main contractor's responsibility to select the sub-contractors, in which case they are termed 'domestic sub-contractors'. Most traditional forms of building contract only permit sub-contracting with the prior written consent of the employer (to be given through the agency of his architect).

There are many different standard forms of building contract used in the construction industry and this book does not intend a detailed analysis of the obligations of employer and main contractor. The basic obligations of the employer under most traditional forms of contract are to give up possession of the site to the contractor (to enable uninterrupted building to commence), not to interfere with the execution of building works, to appoint an architect for the purposes of the contract (ie, to supervise the execution of the works, and to certify when the building has reached the stage of 'practical completion'), to nominate sub-contractors to carry out the works (unless the contractor is to select his own), and to pay the price payable to the contractor as and when the contract requires.

In return, the contractor agrees to complete the work set out in the contract in the form of the architect's plans and specifications. Whether the works have been satisfactorily completed is a matter to be judged by the architect who, if satisfied, will issue a certificate of practical completion which will entitle the contractor to receive full payment of the contract price, and the employer to resume possession of the site for the purpose of granting leases to his tenants. Obligations as to quality and fitness of the building materials are implied under s 4 of the Supply of Goods and Services Act 1982, and s 13 of that Act implies a term that the contractor will exercise reasonable care and skill in the performance of building services. However, notwithstanding his implied obligations, the contractor is likely to have entered into a building contract which contains an express obligation to execute the works in accordance with a standard prescribed by the contract.

It should be noted that there is no privity of contract between the employer and the sub-contractors (whether they are nominated or domestic) since it is the main contractor who engages their services. However, it may be possible to establish an implied collateral contract between them, as in *Shanklin Pier Co Ltd v Detel Products Ltd* [1951] 2 KB 854, and further the main contractor may also be liable under the terms of the main contract in respect of the acts or omissions of the sub-contractors.

Some more modern forms of building contract operate quite differently from the traditional form. Design-and-build contracts are increasingly being used in new developments. In simple terms, all of the design work is carried out by the main contractor's architect and, therefore, the employer does not engage an architect. The employer will enter into a single contract with the main contractor under which the contractor agrees both to design (or cause to be designed), and to build. This means that having indicated his requirements to the main contractor, all the employer has to do is wait for the building to be finished, whereupon he can grant a lease of the completed building to a tenant.

8.2.3   The architect

In a traditional form of contract the architect is engaged by the employer to carry out various tasks in relation to the design of the building. Broadly speaking, the architect prepares plans and specifications of the works required by the employer from which the builders will take their instructions, and he will supervise the execution of those works by the building contractor (or sub-contractors) in accordance with the plans and specifications. When the architect is satisfied that the works required by the building contract have been completed, he will issue a certificate of practical completion.

8.2.4   The quantity surveyor

The quantity surveyor is engaged by the employer (or by the architect on behalf of the employer) to estimate the quantities of the materials to be used, and to set them into bills of quantities. What the quantity surveyor does is to measure the amount of work and materials which will be necessary to complete construction in accordance with the architect's plans and specifications. On the basis of his bills of quantities, building contractors will be able to work out the amount of their tenders.

8.2.5   The engineers

In large construction projects, there may be a team of consulting engineers, including a structural engineer, engaged by the employer to give advice on structural design, and mechanical, electrical, heating and ventilating engineers, who give advice to the employer on matters within their areas of competence.

The architect, quantity surveyor and consulting engineers, as professional people, owe the employer a duty by contract to carry out the work required of them with proper care. The standard of care expected is the standard of the ordinary skilled man exercising and professing to have that special skill. If any one of them falls below that standard, or below any higher standard of care set by the contract of engagement under which he is engaged, he will be liable in damages for breach of contract.

8.3   Duties owed to third parties

If the project results in the employer obtaining a completed building which turns out to be defective by reason of its design, or the materials used, or by reason of the manner in which it was constructed, the employer is likely to have a claim for breach of contract against those members of the design and construction team who caused the defect. Contractual damages are assessed under the rule in *Hadley v Baxendale* (1854) 9 Exch 341 and are likely to enable the employer to recover any costs incurred in carrying out remedial repairs, subject to the normal limitation rules under the Limitation Act 1980.

However, consider the position of a buyer from the employer who discovers a defect after completion of his purchase of the freehold; or that of a mortgagee of the freehold who discovers that the value of his security is seriously impaired because of a hidden design or construction defect; or that of a tenant of the building who enters into a lease on the basis of a full repairing covenant, which therefore obliges him to repair damage caused by such inherent defects. Traditionally, such third parties were unable to bring a claim for breach of contract as they did not have a contractual relationship with the employer's development team. Because of the rules of privity of contract, the practice arose of members of the development team giving a collateral warranty with such parties in order to enable them to bring a claim; as to collateral warranties, see **8.4.1**. In the absence of such a collateral warranty, the only other potential remedy for a third party lay in tort. There are, however, problems in bringing such a claim, as to which, see **8.3.2** below.

8.3.1   Contracts (Rights of Third Parties) Act 1999

This Act came into force on 11 May 2000, and applies to contracts entered into on or after that date. It allows the parties to a contract to confer rights on third parties. A third party, such as a future tenant or mortgage lender, may enforce the contract as if he were a party to it, provided that the contract expressly provides that he may or that it purports to confer a benefit on him. The third party must be expressly identified in the contract by name, as a member of a class or as answering a particular description, but need not be in existence when the contract is entered into. The case of *Avraamides v Colwill* [2006] EWCA Civ 1533 shows that the requirement that the third party must be identified in the contract will be strictly construed by the courts.

In theory, therefore, this Act provides a mechanism whereby third parties would be able to enforce the contractual obligations of the employer's development team, if, for example, the contract was stated to be for the benefit of 'all future tenants' of the building. However, at the time of writing, it seems that virtually all contracts with builders and professionals involved in the development process are expressly excluding this Act. One of the reasons for this is that, under s 2 of the Act, where a third party has been given rights under the Act, the contract cannot be amended or rescinded so as to vary those rights without the third party's consent. This prospect of having to obtain the consent of all relevant mortgage lenders, tenants or purchasers before the employer and the contractor or professionals are able to vary the terms of their original agreements, would be a major obstacle in practice to the efficient management of a development project. It seems likely, therefore, that for the time being at least, traditional forms of protection (eg, tort or collateral warranties) will still need to be relied upon.

Another reason for not using the Act is in a case where a funder or contracting purchaser is to be given step-in rights in case of the insolvency of the developer; these cannot be given under the 1999 Act, because the Act grants only rights, and cannot impose burdens on the third party (such as the obligations to pay outstanding sums due under the original contract).

8.3.2   Liability in tort

In seeking to bring a claim in tort, the problem that the buyer, lender or tenant will encounter is that any loss they sustain as a result of faulty design, materials or workmanship is likely to be classified as pure economic loss and, therefore, generally irrecoverable in tort. For example, in the case of the freehold buyer, if he discovers after completion of his purchase that the foundations of the building have been laid in a negligent fashion, so that the building cannot be used without remedial works first being carried out, he can either execute the repairs himself (thereby incurring repair costs), or dispose of the defective building to someone else (probably at less than the purchase price), or simply abandon the property (thereby wasting the money paid for the building in the first place); but whichever course of action the buyer takes, the loss he incurs is purely economic, and only in limited circumstances will the courts allow the claimant to recover such loss in tort.

To establish a claim in negligence, the claimant will have to show that the defendant owed him a duty of care, that the defendant breached that duty, and that the claimant suffered an actionable form of damage as a result. Following a series of House of Lords' decisions in the late 1980s and early 1990s, it is safe to say that liability in the tort of negligence will only arise if there is a breach of one of two categories of duty. The first duty is based upon the decision in *M'Alister (or Donoghue) (Pauper) v Stevenson* [1932] AC 562 where liability will arise out of a lack of care which results in reasonably foreseeable damage to persons or to property (other than to the property which causes the damage). The second duty is founded upon the case of *Hedley Byrne & Co Ltd v Heller & Partners Ltd* [1964] AC 465 and is concerned with a lack of care which causes non-physical economic loss.

8.3.3   Liability for physical damage

The duty of care under *M'Alister (or Donoghue) (Pauper) v Stevenson* [1932] AC 562 is a duty to avoid physical injury to person or property. It imposes a duty upon the manufacturer of a product (eg, a builder constructing a building) to take reasonable care to avoid damage to person or property through defects in the product. However, it does not impose a duty upon the manufacturer to ensure that the product itself is free from defects. Simply because the design or construction of the building is defective does not necessarily render the person who was responsible for the defect liable in damages, even if a duty was owed, and the damage was foreseeable. The case would turn upon whether the claimant suffered a type of loss recognised by the courts as legally recoverable. Pure economic loss (eg, the cost of repairing the defect, and the loss of profits while repairs are carried out) is not recoverable under *Donoghue v Stevenson* principles.

In *D&F Estates Ltd v Church Commissioners for England* [1989] AC 177, the House of Lords held that liability in tort arises only where there is some physical damage to person, or to some other property, and that damage to the building itself which merely reduced its value, is pure economic loss, and thus irrecoverable in tort, (except under *Hedley Byrne v Heller* principles). In *Murphy v Brentwood District Council* [1990] 2 All ER 908, the House of Lords reaffirmed its earlier decision, and stated that the idea that component parts of the same building could amount to separate species of property, (the 'complex structure' theory) so that, for example, negligently laid foundations could be said to have damaged 'other' property when they led to cracks appearing in the walls, was not correct.

To give an example of what may be recoverable, consider the position where, after completion of his purchase of the freehold, a defectively constructed roof collapses and causes personal injury to a buyer. The buyer may be able to recover damages in respect of his personal injuries, and any economic loss arising out of those injuries (eg, loss of earnings), but he will not be able to recover the cost of repairing the roof itself since that loss is pure economic loss.

8.3.4 Liability for economic loss

Economic loss is a term which can be used to describe any monetary loss. Pure economic loss is monetary loss which is not connected to physical injury to person or property. With one or two isolated and doubtful exceptions (see, eg, *Junior Books v Veitchi* [1983] 1 AC 520), pure economic loss is only recoverable in tort where, in a special relationship of close proximity, a duty of care is owed to avoid loss arising from a negligent misstatement. In *Hedley Byrne & Co Ltd v Heller & Partners Ltd* [1964] AC 465, the House of Lords decided that, in a relationship of close proximity, where a person was seeking information from one who was possessed of certain skills, a duty was owed by the latter to exercise reasonable care if he knew, or ought to have known that reliance was being placed upon his skill and judgment. Put simply, the duty amounts to a duty to prevent pure economic loss arising from the making of a statement, or the giving of advice. In the context of a building project, many statements are made, and much advice is given, but proximity of the parties, and reliance are the fundamental factors.

The extent of this duty has recently been restated and redefined by the House of Lords in *Caparo Industries plc v Dickman* [1990] 2 AC 605. It is now the case that, in order for there to be the requisite degree of proximity between the parties for the duty to arise, the defendant (ie, the person who made the statement, or gave the advice) must have known (both in the preparation of what was said, and in the delivery) that the statement would be communicated to an identified person or group of persons in connection with a transaction of a particular type, and that the recipient would be very likely to rely upon it.

While the employer, by reason of his contractual relationship with his professional advisers (eg, the architect or structural engineer), might easily establish the requisite degree of proximity, and show reliance upon the advice given, his tenant, buyer, or the buyer's lender are unlikely to be able to show the requisite proximity. In other words, the pure economic loss that a successor in title to the employer suffers remains irrecoverable.

As a result of this inability to recover the cost of repairing damage to the building outside a contractual relationship, various devices have been utilised by buyers, their lenders, tenants, and the employer's own financiers.

8.4 Protecting other parties

8.4.1 Collateral warranties

A collateral warranty is an agreement (under hand or by deed) entered into by someone engaged in the construction or design of a building by virtue of which that person assumes a contractual duty of care for the benefit of someone who has an interest in seeing that the building is free from defects, but who does not otherwise have a contractual relationship with the warrantor. Collateral warranties are commonly required to be given by the consultants, the main contractor and the sub-contractors to the freehold buyer, his lender, the developer's financiers, and possibly (if negotiated) the tenant. With one exception, the employer does not need warranties, as he is in a contractual relationship with his design and construction team. However, he will require warranties from the sub-contractors with whom the employer has no direct contractual relationship.

The advantages of warranties are twofold. First, they create the certainty of a contractual relationship, as opposed to the uncertainty that exists in tort. All the claimant would need to show in order to establish a claim is that the contractual duty contained in the warranty had been breached, and that damage had ensued. Secondly, the beneficiary of the warranty is likely to be able to recover in contract loss that can be described as purely economic. All the claimant has to show in this regard is that the loss suffered as a result of the breach of warranty could reasonably be said to have been in the contemplation of the parties at the time the warranty was entered into.

The main disadvantage of collateral warranties appears to be that the Latent Damage Act 1986, which, in certain situations, extends the limitation period for bringing civil claims, does not apply to claims for breach of contract and, therefore, if defects do not manifest themselves until more than six years after the warranty was entered into (or 12 years if by deed), no claim can then be brought.

Many firms of solicitors have their own preferred form of collateral warranty and, although attempts have been made to standardise the type of warranty to be used in the construction industry, those attempts have not always been enthusiastically received. In practice, the terms of collateral warranties are being dictated increasingly by the warrantor's professional indemnity insurers, who are concerned to limit their potential liability.

However, standard forms of collateral warranty are now published by the British Property Federation, the Construction Industry Council and the Joint Contracts Tribunal. They have been approved by the relevant professional bodies and are widely used. This has reduced the need for extensive negotiations.

A collateral warranty will normally contain the following provisions:

(a)   Confirmation that the team member (TM) owes to the third party benefiting from the warranty a similar duty of care to that owed to the person employing him. The TM will already owe a duty of care to the person employing him – normally the developer – by virtue of being appointed under a contract by his employer to carry out the design or construction work. It will oblige the TM to use reasonable skill and care in the performance of his duties under the contract, and he will be negligent if he fails to do so.

(b)   Confirmation that deleterious materials will not be used in the development. A warranty given by the architect will confirm that such materials will not be specified for use in the development, and a warranty given by the building contractor will confirm that such materials will not be used in the development. The materials that are not to be used may be listed in the warranty or the warranty may exclude the use of materials that do not comply with British Standards or are known to be deleterious.

(c)   Confirmation that professional indemnity insurance cover will be maintained by the TM up to a specified amount for a specified period. The period will normally be either six years or 12 years from the date of issue of the certificate of practical completion in relation to the development.

(d)   Confirmation that, on giving appropriate notification to the TM, the person to whom the warranty is given may 'step into the shoes' of the developer and, upon paying to the TM any outstanding fees or sums due, may instruct the TM under the terms of the contract as though the person to whom the warranty is given had in fact been the TM's employer. This is essential for any contracting purchaser of the completed development or any funder. If the developer becomes insolvent during the development process, it will be crucial for the contracting purchaser or funder to ensure that the development is properly completed, and the best way of achieving this is to instruct the team originally appointed to carry out the development.

(e)   In the case of an architect or other person providing design material, a royalty-free licence to use that material in connection with the completion and subsequent maintenance of the development. The copyright in the design material will normally remain with the designer, but the person benefiting from the warranty will be able to use the material but only to the extent that this is needed in connection with the development

(f)   Limitations on the number of parties that can benefit from the warranty. The TM – and his professional indemnity insurer – will wish to limit the number of parties to which a warranty must be given and, although the giving of a warranty to a future purchaser (or two) or a lender will not normally cause any difficulty, a tenant (other than an anchor tenant) will be unlikely to be accepted by the TM or his insurer.

(g)   Similarly there will be limitations/prohibitions on the assignment of the benefit of the warranty.

It is extremely unlikely that warranties will be given after the professional has been engaged. It is therefore essential that the professional is contractually committed to give warranties by the contract of engagement.

It seems that a claim in contract arising out of a breach of a collateral warranty will not exclude an alternative claim in tort (if a cause of action exists). In *Henderson v Merrett Syndicates Ltd* [1994] 3 All ER 506, Lord Goff said that 'an assumption of responsibility, coupled with the concomitant reliance, may give rise to a tortious duty of care irrespective of whether there is a contractual relationship between the parties, and in consequence, unless the contract precludes him from doing so, the [claimant], who has available to him concurrent remedies in contract and tort, may choose that remedy which appears to him to be the most advantageous'.

8.4.2   Other methods

8.4.2.1   Assignment of rights

The employer may consider attempting to satisfy the demands of his financier, buyer or tenant for protection against latent defects by assigning whatever rights the employer may have (primarily under contract law) against the contractor and the consultants. An assignment is probably only appropriate if made in favour of a financier, a buyer or a tenant of the whole of the development site. However, even where a tenant takes a lease of the whole of a development site, a landlord will be reluctant to part with his contractual rights in case the tenant's lease is forfeited or disclaimed.

Building contracts and contracts for the engagement of consultants may contain prohibitions on the assignment of the benefit of the contract without consent and it now seems that, following the House of Lords' decision in *Linden Garden Trust Ltd v Lenesta Sludge Disposals Ltd; St Martins Property Corporation Ltd v Sir Robert McAlpine & Sons Ltd* [1993] 3 WLR 408, most prohibitions will be effective, although each clause will have to be interpreted to discover its exact meaning.

8.4.2.2   Declaring a trust of rights

Declaring a trust of rights may be considered as an alternative to an outright assignment where the employer is retaining an interest in the property and, therefore, does not wish to part with valuable contractual rights. In this way the employer can retain the benefit of the rights he has against the contractor and consultants, but declares that he holds them upon trust for the benefit of himself and his tenants.

8.4.2.3   Latent defects insurances

With residential properties, buyers are anxious to ensure that a newly constructed property is covered by the National House-Building Council (NHBC) Buildmark scheme, or other equivalent insurance. In the commercial field, there are no such standard schemes. However, following the BUILD report (Building Users Insurance against Latent Defects) published in 1988 by the National Economic Development Office, several of the leading insurance companies in the UK have introduced latent defects insurance in respect of commercial properties.

Policies will vary from company to company (and, indeed, from development to development), but the essential elements are likely to be similar across the board. Latent defect insurance commonly provides cover against damage caused by defective design or construction works for a period of 10 years after practical completion of the development (or such longer period as may be agreed with the insurer). The beneficiary of the policy is covered against the cost of making good most (but not necessarily all) damage caused by a design or construction defect (although not other risks), and the policy may cover other items of economic loss such as loss of rent, or loss of use of the building while repairs are being carried out. The policy can be taken out to cover the employer (as initial owner of the building) and his financiers. Most policies will also automatically insure subsequent owners and occupiers, which will obviously be the desired aim from the employer's point of view. The premium is likely to be substantial (perhaps 1.5% of development costs).

The advantages of such a policy is that there is no need for the claimant under the policy to establish legal liability for the damage incurred, and there ought to be easy access to funds to finance repairing costs and, possibly, to cover other economic loss. The disadvantages are that, as with other policies, the insurance may be subject to excesses (meaning that the claimant might have to fund, say, the first £50,000 of a claim), and that the insurer will invariably require some element of supervision over the execution of the works, since the risk he is taking on will be considerable. Such insurance is not something which can be obtained economically after the construction process is complete.

Proposals have been put to the European Commission regarding compulsory insurance of all new residential, commercial and civil engineering construction projects (see the Mathurin Report 1990) and legislation in this area may eventually materialise.

8.4.2.4   Limiting repair covenants

In a landlord and tenant relationship, the tenant should consider limiting the scope of his repairing covenant. The main problem for a tenant is that the landlord is likely to insist upon the tenant entering into a lease which contains a covenant by the tenant to repair the demised premises. Provided the damage amounts to disrepair (see **17.2.6**), the usual repair covenant imposed by the landlord will oblige the tenant to repair damage which is caused by a defect in the design or construction of the building. While the tenant can commission a full structural survey of the premises prior to the grant of the lease in an effort to discover defects, the very nature of a design or construction defect makes it unlikely that it will exhibit itself until some time after the building has been completed and the lease granted.

It is, therefore, suggested that, on the grant of a lease of a relatively new building, the tenant should attempt to limit the scope of his repairing covenant by excluding (either totally, or for a limited period of, say, three or six years after the grant of the lease) liability to repair damage caused by an inherent, or latent, design or construction defect. Not only should the tenant seek to exclude such liability from his own covenant, but he should make sure that no vacuum is left in the repairing obligations under the lease by insisting that the landlord assumes this liability. If this is not done, there is a risk that the property may remain in disrepair. The landlord will be anxious to avoid having to bear any repair costs in respect of the building, and so the limitation of the tenant's repairing obligations is a matter to be negotiated and will depend upon the relative bargaining strengths of the parties. It is most unlikely that the tenant would succeed in his negotiations if, in the agreement for lease, the tenant had insisted upon a degree of control and supervision over the execution of the landlord's works (see **26.3.4**). The landlord would probably argue that the tenant had had every opportunity before the lease was granted to discover defects, and that he should, therefore, consider taking action against his professional advisers.

On the grant of a lease of part of a building, where the tenant would not ordinarily undertake repairing responsibilities in respect of the structure and external parts, but would instead be expected to contribute by way of service charge to the landlord's costs incurred in maintaining those parts, the tenant would seek to ensure that he was not obliged to contribute to the landlord's costs of repairing damage caused by design or construction defects (either throughout the term, or for a limited period). Again, while the tenant could commission a full structural survey, design defects may not be apparent at the time of the survey, or may be hidden in some other part of the building to which the surveyor was unable to gain access.

8.4.2.5   Defect liability periods

In a landlord and tenant relationship, the tenant may seek the benefit of a defect liability period. If the landlord will not agree to exclude the tenant's liability for inherent defects in the lease, the tenant ought to press for the inclusion of a clause in the agreement for lease obliging the landlord to remedy any defects which appear within a short period of time following practical completion of the building. If the landlord agrees to the inclusion of a defects liability period, it is likely to mirror a similar clause in the building contract entered into with the contractor. Quite often, building contracts provide for the contractor to remedy any defects which manifest themselves within, say, the first 6 or 12 months after practical completion. By including a similar clause in the agreement for lease, the landlord is indirectly passing on the benefit of the clause to the tenant.

8.4.2.6   Forced enforcement of remedies

A tenant may seek a side letter, or supplemental deed from his landlord whereby the landlord agrees to enforce any rights he may have against the contractor or the consultants, by way of civil proceedings, in respect of defects which would otherwise render the tenant liable to repair under the repairing covenant. However, whether the landlord suffers any loss upon which a claim could be based is doubtful where the tenant has entered into a full repairing lease.

A buyer, financier or tenant may seek the inclusion of a provision whereby the employer agrees to enforce his rights as original contracting party against the contractor or the consultants in respect of defects where loss or liability to repair would otherwise fall upon the former. Difficulties have arisen in this area in that, if the employer has received full market value on a sale of the property to a buyer, or has secured the inclusion of a full repairing covenant on the grant of a lease of the property to a tenant, he cannot be said to have suffered any loss upon which a claim could be maintained.

However, the House of Lords' decision in the *Linden Garden* case has shown that in a commercial contract where it was in the contemplation of the contracting parties that title to the property which formed the subject matter of the contract might be transferred to a third party before a breach had occurred, the original contracting party is taken to have entered into the contract for the benefit of himself and all persons who may acquire an interest in the property before the breach occurs. What this means is that, in certain circumstances, the employer may be able to recover damages for breach of contract in respect of loss incurred by his buyer, financier or tenant. This area is not without its complications, and the full ramifications of recent developments in this area have not yet been explored.

Part I Summary – Site Acquisition

Topic	Summary	Reference
The need for planning permission	Planning consent from the local planning authority – usually the district council – is required for any 'development'.	Chapter 1
What is development?	Development is widely defined to include building operations, demolition and material changes of use. Certain of these are excluded from the definition and certain types of minor development are permitted by the legislation, subject to various conditions. These include changing a use from one within a particular 'use class' to another in the same class.	Chapter 2
Applying for planning permission	Application should be made on the proper form enclosing the correct fee to (usually) the District Council. Application can be made for full permission, which requires the submission of detailed plans and specifications, or outline permission, which will only give permission in principle and further approval of the details will be required. Planning consents are normally granted subject to conditions which must be complied with in carrying out the development. The kind of conditions which may be imposed are restricted by the courts. The *Newbury* test requires that they must be for a planning purpose, fairly and reasonably relate to the development and not be so unreasonable that no reasonable planning authority would have imposed them. Applicants can appeal to the Secretary of State against refusal of permission or in relation to adverse conditions. There is usually a six-month time limit on making appeals.	Chapter 3
Planning obligations	The types of conditions which may be attached to planning consents are restricted. Sometimes it is necessary for other issues to be dealt with, which are necessary for a planning proposal to be acceptable but cannot be dealt with by a lawful condition. Subject to government guidelines, the developer and the planning authority can enter into a binding agreement under s 106 of the Town and Country Planning Act 1990 covering these matters. The benefits obtained by the local authority under a s 106 agreement are sometimes referred to as 'planning gain'.	Chapter 4

Topic	Summary	Reference
Enforcement of planning law	Building operations in breach of planning control can be enforced within four years; material changes of use and breaches of conditions attached to a planning consent can be enforced for 10 years. A variety of enforcement methods are available to a local authority, including an enforcement notice, a breach of condition notice and a stop notice. There are criminal sanctions for non-compliance. There is an appeal procedure against an enforcement notice. The appeal to the DCLG must be made before the notice takes effect.	Chapter 5
Environmental issues	If land is contaminated, a local authority can serve a remediation notice requiring it to be cleaned up. This can be served on the person who caused or permitted the contamination or on the current occupier. It will also usually be a condition of any planning consent that the land be cleaned up before the development can take place. Clean-up costs can be very high. It is thus essential for a potential buyer to ascertain whether there is any possibility of the land being contaminated. The possibility of asbestos being in a building or Japanese knotweed being on a site must also be considered. Commencing in 2008, energy performance certificates will be required for new commercial buildings or when an existing building is sold or let.	Chapter 6
Matters of contract	The Standard Commercial Property Conditions will often be incorporated into a contract for the sale of commercial property. An option may be granted or a contract conditional on the grant of planning permission may be entered into. The procedure to be followed will be much the same as in a residential transaction, although the impact of VAT will need to be considered and the VAT status of the transaction made clear in the contract. The sale of a new commercial building is standard rated; other commercial transactions are exempt but subject to an option to tax.	Chapter 7
Construction projects	A design and construction team will be employed by the developer. The team will have contractual duties to the developer but potential tenants or buyers of the completed development will want to ensure that duties are also owed to them. Collateral warranties may well be required from the design and construction team.	Chapter 8

Part II
COMMERCIAL LEASES

Chapter 9
Landlord and Tenant Law and Commercial Leases

9.1 Introduction

A thorough knowledge and understanding of landlord and tenant law is essential for all commercial conveyancers; without such an understanding it would be impossible to properly advise clients on their rights and liabilities under the lease. Consequently, this part of the book starts with a consideration of the more important principles governing the relationship between landlords and tenants of business premises.

9.2 Liability of the parties on the covenants in the lease

The detailed rules relating to the enforceability of covenants are considered in **Chapter 12**. The following is intended only as an outline of the main issues involved.

9.2.1 Leases granted before 1 January 1996

9.2.1.1 Position of the original parties

Unless the lease provides to the contrary, the original parties will remain liable on their express covenants in the lease by privity of contract throughout the whole term, despite any disposition of their interests. Thus, the original tenant must appreciate that he will be liable not just for breaches committed while he is the tenant but also for any breach of covenant committed by his successors. This continuing liability may have serious consequences for the original tenant and means, for example, that he will be liable for any arrears of rent occurring throughout the whole term.

In the same way, through privity of contract, the original landlord will remain liable on his covenants to the original tenant for the whole term, despite any assignment by him of the reversion, ie, he will be liable to the original tenant if a buyer of the reversion breaks a covenant.

9.2.1.2 Position of landlord and tenant for the time being

The relationship between an assignee of the lease and the landlord for the time being and between a buyer of the reversion and the tenant for the time being rests on the doctrine of privity of estate. Liability under this doctrine extends only to those covenants which touch and concern the land.

Further, a party is only liable for breaches committed during his period of ownership of the lease or reversion, as the case may be. Thus, for example, an assignee of the lease, for the period while he has the lease, has the benefit of the landlord's covenants and is liable on the tenant's covenants provided, in both cases, the covenants touch and concern the land.

9.2.2 Leases granted on or after 1 January 1996

The Landlord and Tenant (Covenants) Act 1995 (LT(C)A 1995) abolished the concept of privity of contract for leases entered into on or after 1 January 1996. Thus once the original tenant has assigned the lease he is not liable for any future breaches (although he may be required to guarantee his immediate assignee: see **18.2.7**). On a sale of the reversion, the landlord may apply to the tenant for release from the landlord's covenants in the lease (see **12.2.2**).

9.3   Security of tenure

The majority of business tenants will enjoy security of tenure under Pt II of the Landlord and Tenant Act 1954 (LTA 1954) and the importance of this Act in its effect on termination of the lease cannot be overstated. The protection given to tenants covered by the Act is twofold. First, a business tenancy will not come to an end at the expiration of a fixed term, nor can a periodic tenancy be terminated by the landlord serving an ordinary notice to quit. Instead, notwithstanding the ending of the contractual term, the tenancy will be automatically continued under s 24 until such time as it is terminated in one of the ways specified in the Act. Secondly, upon the expiration of a business tenancy in accordance with the Act, business tenants normally have a statutory right to apply to court for a new tenancy and the landlord may only oppose that application on certain statutory grounds (some of which involve the payment of compensation by the landlord if the tenant has to leave). Any new tenancy granted will also enjoy the protection of the Act.

It is possible, in certain circumstances, for the landlord and tenant to contract out of the Act, but certain formalities must be observed.

Further consideration of this Act is dealt with in **Chapter 31**.

9.4   Lease/licence distinction

The security of tenure provisions in the LTA 1954 and other statutory provisions dealt with elsewhere in the book do not apply to licences. It therefore becomes necessary to examine the distinction between a lease and a licence. A lease is an interest in land. A licence, on the other hand, confers no interest in land; it merely authorises that which would otherwise be a trespass. One of the leading cases in this area is *Street v Mountford* [1985] 2 All ER 289. While this case concerned a residential tenancy, similar principles have subsequently been applied to business tenancies. Subject to certain exceptions, for example, lack of intention to create legal relations or occupation pending the grant of a lease, the House of Lords held that as a general rule:

(a)   the grant of exclusive possession,

(b)   for a term,

(c)   at a rent,

will create a tenancy rather than a licence; and the court will ignore any shams or pretences aimed at misleading the court.

In the context of business premises, some arrangements will clearly not confer exclusive possession and will thus remain licences, for example, the 'shop within a shop' sometimes found in department stores, or the kiosks often found in theatres or hotel foyers. Moreover, there seems to be a greater readiness by the courts to find that exclusive possession was not granted than is the case with residential premises (see, eg, *Esso Petroleum Co Ltd v Fumegrange Ltd* [1994] 46 EG 199 and *National Car Parks Ltd v Trinity Development Co (Banbury) Ltd* [2001] EWCA Civ 1686, [2001] 28 EG 144).

To avoid the risk of inadvertently creating a lease, the use of licences needs very careful consideration. As an alternative, the parties should consider the 'contracting out' provisions in the LTA 1954.

Chapter 10

An Outline of Taxation of Commercial Properties

10.1 Value added tax

At the outset of any property transaction, it is essential to consider the impact of VAT legislation, and to advise the client accordingly. One of the aims of the Finance Act 1989 was to bring UK law into line with EU law by bringing many property transactions and the provision of construction and other services within the scope of VAT. The reader will already be aware of the basic principles of VAT, which dictate that VAT may be payable in respect of a supply of goods or services made in the course of a business. Whether VAT is payable depends upon a number of things including whether the supplies in question are exempt, zero-rated or standard-rated. The reader will also be aware of the effects of such supplies, the payment and receipt of input and output tax, and the recovery of VAT incurred.

Supplies of goods and services made in relation to a property transaction can be grouped as follows:

(a) Residential properties:
  (i) sale of a green field site: exempt (but subject to the option to tax);
  (ii) construction services: zero-rated;
  (iii) civil engineering works: zero-rated;
  (iv) professional services (eg, legal and other professional fees): standard-rated;
  (v) sale of a new house: zero-rated;
  (vi) grant of a lease of a new house (for a term exceeding 21 years): zero-rated.

(b) Commercial properties:
  (i) sale of a green field site: exempt (but subject to the option to tax);
  (ii) construction services: standard-rated;
  (iii) civil engineering works: standard-rated;
  (iv) professional services: standard-rated;
  (v) sale of a new freehold building or the grant of an option to purchase such a building: standard-rated;
  (vi) sale of an old freehold building: exempt (but subject to the option to tax);
  (vii) the grant of a lease (for any length of term): exempt (but subject to the option to tax);
  (viii) the assignment of a lease: exempt (but subject to the option to tax);
  (ix) the surrender of a lease: exempt (but subject to the option to tax by the person who receives the consideration);
  (x) repair, alteration and demolition works: standard-rated.

Rules relating to work carried out on listed buildings are not considered in this book, and the particular problems associated with premises of mixed use are also outside the scope of this book.

Some of the supplies listed above are exempt supplies, but are subject to what is called the 'option to tax' (also known as the 'option to waive exemption'). This is dealt with more comprehensively at **10.1.3**. What the option means is that the person who makes the supply can voluntarily convert the supply from one which is exempt and, therefore, gives rise to no VAT liability into a standard-rated supply.

The VAT consequences arising in residential and commercial developments are now considered.

10.1.1 Residential developments

In a typical new residential development, the VAT consequences will not be too complicated. If, for example, a property company, ABC Limited, buys a green field site, the seller is making an exempt supply to ABC Limited which will not be subject to VAT unless the seller, being a taxable person, has elected to waive the exemption. In any event if, as is often the case, the seller is a private individual, he is not likely to be selling the land in the course of a business, and the supply will, therefore, be outside the scope of VAT. Any construction services (such as work provided by builders and the provision of materials) and civil engineering works (such as the construction of the roads and sewers serving the development) supplied to ABC Limited will be supplied at a zero-rate of VAT. It is, therefore, probable that the only significant VAT incurred by the property company in constructing the residential development will be in respect of professional fees paid to surveyors, solicitors, architects and selling agents for services supplied.

On completion of construction, ABC Limited will dispose of the houses. The purchase price payable on the freehold sale of a newly built house, or the premium (or rent) payable in respect of a lease of the house granted for a term exceeding 21 years does not attract VAT. These supplies are zero-rated. However, when zero-rated supplies are made, while no VAT is paid for the supply, tax is deemed to be charged at a nil rate on the output (so that they are still technically regarded as taxable supplies) and therefore related input tax incurred can be recovered. What this means is that ABC Limited will account to HM Revenue & Customs (HMRC) for output tax on supplies made (which will be nil), less input tax on related supplies received (ie, the VAT paid on professional fees). This clearly leads to a deficit which means that a refund of VAT will be due from HMRC.

A subsequent sale of a dwelling (either freehold or leasehold) will be made by a private individual and will not, therefore, be made in the course of a business. In the event that the sale is made in the course of a business (eg, by a relocation company), the supply would be exempt.

10.1.2 Commercial developments

In a typical new commercial development, the same process can be followed, with different VAT consequences. The sale of a green field site to a developer is again an exempt supply, subject to the option to tax. However, the provision of construction services and civil engineering works to a commercial developer are standard-rated supplies, which means that considerable VAT will be incurred in addition to VAT on the standard-rated supply of professional services.

Once the building has been completed, the developer may either sell the freehold, or grant a lease of it to a tenant. The sale of a 'new' or partially completed building is a standard-rated supply. VAT must be charged in respect of the purchase price. In this context, a 'new' building is one which was completed within the three years preceding the sale, and 'completion' of a building takes place on the earlier of either the day upon which the certificate of practical completion was issued by the architect or the day upon which the building was completely occupied. The grant of a lease of all or part of commercial premises (whether new or old) is an exempt supply, subject to the right of the landlord to opt to tax the rents, premium and other sums payable under the lease. In both cases, whether the freehold sale or the grant of a commercial lease, the developer is able to charge VAT, either because it is a standard-rated supply, or because the exemption has been waived. This means that output tax will be received to facilitate recovery of related input tax incurred.

Take, by way of example, a commercial development where the construction costs paid by the developer amount to £2 million (with VAT on a standard-rated supply of £350,000), the cost of roads and sewers amounts to £500,000 (with £87,500 VAT) and professional fees total £100,000 (with £17,500 VAT). The total input tax paid by the developer adds up to £455,000.

If the developer, being a taxable person, is able to sell the 'new' freehold building for £4 million, he will have to charge VAT amounting to £700,000. This output tax can be set against related input tax incurred, resulting in the difference only (£245,000) having to be accounted for to HMRC. The developer suffers from cash flow difficulties in that he is likely to incur the input tax some time in advance of receiving the output tax, but he is not left out of pocket. The same result will be achieved if, instead of selling the freehold, the developer chooses to grant a lease of the building and elects to charge VAT on the sums payable under the lease. The making of the election facilitates immediate recovery of related input tax.

10.1.3   The option to charge VAT

The election to waive exemption or, as it is more commonly called, the option to tax was introduced on 1 August 1989 in order to lessen the impact of the VAT charges on commercial developers. The purpose of the option to tax is to enable the commercial owner to convert what would otherwise be exempt supplies in respect of a particular property into supplies chargeable to VAT at the standard rate, so that the developer will be able to recover the input tax which he incurred when acquiring or developing the property.

The consequence of making the election is that all future grants in the property by the person who makes the election will be subject to VAT at the standard rate.

10.1.3.1   How is the election made?

As a preliminary to waiving the exemption, the owner must check that he is registered for VAT, or else the election will be meaningless. There is no prescribed form or procedure for electing, nor is there any requirement to consult with or notify anyone who might be affected by the election. However, from a practical point of view, it is advisable that a landlord notifies his tenants, since it is the tenants who will bear the VAT. The one procedural requirement that must be followed when making the election is that written notice of the election must be given to HMRC within 30 days of the election.

If an exempt supply (eg, the grant of a lease) has been made by the elector in respect of the relevant property since 1 August 1989, consent of HMRC will be required before the election can be made, and consent will only be granted if HMRC is satisfied that the input tax which the elector will be able to recover as a consequence of his making the election is fair and reasonable. It is therefore advisable for a landlord intending to make an election to do so before he grants a lease of his property.

In all other cases, consent of HMRC is not required.

Since the purpose of making the election is to charge VAT, the elector should ensure that he is registered for VAT.

10.1.3.2   Who or what is affected?

The election is personal, done on a property-by-property basis and, once made, it may only be revoked within three months of the election, or after 20 years (see the Value Added Tax (Buildings and Land) Order 1995 (SI 1995/279)). The fact that the election is personal means that while a landlord who elects to waive the exemption would have to charge VAT on the rents payable by its tenants, its tenants would not, unless they too elected, have to charge VAT to their sub-tenants, and the same applies to a buyer of the landlord's interest. As an exception to the general rule, an election made by a company in respect of a property will bind other companies (in respect of that property) if they are in the same VAT group of companies at the time of the election, or joined the group later, when the property affected was still owned by a group company.

The fact that the election is made on a property-by-property basis means that a commercial owner can pick and choose which of its properties should be voluntarily standard-rated. Once made, the election affects the whole of the property or, if the elector owns an interest in only part of the property, it will affect the entirety of that part. Hence, the elector cannot choose to waive the exemption in respect of the ground floor and not the upper two floors if he owns the entire building. What may appear to be separate buildings, but which are linked together internally or by covered walkways are to be treated as one building. Therefore, if a shopping precinct is owned by one landlord (as is usually the case) an election by that landlord will affect all of the shops in the precinct.

10.1.3.3 Should the election be made?

The reason for making the election is to facilitate the recovery of related input tax incurred on the acquisition or development of the property. If no related input tax has been or is likely to be incurred, there is no reason why the election should be made. If considerable input tax has been or will be incurred, consideration must be given to whether or not the election should be made, but the elector must have regard to the effect that the election will have on the persons to whom supplies are being made.

If a developer-landlord, having incurred VAT on acquisition or development costs, wants to waive the exemption and charge VAT on the rents it will receive from its tenants, and those tenants make mainly standard-rated or zero-rated supplies in the course of their businesses (eg, tenants of retail foodstores, solicitors or surveyors offices), the tenants would not be adversely affected by a charge to VAT on rent, since there will be output tax (actual or deemed) to offset against the input tax. The tenants will not end up out of pocket.

Tenants who make only exempt supplies in the course of their businesses (eg, banks, building societies, insurance companies) will be hard hit by the election. The VAT that these tenants have to pay on the rent will be irrecoverable, and will have to be borne as an overhead of the business. This could have the effect of frightening off a class of tenants whom the developer might have been hoping to attract to the development or lead to their reducing the amount of rent that they would be prepared to pay.

The Finance Act 1997 makes provision for a limited disapplication of the election where the ultimate end-user of the property occupies wholly or mainly for exempt purposes and was involved in some way in the acquisition, construction or financing of the property. The provision is an anti-avoidance device and the circumstances in which the disapplication will apply will be few and far between.

10.1.4 Drafting points

Is the election on its own sufficient to render VAT payable by the person who receives the supply? It is necessary to look at two principal relationships: seller and buyer, and landlord and tenant.

10.1.4.1 Seller and buyer

If a seller sells a 'new' commercial building (whether it is the first sale or a subsequent sale of the still 'new' building) the seller is making a standard-rated supply, and so there will be mandatory VAT on the purchase price. The basic rule is that, unless the contrary appears, the purchase price stated in the contract is deemed to include VAT. It is, therefore, important that the seller includes a clause in the contract obliging the buyer to pay VAT in addition to the purchase price. Failure to do so will result in the seller having to account to HMRC for the VAT out of the purchase price received which, at current rates, will mean that the seller will be left with seven forty-sevenths less than he anticipated. This can result in the seller incurring a huge loss, for which his solicitor would no doubt be liable in negligence. Consider a sale at a price of £1 million. If an express provision is included in the contract, the buyer will have to pay £1.175 million to complete, HMRC will get the VAT on the purchase price, and the seller will be left with £1 million. If the express clause is left out, the buyer need only pay £1 million to complete, out of which HMRC will get £148,936 ($\frac{7}{47} \times$ £1 million) leaving the seller with only £851,064.

If the seller sells an old commercial building (ie, one that is now more than three years old) then the supply which is being made is an exempt supply and the position is different. If the seller waives the exemption before exchange then he converts the supply into a standard-rated supply and the above paragraph would then be applicable. The seller would have to make an express provision in the contract. If the exemption is waived after exchanging contracts then, under s 89 of the Value Added Tax Act 1994 (VATA 1994), the option to tax would operate as a change in the rate of tax from 0% to 17.5% (ie, from an exempt to a standard-rated supply) and accordingly the seller could add VAT to the purchase price, without the need for an express clause in the contract enabling him to do so. In this case, it is important that the buyer's solicitor ensures that the contract makes it clear that the purchase price is inclusive of VAT so that no hardship is felt by the buyer if the seller chooses to elect after exchange. Only if the contract expressly excludes s 89, or the purchase price is expressly stated to be payable inclusive of VAT, will the seller be unable to add VAT to the purchase price.

10.1.4.2 Landlord and tenant

The grant of a commercial lease (of either an old or new building) is an exempt supply, unless the landlord has opted to tax. In respect of existing leases, s 89 of the VATA 1994 again operates so that an election by the landlord after the grant of the lease effects a change in the rate of VAT from 0% to 17.5%. The landlord does not need the benefit of an express clause in the lease, and can simply add VAT to the rent (and other sums payable under the lease) unless there is a clause in the lease (which would not usually be the case) expressly exonerating the tenant from liability to VAT on such payments, or excluding s 89.

If the election is made before the grant of the lease, so that the supply is converted to a standard-rated supply from the outset, s 89 will not operate, and the rent will be deemed to be payable inclusive of VAT. It is, therefore, essential that the landlord's solicitor ensures that the lease contains a covenant by the tenant to pay VAT on the rent (and the other sums payable under the lease). Whenever a lease is drafted, irrespective of whether advantage can be taken of s 89, there ought to be a covenant by the tenant to pay VAT in addition to the sums payable under the lease. This avoids problems for the landlord.

10.1.5 Other areas of concern

VAT is a far-reaching tax in the property world which can impact on other aspects of property transactions.

10.1.5.1 Reverse premiums and rent-free periods

A reverse premium is a payment made by the landlord to a prospective tenant as an inducement to him to enter the lease. Money is passing from landlord to tenant, and is the consideration for a supply being made by the tenant. This payment will be subject to VAT and the tenant should ensure that the terms of the contract allow this to be added to the payment. The landlord will not, however, be able to recover this VAT as input tax if, when granting the lease, he is making an exempt supply. So the cost to the landlord will be increased by 17.5%. The landlord could recover this VAT if he elected to tax in respect of the property, but this would also mean that he would have to charge VAT on the rent. This would then be a particular problem for exempt tenants, such as banks or insurance companies, as the VAT on the rent will not be recoverable and they may wish to try and negotiate a lower rent to compensate for this.

Rent-free periods give rise to difficult VAT problems. It appears that if the rent-free period is being given because the tenant is carrying out work to the premises which will benefit the landlord, or simply because the landlord is trying to induce the tenant to enter into the lease (as an alternative to a reverse premium), then VAT at the standard rate will be payable on the amount of rent forgone. The tenant is making a supply to the landlord (ie, is positively doing something) in consideration of a rent-free period. However, if the rent-free period is given simply because the state of the market means that it is part of the bargain negotiated between landlord and tenant (eg, where it is given to allow the tenant some time in which to fit out the premises for his own benefit, or arrange sub-lettings), there will be no VAT on the rent-free period, since nothing is being done in return for it.

10.1.5.2   Surrenders

When a tenant surrenders his lease to the landlord, consideration may move in either direction, either because the tenant is desperate to rid himself of the liability to pay rent and perform the covenants, or because the landlord is anxious to obtain vacant possession. By virtue of the Value Added Tax (Land) Order 1995 (SI 1995/282), the supply made in either case is an exempt supply, subject to the option to tax by the person who receives the consideration.

Where a surrender is effected by operation of law, it is unclear whether any VAT can be claimed by HMRC. Indeed, it may be difficult to establish the value of the supply being made. If such a surrender is to arise, it may be advisable to ensure that liability for VAT is clearly documented by the parties before surrender occurs.

10.1.5.3   Transfers of going concerns

There are complicated rules regarding the transfer of a going concern, which can include the sale of a tenanted building. However, these rules are outside the scope of this book.

10.1.5.4   VAT on costs

Sometimes, a lease will oblige the tenant to pay the landlord's legal costs incurred on the grant of the lease. Often, a lease will oblige the tenant to pay the landlord's legal costs on an application for licence to assign, or alter, or change use. The position as regards VAT on those costs is complicated by the approach of HMRC, which treats the payment of the landlord's legal costs, in either case, as part of the overall consideration for the grant of the lease. Hence, the VAT position depends upon whether the landlord has opted to waive the exemption.

If the landlord's solicitor charges his client £1,000 plus VAT for legal services provided on the grant of the lease, he will issue his client with a VAT invoice requiring payment of £1,000 plus VAT of £175. The landlord, having waived the exemption in respect of this property, and making use of his VAT invoice, will be able to recover the input tax (£175) from the output tax which he will receive on the rents. If the lease contains a clause obliging the tenant to pay those legal costs, the landlord will look to the tenant for a reimbursement of the outstanding £1,000. However, since HMRC treats such a payment as part of the consideration for the grant of the lease, and since the landlord has waived the exemption, the tenant must pay £1,000 plus VAT, the landlord must issue the tenant with a VAT invoice, and the landlord must account to HMRC for the VAT element received. The tenant may be able to recover the VAT which he has paid, depending on the nature of his business.

If the landlord has not waived the exemption, the position is different. First, he will not be able to recover the VAT charged by his solicitor, since that VAT was incurred in relation to an exempt supply. Secondly, therefore, he will require the tenant to reimburse the full amount of costs and VAT (ie, £1,175), but because this reimbursement is treated as part of the consideration for the grant of the lease, and because the supply made by the landlord is an exempt supply, no VAT invoice can be issued to the tenant (as, in fact, there is no charge to VAT being made to the tenant), and the tenant will be unable to recover any part of the reimbursement.

The same principles are adopted where, during the term, the tenant exercises a right given to him under the lease and pays the landlord's legal costs (eg, on an application for licence to assign pursuant to a qualified covenant (see **18.2.2**)).

10.2 Stamp duty land tax on leases

Ad valorem duty will be assessed on any premium paid and also on the rent. Stamp duty land tax must be paid within 30 days of the execution of the instrument.

The amount of duty payable on the premium is assessed in the same way as on purchases of land. The normal reduced rates of duty are available.

The Finance Act 2003 introduced wide-ranging reforms to the stamp duty regime which came into force on 1 December 2003. These include:

(a)   a change of name to stamp duty land tax (SDLT);

(b)   raising the threshold for the payment of duty from £60,000 to £150,000 for non-residential properties;

(c)   introducing the new regime for the rental element of leases. Duty is now payable at a flat rate of 1% on the 'net present value' (NPV) of the total rent payable over the term of the lease. The NPV is calculated by discounting rent payable in future years by 3.5% per annum;

(d)   where the NPV of the total rent does not exceed £150,000, no duty will be payable;

(e)   duty will not be chargeable on the VAT element of consideration provided the landlord has not opted to charge tax by the time the lease is granted;

(f)   changes to the methods of payment of duty. In particular, there will no longer be a need for a 'stamp' to appear on a document as proof of payment; instead, a Land Transaction Return must be submitted to the Inland Revenue giving details of the transaction.

SDLT has now become an important factor in commercial leases as the amount of duty is directly related to the length of the term, ie, the longer the lease, the more duty is potentially payable. Further, if the tenant remains in possession ('holds over') after the end of a fixed term under the provisions of Part I of the Landlord and Tenant Act 1954 (see **Chapter 31**), a further charge to duty may arise. This will be payable by the current tenant.

Chapter 11
Lease Drafting

11.1 Principles of drafting

A commercial property lawyer will encounter many different types of commercial lease, since every firm of solicitors engaged in property matters is likely to have its own commercial lease precedent which it will adapt for use in each commercial letting in respect of which the firm is instructed. Most firms restrict their office precedent to a document of manageable length. However, it is not uncommon when acting for a tenant to receive a draft lease which runs to 60 or more pages of relatively small print, all of which has to be carefully examined by the tenant's solicitor. Brevity and concise language must always be encouraged in the drafting (and the amending) of a lease. If the draft lease is kept short, less time will be taken in the subsequent negotiation of the terms and, therefore, in the transaction generally. It will also be easier to read for both clients and solicitors, and will result in legal fees being kept to a minimum. However, the draftsman cannot always restrict the length of the document where complex and extensive legal obligations are being entered into. Clauses cannot be left out of the lease simply to reduce its length, and even though the possibility of a clause being relied upon during the term might appear slight, if a reason exists for the inclusion of the clause, it should be retained. There are many matters to be contemplated in a landlord and tenant relationship, all of which require regulation in the lease.

If, following the grant of the lease, the reversion is to be sold to an investment fund (which is the case with many commercial developments, both new and old), the draftsman should always have regard to the requirements of institutional investors who will require the form of lease to be as close to their standard 'institutional' form as possible. If an institutionally preferred form of lease has not been granted, the landlord will have greater difficulty in disposing of the freehold. All leading commercial practices ensure that their office precedent is in an institutional form. An 'institutional' lease is one which places all the costs of repairing and insuring upon the tenant, thereby ensuring that the income derived by the landlord from the rent is subject to as little fluctuation (in terms of outgoings) as possible. It is often granted for a term of 15 years with a five-yearly rent review pattern although in recessionary times, shorter leases are common.

The techniques to be adopted in the drafting of the lease are outlined in the drafting section of the Legal Practice Guide, *Skills for Lawyers* and are not repeated here.

11.2 Rules of construction

The purpose of interpreting any legal contract is to discover the real intention of the parties, but that intention can only be ascertained from the wording of the contract itself, and not from extrinsic evidence.

In construing a lease, the court is always reluctant to hold a clause void for uncertainty and thus, if the court can find a way to interpret the clause, some sense will be given to it. Equally, however, the court is generally unwilling to imply terms into a document which has been entered into after extensive negotiations between legally represented parties (although see the approach of the Court of Appeal in *Royal Bank of Scotland plc v Jennings and Others* [1997] 19 EG 152). Faced with an ambiguity, the court will usually adopt the literal approach to interpretation, unless this would lead to a result so absurd that, in the commercial reality of the situation the parties find themselves in, they could not reasonably have intended it (see *Broadgate Square plc v Lehman Brothers Ltd* [1995] 01 EG 111). The court will not examine the offending clause in isolation, but will construe the lease as a whole, to see if some assistance can be gained from other parts of the deed, where similar words and phrases may have been used in other contexts. Ordinary and technical words of the English language will be given the meanings usually attributed to them by the lay person unless the lease clearly directs some other meaning (eg, by use of a definitions or interpretation clause).

If, owing to a common mistake between the parties, the lease, as executed, does not embody the common intentions of the parties, the remedy of rectification may be available. This is, however, an equitable and discretionary remedy, and there is a heavy burden upon the claimant in a claim for rectification to show the existence of a common mistake. Rectification will not be awarded so as to prejudice a bona fide purchaser of the interest of either landlord or tenant who did not have notice of the right to rectify.

If there is a discrepancy between the executed original lease and counterpart, the former prevails over the latter, unless the original is clearly ambiguous.

11.3   Prescribed clauses leases

The LRA 2002 empowered Land Registry to prescribe a form of lease which would have to be used in all cases where the lease was registrable. This would be necessary to facilitate the registration of the lease and also because of the proposed introduction of electronic conveyancing. After consultation, Land Registry has now decided against a prescribed form of lease as such. However, the Land Registration (Amendment) (No 2) Rules 2005 provide that certain leases must contain prescribed clauses.

Use of the prescribed clauses is compulsory for leases that are dated on or after 19 June 2006, which are granted out of registered land, and are compulsorily registrable. These leases are known as 'prescribed clauses leases'.

A lease will not, however, be a prescribed clauses lease if it arises out of a variation of a lease which is a deemed surrender and re-grant, or if it is granted in a form expressly required by any of the following:

(a)   an agreement entered into before 19 June 2006;

(b)   a court order;

(c)   an enactment;

(d)   a necessary consent or licence for the grant of the lease given before 19 June 2006.

If an applicant claims that a lease is not a prescribed clauses lease due to one of these exceptions, a conveyancer's certificate or other evidence must be supplied with the application for registration.

11.3.1   Required wording

The wording required in a prescribed clauses lease must appear at the beginning of the lease or immediately after any front cover sheet and/or front contents page. A new Sch 1A is inserted into the Land Registration Rules 2005 which sets out the required wording and gives instructions as to how to the prescribed clauses must be completed:

LR1. Date of lease

LR2. Title number(s)

LR2.1 Landlord's title number(s)

Title number(s) out of which this lease is granted. Leave blank if not registered.

LR2.2 Other title numbers

Existing title number(s) against which entries of matters referred to in LR9, LR10, LR11 and LR13 are to be made.

LR3. Parties to this lease

Give full names, addresses and company's registered number, if any, of each of the parties. For Scottish companies use a SC prefix and for limited liability partnerships use an OC prefix. For foreign companies give territory in which incorporated.

Landlord

Tenant

Other parties

Specify capacity of each party, for example 'management company', 'guarantor', etc.

LR4. Property

*Insert a full description of the **land** being leased*
or
Refer to the clause, schedule or paragraph of a schedule in this lease in which the land being leased is more fully described.

Where there is a letting of part of a registered title, a plan must be attached to this lease and any floor levels must be specified.

In the case of a conflict between this clause and the remainder of this lease then, for the purposes of registration, this clause shall prevail.

LR5. Prescribed statements etc.

If this lease includes a statement falling within LR5.1, insert under that sub-clause the relevant statement or refer to the clause, schedule or paragraph of a schedule in this lease which contains the statement.

In LR5.2, omit or delete those Acts which do not apply to this lease.

LR5.1 Statements prescribed under rules 179 (dispositions in favour of a charity), 180 (dispositions by a charity) or 196 (leases under the Leasehold Reform, Housing and Urban Development Act 1993) of the Land Registration Rules 2003.

LR5.2 This lease is made under, or by reference to, provisions of:

Leasehold Reform Act 1967

Housing Act 1985

Housing Act 1988

Housing Act 1996

LR6. Term for which the Property is leased

Include only the appropriate statement (duly completed) from the three options.

NOTE: The information you provide, or refer to, here will be used as part of the particulars to identify the lease under rule 6 of the Land Registration Rules 2003.

From and including

To and including

OR

The term as specified in this lease at clause/schedule/paragraph

OR

The term is as follows:

LR7. Premium

Specify the total premium, inclusive of any VAT where payable.

LR8. Prohibitions or restrictions on disposing of this lease

Include whichever of the two statements is appropriate.

Do not set out here the wording of the provision.

This lease does not contain a provision that prohibits or restricts dispositions.

OR

This lease contains a provision that prohibits or restricts dispositions.

LR9. Rights of acquisition etc.

Insert the relevant provisions in the sub-clauses or refer to the clause, schedule or paragraph of a schedule in this lease which contains the provisions.

LR9.1 Tenant's contractual rights to renew this lease, to acquire the reversion or another lease of the Property, or to acquire an interest in other land

LR9.2 Tenant's covenant to (or offer to) surrender this lease

LR9.3 Landlord's contractual rights to acquire this lease

LR10. Restrictive covenants given in this lease by the Landlord in respect of land other than the Property

Insert the relevant provisions or refer to the clause, schedule or paragraph of a schedule in this lease which contains the provisions.

LR11. Easements

Refer here only to the clause, schedule or paragraph of a schedule in this lease which sets out the easements.

LR11.1 Easements granted by this lease for the benefit of the Property

LR11.2 Easements granted or reserved by this lease over the Property for the benefit of other property

LR12. Estate rentcharge burdening the Property

Refer here only to the clause, schedule or paragraph of a schedule in this lease which sets out the rentcharge.

LR13. Application for standard form of restriction

Set out the full text of the standard form of restriction and the title against which it is to be entered. If you wish to apply for more than one standard form of restriction use this clause to apply for each of them, tell us who is applying against which title and set out the full text of the restriction you are applying for.

Standard forms of restriction are set out in Schedule 4 to the Land Registration Rules 2003.

The Parties to this lease apply to enter the following standard form of restriction [against the title of the Property] *or* [against title number   ]

LR14. Declaration of trust where there is more than one person *comprising the Tenant*	The Tenant is more than one person. They are to hold the Property on trust for themselves as joint tenants.
If the Tenant is one person, omit or delete all the alternative statements.	OR
If the Tenant is more than one person, complete this clause by omitting or deleting all inapplicable alternative statements.	The Tenant is more than one person. They are to hold the Property on trust for themselves as tenants in common in equal shares.
	OR
	The Tenant is more than one person. They are to hold the Property on trust *Complete as necessary*

- All words in italicised text and inapplicable alternative wording in a clause may be omitted or deleted.
- Clause LR13 may be omitted or deleted.
- Clause LR14 may be omitted or deleted where the Tenant is one person.
- Otherwise, do not omit or delete any words in bold text unless italicised.
- Side-headings may appear as headings if this is preferred.
- Vertical or horizontal lines, or both, may be omitted.

Land Registry Practice Guide 64 gives detailed guidance on use of the clauses.

11.4 The structure of the lease

11.4.1 Commencement, date and parties

It is customary to commence the drafting of a document by describing the document according to the nature of the transaction to be effected; for example, a lease will commence with the words 'This Lease'. The date of the lease will be left blank until it is manually filled on completion with the date of actual completion. The draft lease should then set out the names and addresses of each party to the lease (eg, landlord, tenant and any guarantors).

11.4.2 Definitions

Every well-drafted document should contain a definitions section. If a word is to bear a specific meaning in a document, that meaning ought to be clearly defined at the start of the document. If certain phrases or words are likely to recur in the document, those phrases or words ought to be given a defined meaning at the start of the document. The use of a definitions clause in a legal document avoids needless repetition of recurring words and phrases, and permits a more concise style of drafting. If a word or phrase is to be defined in the definitions clause, the first letter of the defined term should be given a capital letter, and every use of that word or phrase thereafter should appear in the same form.

The following words and phrases are commonly used as defined terms in commercial leases:

'Development'

The lease is likely to regulate the carrying on of building, mining, engineering or other operations at the premises, and the making of a material change in the use of the premises. Rather than having to repeat the statutory definition of development at each reference, it is simpler just to refer to 'Development', which can be defined in the definitions clause as having the meaning given to it by s 55 of the TCPA 1990.

'Insured Risks'

There are many risks against which the lease will require the premises to be insured, and there will be several references to those risks in the insurance and repairing provisions of the lease. A full list of risks can be set out in the definitions clause, and then referred to elsewhere as the 'Insured Risks'.

'Interest'

If the tenant delays paying rent or any other sums due to the landlord under the lease, the landlord will want to charge the tenant interest on the unpaid sums. The rate of interest can be set out in the definitions clause. It is usually agreed to be a rate which is between 3 and 5% above the base lending rate of a nominated bank. The landlord usually stipulates that if the base rate of that bank should cease to exist, the interest rate under the lease will be a reasonably equivalent rate of interest.

'Pipes' or 'Conduits'

The tenant may be granted rights to use pipes in other parts of the landlord's building in order to run services to and from the premises. The landlord may reserve the right to use pipes passing through the tenant's premises. The lease should make it clear that 'Pipes' includes all pipes, sewers, drains, watercourses, wires, cables and other conducting media. In this sense the defined term is not so much a definition, as an expansion of the meaning of the word.

'Planning Acts'

The lease will contain several references to the TCPA 1990, the EA 1995, the PCA 1991, and other statutes relating to planning and environmental law, and the tenant will have obligations to comply with them. Those statutes can be grouped together and called 'the Planning Acts'.

'Premises'

There will be many references in the lease to the premises demised to the tenant. The draftsman will not want to repeat anything other than 'the Premises' at each reference. Hence, the definitions clause should define the premises demised by the lease, and a full verbal and legal description should be set out either here, or in the parcels clause (see **11.3.4**), or in one of the schedules to the lease.

'Term'

The term of the lease is one of the phrases most commonly referred to in the lease. Thought should be given to whether the definition should relate just to the contractual term, or whether it should include any extension, holding over or continuation of the term.

'VAT'

In defining value added tax, it should be made clear that 'VAT' also includes any tax replacing VAT, or becoming payable in addition to it, in case the fundamental principles of the tax are changed.

'Rent'

Rent will also be a commonly recurring word. Careful thought should be given as to what 'Rent' is to mean, and in the light of its definition, whether it is appropriate to use the term at every reference to rent in the lease. If the landlord wants to reserve service charge payments, insurance premiums and VAT as rent, so that he enjoys the same remedies for recovery of those sums as he enjoys in respect of rent (eg, distress and forfeiture without the need to serve an LPA 1925, s 146 notice), 'Rent' should be defined to include those items. It should also be made clear that 'Rent' means not only the original contractual rent, but also any revised rent which becomes payable by virtue of the rent review clause, and any interim rent which becomes payable under s 24A of the LTA 1954 during a statutory continuation tenancy. In this manner, it is made clear that, in a case where a tenant's liability continues after assignment, the liability relates to the payment of a rent which may be increased after the date the landlord assigns his interest in the premises. The term 'Rent' is not an appropriate term in every case under the lease. For instance, in the rent review clause, it is the annual rent which is to be reviewed from time to time during the term, not necessarily the 'Rent' as defined. Also, the landlord might be prepared to allow payment of the annual rent to be suspended for a period of time if there is damage to the premises by an insured risk, but he may not wish to have suspended the payment of other sums (eg, service charge) which have been reserved as 'Rent'. This was the point in issue in the case of *P&O Property Holdings Ltd v International Computers Ltd* [2000] 2 All ER 1015, ChD.

'Building'

If the lease is of part only of the landlord's building, the building itself should be identified, as the landlord will probably be entering into covenants in the lease to repair the structure and exterior of the building. There may be other references to the 'Building' with regard to the provision of services and the grant and reservation of easements.

'Common Parts'

Where a lease of part of a building is intended, the tenant will be granted rights to use the 'Common Parts' of the 'Building'. The extent of the 'Common Parts' should be clearly expressed.

11.4.3   The interpretation clause

Certain words or phrases do not require a fixed definition for the purposes of the lease, rather their meaning needs to be expanded or clarified to assist the reader in his interpretation and construction of the lease. Common examples of matters of interpretation are the following:

Joint and several liability

The lease should make it clear that, if the landlord or tenant is more than one person, the obligations placed upon those persons by the lease will be enforceable against either or both of them.

One gender to mean all genders

Section 61 of the LPA 1925 applies in respect of all deeds executed after LPA 1925 came into force so that any reference in a deed to the masculine will include the feminine, and vice versa. However, s 61 does not deal with the neuter (ie, 'it'), and it is therefore common to state, for the avoidance of doubt, that a reference to one gender includes all others.

References to statutes

Leases usually provide that, unless a particular clause expressly provides to the contrary, a reference in the lease to a statute or to a statutory instrument is to be taken as a reference to the Act or instrument as amended, re-enacted or modified from time to time, and not restricted to the legislation as it was in force at the date of the lease.

Expanding the meaning of words or phrases

If one of the tenant's covenants states that the tenant is prohibited from doing a certain act, the tenant will not be in breach of covenant if the act is done by a third party. It is, therefore, usual to state that if the tenant is required by the lease not to do a certain act, neither may he permit nor suffer the act to be done by someone else. If one of the tenant's covenants prohibits the carrying out of a certain act without the landlord's prior consent, and it is stipulated that the landlord's consent cannot be unreasonably withheld, it is usual to stipulate that his consent may not also be unreasonably delayed. Rather than dealing with these matters of drafting as and when the need arises in the lease, both of these points can be concisely dealt with by using an appropriate form of wording in the interpretation clause at the beginning of the lease.

11.4.4 The letting

The letting is the operative part of the lease which will create the tenant's interest, define the size of that interest, reserve rent, impose covenants, and deal with the grant and reservation of rights and easements. The clauses will be set out in the following logical sequence:

The operative words

Sufficient words of grant should be used to show the intention of the landlord to grant an interest in favour of the tenant. The landlord usually either 'demises' or 'lets' the premises to the tenant.

The parcels clause

A full description of the premises, including the rights to be granted to the tenant should be contained in the parcels clause. Often, the description is removed to one of the schedules (see below) so that the parcels clause simply refers to 'the Premises' (which will be a defined term).

Exceptions and reservations

Usually, the rights to be reserved for the benefit of the landlord are only briefly referred to in this part of the lease, and are set out extensively in one of the schedules.

The habendum

The habendum deals with the length of term to be vested in the tenant, and its commencement date.

The reddendum

The reddendum deals with the reservation of rent (which may be varied from time to time by a rent review clause), the dates for payment, and the manner of payment (ie, whether in advance or in arrear).

The covenants

Although the covenants on the part of landlord, tenant and surety are often set out in separate schedules, the parties expressly enter into them in the operative part of the lease.

11.4.5 The provisos

Grouped together under the heading of provisos is a wide variety of clauses which cannot easily be dealt with elsewhere in the lease, being clauses which are neither in the nature of covenants nor easements, and do not impose obligations upon one or other of the parties to the lease. They are clauses which have no common thread except that most of them are inserted into the lease for the landlord's benefit alone.

The provisos usually include the following clauses:

(a)   The proviso for re-entry, (ie, the forfeiture clause). This is dealt with in greater detail in **Chapter 23**.

(b)   An option to determine the lease where the premises are damaged by an insured risk so that they are no longer fit for use or occupation, and the landlord either cannot or, after a period of time, has not reinstated the premises (see **22.7**).

(c)   A rent abatement clause, which provides that the rent (and, possibly, other sums payable by the tenant under the lease) should cease to be payable if the premises are rendered unusable by damage caused by an insured risk (see **22.7.2**).

(d)   A provision which states that the landlord does not, by reason of anything contained in the lease, imply or represent that the tenant's proposed use of the premises is a permitted use under planning legislation. In *Laurence v Lexcourt Holdings Ltd* [1978] 2 All ER 810 (a case at first instance), the landlord had let premises to the tenant as 'offices'. After completion of the lease, the tenant discovered that only part of the premises enjoyed the benefit of planning permission for office use, and that the local planning authority was only prepared to grant planning permission in respect of all of the premises on a temporary basis. The court held that the tenant was entitled to rescind on account of the landlord's misrepresentation, since it was implicit in what was said in the lease that the premises could lawfully be used by the tenant for the intended purpose throughout the term. The landlord should therefore make it clear in the lease that, simply because the lease (or any licence granted subsequently) permits a certain type of business activity at the premises, the landlord does not warrant that permission is available for that use.

(e)   A provision whereby the tenant acknowledges that he has not entered into the lease in reliance upon any statement made by or on behalf of the landlord. This provision seeks to prevent the tenant from pursuing a remedy against the landlord in respect of a misrepresentation, but it will be subject to s 3 of the Misrepresentation Act 1967 (as amended by s 8 of the Unfair Contract Terms Act 1977) and will have to satisfy the test of reasonableness set out in the 1977 Act.

(f)   A provision regulating the method of service of notices under the lease. On occasions during the lease, one party will want or need to serve a notice on the other under one of the provisions in the lease (eg, to implement a rent review clause, or to give notice of an assignment of the lease, or as a preliminary step to the exercise of a right of re-entry). Whether or not a notice has been validly served will be an important issue and should, therefore, be a matter which is capable of conclusive determination. Accordingly, the lease should specify the method of service of notices, either by incorporating the provisions of s 196 of the LPA 1925 (as amended by the Recorded Delivery Service Act 1962) into the lease, or by expressly setting out the methods of service to be permitted by the lease. Section 196(3) provides that service can be effected by leaving the document at the premises or at the person's last-known abode or place of business. Section 196(4) deems service to have been effected if the notice is sent by recorded delivery post, provided that it is not returned through the Post Office as undelivered. The importance of tenants having proper systems in place to deal with notices was emphasised in *Warborough Investments Ltd v Central Midlands Estates Ltd* [2006] PLSCS 139. In this case, a 'trigger' notice initiating a rent review (see **16.6.3**) was held validly served when left at the customer service desk of a supermarket.

(g)   Excluding compensation under the LTA 1954. If the parties agree that the tenant should not be entitled to compensation under s 37 of the LTA 1954 at the end of his lease (see **31.6**), this part of the lease should include a clause whereby the tenant's right to compensation is excluded.

(h)   Fixing a perpetuity period. The landlord commonly reserves rights in the lease to use service pipes which currently pass through the tenant's premises, or which may at some future date be laid through them. The grant of a future right may be void if it infringes the rule against perpetuities. To avoid any possibility of this, the lease may specify a perpetuity period not exceeding 80 years (Perpetuities and Accumulations Act 1964, s 1(1)).

(i)   Excluding the tenant's security of tenure. Occasionally, the parties agree that the security of tenure provisions contained in the LTA 1954, Pt II should not apply to the lease (see

31.1.5). If this is to be the case, the contracting-out provision should appear in this part of the lease. Consent of the court would be required in respect of such an agreement.

(j)   Options to break. If either party is to enjoy the right to terminate the lease early by the exercise of an option to break (see **14.2**), the option is usually contained in this part of the lease.

11.4.6   Schedules

Most of the detail of the lease can be omitted from the main body of the document and placed in separate schedules. This will make the lease easier to read, and from the client's point of view, it makes it easier for him to refer to the various provisions of the lease.

Most leases contain schedules dealing with the following matters:

The premises

The first schedule to the lease often contains a description of the premises, which should be complete and accurate and, where appropriate, refer to plans to be incorporated in the lease.

Rights

If rights are to be granted to the tenant (eg, on a lease of part), they are usually referred to briefly in the body of the lease and set out in detail in a schedule.

Exceptions

Where the landlord is reserving rights (which will usually be the case) those matters will briefly be referred to in the body of the lease, and set out in detail in a schedule.

Rent review

Provisions relating to revisions of the annual rent during the term will either be contained in a separate clause in the body of the lease, or included in a schedule.

Covenants

There will be separate schedules detailing the tenant's covenants, the landlord's covenants and the covenants to be entered into by the tenant's guarantor on the grant of the lease, the assignee's guarantor on the assignment of the lease, and an outgoing tenant as an authorised guarantor (as to which, see **18.2.7**).

Service charge provisions

If there is to be a service charge, it is usual to group all the service charge provisions in one schedule to the lease.

11.4.7   Execution

The lease and its counterpart are deeds and, therefore, the usual rules relating to the execution of deeds are applicable. A testimonium clause is not an essential part of a lease but, if one is included, it ought to appear immediately before the first schedule. Attestation clauses will, of course, be essential.

11.5   The 2007 Code for Leasing Business Premises in England and Wales

The origins of the 2007 Code can be traced back to the *Code of Practice for Commercial Leases in England and Wales*, which was published in April 2002 following government pressure on the property industry. The 2002 Code was drafted by a working party comprising representatives from property and industry and professional advisers. The Government felt that landlords were generally not offering tenants sufficiently flexible lease terms to match their business requirements. The Government was especially concerned that upward-only rent reviews remained prevalent in longer leases and was considering outlawing them.

At the launch of the Code in 2002, Sally Keeble, the then Regeneration Minister, stated that the Code recommended that commercial property owners should, wherever possible, provide a choice of leasing terms to prospective tenants, where this was practicable.

The Government also commissioned a two-year study of the impact of the Code. This was undertaken by the University of Reading and its report, *Monitoring the 2002 Code of Practice for Commercial Leases*, was released in early 2005. The Code was found to be having little direct effect upon lease negotiations. Restrictions on assignment and sub-letting had not been relaxed and were still the subject of complaint by many tenants. The provisions of the Landlord and Tenant (Covenants) Act 1995 (LT(C)A 1995) had, indeed, encouraged landlords to impose detailed restrictions on assignment and to require authorised guarantee agreements (AGAs) from assigning tenants (see **18.2.5.1**). The property industry thus appeared to be ignoring the thrust of the recommendations in the Code that restrictions, beyond the standard 'consent not to be unreasonably withheld', should be imposed on tenants only if that is necessary to protect the landlord's interests and, in particular, that AGAs should be required only where the assignee is of lower financial standing than the present tenant.

In March 2005, Housing and Planning Minister Yvette Cooper stated that the Government was still concerned about inflexibility in the commercial property market. The major problems were assignment and sub-letting provisions, which made it difficult for tenants to dispose of properties that were surplus to requirements. She announced a review of the law of assignment and sub-letting, with the aim of easing the position for tenants while not jeopardising property investment; this included looking at legislative options. There was also continued concern about the prevalence of upward-only rent review clauses in longer leases and further progress in this area was necessary to improve the flexibility of the market. The Government would continue to monitor the situation and retain the option to legislate in future if necessary.

The Government clearly believed that the property industry was providing inadequate flexibility for tenants and that it was time to reconsider the rights given to landlords by the LT(C)A 1995 with regard to assignment and AGAs. Although legislation amending the LT(C)A 1995 or banning upward-only rent reviews has not been ruled out, the Government signalled its desire for change to be achieved voluntarily and for the 2002 Code to be updated. The joint working group that produces the Code was reconvened and a new version of the Code was published in March 2007 (the *Code for Leasing Business Premises*). The 2007 Code provides a step-by-step occupiers' guide to contract negotiations, intended to help tenants avoid the pitfalls of bad contracts and to ensure that landlords operate to industry-agreed standards. It also encourages parties to move away from upward-only rent review clauses, which have enabled landlords to increase rents unchecked.

A number of radical overhauls of leasing practices were recommended, including the following:

(a)   Landlords should price alternative rent review terms on a risk-adjusted basis.

(b)   Preconditions on break clauses should be restricted.

(c)   If sub-letting is allowed, it should be at the market rent.

(d)   At the time of lease negotiations, landlords should disclose known irregular events that would have a significant effect upon the amount of future service charges.

(e)   Unless expressly stated in the heads of terms, tenants will be obliged only to give the premises back at the end of their lease in the same condition as they were in when the lease was granted.

The 2007 Code offers three documents to improve leasing practice:

(a)   a two-page 'Landlords Code', which clarifies what is expected from landlords;

(b)   a step-by-step 'Occupier Guide' for tenants that will take them through the leasing process; and

(c)   a checklist showing tenants at a glance what they are signing up to, which can also be used by all parties, their agents and solicitors during lease negotiations.

Housing and Planning Minister, Yvette Cooper, said: 'The new code will mean all businesses get a better deal on commercial property leases. This is an important step forward by the industry since it sets out clearly and simply best practice and advice for lease negotiations. My challenge to the industry is to make sure that it is used in all lease negotiations. We shall be keeping a close watch on the market to see that it makes a real difference.'

She also said: 'We believe the new code should have a chance to work, but . . . we have legal options if it does not succeed. Industry needs to take the lead here. We will keep an eye on the effect of the code and watch with interest to ensure that there is proper, accountable self-regulation so that legislation is not necessary.'

In July 2009, the Department of Communities and Local Government published a report on the use of the Code conducted by the University of Reading. This shows a disappointing lack of awareness and use of the Code. The Parliamentary Under Secretary of State for Communities and Local Government, Ian Austin, commented on this in a written statement to the House of Commons on 3 July 2009 (*Hansard* col 30WS).

He stated that the Government had 'held back' on legislating to 'give the 2007 Code a chance to work'. He made it clear that if the forthcoming impact assessment on the Code 'shows that the market has not responded, legislation is bound to come back on the agenda'. He firmly placed the onus on the property industry to ensure the Code's success. He stated (*Hansard* col 31WS):

> I call on the property industry, while there is still time, to redouble efforts to disseminate and use the code – every tenant negotiating a lease should have a copy and be encouraged to use it. In particular, the professions – surveyors and solicitors – have a special responsibility for making it available. A professional, modern industry will surely have an interest in ensuring that its customers are fully and properly informed about the leasing choices they are making. The UK commercial property industry should be a world leader, not just in its level of sophistication, but also in the fairness with which it operates.

It is thus clear that to avoid Government intervention, the property industry will now have to be seen to be complying with the 2007 Code.

The 2007 Code is set out in full in **Appendix 2**. A lease prepared by the Practical Law Company (^{PLC}Property) to promote discussion of the 2007 Code is set out in **Appendix 3**. It is intended to be compliant with the Code and also the RICS Code of Practice for Service Charges.

Chapter 12

The Parties to the Lease

12.1 Introduction

Following the date and commencement, the lease will set out details of the parties to the lease, namely the landlord, the tenant and any guarantor (who is also often referred to as a surety).

In respect of a corporate party, the lease should give the company's full name and either its registered office or its main administrative office, and the company's registration number. In respect of an individual party, the full name and postal address of the individual will suffice.

The purpose of this chapter is to examine the extent and duration of liability of the parties to a lease, the Landlord and Tenant (Covenants) Act 1995 (LT(C)A 1995) (which came into force on 1 January 1996) brought about considerable changes in this area. In particular, it abolished the concept of privity of contract in relation to leases which are defined as new leases for the purposes of the Act (see **12.2.2**). Accordingly, this chapter examines the law and practice both in relation to leases already in existence at the date when the Act came into force (the old regime), and those which are new leases (the new regime).

12.2 The landlord

The landlord's primary purpose as a party to the lease is to grant to the tenant the leasehold interest that both parties intend, upon the terms agreed between them. These terms may require the landlord to enter into covenants with the tenant in order to ensure that the tenant peaceably enjoys occupation of the premises, and a certain quality of accommodation (see, more specifically, **Chapter 21**).

12.2.1 The old regime

12.2.1.1 The original landlord

By virtue of the principle of privity of contract, the original landlord, as an original contracting party, remains liable in respect of any covenants entered into in the lease, even after he has sold the reversion. The landlord protects himself against the possibility of being sued for a breach of covenant committed by his successor by obtaining from him an express indemnity covenant in the transfer of the reversion. Such a covenant is not implied at law.

If the landlord has granted a lease of an entire building, it is unlikely that he entered into many covenants with the tenant. If the landlord has granted a lease of part of a building, or of premises forming part of a larger commercial site, the landlord may have entered into covenants to provide services to the tenants. If this is the case, the landlord may have limited expressly the duration of his liability under the covenants to the time the reversion is vested in him, rather than relied upon obtaining an indemnity covenant.

12.2.1.2   A successor to the reversion

The landlord's successor in title is bound during his period of ownership by all covenants imposed upon the landlord which have reference to the subject matter of the lease (see s 142(1) of the LPA 1925). At the same time, he takes the benefit of the tenant's covenants which have reference to the subject matter of the lease under s 141(1) of the LPA 1925. There was some doubt as to whether the benefit of surety covenants contained in the lease would pass to a buyer of the reversion without an express assignment, but it now appears in the light of *P&A Swift Investments v Combined English Stores Group plc* [1988] 3 WLR 313 that it will, provided the lease made it clear that a reference in the lease to the landlord includes his successors in title.

12.2.2   The new regime

12.2.2.1   The original landlord

Under a lease affected by the LT(C)A 1995 (as a general rule, those granted on or after 1 January 1996), on an assignment of the reversion by the original landlord, while there is no automatic release from his obligations under the lease, ss 6 and 8 of the Act provide a procedure whereby the assigning landlord can apply to the tenant to be released from his obligations under the lease. The outgoing landlord may serve a notice (in a prescribed form) on the tenant (either before or within four weeks after the assignment) requesting his release. If, within four weeks of service, the tenant objects by serving a written notice on the landlord, the landlord may apply to the county court for a declaration that it is reasonable for the covenant to be released. If the tenant does not object within that time limit, the release becomes automatic. Any release from a covenant under these provisions is regarded as occurring at the time when the assignment in question takes place. However, in the case of *BHP Great Britain Petroleum Ltd v Chesterfield Properties Ltd* [2001] EWCA Civ 1797, [2002] 2 WLR 672, the Court of Appeal held that the statutory release mechanism did not operate to release the landlord from those covenants which were expressed to be personal. In respect of such covenants, the original landlord would continue to be liable even after the assignment of the reversion had taken place. This decision may have significant implications for landlords.

Once a landlord is released under these provisions, he ceases to be entitled to the benefit of the tenant covenants in the lease as from the date of the assignment of the reversion.

However, the House of Lords decision in *Avonridge Property Co Ltd v Mashru* [2005] UKHL 70 offers a further opportunity for landlords to ensure that they are released from liability on an assignment of the reversion. In that case, it was held that a provision that expressly limited the landlord's liability under the covenants to the time that the reversion was vested in him was not rendered void by the provisions of the LT(C)A 1995. This seems likely to be an attractive provision for landlords to insert in leases, avoiding as it does the reliance on the 'reasonableness' provisions of the LT(C)A 1995. As the facts of that case show, however, tenants should be very cautious in agreeing to it when the landlord's covenants are of substantial value, eg to perform the covenants in the head lease. A transfer of the reversion to an impecunious person could result in the tenant having no effective remedy if the landlord's covenants were not performed.

12.2.2.2   A successor to the reversion

The landlord's successor becomes bound, as from the date of the assignment, by all of the landlord covenants in the lease, except to the extent that immediately before the assignment they did not bind the assignor (eg, covenants expressed to be personal). Similarly, the new landlord becomes entitled to the benefit of the tenant covenants in the lease. Sections 141 and 142 of the LPA 1925 do not apply in relation to new leases, so there is no need to enquire whether the relevant covenant is one which 'has reference to the subject matter of the lease'. The benefit of surety covenants (not being tenant covenants for the purposes of the Act) will pass to an assignee of the reversion in accordance with *P&A Swift Investments* on the basis that the assignee has acquired the legal estate, and the surety covenants touch and concern that estate. In the same manner, the benefit of a former tenant's authorised guarantee agreement (see **18.2.7**) will pass to the assignee.

A successor can apply to be released from his obligations under the lease when, at some future time, he assigns the reversion. If at that time a former landlord is still liable on the lease covenants (because he did not obtain a release from the tenant when he assigned the reversion), he can make another application to the tenant to be released.

12.3   The tenant

The person to whom the lease is granted is known as the original tenant. The person to whom the tenant later assigns his lease is known as the assignee. The original tenant will be required to enter into many covenants in the lease regulating what can be done in, on or at the premises.

12.3.1   The old regime

12.3.1.1   The original tenant – privity of contract

Prior to the LT(C)A 1995, basic principles of privity of contract dictated that the original tenant, as an original contracting party, remained liable in respect of all of the covenants in the lease for the entire duration of the term, even after he assigned the lease. The original tenant under the existing regime is in the undesirable position of being liable for a breach of covenant committed after he has parted with his interest in the premises. If, for example, the tenant was granted a 25-year term which he assigned at the end of the fifth year to an assignee who then failed to pay rent and allowed the premises to fall into disrepair, the landlord could choose to sue, not the assignee, but the original tenant for non-payment of rent and breach of the repairing covenant. It does not matter that since the assignment the rent has been increased under the rent review clause (unless the increase is referrable to a variation of the lease terms agreed between the landlord and assignee – see s 18 of the LT(C)A 1995 and the case of *Friends' Provident Life Office v British Railways Board* [1995] 1 All ER 336).

The effect of privity of contract becomes increasingly significant in recessionary times. If the reason why the assignee has defaulted in his obligations under the lease is that the assignee has become insolvent, instead of pursuing a worthless claim against the assignee, the landlord would look to the original tenant for payment of rent.

12.3.1.2   For how long is the original tenant liable?

The original tenant's liability lasts for the entire duration of the contractual term. Once he has assigned his interest in the lease, his liability will not extend into any continuation of that term that may arise under s 24 of the LTA 1954, unless there is an express provision in the lease to the contrary. As will be seen later (at **31.1.7**), a tenancy which is protected by Pt II of that Act will not come to an end on the expiration of the contractual term. Instead, s 24 continues the tenancy on exactly the same terms, and at the same rent, until the tenancy is terminated in one of the methods prescribed by the Act. Hence, the contractual rent remains payable beyond the expiry date of the lease, but the effect of the House of Lords' decision in *City of London Corporation v Fell* [1993] 49 EG 113 is that, where the original tenant has already assigned his lease before the contractual expiry date of the lease, his liability will cease at that date, and will not be continued.

However, even before *City of London Corporation v Fell*, landlords were drafting leases to include a provision to ensure that the original tenant (and any assignees who entered into a direct covenant with the landlord) would remain liable to perform the covenants during a statutory continuation. This would be done by defining 'the Term' in the lease to include 'the period of any holding over or any extension or continuance whether by agreement or operation of law'. The tenant is then required to pay the rent and perform his covenants during 'the Term'. The one consolation for a tenant who has assigned the lease but remains liable because of the definition of 'the Term' is provided by *Herbert Duncan Ltd v Cluttons* [1992] 1 EGLR 101, which held that the continuing liability to pay rent relates only to the contractual rent under the lease, and not to any interim rent fixed by the court under s 24A of the LTA 1954 unless the lease states otherwise.

12.3.1.3   The need for an indemnity

As a result of the continuing nature of the original tenant's liability under the old regime, it is essential that, on an assignment, the original tenant obtains an indemnity from the assignee against all future breaches of covenant (whether committed by the assignee or a successor in title). An express indemnity may be taken, but this is not strictly necessary since s 77 of the LPA 1925 automatically implies into every assignment for value a covenant to indemnify the assignor against all future breaches of covenant. If the lease is registered at Land Registry, Sch 12 to the Land Registration Act 2002 (LRA 2002) implies a similar covenant for indemnity into a transfer of the lease, whether or not value is given.

From a practical point of view, it should be noted that an indemnity from an assignee (whether express or implied) is worthless if the assignee is insolvent, and this may be the very reason why the landlord is pursuing the original tenant in the first place.

Where there has been a succession of assignments, and the original tenant finds that he is unable to obtain a full indemnity against his immediate assignee, the assignee in possession may be liable at common law to indemnify the original tenant who has been sued for breach of covenant (see *Moule v Garrett and Others* (1872) LR 7 Exch 101), but again the indemnity may be worthless owing to the insolvency of the defaulting assignee.

12.3.1.4   The assignee – privity of estate

By virtue of the doctrine of privity of estate, an assignee under the old regime is liable in respect of all of the covenants in the lease which 'touch and concern' the demised premises, for as long as the lease remains vested in him.

An assignee cannot be sued for a breach of covenant committed prior to the lease being vested in him, save to the extent that the breach in question is a continuing breach (eg, breach of a covenant to repair) which effectively becomes the assignee's breach from the date of the assignment. If, at the time of the assignment there are arrears of rent, the landlord's claim to recover the arrears would be against the assignor, not the assignee. However, from a practical point of view, the landlord is unlikely to give his consent to an assignment (assuming the lease requires his consent) unless the arrears are cleared. Further, the assignee is unlikely to take the assignment while rent is in arrear because of the risk of forfeiture of the lease on account of the outstanding breach.

An assignee is not liable for breaches of covenant committed after he has parted with his interest in the premises, (although he may still be sued in respect of breaches committed while he was the tenant) and he is not liable in respect of covenants which do not touch and concern the premises (but see **12.3.1.5**).

12.3.1.5   Covenants which touch and concern

Under the old regime, an assignee is liable only in respect of those covenants which touch and concern the demised premises. These are covenants which are not in the nature of personal covenants, but have direct reference to the premises in question by laying down something which is to be done or not to be done at the premises, and which affect the landlord in his normal capacity as landlord, or the tenant in his normal capacity as tenant. If the purpose of the covenant is to achieve something which is collateral to the relationship of landlord and tenant, then the covenant does not touch and concern.

Nearly all of the covenants in a typical commercial lease touch and concern the demised premises. For example, the covenants:

(a)   to pay rent,

(b)   to repair,

(c)   to use the premises for a particular purpose,

(d)   not to make alterations without consent,

(e)   not to assign or sublet without consent,

are all covenants which relate to the premises and have reference to the landlord and tenant relationship in respect of those premises.

By contrast, the following covenants do not touch and concern:

(a)   to pay a periodic sum to a third party;

(b)   to build premises for the landlord upon some other land; or

(c)   to repair or renew chattels (as distinct from fixtures, which would form part of the premises).

These covenants do not have any reference to the relationship of landlord and tenant in respect of the land in question and, therefore, would not bind an assignee.

12.3.1.6   Direct covenants

Landlords have never liked the limited duration of an assignee's liability under the doctrine of privity of estate. In practice, therefore, it is common for the landlord to try to extend the liability of an assignee under the old regime by requiring him, as a condition of the landlord's licence to assign, to enter into a direct covenant to observe the covenants in the lease for the entire duration of the term, thereby creating privity of contract between landlord and assignee. This covenant is usually contained in the formal licence to assign (see **27.2**). The landlord will always then have a choice between original tenant and present assignee as to whom to sue for a breach of covenant committed by the latter. Where intermediate assignees have entered into direct covenants in this manner, the landlord's options are increased.

If an assignee has given a direct covenant to the landlord, the extent of his continuing liability is governed by the *City of London v Fell* case, and the definition of 'the Term' in the lease in the same way as applies to the original tenant.

12.3.1.7   The need for an indemnity

The assignee from the original tenant will have covenanted, either expressly or impliedly, with the original tenant to indemnify him against liability for loss arising out of any future breach of covenant (whether committed by the assignee or a successor in title). Irrespective of whether the assignee is affected by privity of estate or contract, because he gave an indemnity covenant to his assignor, he needs to obtain one from his assignee. An express indemnity may be taken, but s 77 of the LPA 1925 and Sch 12 to the LRA 2002 will operate in the same way as before.

12.3.2   The new regime

As stated above, the main purpose of the LT(C)A 1995 was to abolish privity of contract in leases, and it is therefore in the area of tenant liability that the Act has the most significant impact.

12.3.2.1   The original tenant – privity of contract release

The basic rule is that a tenant under a lease which is a new lease for the purposes of the LT(C)A 1995 is only liable for breaches of covenant committed while the lease is vested in him. Thus, on assignment of the lease, the assignor is automatically released from all the tenant covenants of the tenancy (and he ceases to be entitled to the benefit of the landlord covenants).

This means that while the outgoing tenant can be sued for breaches of covenant committed at a time when the lease was vested in him, he cannot be sued for any subsequent breaches.

12.3.2.2   The assignee – liability on covenants

The basic rule applies equally to assignees. As from the date of assignment, an assignee becomes bound by the tenant covenants in the lease except to the extent that immediately before the assignment they did not bind the assignor (eg, they were expressed to be personal to the original tenant), but when he assigns the lease, he is automatically released from all of the tenant covenants. One slight change for leases under the new regime is that an assignee will be liable on all the tenant covenants in the lease whether or not they 'touch and concern' the land. The combination of this slight change, and the statutorily imposed limitation on the duration of an assignee's liability, makes the practice under the old regime of obtaining direct covenants from assignees inapplicable to leases granted under the new regime.

In the same way that the assignee becomes bound by the tenant covenants, so too does the assignee become entitled, as from the date of the assignment, to the benefit of the landlord covenants in the lease.

12.3.2.3   Excluded assignments

Assignments in breach of covenant (eg, where the tenant has not complied with a requirement in the lease to obtain his landlord's consent before assigning) or by operation of law (eg, on the death or bankruptcy of a tenant) are excluded assignments for the purposes of the LT(C)A 1995. On an excluded assignment, the assignor will not be released from the tenant covenants of the lease, and will remain liable to the landlord, jointly and severally with the assignee, until the next assignment, which is not an excluded assignment, takes place.

12.3.2.4   Authorised guarantee agreements

To counterbalance the loss to the landlord of the benefits of the old privity regime, the LT(C)A 1995 allows the landlord to require an outgoing tenant, who will be released from liability under the Act, to enter into a form of guarantee whereby the outgoing tenant guarantees the performance of the tenant covenants by the incoming tenant (see **18.2.7**).

12.3.2.5   Indemnity covenants?

As an assigning tenant is not liable for the breaches of covenant committed by his successor, the LT(C)A 1995 has repealed s 77 of the LPA 1925 and Sch 12 to the LRA 2002 in relation to leases granted under the new regime. However, it should be noted that an outgoing tenant may remain liable to the landlord for an assignee's breaches of covenant under the terms of an authorised guarantee agreement and, in such circumstances, an express indemnity from the assignee should be obtained.

12.4   The guarantor

Much attention in practice is given to the financial status of the proposed tenant, and a consideration of what is called 'the strength of the tenant's covenant'. A tenant is said to give 'a good covenant' if it can be expected that the tenant will pay the rent on time throughout the term, and diligently perform his other obligations under the lease. An established, high performing and renowned public limited company (such as one of the large retail food companies) will be regarded as a good covenant in the commercial letting market, whereas newly formed public limited companies and many private companies, whose reputation, reliability and financial standing are unknown in the property market, will not be perceived as giving a good covenant. If the covenant is so bad that the landlord has reservations about the proposed tenant's ability to maintain rental payments throughout the term without financial difficulties, the landlord will consider not granting a lease to that tenant in the first place.

However, in situations which fall between these two extremes, the landlord often requires a third party, known as a guarantor, to join in the lease to guarantee the tenant's obligations.

12.4.1 Practical points

The landlord's aim is to ensure that he receives the rent due under the lease on time throughout the term, either from the tenant, or if the tenant defaults, from the guarantor. Therefore, just as the landlord ought to investigate the financial status of his proposed tenant, so too should he investigate the status of the guarantor nominated by the tenant.

With private limited companies or newly formed public limited companies (who, even with plc status, may be just as likely to be in breach as any other tenant) many landlords will ask for one or more of the company's directors to guarantee the tenant's performance of its obligations. However, the landlord should not necessarily be so blinkered in his approach, since other options may prove to be more fruitful.

Does a subsidiary company have a parent or sister company which can stand as guarantor? If the directors are not of sufficient financial standing, are the shareholders of the company in any better position to give the landlord the element of reliability he requires? Will the tenant's bank guarantee the obligation of its client?

The guarantor should be advised to seek independent advice, since there is a clear conflict of interests between tenant and guarantor. The conflict arises in that, on the one hand, the advice to be given to the tenant is that, without a guarantor, the tenant will not get a lease, while, on the other hand, the advice to give to the guarantor would be to avoid giving the guarantee. Further, in seeking to make amendments to the surety covenants in the lease on behalf of the guarantor, the solicitor may be prejudicing the negotiation of the lease terms between the landlord and his tenant–client, causing delay or disruption.

12.4.2 The extent of the guarantee

12.4.2.1 The old regime

The purpose of the guarantee is to ensure that the guarantor will pay the rent if the tenant does not, and will remedy or indemnify the landlord against any breaches of covenant committed by the tenant. Two points should be noted. First, it is usual for the landlord in drafting the lease to define 'the Tenant' to include the tenant's successors in title. This means that in guaranteeing the obligations of 'the Tenant', the guarantor has guaranteed the performance of future (and as yet unknown) assignees of the lease. His liability would, therefore, extend throughout the duration of the lease (even after the original tenant had assigned the lease). Secondly, even if the guarantee was limited to a guarantee of the original tenant's obligations, an original tenant remains liable by virtue of privity of contract under the existing regime to perform the covenants in the lease for its entire duration. Should, therefore, the landlord choose to sue, not the assignee in possession, but the original tenant, the guarantee would remain active.

Ideally, the guarantor should seek to limit the extent of his liability so that the guarantee applies only for so long as the lease remains vested in the tenant in respect of whom the guarantee was originally sought. This is a matter for negotiation with the landlord.

12.4.2.2 The new regime

Abolition of the concept of privity of contract in leases applies equally to guarantors. Section 24(2) of the LT(C)A 1995 provides that where a tenant is released under the LT(C)A 1995 from the tenant covenants of the lease, any person (ie, the guarantor) who was bound, before the release, by a covenant imposing liability upon that person in the event of default by the tenant, is released to the same extent as the tenant. Any attempt to extend the liability of a guarantor beyond the duration of the liability of the tenant whose performance was guaranteed is likely to fall foul of the anti-avoidance provisions of s 25 of the LT(C)A 1995. However, it is arguable that a guarantor can be required to undertake a separate obligation to guarantee the tenant's performance under any authorised guarantee agreement he may enter into.

There is some comfort for the guarantor in either regime in that, unless there is an express provision in the lease to the contrary, the liability of the guarantor will cease upon the contractual term date and will not continue during a statutory continuation tenancy under s 24 of the LTA 1954 (see *Junction Estates Ltd v Cope* (1974) 27 P & CR 482). However, it is common practice to define the lease term to include 'the period of any holding over or any extension or continuance whether by agreement or operation of law', and to prolong the guarantor's liability by requiring him to covenant with the landlord throughout 'the term' as so defined.

12.4.3   Discharge or release

The guarantor cannot unilaterally revoke his guarantee, but in certain cases, usually where the landlord acts to the prejudice of the guarantor, the conduct of the landlord might operate as a release.

12.4.3.1   Variations

If the landlord, without obtaining the consent of the guarantor, agrees with the tenant to vary the terms of the lease (eg, by substituting more onerous repairing obligations), the variation of the lease will operate to discharge the guarantor. A guarantor cannot stand as surety and be made liable for the tenant's default in the performance of terms different to those guaranteed to be performed, unless the guarantor has agreed to the variation. However, an immaterial variation of the lease which would not prejudice the guarantor (eg, by substituting less onerous repairing obligations) is not likely to discharge the guarantor, although authority appears to suggest that it is for the guarantor to decide whether or not he would be prejudiced by the proposed variation. In *Holme v Brunskill* (1877) 3 QBD 495, a surrender of part of the premises comprised in the lease (which might not appear in any way to prejudice the guarantor, particularly if the rent is reduced as a result), which was agreed without the consent of the guarantor, operated to discharge the guarantee. However, a variation which does not affect the terms of the (tenant's) principal contract will not affect the guarantor's secondary contract (see *Metropolitan Properties Co (Regis) Ltd v Bartholomew* [1995] 14 EG 143).

A surrender of the whole of the premises comprised in the lease will operate to end the liability of the guarantor as from the date of surrender, but not in respect of any breaches of covenant outstanding at that time.

Increasing the rent by exercising a rent review clause does not amount to a variation and so will not release the guarantor. This means that a guarantor may be guaranteeing the payment in future of an unknown level of rent (although see the protection given to guarantors of former tenants by s 18 of the LT(C)A 1995 and in the case of *Friends' Provident Life Office v British Railways Board* [1995] 1 All ER 336).

12.4.3.2   'Giving time'

'Giving time' to the tenant may operate to discharge the guarantee. A landlord 'gives time' to a tenant if, in a binding way, he agrees to allow the tenant to pay rent late, or not at all. It does not seem that a mere omission to press for payment (eg, due to an oversight, or perhaps to avoid a waiver of the right to forfeit the lease) will amount to the giving of time.

12.4.3.3   Release of co-guarantor

According to general principles of suretyship, if there is more than one guarantor, the release by the landlord of one of them operates as a release of all of them.

12.4.3.4 Death

The death of the tenant is not likely to bring an end to the guarantee, since the lease will vest in the tenant's personal representatives who, as the tenant's successors in title, will become 'the Tenant' under the lease, whose obligations are guaranteed by the guarantor. Under the new regime, such a vesting would be an excluded assignment, and so the guarantor would not be released. Further, the death of the guarantor will not necessarily bring an end to the guarantee since the guarantor's own personal representatives will remain liable under the guarantee to the extent of the deceased's assets passing through their hands. However, it is more common for the landlord to make provision for the possible death of the guarantor by obtaining a covenant from the tenant obliging him to find a suitable replacement.

12.4.3.5 Bankruptcy or liquidation

The bankruptcy or liquidation of the tenant will not operate to release the guarantor. On the bankruptcy of an individual tenant, the lease will vest in the trustee-in-bankruptcy who will become 'the Tenant' for the purposes of the lease (and such a vesting is an excluded assignment under the new regime). On the liquidation of a corporate tenant, the lease will remain vested in the company (unless the liquidator obtains an order under s 145 of the Insolvency Act 1986 (IA 1986)).

Even if the trustee or liquidator chooses to disclaim the lease, the disclaimer will not operate to end the guarantor's liability (see **29.1.2**).

12.4.4 Drafting points for the landlord

The landlord should ensure that the guarantor joins in the lease to give the covenants the landlord requires. A guarantee will be unenforceable if it is not in writing (see *Actionstrength Ltd v International Glass Engineering* [2003] 2 AC 541).

The two basic obligations of a guarantor are to pay the rent (and any other sums payable by the tenant under the lease) if the tenant does not pay, and to remedy, or to indemnify the landlord against loss caused by, any breaches of covenant committed by the tenant. The landlord will ensure that the guarantor is liable for the period in respect of which the tenant is liable under the lease (and, possibly, under any authorised guarantee agreement that the tenant may enter into).

Several other provisions are usually required by the landlord:

(a) A covenant from the tenant to provide a replacement guarantor should one of several unfortunate or undesirable events happen. For instance, if the guarantor is an individual who dies, or becomes mentally incapable (ie, a receiver is appointed under s 99 of the Mental Health Act 1983) or has a petition in bankruptcy presented against him (or is affected by other proceedings under the IA 1986 which the landlord considers serious enough to warrant substitution) the landlord will require the tenant to find a replacement of equivalent financial standing. If the guarantor is a company and a winding-up commences (or, as above, it is affected by other adverse insolvency proceedings), again the tenant will be required to find a reasonably acceptable replacement.

(b) A provision protecting the landlord against the tenant's trustee-in-bankruptcy or liquidator disclaiming the lease to bring the tenant's liability to an end. The effect of a disclaimer is dealt with at **29.1.3**. For present purposes it can be said that, whilst disclaimer does not end the liability of a guarantor, most landlords will nevertheless want the ability to require the guarantor to take a lease from the landlord in the event of disclaimer, for the full unexpired residue of the term then remaining.

(c) A provision to deal with situations which might otherwise operate to release the guarantor. As part of the guarantor's covenants, the landlord will include a declaration that a release will not be effected by the giving of time to the tenant, or by a variation in the terms of the lease (although as a concession, the landlord might accept that a variation prejudicial to the guarantor will still operate as a release unless the guarantor has consented to it). The effect of stating in the lease that the guarantor will not be released 'by any other event which, but for this provision, would operate to release the surety' is doubtful.

12.4.5   Drafting points for the guarantor

If the guarantor has accepted the principle of giving a guarantee, he should make all efforts to minimise his liability. There are several provisions a guarantor can seek to negotiate:

(a)   A limit on the length of his liability; while the LT(C)A 1995 releases a guarantor to the same extent as it releases the tenant, the guarantor should try to ensure that he is not contractually bound to guarantee the tenant under any authorised guarantee agreement (as to which, see **18.2.7**).

(b)   An obligation on the landlord's part to notify the guarantor of any default by the tenant; one would expect the tenant to tell his guarantor if the tenant was experiencing difficulties in meeting his obligations under the lease. However, this might not always be the case, and in order to alert the guarantor to possible claims under the guarantee and, perhaps, to enable him to put pressure on the tenant, he could seek to include a covenant by the landlord to notify him in writing whenever the tenant falls into arrears with the rent, or otherwise breaches a covenant in the lease.

(c)   Participation in rent reviews; as the guarantor guarantees payment of future unascertained rents he may try to persuade the landlord to allow him to play a part in the rent review process. This would necessitate amendments to the usual rent review clause, and would not be attractive to the landlord. Further, the tenant would not be keen either to hand over the review negotiations to the guarantor or to have him involved as a third party in the review process, and an assignee of the lease would certainly see it as an unattractive proposition.

(d)   An ability to demand an assignment of the lease from the tenant where the tenant is in default under the lease. This would enable the guarantor to minimise his liability by being able to call for an assignment and then assign the lease to a more stable assignee.

12.4.6   An assignee's guarantor

The above paragraphs have concentrated on the guarantee to be provided by the original tenant on the grant of the lease. However, as a condition of granting licence to assign the lease, the landlord may require the assignee to provide a suitable guarantor in respect of his obligations (see **18.2.3**). Under the old regime, it will be the landlord's intention to fix the new guarantor with liability for the duration of the contractual term and beyond, in the same way that he tries to fix the liability of the original tenant's guarantor. Under the new regime, liability should not exceed the liability of the assignee.

12.5   Rent deposits

As an alternative (or in addition) to a guarantee, the landlord may require the tenant to enter into a rent deposit deed whereby the tenant is required to deposit with the landlord, on the grant of the lease, a sum of money equivalent to, say, 12 months' rent, which the landlord is allowed to call upon in the event of tenant default. At the end of the lease (or, perhaps, on lawful assignment), the deposit should be returned to the tenant.

Careful thought must be given to the setting up of this arrangement and to the drafting of the rent deposit deed. The following factors should be kept in mind.

(a)   The deed should specify what default by the tenant will trigger access to the deposit (eg, non-payment of rent, VAT or interest, or other breaches of covenant).

(b)   If the deposited money is to be viewed as belonging to the landlord, it will be at risk if the landlord becomes insolvent. For instance, it would fall under the control of the landlord company's liquidator if the company went into liquidation. Equally, if the money is to be viewed as belonging to the tenant, it will be at risk at the precise moment when the tenant is likely to be in default in the performance of the lease terms (ie, the occasion of his insolvency). It is, therefore, usual to place the money in a separate deposit account (managed in such a way that only the landlord and his nominees may draw money out of the account) which is then charged to the landlord in order that the landlord has first call on the money in a liquidation or bankruptcy. If the tenant is a company, the charge it creates will have to be registered at Companies House pursuant to s 860 of the Companies Act 2006.

(c)   Under the old regime, the obligations under the rent deposit deed are personal obligations between the original landlord and the original tenant, and the obligation to repay the deposit at the end of the term will not bind an assignee of the reversion: see *Hua Chiao Commercial Bank Ltd v Chiaphua Industries Ltd* [1987] 1 AC 99. Further, the benefit of the obligation to repay does not pass to an assignee of the lease and thus, if the landlord inadvertently repaid the deposit to an assignee, the obligation to pay to the original tenant would still exist. The deed should deal with the personal nature of the obligations by providing that the landlord should not assign his interest in the reversion other than to a buyer who, by supplemental deed executed in favour of the tenant, expressly takes over the obligations of the landlord contained in the rent deposit deed. It should further provide that, on assignment of the lease, the deposit should be repaid to the tenant if the landlord has consented to the assignment in the usual manner under the alienation covenant. The assignee will be required to enter into a fresh rent deposit agreement.

Under the new regime, unless expressed to be personal, the obligation to repay the deposit will pass to an assignee of the reversion as one of the landlord covenants of the tenancy. Similarly, the benefit of repayment will pass to an assignee of the lease. The original tenant should, therefore, ensure either that the benefit of repayment is expressed to be personal to him, or that the assignee pays to him a sum equivalent to the deposit at the time of the assignment. An assignee of the reversion should ensure that, as he will have the burden of the covenant to repay the deposit, he has control of the deposit itself. An original landlord may be reluctant to part with the deposit unless he is able to secure a release from the covenant to repay the deposit under the LT(C)A 1995. If he is unable to secure a release, he may prefer to retain the deposit (various schemes have been suggested which enable the landlord to keep the deposit under his control but, at the same time, allow the assignee access to it in the event of tenant default).

(d)   The parties should consider to whom the interest earned on the money belongs (usually the tenant), whether the interest can be drawn out of the account, and at what stage the tenant will be required to make up any shortfall in the deposit (if, eg, the level of the account drops below an agreed figure due to the tenant's default). The deed will also have to make clear the situations in which the landlord will be entitled to draw upon the deposit.

One overriding factor that remains is that the tenant may not have sufficient money to put up a deposit in the first place.

Chapter 13
The Parcels Clause

13.1 Purpose

The purpose of the parcels clause is to accurately and unambiguously describe the property being let to the tenant so that it is clear what is included and what is excluded. Where the whole of a building is being let, the parcels clause will contain the same sort of description as in the case of the sale of freehold land. Moreover, provided the boundaries are clearly identifiable it may be possible to adequately describe the premises in words alone. However, where a lease of part only of a building is intended, the parcels clause needs more care and attention and a plan will be essential (see **24.2**).

13.2 Airspace and underground

A lease of land includes the buildings on it and everything above and below the land. Thus, a lease of a building includes the airspace above it to such a height as is necessary for the ordinary use and enjoyment of the land and buildings. However, the parties may limit the extent of the parcels clause by excluding the airspace above the roof. If there is such a limitation, this will prevent the tenant from adding extra floors by extending upwards since to do so would be a trespass. The tenant should also appreciate that problems may be caused if he had to erect scaffolding above roof height to comply with his obligation to repair the roof; that would also amount to a trespass. The tenant should, therefore, ensure that he has any necessary right to enter the airspace above his building to the extent necessary to comply with his obligations under the lease. Without any limitation on the airspace the tenant will be free to extend upwards subject only to obtaining any necessary planning permission and consent under the alterations covenant.

13.3 Fixtures

The point about a fixture is that it is part of the demised premises and prima facie belongs to the landlord. If an article is not a fixture, it will be a chattel. Yet, despite the apparent simplicity of the matter, it is not always easy to distinguish between the two, and over the years the courts have developed a test based on the degree of annexation of the item to the land and the purpose of annexation (see, eg, *Holland and Another v Hodgson and Another* (1872) LR 7 CP 328). However, the application of this test to a given set of facts is notoriously difficult and the reader is referred to one of the standard works on land law for further consideration of this issue (and in particular the House of Lords' judgment in *Elitestone v Morris* [1997] 2 All ER 513).

For the avoidance of doubt, a prospective tenant should always compile a full inventory of the fixtures which are present at the commencement of the lease.

13.3.1 Repair of fixtures

If an article is a fixture, it is treated as part of the demised premises and the tenant will become responsible for its repair under his obligation to repair 'the demised premises'. This can have a significant impact on the tenant bearing in mind that many business premises include expensive fixtures such as central heating and air conditioning plant. For this reason the tenant should always inspect the condition of the fixtures before completion of the lease and if any defects are discovered, the tenant must make sure that he does not become liable to remedy those defects under his repairing obligation. This can be achieved by getting the landlord to do any necessary repairs before the lease commences or by agreeing the state and condition with the landlord and ensuring that the covenant to repair does not require any higher standard than that existing at the date of commencement.

13.3.2 Removal of fixtures

The tenant may have the right to remove fixtures at the end of the lease depending upon whether they are 'landlord's fixtures', which cannot be removed, or 'tenant's fixtures', which the tenant is entitled to remove unless the lease provides to the contrary. Tenant's fixtures are those articles:

(a)   affixed by the tenant;

(b)   for the purpose of his trade; and

(c)   which are capable of removal without substantially damaging the building and without destroying the usefulness of the article.

The terms of the lease may require the tenant to yield up the premises at the end of the term together with all fixtures. Whether this excludes the tenant's right to remove tenant's fixtures depends on the form of wording used; very clear words will be required before the right is excluded. However, it has been held that an obligation to yield up the premises 'with all and singular the fixtures and articles belonging thereto', is sufficient to exclude the right but the tenant should resist such a clause. Where the tenant is entitled to remove fixtures, he must make good any damage he causes by their removal and, as a general rule, the right only exists during the term.

13.4 Rights to be granted and reserved

The tenant may need to be granted rights to enable him to use the demised premises to their full extent. For example, he may need the right to enter upon the landlord's adjoining property to comply with his obligation to repair; this can be particularly important where the walls of the demised premises are flush against the boundary. The tenant may also need the right to connect into services on the landlord's adjoining property.

From the landlord's point of view, he may need to reserve rights such as a right to enter the demised premises to view the state and condition or to repair. The service pipes and cables for the landlord's adjoining property may pass under or through the demised premises and the landlord will thus need to reserve rights in respect of them.

Chapter 14
Term

14.1 Introduction

The duration of a lease for a term of years must be fixed and certain before the lease takes effect. Thus, for example, a tenancy 'until the landlord requires the land for road widening' is void for uncertainty (*Prudential Assurance Co Ltd v London Residuary Body* [1992] 3 All ER 504). This principle applies to all leases, including periodic tenancies. A provision that one party is unable to determine a periodic tenancy, or for it only to be determined in certain circumstances, is inconsistent with the concept of a periodic tenancy. If termination on the happening of an uncertain event is required by either party, this can be achieved by granting a long fixed term with a break clause exercisable only on the happening of the event in question (see **14.2**).

Most business tenancies will be for a fixed term in which case the lease must specify the date of commencement of the term and its duration (eg 'for a term of ten years from and including the 29 September 1994'). There is no need for the commencement of the term to be the same date as the date of completion of the lease. It may be more convenient for the landlord, particularly when he is granting several leases in the same block, to choose one specific date from which the term of each will run. If this is an earlier date than completion then, unless the lease provides to the contrary, the tenant's rights and obligations will only arise on completion, not the earlier date. However, for the avoidance of doubt, the lease should expressly state the precise date from which the rent is to be payable.

In specifying the date of commencement, it is important to avoid any ambiguity so that it is clear beyond doubt when the term expires (but note the effect of the lease being protected under Pt II of the LTA 1954). The presumption is that if the term is stated to run 'from' a particular date, the term begins on the next day. If, however, the term is expressed to begin 'on' a particular date, that day is the first day of the term. To avoid any possible argument, it is always best to use clear words such as 'beginning on', 'beginning with' or 'from and including' (see *Meadfield Properties Ltd v Secretary of State for the Environment* [1995] 03 EG 128).

In recent years, various external pressures have been placed on the term of commercial leases. The changes brought about by stamp duty land tax (SDLT) and Government pressure (see **11.5**) have resulted in shorter lease terms. For example, a 20-year lease at a rent of £250,000 per year will result in a payment of £50,000 in SDLT. Over the past few years, lease terms have fallen from the classic 25-year term of the past to 10 or 15 years or even less – and even then many tenants are insisting on break clauses (see **14.2**) being included in the lease. Short, flexible lease terms are often the order of the day.

14.2 Break clauses

14.2.1 Who may operate them and when?

Either or both parties may be given an option to determine the lease at specified times during the term, or on the happening of certain specified events. For example, the tenant may be given the option to determine a 21-year lease at the end of the seventh and fourteenth years, or if he is prevented from trading due to the withdrawal of any necessary statutory licences. The landlord may be given an option to determine if he, at some future date, wishes to redevelop the premises or to occupy them for his own business purposes. The tenant should try to stipulate that the landlord cannot exercise the option until after a specified number of years as otherwise from the tenant's point of view the venture will be too uncertain in its duration.

Some options to break are expressed to be personal to the original tenant in order to prevent them being exercised by successors in title following an assignment. However, in *Brown & Root Technology v Sun Alliance* [1997] 18 EG 123, the court held that following the assignment of a registered lease to the tenant's parent company, the option was still exercisable by the original tenant until the assignment was completed by registration. It was only on registration of title that the legal estate vested in the assignee; until then the assignor remained the tenant and thus retained the ability to exercise the option. However, the position may be different for those leases granted on or after 1 January 1996, the date the Landlord and Tenant (Covenants) Act 1995 came into force. That Act defines 'assignment' to include an equitable assignment, and thus liability on the lease covenants is not dependent on registration of the title.

14.2.2   How are they exercised?

The break clause must be exercised in accordance with its terms. Thus, it must be exercised at the correct time and in the correct manner (see, eg, *Claire's Accessories UK Ltd v Kensington High Street Associates* [2001] PLSCS 112, as to the correct place of service). If there are any pre-conditions for the exercise of the option, they must be strictly complied with. Consequently, the tenant should be wary of any provision in the lease making compliance of tenant covenants a pre-condition for the exercise of the option. In such a case, even a trivial, immaterial breach of covenant on the part of the tenant may prevent him from validly exercising the option. The tenant should modify such a pre-condition so that it requires 'substantial' or 'material' compliance (see, eg, *Bairstow Eves (Securities) Ltd v Ripley* [1992] 2 EGLR 47 and *Fitzroy House Epworth Street (No 1) v The Financial Times Ltd* [2006] EWCA Civ 329). Similarly, any notice requirements for the exercise of the option must be strictly complied with because, unless the lease states to the contrary, time is of the essence of a break clause (*United Scientific Holdings v Burnley Borough Council* [1978] AC 904). If an incorrect date is specified in the break notice, the court may be prepared to correct it if the mistake would not have misled a reasonable recipient (*Mannai Investment Co Ltd v Eagle Star Life Assurance Co Ltd* [1997] AC 749). Subsequent cases have shown that the courts will adopt a similar approach when dealing with other errors in break notices, but it must always be borne in mind that each case will turn on its own facts (see, eg, the contrasting cases of *Lemmerbell Ltd v Britannia LAS Direct Ltd* [1998] 3 EGLR 67 and *Havant International Holdings Ltd v Lionsgate (H) Investments Ltd* [1999] EGCS 144).

14.2.3   Effect of exercise on sub-tenants

The effect of the exercise of an option in a head-lease may be to terminate any sub-lease granted. This is dealt with further at **30.4**.

14.2.4   Relationship with the LTA 1954, Part II

The landlord must be aware of the interrelationship with Pt II of the LTA 1954 and may wish to give thought to drafting the circumstances giving rise to the exercise of the option in line with the requirements of s 30(1)(f) or (g) of that Act (see **31.5**). This is desirable because the exercise of the option may not necessarily entitle the landlord to recover possession as he must also, where necessary, comply with the provisions of the 1954 Act (see **31.2**). Further, where necessary, regard should be had to the relationship between the notice required under the break clause and the notice provisions of the 1954 Act.

14.3 Options to renew

Options to renew are not often found in business leases because most tenants are protected under Pt II of the LTA 1954 and will, therefore, have a statutory right to a new tenancy which the landlord may only oppose on certain grounds (see **Chapter 31**).

14.4 Impact of SDLT

Because the amount of SDLT payable will increase with the length of the lease (see **10.2**), a tenant will often find it preferable to take a short lease with an option to renew rather than a long lease with a break clause. So a five-year term with an option to renew will pay less SDLT on grant than a 10-year term with a right to break after five years. If the break clause is exercised, there will be no refund of SDLT paid in relation to the final five years of the term. Obviously, if a five-year lease is taken and this is renewed, extra SDLT will be then be payable – but it will only be payable if the lease is renewed.

Chapter 15

Rent

15.1 Introduction

One of the primary purposes in granting the lease is to enable the landlord to receive income in the form of rent. However, the payment of rent by the tenant is not essential to the landlord and tenant relationship and it is not uncommon, when property is difficult to let, for landlords to grant rent-free periods to tenants as an inducement for them to take the lease or to allow the tenant to fit out the premises.

The lease must contain a covenant by the tenant to pay the rent. In certain rare situations the tenant may have the right to deduct sums from the rent payable. For example, the tenant has the right to deduct those sums allowed by statute and, where the landlord is in breach of his repairing obligation, the tenant seemingly has an ancient right to undertake the repairs himself and deduct the expense from future payments of rent (see **28.2**). In addition, the tenant may be able to exercise a right of set-off and deduct an unliquidated sum for damages where the landlord is in breach of covenant and the tenant has thereby suffered a loss. Landlords often seek to counter the tenant's right to make deductions by stating in the covenant to pay rent that rent is to be paid 'without deduction'. However, this will not prevent a tenant from making a deduction authorised by statute, nor from exercising his right of set-off (see *Connaught Restaurants Ltd v Indoor Leisure Ltd* [1993] 46 EG 184). To exclude the tenant's right of set-off, very clear words must be used.

The covenant to pay rent is usually followed by a covenant by the tenant to pay all taxes, rates, assessments and outgoings imposed on the demised premises; this will include rates and water rates. For the avoidance of doubt, the tenant should make it clear that this obligation does not extend to any taxes payable by the landlord arising out of the receipt of the rent or due to any dealing by the landlord with the reversion.

In the definitions clause of the lease the landlord should seek to define 'Rent' as also including any 'interim rent' which may become payable under s 24A of the LTA 1954 (see **31.4**). If this were not done and the original tenant's continuing liability was stated by the lease to extend into the statutory continuation (under s 24), he would remain liable only for the contractual rent during that period and not for any interim rent which an assignee may be ordered to pay as part of any future renewal proceedings under the 1954 Act (*Herbert Duncan Ltd v Cluttons* [1992] 1 EGLR 101).

15.2 Amount

The amount of rent must be certain. However, the actual amount need not be stated as long as some means are provided by which the exact amount can be ascertained. For example, the rent may be fixed at £25,000 per annum for the first five years of a 10-year lease and then at 'such revised rent as may be ascertained'. Provided the means of ascertaining the new rent are clearly stated, this is a valid method of dealing with the rent. Such clauses are dealt with in **Chapter 16** where consideration is also given to the different methods of assessing the revised rent.

15.3   Time for payment

The lease should set out the following:

(a)   The date from which the rent is payable and the date of the first payment. It is usual to state that the first payment, or an apportioned part of it, is payable on the date of the lease unless a rent-free period is to be given.

(b)   The payment dates, otherwise, in the case of a tenancy for a fixed term of years, there is authority for the proposition that the rent will be payable yearly. It is common practice in business leases to make the rent payable on the usual quarter days, ie, 25 March, 24 June, 29 September and 25 December.

(c)   Whether rent is to be payable in advance or arrear. Unless the lease provides to the contrary, which is usual, the general law provides that rent is payable in arrears.

In modern commercial leases, provision is often made for the payment of rent by way of direct debit or standing order to minimise the risk of delay.

15.4   Other payments reserved as rent

It is common for leases to provide for the tenant to make other payments to the landlord such as a service charge, or reimbursement of insurance premiums paid by the landlord. Landlords will often require the lease to state that such sums are payable as additional rent. The advantage to the landlord is that if the tenant defaults, the remedy of distress will be available; a remedy which can only be used for non-payment of rent and not for breaches of other covenants. Further, the landlord will be able to forfeit the lease for non-payment of sums defined as rent without the need to serve a notice under s 146 of the LPA 1925, see **30.5**.

It would also be possible for any VAT payable on the rent to be reserved as additional rent.

15.5   Suspension of rent

In the absence of any contrary provision in the lease, the rent will continue to be payable even if the premises are damaged or destroyed and so cannot be used by the tenant. The contractual doctrine of frustration will only apply to leases in exceptional circumstances (see *National Carriers Ltd v Panalpina (Northern) Ltd* [1981] AC 675). From the tenant's point of view, therefore, he should insist on a proviso that the rent is suspended if the premises become unfit for use. If the lease contains a service charge, provision should also be made for this to be suspended as otherwise it too would continue to be payable. This issue is considered further at **22.7**.

15.6   Interest

Unless there is provision to the contrary, interest cannot be charged by the landlord on any late payment by the tenant of rent or other sums due under the lease (unless judgment is obtained against the tenant for such amounts). The Late Payment of Commercial Debts (Interest) Act 1998 does not apply to leases. It is, therefore, usual for a lease to provide that interest is payable by the tenant on any late payment of money due under the lease (from the due date to the date of actual payment). If, as usual, the rate of interest is geared to the base rate of a named bank (eg, 4% above), a problem may arise if that bank no longer fixes a base rate. It is, therefore, sensible to provide for an alternative rate should this situation arise. For the tenant's protection, this should be stated to be 'some other reasonable rate as the landlord may specify'. Without the addition of the word 'reasonable' the tenant would have no right to dispute any new rate he thought excessive.

From the landlord's point of view, it is preferable for the lease to state that the interest rate is to apply 'both before and after any judgment'.

15.7 VAT

The implications of VAT on business leases has been discussed in **Chapter 10**. The landlord should include an appropriate clause entitling him to add VAT to the rent and other payments due from the tenant by providing that the rent and other sums are payable exclusive of VAT.

Chapter 16
The Rent Review Clause

16.1 The need for review

If the lease is granted for anything longer than about five years, the parties will have to address their minds to the question of whether provision should be made in the lease for varying the annual rent at intervals during the term. Traditionally, rent review clauses are included in commercial leases in order to give the landlord the ability to increase the rent, and this chapter generally proceeds on the basis that only upward revisions of rent are contemplated by the parties. However, in recent years, the Government has repeatedly expressed concerns about upward-only rent review clauses (see **11.5**) and the 2007 *Code for Leasing Business Premises* provides as follows:

> **4 Rent Review**
>
> Rent reviews should be clear and headline rent review clauses should not be used. Landlords should on request offer alternatives to their proposed option for rent review priced on a risk-adjusted basis. For example, alternatives to upward only rent review might include up/down reviews to market rent with a minimum of the initial rent, or reference to another measure such as annual indexation.
>
> Where landlords are unable to offer alternatives, they should give reasons.
>
> Leases should allow both landlords and tenants to start the rent review process.

16.2 Regularity

Reviews are commonly programmed to occur at three- or five-year intervals during the term. In a modern 15-year 'institutional' letting (so called because a 15-year lease, where the tenant is obliged to repair and pay for the insurance of the premises is the type of letting favoured by those institutions which frequently invest in the commercial property market), reviews will be programmed to occur at every fifth anniversary of the term.

It is suggested that computation of the review dates in the lease is best achieved by reference to anniversaries of the term commencement date. However, if this method is adopted, the tenant should check that the term commencement date has not been significantly backdated by the landlord, as this would have the effect of advancing the first review date (eg, if the term runs from 29 September 2001, but the lease is only completed on 1 November 2002, the fifth anniversary of the term is now less than four years away). Instead of calculating the dates as anniversaries of the start of the term, some leases set out the exact review dates in the lease. This, however, ought to be avoided since it can create valuation problems at review if the rent review clause in the lease (with its specific review dates) is incorporated as a term of the hypothetical letting (as to which, see **16.5**).

Landlords may attempt to insert a rent review date on the penultimate day of the term. At first sight this might seem illogical since the term is about to end, but of course the tenant is likely to enjoy a statutory continuation of his tenancy under LTA 1954, s 24(1) whereby his tenancy will continue beyond the expiry date at the rent then payable. Where the tenant enjoys the benefit of a statutory continuation, the landlord may be able to apply to the court under LTA 1954, s 24A for an interim rent to be fixed (see **31.4**) in order to increase the rent payable by the tenant during the continuation. However, many landlords are not content to rely on the provisions of s 24A, preferring instead to achieve a rental uplift by implementing a contractual rent review clause on the penultimate day of the contractual term (ie, just before the statutory continuation is due to begin). In practice, because the contractual method of assessment in the rent review clause is likely to differ from the statutory basis of assessment adopted by the court, a penultimate day rent review usually secures a greater increase in rent and therefore ensures that the rent payable during the statutory continuation is greater than would be the case under the interim rent provisions. An interim rent is often assessed at some 10% to 15% below a full market rent (see **31.4.2**).

The tenant ought to resist a penultimate day rent review for the obvious reason that s 24A is likely to give him a better deal, and that a penultimate day review takes away the 'cushion effect' of s 24A (see **31.4.3**).

16.3   Types of rent review clauses

There are various ways in which rent can be varied during the term.

16.3.1   Fixed increases

The lease could provide, for example, that in a lease for a 10-year term, the rent is set at £10,000 for the first three years of the term, £15,000 for the next three years, and £20,000 for the remainder of the term. This sort of clause would be very rare since the parties to the lease would be placing their faith in the fixed increases proving to be realistic.

16.3.2   Index-linked clauses

Some of the early forms of rent review clauses required the rent to be periodically re-assessed by linking the rent to an index recording supposed changes in the value of money. Indexes such as the General Index of Retail Prices and the Producer Price Index can be used in order to revise the rent either at the review dates, or at every rent payment date. Reference should be made to one of the standard works on landlord and tenant law for information as to how such clauses work in practice.

16.3.3   Turnover and sub-lease rents

A turnover rent is one which is geared to the turnover of the tenant's business, and can only therefore be considered by the landlord where turnover is generated at the premises. A turnover rent would be impractical in the case of office or warehouse premises. The tenant's rent (or at least a proportion of it) is worked out as a percentage of the turnover. If a turnover rent clause is to be used, thought will have to be given in the lease to the definition of the turnover of the business (eg, whether credit sales are to be included with cash sales as part of the turnover or whether internet sales are to be included). Other considerations include whether access will be given to the landlord to inspect the tenant's books, how turnover is to be apportioned if it is generated at the demised premises and other premises and whether the tenant is to be obliged in the lease to continue trading from the premises in order to generate turnover. Reference should be made to one of the standard works on landlord and tenant law for further details of the operation of turnover rent clauses.

Similarly, a sub-lease rent is one where the rent payable is assessed as a percentage of the tenant's income from sub-letting the premises.

16.3.4 Open market revaluation

An open market revaluation review clause requires the rent to be revised in accordance with changes in the property market.

The most common form of rent review clause will provide that at every rent review date (eg, every fifth anniversary of the term) the parties should seek to agree upon a figure that equates to what is then the current open market rent for a letting of the tenant's premises. The aim of the exercise is to find out how much a tenant in the open market would be prepared to pay, in terms of rent per annum, if the tenant's premises were available to let in the open market on the relevant review date. This agreement is achieved either by some form of informal negotiated process between the landlord and the tenant, or by the service of notices and counter-notices which specify proposals and counter-proposals as to the revised rent. If agreement cannot be reached, the clause should provide for the appointment of an independent valuer who will determine the revised rent. The valuer will be directed by the review clause to take certain matters into account in conducting his valuation, and to disregard others, and he will call upon evidence of rental valuations of other comparable leasehold interests in the locality.

A clause which provides for an open market revaluation is the type of review clause most frequently encountered in practice, and is the one upon which the rest of this chapter will concentrate.

16.4 Open market revaluations

First and foremost it should be understood that a valuer of commercial leasehold premises cannot find the rental value of 'the premises' since 'the premises' as such are not capable of rental valuation. It is a leasehold interest in the premises, a lease granted for a particular length of time, for a particular purpose, and upon certain terms and conditions which is capable of rental valuation, and which must fall to be valued.

Having established that it is not the premises, but an interest in the premises which has to be valued at each review date, it must be clearly understood that it is not the tenant's own interest that will be valued but a hypothetical interest in the premises. The reason for this is that valuing the tenant's interest gives rise to many problems, uncertainties and injustices. For example, consider the position of the tenant who, in breach of his obligations under the lease, has allowed the premises to fall into disrepair, which has had the effect of reducing the open market rental valuation (OMRV) of the premises. Is it fair that the landlord should suffer at rent review by having the rent depressed on account of the tenant's breach of covenant? From a tenant's perspective consider the position of a tenant who, in the fourth year of the term, at his own expense, voluntarily made improvements to the premises which had the effect of increasing the OMRV of his interest in the premises. Is it fair that the tenant should suffer at rent review by having to pay an increased rent which reflects in part the rental value attributable to his improvements?

These are just two of the many problems inherent in a valuation of the tenant's actual lease. As a result of these difficulties and injustices connected with such a valuation, it is accepted that the valuer should be instructed by the rent review clause to ascertain the OMRV of a hypothetical interest in the premises. He should be directed by the clause to calculate how much rent per annum a hypothetical willing tenant would be prepared to pay for a letting of the premises, with vacant possession, for a hypothetical term. He is directed by the lease to make certain assumptions about the terms of the letting, and to disregard certain matters which might otherwise distort the OMRV, in order to overcome the difficulties and eradicate the injustices referred to above.

16.5   The hypothetical letting

It is important that the parties ensure that the terms and circumstances of the hypothetical letting (which will form the basis of valuation at review) are clearly stated in the lease, and achieve a fair balance between the parties without departing too far from the reality of the tenant's existing letting.

The lease should make it clear that the date of valuation, when the OMRV is assessed, is the review date itself. A negotiated agreement as to the revised rent between the landlord and the tenant, or a determination by an independent valuer, may occur several months before or after the relevant review date, although the new rent is usually stated to be payable from the review date itself. Irrespective of the date of assessment, the tenant should not allow the valuation date to be capable of variation; it should be fixed at the relevant review date. Any clause which purports to allow the valuation date to be fixed by the service of a notice by the landlord is to be resisted for the simple reason that in a falling market, the landlord would serve his notice early to secure a higher rent, while in a rising market he would serve his notice late at a time when the market was at its peak, safe in the knowledge that the revised rent would be backdated and payable from the review date. In a similar way, any clause which defines the valuation date as the day upon which agreement is reached, or the third-party determination is to be made is to be resisted, as it might encourage the landlord to protract the review process to get the benefit of a later valuation date.

16.5.1   The aim of the exercise

The valuer will be directed by the lease to ascertain the open market rental value of a hypothetical letting of the premises at each review date. Different phrases are used by different clauses to define the rent to be ascertained. Some leases will require the valuer to find a 'reasonable rent' for a letting of the premises, or a 'fair rent', or a 'market rent', or a 'rack rent' or 'the open market rent'. It is submitted that the latter clause is the preferred phrase to adopt, as it is the one most commonly used in practice, and is therefore a phrase with which professional valuers are familiar. Other phrases are less common, and are open to adverse interpretations by valuers and the court.

Most tenants would want to avoid the use of the expression 'the best rent at which the premises might be let' since this might allow the valuer to consider the possibility of what is known as a special purchaser's bid. If, by chance, the market for a hypothetical letting of the premises contains a potential bidder who would be prepared to bid in excess of what would ordinarily be considered to be the market rent, the 'best' rent would be the rent which the special bidder would be prepared to pay. For example, if the premises which are the subject matter of the hypothetical letting are situated next to premises occupied by a business which is desperate to expand, the 'best' rent might be the rent which that business would be willing to pay.

16.5.2   The circumstances of the letting

To enable the valuer to do his job, the rent review clause must clearly indicate the circumstances in which a hypothetical letting of the premises is to be contemplated. For example, he must be able to establish which premises are to be the subject matter of the letting, whether there is a market for such a letting, whether the premises would be available with or without vacant possession, and what the terms of the letting would be. It is common for the clause to require the valuer to find the open market rent of a letting of the tenant's vacant premises, for a specified duration, on the assumption that there is a market for the letting which will be granted without the payment or receipt of a premium, and subject only to the terms of the actual lease (except as to the amount of the annual rent).

16.5.2.1 The premises

Usually, the valuer is required to ascertain the rental value of a hypothetical letting of the premises actually demised by the tenant's lease. The draftsman should therefore ensure that the demised premises are clearly defined by the parcels clause in the lease, and that they enjoy the benefit of all necessary rights and easements to enable them to be used for their permitted purpose.

A valuer uses comparables as evidence in his valuation of a letting of the premises. He draws upon evidence of rents currently being paid by tenants of comparable buildings, let in comparable circumstances, on comparable terms. If the actual premises demised to the tenant are unique or exceptional (eg, an over-sized warehouse) there may be no comparables in the area for the valuer to use. In that case, the lease ought to require the valuer to adopt a different approach to his valuation, perhaps by directing him to take account of rental values of other premises which would not ordinarily count as comparables. This in itself may lead to valuation problems as, for example, in *Dukeminster (Ebbgate House One) Ltd v Somerfield Properties Co Ltd* [1997] 40 EG 157.

16.5.2.2 The market

As the hypothetical letting is an artificial creation, and since leasehold valuations cannot be carried out in the abstract, an artificial market has to be created. If the rent review clause does not create a well balanced hypothetical market in which the letting can be contemplated, it would be open for the tenant (in appropriate cases) to argue at review that no market exists for a letting of the tenant's premises, and that therefore an 'open market' rent for the premises would be merely nominal, or a peppercorn. An example of this could occur if the tenant was occupying premises which were now outdated to such an extent that they were impractical for modern use, or that the premises were so exceptional that only the tenant himself would contemplate occupying them. Only the actual tenant would be in the hypothetical market for such premises, and even he might not be in the market if he can show that he has actively been trying to dispose of his lease. The market might truly be dead.

To create a market, the rent review clause usually requires the valuer to assume that the hypothetical letting is taking place in the open market and being granted by a 'willing landlord' to a 'willing tenant'. In *FR Evans (Leeds) Ltd v English Electric Co Ltd* (1977) 245 EG 657 it was held that where such phrases are used, it means that the valuer must assume that there are two hypothetical people who are prepared to enter into the arrangement, neither of whom is being forced to do so, and neither of whom is affected by any personal difficulties (eg, a landlord with cash-flow problems, or a tenant who has just lost his old premises) which would prejudice their position in open market negotiations. A willing landlord is an abstract person, but is someone who has the right to grant a lease of the premises, and a willing tenant, again an abstraction, is someone who is actively seeking premises to fulfil a need that these premises would fulfil. It is implicit in the use of these phrases that there is at least one willing tenant in the market, and that there is a rent upon which they will agree.

Even if the lease is silent as to whether there is assumed to be a willing tenant, the Court of Appeal has held in *Dennis & Robinson Ltd v Kiossos Establishment* [1987] 1 EGLR 133 that such a creature is in any case to be assumed, since a rent review clause which asks for an open market valuation by its nature requires there to be at least one willing tenant in the market. This means that for rent review purposes, where an open market valuation is required, there will always be someone in the hypothetical market who would be prepared to take a letting of the premises, and therefore the tenant cannot argue that the market is completely dead. However quite how much a willing tenant would be willing to pay is for the valuer to decide.

If the market is well and truly dead, the landlord's only protection is an upwards-only rent review clause.

16.5.2.3   The consideration

Any consideration moving between the parties at the time of the grant is likely to have a bearing on the amount of rent to be paid by the tenant. Such movements are not uncommon in the open market. For example, a landlord may seek to induce a tenant to take the lease at a certain level of rent by offering him a reverse premium without which the tenant might only be prepared to pay rent at a lower level. A rent-free period may be offered by a landlord, either as a straightforward inducement as above, or to compensate a tenant for the costs that he will incur in fitting out the premises at the start of the term. Without the rent-free period, the tenant might only be prepared to pay a lower rent. If the tenant pays a premium to the landlord at the outset, this may be reflected in the tenant paying a rent lower than he would otherwise pay.

As far as the hypothetical letting is concerned, it is common for the rent review clause to assume that no consideration (in the form of a premium) will be moving between the parties on the grant of the hypothetical letting. As seen above, such payments can distort the amount of initial rent payable by a tenant. Therefore to get the clearest indication of what the market rent for the letting would be, it ought to be assumed that no premium is to be paid on the grant of the hypothetical letting.

Furthermore, the landlord may seek to include a provision which states that no inducement in the form of a rent-free period will be given to the hypothetical tenant on the grant of the hypothetical lease. This is an attempt by the landlord to deprive the tenant of the effect of such concessions granted in the market place (thereby keeping the level of rent, on review, artificially high). The landlord is trying to achieve a headline rent rather than an effective rent. For example, if the tenant agrees to take a lease at £100,000 per annum for a term of five years, but is to receive a 12-month rent-free period, while the headline rent (the rent stated to be payable under the lease) remains at £100,000 per annum, the annual rent effectively payable (the 'effective' rent) is only £80,000. At review, therefore, the landlord would argue that the effect of disregarding any rent-free period which might be available in the open market, is that the new rent payable from review should be a headline rent not an effective rent. The tenant would argue that, since the hypothetical tenant is not getting the benefit of a rent-free period, therefore, the revised rent should be discounted to compensate the hypothetical tenant for a benefit he has not received.

There have been several cases on the effect of these types of provisions. The Court of Appeal in *Broadgate Square plc v Lehman Brothers Ltd* [1995] 01 EG 111, applying the purposive approach to the interpretation of the relevant clause said that '... the court will lean against a construction which would require payment of rent upon an assumption that the tenant has received the benefit of a rent-free period, which he has not in fact received ...' (per Leggatt LJ). However, such an approach cannot be adopted in the face of clear, unambiguous language. According to Hoffmann LJ, '... if upon its true construction the clause deems the market rent to be whatever is the headline rent after a rent-free period granted ... the tenant cannot complain because in changed market conditions it is more onerous than anyone would have foreseen'. The presence of such a clause in the hypothetical letting may itself be an onerous provision which justifies a reduction in the OMRV (possibly to the extent that it negates the effect of the landlord's clever drafting).

16.5.2.4   Possession

As the valuer is assessing the rental value of the tenant's existing premises, is he to assume that the tenant is still there (in which case rent to be paid by a hypothetical bidder would be very low), or is he to assume that the tenant has vacated? Naturally, he must assume that the tenant has moved out, and therefore most rent review clauses of this type include an assumption that vacant possession is available for the hypothetical letting.

Care must be taken in making this assumption, because in certain cases it can give rise to problems:

(a)   If the tenant has sub-let all or part of the premises, an assumption that vacant possession is to be available will mean that the effect on rent of the presence of the sub-tenant will have to be disregarded. If the sub-tenant occupies for valuable business purposes (eg, the premises in question are high street offices where the ground floor has been sub-let as a high class shop), the presence of the sub-tenancy would ordinarily increase the rental value of the head leasehold interest since the head tenant would expect to receive lucrative sub-lease rents. The assumption of vacant possession would deny the landlord the opportunity to bring a valuable sub-letting into account at review. If the sub-tenancy was for residential purposes yielding precious little in terms of sub-lease rents, the assumption of vacant possession would allow the landlord to have the sub-letting disregarded and, depending on the other terms of the hypothetical letting, enable the premises to be valued as a whole for the permitted business purpose.

(b)   The assumption of vacant possession means that the tenant is deemed to have moved out of the premises and, as all vacating tenants would do, he is deemed to have removed and taken his fixtures with him. In respect of shop premises, this might mean that all of the shop fittings must be assumed to have been removed, leaving nothing remaining but a shell. (Of course, in reality, the premises are still fully fitted out, but for hypothetical valuation purposes, the tenant's fixtures are assumed to have gone.) If a hypothetical tenant were to bid in the open market for these premises then, depending upon market forces prevalent at the time, he might demand a rent-free period in order to compensate him for the time it will take for him to carry out a notional fitting out of the premises (ie, to restore the fittings that have notionally been removed). Since the revised rent has to be a consistent figure payable throughout the period until the next review date, this notional rent-free period would have to be spread out during the review period, or possibly over the rest of the term, thereby reducing the general level of rent (eg, the valuer finds that the rent for the next five years should be £10,000 per annum, but that an incoming tenant would obtain a rent-free period of 12 months. By spreading the notional rent-free period over the five-year review period the rent would be £8,000 per annum). The landlord can counter this problem by including an assumption that, notwithstanding vacant possession, the premises are fully fitted out for occupation and use (see **16.5.3**).

16.5.2.5   The terms

The valuer, in ascertaining the OMRV of a leasehold interest, must look at all of the proposed terms of the lease. The more onerous the lease terms, the less attractive the lease becomes from a tenant's point of view, and therefore the lower the OMRV of the interest. If the rent review clause is silent, the hypothetical letting will be assumed to be granted upon the terms of the tenant's existing lease, since the court does not like to stray too far away from reality, and there is a general preference by the court to construe rent review clauses in such a way as to ensure that the tenant does not end up paying in terms of rent for something that he is not actually getting. Usually, however, the clause directs the valuer to assume that the letting is to be made upon the terms of the tenant's actual letting, as varied from time to time. (The fact that the valuer must take account of variations means that it is imperative that, when conducting the review, the valuer checks the terms of all deeds of variation entered into, and all licences granted since the date of the lease to see if the terms of the actual lease have been changed.)

Each of the terms of the lease will be analysed by the valuer at review to see if they will have any effect on the rental value. If either party, with sufficient foresight, feels that a particular term will have a detrimental effect on the rental value (because the term is too wide, or too narrow, or too onerous) that party may seek to have the term excluded from the hypothetical letting, by use of an assumption or a disregard (see **16.5.3**).

The valuer will look closely at all of the terms of the lease, but in particular at the following.

The alienation covenant

If the alienation covenant in the actual lease is too restrictive (eg, by prohibiting all forms of alienation), its incorporation as a term of the hypothetical letting will lead to a decrease in the OMRV of that interest. Similarly, if the actual lease allows only the named tenant to occupy the premises (or only companies within the same group of companies as the tenant), this will have a negative impact on the OMRV. In these cases it will be advisable for the landlord to exclude the excessive restrictions on alienation from the terms of the hypothetical letting. The tenant might consider this to be unfair and, perhaps, a compromise would be to widen the alienation covenant in the actual lease.

The user covenant

If the actual lease narrowly defines the permitted use of the premises and allows little or no scope for the tenant to alter that use, a tenant bidding for the lease in the open market is likely to reduce his rental bid to reflect the fact that he would be severely hindered should he wish to dispose of the premises during the term, or change the nature of his business. It became clear in *Plinth Property Investments Ltd v Mott, Hay & Anderson* [1979] 1 EGLR 17 (a Court of Appeal decision) that the possibility of the landlord agreeing to waive a breach of covenant (eg, by allowing a wider use of the premises than the covenant already permits) has to be ignored. This principle is not just applicable to user covenants (although the *Plinth* case specifically concerned a user covenant) but to all covenants where the landlord is freely able to withhold his consent to a change. It is not open to the landlord at review to disregard the detrimental effect on rent of a restrictive clause which has been incorporated into the hypothetical letting by saying that he is or might be prepared to waive the restriction. Further, a landlord cannot unilaterally vary the terms of the lease (see *C&A Pension Trustees Ltd v British Vita Investments Ltd* (1984) 272 EG 63). If the landlord is intent on tightly restricting the tenant in the user clause in the actual lease, but wants to maximise the rental value of the hypothetical letting at review and is concerned that the incorporation of the restrictive clause into the hypothetical letting will harm the OMRV, he should draft the review clause so that the actual user covenant is to be disregarded, and an alternative permitted use is to be assumed. Obviously, the tenant should strongly resist such an approach, since he would find himself paying a rent from review assessed on the basis of a freedom that he does not in fact possess. Again, a compromise might be to widen the user covenant in the actual lease.

If the lease allows only the named tenant to use the premises for a named business (ie, a very restrictive user covenant), the landlord should try to have the user covenant disregarded at review. If he fails to do so, the court might be prepared to step in to assist the landlord as in *Sterling Land Office Developments Ltd v Lloyds Bank plc* (1984) 271 EG 894 where a covenant not to use the premises other than as a branch of Lloyds Bank plc was incorporated into the hypothetical letting, but with the name and business left blank, to be completed when the name and business of the hypothetical tenant were known.

Rent and rent review

The review clause will state that the hypothetical letting is to be granted upon the same terms as the actual lease save as to the amount of rent. As the aim of the review exercise is to vary the amount of rent, it is clear that the rent initially reserved by the lease must not be incorporated into the hypothetical letting. However, the tenant must be alert to guard against any form of wording which has the effect of excluding from the hypothetical letting not only the amount of rent reserved, but also the rent review clause itself. It is a commonly held view that a tenant bidding for a medium- or long-term letting of premises in the open market, where the annual rent cannot be increased during the term, is likely to pay more than if the letting contained a rent review clause. The tenant would pay a rent in excess of the current market rent in return for a guarantee that the rent will not rise but would be fixed at the initial rent for the entire duration of the term. A long series of cases followed the decision in *National Westminster Bank plc v Arthur Young McClelland Moores & Co* [1985] 1 WLR 1123 where the provisions of a rent review clause were interpreted in such a way as to exclude from the hypothetical letting the rent review provisions. This alone led to the annual rent being increased from £800,000 to £1.209 million, instead of £1.003 million if the rent review clause had been incorporated. Courts today tend to shy away from interpreting a rent review clause in such a way as to exclude a provision for review from the hypothetical letting. In the absence of clear words directing the rent review clause to be disregarded, the court will give effect to the underlying purpose of the clause and will assume that the hypothetical letting contains provisions for the review of rent. However, the tenant must always check carefully that the review clause is not expressly excluded from the hypothetical letting, since the court would be bound to give effect to such clear words. Ideally, the hypothetical letting should be '... upon the terms of this lease, other than the amount of rent'.

The length of term

Whether the lease is for a short term or a long term will affect how much rent a tenant is prepared to pay. While a landlord often needs to guarantee rental income by granting a long-term lease, in times of uncertain trading tenants often prefer shortterm lettings in order to retain a degree of flexibility, and to avoid long-term liability in the event of business failure. If a short-term letting is more attractive to tenants in the current market, it follows that a tenant would be prepared to bid more in terms of rent per annum for such a letting than if a longer term was proposed. On the other hand, other tenants with long-term business plans and a desire for stability and security would be prepared to increase their rental bid in return for a longer letting.

The rent review clause must define the length of the hypothetical letting. The landlord will want to maximise the rental value of the hypothetical letting by specifying as the hypothetical term a length which is currently preferred in the market by prospective tenants of premises of the type in question. The landlord will have to ask his surveyor for advice in this regard, since the term to be adopted is purely a matter of valuation, which will differ from lease to lease.

As well as stating the length of the hypothetical term, the rent review clause should also state the starting date of that term. If the term is stated but the commencement date is not, the result is unclear. In *Lynnthorpe Enterprises Ltd v Sydney Smith (Chelsea) Ltd* [1990] 2 EGLR 131, it was held that the commencement date was to be assumed to be the same day as the actual lease. However, in *Canary Wharf Investments (Three) v Telegraph Group Ltd* [2003] 46 EG 132, the judge applied a 'presumption of reality' and held that it was to be assumed that the term was to commence on the review date.

When the valuer makes his valuation, he is allowed to take into account the prospect of the term being renewed under the LTA 1954 (see *Secretary of State for Employment v Pivot Properties Limited* (1980) 256 EG 1176). Obviously, the rent will turn out to be higher if there is a strong possibility of renewal. In the *Pivot* case, that possibility led to an uplift in the rent of £850,000 per annum.

16.5.3 Assumptions to be made

Several assumptions have already been considered in respect of the circumstances of the hypothetical letting. Certain other assumptions are also commonly made:

(a) An assumption that the premises are fully fitted out and ready for immediate occupation and use by the incoming tenant. An assumption of vacant possession necessarily leads to an assumption that the tenant has moved out and taken all his fixtures with him. The assumption that the premises are fully fitted out attempts to counter the deemed removal of fixtures by assuming that the hypothetical tenant would be able to move straight into the premises without asking for a rent-free period in which he could carry out his notional fitting-out works. Hence the assumption removes any discount the tenant would claim at review in respect of the rent-free period that the hypothetical tenant might have claimed. The phrase 'fit for occupation' does not appear to go as far as 'fully fitted out' since the former assumption anticipates a stage where the premises are simply ready to be occupied for fitting out purposes, in which case the hypothetical tenant might still demand a rent-free period (see *Pontsarn Investments Ltd v Kansallis-Osake-Pankki* [1992] 22 EG 103). Some solicitors prefer to deal with this problem in a different way by including an assumption that '... no reduction is to be made to take account of any rental concession which on a new letting with vacant possession might be granted to the incoming tenant for a period within which its fitting out works would take place'.

(b)   An assumption that the covenants have been performed. Most rent review clauses include an assumption that the tenant has complied with his covenants under the lease. In the absence of such a provision, a court is willing to imply one in any case, since it is a general principle that a party to a transaction should not be allowed to profit from its own wrongdoing (see *Family Management v Grey* (1979) 253 EG 369). This is particularly important when considering the tenant's repairing obligation. Clearly the hypothetical tenant can be expected to pay more in terms of rent if the premises are in good repair and, conversely, less if they are in a poor condition (for whatever reason). A tenant should not be allowed to argue in reduction of the rent at review that the premises are in a poor condition, if it is through his own default that the disrepair has come about and hence the reason for the assumption under consideration.

The landlord may try to include an assumption in respect of his own covenants (ie, that the landlord has performed his covenants). The tenant ought to resist this, especially where the landlord will be taking on significant obligations in the actual lease. For example, in a lease of part of the landlord's premises, the landlord may be entering into covenants to perform services, and to repair and maintain the structure, exterior and common parts of the building. If the landlord fails to perform his covenants, the likely result is that the rental value of an interest in the building will decrease, since the building will be less attractive to tenants in the market. Accordingly, the rent at review would be adjusted to reflect this. However, an assumption that the landlord has performed his covenants enables the landlord to have the review conducted on the basis that the building is fully in repair (without regard to his own default), which means that the tenant would be paying for something at review (ie, a lease of premises in a building which is in first-rate condition) that he does not in fact have. Such an assumption should be resisted by the tenant.

However, the landlord will not concede the tenant's argument easily. Landlords will argue that, without it, the valuer will assess the new rent at a lower level, even though immediately afterwards the tenant might bring proceedings against the landlord in respect of the landlord's breach of covenant, forcing the landlord to put the building into repair. They argue that it is unfair that the rent will be set at a low level for the entire review period on the basis of a temporary breach of covenant, which the landlord might soon be required to remedy. The tenant's counter-argument is that a claim for breach of covenant is no substitute for a dilapidated building.

(c)   If the landlord has waived the VAT exemption in respect of the premises, so that VAT is payable in addition to the rent, this will negatively affect a tenant who has an adverse VAT status. Organisations such as banks, building societies and insurance companies make exempt supplies in the course of their business and therefore do not receive any output tax which can be set off against the input tax to be paid on the rent. These organisations have to bear the VAT on the rent as an overhead of the business. Arguably, such tenants in the market would reduce their bids in order to compensate for the VAT overhead that they will have to absorb. Some landlords counter this by including an assumption that the hypothetical tenant will be able to recover its VAT in full (thereby removing the need for the hypothetical tenant to ask for a discount on rent to cover his VAT overhead), or by ensuring that the hypothetical letting includes a covenant by the landlord not to waive the exemption for VAT purposes. Tenants ought to try to resist such a provision, leaving the valuer to value the lease on the basis of the reality of the actual letting.

16.5.4 Matters to be disregarded

In order to be fair to the tenant, the landlord usually drafts the review clause so that certain matters which would otherwise increase the OMRV of a letting of the premises are disregarded.

16.5.4.1 Goodwill

A letting of premises will be more attractive in the open market if there is existing goodwill at the premises, in the shape of a regular flow of clients or customers, or the benefit of a good reputation. The letting would command a higher rent than could otherwise be expected, as tenants will be eager to obtain possession of the premises in order to take advantage of the goodwill. However, it is the tenant who generates such goodwill and so it is only fair that any effect on rent of that goodwill ought to be disregarded at review.

16.5.4.2 Occupation

The fact that the tenant, his predecessors or his sub-tenants have been in occupation of the premises is usually disregarded. It is accepted that, if the tenant was bidding for a letting of his own premises, he would bid more than most others in the market in order to avoid the expense of having to move to other premises. The rental effect of occupation should therefore be disregarded. In appropriate cases, where the tenant also occupies adjoining premises, his occupation of those premises should also be disregarded, to avoid the argument that the tenant would increase his bid for the demised premises to secure a letting of premises which are adjacent to his other premises.

If the rent review clause requires occupation by the tenant to be disregarded, but makes no similar requirement as regards his goodwill (see above), the valuer should nevertheless disregard the rental effect of the tenant's goodwill, since goodwill must necessarily be the product of the tenant's occupation (see *Prudential Assurance Co Ltd v Grand Metropolitan Estate Ltd* [1993] 32 EG 74).

16.5.4.3 Improvements

If the tenant improves the premises, then he usually does so at his own expense, but the result will inevitably be that the rental value of an interest in the premises will increase. It is unfair for the landlord to ask that the rent be increased at review to reflect the increase in rental value brought about by the tenant's improvements. If improvements were to be taken into account, the tenant would be paying for his improvements twice over (once on making them, and once again when the revised rent becomes payable). The landlord usually drafts the rent review clause so that the effect on rent of most of the tenant's improvements are disregarded.

Which improvements are to be disregarded? The tenant will want to make sure that the effect on rent of all improvements that have been carried out either by him or his sub-tenants or his predecessors in title are disregarded, whether they were carried out during the term, during some earlier lease or during a period of occupation before the grant of the lease (eg, during a pre-letting fitting out period). He will also want to have disregarded the effect on rent of improvements executed by the landlord, but which were carried out at the tenant's expense. The landlord will want to make sure that any improvements that the tenant was obliged to make are taken into account. These will include improvements made under the lease granted in consideration of the tenant carrying out works to the premises, or improvements the tenant was obliged to carry out under some other document, such as an agreement for lease, or by virtue of a statutory provision requiring the tenant to carry out work (eg, the installation of a fire escape and doors). An obligation in a licence to alter, that the tenant execute permitted works in accordance with agreed drawings, or by a stipulated time, is not an obligation in itself to do the works in a particular way (see *Historic Houses Hotels Ltd v Cadogan Estates* [1997] AC 70).

16.5.4.4 User, alienation and improvements

It is possible that for his own benefit the landlord might try to have disregarded some of the more restrictive covenants contained in the actual lease such as user, alienation and improvements. This is unfair to the tenant who ought to be advised to resist such a disregard.

16.6 The mechanics of the review

There are two principal ways in which the review process can be conducted:

(a)   by negotiations between the parties, but in default of agreement, by reference to an independent third party for determination (see **16.6.2**);

(b)   by the service of trigger notices and counter-notices in an attempt to agree the revised rent, but in default, by reference to a third party (see **16.6.3**).

Whichever method is to be adopted, the first consideration to be dealt with is whether time is to be of the essence in respect of any time limits contained in the clause, or in respect of the rent review dates.

16.6.1 Is time of the essence?

As a general rule, if time is of the essence of a particular clause, a party who fails to act by the time limit specified loses the right given by that clause. If time is of the essence of the whole rent review clause, the slightest delay will mean that the landlord will be denied the opportunity to increase the rent until the next review date, (or, indeed, the tenant will be denied the opportunity to decrease the rent until the next review date if the clause permits downward reviews).

The House of Lords in *United Scientific Holdings Ltd v Burnley Borough Council* [1977] 2 All ER 62 held that, in the absence of any contrary indications in the express wording of the clause, or in the interrelation of the rent review clause with other clauses in the lease, there is a presumption that time is not of the essence of the clause and that the review can still be implemented and pursued, even though specific dates have passed (see, eg, *McDonald's Property Co Ltd v HSBC Bank plc* [2001] 36 EG 181). It follows from this decision that there are three situations where time will be of the essence, either of the whole clause, or in respect of certain steps in the review procedure.

16.6.1.1 An express stipulation

Time will be of the essence in respect of all or any of the time limits in the review clause if the lease expressly says so.

16.6.1.2 Any other contrary indication

The phrase 'time is of the essence' may not have been used in the lease, but there are cases where other forms of wording used by the draftsman have been sufficient to indicate an intention to rebut the usual presumption. In *First Property Growth Partnership v Royal & Sun Alliance Services Ltd* [2002] EWHC 305 (Ch), [2002] 22 EG 140, the clause required the landlord to serve notice of intention to review upon the tenant 12 months before the relevant review date 'but not at any other time'. This was held to make time of the essence and thus the landlord's notice served after the relevant review date was invalid. In *Starmark Enterprises Ltd v CPL Distribution Ltd* [2001] 32 EG 89 (CS), the lease provided for service of a trigger notice by the landlord specifying the amount of rent payable for the following period but went on to provide that if the tenant failed to serve a counter-notice within one month the tenant would be 'deemed to have agreed to pay the increased rent specified in that notice'. The Court of Appeal held that time was of the essence; the 'deeming' provision was a sufficient contra-indication to rebut the usual presumption. Reference should be made to one of the standard works on landlord and tenant law for further consideration of the many cases dealing with this issue.

16.6.1.3   The interrelation of the review clause with other clauses in the lease

The usual way in which a clause might interrelate with the review clause in such a way as to make time of the essence is if the tenant is given an option to break the term on or shortly after each review date. The inference in such an interrelation is that, if the tenant cannot afford to pay the revised rent or, where the level of rent is not yet known, he does not envy the prospect of an increase, he is given an opportunity to terminate the lease by exercising the break clause. Since time is usually of the essence in respect of the exercise of a break clause, time may also be construed to be of the essence of the rent review clause. It does not matter that the review clause and the option are separate clauses in the lease; the court simply has to be able to infer a sufficient interrelation. Nor, apparently, does it matter that the option to break is mutual and linked to only one of several rent review dates (*Central Estates Ltd v Secretary of State for the Environment* [1997] 1 EGLR 239).

Unless a rigid timetable for conducting the review is required by either party, it is not often that time will be made of the essence, because of the fatal consequences arising from a delay. It might be advisable to state expressly that time is not of the essence. However, in most leases the timetable is so flexibly drafted that the parties do not feel the need to make express declaration that time is not of the essence, preferring instead to rely upon the usual presumption (but see *Barclays Bank plc v Savile Estates Ltd* [2002] EWCA Civ 589, [2002] 24 EG 152). If any time clauses are intended to be mandatory, the lease should clearly say so.

16.6.2   The negotiated revision

The informal approach to arriving at a revised rent usually provides for the new rent to be agreed between the parties at any time (whether before or after the relevant review date), but if agreement has not been reached by the review date, either or both of the parties will be allowed by the clause to refer the matter to an independent third party for him to make a determination as to the new rent. If such an approach is adopted, the tenant should ensure that the rent review clause does not reserve the right to make the reference to the third party exclusively to the landlord. The tenant must ensure that he also has the ability to make the reference. Even though the rent review clause may permit only upward revisions, it may be in the tenant's interests to have a quick resolution of the review, particularly if he is anxious to assign his lease or sell his business. In exceptional cases (eg, *Royal Bank of Scotland plc v Jennings and Others* [1997] 19 EG 152), the court might be prepared to imply an obligation upon the landlord to refer a review to the third party to give business efficacy to the clause.

16.6.3   Trigger notices

The service of a trigger notice is the more formal approach, which usually requires the parties to follow a rigid timetable for the service of notices. One party sets the review in motion by the service of a trigger notice, specifying his proposal for the revised rent, and the other party responds by the service of a counter-notice. A typical clause might provide for the landlord to implement the review by the service on the tenant of a trigger notice, between 12 and 6 months before the relevant review date, in which the landlord specifies a rent that he considers to be the current market rent for the premises. The tenant should be given the right to dispute the landlord's proposal by serving a counter-notice within, say, three months of the service of the trigger notice. The parties would then be required to negotiate, but in default of agreement within, say, three months of the service of the counter-notice, either or both parties may be given the right to make a reference to a third party for a determination. Time may be stated to be of the essence in respect of all or part of the timetable.

Great care must be taken with this more rigid style of approach, particularly if time is of the essence (see **16.6.1**). Problems can easily arise as follows:

(a) There is no requirement for the landlord to be reasonable when he specifies his proposal for the revised rent in his trigger notice (see *Amalgamated Estates Ltd v Joystretch Manufacturing Ltd* (1980) 257 EG 489). This is very dangerous for the tenant where time is of the essence in respect of the service of the tenant's counter-notice. If the tenant fails to respond within the time limit required by the lease, he will be bound by the rent specified in the landlord's notice. A well advised tenant should avoid such a clause.

(b) There has been much litigation surrounding the question of whether a particular form of communication, often in the form of a letter between the parties' advisers, suffices as a notice for the purposes of the review clause. If a communication is to take effect as a notice it ought to be clear and unequivocal, and must be worded in such a way as to make it clear to the recipient that the sender is purporting to take a formal step, or exercise some right under the review clause. Phrases such as 'subject to contract' and 'without prejudice', although not necessarily fatal to the notice, are to be avoided.

(c) For the same reasons stated in connection with informally negotiated reviews, the tenant must ensure that the review timetable allows him to implement the review and to refer the rent revision for determination by the third party. These rights must not be left exclusively with the landlord.

Unless there is some compelling reason to the contrary, the informal approach is to be preferred.

16.6.4 The third party

A surveyor usually acts as the independent third party. The lease will provide for the parties to agree upon a surveyor, failing which one or both of the parties will be allowed to make an application to the President of the Royal Institution of Chartered Surveyors (RICS) for the appointment of a surveyor to determine the revised rent. RICS operates a procedure to deal efficiently with such applications, and will appoint a surveyor with knowledge and experience of similar lettings in the area. It is important that the lease makes it clear in which capacity the surveyor is to act; as an arbitrator between the parties, or as an expert. There are considerable differences between the two.

(a) An arbitrator seeks to resolve a dispute by some quasi-judicial process, whereas an expert imposes his own expert valuation on the parties.

(b) The arbitrator is bound by the procedure under the Arbitration Act 1996, which deals with hearings, submission of evidence and the calling of witnesses. An expert is not subject to such external controls, and is not bound to hear the evidence of the parties. Whilst an arbitrator decides on the basis of the evidence put before him, an expert simply uses his own skill and judgment.

(c) There is a limited right of appeal to the High Court on a point of law against an arbitrator's award, whereas an expert's decision is final and binding unless it appears that he failed to perform the task required of him.

(d) An arbitrator is immune from suit in negligence, whereas an expert is not.

Using an expert tends to be quicker and cheaper and is, therefore, often provided for in lettings of conventional properties at modest rents. Where there is something unorthodox about the property, which might make it difficult to value, or where there is a good deal of money at stake in the outcome of the review, an arbitrator is to be preferred so that a fully argued case can be put. Alternatively, the review clause could leave the capacity of the third party open, to be determined by the party who makes the reference at the time the reference is made.

16.7 Ancillary provisions

The landlord invariably includes additional provisions to deal with:

(a)   payment of the revised rent where the review is implemented after the review date;

(b)   recording a note of the revised rent.

16.7.1 The late review

If time has not been made of the essence of the rent review date, the landlord can attempt to increase the rent by implementing the clause after the date for review has passed. To deal with this possibility, the review clause is usually drafted to include the following types of provisions:

(a)   that the existing rent (the old rent) continues to be payable on account of the new rent until the new rent has been ascertained;

(b)   that the new rent, once ascertained, becomes payable from, and is backdated to the rent review date;

(c)   that as soon as the new rent has been ascertained, the tenant is to pay to the landlord the amount by which the old rent paid on account of the new rent since the review date actually falls short of the new rent, and because the landlord has been denied the benefit of this shortfall pending the outcome of the review, the tenant is to pay it with interest calculated from the rent review date until the date of payment.

The tenant should check the operation of these provisions. If the rent review clause permits both upward and downward reviews, he should ensure that there is some equivalent provision for the landlord to pay any shortfall (with interest) to the tenant if the new rent turns out to be lower than the old rent (although in *Royal Bank of Scotland v Jennings* (above) the court was prepared to imply such a term in any case). He should also check that the rate of interest at which the shortfall is to be paid is not set at the usual interest rate under the lease (4% or 5% above base rate, see **15.6**). The usual rate is intended to operate on the occasion of tenant default, whereas in the case of a late rent review, the fault may lie with a delaying landlord as much as a delaying tenant. The interest rate should be set at base rate itself or, perhaps, 1% or 2% above base rate. Finally, the tenant should check that the review clause allows the tenant to instigate the review process, and to force negotiations or the third party reference, since the tenant might prefer a speedy settlement of the review as an alternative to facing a future lump sum payment of a shortfall with interest.

16.7.2 Recording the review

It is good practice to attach memoranda of the revised rent to the lease and counterpart as evidence for all persons concerned with the lease of the agreement or determination. The rent review clause usually obliges both parties to sign and attach identical memoranda to their respective parts of the lease. It is usual for both parties to bear their own costs in this regard.

Chapter 17

Repairing Covenants

17.1 Introduction

Responsibility for repairs is one of the most common sources of dispute between landlord and tenant and unless the matter is dealt with expressly in the lease there is a danger that neither party will be liable to repair. While it is true that certain obligations will be implied, these are of relatively little practical importance; they include the following:

(a) the tenant is under a duty to use the premises in a tenant-like manner (and see *Dayani v Bromley London Borough Council* [1999] 3 EGLR 144);

(b) the landlord may be liable if he fails to take care of the common parts of the building, for example, the neglect of a lift or staircase in a high rise block, but much will depend on the surrounding circumstances (see *Liverpool City Council v Irwin* [1977] AC 239, a case concerning a block of residential flats);

(c) in rare situations the landlord may be under an implied obligation to repair so as to give business efficacy to the agreement between the parties (see *Barrett v Lounova (1982) Ltd* [1990] QB 348).

Thus, in the absence of a comprehensive code of implied obligations, it is imperative that the responsibility for repairs is dealt with expressly in the lease. The landlord's objective on granting anything more than a short-term letting will be to obtain a 'clear' lease, under which the rent always represents the landlord's clear income so that the tenant ends up paying the cost of any repairs, regardless of who carries them out. If the lease is of the whole of a building, the landlord will usually impose a full repairing covenant on the tenant. If, however, the lease is of only part of a building, the responsibility for repairs will usually be divided between the parties. For example, the tenant may be made liable for internal non-structural repairs while the landlord covenants to repair the remainder of the building. However, any expense incurred by the landlord in complying with his obligation will be recovered from the tenant under the service charge provisions. The special problems associated with a lease of part of a building and service charges are dealt with in **Chapter 24**.

17.1.1 The 2007 Code for Leasing Business Premises

The 2007 Code provides:

> **7 Repairs**
>
> Tenants' repairing obligations should be appropriate to the length of term and the condition of the premises.
>
> Unless expressly stated in the heads of terms, tenants should only be obliged to give the premises back at the end of their lease in the same condition as they were in at its grant.

17.2 Tenant's covenant to repair

17.2.1 Subject matter of the covenant

In the lease the tenant will invariably covenant to repair the demised premises and, therefore, it must be made clear what the subject matter of the covenant is, ie, what is the covenantor liable to repair? Thus, it will be necessary to read the repairing covenant in conjunction with the definition of the 'demised premises' in the parcels clause. On the grant of a lease of the whole of a building there should not be any difficulty as the responsibility for repairs will doubtless extend to the whole of the demised premises. On the grant of a lease of part of a building where the responsibility for repairs is to be divided between the parties it must be made clear who is to be responsible for repairing each part of the building. This will require very careful drafting of both the parcels clause and the repairing covenant (see **24.3** where this matter is dealt with in more detail).

As general rule, a covenant to repair the demised premises will also extend to:

(a)   any landlord's fixtures attached to them;

(b)   any buildings erected after the date of the lease. If, however, the covenant is to repair 'the buildings demised', it will only extend to the buildings existing at the date of the lease.

One further issue which requires clarification is the question of responsibility for site contamination. If the site is subsequently discovered to be contaminated, can the tenant be required to remove the contamination under a simple repairing covenant? As yet there is a lack of judicial authority but it is submitted that there may be a problem for the landlord in persuading the court that a simple repairing covenant can be extended to the soil as well as the buildings. In the absence of judicial guidance the matter should be dealt with expressly in the lease; perhaps by defining the term 'repair' to include the remediation of site contamination.

17.2.2 Extent of liability

In examining the extent of the tenant's liability, a number of important matters need to be considered. For example, are the premises in disrepair? What is the standard of repair? Does the covenant require the tenant to renew or improve the premises? Is the tenant liable for inherent defects? Each of these is considered in turn.

17.2.3 Are the premises in disrepair?

If the tenant is under an obligation to repair the premises, he will only be liable if it can be shown that there is damage or disrepair to them. In other words, before the tenant incurs any liability, the landlord will need to show that the premises have deteriorated from their previous physical condition so that they are in a worse condition now, than when they were let. This requirement led to the downfall of the landlord in *Post Office v Aquarius Properties Ltd* [1987] 1 All ER 1055, where the basement of a building flooded due to a defect in the structure. The landlord's problem in fixing the tenant with responsibility for repair was the fact that the defect had caused no damage to the building itself. This being so, the court held that the tenant was not liable to remedy the defect under his covenant to repair.

17.2.4 The standard of repair

Sometimes the word 'repair' is qualified by the addition of the word(s), 'good', 'tenantable', or 'sufficient', but it would appear that these additions add little to the word 'repair' itself (*Anstruther-Gough-Calthorpe v McOscar and Another* [1924] 1 KB 716). The standard of repair required is 'such repair as having regard to the age, character and locality would make it reasonably fit for the occupation of a reasonably minded tenant of the class likely to take it' (per Lopes LJ in *Proudfoot v Hart* (1890) 25 QBD 42). Further, the standard will be determined by reference to the age, character and condition of the premises at the time the lease was granted. It makes no difference that the neighbourhood now attracts a superior or inferior class of tenant; the tenant need only keep them in the same condition as they were when let to him. If, however, the premises are in disrepair at the date of the lease, a covenant to keep in repair will require the tenant to first put the premises into repair (according to their age, character and locality), and then to keep them in repair.

17.2.5 Is the tenant liable to renew or improve the premises?

If the tenant is just under an obligation to 'repair', difficult questions can arise as to the meaning of that word. Do the works contemplated fall within the obligation, or are they more properly classified as works of renewal or improvement, for which the tenant is not responsible under a simple covenant to repair? It was said in *Lurcott v Wakeley & Wheeler* [1911] 1 KB 905 that 'Repair is restoration by renewal or replacement of subsidiary parts of a whole. Renewal, as distinguished from repair, is the reconstruction of the entirety, meaning by the entirety not necessarily the whole but substantially the whole ...'. Thus, the fundamental question is whether the work done can properly be described as repair, involving no more than renewal or replacement of defective parts, or whether it amounts to renewal or replacement of substantially the whole. This will be a question of degree in each case. In *Lurcott v Wakeley*, the rebuilding of a defective wall of a building was held to be within the tenant's covenant because it was the replacement of a defective part rather than the replacement of the whole. However, the tenant may be required to replace part after part until the whole is replaced. On the other hand, in *Lister v Lane & Nesham* [1893] 2 QB 212, the tenant was held not to be liable for the cost of rebuilding a house which had become unsafe due to poor foundations: 'a covenant to repair ... is not a covenant to give a different thing from that which the tenant took when he entered into the covenant. He has to repair that thing which he took; he is not obliged to make a new and different thing ...', per Lord Esher MR. In deciding whether the tenant is being asked to give back to the landlord a wholly different thing from that demised, guidance may sometimes be found by considering the proportion which the cost of the disputed work bears to the value or cost of the whole premises (see also *Elite Investments Ltd v TI Bainbridge Silencers Ltd* [1986] 2 EGLR 43). It must be stressed, however, that decided cases can do no more than lay down general guidelines and each case will turn on its own facts.

In the same way that the tenant need not renew the premises, a covenant to repair does not impose any obligation on the tenant to improve them. A tenant may sometimes be concerned that his landlord is trying to get him to upgrade or improve the premises under the guise of carrying out repairs. The distinction is not always easy to make but Lord Denning stated in *Morcom v Campbell-Johnson* [1955] 3 All ER 264 that 'if the work which is done is the provision of something new for the benefit of the occupier, that is, properly speaking, an improvement; but if it is only the replacement of something already there, which has become dilapidated or worn out, then, albeit that is a replacement by its modern equivalent, it comes within the category of repairs and not improvements' (see also *New England Properties plc v Portsmouth News Shops Ltd; Sterling Surveys v New England Properties; New England Properties v Ex-Eltronics (UK) Ltd* [1993] 23 EG 130).

17.2.6 Inherent defects

At one time it was thought that a covenant to repair did not require the tenant to repair damage caused by 'inherent defects' (ie, defects in design or construction of the building). However, it now seems that this approach was wrong and that there are no special rules relating to damage caused by inherent defects. As with all kinds of disrepair it will, therefore, be a question of degree as to whether what the tenant is being asked to do can properly be described as repair or whether it would involve giving back to the landlord something wholly different from that which he demised (*Ravenseft Properties Ltd v Davstone (Holdings) Ltd* [1980] QB 12). Even the possibility of the tenant being liable for damage caused by such defects will alarm the tenant as it may require, not only repair of the damage, but also eradication of the defect itself if this is the only realistic way of carrying out the repairs (see **17.2.7**).

If the inherent defect has not caused any damage to the premises, they are not in disrepair and thus the tenant is not liable on his covenant.

17.2.7 Varying the obligation

In drafting the repairing obligation, it is possible to restrict or widen its scope from that imposed by a simple covenant to repair. Looked at from the landlord's point of view, it is possible to extend the liability of the tenant by the use of clear words which make the tenant liable to renew or improve the demised premises (see, eg, *Credit Suisse v Beegas Nominees Ltd* [1994] 11 EG 151). In *Welsh v Greenwich London Borough Council* [2000] PLSCS 149, the Court of Appeal held that a reference to keeping the premises in 'good condition' in the repairing obligation was a significant addition and would extend the obligation to defects which had not caused any damage to the structure of the premises (on the facts, damage caused by condensation).

From the tenant's point of view, there are a number of ways in which he may seek to reduce his liability.

(a)   The tenant may be alarmed at the prospect of having to repair inherent defects. For that reason, tenants of new buildings will often seek to limit their liability by excluding from their obligation liability for defects caused by design or construction faults, at least for a specified period of time. From the tenant's point of view, the landlord should covenant to repair damage caused by these defects (see **8.4.2**).

(b)   In most leases the landlord will insure the premises against a number of stated risks. The tenant should always insist that his repairing covenant does not render him liable to repair damage caused by a risk against which the landlord has or should have insured. The landlord should not object since he will be able to claim on the insurance policy. However, the landlord will insist that the tenant remains liable if the insurance is avoided because of an act or omission of the tenant or someone at the premises with the tenant's consent (see **22.7.1**).

(c)   If the premises are in disrepair at the commencement of the lease but it has been agreed between the parties that the tenant need not repair the premises to a higher standard, this should be expressly stated in the covenant. Further, for the avoidance of future disputes, a detailed schedule of condition, with appropriate photographic evidence, should be prepared by a surveyor, agreed by the parties and annexed to the lease.

(d)   The covenant to repair may be qualified by a proviso 'fair wear and tear excepted'. This will exclude from the obligation to repair damage attributable to the normal effects of time and weather and of normal and reasonable use of the premises but it will not exclude liability for consequential damage.

17.2.8 Access by landlord to execute works in default

A covenant to repair given by the tenant is often followed by a covenant to permit the landlord to enter the demised premises, upon reasonable notice, to ascertain their state and condition. This covenant should make two further provisions. First, a provision for the landlord to serve a notice of disrepair on the tenant if he is found to be in breach of his repairing obligation. Secondly, a covenant to repair by the tenant upon receipt of the notice followed by a right for the landlord to enter upon the premises to carry out the repairs, at the tenant's expense, if the tenant fails to do so within a specified time. The expense incurred by the landlord acting under such a power should be expressed to be recoverable 'as a debt'. This is an attempt to avoid the restrictions imposed by the Landlord and Tenant Act 1927 (LTA 1927) and the Leasehold Property (Repairs) Act 1938 on the recovery of damages, as opposed to a debt, for disrepair (see **28.1.2.1**).

The landlord should be aware, however, that if he reserves the right to enter the demised premises to carry out repairs in default, he will, in certain circumstances, become liable under the Defective Premises Act 1972 (see **17.3**).

17.3 Landlord's covenant to repair

The only common situation in which a landlord will covenant to repair is on the grant of a lease of part of a building, where the landlord will be able to recover his expenditure under the service charge provisions. A landlord's covenant to repair will be subject to the same rules of construction as a tenant's covenant and thus, for example, the landlord need not carry out works so as provide the tenant with something wholly different from that originally demised.

Where the covenant is to repair the demised premises, it is implied that the landlord is not liable until he has had notice of the disrepair (see, eg, *O'Brien v Robinson* [1973] AC 912). This requirement of notice is not affected by the fact that the landlord has a right of entry onto the premises. Once the landlord has notice, he must take steps to carry out the necessary repairs. If immediate permanent repairs are not possible, the landlord must take immediate steps to render the premises temporarily safe. If, on the other hand, the landlord's obligation is to keep in repair some part of the building not comprised in the demise (eg, the common parts), the landlord's liability runs from the moment the disrepair occurs, regardless of the question of notice (*British Telecommunications plc v Sun Life Assurance Society plc* [1995] 45 EG 133).

Where the landlord is under an obligation to repair, there is an implied right for him to enter upon the demised premises to carry out those repairs (but this should always be dealt with expressly).

Under the Defective Premises Act 1972, a landlord who is under an express or implied obligation for the repair of the demised premises owes to all persons who might reasonably be expected to be affected by defects in the state of the premises a duty to take such care as is reasonable in all the circumstances to see that they are reasonably safe from personal injury or damage to their property. This duty arises as soon as the landlord knows or ought to have known of the defect (see *Sykes v Harry* [2001] EWCA Civ 167, [2001] 3 WLR 62). Further, even where the landlord is under no obligation to repair but merely has a right to do so, he is made subject to the same duty, although he will not be liable to the tenant if the defect arose from the tenant's failure to comply with an express covenant to repair.

17.4 Covenant to yield up in repair

The tenant will often enter into a covenant to yield up the premises in repair at the end of the term. This covenant, which requires the tenant to leave the premises in repair, is entirely independent of the covenant to repair by the tenant. Thus, if the landlord had previously obtained judgment against the tenant for breach of the repairing covenant, yet the premises remain in disrepair, he will still be able to bring a claim at the end of the term on the covenant to yield up in repair (but obviously the amount of damages will be affected).

17.5 Decorating

Because some doubt exists as to the amount of decoration required by a covenant to repair, the matter is best dealt with expressly in the lease. The usual form of covenant requires the tenant to decorate the exterior and interior of the demised premises at specified intervals during the term, and during the last year of the term. The obligation to decorate in the last year could require the tenant to decorate in two consecutive years depending on when the lease is terminated (eg, in a 10-year lease with a decorating obligation every three years). The tenant may, therefore, wish to provide that the obligation to decorate in the last year shall not apply if he has decorated in the previous, say, 18 months. The landlord may wish to retain some control by requiring the tenant to obtain consent (not to be unreasonably withheld) before any change in the colour scheme is made.

Some covenants specify the materials to be used, for example, 'with two coats of good quality oil paint'. Care should be taken to ensure that the materials specified are appropriate to the type of building concerned as it is not uncommon to find that the specified materials are wholly inappropriate to the nature of the building and its method of construction. More modern covenants simply require the tenant to carry out his obligation 'in a good and workmanlike manner with good quality materials'.

On the grant of a lease of part of a building the exterior decoration would normally be undertaken by the landlord who would recover his expenses under the service charge.

17.6 Statutory curtailment

Oppressive enforcement of a tenant's repairing obligations may be curtailed as follows:

(a)   A landlord's right to bring a claim for damages in respect of the tenant's breach of a repairing covenant may be limited by the operation of the Leasehold Property (Repairs) Act 1938 (see **28.1.2.1**).

(b)   Under s 147 of the LPA 1925, the court may, in certain circumstances, relieve a tenant of his obligations in respect of a covenant relating to internal decorative repairs (see **30.5.3**).

Chapter 18
Alienation

18.1 Introduction

Unless the lease contains some restriction, the tenant will be free to deal with his interest in any way he wishes. He will be able to assign the lease, grant sub-leases of the whole or part, charge the lease and part with possession of the premises, without obtaining his landlord's consent. Complete freedom like this is unlikely to prove acceptable to the landlord for a number of reasons and thus a fair balance between the competing concerns and aims of both parties will have to be reached.

18.1.1 Assignment

From the tenant's point of view, the lease may become a burden if he is unable to dispose of it freely when he no longer has any use for the premises. This situation may arise, for example, where the premises have become surplus to his requirements or because they are no longer suitable for his needs. The tenant would also be in difficulty if his business venture failed and he could no longer afford the rent. However, from the landlord's point of view, close control over assignment is essential, because without it the landlord may find his premises occupied by an unsatisfactory tenant, and the value of his reversionary interest may be reduced. The assignee will become responsible for the rent and the performance of the other covenants in the lease, and the landlord will want to ensure that he is of good financial standing. The identity and status of any potential assignee is, therefore, important to the landlord for financial reasons. Further, there may be estate management reasons why the landlord will wish to exercise some control over assignees, for example, where the landlord owns the adjoining premises.

A covenant against assignment is not broken by an involuntary assignment such as occurs on the death or bankruptcy of the tenant. Nor is a restriction on assignment broken by a sub-letting of the premises.

18.1.2 Sub-letting

In some situations the tenant may wish to grant a sub-lease of the demised premises (see **25.2**). The landlord will want the ability to control sub-letting because in certain circumstances the head tenancy may cease to exist and the sub-tenant will become the immediate tenant of the landlord. This could happen, for example, on the surrender of the head-lease or on the forfeiture of the head-lease followed by the sub-tenant's successful application for relief. A similar situation could arise at the end of the contractual term if the head tenant does not apply (or is unable to apply) for a new tenancy under Pt II of the LTA 1954 but the sub-tenant does; the sub-tenant may be granted a new tenancy of his part against the head landlord. In all these situations the landlord would want to be sure that the sub-tenant was able to pay the rent and perform the covenants and will, therefore, wish to have some control over the identity and status of any proposed sub-tenant. Where a tenant mortgages his lease by way of sub-lease, this has been held to be a breach of the covenant, though possibly not where the mortgage is by way of legal charge (see *Re Good's Lease* [1954] 1 All ER 275). However, a covenant against sub-letting will not prevent the tenant from granting licences. Similarly, a covenant against sub-letting 'the demised premises' will not be broken by a sub-lease of part only (*Cook v Shoesmith* [1951] 1 KB 752). If such a restriction is intended, it must be dealt with expressly.

18.1.3   Parting with/sharing possession

A covenant preventing the tenant from parting with possession of the premises is wider in its effect than the two provisions mentioned above but it will not prevent the tenant from allowing another person to use the premises provided the tenant retains legal possession. It will not, therefore, prohibit a tenant from granting a licence of the premises to another unless the licence confers exclusive possession on the licensee (see *Street v Mountford* [1985] AC 809).

Arrangements under which a business tenant shares his premises with someone else are not uncommon with 'shops within shops' being frequently encountered. However, such an arrangement would not be possible if there was a covenant against sharing possession in the lease, forbidding, as it does, the granting of licences by the tenant. The tenant should try to resist the imposition of such a wide restriction, particularly where the tenant is a member of a group of companies and intends to share the premises with other members of the group.

18.1.4   The landlord's concerns on a dealing of part of the demised premises

Landlords often impose much stricter control on a dealing with part only of the demised premises because of the estate management problems which dealings of part can create. A sub-tenant can in certain circumstances become the immediate tenant of the head landlord. If a number of sub-leases have been granted, a landlord who had let a building as a whole to a single tenant could, at some future date, be faced with the estate management problems associated with having a number of different tenants each with a lease of a different part of the building.

Further, if the tenant was allowed to grant a sub-lease of part only of the premises, this could lead to the division of the demised premises into commercially unattractive units. If, in the future, the head-lease was forfeited and the sub-tenant successfully applied for relief in respect of his part, the head landlord might have difficulty in re-letting the vacant part if that part is no longer attractive to the market because of the way in which the premises have been sub-divided.

18.2   Restrictions on alienation

For the reasons mentioned above, it is common for the landlord to impose restrictions on dealing, such restrictions being either absolute in effect, ie, an unqualified (absolute) covenant by the tenant not to assign, underlet, part with possession, etc or alternatively, in the form of a qualified covenant, not to deal with the premises without the landlord's consent.

18.2.1   Absolute covenants against dealings

If the covenant is absolute, the tenant cannot assign or underlet without being in breach of covenant. While the landlord may be prepared to waive the covenant in a given case, the tenant will be entirely at the mercy of his landlord who may refuse consent quite unreasonably subject only to the restrictions imposed by the Sex Discrimination Act 1975, Race Relations Act 1976 and Disability Discrimination Act 1995. Also, if the covenant is absolute, the landlord is not obliged to give any reason for his refusal. An absolute covenant against dealings is unusual in business leases, except in very short-term leases, or to the extent that it prohibits dealings with part of the premises (see **18.2.3**). Any wider form of absolute restriction should be resisted by the tenant and if, exceptionally, there is such a restriction, the tenant should make sure its presence is reflected in the rent he has to pay.

18.2.2   Qualified covenants against dealings

A qualified covenant prohibits alienation by the tenant without the landlord's consent. Sometimes, the covenant will state that the landlord's consent is not to be unreasonably withheld; this is known as a fully qualified covenant.

18.2.3   A common form of covenant

The form of covenant encountered in practice will contain elements of both the absolute and qualified restrictions by prohibiting absolutely dealings in relation to part only of the premises, and dealings which stop short of an assignment or sub-letting of the whole (eg, parting with possession or sharing occupation of the premises), and then prohibiting without the landlord's prior written consent assignments or sub-lettings of the whole.

Such a clause attempts to strike a fair balance between both landlord and tenant as it will allow the tenant to assign or sub-let the whole of the premises subject to obtaining the landlord's prior consent (and the landlord will not be able to unreasonably withhold his consent). This should meet the tenant's main concern of being unable to divest himself of the lease should his circumstances change. At the same time, it will allay the landlord's fears by imposing an absolute prohibition on dealings with part only of the premises.

Other provisions will be found in a common form of alienation covenant. For example:

(a)   *Assignments.* In relation to leases granted before 1 January 1996, the lease will invariably require the assignee to enter into a direct covenant with the landlord to perform the covenants in the lease. This will make the assignee liable on the covenants in the lease during the whole term, rather than just during the currency of his ownership. Further, on an assignment to a limited company, the alienation clause may require the assignee company to provide sureties.

(b)   *Sub-leases.* If the landlord is prepared to permit sub-letting, the terms of the sub-lease will often be dictated by the alienation clause. In particular, the landlord will wish to ensure that any sub-lease is at a rent no less than that in the head-lease and with similar review provisions; that the sub-tenants enter into direct covenants with the head landlord; and that no further sub-letting is allowed. Sometimes, the prohibition against sub-letting part will be absolute only in so far as it applies to sub-leases of less than a certain area; for example, in and office block to sub-leases of less than one floor (sub-leases are dealt with in more detail in **Chapter 25**).

(c)   *Conditions on assignment.* In relation to commercial leases granted on or after 1 January 1996, the lease will usually stipulate conditions which must be satisfied, or circumstances which must exist before the landlord will give his consent to the assignment (see below).

18.2.4   Consent not to be unreasonably withheld

Section 19(1)(a) of the LTA 1927 provides that, notwithstanding any contrary provision, a covenant not to assign, underlet, charge or part with possession of the demised premises or any part thereof without the landlord's licence or consent, is subject to a proviso that such licence or consent is not to be unreasonably withheld. In other words, a qualified covenant can be converted into a fully qualified covenant by the operation of s 19(1). The section has no application to the operation of an absolute covenant, where the landlord remains free to refuse his consent to an assignment quite unreasonably. Furthermore, the section has to be read in the light of s 19(1A) of the LTA 1927 (introduced by s 22 of LT(C)A 1995) as regards covenants against assigning.

The Landlord and Tenant Act 1988 (LTA 1988) further strengthens the position of a tenant seeking consent to assign or sub-let. The Act applies where the lease contains a fully qualified covenant against alienation (whether or not the proviso that the landlord's consent is not to be unreasonably withheld is express or implied by statute). When the tenant has made written application for consent, the landlord owes a duty, within a reasonable time:

(a)   to give consent, unless it is reasonable not to do so (see below). Giving consent subject to an unreasonable condition will be a breach of this duty; and

(b)   to serve on the tenant written notice of his decision whether or not to give consent (see LTA 1988, s 1(3)(b), and *Footwear Corporation Ltd v Amplight Properties Ltd* [1999] 1 WLR 551), specifying in addition:

(i)   if the consent is given subject to conditions, the conditions; or

(ii)   if the consent is withheld, the reasons for withholding it.

The burden of proving the reasonableness of any refusal or any conditions imposed is on the landlord. The sanction for breach of this statutory duty is liability in tort for damages. The LTA 1988 does not specify what is to be regarded as a reasonable time nor when refusal of consent is to be deemed reasonable. Again, this Act has to be read in the light of s 19(1A) of the LTA 1927. The operation of the LTA 1988 is further considered in **Chapter 27**.

18.2.5   Can the landlord refuse consent?

Whether the landlord can refuse consent will depend upon whether the landlord has made use of s 19(1A) of the LTA 1927 or, if not, his reasonableness in the circumstances of the case.

18.2.5.1   Making use of section 19(1A)

Section 19(1A) of the 1927 Act (which operates only in relation to qualified covenants against assigning) allows the landlord, in commercial leases granted on or after 1 January 1996, to stipulate in the lease (or in a written agreement entered into with the tenant at any time before he applies for licence to assign) conditions which need to be satisfied, or circumstances which must exist, before the landlord will give his consent to the assignment. It is provided by s 19(1A) that if the landlord withholds his consent on the grounds that the specified circumstances do not exist, or that the specified conditions have not been satisfied, then the landlord will not be unreasonably withholding his consent. If the landlord withholds his consent on grounds other than those specified, s 19(1)(a) of the LTA 1927 will apply in the usual way (see **18.2.4** and below). However, it can be seen that the effect of s 19(1A) is to reduce the protection afforded to tenants by s 19(1)(a).

The nature and type of condition to be satisfied (or circumstances which must exist) is left to the parties to decide, but s 19(1C) of the LTA 1927 envisages their falling in two categories: those which can be factually or objectively verified; and those where the landlord has a discretion.

Factual conditions or circumstances might include a requirement that the proposed assignee is a publicly quoted company on the London Stock Exchange, or has pre-tax net profits equal to three times the rent, or a requirement that the assignor enter into an authorised guarantee agreement (see **18.2.7**), or that the assignee procure guarantors.

Discretionary circumstances or conditions are those which cannot be verified objectively, and a judgment or determination will have to be made as to whether they have been satisfied. This type of condition will be valid only if either it provides for an independent third-party reference (in the event of the tenant disagreeing with the landlord's determination), or the landlord commits himself to making a reasonable determination. Typical examples of discretionary circumstances or conditions may include a provision that the proposed assignee must, in the opinion of the landlord, be of equivalent financial standing to the assignor, and should the tenant not agree, the matter is to be referred to an independent third party; or a provision that the assignee must not, in the reasonable opinion of the landlord, be in competition with other tenants in the same development.

Note that the 2007 *Code for Leasing Business Premises* provides:

> Leases should . . . not refer to any specific circumstances for refusal, although a lease would still be Code compliant if it requires that any group company taking an assignment, when assessed together with any proposed guarantor, must be of at least equivalent financial standing to the assignor (together with any guarantor of the assignor).
>
> Authorised Guarantee Agreements should not be required as a condition of the assignment, unless at the date of the assignment:
>
> - the proposed assignee, when assessed together with any proposed guarantor, is of lower financial standing than the assignor (and its guarantor); or
> - is resident or registered overseas.
>
> For smaller tenants a rent deposit should be acceptable as an alternative.

18.2.5.2   Where section 19(1A) does not apply

Section 19(1A) has no application to covenants against sub-letting, charging or mortgaging, and does not apply in relation to leases granted before 1 January 1996. In such cases, s 19(1)(a) of the LTA 1927 applies in the usual way, meaning that, notwithstanding any express provision to the contrary, the landlord cannot unreasonably withhold his consent where the covenant is a qualified one. Whether the landlord is acting reasonably in such cases has to be judged from the circumstances existing at the time of the landlord's decision. Here, the parties to the lease cannot lay down in advance that refusal of consent for a particular reason shall be deemed to be reasonable since that is for the court to decide. However, it is open to the landlord to agree that he will not refuse his consent to an assignment or sub-letting in favour of, for example, 'a respectable and responsible person'. If the proposed assignee or sub-tenant is respectable and responsible, the landlord will be unable to refuse his consent, even on other reasonable grounds (*Moat v Martin* [1950] 1 KB 175). Further, it has been held that a lease may validly provide that, before applying for consent to assign or sub-let, the tenant shall first offer to surrender the lease. Such a requirement does not contravene s 19(1)(a), since if the landlord accepts the offer to surrender, no question of consent to assign arises. However, if the lease is protected under Pt II of the LTA 1954, the landlord's acceptance of the tenant's offer may be void. Even so, the tenant may still have to make his offer if he is not to be found in breach of covenant (see *Allnatt London Properties Ltd v Newton* [1984] 1 All ER 423, and **31.1.5**).

The Court of Appeal laid down a number of guidelines on the issue of the landlord's reasonableness under s 19(1)(a) in *International Drilling Fluids Ltd v Louisville Investments (Uxbridge) Ltd* [1986] 1 All ER 321:

(a)   the purpose of a fully qualified covenant against assignment is to protect the landlord from having his premises used or occupied in an undesirable way, or by an undesirable tenant or assignee;

(b)   a landlord is not entitled to refuse his consent to an assignment on grounds which have nothing whatever to do with the relationship of landlord and tenant in regard to the subject matter of the lease;

(c)   it is unnecessary for the landlord to prove that the conclusions which led him to refuse to consent were justified, if they were conclusions which might be reached by a reasonable man in the circumstances;

(d)   it may be reasonable for the landlord to refuse his consent to an assignment on the ground of the purpose for which the proposed assignee intends to use the premises, even though that purpose is not forbidden by the lease;

(e)   while a landlord need usually only consider his own relevant interests, there may be cases where there is such a disproportion between the benefit to the landlord and the detriment to the tenant if the landlord withholds his consent to an assignment, that it is unreasonable for the landlord to refuse consent;

(f)   subject to the above propositions, it is, in each case, a question of fact, depending on all the circumstances, whether the landlord's consent to an assignment is being unreasonably withheld.

The following are examples of situations where consent has been held to have been reasonably withheld:

(a)   Where the proposed assignee's references were unsatisfactory (*Shanley v Ward* (1913) 29 TLR 714). A landlord is rightly concerned that any assignee should be in a position to pay the rent and perform the covenants in the lease. Can the landlord, therefore, require the provision of a surety by the assignee as a condition of consent? If the lease does not require the provision of sureties, the reasonableness of the landlord's request for one will depend to a large extent on the financial strength of the assignee. The landlord will wish to see a bank reference and, usually, three years' audited accounts, but if he still entertains reasonable doubts, it may not be unreasonable for him to require a surety in which case the landlord will wish to be satisfied that their combined strength is sufficient to secure compliance with the lease terms. However, it has been held that the provision of a surety is not always a substitute for a satisfactory and responsible tenant in possession (*Warren v Marketing Exchange for Africa* [1988] 2 EGLR 247). In cases where s 19(1A) of the LTA 1927 has not been used, if the alienation covenant in the lease expressly required the production of sureties, the question arises as to whether the landlord can insist on a surety, however unreasonable that may be. There are conflicting views on the issue but the case of *Vaux Group plc v Lilley* [1991] 1 EGLR 60, contains obiter remarks suggesting that this may be possible, at least if the requirement was appropriately drafted.

(b)   Where there was a long-standing and extensive breach of the repairing covenant by the assignor and the landlord could not be reasonably satisfied that the assignee would be in a position to remedy the breach (*Orlando Investments v Grosvenor Estate Belgravia* [1989] 2 EGLR 74).

(c)   Where the assignee would be in a position to compete with the landlord's business.

(d)   Where the assignment would reduce the value of the landlord's reversion (but see *International Drilling Fluids Ltd v Louisville Investments (Uxbridge) Ltd* above).

(e)   Where the proposed assignee intends to carry on a use detrimental to the premises or a use inconsistent with the landlord's 'tenant mix' policy (see *Moss Bros Group plc v CSC Properties Ltd* [1999] EGCS 47).

(f)   Where the assignee would, unlike the assignor, acquire protection under Pt II of the LTA 1954.

The following are examples of situations where consent has been held to have been unreasonably withheld:

(a)   Where the landlord has refused consent in an attempt to obtain some advantage for himself, for example, the surrender of the lease by the tenant.

(b)   Where there are minor breaches of the repairing covenant.

(c)   Where, on an application to sub-let the premises, the landlord refused consent because the underlease rent was to be less than the market value (something which was not prohibited by the terms of the lease). The landlord argued that a sub-letting below market value, while not affecting the value of the reversion of the demised premises, would adversely affect the reversionary value of neighbouring properties it owned. The court held this to be a case of the landlord seeking a collateral advantage unconnected with the demised premises (*Norwich Union Life Insurance Society v Shopmoor Ltd* [1999] 1 WLR 531).

An issue which has been before the court on more than one occasion is whether the landlord would be acting unreasonably in refusing consent where he anticipated a breach of the user covenant by the assignee. In *Ashworth Frazer Ltd v Gloucester City Council* [2002] 05 EG 133, the landlord refused consent in these circumstances. The earlier Court of Appeal case of *Killick v Second Covent Garden Property Co Ltd* [1973] 1 WLR 658 had seemed to suggest that refusal of consent because of an anticipated breach of covenant would be unreasonable because the landlord would retain his remedies for breach of covenant and thus be in no worse position than if the current tenant breached the clause. The House of Lords in *Ashworth Frazer* rejected this approach saying:

> ... it could not be said, as a matter of law, that a refusal of consent was necessarily unreasonable where it was founded on the landlord's belief, reasonable or otherwise, that the proposed assignee intended to use the demised premises for a purpose which would give rise to a breach of the user covenant. (per Lord Rodger)

In other words, each case will be looked at on its own merits in light of what a reasonable landlord would do.

Under the provisions of the Race Relations Act 1976, the Sex Discrimination Act 1975 and the Disability Discrimination Act 1995, any discrimination in withholding consent for the disposal of the demised premises on grounds of race, sex or disability is generally unlawful.

18.2.5.3   What if consent is refused?

If, having applied for consent to assign or sub-let, the tenant thinks his landlord is being unreasonable in his refusal to give such consent, the tenant has a number of options open to him. These are dealt with at **27.1**.

18.2.6   Restrictions on charging for consent to assign or sub-let

In the case of a qualified covenant against dealings, s 144 of the LPA 1925 implies a proviso that no fine or like sum of money shall be charged for giving such consent to assignment or sub-letting, unless the lease expressly provides for this. However, this does not prevent a landlord from requiring his tenant to pay a reasonable sum for legal and other expenses incurred in connection with the grant of consent.

18.2.7   Authorised Guarantee Agreements

Although the LT(C)A 1995 has abolished privity of contract in relation to leases caught by the Act, an outgoing tenant may sometimes be required to guarantee his immediate assignee's performance of the obligations contained in the lease. This is achieved by the outgoing tenant entering into an Authorised Guarantee Agreement (AGA) with the landlord. The landlord may require an AGA from an outgoing tenant in the following circumstances, where:

(a)   the lease provides that the consent of the landlord (or some other person) is required to the assignment;

(b)   such consent is given subject to a condition (lawfully imposed) that the tenant is to enter into the AGA. For example, the requirement of an AGA may be one of the conditions which the parties had previously agreed had to be satisfied before the landlord was prepared to give his consent to an assignment (see **18.2.5**);

(c)   the assignment is entered into by the tenant pursuant to that condition.

The terms of the guarantee are left to the parties (provided that the purpose of the LT(C)A 1995 is not frustrated) but the Act specifically permits the guarantee to require the outgoing tenant to enter into a new lease should the current lease be disclaimed following the assignee's insolvency (as to which, see **29.1.2**).

Note that the 2007 *Code for Leasing Business Premises* provides that:

> Authorised Guarantee Agreements should not be required as a condition of the assignment, unless at the date of the assignment:

- the proposed assignee, when assessed together with any proposed guarantor, is of lower financial standing than the assignor (and its guarantor); or

- is resident or registered overseas.

For smaller tenants a rent deposit should be acceptable as an alternative.

18.3 Notice of assignment or sub-letting

There is no common law obligation for a tenant to give his landlord notice of any dealing with the lease, but a well-drafted lease will provide for this so that the landlord knows at any given time in whom the lease is vested and whether any sub-lease has been granted. The clause should specify the occasions on which the covenant is to operate (eg, assignment, sub-letting, mortgage). The tenant is usually required to pay a registration fee to the landlord with each notice served.

In the case of assignment, it will fall to the assignee to give notice (and pay any registration fee prescribed by the lease), since it will be his interest which will be jeopardised by the breach of covenant involved in failing to give notice.

For a more detailed consideration of the practical implications of the LT(C)A 1995, see Fogel et al, *Leasehold Liability* (Jordans, 2000).

18.4 Virtual assignments

The usual leasehold covenants preventing assignment, etc without the landlord's consent often prove inconvenient to tenants, eg on the sale of leasehold portfolios, where time is tight and consents would have to be obtained from a multiplicity of landlords. Hence, the virtual assignment was born.

A virtual assignment is an arrangement under which all the economic benefits and burdens of a lease are transferred to a third party, but without any actual legal (or equitable) assignment of the lease itself or any change in the occupation of the premises. Thus, as far as the landlord is concerned, the virtual assignor remains the tenant. However, as between the parties to the virtual assignment, responsibility for the premises passes to the virtual assignee.

But the question is whether such an arrangement is in breach of the terms of the lease. In *Clarence House Ltd v National Westminster Bank plc* [2009] EWHC 77 (Ch), the High Court held that although the virtual assignment did not amount to an assignment, subletting or declaration of trust, it was a breach of a provision in the lease preventing the parting with or sharing of *possession*. At the time of writing, the question is before the Court of Appeal.

Chapter 19

User Covenants

19.1 The need for a user covenant

There are several ways outside the terms of the lease in which the tenant's use of the premises may be restricted:

(a) *Planning legislation.* The tenant may not be able to carry out any building or other operations at the premises, and he will not be able to make a material change in the use of the premises without obtaining planning permission from the local planning authority. Generally, there is no implied warranty by the landlord that the tenant's use of the property is an authorised use under the planning legislation. It is, therefore, for the tenant to satisfy himself that planning permission is available for the use intended.

(b) *Covenants affecting a superior title.* There may be restrictive covenants affecting the landlord's reversionary title (or if the landlord is himself a tenant, affecting a superior title) which bind the tenant and prevent him from carrying out certain activities at the premises. Despite being restricted by statute as to the evidence of title he can call for, the tenant should always press the landlord for evidence of all superior titles.

(c) *Common law restraints.* The law of nuisance may prevent the tenant from using the premises in a such a way as to cause disturbance to a neighbour.

While these restraints operate to exert some degree of control over the tenant, they do not provide the landlord with any remedy should the tenant act in breach. A user covenant (together with several ancillary clauses) will, therefore, be required to give the landlord the desired level of control.

19.1.1 The landlord's concerns

There are various financial and estate management reasons why a landlord will wish to control use of the premises by the tenant:

(a) to maintain the value of the landlord's interest in the premises;

(b) to maintain the rental value of the premises;

(c) to avoid damaging the reputation of the premises by immoral or undesirable uses;

(d) to maintain the value of adjoining premises owned by the landlord;

(e) to avoid the tenant competing with other premises of the landlord in the vicinity;

(f) to maintain a good mix of different retail uses in a shopping precinct owned by the landlord.

The landlord has to be careful when drafting the user covenant to ensure that he does not restrain the tenant's use of the premises any more than is strictly necessary for the landlord's purposes, since a tight user covenant may have an adverse impact from the landlord's point of view on rental values both initially and at rent review. The wider the scope of the user covenant, the more attractive would be a letting of the premises on the open market and, therefore, the higher the rental value may be, both initially and at review. The tighter the covenant, the less attractive would be a letting of the premises on the open market (since the number of potential bidders for this letting would be restricted by the narrowness of the user covenant) and, therefore, the lower the rental value would be. The landlord is not able to argue at rent review that the valuer should assess the revised rent on the basis that the landlord might be prepared to waive a breach of the user covenant in order to permit a more profitable use (thereby increasing the rental value of the tenant's interest), nor is he allowed to vary the lease unilaterally in order to gain a benefit at review (see *Plinth Property Investments Ltd v Mott, Hay & Anderson* [1979] 1 EGLR 17 and *C&A Pension Trustees Ltd v British Vita Investments Ltd* [1984] 2 EGLR 75 and the comments made at **16.5.2.5**).

The landlord will, therefore, need to perform a balancing act between control of the tenant and good estate management on the one hand, and maximisation of rental values on the other. Valuation advice may be necessary here.

19.1.2   Tenant's concerns

From the tenant's point of view, a narrow user covenant ought to be avoided since, although the clause would work favourably for the tenant on rent review, his ability to dispose of the premises at some stage in the future will be hampered in that he will only be able to assign or sub-let to someone who is capable of complying with the covenant and who does not require any greater flexibility.

Additionally, the tenant must have regard to his own future use of the premises. There is a risk that the nature of the tenant's business may change to such a degree that he is taken outside the scope of the user covenant and, therefore, finds himself in breach. The tenant must ensure that sufficient flexibility is built into the covenant to permit future diversification of the tenant's business. However, he should not allow the landlord to insert a covenant that is wider than is strictly necessary for his purposes, since this may penalise the tenant at rent review by increasing the rental value of the tenant's interest. Once again a balancing act is required.

The user clause usually contains a principal covenant by the tenant governing the permitted use of the premises, followed by a range of ancillary clauses prohibiting or controlling a range of other activities.

19.1.3   The 2007 Code for Leasing Business Premises

The 2007 Code provides:

> **8 Alterations and Changes of Use**
> Landlords' control over alterations and changes of use should not be more restrictive than is necessary to protect the value, at the time of the application, of the premises and any adjoining or neighbouring premises of the landlord.

19.2   The permitted use

There are several ways in which the permitted use can be defined in the lease. First, the landlord may be prepared to permit a wide range of uses by broadly stipulating the type of use to be permitted on the premises, for example, use as offices, or as a retail shop, or for light industrial purposes. This would give the tenant a large degree of flexibility and enable him to diversify his business operations within the broad range permitted.

Alternatively, the landlord may choose to restrict the tenant to a very narrow range of uses by defining the permitted use by reference to the nature of the business to be carried on at the premises, for example, use as offices for the business of an estate agency, or as a retail shop for the sale of children's footwear, or as a factory for the manufacture of computer software. This would give the tenant no flexibility to diversify and would hamper the tenant in any efforts to assign his lease, or sub-let the premises to someone who was not in the same line of business.

As a third possibility, the landlord may adopt an approach which is mid-way between the first two by restricting the tenant's use of the premises to a class of similar uses by, for example, defining the permitted use as offices for the business of a solicitor, accountant, architect or other professional person. If the landlord intends permitting the tenant to use the premises for one of a number of similar uses, he may consider defining the use by reference to the Town and Country Planning (Use Classes) Order 1987 (SI 1987/764) (as amended).

19.2.1 Making use of the Town and Country Planning (Use Classes) Order (UCO)

It is often considered desirable that the permitted user is linked to available planning permission. For example, if planning permission is available for any office use within class B1 of the UCO, then the landlord, being quite happy for the premises to be used for any such office purposes, may choose simply to prohibit any use other than B1 office use. However, if this approach is to be adopted, the landlord should check carefully to ensure that there are no uses which could conceivably fall within the definition of B1 office use which the landlord would consider to be unattractive. The same principle is more clearly demonstrated if the lease prohibits any use other than as a retail shop within class A1. This is a very wide-ranging class of uses and there are likely to be several types of shop uses within that class which the landlord would not be prepared to tolerate at the premises.

If the landlord is to make use of the UCO in the user covenant, he should ensure that the lease clearly states that any reference to the UCO is intended to refer to the Order as enacted at the time the lease was granted. The danger is that at some stage during the term the UCO could be amended to bring within the class of use permitted by the lease a use which the landlord considered to be undesirable, thereby converting that use into a permitted use under the lease.

19.2.2 A covenant that names the tenant

It is sometimes difficult to define the type of business to be carried on by the tenant at the premises because of its peculiar nature, and so the landlord feels inclined to restrict use of the premises to the tenant's particular business. This is a dangerous approach to adopt, and it can lead to problems for the tenant (in terms of his ability to dispose of the premises) and can give rise to complicated valuation problems at rent review (*Sterling Land Office Developments Ltd v Lloyds Bank plc* (1984) 271 EG 894 and *Post Office Counters Ltd v Harlow District Council* [1991] 2 EGLR 121).

If the user covenant restricts the use of the premises to, for example, the offices of a particular company which is named in the lease, this would effectively prevent an assignment or sub-letting by the original tenant, even if the lease otherwise anticipated alienation (*Law Land Co Ltd v Consumers Association Ltd* (1980) 255 EG 617).

If the user covenant, without specifically naming the tenant, restricts use of the premises to 'the tenant's business', problems of interpretation will arise. Does the clause refer to the original tenant, or the current tenant? Does it refer to the business being conducted at the outset or the business being conducted from time to time? The danger from the landlord's point of view is that if, as is usually the case, the lease defines 'the Tenant' to include his successors in title, such a clause is likely to be construed by the court as permitting whatever business is currently being carried on by whoever is then the tenant. In other words, the landlord will have lost control. If reference is made to 'the tenant's business as a solicitor', does that mean that only the original tenant can comply with the covenant, or can an assignee? Would sub-letting be impossible since a sub-tenant, not being a tenant under the lease, would inevitably be in breach?

In view of these complications, it is advisable to avoid the use of covenants which either name the tenant, or refer to the tenant's business without sufficient clarity.

19.2.3   A positive or negative covenant?

If the covenant is positive, it will require the tenant 'to use the premises for the purposes of [the named permitted use]'. The benefit from the landlord's point of view is that non-use (eg, because of a temporary shut-down during a recession) will amount to a breach of covenant entitling the landlord to damages should the landlord suffer loss. Loss can arise if the premises form part of a shopping precinct which is dependent upon the continued presence of the tenant's shop in order to generate a flow of shoppers into the precinct. If the tenant's shop is a large food store, its closure will reduce the number of shoppers in the precinct, thereby affecting the profitability of other shops in the precinct and resulting eventually in an adverse effect on the value of the landlord's reversion. The tenant ought to resist a positive covenant (see **28.1.3**).

Most user covenants are negative obliging the tenant 'not to use the premises other than for the purposes of ... [permitted purpose]' in which case a breach is committed by the tenant only if he uses the premises for a purpose not authorised by the landlord. A negative user covenant is not breached by non-use.

Neither form of covenant will be breached if the tenant uses the premises for a purpose ancillary to the permitted use. For example, use of some rooms in a shop for storage purposes where the user covenant permits the retail sale of books, magazines and periodicals would not amount to a breach.

19.3   The extent of the landlord's control

The principal covenant may be absolute, qualified or fully qualified.

19.3.1   Absolute covenants

An absolute covenant gives the landlord absolute control over any change in the use of the premises in that it permits the tenant to use the premises for the purpose of the permitted use and no other. The tenant will not be able to use the premises for a use falling outside the scope of the covenant without obtaining from the landlord a waiver of the tenant's breach, or getting the landlord to agree to a variation of the lease. If the permitted use is narrowly defined, the tenant should be advised to resist an absolute covenant, unless he is sure that he will not want to assign or sub-let the premises, or diversify his business. If the permitted use is sufficiently widely defined (eg, use as offices only), then an absolute covenant should not unduly concern the tenant.

19.3.2   Qualified covenants

A qualified covenant allows the tenant to alter the use of the premises from a permitted use to some other use with the landlord's prior consent, which is usually required to be given in writing. However, such a covenant gives the tenant little extra comfort than is afforded by an absolute covenant since, unlike qualified covenants relating to alienation and improvements, there is no statutorily implied proviso that the landlord's consent is not to be unreasonably withheld. This means that, despite the additional wording added to the covenant, the tenant is still at the mercy of the landlord who may decline the request for a change of use for whatever reason he chooses. The only benefit from the tenant's point of view of a qualified covenant is derived from s 19(3) of the LTA 1927 which states that, provided the change of use will not entail any structural alterations to the premises (which would not often be the case), the landlord is not allowed to demand as a condition of his giving consent the payment of a lump sum or an increased rent (as to which, see *Barclays Bank plc v Daejan Investments (Grove Hall) Ltd* [1995] 18 EG 117). However, s 19(3) does allow the landlord, as a condition of his consent, to insist upon the payment of reasonable compensation in respect of damage to or diminution in the value of the premises or any neighbouring premises belonging to the landlord (which might occur if a valuable use of the premises is abandoned), and the payment of expenses incurred in the giving of consent, such as legal and surveyor's fees.

Section 19(3) does not apply to agricultural or mining leases.

19.3.3 Fully qualified covenants

A fully qualified covenant allows the tenant to change the use of the premises from a permitted use to some other use with the prior consent (in writing) of the landlord, whose consent is not to be unreasonably withheld. Most covenants of this kind will also stipulate (either in the wording of the covenant, or in the interpretation section of the lease) that the landlord cannot unreasonably delay giving consent. Should the landlord, in the tenant's opinion, be guilty of an unreasonable refusal of consent, the tenant may, if he is certain of his ground, change the use of the premises without the landlord's consent. However, this course of action carries a risk and, therefore, most tenants would prefer to follow the safer course of action which is to apply to the court for a declaration that the landlord is acting unreasonably, and then proceed without the landlord's consent. The question of the landlord's reasonableness is ultimately left in the hands of the court. The only potential drawbacks of such a clause for the tenant are that, without an express provision in the lease, there is no obligation on the landlord to provide the tenant with reasons for refusing consent (making it difficult for the tenant to assess whether he has a good chance of success in his application for a declaration) and there is no positive duty upon the landlord to give consent along the lines of the statutory duty imposed by the LTA 1988 in respect of alienation covenants, which means that the tenant does not have a remedy in damages if he suffers loss as a result of an unreasonable refusal.

Section 19(3) of the LTA 1927 applies equally to fully qualified covenants.

19.4 Ancillary clauses

It is usual for the landlord to impose many other covenants upon the tenant which also impact upon user, obliging the tenant:

(a) to comply in all respects with the Planning Acts (as defined in the definitions section of the lease). It is important for the landlord to have the benefit of this covenant since enforcement action for a breach of planning control committed by the tenant could be taken against the landlord, resulting in a possible fine;

(b) not to apply for planning permission, or to carry out acts of development at the premises. This covenant may be absolute, qualified or fully qualified. The landlord will not want the tenant to have freedom to change the authorised use of the premises as this may result in an existing profitable use being lost, thereby reducing the value of the premises. Although, as owner of the reversion, the landlord may be able to raise objections at the application stage, he would prefer to be able to veto the application under the terms of the lease in the first place. It should be noted that such a covenant may restrict the tenant's ability to alter or change the use of the premises even if elsewhere in the lease such action is more freely permitted;

(c) where the landlord has consented to an application for planning permission, and development has commenced, to fully implement all permissions obtained before the end of the term in accordance with any conditions attached to the permission;

(d) not to cause a nuisance, annoyance or inconvenience to the landlord or the tenants of adjoining premises. Whether an activity amounts to a nuisance is to be determined on the basis of ordinary tortious principles. An annoyance is anything which disturbs the reasonable peace of mind of the landlord or an adjoining occupier, and is a wider concept than nuisance. The concept of inconvenience is probably wider still;

(e) not to use the premises for any immoral or illegal use (since such uses may tarnish the reputation of the building and reduce its value);

(f)   not to carry out any dangerous activities, or bring any noxious or inflammable substances onto the premises. The landlord's primary purpose behind this covenant is to preserve the premises. One consequence of a breach by the tenant might be an increase in the insurance premium for the premises, and although the tenant is likely to be obliged to pay the increased premium by virtue of the insurance covenant, the landlord would not want the level of insurance premiums to rise;

(g)   not to overload the premises in any way. The landlord is simply trying to preserve the premises with this covenant;

(h)   not to allow anyone to sleep or reside at the premises;

(i)   not to allow any licence which benefits the premises to lapse (eg, gaming licences, liquor licences). If the premises consist of a betting shop, the value of those premises will depend to a large extent on the continued existence of a betting office licence. The tenant will, therefore, be obliged by the landlord to maintain and where necessary renew the licence.

Chapter 20

Alterations

20.1 Existing restrictions

As with user covenants, there are external restraints, outside the scope of the lease, which may prevent the tenant from altering the premises, or may at least regulate the way in which they are carried out, for example:

(a) *Planning legislation.* If the alterations proposed by the tenant amount to development within the meaning of s 55 of the TCPA 1990 then planning permission will be required.

(b) *The Building Regulations.* Any works to be carried out by the tenant will have to comply with the Building Regulations.

(c) *Covenants affecting a superior title.* The tenant's proposed works may be prohibited by the terms of a covenant affecting the landlord's reversion (which may either be the freehold title, or a leasehold title if the landlord is himself a tenant), or may require the consent of the person currently benefited by the covenant.

(d) *The common law.* The tenant will have to ensure that any works he carries out at the premises do not give rise to a cause of action in the tort of nuisance. He will also have to ensure that he will not, in executing his works, infringe an easement benefiting an adjoining property (eg, a right to light or air over the tenant's premises).

(e) *Other legislation.* The tenant, in altering the premises, will have to bear in mind any requirements of the fire authority in regard to fire safety, and if his works are more than just minor works, the tenant must have regard to environmental legislation regarding noise and other kinds of pollution.

20.2 The need for an alterations covenant

20.2.1 The landlord's concerns

There are various reasons why the landlord will want to control the ability of the tenant to make alterations to the premises:

(a) to ensure that the tenant does not breach the external restraints set out at **20.1**, which may well lead to action being taken against the landlord;

(b) to ensure that at the end of the lease the tenant would not be giving back to the landlord premises differing substantially from those demised;

(c) to maintain the character, appearance and reputation of the building and, therefore, the value of the landlord's interest in the building and any adjoining premises;

(d) to maintain the rental value of the premises;

(e) to preserve the physical state of the premises.

In a short-term letting the landlord will probably want to exercise tight control over the tenant's ability to make alterations to the premises. However, in a longer-term letting, where the tenant may need to adapt the premises during the term to suit his changing business needs, the landlord will be prepared to allow the tenant a greater degree of freedom. In the commercial letting market, a lease for a term of 15 years will not be an attractive prospect for a tenant if there are severe restrictions in the lease on his ability to make alterations. Such restrictions would give the landlord problems at the outset in securing a letting of the premises, and later on at rent review where the restrictive alterations covenant may be taken into account in reduction of the rental value of the premises.

20.2.2   The tenant's concerns

The tenant will be anxious to ensure that the lease gives him the right degree of flexibility. In considering the alterations covenant, the tenant must bear in mind four things.

(a)   Will the tenant need to make any immediate alterations to the premises, before occupying them for the purposes of his business? For example, if the premises form the shell of a large shop, and the tenant has not been allowed access to the premises before completion of the lease, the tenant will need to fit out the premises before being able to trade. If the premises are open-plan offices, the tenant may need to install internal partition walls. If the premises in their present state are unsuited to the tenant's needs, the tenant may need to convert them. The tenant should ensure that the alterations covenant does not prohibit these works, or if the covenant permits them with the consent of the landlord, the tenant should ensure that such consent will be forthcoming.

(b)   Does the tenant anticipate that his business needs may change during the term in such a way that he will need to alter the premises to accommodate these changes?

(c)   Will the tenant's assignee be content with the restrictions on alterations in the lease? Even if the tenant does not anticipate the need to make any changes during the term, an assignee might need to make changes, and if the alterations covenant is too restrictive, an assignee might be dissuaded from taking an assignment of the lease.

(d)   Will the tenant suffer at rent review? If the tenant secures a covenant that is too flexible, in that it gives the tenant extensive freedom to alter and improve the premises as he sees fit, the rental value of the letting may be increased at review as a result.

The tenant should ensure that, in the light of the above points, he has sufficient flexibility, but he should not let the landlord give him any more freedom than is strictly required, or else the tenant might suffer at review.

The covenant against alterations is usually drafted by the landlord to prohibit all alterations and additions to the premises save those expressly permitted by the terms of the lease, or those in respect of which written consent of the landlord has been obtained.

20.2.3   The 2007 Code for Leasing Business Premises

The 2007 Code provides:

8 Alterations and Changes of Use

Landlords' control over alterations and changes of use should not be more restrictive than is necessary to protect the value, at the time of the application, of the premises and any adjoining or neighbouring premises of the landlord.

Internal non-structural alterations should be notified to landlords but should not need landlords' consent unless they could affect the services or systems in the building.

Landlords should not require tenants to remove permitted alterations and make good at the end of the lease, unless reasonable to do so. Landlords should notify tenants of their requirements at least six months before the termination date.

20.3   The extent of the landlord's control

As with other covenants, the covenant against alterations may be absolute, qualified or fully qualified.

In all cases, the landlord must first consider the type of premises involved, and the length of term proposed. In a short-term letting of, say, three years or less, an absolute prohibition against all alterations may be appropriate. In a letting of a large warehouse or factory or other industrial premises, the landlord may only require absolute control over alterations affecting the structure and exterior of the premises, leaving the tenant free to do more or less as he pleases on the inside. In a shopping parade, in order to maintain the general appearance of the parade and the quality of the development, the landlord may feel that he wants to have a very tight control over all alterations, inside and out.

On occasions, the landlord may allow the tenant unrestricted freedom to carry out certain types of alterations or additions. In office leases, where the initial design of the building is open-plan, the lease often allows the tenant to erect internal partitioning walls without having to obtain the landlord's prior consent. The lease would merely require the tenant to notify the landlord of the additions, and to remove them if required to do so by the landlord at the end of the term.

However flexible the landlord proposes to be, in many cases the landlord will consider imposing an absolute covenant against structural alterations for the simple reason that the structure, being such a fundamental part of the building, should not be tampered with by the tenant.

20.3.1   Absolute covenants

If the lease contains an absolute covenant against the making of any alterations, or against the making of a particular type of alteration, the landlord will have total control over the tenant in that regard. As was the case with user covenants, this does not necessarily mean that the tenant will be unable to carry out prohibited alterations, since, although the tenant is at the mercy of the landlord, at some later date the landlord may be prepared to agree to vary the lease, or grant a specific waiver in respect of the tenant's proposed breach of covenant.

Sometimes, the requirements of a particular statute permit the tenant to obtain a court order varying the terms of an absolute covenant where the tenant has been required to carry out works to the premises by a body acting under statutory authority (eg, a fire authority ordering the tenant to install a fire escape, see the Fire Precautions Act 1971). Further, the provisions of the LTA 1927 can, in certain circumstances, enable the tenant to alter the premises notwithstanding an absolute covenant.

The tenant should be advised to avoid an absolute covenant except, perhaps, where the covenant only relates to structural or external alterations (in which case the tenant may agree that it is reasonable that he should not be allowed to tamper with the structural parts of the building) or where the letting is for a short term and the tenant is confident that he will not need to alter the premises in the future to accommodate changes in his business, and that he will not need or want to assign the lease during the term. However, the longer the term, the more the tenant should ensure that he has sufficient flexibility to alter the premises.

20.3.2   Qualified covenants

A qualified covenant against alterations prohibits alterations to the premises by the tenant without the landlord's prior consent (which is usually required to be given in writing). A typical lease of office premises might be drafted to contain an absolute covenant against all alterations to the premises 'except those expressly permitted by this clause'. This absolute covenant would then be followed by a qualified covenant obliging the tenant 'not to make any internal non-structural alterations without the prior written consent of the landlord'.

Section 19(2) of the LTA 1927 implies into a qualified covenant against making improvements a proviso that the landlord's consent is not to be unreasonably withheld. The proviso cannot be excluded by the landlord. However, under s 19(2), the landlord can, as a condition of his giving consent, require payment by the tenant of reasonable compensation in respect of damage to or diminution in the value of the premises or any adjoining premises belonging to the landlord, payment of any legal and other expenses (eg, legal and surveyor's fees) properly incurred in the giving of consent and, where it is reasonable to do so, an undertaking from the tenant to reinstate the premises at the end of the term to the condition they were in prior to the execution of the improvement.

Section 19(2) leaves the tenant with three questions which are discussed below.

20.3.2.1 When does an alteration amount to an improvement?

In deciding whether the tenant's proposed works amount to improvements to the premises, the matter is to be viewed through the eyes of the tenant, not the landlord (see *Lambert v FW Woolworth & Co Ltd (No 2)* [1938] 2 All ER 664). Provided the alteration has the effect of increasing the value or usefulness of the premises from the tenant's point of view, it is irrelevant that the alterations will inevitably lead to a decrease in the value of the landlord's reversionary interest. The tenant may propose knocking through a party wall to an adjacent building which is also in the occupation of the tenant, but which is not owned by the landlord. If such alterations increase the usefulness of the premises to the tenant (which they surely will), they will amount to improvements, and the landlord will not be able to withhold his consent unreasonably. As a consequence of the judicial interpretation of 'improvements', most disputes arising under s 19(2) revolve around the amount of compensation payable to the landlord rather than the classification of the tenant's works, since the tenant should always to be able to show that his alterations will improve the premises from his point of view.

20.3.2.2 When will the landlord be acting unreasonably in withholding his consent?

First of all, the tenant must have supplied the landlord with all the information necessary for the landlord to reach an informed decision (*Kalford Ltd v Peterborough City Council* [2001] EGCS 42. Assuming this has been done, a landlord will only be acting reasonably in refusing consent where his reasons relate to the relationship of landlord and tenant in regard to the premises in question. Withholding consent on the grounds that the premises, if improved, would be more attractive and, therefore, likely to take trade away from the landlord's own premises in the neighbourhood would appear to be unreasonable on the grounds that the landlord is seeking to gain some collateral advantage outside the landlord and tenant relationship.

Since s 19(2) allows the landlord to be compensated for a reduction in the value of the reversion, a landlord would be acting unreasonably if he withheld consent to improvements on the ground of the reduction. The correct approach for the landlord would be to seek reasonable compensation under s 19(2). However, should the tenant refuse to pay a reasonable sum in compensation, or should he refuse to give an undertaking to reinstate the premises at the end of the term where it is reasonable for the landlord to ask for this (eg, in the example above, where the tenant is uniting the premises with other premises not owned by the landlord), the landlord would be acting reasonably in withholding consent.

If the landlord gives his consent, but subject to an unreasonable condition (eg that the tenant pays an excessive amount of compensation to the landlord, or that the tenant agrees to surrender his lease one year earlier than the end of the term), the landlord will be unreasonably withholding his consent.

20.3.2.3   What remedies does the tenant have?

If the landlord, in the tenant's opinion, unreasonably withholds consent to improvements, the tenant may seek a declaration from the court that the landlord is acting unreasonably and that the tenant may, therefore, proceed without the landlord's consent. Alternatively, confident in the belief that the landlord is acting unreasonably the tenant may decide to take a risk by proceeding to execute his proposed works without waiting for the landlord's consent. If subsequently sued for a breach of covenant for altering the premises without the landlord's consent, the tenant can use the landlord's alleged unreasonable withholding of consent as a defence to the claim. However, unless there is an express provision in the lease, there is no obligation on the landlord to give any reasons for refusing consent, and so it may be difficult for the tenant to assess his chances of succeeding either in his application for a declaration, or in the defence of the landlord's claim for breach if the tenant proceeds without waiting for the landlord's consent.

The tenant does not have a claim in damages against the landlord if the refusal of consent results in loss to the tenant (eg, where the tenant's well-advanced business plans are thwarted by the landlord's refusal) since, unlike alienation covenants, there is no positive duty on the landlord to give consent.

Section 19(2) does not apply to mining or agricultural leases.

20.3.3   Fully qualified covenants

Section 19(2) converts a qualified covenant against alterations into a fully qualified covenant in so far as improvements are intended by the tenant. However, to avoid the argument that the tenant's works are not improvements, most tenants will insist on converting a qualified covenant into a fully qualified covenant expressly by adding to the qualified covenant drafted by the landlord the words 'such consent not to be unreasonably withheld or delayed'. That having been done, the landlord may not now unreasonably withhold, nor delay giving his consent in respect of an application by the tenant to carry out any alterations of a kind permitted by the clause.

20.4   Other lease clauses

The landlord is likely to include many other covenants in the lease which have a bearing on what the tenant will be allowed to do to the premises.

(a)   If the terms of the lease permit certain alterations (either with or without the landlord's consent), the landlord may include a provision requiring all alterations and additions to be removed and the premises reinstated at the landlord's request at the end of the term. Section 19(2) of the LTA 1927 allows the landlord to impose this requirement as a condition of the licence to alter where it is reasonable to do so. By including the requirement in the lease, the landlord is trying to avoid the argument that he is attaching an unreasonable condition to his consent. Further, by obliging the tenant to reinstate the premises at the end of the term, the landlord may be able to avoid paying compensation to the tenant on account of his improvements (see **20.5**) on the basis that, if the improvements have been removed, there will be nothing in respect of which compensation can be paid at the end of the term.

(b)   In the same way that the licence to alter may impose a requirement to reinstate, the landlord may also impose a condition obliging the tenant to allow the landlord access to the premises to view the tenant's works. To avoid the argument that such a condition is an unreasonable one to impose, many landlords prefer to insert in the lease an express right of entry for inspection.

(c)   The doctrine of waste may operate to prevent the tenant from altering the premises. Waste is any act which changes the nature of the premises, and can be voluntary, permissive, ameliorating or equitable. Reference should be made to textbooks on land law for a more detailed consideration of the doctrine of waste. It is common to find a prohibition on waste (save to the extent that it might otherwise be permitted in the lease) in the alterations covenant.

(d)   Many landlords impose a covenant on the tenant not to tamper with the electrical supply or installations, especially in a lease of part of a building.

(e)   The landlord will want to control the tenant's ability to make applications for planning permission. This covenant may be absolute, qualified or fully qualified. If the tenant is allowed to obtain planning permission, the landlord is likely to require the tenant to fully implement all permissions obtained before the end of the term where development has been commenced by the tenant.

(f)   The landlord will usually require a covenant by the tenant not to display any signs or advertisements at the premises without the landlord's prior written consent, since a proliferation of signs or advertising hoardings can give the premises an unsightly appearance, thereby reducing the value of the landlord's interest in the building. In a shopping precinct, some landlords want to prevent tenants emblazoning 'sale' signs in shop front windows, as they feel that a 'sale' can sometimes imply that the business of the shop is suffering, which might be interpreted by some people as an indication that the shop is badly situated in the precinct. This can in turn lead to a reduction in the rental value of the premises, and a possible reduction in the value of the landlord's reversion. The tenant will normally ask, and is usually able to negotiate that the covenant is fully qualified.

(g)   The decorating covenant can be said to control the manner in which the tenant may alter the premises since it may dictate that the tenant is not to change the colour of the premises (either inside, outside or both) without the landlord's prior consent.

20.5   Compensation for improvements

Part I of the LTA 1927 (as amended by Pt III of the LTA 1954) makes provision for the tenant to claim compensation from the landlord upon the termination of the lease in respect of improvements which the tenant (or his predecessor) has carried out to the premises. The concept is fair in that the tenant will be returning to the landlord an asset that has increased in value as a result of the tenant's expenditure.

In addition, the LTA 1927 provides a mechanism whereby the tenant may obtain permission for improvements he would like to carry out to the premises even in the face of an absolute covenant.

The LTA 1927 provides that a tenant of business premises (defined under the LTA 1927 as any premises held under a lease and used wholly or partly for the carrying on upon them of a trade or business) is entitled to compensation upon quitting the premises at the end of his lease (no matter how it is terminated) in respect of certain improvements.

20.5.1   Qualifying improvements

To qualify as an improvement for the purposes of the compensation provisions:

(a)   it must be one which, at the termination of the lease, adds to the letting value of the premises;

(b)   it must not consist of trade or other fixtures which the tenant is entitled to remove at the end of the lease;

(c)   it must be reasonable and suitable to the character of the premises;

(d)   it must not diminish the value of any adjoining premises belonging to the landlord; and

(e)   it must not be made in pursuance of a contract made for valuable consideration (where, eg, the lease obliged the tenant to make the improvement, or the improvement was made under some statutory obligation and the tenant was bound by the lease to perform all statutory obligations affecting the premises, or the landlord paid for the tenant to improve the premises, or reduced his rent).

In order to be entitled to compensation on quitting, the tenant must have obtained prior authorisation for his improvements by using the statutory procedure, and he must claim within the statutory time limits.

20.5.2 Authorisation

To obtain authorisation, the tenant must serve upon the landlord notice of intention to make improvements. It does not matter that the covenant in the lease is absolute, or is qualified and the landlord has reasonable grounds to withhold consent. There is no prescribed form for the tenant's notice and, therefore, a letter would suffice, but the tenant should submit with his notice plans and specifications of his proposed works. The landlord has three months from receipt to serve written notice of objection upon the tenant. If the landlord fails to object, the improvements are treated as automatically authorised and will, therefore, attract compensation under the LTA 1927. If the landlord does object in time, the tenant may apply to the court for a certificate that the improvement is a proper one to make. The court will grant the certificate if satisfied that the improvement qualifies as an improvement for the purposes of the LTA 1927 (see **20.5.1**). The tenant is then authorised to make the improvements in accordance with his plans and specifications. Again, it does not matter that the improvements are prohibited by the lease, since it is provided that if the tenant has received no objection from the landlord, or has obtained the certificate of the court, he can carry out the improvements notwithstanding 'anything in any lease of the premises to the contrary'.

20.5.3 Amount of compensation

The amount of compensation that the tenant is to receive must not exceed either the net addition to the value of the premises directly resulting from the improvements or the reasonable cost (as at the date of termination of the tenancy) of carrying out the improvement. It follows, therefore, that if the improvement does not add to the value of the premises, no compensation will be payable.

20.5.4 Time limits

If the landlord does not voluntarily pay compensation to the tenant, the tenant must apply to the court for compensation within three months of the service of the landlord's s 25 notice, or counter-notice to the tenant's s 26 request (see **31.2**) or within three months of the forfeiture of the lease (either by re-entry, or court order). If the lease is to expire by effluxion of time, application must be made between three and six months before the expiry date of the lease.

The parties cannot contract out of the provisions relating to compensation for improvements.

The Law Commission has recommended abolition of compensation for improvements.

20.6 Impact of the Disability Discrimination Act 1995

20.6.1 Introduction

The Disability Discrimination Act 1995 (DDA 1995) came into force on 2 December 1996. It makes it unlawful to discriminate against disabled persons in connection with employment, the provision of goods, facilities and services or the disposal or management of premises. Since 1 October 2004, service providers may have to make 'reasonable adjustments' in relation to the physical features of their premises to overcome physical barriers to access.

20.6.2 Definitions

20.6.2.1 'Disability'

The DDA 1995, s 1 defines a person as having a disability if that person has 'a physical or mental impairment which has a substantial and long-term adverse effect on his ability to carry out normal day-to-day activities'. The definition is very wide. Examples of disabilities include:

(a)   deafness;

(b)   blindness or partial sight;

(c)   mental illness or mental health problems;

(d)   partial or limited mobility;

(e)   learning disabilities, such as dyslexia;

(f)   conditions such as arthritis, diabetes and epilepsy.

20.6.2.2 'Disabled person'

A disabled person is a person who has a disability.

20.6.2.3 'Service' and 'service provider'

A person will be a 'provider of services' where a service is provided to the public or any section of the public.

20.6.2.4 'Discrimination'

A service provider discriminates against a disabled person in two ways:

(a)   by treating a disabled person less favourably without justification;

(b)   by failing to make reasonable adjustments under s 21 without justification.

20.6.3 Duty to make reasonable adjustments

The DDA 1995 imposes duties on a service provider who offers services to the public to make reasonable adjustments in the provision of its services. Since 1 October 2004 this has included taking reasonable steps in relation to a physical feature by removing it or altering it.

20.6.4 Is the landlord or the tenant the service provider?

The DDA 1995 makes no distinction between landlords and tenants.

Instead, the duties under the DDA 1995 apply to a service provider. Essentially, the duties fall upon whoever is providing services to members of the public. Depending on the context, this may be the tenant, the landlord or both.

A landlord may be a service provider for the purposes of the DDA 1995. An example could be the landlord of a multiple let shopping centre where the landlord is responsible for maintaining the public areas which provide access to independent shopping units. As members of the public are permitted to enter the shopping centre premises, then the landlord is likely to be a service provider in respect of those premises as he is providing a service of access to and use of its shopping centre.

20.6.5 The terms of the lease

20.6.5.1 Service charges

Landlords will want to pass on to their tenants through the service charge any costs incurred in making adjustments to physical features in the common parts to comply with s 21 of the DDA 1995. The landlord will need to ensure that the service charge provision allows for this.

20.6.5.2 Rent review

It is unclear at present how any works undertaken by a landlord or tenant to comply with s 21 of the DDA 1995 will be treated upon review.

In the case of the tenant, this will involve an assessment of whether the works were carried out under a duty owed to the landlord (the duty to comply with statute) and whether such works are ignored upon review. A tenant could possibly find himself exposed not only to an obligation to undertake expensive works, but to a substantial increase in his rent upon review.

In the case of a landlord, only those works undertaken to comply with statute will be of relevance. If a landlord undertakes expensive works of physical alteration, when a simpler, cheaper alternative would have sufficed, then the expensive works may be disregarded for the purposes of any review.

20.6.6 Compelling a landlord to make physical alterations

Where a physical obstacle exists in the common parts making it unreasonably difficult or impossible for a disabled person to use the tenant's service, the tenant is likely to have to ask the landlord to alter or remove that physical feature to comply with his duties under s 21(2).

However, if the landlord refuses, the tenant will be unable to compel the landlord to make adjustments unless he has specific contractual rights under the lease.

Making a request of the landlord, however, does not mean that the tenant has fulfilled his duties under the DDA 1995. The tenant will have to consider:

(a)   providing a reasonable means of avoiding the feature; or

(b)   providing a reasonable alternative method of making the service available.

Tenants of new leases in multiple let buildings should consider asking for provisions in the lease requiring the landlord to ensure that common parts are accessible under the DDA 1995, and that the allocation of the responsibility of cost for doing this is agreed.

The landlord is likely to seek provisions in the service charge clause allowing him to charge all tenants equally for any works that he undertakes to the common parts.

20.6.7 Compelling a tenant to make physical alterations

Whether a landlord can compel a tenant to carry out physical alterations will depend upon the terms of the lease in each case. Often a lease will contain a provision requiring the tenant to comply with any relevant statutory duties. However, since the duty under s 21(2) is not an absolute obligation to carry out physical alterations (but only to make reasonable adjustments), this provision will not in itself be sufficient to compel a tenant to make physical alterations.

A clause in a lease which required physical adjustments to be made for the purposes of complying with s 21(2) of the DDA 1995 would be narrower, and more onerous, than the duties prescribed by the DDA 1995. This would affect the marketability of the lease, and would be likely to have a negative effect upon any rent review.

20.6.8 Prospective tenants' concerns

Complying with the duties under s 21(2) may necessitate making physical adjustments at significant cost. Consequently, before taking a lease of premises, a disability audit should be conducted as part of any survey.

20.6.9   Landlord's consent to alterations

Where a service provider occupies premises under a lease, then consent from the landlord may be required under the terms of the lease, before the service provider can make alterations within his demise to comply with his duties under s 21 of the DDA 1995.

Whilst most leases include provisions entitling a tenant to undertake alterations, some do not, or are restrictive in what they permit. However, if the only way in which a tenant can comply with his duties under s 21 is to carry out physical alterations, what happens where the lease restricts or prohibits such works?

In such circumstances, s 27 of the DDA 1995 applies.

20.6.9.1   The DDA 1995, s 27

If the terms and conditions of a lease:

(a)   impose conditions which apply if the occupier alters the premises; or

(b)   entitle the landlord to impose conditions when granting consent to an alteration,

the occupier is to be treated for the purposes of s 27(1) of the DDA 1995 as not being entitled to make the alteration.

20.6.9.2   The effect of s 27

Where s 27 of the DDA 1995 applies then, except to the extent to which it expressly so provides, a lease will have effect as if it provided that:

(a)   the occupier is entitled to make the alteration with the written consent of the landlord;

(b)   the occupier must make written application to the landlord for consent to the alterations;

(c)   the landlord is not to withhold his consent unreasonably;

(d)   the landlord is entitled to grant his consent subject to reasonable conditions.

20.6.9.3   Withholding consent unreasonably

Whether the withholding of consent is unreasonable will depend on the circumstances in question. The landlord's consent is likely to have been reasonably withheld where the proposed alterations cause, or would be likely to cause, either:

(a)   a significant reduction in the value of the landlord's interest in the premises; or

(b)   significant disruption or inconvenience to other tenants of the landlord (for example, where the premises consist of multiple adjoining units).

If a landlord unreasonably withholds his consent to an alteration that a tenant wishes to undertake to comply with his duties under s 21(2) of the DDA 1995, then the tenant can:

(a)   refer the matter to court; or

(b)   join the landlord as a party to any proceedings instituted against the tenant.

20.6.9.4   Withholding consent reasonably

A landlord is to be taken, for the purposes of s 27 of the DDA 1995, to have acted reasonably in withholding consent to alterations requested by a tenant where:

(a)   there is a binding obligation requiring the consent of any person to the alteration (for example, the consent of a superior landlord);

(b)   the relevant landlord has taken steps to seek that consent; and

(c)   that consent has not been given, or has been given subject to a condition making it reasonable for the landlord to withhold its consent; or

(d)   the relevant landlord does not know, and could not reasonably be expected to know, that the alteration is one which the occupier proposes to make in order to comply with a s 21 duty.

For example, the landlord's interest in the property may be mortgaged and the terms of the mortgage may prohibit any alterations without the mortgagee's consent. If the landlord seeks his mortgagee's consent, but that consent is refused, then the landlord is likely to have reasonably withheld his consent for the purposes of s 27 of the DDA 1995.

20.6.9.5 Sub-leases

Where a landlord requires the consent of a superior landlord before he can consent to a request by his tenant to execute alterations, that superior landlord may not withhold consent unreasonably. The superior landlord may, however, attach reasonable conditions to the consent.

Chapter 21
The Landlord's Covenant for Quiet Enjoyment

21.1 Nature of the covenant

Most leases will contain an express covenant for quiet enjoyment by the landlord (and, even in the absence of an express covenant, one will be implied). The usual form of express covenant provides that if the tenant pays the rent and performs his covenants, he may quietly hold and enjoy the demised premises without interruption by the landlord or anyone lawfully claiming under him. This usual form of covenant is restricted in that it only extends to interruption of or interference with the tenant's enjoyment of the demised premises by the landlord or any person lawfully claiming under him; it does not extend to the acts of anyone with a title superior to that of the landlord. However, the parties are free to negotiate a more extensive covenant for quiet enjoyment which does extend to the acts of those with a superior title, thereby providing the tenant with a greater degree of protection.

The covenant only extends to the lawful acts of those claiming under the landlord since, if they are unlawful (eg, trespass) the tenant will have his own remedies against the person committing the act. This means that there is no breach of the covenant in the event of an interruption by an adjoining tenant which is unauthorised by the landlord.

21.2 Acts constituting a breach

The covenant will provide the tenant with a remedy in the case of unlawful eviction or where there is substantial interference with the tenant's use or enjoyment of the demised premises. While this is a question of fact in each case, the following situations have given rise to a breach:

(a) Where the landlord erected scaffolding on the pavement in front of a shop which blocked the access to the shop (*Owen v Gadd* [1956] 2 QB 99). This illustrates that it is not necessary for there to be any physical intrusion into the demised premises provided (it would seem) that there is physical interference with the enjoyment of the premises.

(b) Where the demised premises were flooded due to the landlord's failure to repair a culvert on his adjoining land (*Booth v Thomas* [1926] Ch 397).

(c) Where the landlord carried out work to the building in a manner which caused prolonged and substantial interference to the tenant by reason of 'dust, noise, dirt ... deterioration of common parts ... general inconvenience ... and water penetration' (see *Mira v Aylmer Square Investments Ltd* [1990] 1 EGLR 45). If the landlord is under an obligation to repair the premises, he must take all reasonable precautions to prevent disturbance (*Goldmile Properties Ltd v Lechouritis* [2003] EWCA Civ 49, [2003] 15 EG 143).

Until recently, it had been thought that the word 'quiet' in the covenant did not refer to the absence of noise and that some direct and physical interference was required before the landlord incurred liability under it. However, in the case of *Southwark London Borough Council v Mills and Others; Baxter v Camden London Borough Council* [1999] 3 WLR 939, the House of Lords held that no such limitation exists. The fact that the tenant was complaining of noise from adjoining premises in the block due to poor sound insulation did not in itself preclude a claim for breach of the covenant for quiet enjoyment. However, it was also held that the covenant applies only to the subject matter of the lease at the date of the grant. If, at that date, the premises already suffer from poor soundproofing qualities, the covenant is one not to interfere with the tenant's use or enjoyment of premises with that feature.

The covenant for quiet enjoyment is closely linked with the landlord's implied obligation not to derogate from his grant. This requires a landlord not to do anything which substantially interferes with the use of the demised premises for the purpose for which they were let. (See **28.2.2.2**).

Chapter 22

Insurance

22.1 Introduction

There is no implied obligation on either party to insure the demised premises. However, it is very important to both parties and their lenders that their respective interests are fully protected and it is, therefore, essential for the lease to make express provision for insurance. There are a number of important issues which will need to be addressed by the draftsman.

22.1.1 The 2007 Code for Leasing Business Premises

The 2007 Code provides:

> **9 Insurance**
>
> Where landlords are insuring the landlord's property, the insurance policy terms should be fair and reasonable and represent value for money, and be placed with reputable insurers.
>
> Landlords must always disclose any commission they are receiving and must provide full insurance details on request.
>
> Rent suspension should apply if the premises are damaged by an insured risk or uninsured risk, other than where caused by a deliberate act of the tenant. If rent suspension is limited to the period for which loss of rent is insured, leases should allow landlords or tenants to terminate their leases if reinstatement is not completed within that period.
>
> Landlords should provide appropriate terrorism cover if practicable to do so.
>
> If the whole of the premises are damaged by an uninsured risk as to prevent occupation, tenants should be allowed to terminate their leases unless landlords agree to rebuild at their own cost.

22.2 Who is to insure?

In a lease of business premises, it is common practice for the landlord to effect the insurance cover. On a lease of part of a building (eg, one unit in a shopping centre, or a suite of offices in a block) it is more appropriate for the landlord to arrange insurance for the whole building including any car parks, pedestrian areas etc, as in this way only one policy is needed. Further, all the common parts of the building will be covered under the same policy and there is no danger of any parts of the building being left uninsured. On the grant of a lease of the whole of a building, either party could be made to insure but the landlord will usually wish to assume the responsibility, rather than face the risk of the tenant failing to comply with his covenant to insure. While the landlord would be able to sue the tenant for breach of covenant, the tenant may have insufficient funds to satisfy the judgment.

If the landlord effects the insurance, before completion the tenant should ask to see a copy of the policy so that he can satisfy himself as to the amount and terms of cover. As the tenant has a continuing interest in the insurance of the demised premises he should also require the landlord to produce evidence of the terms of the policy and of payment of the premiums, at any time during the term of the lease.

22.3   Who is to pay?

Where the landlord has insured the demised premises, there will be a covenant in the lease requiring the tenant to reimburse the cost of insurance to the landlord. This sum is likely to be reserved as rent in order to give the landlord better remedies for recovery. If the demised premises are part of a larger building which the landlord has insured, recovery can either be through the service charge provisions or, alternatively, there may be a separate covenant by the tenant to reimburse an apportioned part of the premium. The tenant must ensure that the apportionment of the premium between the tenants is fair, particularly if the business of some of the tenants involves hazardous activities which lead to an increase in the premium.

It should be noted that a covenant by the tenant to reimburse premiums that the landlord 'shall from time to time properly expend' does not impose an obligation on the landlord to shop around for a reasonable level of premium (see *Havenridge Ltd v Boston Dyers Ltd* [1994] 49 EG 111).

22.4   In whose name?

Where the landlord is to insure, the tenant should press for it to be effected in the joint names of the landlord and tenant. This will be to the tenant's advantage because the insurance company will not allow the policy to lapse unless both parties have been given notice. It will also ensure that the proceeds of the policy will be paid out to both parties jointly, and thus give the tenant some control over how they are laid out.

Another advantage to the tenant is that insurance in joint names will prevent subrogation. This is the right of the insurer to step into the shoes of the insured and pursue any claims that the insured has against third parties to recover the loss. This means that if the landlord had a cause of action against the tenant arising out of some default on the tenant's part which caused the damage, the insurers would be able to pursue that claim. If, however, the insurance is in the joint names of the landlord and tenant, subrogation will not be possible. Even in those cases where the insurance is in the landlord's name alone, the tenant may still be able to prevent subrogation occurring where it can be shown that the insurance has been taken out for the mutual benefit of both parties (eg, see *Mark Rowlands Ltd v Berni Inns Ltd* [1986] 1 QB 211, where the tenant agreed to reimburse the landlord the premiums paid; see also *Lambert v Keymood Ltd* [1997] 43 EG 131).

If the landlord objects to insurance in joint names, or if it is not a realistic possibility, for example, where the demised premises consist of one shop in a large shopping centre, the tenant should seek to have his interest 'noted' on the landlord's policy so that he will be notified before the policy lapses.

22.5   Risks covered

The lease should contain a comprehensive definition of the insured risks listing, for example, fire, lightning, explosion, impact, storm, tempest, flood, overflowing and bursting of water tanks or pipes, riot, civil commotion, and many other risks commonly included in a buildings insurance policy. To give the landlord flexibility, at the end of the definition there should be a 'sweeping up' provision along the lines 'and such other risks as the landlord may from time to time reasonably consider to be necessary'.

Consideration also needs to be given to the issue of insurance cover against terrorist acts and reference should be made to one of the specialist texts on drafting leases for further information on this topic.

22.6   The sum insured

While the demised premises could be insured for their market value, the better approach for the tenant is to require cover for the full reinstatement cost. This will allow the landlord to replace the building should it be totally destroyed. Care must be taken to ensure that site-clearance costs, professional fees and fees for any necessary planning applications, and any VAT are also recoverable. As to the actual amount of cover, specialist advice will be needed and the insuring party should consult experienced insurance brokers.

22.7   What if the premises are damaged?

Although the doctrine of frustration is capable of applying to leases (*National Carriers Ltd v Panalpina (Northern) Ltd* [1981] AC 675), it will only do so in exceptional circumstances. Accordingly, unless the doctrine applies, the lease will continue notwithstanding any accidental damage to the demised premises, and the loss will fall on the party obliged to repair.

22.7.1   Will the tenant have to repair?

Since the tenant will be paying for the insurance taken out by the landlord, he should ensure that he is not obliged to repair the premises if they are damaged by one of the insured risks. It is common practice to exclude from the tenant's repairing covenant liability for damage caused by an insured risk, unless the insurance policy had been invalidated, or the insurance proceeds are not fully paid out by reason of the act or omission of the tenant (or some other person who was at the premises with the tenants' authority).

It is important that the tenant carefully checks the definition of insured risks, since, if there were significant omissions from the definition, the benefit of the limitation of the tenant's repair covenant would be seriously eroded. To take an extreme example, if fire was not an insured risk, the tenant would remain liable to repair damage caused by fire under the basic obligation to repair. The tenant must, therefore, make sure that the definition of insured risks includes all risks normally covered by a comprehensive buildings insurance policy.

22.7.2   Will the rent be suspended?

Unless the lease is frustrated, rent continues to be payable where the premises are damaged, even if the damage is extensive. It is, therefore, common to include a provision in the lease that if the demised premises are damaged by an insured risk, and become unfit for occupation or use by the tenant, the rent (or a fair proportion of it, depending on the extent of the damage) should cease to be payable.

The landlord will agree to a rent suspension only if the damage results from an insured risk, so that the tenant will remain liable for rent where the demised premises become unusable as a result of damage for which the tenant is ordinarily liable under his repair covenant. Again, it is important that the tenant examines the defined list of insured risks to ensure that the rent abatement clause operates on the occasion of damage by all usual insurable risks. The landlord will want to further qualify the suspension by stipulating that rent continues to be payable where the landlord's insurance policy has been invalidated by the act or omission of the tenant (or someone at the premises with the tenant's consent). If this were not the case, the landlord might lose both the rent, and the insurance proceeds.

The suspension will continue for such period as is specified in the lease. The landlord usually seeks to limit it to a period of two (or perhaps three) years, or, if earlier, until the premises have been reinstated and are again fit for use and occupation, for the purpose permitted by the lease. It should be noted that there is a subtle difference between premises being fit for occupation and use, and the premises being fit for occupation or use.

The tenant should press for a similar suspension in respect of other payments under the lease, such as the service charge, because if the premises are damaged, and the tenant is unable to occupy them, he will not be able to take advantage of the services provided by the landlord. However, the landlord will not give way to the tenant easily. If damage is occasioned to the tenant's premises alone, this is not likely to reduce significantly the level of services provided to the rest of the tenants, and the landlord will, therefore, argue that he is not prepared to suffer any reduction in the amount of service charge income.

If the demised premises are damaged, and the rent abatement clause operates, the landlord will lose rental income. The landlord will, therefore, require insurance against loss of rent during the period of suspension, and since the tenant is getting the benefit of the rent abatement clause, he will require the tenant to pay the premiums. If a rent review is possible during the period of suspension, the review clause will almost certainly require the rent to be revised on the assumption that the demised premises have been fully restored. This being so, the insurance against loss of rent should be for a sum which anticipates an increased rent on review. Valuation advice will be needed in this regard.

22.7.3   Who will reinstate?

If the insurance is in the joint names of landlord and tenant, the proceeds of the policy will be paid to both of the insured who have equal control over the application of the proceeds and, therefore, the reinstatement of the premises. However, where the policy is in the sole name of the landlord, unless the lease provides to the contrary, there is no obligation on the landlord to use the proceeds of the policy to reinstate the demised premises. While the Fires (Prevention) Metropolis Act 1774 (which applies throughout England and Wales) entitles any person interested in a building (whether as landlord or tenant) to require the insurers to apply the proceeds of a fire policy for that building towards its repair or replacement, the Act has no application to damage other than by fire, and the requirement must be made clear before the moneys are paid out. In those cases where the tenant is under an obligation to pay the cost of the insurance, it has been held that the landlord may be presumed to have insured on behalf of the tenant as well as himself, and thus the tenant can require the proceeds to be laid out on reinstatement (*Mumford Hotels Ltd v Wheler and Another* [1964] Ch 117). Notwithstanding this, where the landlord insures in his sole name, the tenant should always insist on an express covenant from the landlord to apply the proceeds of the policy in reinstating the demised premises.

A covenant by the landlord to reinstate often provides that in the event of damage to or destruction of the premises by an insured risk, the landlord will use the insurance proceeds in reinstating the premises. The landlord should make it clear that any insurance money in respect of loss of rent is not to be applied in the reinstatement of the premises. From the tenant's point of view, he should pay particular attention to the wording of the covenant which is often an obligation just to lay out the insurance moneys received in respect of damage to the premises in the reinstatement. This does not deal with the situation where the insurance proceeds are insufficient to cover the entire cost of reinstatement. Although the landlord might be in breach of covenant for underinsuring the premises, the tenant should nevertheless press for a covenant by the landlord to make up the difference, or, more effectively, an unqualified covenant to reinstate. Where this latter form of covenant is chosen, the landlord should qualify the absolute nature of his obligation by providing that he is not liable in the event that the policy is invalidated, or the proceeds irrecoverable by reason of the act or omission of the tenant (or anyone at the premises with the tenant's consent).

In any event, the landlord would not want to be liable to reinstate the premises if circumstances beyond the landlord's control contrive to prevent him from doing so (eg, strikes, lock-outs, shortages of materials).

22.7.4 What if reinstatement is impossible?

The tenant should try to specify a reasonable period (eg, two or three years) within which reinstatement must take place. If reinstatement has not been completed within that period, so that the premises are still incapable of use, or if reinstatement simply proves to be impossible, for example, because the landlord is unable to obtain the necessary planning and other consents required for reinstatement, the lease may provide for either party to serve notice to terminate the lease. Indeed, the tenant may consider it appropriate to negotiate a provision allowing him to terminate the lease immediately the premises are rendered unfit for occupation or use by an insured risk, so that he may relocate his business without delay. The landlord should always bear in mind that the tenancy may be protected by Pt II of the LTA 1954, and consequently the lease would need to be terminated in accordance with the provisions of that Act (see **Chapter 31**).

If reinstatement is not possible (or the parties do not desire it), in the absence of an express provision in the lease, it is unclear as to whom the insurance proceeds will belong, and it will be left to the court to ascertain the intention of the parties by looking at the lease as a whole.

22.7.5 Damage by uninsured risks

Historically, the risk of damage caused by an uninsured risk has been carried by the tenant. The landlord would not be obliged to reinstate the property, there would be no rent suspension and the terms of the tenant's repairing covenant would probably be wide enough to require him to carry out the necessary remedial work. However, para 9 of the 2007 *Code for Leasing Business Premises* contains a number of recommendations in respect of uninsured risks, namely:

> If the whole of the premises are damaged by an uninsured risk so as to prevent occupation, tenants should be allowed to terminate their leases unless landlords agree to rebuild at their own cost.
>
> Landlords should provide appropriate terrorism cover if practicable to do so.
>
> Rent suspension should apply if the premises are damaged by an uninsured risk other than where caused by a deliberate act of the tenant.

22.8 Additional provisions

Certain other covenants on the part of the tenant are commonly included in relation to the insurance of the premises:

(a)   not to cause the insurance to be invalidated;

(b)   to pay any increased or additional premiums that become payable by reason of the tenant's activities at the premises;

(c)   to pay the cost of annual valuations for insurance purposes; the tenant should beware the cost of such regular valuations;

(d)   not to bring dangerous or explosive items onto the premises;

(e)   to comply with the requirements and recommendations of the landlord's insurers and the fire authority;

(f)   to insure and reinstate any plate glass at the premises;

(g)   to bear the responsibility of any excess liability under the landlord's insurance policy.

22.9 Insurance by the tenant

If, exceptionally, the tenant covenants to insure the demised premises, the landlord must make sure his interest as landlord is fully protected. The landlord will have similar concerns to those expressed above on behalf of the tenant and so will wish to ensure:

(a)   that insurance be effected in the joint names of the landlord and tenant, with insurers to be approved by the landlord;

(b)   that the insurance is effected upon terms to be approved by the landlord (eg, as to the basis of cover, the risks insured and amount);

(c)   that in the event of damage or destruction the tenant covenants to reinstate the demised premises.

There will not be a rent abatement clause.

Chapter 23
Proviso for Re-entry

The lease should always contain a proviso enabling the landlord to re-enter the demised premises and prematurely end the lease on breach by the tenant of any of his covenants, or upon the happening of certain specified events. The right to forfeit the lease is a valuable remedy for the landlord but the right is not automatic; it only exists where the lease expressly includes such a right (or where, rarely, the lease is made conditional upon the performance by the tenant of his covenants; or where the tenant denies his landlord's title).

The proviso for re-entry should specify the events giving rise to the right. These are commonly:

(a)   where the rent reserved by the lease is in arrear for 21 days after becoming payable (whether formally demanded or not);

(b)   where there is a breach by the tenant of any of the covenants, agreements and conditions contained in the lease;

(c)   where the tenant has execution levied on his goods at the demised premises;

(d)   upon the bankruptcy or liquidation of the tenant, or the happening of other insolvency events such as:

    (i)   the presentation of a petition in bankruptcy;

    (ii)   the presentation of a petition for a winding-up order, or the passing of a resolution for a voluntary winding up;

    (iii)   the presentation of a petition for an administration order, or the making of such an order;

    (iv)   the creation of a voluntary arrangement; or

    (v)   the appointment of a receiver or an administrative receiver.

The landlord's intention is to give himself as many opportunities as possible to forfeit the lease where the tenant is in financial difficulty. In some insolvency proceedings, the landlord will want to give himself two attempts at forfeiting the tenant's lease (eg, once on the presentation of the petition in bankruptcy and once on the making of the bankruptcy order) in case the landlord inadvertently waives his right to forfeit on the first occasion.

A tenant should resist the inclusion of some of the less serious events (eg, the mere presentation of the petition) or those insolvency events which are designed to cure insolvency (eg, administration proceedings, voluntary arrangements, liquidations for the purpose of restructuring). Further, if the tenant's lease is likely to possess sufficient capital value to provide security for a loan (though this may be unlikely), the tenant should try to restrict the landlord's right to forfeit in these circumstances.

Despite the existence of a right of forfeiture and the happening of one of the above events, the lease does not end automatically; but the landlord will have the right to end the lease. The way in which that right is exercised, and the complex formalities surrounding its exercise, are dealt with at **30.5**.

Chapter 24
Lease of Part

24.1 Introduction

The purpose of this chapter is not to deal with every single issue of relevance on the lease of part of a building; some can only be dealt with in the context of particular clauses. The reader will, therefore, find references to leases of parts elsewhere in this book. However, there are some important issues which can be dealt with separately and by drawing these together in this chapter, particularly the service charge provisions, the reader will become aware of the special considerations which apply whenever a lease of part of a building is contemplated.

24.2 Boundaries and easements

It is important that the parcels clause fully and accurately identifies the boundaries of the property to be let. This is particularly important bearing in mind that the tenant's liability to repair is often co-extensive with the demise; if he has to repair the 'demised premises' it must be clear where they start and finish.

As far as easements are concerned, the tenant will usually need to be granted rights over the parts of the building retained by the landlord or let to other tenants. The case of *B&Q plc v Liverpool and Lancashire Properties Ltd* [2000] EGCS 101, illustrated the way in which rights granted to tenants may hinder the landlord's future development proposals. In the same way, the landlord will wish to reserve certain rights over the property being let.

These matters are more fully considered in the Legal Practice Guide, *Property Law and Practice*.

24.3 Responsibility for repairs

On the grant of a lease of part of a building, for example, one floor in an office block or one unit in a shopping precinct, it would be unusual to impose the responsibility for repairing the demised premises on one party alone. It is more practical for the responsibility to be shared between the parties. While every lease and building is different, a common division of the repairing obligation in a large multi-occupied building is to make the tenant responsible for the internal non-structural parts of the demised premises while the landlord covenants to repair the remainder of the building. Any expense incurred by the landlord in complying with this obligation will usually be recoverable under the service charge provisions, see **24.4**.

Great care must be exercised in drafting the appropriate obligations.

24.3.1 Drafting considerations

The whole building must be covered; there must be no doubt over who is responsible for the repair of each part of the building. If the tenant's covenant is limited, as it often is, to repairing the internal non-structural parts of the demise, he must make sure that the landlord assumes responsibility for the structure (including the roof, main loadbearing walls and foundations), the common parts, the conducting media, and the exterior (including any landscaped areas, forecourts, roadways and fences). To guard against the inadvertent omission of a part of the building from the landlord's repairing obligation, many repairing covenants begin by obliging the landlord generally to repair the 'Building and Grounds' (as defined in the lease) and then go on to list the items intended to be covered, adding 'without prejudice to the generality of the foregoing'. The following are some of the matters which will need consideration:

(a)   Walls. It must be made clear who is responsible for each wall in the building. Often the landlord will assume responsibility for the structural walls and possibly the outer half of the internal non-structural walls dividing the demised premises from the other parts of the building. The obligation to repair should be attributed as regards each physical layer of the wallcovering, plaster, brick etc.

(b)   The same meticulous approach is required for floors, ceilings and the joists and girders, etc, which lie between them.

(c)   Windows. There are conflicting authorities on the responsibility for the repair of windows and thus the matter should be dealt with expressly in the lease, usually by making the tenant responsible.

(d)   Roofs and roof spaces. Again, this is a notoriously grey area and the matter must be dealt with expressly in the lease.

(e)   Conducting media. Often the landlord will be made responsible (unless perhaps the conduits exclusively serve the demised premises), but the lease must put the matter beyond doubt.

(f)   The plant, including all heating and cooling systems, generators, boilers etc.

(g)   Decorative repairs. The landlord will usually assume responsibility for the exterior decoration and recover his costs under the service charge (see **24.4**).

The obligation to repair is often co-extensive with ownership, and care must be taken to link together the repairing obligations with the definition of the demised premises in the parcels clause.

The draftsman must also appreciate the precise meaning of certain words and phrases which have been judicially defined in a plethora of case law. Thus, for example, 'structural repairs', 'main walls', 'external walls' and 'exterior' have all been judicially considered; and reference should be made to one of the standard works on landlord and tenant law for a more detailed analysis of such technicalities.

24.3.2 Other considerations

The lease should attribute responsibility for repair of every part of the building. If, however, the lease is silent on a particular point the question arises as to whether the courts will imply a repairing obligation on behalf of either the landlord or tenant? In this regard there are a number of cases in which the landlord of residential properties have been held impliedly liable to carry out various repairs. For example, in *Barrett v Lounova (1982) Ltd* [1990] QB 348, it was held that a covenant by a periodic tenant of an old house to keep the interior in repair would lack business efficacy unless there were implied a corresponding obligation on the landlord to maintain the structure and exterior. It remains to be seen to what extent cases like this will be applied to business leases. See **Chapter 17** for a discussion of repairing covenants in general.

24.4 Service charges

In a letting of the whole of a property the landlord will normally wish to impose all responsibility for the repair and maintenance of the property on the tenant. This will not usually be possible in the case of lettings of part of a building, but the landlord will seek to achieve the same economic effect by the use of a service charge. The landlord will be responsible for repair and maintenance and the provision of services but will require the costs he incurs on these matters to be reimbursed by the tenants. The landlord could charge a higher inclusive rent to cover his anticipated costs, but he then runs the risk of inflation or unexpected outgoings making his estimate incorrect. The inclusive rent method is unpopular with institutional landlords and lenders who prefer a 'clear lease', where the rent will always represent the landlord's clear income from the property and the landlord is reimbursed for the expenditure on the provision of services by means of a service charge which fluctuates annually according to the actual costs incurred.

From the landlord's point of view, it is necessary to decide whether the service charge should be reserved as additional rent. The advantages of reserving it as rent have already been considered (see **15.4**).

24.4.1 Services to be provided

Tenants need only pay for the provision of those services specified in the lease. If there is no provision for the tenant to pay, the landlord cannot recover his expenditure. Therefore, when drafting the service charge provisions, the landlord's solicitor needs to be careful to include all the expenditure to be laid out on the building (excluding those parts for which the tenant is made responsible). This will require a thorough examination of all the lease terms. The following is not a comprehensive list of items to be included in a service charge as each lease needs individual consideration. However, some common items of expenditure are set out below.

24.4.1.1 Repairs and decoration

The clause should allow the landlord to recover all his expenses in performing his repairing obligation. Thus it may need to allow him to recover his expenses in inspecting, cleaning, maintaining, repairing and decorating the common parts and any other parts of the building for which he is responsible, for example, the conducting media, roof, structural parts, plant, etc. Whether the landlord can go beyond 'repair', and rebuild or carry out improvements is a question of construction of the relevant clause but the tenant must be aware of the danger of having to contribute to work which would be outside a simple covenant to 'repair', for example, the replacement of defective wooden window frames with modern double glazed units. In such a case the landlord would be unduly profiting at the tenant's expense. Another concern of the tenant is that the clause may require his contribution to expenditure incurred by the landlord in remedying inherent defects in the building, for example, those caused by a design defect or through the use of defective materials. The tenant should resist such an onerous obligation.

The landlord should pay particular attention to the wording of the service charge provision. In *Northways Flats Management Co v Wimpey Pension Trustees* [1992] 31 EG 65, the clause required the landlord, before carrying out the work, to submit details and estimates to the tenants. The court held that this was a pre-condition to the recovery of the service charge and since it had not been complied with, the landlord was unable to recover his expenditure.

24.4.1.2 Heating, air-conditioning, etc

The landlord will wish to recover his costs in supplying heating, air-conditioning and hot and cold water to the common parts of the building and possibly the demised premises as well. Sometimes, the landlord will restrict the provision of heating to the winter months. The tenant may want some minimum temperature to be specified but the landlord may be unwise to agree to this, preferring to provide heating to a temperature which the landlord considers adequate. The landlord should also ensure that he is not liable to the tenant for any temporary interruption in supply due to a breakdown.

24.4.1.3   Staff

The landlord will wish to recover his costs in employing staff in connection with the management of the building such as receptionist, maintenance staff, caretakers and security personnel. The clause should also extend to any staff employed by the managing agents for the purpose of providing services at the building. From the tenant's point of view he should guard against having to pay the full-time wages of staff who are not wholly engaged in providing the services.

24.4.1.4   Managing agents

If the landlord employs managing agents to provide the services, he should ensure that the service charge allows him to recover their fees since in the absence of an express provision it is unlikely that the landlord would be able to recover those fees. A company owned by the landlord can be employed as managing agents provided such an arrangement is not a sham (*Skilleter v Charles* [1992] 13 EG 113).

The tenant must make sure that the amount of fees recoverable is reasonable and may want some restriction placed on them in the lease.

If the landlord performs his own management services, the service charge should enable him to recover his reasonable costs for so doing.

24.4.1.5   Other common items of expenditure

Other common items of expenditure include:

(a)   maintaining the lifts, boilers and other plant and machinery;

(b)   lighting of the common parts;

(c)   refuse removal;

(d)   fire prevention equipment;

(e)   window cleaning;

(f)   legal and other professional fees;

(g)   service staff accommodation;

(h)   insurance (although sometimes this is dealt with outside the service charge provisions);

(i)   interest on the cost of borrowing money to provide the services;

(j)   maintenance of landscaped areas;

(k)   outgoings payable by the landlord;

(l)   advertising and promotion costs, in the case of a shopping centre.

24.4.1.6   'Sweeping-up' clause

No matter how comprehensive the landlord thinks he has been in compiling the list of services to be provided, it is advisable to include a sweeping-up clause to cover any omissions and to take account of any new services to be provided over the lifetime of the lease. However, careful drafting of such a clause is required as the courts construe them restrictively (see *Mullaney v Maybourne Grange (Croydon) Ltd* [1986] 1 EGLR 70). From the tenant's point of view he should guard against the clause being drafted too widely and insist on the service being of some benefit to him before having to pay for it.

24.4.2   Landlord's covenant to perform the services

The services to be provided often fall into two categories: essential services which the landlord should be obliged to provide (eg, heating and lighting the common parts and repairing and maintaining the structure) and other non-essential services which he has a discretion to provide. From the tenant's point of view, he must make sure that, in return for paying the service charge, the landlord covenants to provide the essential services. Without such an express provision, it is by no means certain that one would be implied, leaving the tenant with no remedy if the services were not provided (see, however, *Barnes v City of London Real Property Co; Webster v City of London Real Property Co; Sollas v City of London Real Property Co; Oakley, Sollas & Co v City of London Real Property Co* [1918] 2 Ch 18).

In drafting the covenant the tenant should require the services to be provided in an efficient and economical manner; and to a reasonable standard, rather than a standard the landlord considers adequate. The Supply of Goods and Services Act 1982 provides that where a service is provided in the course of a business there is an implied term that the supplier will carry out the service with reasonable care and skill but it is obviously better for the tenant to deal with the matter expressly. In *Finchbourne v Rodrigues* [1976] 3 All ER 581, the view was expressed that the costs claimed should be fair and reasonable to be recoverable under the service charge. However, this view may no longer reflect current judicial thinking (see *Havenridge Ltd v Boston Dyers Ltd* [1994] 49 EG 111) and therefore, again, an express provision is preferable. From the landlord's point of view, he may wish to restrict the covenant so that he is liable to use only 'reasonable endeavours' or 'best endeavours' to provide the services, rather than be under an absolute obligation to do so. In any event, the covenant should be limited so that the landlord is not liable to the tenant for failure to provide the services due to circumstances outside his control such as industrial action.

Another consideration for tenants is the length of the unexpired residue of their lease as they will be understandably reluctant to pay for works which are calculated to benefit future interests in the property rather than tenants under the current lease. This was held to be a relevant factor in deciding what was recoverable by the landlord under the service charge provisions in the case of *Fluor Daniel Properties Ltd v Shortlands Investments Ltd* [2001] PLCS 10 (although much will, of course, depend on the exact form of wording used).

As a general rule, the obligation to provide the services is independent of the obligation to pay for them. Therefore, in the event of non-payment by the tenant, the landlord cannot withdraw services (and in any event it is unlikely that the landlord could withdraw services from one tenant alone).

24.4.3 The tenant's contribution: basis of apportionment

In addition to setting out the items which can be charged to the tenant, the clause must deal with how the total cost is to be apportioned between the tenants in the building. The following are some commonly used methods:

(a) By reference to rateable value. This can be arbitrary since rateable values can vary for reasons which bear no relationship to the amount of services consumed.

(b) According to floor area. This can be a reasonable method, depending on the nature of the building, but some method of measurement will have to be agreed.

(c) According to anticipated use of services. This can be difficult to assess and depends on the nature of each tenant's business and its location within the building.

(d) As a fixed percentage. This provides certainty for both parties but is inflexible. Further, the landlord must make provision for any future enlargement of the building which would necessitate a recalculation of the percentages.

Each method has its own advantages and disadvantages and reference should be made to one of the standard works on the drafting of business leases for further consideration of the matter. Whatever method is adopted, the tenant will want to ensure that he does not become liable for any unlet units; the landlord should be required to pay the service charge for these.

24.4.4   Payment of the charge

24.4.4.1   Advance payments

Typical service charge provisions stipulate that the service charge is to be paid by the tenant periodically in advance (usually on rent days). Advance payments are necessary because otherwise the landlord would have to fund the provision of work and services out of his own resources and recoup his expenditure from the tenants later. The amount of the advance payments can give rise to disputes between the parties unless the tenant can be sure such payments are not excessive. There are different ways of calculating the payments, for example, it can be based on the previous year's actual expenditure or on an estimate of the likely expenditure in the current year. If the latter method is adopted, the tenant should insist on the amount payable being certified by, for example, the landlord's surveyor, and that the payment is only to be made upon receipt of such a certificate (see **24.4.4.3**).

The tenant may wish to consider a requirement that the landlord is to pay the advance payments into a separate account to be held on trust in order to avoid the problems which will arise if the landlord becomes insolvent.

24.4.4.2   Final payments and adjustments

At the end of the year the service charge provisions will, typically, require the landlord to prepare annual accounts showing his actual expenditure in the year: such accounts to be certified by the landlord's accountant (see **24.4.4.3**). Where advance payments have been made an adjustment will be necessary to correct any over or underpayment. In the case of underpayment the tenant will be required to pay this amount within a specified time. If there is an overpayment, the lease may provide for its refund to the tenant or, more usually, it will be credited to the following year's payments.

24.4.4.3   Certification of amounts due

It is common for the service charge provisions to stipulate that the landlord provides a certificate given by his surveyor or accountant, acting as an expert, in connection with the amount of both the advance and end of year payments. Unless the lease provides to the contrary, the expert must be independent from the landlord (*Finchbourne v Rodrigues* above), although the tenant may wish this to be expressly stated in the lease. If the certificate is said to be 'final and conclusive as to the facts stated', its finality is likely to be upheld by the courts. If the lease makes the expert's certificate conclusive on matters of law, for example, as to the construction of the lease, there are conflicting views on its validity but it may be that it will be upheld if the expert is given the exclusive right to determine the issue and the lease is clear on the party's intention to exclude the jurisdiction of the courts (see *National Grid Co plc v M25 Group Ltd* [1999] 08 EG 169 and *Morgan Sindall v Sawston Farms (Cambs) Ltd* [1999] 1 EGLR 90).

24.5   Sinking and reserve funds

The object of sinking and reserve funds is to make funds available when needed for major items of irregular expenditure. A sinking fund is a fund established for replacing major items such as boilers and lifts which may only be necessary once or twice during the lifetime of the building. A reserve fund is established to pay for recurring items of expenditure such as external decoration which may need attending to, not annually, but perhaps every four or five years. The estimated cost of such decoration will be collected over each five-year period to avoid the tenants from being faced with a large bill every five years.

The advantage of such funds is that money is available to carry out these major works when needed without any dramatic fluctuations in the service charge payable from one year to another. However, the creation of such a fund needs careful thought and many difficult questions will need to be addressed at the drafting stage. Who is to own the fund? Is it to be held absolutely or on trust? What is to happen to the fund when the landlord sells the reversion? What will be the position upon termination of the lease? (See *Secretary of State for the Environment v Possfund (North West) Ltd* [1997] 39 EG 179.) Further, there may be considerable tax disadvantages. Such matters are beyond the scope of this book, but the parties will need specialist advice about these matters.

24.6 Insurance

On a lease of part of a building in multi-occupation the landlord will usually insure the whole building and recover the premium from the tenants under the service charge provisions or in a separate insurance clause. Insurance is dealt with in **Chapter 22**.

24.7 RICS Code of Practice for Service Charges

Unfortunately, disputes over service charges in commercial properties are commonplace. Because of such problems, the RICS has published a new *Code of Practice for Service Charges* which came into force on 1 April 2007. This is aimed at surveyors who administer the services on a day-to-day basis and represents best practice. It cannot override the terms of existing leases, but does require that such leases should, as far as possible, be read in a way that is consistent with the Code. The Code also requires surveyors to try to ensure that the service charge provisions in leases granted or renewed on or after 1 April 2007 reflect the provisions of the Code.

The Code gives much greater protection for tenants, including the following:

(a) use of alternative dispute resolution (ADR) in relation to any disputes;

(b) better communication, including consultation on proposed expenditure;

(c) a right to challenge unreasonable expenditure;

(d) 'transparency' in the accounts, particularly in relation to management and other charges;

(e) management charges should not be linked to a percentage of the total expenditure;

(f) costs should be reasonable and works carried out to a reasonable standard;

(g) the apportionment of costs to each tenant should be fair and reasonable;

(h) sinking funds should be held on trust in an interest bearing account.

It remains to be seen how far these matters will be incorporated into the drafting of new leases, but the existence of the Code should give those negotiating and approving leases on behalf of tenants strong grounds for resisting any service charge terms not complying with the Code.

To reinforce this, the 2007 *Code for Leasing Business Premises* provides:

> **6 Service Charges**
>
> Landlords must, during negotiations, provide best estimates of service charges, insurance payments and any other outgoings that tenants will incur under their leases.
>
> Landlords must disclose known irregular events that would have a significant impact on the amount of future service charges.
>
> Landlords should be aware of the RICS 2006 Code of Practice on Service Charges in Commercial Property and seek to observe its guidance in drafting new leases and on renewals (even if granted before that Code is effective).

Chapter 25

Underleases

25.1 Liability of sub-tenants

Ordinarily, there is neither privity of contract nor privity of estate between a head landlord and a sub-tenant and, therefore, the head landlord is unable to sue a sub-tenant in respect of any breaches of the terms of the head-lease. However, it is a common practice for the head landlord to require a sub-tenant as a condition of granting consent to the sub-letting, to enter into a direct covenant with the head landlord to observe and perform the covenants in the head-lease. This will make the sub-tenant liable to the head landlord in contract. Further, a sub-tenant may be bound by those restrictive covenants in the head-lease of which he had notice when he took his sub-lease. As the sub-tenant is entitled to call for production of the head-lease on the grant of his sub-lease (LPA 1925, s 44), he will be deemed to have notice of the contents of the head-lease even if he does not insist on his right to inspect it (see the Legal Practice Guide, *Property Law and Practice* for further consideration of this matter).

25.2 Reasons for sub-letting

There are many reasons why a tenant may want to grant an underlease of all or part of the premises demised by the head-lease. It may be that the tenant finds that he has surplus accommodation which is not required for the purpose of his business and, therefore, instead of leaving that part vacant (thereby wasting money) the tenant may try and cut his losses by finding a sub-tenant. Indeed, the tenant may well seek to create space for a sub-letting in the knowledge that the current market would lead to the sub-tenant paying a rent per square foot in excess of what the tenant is paying to the head landlord.

On other occasions, the tenant may be sub-letting the premises as an alternative to assigning the lease. Where a tenant has a continuing liability (either under privity of contract or under an authorised guarantee agreement), despite his ability to call for an overriding lease in the event of later default by an assignee (see **28.1.4**), the tenant might prefer to retain control of the premises by sub-letting rather than assigning.

25.3 Drafting points

Where the tenant proposes to grant an underlease of all or part of the premises, he must have regard to the terms of his own lease, and in particular to the terms of the alienation covenant which is likely to control or regulate in some way the content of the underlease. The head-lease will usually require the tenant to obtain the consent of the head landlord before granting the sub-lease. Section 19(1)(a) of the LTA 1927 and s 1 of the LTA 1988 apply to qualified covenants against sub-letting.

In drafting the sub-lease, the tenant should bear in mind the following matters.

25.3.1 The term

The tenant should ensure that the term of the sub-lease is at least one day shorter than the unexpired residue of his head-lease term, since a sub-lease for the whole residue of the head-lease term will take effect as an assignment of that term. Not only will this be contrary to the tenant's intention, it will also probably breach the alienation covenant in the head-lease, as the landlord will have given his consent to a sub-letting, but not an assignment.

In taking up possession, the sub-tenant will be in occupation for the purpose of a business and may, therefore, enjoy security of tenure under Pt II of the LTA 1954 (see **Chapter 31**). The tenant may want to consider excluding the sub-letting from the protection of the Act so that he can be sure to resume occupation at the end of the sub-lease. Indeed, it may be a requirement of the alienation covenant in the head-lease that any sub-leases are to be contracted-out of the LTA 1954, so that if the tenant's interest is terminated in circumstances which result in the sub-tenant becoming the immediate tenant of the head landlord, the head landlord will be guaranteed possession at the end of the sub-lease.

25.3.2 The rent

The tenant will want to ensure that the rent to be paid by the sub-tenant is as high as the market will currently allow, and if the sub-lease is to be granted for anything longer than a short term, the tenant will want to review the rent from time to time. Careful attention must again be paid to the alienation covenant in the head-lease which might dictate the terms upon which any sub-lettings are to be granted.

It is common for the head landlord to attempt to include several requirements in the head-lease:

(a) that any sub-letting by the tenant is granted at a rent which is the greater of the rent payable under the head-lease, and the full open market rent for the premises;

(b) that any sub-letting is granted without the payment of a premium; and

(c) that the sub-letting contains provisions for the review of rent (in an upwards direction only) which match the head-lease review provisions in terms of frequency, timing and basis of review.

The reason the landlord seeks to impose such conditions is that at some future date, the interest of the intermediate tenant might determine (eg, by reason of surrender) leaving the sub-tenant as the landlord's immediate tenant upon the terms of the sub-lease. However, if the tenant, at the grant of his lease, had agreed to excessively restrictive conditions on sub-letting, he may now find it difficult to arrange a sub-letting, particularly at a time when the market is falling and potential sub-tenants are only prepared to pay a rent below the current rent payable under the head-lease. One popular way around this was for the tenant to enter into a side letter or collateral agreement with the proposed sub-tenant in which the tenant agrees to reimburse the sub-tenant the difference between the head-lease rent and the current market rent. However, the case of *Allied Dunbar Assurance plc v Homebase Ltd* [2002] EWCA Civ 666, [2002] 27 EG 144 has ruled that this is not a valid way of avoiding restrictions in the head-lease preventing sub-letting below the head-lease rent.

The sub-tenant should be wary of an obligation in the sub-lease which simply requires him to pay the rents payable from time to time under the head-lease, since such a provision would give him no input into any negotiations for the review of rent during the term, and is likely to give little incentive to the tenant to argue with any vigour against the landlord at review, since he knows that whatever figure is agreed, it will be paid by the sub-tenant.

If the head landlord has elected to waive the exemption for VAT purposes, so that VAT is payable by the tenant, the election in no way affects the sub-lease rents. It would, therefore, be wise for the tenant to waive the exemption in respect of these premises so that VAT can be charged to the sub-tenant, although careful consideration must always be given to the effect of waiving the exemption.

Note that the 2007 *Code for Leasing Business Premises* requires that if sub-letting is allowed, the rent should be the market rent as at the time of sub-letting.

25.3.3 The covenants

In drafting the sub-lease, the tenant will attempt to mirror the provisions of the head-lease. He should be careful not to allow the sub-tenant scope to do anything at the premises which is forbidden under the provisions of the head-lease.

Particular attention should be paid to:

(a) *Alienation.* It is unlikely that the head-lease will allow any further sub-letting of the premises. Care should, therefore, be taken to impose appropriate restrictions in the sub-lease. There ought to be an absolute covenant against sub-letting (or sharing or parting with possession of the premises), with a qualified covenant against assigning the sub-lease.

(b) *Repair.* The same repairing obligation as affects the tenant (or an even tighter one) ought to be imposed upon the sub-tenant. In interpreting a repair covenant, regard is to be had to the age, character and locality of the premises at the time the lease was granted. If there has been a considerable lapse of time between the grant of the head-lease, and the grant of the sub-lease, different standards of repair might be required by the respective repair covenants, leading to a possible residual repair liability on the part of the tenant. The sub-tenant's obligation will be to repair 'the premises'. The tenant must make sure that 'the premises' are defined in the sub-lease to include all of the premises demised by the head-lease, or if a sub-letting of part is contemplated, that the division of responsibility is clearly stated.

(c) *Insurance.* In all probability, the head landlord will be insuring the premises, with the tenant reimbursing the premium. The sub-lease should, therefore, provide that the sub-tenant reimburses the premiums paid by the tenant (or a proportionate part if a sub-lease of part is contemplated).

(d) *Decoration.* The tenant should ensure that the sub-lease obliges the sub-tenant to decorate the premises as frequently as, and at the times, and in the manner required by the head-lease.

25.3.4 Rights of access

The tenant is unlikely to extend the usual covenant in the sub-lease for quiet enjoyment to cover liability for the acts and omissions of someone with a title paramount (eg, the head landlord). If he did so, he would be in breach of the covenant if the head landlord disturbed the sub-tenant's occupation by exercising a right of entry contained in the head-lease. However, in any case, to avoid a possible dispute, the tenant should ensure that in reserving rights of entry onto and access over the sub-let premises, those rights are reserved for the benefit of the tenant and any superior landlord.

25.3.5 An indemnity

Despite imposing broadly similar covenants in the sub-lease to those contained in the head-lease, the tenant will also want to include a sweeping-up provision obliging the sub-tenant to perform all of the covenants in the head-lease in so far as they affect the sub-let premises, and to indemnify the tenant against liability for breach. The sub-tenant might prefer, however, to enter into a negative obligation not to cause a breach of the head-lease covenants. Care must be taken on a sub-lease of part to ensure that a correct division of liability is made between tenant and sub-tenant in respect of the head-lease covenants.

25.4 The sub-tenant's concerns

Before the sub-lease is granted, the sub-tenant must ensure that the consent of the head landlord (if required) has been obtained. The usual condition of granting consent is that the sub-tenant is to enter into a direct covenant with the head landlord to perform the covenants in the head-lease (at least in so far as they relate to the sub-let premises). Ordinarily, there is no privity of contract or estate between a head landlord and a sub-tenant, but the direct covenant creates a contractual relationship.

As the head landlord is likely to be giving a direct covenant, and as he is also likely to covenant with the tenant in the sub-lease to perform the head-lease covenants, it is essential that the sub-tenant inspects the head-lease (including all licences and supplemental deeds which may have effected a variation of its terms). The sub-tenant's liability under the direct covenant with the head landlord should not extend beyond his liability on the tenant covenants in the sub-lease.

As an alternative to requiring the sub-tenant to enter into a direct covenant with the head landlord, use could be made of the Contracts (Rights of Third Parties) Act 1999. Under the provisions of this Act, a non-contracting party has the right to enforce a contract term if the contract expressly provides that he may or, subject to contrary intention, the term purports to confer a benefit on him. In the context of sub-leases, the head-lease could be drafted to require any permitted sub-lease to contain a covenant by the sub-tenant to observe and perform the head-lease covenants and conferring upon the head landlord the right to enforce that covenant. Such a covenant would be a tenant covenant of the sub-lease and thus the sub-tenant would be released from future liability following a lawful assignment (and, of course, the assignee would become bound by it). In the same way, the landlord's obligations in the head-lease may be expressed to be for the benefit of sub-tenants, thus giving sub-tenants the right to enforce, for example, the head landlord's obligation in the head-lease to provide services.

With regard to the drafting of the sub-lease, the following points may be borne in mind.

(a)   Where there is to be a direct covenant in the licence to sub-let, it is important for the sub-tenant to remember that it will not work both ways, and so the sub-tenant does not have any means of enforcing a breach of covenant by the head landlord. The sub-tenant should consider insisting upon a covenant by the tenant in the sub-lease obliging the tenant to enforce a breach of covenant by the head landlord as and when required by the sub-tenant. The sub-tenant is likely to concede that he should bear the cost of any claim.

(b)   The usual covenant for quiet enjoyment exempts an intermediate landlord from liability in respect of the acts or omissions of a superior landlord. The sub-tenant may consider extending the usual covenant.

(c)   The sub-tenant should ask the tenant to covenant with him to pass on to him any notices received from the head landlord (eg, LPA 1925, s 146 notices).

(d)   The sub-tenant should explore the possibility of having his interest noted on the head landlord's insurance policy. He should ask for details of the policy and ensure that provision is made to enable the policy to be produced to him from time to time. The provision referred to at (a) above should enable the sub-tenant to force the tenant to force the landlord to reinstate the premises if they are damaged by an insured risk.

Chapter 26
Agreements for Lease

26.1 Introduction

The agreement for lease, if used, will be drafted by the landlord's solicitor in duplicate, and submitted to the tenant's solicitor for approval together with the draft lease in duplicate (attached to each part of the draft agreement). If the landlord requires the tenant to pay the landlord's costs of drafting, negotiating and executing the lease, he is also likely to require the tenant to pay his costs in connection with the agreement for lease. In recessionary times, the tenant is likely to resist such requirements.

The agreement for lease is an estate contract and can be protected by way of a C(iv) land charge against the landlord's name, or by notice against the landlord's registered title. The circumstances in which an agreement may be used will necessarily involve a delay between exchange and completion, in which case it might be considered advisable to protect the agreement against the possibility of the landlord selling the reversion and defeating the tenant's interest.

26.2 When are they used?

In most commercial letting transactions, the parties proceed straight to the completion of the lease without concerning themselves with the formality of entering into an agreement for lease. The reason for this is that the agreement would simply exist as a contractual commitment between the parties to enter into a lease, the form and content of which had already been agreed by negotiation. With the terms of the lease already agreed, why bother to embody them in an agreement for lease, when the parties could proceed immediately to the execution and exchange of the lease and counterpart? There is little risk in either party backing out of the arrangement in the time between the conclusion of negotiations and completion of the lease, especially since both parties will have invested considerable time and resources in the negotiation process.

The circumstances when an agreement for lease is used are usually limited to occasions where one (or both) of the parties is required to do something to the premises prior to the grant of the lease.

Typically, an agreement for lease is used where the landlord has commenced, or is about to commence constructing the premises. The landlord's aim is to secure an agreed letting of the premises to a prospective tenant as soon as possible so that, when construction has been completed, the tenant will be bound to complete the lease, and rent will become payable to the landlord to provide income to offset his building costs. On other occasions, an agreement may be used where the landlord, at the request of the tenant, is carrying out substantial works of repair or refurbishment to the premises prior to the grant of the lease. In this kind of situation the landlord would not want to go to the expense of executing works without a commitment from the tenant to enter into a lease once the works have been carried out. An agreement may also be used where it is proposed that the tenant carries out major works to the premises prior to the grant of the lease, in which case both parties would ideally like the security of a binding commitment to enter into a lease upon completion of the works.

The main aim of the agreement, apart from recording the agreed terms of the lease to be entered into, is to stipulate the nature of the works to be carried out to the premises, the time in which they are to be carried out, and the manner in which they will be executed. There is little point in the landlord agreeing to grant a lease of premises to the tenant upon the completion of the construction of a building if the agreement does not state, amongst other things, who will construct the building, and by when, and to what specifications.

26.3   A typical agreement

In order to consider the type of clauses commonly found in an agreement for lease where works are required to be carried out, this part of the book concentrates on an agreement in which the landlord will be obliged to construct a building prior to the grant of the lease. Many of the points raised will be equally applicable, or can be adapted to a situation where it will be the tenant who is carrying out works to the premises before completion.

The basic thrust of the agreement will be that the landlord, as the owner of the site, will construct (or, by engaging building contractors, cause to be constructed) premises for occupation by the tenant. Once the premises reach a stage of 'practical completion' (see **26.3.5**) the tenant will be obliged to enter into the form of lease attached to the agreement. Rent will then become payable under the terms of the lease, giving the developer/landlord a return on his investment. Naturally, the terms of the agreement are open for negotiation. In particular, negotiations will revolve around the extent of control, input or supervision the tenant will be allowed to have in respect of the execution of the works, and how much protection he will have if, after completion of the lease, the works turn out to be defective.

The following is a list of some of the problems to be addressed in the drafting and negotiation of the agreement.

26.3.1   What works will be carried out by the landlord?

In the type of agreement under consideration, the works will involve the construction of the entire building which will house the premises to be demised by the lease. The extent of works proposed by the landlord must be clearly indicated in the agreement.

It will, therefore, be necessary for detailed plans and specifications, recording exactly what is to be constructed, to be attached to the agreement for lease, and for the agreement to stipulate that the landlord is to develop in accordance with them.

26.3.2   Will the landlord be able to depart from the agreed plans and specifications?

The tenant will not want the agreement to permit the landlord's development to vary from the plans and specifications, since this might result in the tenant being obliged to take a lease of premises differing radically from those originally planned. On the other hand, the landlord would like to build into the agreement a degree of design and construction flexibility, so that if, as the development proceeds, it becomes apparent to the architect that a variation in design or construction is necessary or desirable (either on economic, architectural, or purely aesthetic grounds), the agreement will permit a variation to be made. This is a matter for negotiation between the parties. A possible compromise might be reached if the agreement allows certain 'permitted variations', which could be defined to mean those required by the local planning authority under the terms of any planning permission for the development of the site, or those which are insubstantial and are reasonably required by the landlord.

It should be noted that if a contract is varied in a material manner, outside the scope of existing contractual provisions, a new contract will come into being which will have to satisfy the requirements of s 2 of the Law of Property (Miscellaneous Provisions) Act 1989 (LP(MP)A 1989) (see *McCausland v Duncan Lawrie Ltd* [1996] 4 All ER 995).

26.3.3 What standard of works is required?

It is usual to include an obligation in the agreement on the landlord's part to ensure that the works described in the agreement are carried out with reasonable skill and care, and in accordance with all relevant statutory approvals (eg, planning permission, Building Regulations).

26.3.4 Is there to be any degree of supervision?

The landlord will want complete freedom to enable his builders to progress the development of the site without any interference from the tenant, and may be able to insist upon this in his negotiations. However, the tenant may have sufficient bargaining strength to demand a degree of control and supervision over the execution of the landlord's works. He may require the agreement to make provision allowing a surveyor, appointed by the tenant, to inspect the works as they are being carried out, in order to make comments and representations to the landlord (or his architect), and to point out errors in the works, and variations not permitted by the agreement. The issue of whether the tenant is to have any involvement in the development and, if so, the degree of control to be allowed, is a matter which will depend heavily upon the relative bargaining strengths of the parties.

26.3.5 Who decides when the building is ready for occupation?

The determination of the date upon which the building is completed is important since it will trigger the commencement of the lease (and therefore liability for rent).

A landlord is interested in achieving completion as soon as possible in order to obtain rent, whereas the tenant may have an interest in delaying completion (unless he is especially keen to gain possession). The tenant will not want the agreement to force him to complete the lease until the premises have been fully completed to his satisfaction, and are ready for immediate occupation and use. However, the landlord will not want to give the tenant any scope for delaying the transaction beyond a date when the premises are sufficiently ready. The landlord will want to be able to force the tenant to complete the lease notwithstanding one or two imperfections. It is, therefore, a representative of the party who is carrying out the works who usually certifies that the building has reached the stage of 'practical completion' for the purposes of the agreement.

Practical completion occurs when the building works have been sufficiently completed to permit use and occupation for the intended purpose, even though there may be some minor matters outstanding.

The certificate of practical completion, in the type of agreement under consideration, will be given by the landlord's architect (as defined by the agreement). Care should be taken where the agreement is drafted 'back-to-back' with a design-and-build building contract, where the landlord will not have engaged the architect (see **8.2.3**). Issues which will concern the tenant are whether the tenant should have any control over who should act as the architect, whether the architect is to be independent (ie, whether he may be someone who is in the employ of the landlord), and whether, at the final inspection of the works, the tenant can insist upon the attendance of his own representative to make representations to the landlord's architect, or to carry out a joint inspection for the purpose of issuing the certificate. The tenant's main aim in this regard is to be able to object to and delay the issue of the certificate of practical completion (which triggers completion) if in his opinion the works have not yet been satisfactorily completed. As ever, this is a matter upon which negotiations are required.

26.3.6   Will the agreement specify a completion date?

If the building is being built between exchange and completion, there will not be a fixed date for completion. The agreement will provide for the lease to be completed within a specified number of days after the issue of the certificate of practical completion. The landlord would seek to resist being obliged to complete his building works within a fixed time-scale, since there are any number of reasons why the execution of the works might be delayed. However, on the other hand, the tenant would like the agreement to impose some time restraints upon the landlord, as he will not want to be kept waiting indefinitely for the building to be completed. Presumably the tenant would be anxious to obtain possession of a completed building as soon as possible in order to satisfy his business needs. The tenant may press for the inclusion of a clause which requires the landlord to use his best (or reasonable) endeavours to ensure that the building is completed by a certain date. The landlord may be prepared to accept such a clause provided he is not liable for delays caused by matters outside his control.

26.3.7   Is the person carrying out the works to be liable for any delay?

It is usual for the agreement to include what is called a 'force majeure' clause to ensure that the person executing the works will not be in breach of the requirement to complete the works by a certain date if the delay is caused by matters which are outside his control. A force majeure clause covers delaying factors such as adverse weather conditions, strikes, lock-outs, or other industrial action, civil commotion, shortages of labour or materials and others.

26.3.8   Will there be any penalties for delay?

Usually, the tenant can only delay the transaction by failing to complete the lease within the stipulated number of days after the issue of the certificate of practical completion. To discourage the tenant from delaying completion, and to compensate the landlord, the agreement should stipulate a 'rent commencement date' from which rent will become payable under the lease, regardless of whether the tenant has completed the lease. If the tenant delays completion beyond the rent commencement date, he will still be bound to pay rent to the landlord on completion of the lease calculated from the earlier rent commencement date. In this way the tenant is penalised for his delay by having to pay rent in respect of a period when he was not in occupation of the premises, and the landlord is thus not left without income. The rent commencement date is usually stated to be the day upon which the lease is due to be completed (ie, a certain number of days after the issue of the certificate of practical completion) or, if a rent-free period is being given to the tenant, a certain number of months after the day upon which completion is due.

If the landlord fails to complete the building by any long-stop date inserted in the agreement, and is unable to avail himself of the force majeure clause, the tenant could just sit tight and await completion, in the knowledge that rent will not become payable until then. However, most tenants will not want to be kept waiting indefinitely, since premises are usually required for immediate business needs. Therefore, as an incentive to the landlord to build within the timescale specified by the agreement, the tenant should insist upon a clause providing for liquidated damages to be payable by the landlord if he delays beyond the long-stop date. The agreement ought to state a daily rate of damages payable to the tenant in the event of a delay. The landlord should ensure that the building contract entered into with his building contractors runs 'back-to-back' with the agreement for lease so that he may claim liquidated damages from his contractors in the event of a delay. The tenant may want a further provision enabling him to terminate the agreement in the event of a protracted delay.

26.3.9   What if there are any defects in the works or materials?

If, after completion, the tenant discovers that there are defects in the design or construction of the premises, or in the materials used, then in so far as the defects amount to disrepair (see

17.2.6) the tenant will be bound to remedy them under the repairing covenant in the lease. A well-advised tenant will have instructed a surveyor to look for defects in the works prior to the grant of the lease. However, the nature of a design or construction defect is such that it rarely manifests itself until some time after the lease has been completed. The tenant should, therefore, ask for some protection in the agreement (or in the lease itself) against the prospect of such 'latent' or 'inherent' defects arising. There are several ways in which this can be done.

(a)   In negotiating the terms of the repairing covenant, the tenant could seek to exclude liability (either absolutely, or during the first few years of the term) in respect of any disrepair which arises out of a defect in the design or construction of the building, or in the materials used. Liability for repair necessitated by latent defects, if excluded from the tenant's covenant, ought to be transferred to the landlord under the lease.

(b)   In the agreement for lease, the tenant could negotiate the inclusion of a clause which creates a 'defects liability period' to oblige the landlord to put right any defects which become apparent within, for example, the first 12 months after practical completion.

(c)   In the agreement, the tenant could insist upon a provision obliging the landlord to enforce a clause in the building contract entered into by the landlord with his building contractor whereby the contractor had undertaken to remedy any defects becoming apparent within an initial defects liability period. Similarly, the agreement could oblige the landlord to pursue, for the tenant's benefit, any other contractual remedies the landlord may have against the other members of his design and construction team (eg, architects, engineers, surveyors) under their contracts of engagement.

(d)   The tenant could either take out, or require the landlord to take out insurance for the benefit of the tenant and his successors in title against damage caused by design of construction defects.

(e)   In the agreement the tenant could insist that the landlord procures collateral warranties for the tenant from the landlord's design and construction team (eg, builders, architects, engineers and surveyors) whereby those persons who have been involved in developing the site enter into a warranty with the tenant (and successors in title) that they have exercised reasonable skill and care in performing their duties under their respective contracts of engagement. The reason for this is that the tenant has no contractual relationship with the landlord's builders and designers, and so would be without a remedy in contract if their contractual obligations were not met.

26.3.10   Who is to be responsible if the premises are damaged after practical completion, but before completion of the lease?

If the premises are damaged before practical completion, then the certificate will not be issued, for the obvious reason that the premises will not have reached the stage of practical completion. The landlord will have to put right the damage before the certificate can be issued. If the premises are damaged after practical completion, but before actual completion, the agreement ought to stipulate that the premises remain at the landlord's risk since the tenant is not yet entitled to possession. The landlord ought to maintain insurance cover until the premises are handed over, and the agreement may make this a requirement.

26.3.11   What form will the lease take?

Before the agreement is entered into, the final form of the lease which the tenant will be required to enter into must have been agreed between landlord and tenant. Full negotiations must have taken place regarding the terms of the lease. The agreed form of draft should be appended to the agreement, with an obligation in the agreement upon the tenant to take a lease in that form on the date of actual completion. It is unwise to attach the original draft lease which, after amendments and counter-amendments, may now be untidy and difficult to interpret. A fair copy of the agreed draft should be prepared and attached to the agreement.

There seems little point in the parties entering into an agreement for lease unless all negotiations regarding the lease terms have been concluded.

26.3.12   To which premises will the agreement relate?

The agreement will normally describe the premises by reference to the parcels clause in the draft lease, which in turn will refer to plans attached to the agreement showing the exact extent of the premises. Plans will be essential where a lease of part is intended.

26.3.13   Should any conditions of sale be incorporated?

The terms of the agreement for lease ought to set out extensively the rights and obligations of the landlord and tenant, in which case there may be no need to incorporate a set of conditions of sale. However, safety ought to dictate that they be incorporated in any case, with a provision that they apply except in so far as they are inconsistent with any other terms of the agreement.

26.3.14   Will the agreement require the landlord to deduce title, and will he disclose incumbrances in the agreement?

If title is deduced to the tenant, the agreement will usually prohibit requisitions after exchange.

26.3.15   Will the agreement merge with the lease?

The usual conveyancing doctrine of merger applies to an agreement to grant a lease, but it is common practice to include a clause excluding the doctrine since many of the contractual obligations are intended to continue in operation post-completion.

In so far as they do continue in operation, they may be construed as landlord or tenant covenants of the tenancy, and therefore binding upon successors in title (see the definition of 'covenant' and 'collateral agreement' in s 28(1) of the LT(C)A 1995).

Chapter 27
Selling the Lease

27.1 Applications for consent to assign

It will nearly always be the case that the lease will restrict the tenant's right to assign the lease. There may be an absolute covenant against assignment, in which case the tenant is absolutely prohibited from assigning his lease. The landlord may (or may not) agree to waive the breach in a particular case but the tenant will be entirely at the mercy of his landlord. An assignment in breach of an absolute covenant will be effective, but the lease will be liable to forfeiture by the landlord because of the breach of covenant. More commonly, there will be a qualified covenant, ie, not to assign without the landlord's prior written consent. In the case of a qualified covenant against assignment, s 19(1)(a) of the LTA 1927 implies a proviso that, notwithstanding any contrary provision, the landlord's licence or consent is not to be unreasonably withheld. The reasonableness of the landlord's refusal of consent has been dealt with earlier in this book (see **18.2.5),** and it will be recalled that if the parties have specified for the purposes of s 19(1A) of the LTA 1927 conditions to be satisfied, or circumstances to exist, before consent is to be given, a refusal of consent on the grounds that they are not satisfied, or they do not exist, is not an unreasonable withholding of consent.

Assuming the alienation covenant is qualified, the first step is for the tenant to make written application to his landlord for consent to assign. If the landlord consents, the tenant can proceed with the assignment. If the landlord unreasonably refuses consent, the tenant can proceed to assign and will not be deemed in breach of covenant. The danger for the tenant is in knowing whether the landlord's refusal is unreasonable or not, because if the landlord's refusal turns out to have been reasonable, the landlord will have the right to forfeit the lease. Further, for the purposes of the LT(C)A 1995, the assignment will be an excluded assignment, meaning that the assignor will not be released from the tenant covenants in the lease. Alternatively, the tenant may pursue the safer course of action by seeking a court declaration that the landlord is acting unreasonably in withholding consent, but this may prove costly and time-consuming. A further problem, prior to the passing of the LTA 1988, was that the tenant could not, in the absence of an express covenant by the landlord, obtain damages if the landlord withheld consent unreasonably.

Section 1 of the LTA 1988 (which only applies to qualified covenants) provides that where the tenant has made written application to assign, the landlord owes a duty, within a reasonable time:

(a)   to give consent, unless it is reasonable not to do so. Giving consent subject to an unreasonable condition will be a breach of this duty; and

(b)   to serve on the tenant written notice of his decision whether or not to give consent, specifying in addition:

   (i)   if the consent is given subject to conditions, the conditions; or

   (ii)   if the consent is withheld, the reasons for withholding it.

No doubt the landlord will wish to see a bank reference, audited accounts (eg, for the last three years) and, if appropriate, trade references for the proposed assignee and these should accompany the tenant's application. If the landlord needs any further information to enable him to process the application, he should request this from the tenant.

The LTA 1988 does not define what amounts to a reasonable time and each case will turn on its own facts. However, in *Go West Ltd v Spigarolo* [2003] EWCA Civ 17, [2003] 07 EG 136, the judge commented:

> I find it hard to imagine that a period of ... almost four months could ever be acceptable, save perhaps in the most unusual and complex situations ... it may be that the reasonable time ... will sometimes have to be measured in weeks rather than days; but, even in complicated cases, it should be measured in weeks rather than months.

In *Blockbuster Entertainment Ltd v Barnsdale Properties Ltd* [2003] EWHC 2912, a landlord who was asked for consent on 28 May and gave it on 15 July was held to have unreasonably delayed in giving that consent. Similarly, in *Mount Eden Land Ltd v Folia Ltd* [2003] EWHC 1815, the judge, while emphasising that each case turned on its own facts, thought that a period of four to five weeks was 'generous'.

As to whether the landlord is unreasonably withholding his consent, this is left to the general law. The burden of proving the reasonableness of any refusal or any conditions imposed is on the landlord and the sanction for breach of the statutory duty is liability in tort for damages. As a result of the Act, landlords must give careful consideration to the financial consequences of having delayed or refused consent unreasonably and they should set up efficient procedures to ensure that each application for consent is dealt with expeditiously and in accordance with the Act.

If the landlord is himself a tenant and the applicant for consent is the sub-tenant, then if the head-lease requires the superior landlord's consent to the assignment, the Act imposes a duty on the immediate landlord to pass on a copy of the application to the superior landlord within a reasonable time.

Section 3 of LTA 1988 deals with the situation where a head-lease contains a covenant by the tenant not to consent to a disposition by a sub-tenant without the consent of the head landlord, such consent not to be unreasonably withheld. In such circumstances, a similar duty to that contained in s 1 is imposed on the head landlord towards the sub-tenant.

In considering whether or not to give consent, the landlord does not owe earlier tenants a duty of care to ensure that the assignee is of sufficient financial standing. If the assignee turns out to be unsatisfactory, the landlord will still be able to serve a default notice on those former tenants who may still be liable to the landlord (according to whether it is an 'old' or 'new' lease for the purposes of the LT(C)A 1995) (*Norwich Union Life Insurance Society v Low Profile Fashions Ltd* (1992) 21 EG 104). In such a situation, the earlier tenants may then be able to secure an overriding lease under the provisions of the LT(C)A 1995 (see **28.1.4**).

The landlord's solicitor, on receiving the tenant's application to assign, will often seek an undertaking from the tenant's solicitor to pay the landlord's legal and other costs of dealing with the application and preparing the licence (plus VAT) (see *Dong Bang Minerva (UK) Ltd v Davina Ltd* [1996] 31 EG 87). This does not infringe s 144 of the LPA 1925. Care should be taken in drafting the undertaking to make it clear whether the obligation to pay the landlord's costs applies in the event of the licence not being granted; this may be a requirement of the lease in any case.

To prevent the court from finding that consent has been given before the licence to assign is entered into, the landlord must ensure that any correspondence with the tenant's advisers is expressly stated to be subject to the parties entering into a licence to assign. Heading the correspondence 'subject to contract' or 'subject to licence' will not be sufficient (see *Next plc v National Farmers Union Mutual Insurance Co Ltd* [1997] EGCS 181).

27.2 The landlord's licence

If the landlord is prepared to give his consent to the assignment, a licence to assign will usually be prepared by the landlord's solicitor in which the landlord will formally grant his consent. If the tenant and assignee are to enter into covenants in the licence then all three (ie, landlord, tenant and assignee) will be parties to the licence, which will be in the form of a deed. The licence will include various covenants and conditions such as:

(a)   A direct covenant with the landlord to observe and perform the covenants in the lease. However, because of the provisions of the LT(C)A 1995, the licence to assign should not make the assignee liable on the lease covenants for the entire duration of the lease, but only for the period he is actually the tenant. The provisions of the LT(C)A 1995 in this regard are dealt with in **Chapter 18.** However, in an old lease, a covenant by the assignee to observe and perform the covenants in the lease for the entire duration of the term would be permitted and is usual.

(b)   A covenant by the tenant:

(i)   to pay the landlord's costs and expenses in dealing with the tenant's application;

(ii)   not to allow the assignee to take up possession until the assignment has been completed.

(c)   That the licence extends only to the transaction specifically authorised.

(d)   That the licence is not to act as a waiver of any breach committed by the tenant prior to the date of the licence.

(e)   That the licence shall cease to be valid unless the assignment is completed within, say, two months. This is because, although the proposed assignee is now acceptable to the landlord, the assignment might otherwise be delayed to a time when the assignee is of a poorer financial standing.

(f)   In a new lease, the landlord will probably require the assignor to enter into an Authorised Guarantee Agreement (see **18.2.7**). (This may well be a requirement set out in the lease under s 19(1A) of the LTA 1927 and which thus must be complied with before the landlord need give consent (see **18.2.5.1**).) Note, however, the recommendations of the 2007 *Code for Leasing Business Premises* (set out at **18.2.5.1**), which provide that an Authorised Guarantee Agreement should not be an automatic requirement on an assignment.

27.3 Authorised Guarantee Agreements

It is currently standard practice for a landlord to insist on an outgoing tenant entering into an Authorised Guarantee Agreement on an assignment of a new lease guaranteeing that the assignee will perform the covenants in the lease. This is often a requirement set out in the lease in accordance with s 19(1A) of the LTA 1927. If it is not set out in the lease, it would be lawful to require an AGA provided that this was reasonable in the circumstances.

As noted (at **18.2.5.1**) the 2007 *Code for Leasing Business Premises* provides that an AGA should not be an automatic requirement on an assignment, but necessary only if the proposed assignee is of a lower financial standing than the assignor or is resident or registered overseas. Assignors should, therefore, cite the 2007 *Code* to landlords insisting on an AGA, but may well find that most landlords will not be sympathetic and will still insist on the guarantee.

27.3.1 Content of an Authorised Guarantee Agreement

A specimen AGA is set out in **Appendix 4**. It will typically contain covenants by the assignor:

(a)   guaranteeing that the assignee will perform the tenant's covenants in the lease;

(b)   promising to perform such covenants if the assignee does not;

(c)   promising to take a new lease if the liability of the assignee is disclaimed on insolvency.

It should be ensured that the assignor's liability does not extend beyond that of the assignee, and it should be provided that on the assignee being released from liability under the LT(C)A 1995 (see **12.3.2**), so is the assignor.

27.3.2 LTA 1954 considerations

If the original lease is contracted out of the security of tenure provisions of the LTA 1954 (see **Chapter 31**), it is likely that the landlord will require any new lease taken by the assignor under the terms of the AGA to be similarly excluded from the security of tenure provisions. The landlord must, therefore, ensure that the assignor signs the appropriate notice under s 38A of the LTA 1954 before the AGA is entered into (see **31.1.6**).

Chapter 28
Remedies for Breach of Covenant

28.1 Landlord's remedies

Before the landlord takes any steps against a defaulting tenant, he should first consider whether any other party is also liable. For example, are there any sureties or guarantors, is the original tenant under a continuing liability, or did any of the previous assignees give the landlord a direct covenant on assignment, upon which they may still be liable? The reader will recall that the ability of the landlord to proceed against some of these other parties is affected by the Landlord and Tenant (Covenants) Act 1995 (LT(C)A 1995). These issues have been dealt with earlier in the book.

Before proceeding against a former tenant or his guarantor for a 'fixed charge', that is:

(a)   rent; or

(b)   service charge; or

(c)   any liquidated sum payable under the lease; or

(d)   interest on such sums,

the LT(C)A 1995 requires the landlord to serve a notice of the claim (usually referred to as a 'Default Notice') upon the former tenant or his guarantor, as the case may be, within six months of the current tenant's default (there is no requirement to serve a notice also on a former tenant before serving a notice on that tenant's guarantor (*Cheverell Estates Ltd v Harris* [1998] 02 EG 127)). Failure to serve a valid notice will mean that the landlord is unable to recover that sum from the person concerned. This requirement applies to all leases and not just those granted after the commencement of the LT(C)A 1995.

The Court of Appeal, in *Scottish & Newcastle plc v Raguz* [2007] EWCA Civ 150, had held that a s 17 notice had to be served by a landlord where a rent review date had passed without the new rent having been assessed, whether or not there were actually any arrears outstanding. The House of Lords ([2008] UKHL 65) has now reversed this decision. Should the delayed fixing of the new rent result in an increased amount being payable (which would be backdated to the review date), this would normally be due as a lump sum on the date specified in the lease. The landlord would then have six months from that date to serve a s 17 notice should it not be paid by the current tenant.

Where the landlord does proceed against a former tenant or his guarantor, that person may be able to regain some control over the property by calling for an overriding lease (see **28.1.4**).

28.1.1 For non-payment of rent

Only six years' arrears of rent are recoverable, whether by claim or distress (Limitation Act 1980).

28.1.1.1 By claim

If the tenant, or one of the parties mentioned above, is liable for the rent, the landlord may pursue his normal remedies for recovery through the High Court or county court. As to the choice of court and type of proceedings, see the Legal Practice Guide, *Civil Litigation*.

28.1.1.2 Bankruptcy and winding up

If the sum owed exceeds £750, the landlord, as an alternative to a claim, may wish to consider the possibility of serving a statutory demand on the tenant with a view to commencing bankruptcy or winding-up proceedings, in the event of non-compliance with the demand (IA 1986). The landlord must bear in mind that the enforced bankruptcy of the tenant may reduce the chances of payment in full since he will become an ordinary unsecured creditor.

28.1.1.3 Distress

Distress is the landlord's ancient common law right, when the tenant is in arrears with his rent, to enter upon the demised premises and seize chattels to the value of the debt. The remedy is lost once the landlord has obtained judgment for the outstanding sum and the remedy should, therefore, be regarded as an alternative to proceeding by way of a claim. The distress can be carried out by the landlord personally, or as is more often the case, by a certificated bailiff acting on the landlord's behalf.

The rules concerning entry onto the demised premises are technical and easily broken, for example, entry can be gained through an open window but a closed window must not be opened. Such rules are beyond the scope of this book. Once on the demised premises, the landlord (or bailiff) may seize goods to satisfy the outstanding debt. The seized goods are then impounded either on or off the premises. If they are impounded on the premises, they may be left there and the tenant will be asked to sign a 'walking possession agreement' to avoid any argument that the landlord has abandoned the distress. This agreement will list the goods against which distress has been levied. If the tenant removes the goods, he commits 'pound-breach' and will become liable for treble damages. After the expiry of five days the landlord may remove the goods and sell them to pay off the arrears and the costs of distress. While a public auction is not essential, the landlord must obtain the best price and for that reason most landlords will auction the goods.

Certain goods which are on the premises cannot be distrained against, for example, cash, perishable goods, tools of the tenant's trade up to £150 in value, things in actual use and goods delivered to the tenant pursuant to his trade. In addition, there are provisions to protect the goods of third parties contained in the Law of Distress Amendment Act 1908.

Special rules apply in the event of the bankruptcy or winding up of the tenant.

The Law Commission has recommended the abolition of the remedy and the above is only intended as an outline of the subject. Moreover, it may be the case that the remedy will not survive a challenge under the Human Rights Act 1998 (see *Fuller v Happy Shopper Markets Ltd* [2001] 1 WLR 1681, ChD). More detailed coverage is contained in the standard works on landlord and tenant law.

28.1.1.4 Collecting the rent from a sub-tenant

If the premises have been sub-let, the superior landlord can serve notice on the sub-tenant under s 6 of the Law of Distress Amendment Act 1908, requiring the sub-tenant to pay his rent to the superior landlord until the arrears are paid off.

28.1.1.5 Forfeiture

Forfeiture for non-payment of rent is dealt with at **30.5.2**.

28.1.2 Breach of tenant's repairing covenant

From a practical point of view, and as a first step, the landlord, exercising his right of entry in the lease, should enter onto the demised premises with his surveyor to draw up a schedule of dilapidations. This should be served on the tenant with a demand that the tenant comply with his repairing obligation. If the tenant remains in breach of his obligation to repair the demised premises, the landlord has various remedies available to him.

28.1.2.1   Claim for damages

The measure of damages

The landlord may bring a claim for damages against the tenant either during the term or after its expiry. Section 18 of the LTA 1927 limits the maximum amount recoverable in all cases by providing that the damages cannot exceed the amount by which the value of the reversion has been diminished by the breach. It follows that the cost of repairs will be irrecoverable to the extent that they exceed this statutory ceiling.

Where proceedings are commenced during the term of the lease the reduction in the value of the reversion will be influenced by the length of the unexpired residue: the longer the unexpired term, the less the reduction should be.

In proceedings commenced at or after the end of the lease the court may be prepared, at least as a starting point, to accept the cost of repairs as evidence of the measure of damages, subject to the ceiling imposed by s 18 (see *Smiley v Townshend* [1950] 2 KB 311). See also *Ultraworth Ltd v General Accident Fire and Life Assurance Corporation* [2000] 2 EGLR 115, a case where the diminution in the value of the reversion was unaffected by the tenant's breach of the repairing obligation.

If a sub-tenant is in breach of a repairing covenant in the sub-lease, the measure of damages is the reduction in value of the intermediate landlord's reversion. If the sub-tenant knows of the terms of the superior tenancy, the intermediate landlord's liability to the superior landlord will be relevant in assessing these damages.

Section 18 further provides that no damages are recoverable for failure to put or leave the premises in repair at the termination of the lease, if the premises are to be pulled down shortly after termination or if intended structural alterations would render the repairs valueless. To benefit from this provision the tenant must show that the landlord had a firm intention (to pull down or alter) at the end of the lease.

It is important to appreciate that s 18 applies only to claims for damages by the landlord and has no application where the sum owed by the tenant is in the nature of a debt. If, therefore, the tenant covenants to spend £X per year on repairs, but fails to do so, the landlord may recover the deficiency as a debt without regard to the statutory ceiling in s 18.

The need for leave to sue

If the lease was granted for seven years or more and still has at least three years left to run, the Leasehold Property (Repairs) Act 1938 lays down a special procedure which the landlord must follow before being able to sue for damages (or forfeit the lease) for breach of the tenant's repairing covenant. Where the Act applies, it requires the landlord to serve a notice on the tenant under s 146 of the LPA 1925. Apart from the normal requirements of such a notice (see **30.5.3**), it must in addition, contain a statement informing the tenant of his right to serve a counter-notice within 28 days claiming the benefit of the Act. If such a counter-notice is served, the landlord cannot proceed further without leave of the court, which will not be given unless the landlord proves (and not just shows an arguable case):

(a)   that the value of the reversion has been substantially diminished; or

(b)   that the immediate remedying of the breach is required for preventing substantial diminution, or for complying with any Act or by-law, or for protecting the interests of occupiers other than the tenant, or for the avoidance of much heavier repair costs in the future; or

(c)   that there are special circumstances which render it just and equitable that leave be given.

Even if the landlord makes out one of the grounds, the court still has a discretion to refuse leave but this should only be exercised where the court is clearly convinced that it would be wrong to allow the landlord to continue. The court may, in granting or refusing leave, impose such conditions on the landlord or tenant as it thinks fit. The relevant date for determining whether the grounds are established is the date of the hearing; see *Landmaster Properties Ltd v Thackeray Property Services* [2003] 35 EG 83.

The Act does not apply to breach of a tenant's covenant to put premises into repair when the tenant takes possession or within a reasonable time thereafter.

28.1.2.2   Self-help

If the tenant is in breach of his repairing obligations, can the landlord enter the demised premises, carry out the necessary works and recover the cost from the tenant? In the absence of a statutory right or an express provision in the lease, the landlord has no general right to enter the demised premises even where the tenant is in breach of his obligations. Indeed, the tenant may be able to obtain an injunction to restrain the landlord's trespass. For that reason most leases will contain an express right for the landlord to enter the demised premises and carry out any necessary repairs at the tenant's expense, in default of the tenant complying with a notice to repair. In the case of *Jervis v Harris* [1996] Ch 195, the court accepted the landlord's argument that his claim against the tenant to recover this expenditure was in the nature of a debt claim rather than one for damages. Thus, the landlord was able to evade the statutory restrictions in the 1927 and 1938 Acts, mentioned above. However, in exceptional circumstances the court may refuse the landlord an injunction to enforce his right of entry in the lease (see *Creska Ltd v Hammersmith and Fulham London Borough Council (No 2)* (1999) 78 P & CR D46).

28.1.2.3   Specific performance

In *Rainbow Estates Ltd v Tokenhold Ltd* [1999] Ch 64, the court held that, in principle, there is no reason why the equitable remedy of specific performance should not be available to enforce compliance by a tenant with his repairing obligation. However, other remedies are likely to be more appropriate and the court stressed that specific performance will only be awarded in exceptional circumstances. In this case there was no alternative remedy for the landlord – unusually, the lease contained no forfeiture clause nor a provision allowing the landlord to enter and carry out the repairs himself.

28.1.2.4   Forfeiture

The landlord may be able to forfeit the lease for breach of the tenant's covenant to repair; forfeiture is dealt with at **30.5**.

28.1.3   Breaches of other covenants by the tenant: an outline

28.1.3.1   Damages

Damages for breach of covenant are assessed on a contractual basis, the aim being to put the landlord in the same position as if the covenant had been performed. The general principle is that the landlord may recover as damages all loss which may be fairly and reasonably considered as arising in the natural course of things from the breach, or such as may be reasonably supposed to have been in the contemplation of both parties, at the time of entering into the lease as the probable result of that breach (*Hadley v Baxendale* (1854) 9 Exch 341). In the majority of cases the damages will be equal to the diminution in the value of the reversion.

The breach of some particular covenants will now be considered.

Covenant to insure

The landlord usually assumes responsibility for insurance. If, however, the tenant has covenanted to insure, there will be a breach of covenant if the premises are uninsured or under-insured at any time during the term. If the premises are damaged during the period of default, the measure of damages will be the cost of rebuilding (*Burt v British Transport Commission* (1955) 166 EG 4).

Covenant against dealings

There is little authority on the measure of damages obtainable by a landlord where, for example, the tenant has assigned the lease without consent. However, the landlord will probably be entitled to compensation for the fact that his new tenant is less financially sound than the assignor and the value of his reversion is thus reduced.

User covenant

Damages may be awarded for breach by the tenant of a positive covenant to keep the premises open. For example, if the anchor tenant, in breach of covenant, closes its shop premises in a shopping centre, it may have such an adverse effect on the profitability of the other shops in the centre that the landlord may be forced to offer rental consessions to the other tenants. The landlord should be compensated for this loss by an award of damages; but there may be difficult problems in quantifying the amount of the damages. If the landlord can prove that his financial loss arises wholly from the tenant's breach, there should be no difficulty for the landlord. However, it may be the case that the centre was already in decline long before the tenant ceased trading so that the defaulting tenant's breach merely contributed to the already falling profitability of the centre (see, generally, *Transworld Land Co Ltd v J Sainsbury plc* [1990] 2 EGLR 255).

28.1.3.2   Injunction

In certain circumstances, the landlord may be able to obtain an injunction against the tenant. An injunction is an equitable remedy and thus at the discretion of the court which may award damages instead. In an appropriate case the landlord may be able to obtain an interim injunction pending the full hearing. There are two types of injunction:

(a)   *Injunctions prohibiting a breach of covenant.* The landlord may consider the use of such an injunction to prevent, for example:

    (i)   an assignment in breach of covenant;

    (ii)   the carrying out of unauthorised alterations;

    (iii) an unauthorised use.

(b)   *Mandatory injunctions.* These injunctions compel the tenant to do something to ensure the performance of a covenant. The court is cautious in its grant of mandatory injunctions.

Standard works on landlord and tenant law contain a more detailed consideration of the subject of injunctions.

28.1.3.3   Specific performance

Like the injunction, this is an equitable remedy and is therefore discretionary. The House of Lords has confirmed that specific performance is not available against a tenant who is in breach of his 'keep open' covenant (*Co-operative Insurance Society Ltd v Argyll Stores (Holdings) Ltd* [1997] 23 EG 137).

28.1.3.4   Forfeiture

Often the landlord's most effective remedy will be to commence (or threaten to commence) forfeiture proceedings against the tenant with a view to ending the lease. This remedy is dealt with at **30.5**.

28.1.4   Right of former tenant or his guarantor to an overriding lease

If a former tenant, or guarantor, is served with a notice by the landlord requiring payment of a fixed charge (see **28.1**), the LT(C)A 1995 allows him to call for an overriding lease within 12 months of payment. For example, L granted a lease to T in 1980. The lease is now owned by A who fell into arrears with his rent. L served notice on T requiring T to pay this sum. T duly made full payment and now claims an overriding lease from L. This will be a head-lease 'slotted in' above the lease of the defaulting tenant. The lease of the defaulting tenant moves one step down the reversionary line and becomes a sub-lease. Thus, T will become the immediate landlord of A and in the event of continued default by A can decide what action to take against him, eg, forfeiture of the occupational lease (sub-lease). Under the overriding lease, T now has some control over the premises for which he is being held liable. The same situation would arise in leases granted on or after 1 January 1996 where the former tenant had been required under an authorised guarantee agreement to guarantee the performance of his immediate assignee, and that assignee is now in default (see **18.2.7**).

The terms of the overriding lease will be on the terms of the defaulting tenant's lease (with consequential adjustments to add a small reversionary period).

Before deciding to call for an overriding lease, a former tenant (or guarantor) should be made aware that he may become liable for landlord's covenants (eg, repairing obligations).

28.2   Tenant's remedies

28.2.1   Breach of an express covenant

In general, a breach by the landlord of one of his covenants in the lease will entitle the tenant to bring a claim for damages. The measure of damages will usually be the difference between the value of the tenant's interest in the premises with the covenant performed and the value with the covenant broken. In certain circumstances, the tenant may seek a more appropriate remedy, such as specific performance or an injunction.

Particular attention should be paid to the landlord's repairing covenant.

28.2.1.1   Breach of landlord's repairing covenant

Unless the lease is of part of a building, it is unusual for the landlord to enter into a covenant to repair. Even where the landlord has assumed the responsibility for repairs, he will generally only be liable if he has notice of disrepair. If the landlord fails to carry out the repairs for which he is liable, the tenant has various remedies available to him. These include the following.

Claim for damages

The tenant's normal remedy will be to bring a claim against his landlord for damages for breach of covenant. Section 18 of the LTA 1927, which restricts a landlord's claim for damages (see **28.1.2.1**), is not relevant to a tenant's claim. Here, damages will be assessed by comparing the value of the premises to the tenant at the date of assessment with their value if the landlord had complied with his obligation. The tenant will also be entitled to damages for consequential loss such as damage caused to the tenant's goods. If the disrepair was such that the tenant was forced to move into temporary accommodation, the cost of this should also be recoverable, provided the tenant had acted reasonably to mitigate his loss.

Self-help

Subject to notifying the landlord and giving him a reasonable opportunity to perform his covenant, the tenant is entitled to carry out the repair himself and deduct the reasonable cost of so doing from future payments of rent (*Lee-Parker v Izzet* [1971] 1 WLR 1688). If the landlord sues the tenant for non-payment of rent, the tenant will have a defence (see **15.1**).

Specific performance

The tenant, unlike the landlord, may be able to obtain an order of specific performance. The granting of the order is entirely at the discretion of the court, and being an equitable remedy it will not be granted if damages are an adequate remedy. Further, there must be a clear breach of covenant and must be no doubt over what is required to be done to remedy the breach.

Appointment of receiver

In the tenant's claim against the landlord for breach of covenant, the tenant may seek the appointment of a receiver to collect the rents and manage the property in accordance with the terms of the lease (including the performance of the landlord's covenants). The court has this power whenever it appears just and convenient to make such an appointment (Supreme Court Act 1981, s 37). The power has been exercised not only where the landlord had abandoned the property but also where he has failed to carry out urgently needed repairs in accordance with his covenant (see *Daiches v Bluelake Investments Ltd* [1985] 2 EGLR 67).

The tenant must nominate a suitably qualified person to act as receiver, for example, a surveyor and before agreeing to act, the potential appointee should ensure that the assets of which he will have control will be sufficient to meet his fees or that he obtains an indemnity in respect of them from the applicant.

A receiver may also be appointed where the landlord collects a service charge from the tenants but fails to provide the services he has promised.

28.2.2 Breach of an implied covenant

28.2.2.1 Covenant for quiet enjoyment

Most leases will contain an express covenant by the landlord for quiet enjoyment (see **Chapter 21**). In the absence of an express covenant one will be implied arising out of the relationship of landlord and tenant. The implied covenant extends only to interruption of or interference with the tenant's enjoyment of the demised premises by the landlord or any person lawfully claiming under him; it does not extend to acts done by anyone with a title superior to that of the landlord. Express covenants are often similarly restricted, in which case the only significant difference between the express and the implied covenant is that under an express covenant the landlord will remain liable throughout the term granted, whereas under an implied covenant the landlord's liability operates only during the currency of his ownership of the reversion.

The covenant will provide the tenant with a remedy in the case of unlawful eviction or where there is any substantial interference with the tenant's use and enjoyment of the premises either by the landlord or by the lawful (rightful) acts of anyone claiming under him. The acts likely to amount to a breach of the covenant are discussed at **21.2**. The normal remedy will be damages, assessed on a contractual basis, to compensate the tenant for the loss resulting from the breach.

28.2.2.2 Derogation from grant

A landlord is under an implied obligation not to derogate from his grant. This covenant complements the covenant for quiet enjoyment and sometimes the two overlap. The landlord will be in breach of his obligation if he does anything which substantially interferes with the use of the demised premises for the purpose for which they were let. Having given something with one hand the landlord cannot take away its enjoyment with the other. The principle is often used to prevent the landlord from using his retained land in a way which frustrates the purpose of the lease. Thus, it has been held to be a derogation from grant for a landlord to grant a lease for the purpose of storing explosives and then to use his retained land in such a way as to render the storage of explosives on the demised premises illegal (*Harmer v Jumbil (Nigeria) Tin Areas Ltd* [1921] 1 Ch 200; see also *Petra Investments Ltd v Jeffrey Rogers plc* [2000] 3 EGLR 120, a case concerning the landlord's ability to alter the original concept of a shopping centre). Similarly, if the landlord uses machinery on his retained land which by reason of vibration affects the stability of the demised premises there will be a breach of the implied covenant. However, there will be no derogation from grant where the landlord's use of the adjoining land merely makes the user of the demised premises more expensive, for example, by letting the adjoining premises to a business competitor of the tenant (*Port v Griffith* [1938] 1 All ER 295 and *Romulus Trading Co Ltd v Comet Properties Ltd* [1996] 2 EGLR 70; but see also *Oceanic Village Ltd v Shirayama Shokusan Co Ltd* [2001] All ER (D) 62 (Feb) in which the High Court was prepared, exceptionally, to find the landlord in breach of the obligation in such circumstances).

Until the decision in *Chartered Trust plc v Davies* [1997] 49 EG 135, it was generally believed that it was insufficient to amount to derogation from grant for a landlord to stand back while tenant A, in breach of covenant, committed acts of nuisance against tenant B thus driving tenant B out of business. Just because the landlord failed to take action against tenant A to prevent the nuisance did not, so it was thought, amount to a repudiation of B's lease. However, the Court of Appeal held that inaction by the landlord in these circumstances may amount to derogation from grant. The implications of this decision will be felt most where, as in the instant case, the landlord has retained management control of a shopping centre and is responsible for the common parts. If, in breach of covenant, one of the tenants does something in the common parts which adversely affects another tenant, the landlord will have to consider acting to enforce the lease obligations or else run the risk of being found to have derogated from grant (see also *Nynehead Developments Ltd v RH Fibreboard Containers Ltd and Others* [1999] 9 EG 174).

Chapter 29
The Effect of Insolvency

29.1 Bankruptcy of the tenant

29.1.1 The trustee-in-bankruptcy

On the making of a bankruptcy order, the Official Receiver assumes control of the bankrupt tenant's property pending the appointment of a trustee-in-bankruptcy at a meeting of the bankrupt's creditors. As soon as he is appointed, the estate of the bankrupt automatically vests in the trustee to enable the trustee to realise the bankrupt's assets and pay off the creditors. Since he becomes the owner at law of the bankrupt's property, the trustee incurs personal liability in respect of that property until he disposes of it, or unless he exercises his right of disclaimer (see **29.1.2**). The leasehold interest of a bankrupt tenant will vest in the trustee, but not, therefore, without the obligation to pay the rent and the liability to repair the premises and observe the other covenants in the lease. The automatic vesting of the lease in the trustee is an involuntary assignment and does not breach the covenant against assigning without consent.

If the lease has some value attached to it (ie, a premium could be demanded on an assignment), the trustee will seek to sell the lease to raise some money for the benefit of the creditors. He will have to comply with the alienation covenant in the lease which will probably involve obtaining the consent of the landlord, and he will be liable to pay rent until the assignment is completed. More often than not the lease does not have any value and amounts to a burden on the bankrupt's estate owing to the continuing obligation to pay rent and perform the covenants. In this case the trustee would prefer to disclaim the lease.

29.1.2 Disclaimer

Section 315 of the Insolvency Act 1986 (IA 1986) gives the trustee power to disclaim onerous property. Onerous property is defined as including any property comprised in the bankrupt's estate which is such that might give rise to a liability to pay money or perform any other onerous act. This clearly covers the typical commercial lease, which by its nature contains onerous continuing obligations. The trustee disclaims the lease by giving to the landlord notice of disclaimer in the prescribed form.

Initially, the landlord will not know whether the trustee intends retaining the lease, with a view to selling it at a premium, or disclaiming it. However, under s 316, the landlord can force the hand of the trustee by requiring him to decide whether or not he is going to disclaim the lease. If the trustee does not give notice of disclaimer within 28 days of receiving a written application from the landlord under s 316, he cannot then disclaim. Section 316 is of no relevance to a landlord who has decided to forfeit the lease (see **29.5**).

29.1.3 The effect of disclaimer

The effect of disclaimer is that it operates to determine the rights, interests and liabilities of the bankrupt and his estate in respect of the disclaimed property, and it discharges the trustee from all personal liability in respect of that property as from the date of his appointment. The lease will no longer form part of the bankrupt's estate; the trustee will no longer be liable to pay the rent or perform the covenants; the bankrupt and his trustee will have washed their hands of the lease. Any claims the landlord may have in respect of unpaid rent up until the date of disclaimer, or other breaches of covenant, or any loss arising out of the disclaimer (including future rent) will have to be proved for in the bankruptcy.

If the bankrupt tenant was the original tenant (with no sub-tenancies having been created, and no guarantor backing up the original tenant's obligations), disclaimer ends the lease itself and the landlord is entitled to recover possession. If the bankrupt tenant was an assignee, while disclaimer ends the lease, it does not destroy the liability of any other persons still liable to the landlord (eg, the original tenant, his guarantor, any intermediate assignees who have given direct covenants to the landlord and their respective guarantors, and any former tenant under an Authorised Guarantee Agreement (AGA)). To this extent, there is a deemed continuing tenancy for the purpose of preserving the liability of others (see *Hindcastle Ltd v Barbara Attenborough Associates Ltd* [1996] 15 EG 103 and *Doleman v Shaw* [2009] EWCA Civ 283). This leaves the landlord in the position of being able to pursue those persons for payment of the rent for the remainder of the term, unless and until the landlord takes steps to bring the deemed continuing tenancy to an end.

One option available to a predecessor who finds himself in this invidious position is to make an application to court under s 320 of the IA 1986. Under that section, any person who claims an interest in, or who is under any liability in respect of the disclaimed property (such as the original tenant who is under a liability to pay the rent), may apply to the court for an order vesting the lease in him. Having to pay the rent is bad enough, but not having possession of the leasehold interest out of which that liability arises is unacceptable. Once the lease is vested in him, the predecessor can either resume possession or, as will more often be the case, try to curtail his continuing liability to meet the rent by assigning the lease, with the landlord's consent, to a more reliable assignee.

While the effect of a disclaimer on the bankrupt tenant's guarantor (including an authorised guarantor under an AGA) is that it does not release the guarantor from the guarantee it is common to include a provision in the lease (or in the AGA) requiring the guarantor to take a lease from the landlord in the event of disclaimer.

The IA 1986 does not deal with the effect of a disclaimer on a sub-lease in an entirely satisfactory manner. Section 315(3) provides that disclaimer 'does not … affect the rights or liabilities of any other person'. Arguably, if disclaimer results in the lease ceasing to exist, the sub-lease must also end. However, this is subject to the principle of the deemed continuing lease established by the House of Lords in the *Hindcastle* case. Furthermore, the sub-tenant can apply under s 320 for a vesting order, and indeed the landlord can require the sub-tenant to take a vesting order and if the sub-tenant declines to accept it, his right to remain will cease. The court will grant the order on such terms as it thinks fit and the effect of the order will be to make the sub-tenant the immediate tenant of the landlord.

29.2 Liquidation of the tenant

Liquidation (or 'winding up') is the process by which all the company's assets are collected, realised and distributed amongst those entitled to them. The company's existence is then terminated. This usually occurs because of the company's poor financial position. Winding up can either be accomplished voluntarily or compulsorily following a court order.

Unlike bankruptcy, title to the lease does not vest in the liquidator (unless the liquidator takes the unusual step of applying for an order under s 145 of the IA 1986 to vest title in him) and the liquidator does not, therefore, incur any personal liability under the lease. It is the company that remains liable to pay the rent, but it may have stopped doing so, owing to its insolvency. However, if the liquidator is making efforts to assign the lease at a premium, and in the meantime pays rent under the lease, the rent may be considered to be an expense of the liquidation and, therefore, recoverable by the liquidator in priority to other debts.

The liquidator has the same power of disclaimer as the trustee-in-bankruptcy (IA 1986, s 178(2)). There are similar provisions allowing the landlord to force the liquidator to decide whether or not he will disclaim (s 178(5)), providing for notice of disclaimer to be served on any sub-tenants (s 179), and enabling persons having an interest in or being subject to a liability in respect of the premises to apply to the court for a vesting order (s 181).

Disclaimer is a possibility in a compulsory liquidation and a creditors' voluntary liquidation, but is unlikely in a members' voluntary liquidation where it is thought that the directors would either have to assign the lease, or quantify the company's liability under the lease by negotiating a surrender of it before making the declaration of solvency required by such a liquidation. If the liquidator in a members' voluntary liquidation disclaimed the lease, the landlord would be able to claim for his loss arising out of the disclaimer. This unliquidated claim would upset the declaration of solvency.

29.3   The tenant in administration

Administration is a process available to assist ailing companies. It is a short-term intensive care operation supervised by the court aimed at putting an insolvent company back on its feet. Previously, an administrator could only be appointed at the discretion of the court, on an application by the company, its directors or its creditors. However, the Enterprise Act 2002 has introduced a faster and simpler administration procedure whereby an administrator can be appointed by the holder of a qualifying floating charge, the company, or its directors, as well as by the court. However, while a company is in administration, a general moratorium is placed on all proceedings against the company without the administrator's consent or leave of the court.

The administrator is appointed to do all such things as may be necessary for the management of the affairs, business and property of the company with a view to achieving the survival of the company. He has no power to disclaim the company's property, but ordinarily he should not want to, since his purpose is to revive the company, and this would be frustrated by the loss of the company's operating premises. If the company does have surplus leasehold premises which are a drain on the limited resources of the company, the administrator should seek licence to assign the lease, and dispose of the lease in the usual way.

An administrator incurs no personal liability under the lease. The lease does not vest in him; his status is merely as the agent of the company.

29.4   The tenant in receivership

Receivership is a state of affairs which exists when a person is appointed to enter onto another's property to seize and sell assets charged by a mortgage or debenture deed in order to secure repayment of a debt, interest and costs. Usually, the receiver will be either an administrative receiver or a Law of Property Act receiver. A Law of Property Act receiver is appointed to take possession of and receive the income of a specific asset charged by an individual or a company. However, landlords will not often be faced with a Law of Property Act receiver since lenders rarely accept rack-rent leases (having precious little capital value) as security for a loan. An administrative receiver is appointed to take possession of the whole (or substantially the whole) of a company's assets which have been charged to the lender under a floating charge. A company tenant's main charge to the bank will contain a floating charge over all the assets of the company, including the lease of the company's premises and, therefore, a landlord is likely to have to deal with this type of receiver. However, under the Enterprise Act 2002, the holder of a qualifying floating charge created on or after the commencement date of that Act may not appoint an administrative receiver of the company (see **29.3**). Holders of floating charges already in existence at the commencement date will continue to have the right to appoint a receiver without any time limit.

Both types of receiver act as agent of the borrower-tenant and do not, therefore, incur any personal liability for rent. There is no question of the receiver disclaiming the lease and nor should there be. The principal task of the receiver is to sell the assets charged in order to realise cash and repay the borrowings. Licence to assign will be required in the usual way, provided the landlord has not already forfeited the lease. If the lease is particularly onerous, the receiver will either negotiate a surrender or advise his appointor to release the asset from the charge.

There are no restrictions on a landlord's remedies when his tenant is in receivership.

29.5 Effect of a company voluntary arrangement

Company voluntary arrangements (CVAs) were introduced by Part I of the Insolvency Act 1986. They provide a means whereby financially troubled companies can reach a legally binding agreement with their creditors in satisfaction of their debts or a scheme of arrangement of their affairs.

Once the CVA has been entered into, a landlord creditor is bound by its terms regarding the debt owed by the tenant. However, the landlord or other creditor has a window of opportunity to apply to put the company into liquidation, for example, before the CVA is entered into.

One feature of a CVA is the CVA moratorium for small companies, namely those with: (a) a turnover of less than £5.6m; (b) balance sheet assets of no more than £2.8m; and (c) fewer than 50 employees. This will protect the company against action by a landlord or other creditor that could jeopardise its recovery. The moratorium initially lasts for 28 days, but it can be extended. A landlord cannot take any action in respect of arrears where a tenant company falls into the small company definition and it has applied for a moratorium. Instead, the landlord must wait to see what the terms of the CVA, when granted, will permit it to do.

29.6 Insolvency and forfeiture

Earlier chapters have dealt with the drafting issues relating to forfeiture clauses. The landlord will probably have drafted the clause to enable forfeiture to be effected upon non-payment of rent, breach of covenant, or the happening of one of several insolvency events.

If the tenant is insolvent, all three elements of the clause may be operative in that the tenant may have stopped paying rent, allowed the premises to fall into disrepair and a winding-up petition may have been presented to the court. A tenant in financial difficulties in a shopping precinct may close down its premises in breach of a covenant to keep open for trade, withhold rent, and suffer the appointment of a receiver.

On the occasion of insolvency events, the landlord will wish to ensure that the forfeiture clause gives him more than one attempt at forfeiting the lease in the event of insolvency proceedings being instigated, where the landlord inadvertently waives one right to forfeit the lease, when, with knowledge of circumstances giving rise to his right to forfeit, he demands or accepts rent. Hence, the landlord will reserve the right to forfeit both on the occasion of the presentation of the petition (for a winding up, bankruptcy or administration order as the case may be), and on the making of the order itself. Not only does this protect the landlord against an inadvertent waiver, but it also allows him to act at the earliest opportunity, on the presentation of a petition, in order to recover the premises before the insolvency proceedings are brought fully into operation.

However, it must be established how each insolvency event affects the right of the landlord to forfeit the lease.

29.6.1 Individual insolvency

At any time after the presentation of a petition in bankruptcy (or a petition for an interim order in bankruptcy), the court may, on application, order a stay on any action, execution or other legal process against the property of the debtor (s 285(1) of the Insolvency Act 1986). Once a bankruptcy order (or an interim order) has been made, no creditor may have a remedy against the property of the bankrupt in respect of a debt provable in the bankruptcy without the leave of the court (s 285(3) of the IA 1986). There is, however, a suggestion in *Ezekiel v Orakpo* [1976] 3 WLR 693 (which was decided in relation to similar provisions contained in the Bankruptcy Act 1914) that forfeiture does not come within the scope of the latter provision. This case was followed in *Razzaq v Pala* [1997] 38 EG 157. If this proposition is correct, and leave is not required to obtain possession by forfeiture after the bankruptcy order has been made, it is difficult to see how the court could be justified in restraining a forfeiture before the order is made.

29.6.2 Corporate insolvency

After the presentation of a winding-up petition, the court may, on application, order a stay on any existing forfeiture proceedings. Once the winding-up order is made, forfeiture proceedings cannot be continued without leave of the court although peaceable re-entry is probably still possible. If the company is in voluntary liquidation, application can be made to the court for a stay on forfeiture proceedings at any time after the commencement of the winding up, as if the company were being wound up by the court.

Once a petition for an administration order has been lodged at court, and during the period of administration, while there are no restrictions on the landlord's ability to serve an LPA 1925, s 146 notice, the landlord cannot forfeit the lease by court proceedings without leave of the court or peaceable re-entry.

The court will grant leave as a matter of course in liquidation cases (and presumably also in bankruptcy cases) since the landlord, in enforcing a forfeiture, is seeking to recover only his own property. In administration cases, leave should not be refused unless it would seriously impede the achievement of the purposes of the administration, or inflict a loss upon others which is substantially greater than the loss to be inflicted upon the landlord if leave were denied.

If the tenant company is in receivership, the landlord's ability to forfeit is unaffected.

29.7 Insolvency and claims for rent or damages

As an alternative to forfeiting the lease (or possibly in addition) the landlord may pursue other remedies. For instance, if the tenant fails to pay the rent, the landlord may bring a civil claim for the arrears, exercise his right to distrain for the arrears, or, if the tenant has created a sub-tenancy, he may serve notice on the sub-tenant under s 6 of the Law of Distress Amendment Act 1908 requiring the sub-tenant to pay rent direct to the head landlord until rent arrears under the head-lease have been paid off. If the tenant is in breach of any of the other covenants under the lease, the landlord may bring a claim for damages against the tenant.

If the tenant company is in receivership, the landlord's remedies for non-payment of rent or breach of covenant are unaffected, although he may find that the only time any judgment he obtains is met by the receiver is when the receiver applies to the landlord for licence to assign. The landlord would be likely to impose a condition on assignment that all arrears of rent, and any sums in respect of loss arising out of any other breaches of covenant are paid to the landlord before consent is given. The receiver incurs no personal liability for the company's debts, unless, being an administrative receiver, he specifically adopts any of the liabilities of the company.

When an administrator is appointed, the landlord may not exercise a right of forfeiture by way of peaceable re-entry without the consent of the administrator or the court. Further, no proceedings or execution or other legal process may be commenced or continued, nor can any distress be levied without the consent of the administrator or the court. It can thus be seen that a landlord's remedies are very restricted. The landlord cannot sue for arrears of rent or levy distress or forfeit without consent.

In a compulsory liquidation, on the making of the winding-up order, no actions may be commenced or proceeded with against the company without leave of the court. This general stay on proceedings prevents the landlord from distraining for rent, but would not, it appears, prevent him from serving a s 6 notice on any sub-tenants. In a voluntary liquidation, the court may stay any proceedings upon application by the liquidator. In so far as the landlord is a creditor of the company, he must prove for his debt in the liquidation as an ordinary unsecured creditor. However, if the liquidator decided to retain possession of the premises for the purposes of the winding up, rent accrued since the commencement of the winding up will be payable in full by the liquidator as an expense of the liquidation.

In a bankruptcy, since the trustee-in-bankruptcy incurs personal liability, he is likely to disclaim the lease unless it has a capital value. Any actions the landlord may have against the individual tenant may be stayed on application by the trustee in those proceedings, although the landlord is still permitted to distrain for arrears of rent accrued due in the six months preceding the date of the bankruptcy order.

29.8 Landlord's insolvency

In many cases the insolvency of the landlord will not greatly affect the tenant since the landlord's receiver, liquidator, administrator or trustee-in-bankruptcy will be keen to continue receiving the income generated by the lease. Problems will arise where the tenant wishes to take action for breach of covenant against an insolvent landlord, or where the landlord ceases to perform services in accordance with service charge provisions, or apply advance service charge payments made by the tenants. These problems are beyond the scope of this book.

Chapter 30
Methods of Termination

30.1 Introduction

There are a number of ways at common law in which a lease may be ended. Before looking at these in detail, it is important to appreciate that if the tenant enjoys the protection of the security of tenure provisions under Pt II of the LTA 1954, the lease may be ended only in one of the ways specified by that Act. For example, a protected fixed term will not come to an end on the expiry of that term; a protected periodic tenancy will not come to an end by the service of a landlord's common law notice to quit. Such tenancies can only be terminated in one of the ways specified in the Act. These restrictions on termination are dealt with in **Chapter 31**. The methods of termination to be considered here are:

(a) expiry;

(b) notice to quit;

(c) operation of break clause;

(d) forfeiture;

(e) surrender;

(f) merger.

30.2 Expiry

A fixed-term tenancy will terminate at the end of that term; there is no need for either party to take any steps at all. If the tenant remains in possession beyond the expiry date with his landlord's consent, he holds over as a tenant at will, ie, on terms that either party may end the tenancy at any time. A tenancy at will may be converted into an implied periodic tenancy by the payment and acceptance of rent.

30.3 Notice to quit

A periodic tenancy may be determined by service of a notice to quit by either party. There are many technical rules surrounding the drafting and service of such notices and reference should be made to one of the standard works on landlord and tenant law for a consideration of these. What follows is only intended as a reminder of some of the more important rules.

In the absence of contrary agreement, the minimum length of notice required is as follows:

(a) yearly tenancy: half a year's notice (or two quarters if the tenancy expires on a quarter day);

(b) monthly tenancy: one month's notice;

(c) weekly tenancy: one week's notice.

Not only must the length of notice be correct, it must also expire at the end of a completed period of the tenancy. In the case of a yearly tenancy, this means that the notice must expire on the anniversary of the commencement of the tenancy or on the day before the anniversary. For example, with a yearly tenancy beginning on 1 January in one year, the notice should expire on 1 January or 31 December in any subsequent year. A similar rule applies to other periodic tenancies.

At common law, no particular form of notice is required but it must be unambiguous and, for the avoidance of doubt, in writing.

As a general rule, unless the lease provides to the contrary, a notice to quit must relate to all of the land in the lease and not just part.

30.4   Operation of break clause

The lease may contain an option by which one or both parties may determine the lease, at a particular time or on the happening of a specified event, before it has run its full term. This is known as a break clause. If there are any conditions precedent to the exercise of the option, these must be strictly observed (*Bairstow Eves (Securities) Ltd v Ripley* [1992] 2 EGLR 47). If, for example, the option is only exercisable provided the tenant has performed all of his obligations, he will not be able to exercise it while in arrears or in breach of his repairing covenant. However, the exact wording of the option should be examined to see whether such conditions have to be satisfied at the date the notice exercising the option is served, or at the date when it expires. While great care should always be taken in drafting the break notice, minor errors which would not mislead a reasonable recipient may not render the notice invalid (see *Mannai Investment Co Ltd v Eagle Star Life Assurance Co Ltd* [1997] AC 749 and **14.2.2**).

The exercise of a break clause in a head-lease may operate to terminate any sub-lease which has been created (this is certainly the case in the event of exercise by the superior landlord; see *Barrett v Morgan* [2000] 2 AC 264). However, the sub-tenant may have the right to remain in possession if he is protected under Pt II of the LTA 1954.

30.5   Forfeiture

Forfeiture is the landlord's right to re-enter the premises and determine the lease on breach by the tenant of any of his covenants, or upon the happening of certain specified events. However, the right to forfeit is not automatic; it exists only where the lease expressly includes such a right (or if the lease is made conditional upon the performance of the covenants). The drafting of an appropriate provision is dealt with in **Chapter 23**.

Before the landlord proceeds to forfeit the lease, he should consider carefully the consequences of so doing. In a rising market the landlord should have no difficulty in subsequently re-letting the premises, possibly at a higher rent. If, however, the landlord is faced with a falling market, re-letting the premises may not be so easy. As a result of forfeiture the landlord may be left with an empty property on his hands for a long time. This will lead to a loss of income and may have a detrimental effect on any adjoining property of the landlord, for example, other shops in a parade.

The right of forfeiture is enforced by the landlord in one of two ways. First, the landlord may issue and serve proceedings for recovery of possession or, secondly, the landlord may peaceably re-enter the premises. Landlords are sometimes reluctant to adopt the second alternative because an offence will be committed if any violence is used or threatened and the landlord knew that there was someone on the premises opposed to the entry (Criminal Law Act 1977, s 6). Furthermore, there is a feeling that peaceable re-entry may be open to significant challenge under the Human Rights Act 1998. There are further statutory restrictions on the right of peaceable re-entry where the premises are let as a dwelling (Protection from Eviction Act 1977 (PEA 1977)).

30.5.1 Waiver of the right to forfeit

A landlord will be prevented from forfeiting a lease if he has expressly or impliedly waived the right to forfeit. The landlord will still be able to pursue his other remedies but will have lost his right to forfeit. Waiver will be implied where the landlord, knowing of the breach, does some unequivocal act which recognises the continued existence of the lease. It is not, however, a question of intention. So long as the act is inconsistent with an intention to determine the lease, the motive for the act is irrelevant. Thus, a demand for rent, or receipt of rent falling due *after* the right to forfeit has arisen, will amount to waiver notwithstanding a clerical error by the landlord's agent, receipt of rent paid under a standing order, or that the rent is demanded or received 'without prejudice to the landlord's right to forfeit'.

Waiver operates only in respect of past breaches of covenant. Where the landlord waives a 'once and for all' breach (eg, breach of a covenant against sub-letting) his right to forfeit is lost for ever. If, however, the breach is of a continuing nature (eg, breach of a repairing covenant) the right to forfeit, though waived on one occasion, will arise again, as the property continues to be in disrepair (see *Greenwich London Borough Council v Discreet Selling Estates Ltd* [1990] 48 EG 113; as to the need for a fresh s 146 notice).

30.5.2 Forfeiture for non-payment of rent

That the tenant owes rent to his landlord may seem a necessary pre-condition of the landlord's right to forfeit. Yet, exceptionally, this may not be the case. If, on an assignment of the reversion, the tenant is in arrears with payment of the rent, the 'old' and 'new' landlords often come to some arrangement as to who has the right to sue for the outstanding arrears. Such was the situation in *Kataria v Safeland plc* [1998] 05 EG 155, where it was agreed that, on completion, the right to receive the arrears of rent and all rights of action relating thereto were vested in the 'old' landlord. Notwithstanding this, it was held that the 'new' landlord, following completion, was entitled to forfeit the lease for non-payment of rent (even though the arrears were owed to the 'old' landlord). Hence it becomes important to distinguish the right to forfeit from the right of action in respect of the arrears.

The landlord must make a formal demand for the rent before forfeiting unless the lease exempts him from this obligation. To avoid the technicalities of a formal demand, most leases will provide for forfeiture if the tenant is, for example, 21 days or more in arrears 'whether the rent is formally demanded or not' (see also s 210 of the Common Law Procedure Act 1852). If the rent falls into arrears, the landlord may proceed to forfeit either by court proceedings, or by peaceable re-entry.

However, the tenant may have the right to apply to court for relief from forfeiture which, if granted, will mean that the tenant continues to hold under the existing lease. Where the landlord is proceeding by way of court action, those proceedings will be stayed if the tenant pays all the arrears plus the landlord's costs before the hearing. In certain cases, the tenant may also apply for relief within six months from the landlord's recovery of possession, although the rules differ between the High Court and county court. Where the landlord is proceeding by way of peaceable re-entry, the tenant may still apply to the court for relief. Again, the tenant will have to pay the arrears and must, as a general rule, apply within six months of re-entry by the landlord (although in exceptional circumstances the court may be prepared to grant relief outside this period: *Thatcher v CH Pearce & Sons (Contractors) Ltd* [1968] 1 WLR 748).

30.5.3   Forfeiture for breach of other covenants

Before a landlord is able to forfeit for a breach of covenant, other than for the payment of rent, the landlord must normally serve a notice on the tenant under s 146 of the LPA 1925. Where there has been an unlawful assignment, the notice should be served on the unlawful assignee.

A s 146 notice must:

(a)   specify the breach;

(b)   require it to be remedied within a reasonable time, if it is capable of being remedied; and

(c)   require the tenant to pay compensation for the breach, if the landlord so requires.

As far as the second requirement is concerned, the notice will be invalid if the landlord wrongly takes the view that the breach is irremediable and, therefore, does not require the tenant to remedy it within a reasonable time. Whether a breach is remediable is a question of fact in each case. As a general rule, breach of a positive covenant is usually remediable by the tenant doing that which he has left undone. Thus, for example, it has been held that breach of a covenant requiring the tenant to reconstruct the premises by a stated date, was capable of being remedied by the tenant carrying out the work within a reasonable time (*Expert Clothing Service & Sales Ltd v Hillgate House Ltd* [1986] Ch 340). With negative covenants the issue is less clear. Views have been expressed in the past that breaches of negative covenants can never be remedied; once the forbidden act has been done it cannot be undone. However, current thinking is that the breach of some negative covenants can be remedied. Where, for example, the tenant has erected advertisement hoardings in breach of covenant, the removal of them would, it is submitted, remedy the breach. On the other hand, it has been held that certain breaches of negative covenants cannot be remedied. Thus, the breach of an alienation covenant, a covenant against immoral user and a covenant against trading without the appropriate licences have all been held to be irremediable (see, generally, *Expert Clothing Service & Sales Ltd v Hillgate House Ltd* above, and *Scala House & District Property Co Ltd v Forbes* [1974] QB 575). If the landlord is in any doubt about whether a particular breach can be remedied, the notice should require the tenant to remedy the breach 'if it is capable of remedy'.

What is a 'reasonable' period for compliance has always been a grey area. Guidance on this is now provided by *Albany Holdings Ltd v Crown Estate Commissioners* [2003] EWHC 1480. Here the court held that a period of one month would normally be sufficient. However, where the work required to remedy a breach would take longer than one month to carry out, then a longer period may be necessary.

If the tenant does not comply with the requirements of a valid s 146 notice, the landlord may proceed to forfeit the lease by court proceedings or peaceable re-entry. In either case the tenant may be able to seek relief from forfeiture but there is a vital difference between the two methods. If the landlord takes court proceedings, the tenant can seek relief at any time before the landlord actually re-enters the premises: no relief can be granted afterwards. However, if the landlord re-enters peaceably, the tenant can seek relief even after the landlord has re-entered, though the court will take into account all the circumstances including any delay by the tenant in seeking relief (*Billson v Residential Apartments Ltd* [1992] 1 AC 494).

In deciding whether or not to grant relief, the court will have regard to the conduct of the parties and all other relevant circumstances. If relief is granted, it will be granted on such terms as the court thinks fit (LPA 1925, s 146(2)). This gives the court a very wide discretion and the House of Lords has refused to lay down any rigid rules on its exercise. Relief is usually granted where the breach has been remedied and is unlikely to re-occur.

Where the s 146 notice relates to internal decorative repairs, the tenant has a special right to apply to the court for relief under s 147 of the LPA 1925. This is separate from the general right to apply for relief under s 146. Under s 147, the court may wholly or partially relieve the tenant from liability for internal decorative repairs if, having regard to all the circumstances of the case and in particular the length of the tenant's term still unexpired, it thinks the notice is unreasonable. However, s 147 does not apply:

(a)   where the liability is under an express covenant to put the property in a decorative state of repair which has never been performed; or

(b)   to any matter necessary or proper for keeping the property in a sanitary condition, or for the maintenance or preservation of the structure; or

(c)   to any statutory liability to keep a house fit for human habitation; or

(d)   to any covenant to yield up the premises in a specified state of repair at the end of the term.

30.5.3.1   Three special cases

(a)   Where the breach by the tenant is of a repairing covenant, a special procedure may apply. If the lease was granted for seven or more years and still has three or more to run, the s 146 notice must also contain a notice of the tenant's right to serve a counter-notice within 28 days. If this is served, the landlord cannot proceed to forfeit without leave of the court. Such leave is only granted on specified grounds (Leasehold Property (Repairs) Act 1938, see **28.1.2.1**).

(b)   A lease will usually give the landlord the right to forfeit upon the tenant's bankruptcy (or liquidation) or having the lease taken in execution. If the landlord wishes to forfeit, he need only serve a s 146 notice and the tenant may only apply for relief during the first year following the bankruptcy or taking in execution. However, there is an important exception to this rule. If, during that first year, the trustee or liquidator sells the lease, the s 146 protection lasts indefinitely. Without such an exception, it would be difficult for the trustee or liquidator to find a buyer for the lease because of the risk of forfeiture taking place after the expiration of the first year without the service of a s 146 notice and with no right to seek relief.

(c)   Exceptionally, there is no need for the landlord to serve a s 146 notice following bankruptcy, liquidation or taking in execution, and the tenant has no right to apply for relief if the lease is of:

(i)   agricultural land;

(ii)   mines or minerals;

(iii)   a public house;

(iv)   a furnished house;

(v)   any premises where the personal qualifications of the tenant are important for the preservation of the nature or character of the premises or on the ground of neighbourhood to the landlord or anyone holding under him (as to the meaning of 'neighbourhood to the landlord', see *Hockley Engineering Ltd v V & P Midlands Ltd* [1993] 1 EGLR 76).

30.5.4   Position of sub-tenants and mortgagees on forfeiture

If the head-lease is forfeited, this will automatically end any sub-lease. This is unfair to sub-tenants who stand to lose their interest through no fault of their own. In order to protect sub-tenants in this situation, s 146(4) enables them to apply for relief against forfeiture of the head-lease even in those cases where the head tenant is unable to do so. The granting of relief is entirely at the discretion of the court which can impose such conditions as it thinks fit and may, for example, require the sub-tenant to comply with the terms of the head-lease. If the court grants relief, the sub-tenant will become the immediate tenant of the landlord but cannot be granted a longer term than that remaining under the sub-lease. Difficult problems can arise where the sub-lease is of part only of the premises comprised in the head-lease. The view has sometimes been expressed that the sub-tenant may, as a condition of granting relief, have to take a new lease of all the property comprised in the head-lease or pay the arrears of rent relating to the whole.

An important example of the operation of s 146(4) arises in the case of a mortgagee of a lease. Lenders (whether by sub-demise or legal charge) are sub-tenants for the purposes of the subsection and can thus apply for relief from forfeiture of the lease (see *United Dominion Trust Ltd v Shellpoint Trustees* [1993] EGCS 57, as to the time within which relief must be sought by lenders).

30.6   Surrender

Surrender occurs where a tenant relinquishes his lease to his immediate landlord, with his landlord's consent. The lease will merge in the reversion and be extinguished. Surrender can be express or by operation of law. An express surrender must generally be made by deed. Surrender by operation of law occurs where the parties act in a way which is inconsistent with the continuance of the lease. For example, a surrender will occur if the parties agree a new lease to commence during the currency of the existing lease. A similar situation occurs if the tenant gives up possession and returns the key to the landlord and the landlord accepts this as surrender. However, surrender requires the agreement of both parties. If the key is merely left with the landlord, this in itself will not amount to surrender unless the landlord accepts it as surrender, for example, by re-letting the premises (see *Arundel Corporation v The Financial Training Co Ltd* [2000] 3 All ER 456).

If a lease protected under Pt II of the LTA 1954 requires the tenant to offer to surrender the lease before seeking consent to assign, the landlord's acceptance of that offer may be void under s 38 of the LTA 1954 (*Allnatt London Properties Ltd v Newton* [1984] 1 All ER 423, and see **31.1.5**).

30.6.1   Effect of surrender

A surrender will release the tenant from any future liability under the lease but not in respect of past breaches. A well-advised tenant should, therefore, seek a release from all breaches.

The surrender of a head-lease will not affect any sub-lease. The sub-tenant will become the immediate tenant of the head landlord on the terms of the sub-lease. Sometimes, a head tenant will agree to surrender his head-lease with a view to taking a new fixed term from his landlord; this may happen where the head-lease is coming to the end of its fixed term. In this situation, any new head-lease granted following the surrender will be subject to the sub-lease (LPA 1925, s 150).

30.7   Merger

Merger occurs where a tenant acquires his immediate landlord's reversion or a third party acquires both the lease and the immediate reversion. In such a case the lease will end. However, merger will only take place where the person acquiring both the lease and immediate reversion holds both estates in the same capacity and intends merger to take place.

As with surrender, merger of a lease will not affect the position of any sub-tenant.

Chapter 31

The Landlord and Tenant Act 1954, Part II

31.1 Introductory matters

31.1.1 The protection of the Act

The principal Act conferring security of tenure on business tenants and regulating the manner in which business tenancies can be terminated is Pt II of the LTA 1954 (statutory references in this chapter are to this Act, unless otherwise stated). The protection given to tenants covered by the Act is twofold. First, a business tenancy will not come to an end at the expiration of a fixed term, nor can a periodic tenancy be terminated by the landlord serving an ordinary notice to quit. Instead, notwithstanding the ending of the contractual term, the tenancy will be automatically continued under s 24 until such time as it is terminated in one of the ways specified in the Act. Secondly, upon the expiration of a business tenancy in accordance with the Act, business tenants normally have a statutory right to apply to court for a new tenancy and the landlord may only oppose that application on certain statutory grounds. Any new tenancy granted will also enjoy the protection of the Act.

Major changes to the provisions of the Act were brought into force on 1 June 2004 by the Regulatory Reform (Business Tenancies) (England and Wales) Order 2003 (SI 2003/3096). This book reflects the amended provisions.

Selected extracts from the Act are set out in **Appendix 5**.

31.1.2 The application of the Act

Section 23(1) provides that:

> this Act applies to any tenancy where the property comprised in the tenancy is or includes premises which are occupied by the tenant and are so occupied for the purposes of a business carried on by him or for those and other purposes.

This involves a number of elements.

31.1.2.1 There must be a 'tenancy'

Tenancy includes an agreement for a lease and an underlease (even an unauthorised one). However, licences are not protected. The lease/licence distinction is further considered at **9.4**. In view of the danger for landlords in inadvertently creating a protected tenancy, the use of licences as a means of avoiding the Act needs very careful consideration. Certain tenancies are specifically excluded from the protection of the Act and these are dealt with at **31.1.3**.

31.1.2.2 The premises must be occupied by the tenant

Occupation need not be by the tenant personally. It has been held that occupation may be sufficient where it is conducted through the medium of a manager or agent provided that such representative occupation is genuine and not a sham arrangement. Similarly, s 23(1A) and (1B) provides that the Act will apply where an individual is the tenant but the premises are then occupied by a company in which the tenant has a controlling interest. 'Controlling interest' is defined by s 46(2). There are also special rules as to occupation in ss 41, 41A and 46 where a tenancy is held on trust, vested in partners as trustees, or held by one member of a group of companies but occupied by another member of the same group. Occupation need not be continuous provided that the 'thread of continuity' of business user is not broken (*Hancock & Willis v GMS Syndicate Ltd* (1982) 265 EG 473 and *Flairline Properties Ltd v Hassan* [1997] 1 EGLR 138). In *Pointon York Group plc v Poulton* [2006] EWCA Civ 1001, it was held that parking a car in a car parking space during normal business hours could amount to occupation for the purposes of the LTA 1954.

Problems may arise where a business tenant sub-lets part of the property to a business sub-tenant. In such a situation, they cannot both qualify for protection in respect of the sub-let part; there can be no dual occupation for the purposes of the Act. In normal circumstances, it will be the sub-tenant who enjoys the protection of the Act although in an exceptional case the head tenant may reserve sufficiently extensive rights over the sub-let part that he remains the occupier (see *Graysim Holdings Ltd v P&O Property Holdings Ltd* [1995] 3 WLR 854). The case of *Pointon York Group plc v Poulton* [2006] EWCA Civ 1001 shows the problems landlords can face due to the rule that any sub-lease must of necessity be shorter than the head lease out of which it is granted. In this case, the head tenant moved back into occupation in the short period between the end of the sub-lease and the later ending of the head lease and was thus enabled to claim the protection of the Act. It is arguable that a landlord cannot serve a s 25 notice at a time when the tenant is not in business occupation, and so in situations like the *Poulton* case the landlord would not be able to serve the s 25 notice until the tenant actually took up occupation. This would seriously delay the landlord's ability to obtain possession or grant a renewal lease at an increased rent.

31.1.2.3   The premises must be occupied for the purposes of a business carried on by the tenant

'Business' is widely defined in s 23 to include a 'trade, profession or employment and includes any activity carried on by a body of persons, whether corporate or unincorporate'. Where the business is carried on by an individual, it must amount to a trade, profession or employment; but where it is carried on by a body of persons (corporate or unincorporate) 'any activity' may suffice. Thus, it has been held that the organising of a tennis club and the activities of the governors in running a hospital, both amounted to a business use (*Addiscombe Garden Estates v Crabbe* [1958] 1 QB 513 and *Hills (Patents) Ltd v University College Hospital Board of Governors* [1956] 1 QB 90). This does not mean however that the Act will apply whenever the tenant is a body of persons; the 'activity' must be correlative to the conceptions involved in the words 'trade, profession or employment'.

Two problem areas may arise with this requirement.

(a)   The demised premises will sometimes be used for two purposes, only one of which is a business user. For example, the letting may consist of a shop on the ground floor with living accommodation above. Does the Act still apply? In cases of mixed user the Act will apply provided the business activity is a significant purpose of the occupation and not merely incidental to the occupation of the premises as a residence (*Cheryl Investments Ltd v Saldhana* [1978] 1 WLR 1329 and *Gurton v Parrot* [1991] 1 EGLR 98). In the example mentioned, the Act is likely to apply. If, however, a residential tenant occasionally brought work home with him this would not result in his tenancy being protected under the Act.

(b)   The business user may be in breach of a covenant of the lease. How does that affect the tenant's rights? If the lease merely forbids a specific business use (eg, not to use the shop as a newsagents), or any use except the business use specified (eg, not to use the premises for any purpose other than as a newsagents), a business use in breach of such a provision will not deprive the tenant of the protection of the Act. However, s 24(3) does exclude from protection any tenancy where the use of the premises for business purposes is in breach of a general prohibition preventing all business use (eg, not to carry on any business, trade, profession or employment) although if the landlord had consented to or acquiesced in the breach, the Act would still apply.

31.1.3   Exclusions from the Act

Apart from those tenancies which fail to satisfy the requirements of s 23, there are other tenancies which are not protected by the Act. These include:

(a)   Tenancies at will. In *Javad v Aqil* [1991] 1 WLR 1007, a prospective tenant who was allowed into possession while negotiations proceeded for the grant of a new business lease was held, on the facts, to be a tenant at will, and thus excluded from protection. A similar decision was reached in *London Baggage Co (Charing Cross) Ltd v Railtrack plc* [2000] EGCS 57, where a tenant holding over after the expiry of its lease, pending the negotiation of a new lease, was held to be a tenant at will.

(b)   Tenancies of agricultural holdings: these have their own form of protection under the Agricultural Holdings Act 1986.

(c)   A farm business tenancy.

(d)   Mining leases.

(e)   Service tenancies. These are tenancies granted to the holder of an office, appointment or employment from the landlord and which continue only so long as the tenant holds such office, etc. For the exclusion to apply the tenancy must be in writing and express the purpose for which it was granted.

(f)   Fixed-term tenancies not exceeding six months. These tenancies are excluded unless the tenancy contains provisions for renewing the term or extending it beyond six months, or the tenant (including any predecessor in the same business) has already been in occupation for a period exceeding 12 months (see *Cricket Ltd v Shaftesbury plc* [1999] 3 All ER 283).

(g)   'Contracted out' tenancies (see **31.1.5**).

31.1.4   Two important definitions

31.1.4.1   The competent landlord

It is between the tenant and the competent landlord that the procedure under the Act must be conducted. It is important, therefore, that the tenant identifies his competent landlord and deals with him. Where a freeholder grants a lease, there is no cause for concern as the tenant's competent landlord can be no other than the freeholder. However, where the tenant is a sub-tenant, the statutory definition of competent landlord means that the sub-tenant's immediate landlord may not be his competent landlord. Using s 44 of the Act, the sub-tenant must look up the chain of superior tenancies for the first person who either owns the freehold or who has a superior tenancy which will not come to an end within 14 months. The following examples may assist:

As the first example involves a sub-letting of the whole of the premises, T will not be in occupation, and will not, therefore, enjoy the protection of the Act. This means that the head-lease will come to an end on its contractual expiry date, with the result that as soon as the head-lease has entered the last 14 months of its contractual term, ST's competent landlord will be the freeholder. However, in the second example, because it is a sub-letting of part only, then provided T occupies the remaining part for business purposes, the head-lease will be protected. Therefore, it will not expire by effluxion of time. So even if the head-lease has entered the last 14 months of its contractual term, the sub-tenant's competent landlord will still be T (unless, eg, the freeholder has served an appropriate notice terminating the head-lease within 14 months, see **31.2.1**).

It is, therefore, very important for sub-tenants to identify their competent landlord and this can be done by serving a notice on their immediate landlord under s 40 of the Act seeking information about the landlord's interest. A s 40 notice should always be served by a sub-tenant before taking any other steps under the Act. The prescribed form is set out in **Appendix 1**.

31.1.4.2   The 'holding'

The definition of the holding is important because the tenant's right to a new lease normally extends to only that part of the premises known as the 'holding'. Further, many of the landlord's grounds of opposition refer to the holding. This term is defined in s 23(3) of the Act as being the property comprised in the current tenancy excluding any part which is not occupied by the tenant or a person employed by the tenant for the purposes of the tenant's business. In practice, in the majority of cases, it is correct to describe the holding as comprising all the premises originally let except those parts which the tenant is currently sub-letting.

31.1.5   Contracting out – before 1 June 2004

As a general rule, s 38(1) forbids any contracting out of the Act. This means that any agreement purporting to exclude or modify the tenant's security of tenure is void. However, under s 38(4) of the Act the court was empowered to make an order excluding the security of tenure provisions, provided certain conditions were satisfied:

(a)   The proposed letting must have been for a term of years certain. Care must be taken not to fall foul of this requirement. In *Nicholas v Kinsey* [1994] 16 EG 145, a tenancy for 12 months and thereafter from year to year was held to be outside it. More controversially, in *Newham London Borough Council v Thomas-Van Staden* [2008] EWCA Civ 1414, the landlord had granted its tenant a lease for a term beginning on 1 January 2003 and ending on 28 September 2004. The lease defined this period as 'the Term, which expression shall include any period of holding over or extension of it whether by statute or at common law or by agreement'. The Court of Appeal decided that was not for a 'term of years certain', as required by the legislation, because the term had been defined to include a subsequent indefinite period. This again rendered the contracting out void.

(b)   There must have been a joint application to court by both parties.

(c)   The lease entered into must have been substantially the same as the draft lease attached to the court order (*Receiver for Metropolitan Police District v Palacegate Properties Ltd* [2001] 2 Ch 131).

Further, and most importantly, the court's approval must have been obtained before the tenancy was granted (*Essexcrest Ltd v Evenlex Ltd* [1988] 1 EGLR 69).

These provisions have now been changed with regard to leases entered into on or after 1 June 2004. However, the old rules will still be relevant in the case of a dispute between the parties to a contracted out lease if the tenant were to claim that the contracting out procedures were not correctly followed and that the lease does have security of tenure. Equally, any potential purchaser of the landlord's reversion to a contracted out lease will need to check carefully that the correct procedures were followed in order to avoid as far as possible any such claim by a tenant.

31.1.6   Contracting out – on or after 1 June 2004

The new rules no longer require the need to obtain a court order, but still require the proposed letting to be for a term of years certain. Instead the landlord must serve a notice on the tenant in the prescribed form and the tenant (or someone duly authorised by the tenant) must sign a declaration that he has received the notice and accepts the consequences of the agreement to contract out. If the notice is served within the 14 days prior to the grant of the tenancy, the tenant must make a statutory declaration as to this before an independent solicitor. The prescribed form of notice contains a 'health warning' advising the tenant that he is giving up the right to security of tenure and advising him to seek advice not only from a solicitor or surveyor but also from his accountant. The 'instrument creating the tenancy', ie, normally the lease, must then contain reference to the exclusion agreement, the notice and the declaration. The prescribed form of notice is set out overleaf:

IMPORTANT NOTICE

You are being offered a lease without security of tenure. Do not commit yourself to the lease unless you have read this message carefully and have discussed it with a professional adviser.

Business tenants normally have security of tenure – the right to stay in their business premises when the lease ends.

If you commit yourself to the lease you will be giving up these important legal rights.

- You will have **no right** to stay in the premises when the lease ends.
- Unless the landlord chooses to offer you another lease, you will need to leave the premises.
- You will be unable to claim compensation for the loss of your business premises, unless the lease specifically gives you this right.
- If the landlord offers you another lease, you will have no right to ask the court to fix the rent.

It is therefore important to get professional advice – from a qualified surveyor, lawyer or accountant – before agreeing to give up these rights.

If you want to ensure that you can stay in the same business premises when the lease ends, you should consult your adviser about another form of lease that does not exclude the protection of the Landlord and Tenant Act 1954.

If you receive this notice at least 14 days before committing yourself to the lease, you will need to sign a simple declaration that you have received this notice and have accepted its consequences, before signing the lease.

But if you do not receive at least 14 days' notice, you will need to sign a 'statutory' declaration. To do so, you will need to visit an independent solicitor (or someone else empowered to administer oaths).

Unless there is a special reason for committing yourself to the lease sooner, you may want to ask the landlord to let you have at least 14 days to consider whether you wish to give up your statutory rights. If you then decided to go ahead with the agreement to exclude the protection of the Landlord and Tenant Act 1954, you would only need to make a simple declaration, and so you would not need to make a separate visit to an independent solicitor.

It is clear that the Government anticipated that the 14 day 'ordinary' notice would be the one most used (see, for example, the guidance note, 'Business Tenancies: new procedures under the Landlord & Tenant Act 1954, Part 2', published by the then Office of the Deputy Prime Minister in April 2004). However, in practice, the statutory declaration procedure is the one most used. This is largely because solicitors are reluctant to serve the notice until the form of the lease has been finalised – and once it has been finalised, parties do not want to have to wait 14 days before the tenant can take up occupation and start paying rent.

The reason for the reluctance stems from a lack of clarity in the new procedure. Under the old law, it had been held (see **31.1.5**) that the lease entered into must be in substantially the same form as the one approved by the court for contracting out. It was not made clear under the new provisions whether a similar rule might apply. What if the contracting out notice was signed and then the terms of the lease were substantially renegotiated. Would that original notice still be valid? In order to avoid any possible problems, it is usual practice for the notice not to be signed until the terms of the lease have been substantially agreed.

Other problems have been identified. What if the identity of the landlord or the tenant were to change during negotiations, but after the service of the notice? This is not unknown where businesses operate through a web of inter-related companies, each of which is, however, a separate legal entity.

Another problem to bear in mind with the procedure is the position of any guarantors. It is not unusual in a guarantee agreement to find a covenant by the guarantor that it will enter into a new lease of the premises if the tenant should become insolvent and the liquidator should then disclaim the lease. If it is intended that such lease is also to be contracted out of the Act, notice must be served on and signed by the guarantor before he is legally obliged to take that lease, ie before he signs the guarantee agreement, *not* before the lease itself is granted. Similar principles must be applied where an outgoing tenant is entering into an Authorised Guarantee Agreement (see **18.2.7**). It is likely that this will require the tenant to take a new lease on disclaimer.

In *The Chiltern Railway Co Ltd v Patel* [2008] EWCA Civ 178, another potential problem with the procedure was identified by a tenant. A statutory declaration had been used, even though the notice was served more than 14 days before the commencement of the lease and so a simple signature would have been sufficient. The tenant's claim that the lease was fully protected as the correct procedure for contracting out had not been used was rejected by the Court of Appeal.

31.1.7 Continuation tenancies

A business tenancy protected by the Act will not come to an end on the expiry of the contractual term. Instead, s 24 continues the tenancy on exactly the same terms (except those relating to termination) and at exactly the same rent until it is terminated in accordance with the Act. However, the landlord may be able to obtain an increased rent by asking the court to fix an interim rent under s 24A (see **31.4**).

Section 24 continues the tenancy, but does it also continue the liability of the original tenant (or any previous assignees who have given direct covenants) for breaches committed by an assignee during the continuation tenancy? This was the question which arose in *City of London Corporation v Fell* [1993] 49 EG 113 and *Herbert Duncan Ltd v Cluttons* [1992] 1 EGLR 101. In both these cases the original tenant was sued by the landlord for arrears of rent that had accrued during the continuation tenancy due to non-payment by an assignee. The court decided that if the original tenant had covenanted to pay rent during the contractual term only, the landlord was unable to recover from him any rent accruing after that date. However, had the covenant been worded so that the original tenant was liable to pay rent during any statutory extension of the contractual term, the landlord would have been able to recover accordingly. Further, even if the lease had been drafted so that the tenant was bound to pay rent during the statutory continuation, this did not extend to any interim rent ordered by the court. Landlords must bear these points in mind when defining the term of the lease.

If the tenant ceases occupation of the premises on or before the contractual termination date then one of the qualifying conditions for the Act to apply is no longer fulfilled (see **31.1.2**). In these circumstances a fixed-term tenancy will come to an end by effluxion of time and no continuation tenancy will arise (see the new s 27(1A) inserted by art 25 of the 2003 Order, confirming the decision in *Esselte AB v Pearl Assurance plc* [1997] 1 WLR 891; see also *Surrey County Council v Single Horse Properties Ltd* [2002] EWCA Civ 367, [2002] 1 WLR 2106). In this situation the tenant will not incur any further liability for rent (the tenant may also choose to serve a s 27 notice in these circumstances, see **31.2**).

31.2 Termination under the Act

A tenancy protected under the Act will not end automatically at the expiration of a lease for a fixed term nor, if it is a periodic tenancy, can it be ended by an ordinary notice to quit given by the landlord. Instead, such a tenancy can only be terminated in one of the ways prescribed by the Act:

(a) By the service of a landlord's statutory notice (a 's 25 notice').

(b) By the tenant's request in statutory form (a 's 26 request').

(c) Forfeiture (or forfeiture of a superior tenancy).

(d) Surrender. To be valid the surrender must take immediate effect.

(e) By the tenant giving the landlord a notice to quit, unless this was given before the tenant has been in occupation for a period of one month.

(f) Where the lease is for a fixed term, by written notice under s 27 of the Act, served by the tenant upon the landlord at least three months before the contractual expiry date. However, as noted above, the new s 27(1A), confirming the case of *Esselte AB v Pearl Assurance plc* [1997] 1 WLR 891, provides that if a tenant ceases to occupy the premises for business purposes on or before the contractual expiry date, the lease will come to an end by effluxion of time and a s 27 notice is not needed. *Esselte* (and s 27(1A)) must now be read in the light of subsequent cases (*Bacchiocci v Academic Agency Ltd* [1998] 1 WLR 1313 and *Sight and Sound Education Ltd v Books etc Ltd* [1999] 43 EG 61) which have created uncertainty over the period of absence required before it can be established that the tenant has ceased occupation for the purposes of the Act. In light of these cases it may be safer for a tenant to proceed by service of a s 27 notice (see also *Arundel Corporation v The Financial Training Co Ltd* [2000] 3 All ER 456 which, again, emphasises the desirability of a s 27 notice).

It is the first two of the above methods, the s 25 notice and s 26 request, which are the usual methods of terminating a protected business tenancy.

31.2.1 Section 25 notices

31.2.1.1 Form

If such a notice is to be effective, it must be in the prescribed form and be given to the tenant by the competent landlord not less than six months, nor more than 12 months, before the date of termination specified in it. The prescribed forms are contained in the Landlord and Tenant Act 1954, Part II (Notices) (England and Wales) Regulations 2004 (SI 2004/1005), although a form 'substantially to the like effect' can be used instead. Two slightly different forms are prescribed: one for use where the landlord does not oppose the grant of a new tenancy; and one for use where he does. The forms are set out in **Appendix 1**.

A tenant will often seek to attack the validity of his landlord's notice on the ground that it is not in the correct form. The task of the court in these circumstances is to ascertain whether the notice served is substantially the same as the prescribed form. In doing this, any omission from the notice of matters irrelevant to the tenant's rights or obligations may not affect the validity of the notice. However, if the court decides that the notice is not the same as, or substantially to the same effect as, the prescribed form, it is irrelevant that the recipient did not suffer any prejudice: the notice will be invalid (*Sabella Ltd v Montgomery* [1998] 09 EG 153).

In *Smith v Draper* [1990] 2 EGLR 69, it was held that a landlord who had served what turned out to be an invalid notice, could withdraw it and serve a second valid notice.

31.2.1.2   Content

The notice must comply with the following requirements:

(a)   The notice must state the date upon which the landlord wants the tenancy to end. The specified termination date must not be earlier than the date on which the tenancy could have been terminated at common law (and, as mentioned above, the notice must be given not less than six months, nor more than 12 months, before this specified termination date).

For a periodic tenancy or a fixed term with a break clause, the specified termination date cannot be earlier than the date upon which the landlord could have ended the tenancy with an ordinary common law notice. If there is a break clause, it would appear that a separate contractual notice is unnecessary provided the s 25 notice states a date for termination no earlier than the date the break clause would operate (*Scholl Manufacturing Ltd v Clifton (Slim-Line) Ltd* [1967] Ch 41). If the tenancy is for a fixed term without a break clause, the specified termination date cannot be earlier than the last day of the contractual term. If, however, the contractual tenancy has already expired and the tenancy is being continued under the Act, the s 25 notice need only comply with the six–12-month rule mentioned above.

(b)   The notice must state whether or not the landlord will oppose an application to court by the tenant for the grant of a new tenancy and, if so, on which statutory ground(s). The tenant has the right to apply to court for a new tenancy but the landlord can oppose that application on one or more of the seven grounds of opposition set out in s 30 of the Act (see **31.5**). If this is the landlord's intention, he must state in his s 25 notice the ground(s) upon which he intends to rely. As there is no provision in the Act allowing the landlord to amend his notice, the choice of ground(s) is a matter which must be given very careful consideration.

It will not be in every case that the landlord states a ground of opposition. Often the landlord will be quite happy with the tenant's presence and is seeking to end the current tenancy simply with a view to negotiating a new tenancy upon different terms, for example, at an increased rent. In this type of situation the landlord should consult a valuer and obtain expert advice before proceeding further. Where the landlord is not opposing the grant of a new tenancy, the landlord's notice must set out his proposals for the new tenancy, including the property to be comprised in it (ie, all or part of the property contained in the existing tenancy), the rent to be payable and the other terms proposed.

(c)   The notice must relate to the whole of the premises contained in the lease. A s 25 notice cannot relate to part only of the demised premises (*Southport Old Links Ltd v Naylor* [1985] 1 EGLR 66 and see also *M&P Enterprises (London) Ltd v Norfolk Square Hotels Ltd* [1994] 1 EGLR 129).

(d)   The notice must be given and signed by, or on behalf of, the landlord. If there are joint landlords, all their names must be given (*Pearson v Alyo* [1990] 1 EGLR 114).

31.2.2   Section 26 requests

Rather than wait for the landlord to serve a s 25 notice, the tenant can sometimes take the initiative and request a new tenancy from his landlord under s 26 of the Act. However, the tenant must remember that the sooner there is a new tenancy, the sooner the new rent will be payable, which may be higher than the rent payable under the old tenancy. Nevertheless, there are situations where the service of a request by the tenant has tactical advantages for him.

Not all tenants can request a new tenancy. A request cannot be served if the landlord has already served a s 25 notice. Further, a request is only possible where the tenant's current lease was granted for a term of years exceeding one year (or during its continuance under s 24). This will exclude both periodic tenants and those with fixed terms of one year or less; although these tenants still enjoy security of tenure.

31.2.2.1   Form

To be valid, the request must be in the prescribed form as laid down in the Landlord and Tenant Act 1954, Part II (Notices) (England and Wales) Regulations 2004 (SI 2004/1005) and served on the competent landlord. As with the s 25 notice, a form 'substantially to the like effect' can be used instead. The prescribed form is set out in **Appendix 1**.

31.2.2.2   Content

The request must comply with the following requirements:

(a)   It must state the date on which the new tenancy is to begin. The current tenancy will terminate on that date. This date must not be more than 12 months nor less than six months after the making of the request, and cannot be earlier than the date on which the tenancy could have been terminated at common law.

(b)   It must give the tenant's proposals as to:

    (i)   the property to be comprised in the new tenancy, which must be either the whole or part of the property comprised in the current tenancy;

    (ii)   the proposed new rent (this issue requires the advice of a valuer);

    (iii)   the other terms of the tenancy (eg, as to duration).

(c)   The request must be signed by or on behalf of all the tenants.

A landlord who is unwilling to grant a new tenancy must, within two months of receipt of the request, give notice to the tenant that he will oppose any application to court for a new lease stating on which statutory ground(s) of opposition he intends to rely. This is effected by means of a landlord's counter-notice (see **31.2.3**).

As with a s 25 notice, the landlord must choose his ground(s) of opposition with care because he will be confined to those stated in his counter-notice.

If the tenant serves a valid s 26 request and then fails to apply to court for a new tenancy within time (see **31.3**), he will not be allowed to withdraw it and serve a new one with a view to complying with the time limit the second time since the effect of the s 26 request was to fix the date of termination of the tenancy (*Stile Hall Properties Ltd v Gooch* [1979] 3 All ER 848).

31.2.2.3   Reasons for making a request

Usually a tenant is best advised not to make a request because it is not always in a tenant's interest to bring his current tenancy to an end. However, there are some situations in which it might be advisable. For example:

(a)   If the rent payable under the current tenancy is more than that presently achievable in the open market. In a falling market like this the landlord is unlikely to serve a s 25 notice, as it is in his interests to let the existing tenancy continue under the Act.

Therefore, the tenant should give careful consideration to ending the current tenancy and obtaining a new one at a reduced rent.

(b)   If, as is more often the case, the current rent is less than the present market rent, it is in the tenant's interest to prolong the tenancy for as long as possible. In this case the tenant may be able to make what is sometimes called a pre-emptive strike. Say the lease is contractually due to expire on 30 September. In the previous March the landlord is considering serving a s 25 notice with a view to bringing the tenancy to an end on 30 September and negotiating a new tenancy at an increased rent. If the tenant knows or suspects the landlord's plans, he can, before the landlord has acted, serve a request specifying sometime in the following March as the date for the new tenancy. The tenant has thus achieved an extra six months at the old rent.

(c)   If the tenant has plans to improve the premises, he may prefer the certainty of a new fixed term as opposed to the uncertainty of a statutory continuation.

(d)   If the tenant has plans to sell the lease, a buyer would prefer the security of a new fixed term rather than the uncertainty of a statutory continuation.

31.2.3   Counter-notices

31.2.3.1   The tenant's counter-notice

Under the procedure applicable prior to 1 June 2004 both landlord and tenant had to serve a counter-notice following receipt of a s 26 request or a s 25 notice respectively. However, the requirement for a tenant to serve a counter-notice on receipt of a s 25 notice has now been abolished. The requirement for a landlord to serve a counter-notice remains, however.

31.2.3.2   The landlord's counter-notice

The service of a s 26 request by the tenant will require a counter-notice by the landlord if he wishes to oppose the tenant's application to court for a new tenancy. This must state any ground(s) of opposition that the landlord intends to rely on to oppose the tenant's application (see **31.5**). If the landlord fails to serve a counter-notice within two months of receipt of the tenant's request, he will lose his right to raise any ground of opposition to the tenant's application to court for a new tenancy although he will be allowed to raise issues relating to the terms of the new tenancy.

A landlord who has served a counter-notice stating that he will not oppose the tenant's application for a new tenancy will be bound by that decision. Similarly, the landlord cannot later amend his stated grounds of opposition.

There is no prescribed form of counter-notice but it should be unequivocal and in writing.

31.2.4   Service of notices and requests

Notices and requests given under the Act require service. Section 23(1) of the LTA 1927 provides for personal service or by leaving the notice at the last known place of abode (which includes the place of business of the person to be served; *Price v West London Investment Building Society* [1964] 2 All ER 318), or by sending it through the post by registered or (as now applies) recorded delivery. Service on a company may be effected at its registered office (s 1139 of the Companies Act 2006). The effect of complying with one of the methods of service laid down in the LTA 1927 is that there is a presumption of service so that it does not matter that the recorded delivery letter may not have been received by the intended recipient because it went astray in the post. Other methods of service may be effective (eg, the ordinary post) if in fact the notice is received by the person to whom it has been given. But the risk is that the letter may be lost in the post, in which case, notice will not have been given. The question also arises as to the date on which the notice is treated as having been served. In *Railtrack plc v Gojra* [1998] 08 EG 158, it was held that if the registered or recorded delivery method is used (both being methods laid down in the LTA 1927), the notice (or request) is served on the date on which it is posted. This decision was confirmed by the Court of Appeal in *CA Webber Transport Ltd v Railtrack plc* [2004] 1 WLR 320. When, however, notice is sent through the ordinary post, it is served on the date it would have been delivered in the ordinary course of post.

31.3 The application to court

31.3.1 The need for an application

It will become apparent after service of a s 25 notice or counter-notice to a s 26 request, whether or not the landlord is willing to grant a new tenancy. Where a s 25 notice has been served, the contents will have told the tenant whether or not the landlord intends to oppose his application. If the tenant initiated the termination procedure with a s 26 request, the landlord will have responded with a counter-notice if he is not prepared to grant a new tenancy.

The 2003 Order makes provision for either the landlord or the tenant to apply to the court (although, of course, one cannot make an application if the other has already done so). It will usually be the tenant who will apply to the court. Even if the landlord has stated that he is prepared to grant a new tenancy, the tenant will lose his entitlement unless an application is made to the court within the prescribed time limits (see **31.3.2**), or the parties have entered into a legally binding contract for a new lease. Where the landlord is opposing the grant, there is obviously little possibility of such an agreement and so an application must be made.

The landlord will normally only apply to the court where he is opposing the grant and wants an order determining the tenancy on one of the s 30 grounds to be made as quickly as possible. He could wait for the tenant to apply for a new tenancy, but making his own application would mean the matter could be brought before the court as soon as possible. A tenant who fears he will lose in court may delay making his own application for as long as possible in order to gain an extra few weeks or months in the premises. The landlord can only make such application if he has served a s 25 notice opposing renewal or served a counter-notice to a tenant's s 26 notice to that effect.

Where a landlord is not opposing the grant, he can again apply to the court for the grant of that new lease, again in order to have the matter determined as soon as possible. Otherwise, a tenant may delay his own application for as long as possible in order to enjoy the benefit of the more favourable terms of the old lease for as long as possible.

Unless the parties have already entered into a binding lease, the tenant must always apply to court at the appropriate time otherwise he will lose the right to a new tenancy.

31.3.2 The application

Applications may be commenced in either the High Court or, as is more usual, in the county court.

The application must be made within the 'statutory period'. This is defined in s 29A(2) to mean a period ending, where the landlord served a s 25 notice, on the date specified in his notice; and, where the tenant made a s 26 request, a period ending immediately before the date specified in his request.

However, where the tenant has made a s 26 request, the court cannot entertain an application which is made before the end of the period of two months beginning with the date of the making of the request, unless the application is made after the landlord has served his counter-notice.

31.3.3 Agreements extending time limits

By s 29B the parties can by written agreement extend the time limit for applications and they may do so any number of times. The only provisos are that the first agreement to extend must be made prior to the end of the statutory period and any subsequent agreement must be made before the expiry of the period of extension agreed in the previous agreement.

Following the tenant's application to court it is advisable to protect the application by registration of a pending land action under the Land Charges Act 1972. This will make the tenant's application binding on a buyer of the reversion. Where the landlord's title is registered, the application may be an overriding interest under the Land Registration Act 2002, Sch 3, but it would nevertheless be prudent to register a unilateral notice against the reversionary title.

31.4 Interim rents

31.4.1 The need for an interim rent

Where the tenant validly applied to court for a new tenancy, his current tenancy did not terminate on the date specified in the s 25 notice or s 26 request. Instead, s 64 of the Act provided that the current tenancy would be continued at the old contractual rent until three months after the proceedings were concluded. As the Act was originally drafted there was thus an incentive for tenants to delay proceedings as much as possible, because the longer the current tenancy lasted the longer the old rent (which was usually below current market rents) remained payable. This was unfair to landlords particularly in those cases where, due to the effects of inflation, there was a substantial difference between the old contractual rent and the rent achievable in the open market. As a result of this unfairness, s 24A was inserted into the Act by the Law of Property Act 1969. This gave the court a discretion, on the application of the competent landlord, to determine an 'interim rent' to be substituted for the old contractual rent until such time as the current tenancy ceased.

These provisions have now been entirely replaced by a new s 29A inserted by art 18 of the 2003 Order. The interim rent will be payable from the earliest date for the termination of the existing tenancy that could have been specified in the s 25 notice or s 26 request that was served to bring the tenancy to an end. So a tenant who serves a s 26 request but states a commencement date for the new tenancy 12 months after service when the contractual termination date is only six months away (and so he could have served six months' notice) will find that the interim rent will be payable from that earlier date. Either landlord or tenant can apply for an interim rent. Normally, it will be the landlord who will apply as the interim rent is likely to be higher than the existing rent which may have been fixed several years previously. However, in times on falling property values, it might be advantageous for the tenant to apply if the current market rent will be below that being paid under the lease.

31.4.2 Amount

The interim rent will normally be the same as the rent payable under the new tenancy, ie, an open market rent assessed as set out at **31.7.3**. However, this will not be the case where there is a significant movement in the market (upwards or downwards) in the intervening period or where the terms of the new tenancy are so different from the terms of the old one to make a substantial difference in the rent. (Bear in mind here that normally the new lease will be on very similar terms to the old lease; see **31.7.4**.) Nor will this be the case where the landlord opposes the grant of a new tenancy. In both cases, the following provisions apply:

(a)   Section 24A requires the court to assess the interim rent on the basis of a yearly tenancy, while the rent payable under the new lease is usually assessed on the basis of a term of years. And market rents under yearly tenancies are usually less than under fixed terms, since the latter guarantee tenants a more substantial period of occupation.

(b)   The court is obliged to have regard to the rent payable under the current tenancy. This is so that the court can exercise a discretion to 'cushion' the tenant from too harsh a blow in moving from the old out-of-date contractual rent to the new rent (see *English Exporters (London) Ltd v Eldonwall Ltd* [1973] Ch 415). However, a 'cushion' does not have to be provided in every case. The court has a discretion which it may use to specify the full market rent, especially in those cases where the tenant has already benefited from a low contractual rent for a long time (see, eg, *Department of the Environment v Allied Freehold Property Trust Ltd* [1992] 45 EG 156).

31.4.3   Avoiding s 24A

While the introduction of interim rents has been a step in the right direction for landlords, many still feel that the application of the 'cushion' can produce unfairness. Accordingly, the landlord may wish to avoid s 24A altogether by including a penultimate day rent review in the lease. This would revise the contractual rent just before the contractual term expired. In such a case the harshness of changing from the old rent to the new rent would be suffered during the contractual term without the imposition of any 'cushion'. Tenants, on the other hand, will wish to resist such a clause.

Another way of avoiding s 24A would be for the landlord, at the lease-drafting stage, to make it clear that the contractual rent review provisions are to continue to apply notwithstanding the ending of the contractual term. Careful drafting would be required to achieve this but the case of *Willison v Cheverell Estates Ltd* [1996] 26 EG 133 indicates that this is another possibility for the landlord.

31.5   Grounds of opposition

When the landlord serves his s 25 notice or counter-notice in response to the tenant's s 26 request, he must, if he is intending to oppose the grant of a new tenancy, set out one or more of the seven grounds of opposition in s 30 of the Act. The landlord can rely only on the stated ground(s); no later amendment is allowed.

If the landlord has stated a ground of opposition and the tenant's application proceeds to a hearing, a 'split trial' will usually be ordered with the question of opposition being dealt with first as a preliminary issue. Only if the ground is not made out will the terms of the new tenancy be dealt with.

The statutory grounds of opposition are all contained in s 30(1) of the Act and, as will be seen, some of the grounds ((a), (b), (c) and (e)), confer a discretion on the court whether or not to order a new tenancy even if the ground is made out.

31.5.1   Ground (a): tenant's failure to repair

The landlord can oppose the tenant's application for a new tenancy on the ground of the tenant's failure to repair the holding. To succeed, the landlord will have to show that the tenant was under an obligation to repair or maintain the holding and that the tenant is in breach of that obligation. Problems can arise where the repairing obligation is divided between the landlord and tenant, for example, where the landlord is responsible for the exterior and the tenant for the interior of the premises. In such cases, an inspection will be necessary to determine the party in breach. The ground only applies to failure to repair the holding, and not to the disrepair of another part of the demised premises not forming part of the tenant's holding (eg, where the tenant has sub-let part and it is that part which is in disrepair).

This is one of the discretionary grounds and the landlord is only likely to succeed if the tenant's breaches are both serious and unremedied at the date of the hearing.

As an alternative, the landlord may be able to commence forfeiture proceedings to terminate the tenancy; this being one of the permitted methods of termination under the Act. This remedy may be available throughout the term and while the tenant may apply for relief, this will usually only be granted if the tenant rectifies the breach.

31.5.2   Ground (b): persistent delay in paying rent

The requirement of 'persistent delay' suggests that the tenant must have fallen into arrears on more than one occasion. However, the rent need not be substantially in arrears nor need the arrears last a long time. Indeed, there need not be any arrears at the date of the hearing; the court will look at the whole history of payment (see *Hazel v Akhtar* [2002] EWCA Civ 1883, [2002] 07 EG 124). Again, this is one of the discretionary grounds and the court is entitled to take into account the likelihood of future arrears arising should a new tenancy be ordered. The tenant should, therefore, consider offering to provide a surety for any new lease ordered.

31.5.3   Ground (c): substantial breaches of other obligations

Discretionary ground (c) requires other substantial breaches by the tenant of his obligations in the lease, or some other reason connected with the tenant's use or management of the holding. Any breach of an obligation may be relied upon by the landlord (eg, breach of the user covenant) but the breach must be substantial and this will be a question of fact and degree. The ground also extends to reasons connected with the tenant's use or management of the holding and this has been held to include carrying on a use in breach of planning control.

31.5.4   Ground (d): alternative accommodation

The landlord must have offered and be willing to provide or secure alternative accommodation for the tenant. The accommodation must be offered on reasonable terms having regard to the terms of the current tenancy and all other relevant circumstances. Further, the accommodation must be suitable for the tenant's requirements, (including the requirement to preserve goodwill) bearing in mind the nature and type of his business and the location and size of his existing premises. It seems that offering the tenant part only of his existing premises may qualify as alternative accommodation.

This ground, unlike the three previously mentioned, is not discretionary. If the landlord proves the requirements of the ground, the court must refuse the tenant's application.

31.5.5   Ground (e): current tenancy created by sub-letting of part only of property in a superior tenancy

Ground (e) is the least used ground because the necessary requirements are seldom fulfilled. It only applies where the current tenancy was created by a sub-letting of part of the property in a superior tenancy, and the sub-tenant's competent landlord is the landlord under the superior tenancy. The competent landlord will succeed if he can show that the combined rents from the sub-divided parts of a building are substantially less than the rent to be obtained on a single letting of the whole building, and that he requires possession to let or dispose of the whole.

This is the last of the discretionary grounds.

31.5.6   Ground (f): demolition or reconstruction

Ground (f) is the most frequently used ground. The landlord must show that on termination of the tenancy:

(a)   he has a firm intention;

(b)   to demolish or reconstruct the premises in the holding (or a substantial part of them), or to carry out substantial work of construction on the holding (or part of it); and

(c)   that he could not reasonably do so without obtaining possession of the holding.

Each of these elements is considered in turn.

31.5.6.1   The landlord's intention

The landlord must prove a firm and settled intention to carry out relevant work. It has been said that the project must have 'moved out of the zone of contemplation ... into the valley of decision' (per Asquith LJ in *Cunliffe v Goodman* [1950] 2 KB 237, approved in *Betty's Cafes Ltd v Phillips Furnishing Stores Ltd* [1959] AC 20). Not only must the landlord have made a genuine decision to carry out relevant work, he must also show that it is practicable for him to carry out his intention. This will be a question of fact in each case but the landlord's position will be strengthened if he has:

(a)   obtained (or shown a reasonable prospect of obtaining) planning permission and building regulation approval (if necessary);

(b)   instructed professional advisers;

(c)   prepared the necessary drawings and contracts;

(d)   obtained quotations and secured finance; and

(e)   obtained the consent of any superior landlord (if necessary).

Where the landlord is a company, intention is normally evidenced by a resolution of the board of directors. Similarly, local authority landlords should pass an appropriate resolution and have it recorded in their minutes.

The landlord's intention must be established at the date of the hearing (*Betty's Cafes Ltd v Phillips Furnishing Stores Ltd*, above). It is thus irrelevant that the s 25 notice (or s 26 counter-notice) was served by the landlord's predecessor who did not have the necessary intention. See also *Zarvos v Pradhan* [2003] 2 P & CR 9 where a landlord failed at the hearing because the judge was not satisfied that it would be able to finance the project. The landlord appealed and by the time of the appeal has received assurances from its bank that finance would be available. The Court of Appeal refused to allow the landlord to adduce this evidence at the appeal as this would be unfair to the tenant.

If the court is not satisfied that the landlord's intention is sufficiently firm and settled at the date of the hearing, a new tenancy will be ordered. In such cases, however, the court, in settling the terms of the new tenancy, may take into account the landlord's future intentions, and limit the duration of the new tenancy so as not to impede development later when the landlord is able to fully establish intention and the ability to carry it out (see **31.7.2**).

31.5.6.2   The nature of the works

The landlord must prove an intention to do one of six things:

(a)   Demolish the premises comprised in the holding (see *Coppin v Bruce-Smith* [1998] EGCS 45).

(b)   Reconstruct the premises comprised in the holding. For the works to qualify as works of reconstruction it has been held that they must entail rebuilding and involve a substantial interference with the structure of the building but need not necessarily be confined to the outside or loadbearing walls (*Romulus Trading Co Ltd v Henry Smith's Charity Trustees* [1990] 2 EGLR 75).

(c)   Demolish a substantial part of the premises comprised in the holding.

(d)   Reconstruct a substantial part of the premises comprised in the holding.

(e)   Carry out substantial work of construction on the holding. It has been held that such works must directly affect the structure of the building and must go beyond what could be more properly classified as works of refurbishment or improvement (*Barth v Pritchard* [1990] 1 EGLR 109).

(f)   Carry out substantial work of construction on part of the holding.

31.5.6.3   The need to obtain possession

The landlord must show that he could not reasonably execute the relevant work without obtaining possession of the holding. This means the landlord must show that he needs 'legal' (not just 'physical') possession of the holding. He has to show that it is necessary to put an end to the tenant's interest, and this may not always be the case. Accordingly, if the lease contains a right of entry for the landlord which is sufficiently wide to enable him to carry out the relevant work, his ground of opposition will fail. In such a situation, the tenant will be able to argue that the work can be carried out under the terms of the lease and there is thus no need to end it.

Even if the lease does not include a right of entry, the landlord may still fail in his opposition if the tenant is able to rely on s 31A of the Act. This provides that the court shall not find ground (f) to be established if the tenant will either:

(a)   agree to a new lease which includes access and other rights for the landlord, which enable the landlord to reasonably carry out the relevant work without obtaining possession and without substantially interfering with the use of the holding for the tenant's business; or

(b)   accept a new lease of an economically separable part of the holding with, if necessary, access rights for the landlord.

31.5.7   Ground (g): landlord's intention to occupy the holding

Ground (g) is another frequently used ground. The landlord must prove that on the termination of the current tenancy he intends to occupy the holding for the purposes, or partly for the purposes, of a business to be carried on by him, or as his residence. There are a number of elements to this ground which will be considered in turn.

31.5.7.1   The landlord's intention

As with ground (f), the landlord's intention must be firm and settled, and many of the matters discussed at **31.5.6** will be equally relevant here. Therefore, not only must the landlord be able to show a genuine intention to occupy the holding, he must also show that he has a reasonable prospect of being able to do so. It is, therefore, necessary for the court to take into account, for example, whether planning permission would be required to use the premises for the landlord's business and, if so, whether it would be likely to be granted. In some cases, the court has accepted as evidence of intention to occupy, an undertaking to do so given by the landlord. Such an undertaking is not conclusive but it is a relevant consideration when the court is determining the issue (see, eg, *London Hilton Jewellers Ltd v Hilton International Hotels Ltd* [1990] 1 EGLR 112). As with ground (f), the landlord's intention must be shown to exist at the date of the hearing.

The court will not assess the viability of the landlord's proposed business venture provided his intention to occupy is genuine. Thus, the court has held the ground to be established even where they thought the landlord's business plans to be ill thought out and likely to fail; his intention was nevertheless genuine. See, for example, *Dolgellau Golf Club v Hett* [1998] 2 EGLR 75, CA, but also the contrasting case of *Zarvos v Pradhan* [2003] EWCA Civ 208, where possession was refused as the landlord could not establish a reasonable prospect of being able to raise finance.

31.5.7.2   The purpose of occupation

Occupation must be for the purpose of the landlord's business or as his residence. The landlord need not intend to occupy all the holding immediately, provided that within a reasonable time of termination he intends to occupy a substantial part of the holding for one of these purposes.

The wording of this ground refers to a business to be carried on by the landlord. However, the landlord need not physically occupy the premises and it will be sufficient if occupation is through a manager or agent provided that the arrangement is genuine. Further, the ground is still available where the landlord intends to carry on the business in partnership with others. Where the landlord has a controlling interest in a company, any business to be carried on by the company, is treated as a business carried on by the landlord. The landlord has a controlling interest for this purpose, either if he beneficially holds more than half of the company's equity share capital, or if he is a member and able, without consent, to appoint or remove at least half of the directors (s 30(3)). Where the landlord is a company in a group of companies, it may rely on ground (g) where another member of the group is to occupy the premises (s 42). If the landlord is a trustee, he may be able to rely on an intention to occupy by a beneficiary (s 41).

31.5.7.3   The five-year rule

The most important limitation on the availability of this ground of opposition is the 'five-year rule' in s 30(2) of the Act. A landlord cannot rely on ground (g) if his interest was purchased or created within five years before the end of the current tenancy, ie, the termination date specified in the s 25 notice or s 26 request. However, the restriction only applies if, throughout those five years, the premises have been subject to a tenancy or series of tenancies within the protection of the Act.

The idea behind the provision is to stop a landlord buying a reversion within five years of the end of the lease, and then using this ground to obtain possession for himself at the end of the term. Thus, a landlord will not be able to rely on this ground if he purchased the premises subject to the tenancy within the last five years. However, the restriction does not apply where a landlord buys premises with vacant possession, grants a lease, and then seeks to end the lease within five years relying on this ground.

The wording of the provision refers to the landlord's interest being 'purchased' and this is used in its popular sense of buying for money (*Bolton (HL) Engineering Co Ltd v Graham & Sons Ltd* [1957] 1 QB 159). Thus, it will not cover a freeholder who has accepted the surrender of a head-lease without payment, and then seeks to use this ground against the sub-tenant.

Finally, a landlord who is unable to rely on ground (g) because of this restriction, may be able to rely on ground (f) if he intends to demolish or reconstruct the premises. This remains so even if the landlord then intends to use the reconstructed premises for his own occupation.

31.6   Compensation for failure to obtain a new tenancy

On termination, a tenant may be entitled to compensation for any improvements he has made. Additionally, if the tenant is forced to leave the premises he may lose the goodwill which he has built up and he will be faced with all the costs of relocation. This is particularly unfair to those tenants who are forced to leave the premises through no fault of their own, ie, if the landlord establishes one of the grounds of opposition (e), (f) or (g). In certain circumstances, therefore, the tenant may be entitled to compensation for failing to obtain a new tenancy where the landlord establishes one of these 'no fault' grounds.

31.6.1   Availability

Compensation is only available on quitting the premises in one of the following situations:

(a)   Where the landlord serves a s 25 notice or counter-notice to a s 26 request stating one or more of the grounds of opposition (e), (f) or (g) but no others, and the tenant either:

   (i)   does not apply to court for a new tenancy or does so but withdraws his application; or

   (ii)   does apply to court for a new tenancy, but his application is refused because the landlord is able to establish his stated ground.

(b)   Where the landlord serves a s 25 notice or counter-notice to a s 26 request specifying one or more of the grounds (e), (f) or (g) and others; the tenant applies to court for a new tenancy but the court refuses to grant a new tenancy solely on one or more of the grounds (e), (f) or (g). Here the tenant must apply to court for a new tenancy and ask the court to certify that a new tenancy was not ordered solely because one of these three 'no fault' grounds has been made out.

31.6.2   Amount

The amount of compensation is the rateable value of the holding multiplied by the 'appropriate multiplier' which is a figure prescribed from time to time by the Secretary of State, and is currently 1. In some cases, the tenant will be entitled to double compensation.

31.6.3   Double compensation

Sometimes the appropriate multiplier is doubled. This happens when the tenant or his predecessors in the same business have been in occupation for at least 14 years prior to the termination of the current tenancy. These provisions are summarised in the illustration below.

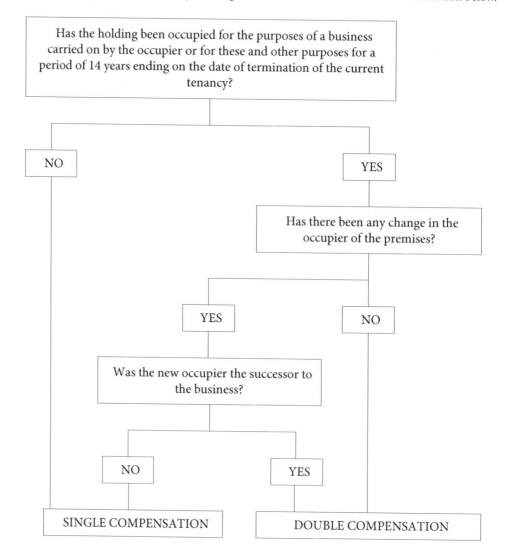

31.6.4   Contracting out

In some situations the tenant's right to compensation can be excluded by agreement between the parties. This agreement is often in the lease itself. However, s 38(2) of the Act provides that where the tenant or his predecessors in the same business have been in occupation for five years or more prior to the date of quitting, any agreement to exclude or reduce the tenant's right to compensation is void.

31.7   The renewal lease

If the tenant follows all the correct procedures and properly applies to court for a new tenancy, the court will make an order for a new lease in two situations:

(a)   if the landlord fails to make out his s 30 ground of opposition; or

(b)   if the landlord did not oppose the tenant's application for a new tenancy.

The terms of this new lease are usually settled by agreement between the parties and it is only in default of such agreement that the court will be called upon to decide the terms. In either event, any new lease will also enjoy the protection of the Act.

The court has jurisdiction over the premises, duration, rent and the other terms.

31.7.1   The premises

The tenant is entitled to a new tenancy of the holding only as at the date of the order. This term was defined in **31.1.4.4**, and excludes any part of the premises which have been sub-let. However, the landlord (but not the tenant), has the right to insist that any new tenancy to be granted shall be a new tenancy of the whole of the demised premises including those parts sub-let.

The court may grant a new lease of less than the holding under s 31A, where the landlord establishes ground (f), the redevelopment ground, but the tenant takes a new lease of an 'economically separable part' of the holding (see **31.5.6**).

The new lease may also include appurtenant rights enjoyed by the tenant under the current tenancy.

31.7.2   The duration

The length of any new lease ordered by the court will be such as is reasonable in all the circumstances but cannot exceed 15 years (often it is much less than this). In deciding this issue the court has a very wide discretion and will take into account matters such as:

(a)   the length of the current tenancy;

(b)   the length requested by the tenant;

(c)   the hardship caused to either party;

(d)   current open market practice;

(e)   the landlord's future proposals.

It may be that the landlord was unable to rely on ground (f) because he could not prove that his intention to demolish or reconstruct was sufficiently firm and settled at the date of the hearing (see **31.5.6**). If, however, the court is satisfied that he will be able to do so in the near future, it may order a short tenancy so as not to impede development later. Similarly, if the premises are shown to be ripe for development, the new lease may be granted subject to a break clause (*National Car Parks Ltd v The Paternoster Consortium Ltd* [1990] 15 EG 53). In the same way, where the landlord has narrowly missed being able to rely on ground (g) because of the five-year rule, the court may be prepared to grant a short tenancy.

31.7.3   The rent

The amount of rent to be paid is the greatest source of disagreement between the parties and specialist valuation advice will be essential. If the question of rent comes before the courts, they will assess an open market rent having regard to the other terms of the tenancy. However, in assessing the rent the court is obliged to disregard certain factors which may otherwise work to the detriment of the tenant, ie:

(a)   Any effect on rent of the fact that the tenant or his predecessors have been in occupation. The classic landlord's argument would be that the tenant, being a sitting tenant, would pay more in the open market for these premises simply to avoid relocation. This would inflate an open market rent and is thus to be disregarded.

(b)   Any goodwill attached to the holding due to the carrying on of the tenant's business. The tenant should not have to pay a rent assessed partly on the basis of goodwill he generated.

(c)   Any effect on the rent of improvements voluntarily made by the tenant (certain conditions must also be satisfied).

(d)   Where the holding comprises licensed premises, any addition in value due to the tenant's licence.

Where the premises are in disrepair due to the tenant's failure to perform his repairing obligation, conflicting views have been expressed on whether the court should disregard this in setting the rent of the new tenancy. One view is that the premises should be valued in their actual condition. This will probably produce a lower rent but the landlord may be able to sue the tenant for breach of his repairing obligation.

The other view is that the premises should be valued on the basis that the tenant has complied with his obligation, thus preventing the tenant benefiting from his own breach. This view is supported by cases such as *Crown Estate Commissioners v Town Investments Ltd* [1992] 08 EG 111.

In *Fawke v Viscount Chelsea* [1980] QB 441, the premises were in disrepair because the landlord was in breach of his repairing obligation. The court decided that the premises should be valued in their actual condition and, therefore, fixed a new rent which was below open market value but which increased once the landlord had complied with his obligation.

Under s 34(3), the court has power to insert a rent review clause in the new lease whether or not the previous lease contained such a provision. The frequency and type of review is at the discretion of the court which may be persuaded by the tenant to make provision for downward revisions as well as upward (see *Forbuoys plc v Newport Borough Council* [1994] 24 EG 156).

As to the effect of the LT(C)A 1995, see **31.7.4**.

Finally, the court does have power to require the tenant to provide guarantors.

31.7.4   Other terms

It will only fall to the court to decide other terms in the absence of agreement between the parties. In fixing the other terms the court must have regard to the terms of the current tenancy and all other relevant circumstances. For that reason, the terms will be much the same as before. The leading case in this area is *O'May v City of London Real Property Co Ltd* [1983] AC 726 which held that if one of the parties seeks a change in the terms, it is for that party to justify the change. Further, the change must be fair and reasonable and 'take into account, amongst other things, the comparatively weak negotiating position of a sitting tenant requiring renewal, particularly in conditions of scarcity' (per Lord Hailsham in *O'May*). Therefore, the tenant should be on his guard against any attempt by the landlord to introduce more onerous obligations into the new lease (eg, a more restrictive user covenant). In the *O'May* case the landlord was, in effect, trying to transfer the responsibility for the repair and maintenance of office premises to the tenant. This would have increased the value of the reversion by more than £1 million but the House of Lords held that the landlord was not entitled to do this. Notwithstanding the effect of the *O'May* case, variations may be made in the renewal lease to reflect the changes introduced by the LT(C)A 1995. The renewal lease will, of course, be subject to the provisions of that Act. This will often mean that under the current lease (granted before 1 January 1996) the original tenant was liable for the entire duration of the term through privity of contract; whereas for the renewal lease, privity of contract will not apply. This change is one of the circumstances to which the court must have regard in fixing the rent and other terms of the new lease. For example, the landlord may wish to alter the terms of the alienation covenant to balance the effect of the loss of privity of contract (see *Wallis Fashion Group Ltd v General Accident Life Assurance Ltd* [2000] EGCS 45; and **18.2.5**).

31.8 The order for the new lease

Any new lease ordered by the court will not commence until three months after the proceedings are 'finally disposed of'. This is when the time for appeal has elapsed, and for appeals to the Court of Appeal the time limit is four weeks from the date of the order. The tenant continues to occupy under his old tenancy during this period. Either party may appeal.

If the court makes an order for a new tenancy upon terms which the tenant finds unacceptable (eg, as to rent), the tenant may apply for revocation of the order within 14 days. In such a case, the existing tenancy will continue for such period as the parties agree or the court determines as necessary to enable the landlord to re-let the premises.

Part II Summary – Commercial Leases

Topic	Summary	Reference
Landlord and tenant law	Commercial property requires knowledge of landlord and tenant law. Successors to the original landlord and tenant will normally be liable on and able to enforce covenants in the lease. In 'old' leases (granted pre-1 January 1996) the original tenant will remain liable even after disposing of the lease. In new leases, the original tenant's liability will cease on assignment, although he may be required to enter into an authorised guarantee agreement to guarantee the performance of his immediate successor.	Chapter 9
Taxation of commercial leases	VAT may be chargeable. The sale of a new commercial building is standard rated; other commercial transactions are exempt but subject to an option to tax. Stamp duty land tax is chargeable both on any premium paid and also on the rent. It is charged on the net present value of the rent payable over the term of the lease.	Chapter 10
Lease drafting	Leases should be drafted in precise clear English. If the lease will lead to registration at Land Registry, prescribed clauses should appear at the beginning of the lease. Landlords and tenants should abide by the recommendations of the 2007 Code for Leasing Business Premises.	Chapter 11
The parties to the lease	The parties will always include the landlord and the tenant. Sometimes a guarantor (or surety) may be required to join in to guarantee the performance of the tenant's obligations, eg as to the payment of rent. Successors to the original landlord and tenant will normally be liable on and able to enforce covenants in the lease. In 'old' leases (granted pre-1 January 1996) the original tenant will remain liable even after disposing of the lease. In new leases, the original tenant's liability will cease on assignment, although he may be required to enter into an authorised guarantee agreement to guarantee the performance of his immediate successor. Sometimes the tenant may be required to deposit a sum with the landlord as security for future rental payments.	Chapter 12

Topic	Summary	Reference
The parcels clause	The property let should be clearly defined – particularly if the tenant is being obliged to repair the demised premises. Care should be taken as to whether roof and airspace above and the sub-soil beneath are to be included. The tenant should also ensure that all necessary easements, eg for access and the provision of services, are included.	Chapter 13
Term	This will be the subject of negotiation between the parties. Shorter leases are now more common then previously. Sometimes, a break clause is inserted into the lease. This allows the party with the benefit of the clause to terminate the lease prematurely, as long as the conditions laid down in the clause are complied with. In the *Mannai* case the House of Lords held that strict compliance with the notice provisions in relation to a break clause was not necessary, provided that a reasonable recipient would understand what was intended. A landlord's break clause may not be effective due to the impact of the security of tenure legislation. The 2007 Code for Leasing Business Premises recommends that landlords should offer tenants a choice of term.	Chapter 14
Rent	The amount of the rent will be settled by the parties' valuers. The lease will state the payment intervals (often quarterly) and whether it is payable in advance (usual) or arrears. Any insurance premiums and service charges payable to the landlord are also normally reserved as rent. This is because the remedies for non-payment of rent are more favourable than for breach of other covenants. Interest is normally made payable on any late payments. There should also be a provision requiring the payment of rent to be suspended should the premises be so badly damaged or destroyed so as to be incapable of use, in full or in part. The lease should also make clear whether the rent is inclusive or exclusive of VAT.	Chapter 15

Topic	Summary	Reference
Rent review	In a lease of more than two or three years in length, provision must be made for the rent to be reviewed so as to take account of inflation and changing property values. This is normally accomplished by requiring a valuer to assess the rent as if there was to be the grant of a new lease of the premises as at the date of the review. The lease will require the valuer to make various assumptions (for the benefit of the landlord) and to disregard various matters (for the benefit of the tenant) when assessing the rent for this hypothetical lease. There will be ancillary provisions relating to the commencement of the review process – normally either party should be able to initiate it – and for the payment of the old rent until the new rent is fixed. The 2007 Code for Leasing Business Premises recommends that landlords should offer alternatives to upward-only rent reviews.	Chapter 16
Repairing covenants	The lease should state clearly who is responsible – there are no implied obligations. Usually the landlord will want the tenant to be responsible for the cost of repair. In a lease of the whole of a building, the tenant will covenant to repair, decorate etc. In a lease of part, eg a unit in a shopping centre, the landlord will normally accept the responsibility for repair etc, but will require each of the tenants to contribute to the cost of this through a service charge.	Chapter 17
Alienation	The tenant will want to be allowed to assign and/or sublet/ and or part with the possession of the property in order to give sufficient flexibility should he not wish to remain in the premises for the full term. The landlord will, however, want control over who is in occupation of his premises – and who is liable to perform the covenants. Often assignment will be permitted subject to the landlord's consent being obtained, such consent not to be unreasonably withheld. Other forms of alienation will often be completely prohibited, particularly sub-letting of part.	Chapter 18

Topic	Summary	Reference
User covenants	The landlord will wish to control the use to which the tenant can let out the premises in order to prevent any 'bad' uses affecting the value of the premises or adjoining property. The tenant will not only need to ensure that any possible use to which he might want to put the premises is permitted, but will also be concerned as to the impact any restrictive user covenant will have on his ability to assign the lease. Note that the user covenant will impact on the rent. A wide permitted use will result in a higher rent; a very narrow use will result in a lower rent, as the property will be less attractive to potential tenants. The use of the premises may also be constrained by the need for planning permission.	Chapter 19
Alterations	The tenant will want some flexibility to allow him to alter the premises should this be required for his business purposes. The landlord will, however, want to ensure that no damage is caused to the structure of the building or which will inhibit the re-letting of the property after the end of the lease. The 2007 Code for Leasing Business Premises recommends that non-structural alterations should be permitted without the need to obtain the landlord's consent. The need for planning consent and to comply with building regulations will also impose restraints on the tenant's ability to undertake alterations. In some circumstances, tenants will be able to obtain compensation for alterations which amount to improvements at the end of the lease.	Chapter 20
Landlord's covenant for quiet enjoyment	The landlord promises that the tenant's occupation of the premises will not be interrupted by actions of the landlord or of those claiming title through him.	Chapter 21

Topic	Summary	Reference
Insurance	It is essential from both the landlord's and the tenant's points of view to ensure that the property is insured. This will usually be at the tenant's expense, although the landlord may prefer to effect the insurance himself. The tenant in particular needs to read the insurance provisions in the light of his repairing obligations and ensure that the property will be insured against all necessary risks. The tenant may well be obliged under his repairing obligations to make good any damage caused other than by an insured risk as defined in the lease. The rent suspension clause is also normally only going to come into effect if damage is caused by an insured risk.	Chapter 22
Proviso for re-entry	Such a 'forfeiture' clause included in the lease allows a landlord to terminate the lease during the fixed term in the case of a breach of the terms of the lease. In the case of non-payment of rent, the lease will normally provide that no formal demand is required. In the case of other breaches of covenant, the landlord must normally serve a notice under s 146 of the LPA 1925 requiring the breach to be remedied, if it is capable of being remedied. Only if the breach is not remedied can forfeiture then take place. There is a special procedure for breaches of repairing covenants. The landlord can either obtain a court order for possession, or re-enter peaceably. Even after possession has been obtained, a tenant can in certain circumstances apply to the court for 'relief' from forfeiture, ie for the lease to be restored to him.	Chapter 23
Leases of part	The boundaries of the property to be let and the grant and reservation of all necessary easements will need careful consideration. The responsibility for repairs etc and insurance will probably fall on the landlord, but with the costs passed to the tenants by means of a service charge.	Chapter 24
Underleases	Although at common law a sub-tenant is not liable to the head landlord for breaches of terms of the head lease, he is normally made to accept such liability as a condition of the grant of the sub-lease. The head lease will often restrict the granting of sub-leases and the terms on which they can be granted.	Chapter 25
Agreements for lease	These are typically used when the premises are in the course of construction. The tenant will need to consider whether there will be any liability on the landlord for delay in completion and also ensure that the tenant is not going to be liable under the repairing covenant for repairs caused by defects in the construction.	Chapter 26

Topic	Summary	Reference
Selling the lease	The landlord's consent to the assignment will usually be required. The LTA 1927 implies that such consent cannot be unreasonably withheld, and the LTA 1988 that it cannot be unreasonably delayed.	Chapter 27
Remedies for breach of covenant	Normal contractual remedies will be available for both parties, ie damages and injunctions/specific performance. When proceeding to enforce a 'fixed charge' against a former tenant or his guarantor, a landlord must give notice under the Landlord and Tenant (Covenants) Act 1995 within six months of the money becoming due. Distress may also be available to a landlord against a tenant for non-payment of rent. The availability of forfeiture should also be considered.	Chapter 28
The effect of insolvency	If the tenant becomes insolvent the trustee in bankruptcy or liquidator has the power to disclaim the lease as an onerous contract. The lease will normally have been drafted to allow forfeiture on the happening of one of several insolvency events.	Chapter 29
Methods of termination	Periodic tenancies can be terminated by notice – usually a full period is required. Fixed term tenancies will expire automatically at the end of the term and can be terminated during the term by agreement between landlord and tenant – known as 'surrender' – or by the landlord exercising a right of re-entry (forfeiture) on the tenant's breach of the terms of the lease. Sometimes, a break clause is inserted into the lease. This allows the party with the benefit of the clause to terminate the lease prematurely, as long as the conditions laid down in the clause are complied with. In the *Mannai* case the House of Lords held that strict compliance with the notice provisions in relation to a break clause was not necessary, provided that a reasonable recipient would understand what was intended. A landlord's break clause may not be effective due to the impact of the security of tenure legislation.	Chapter 30

Topic	Summary	Reference
Landlord and Tenant Act 1954, Part II	Most commercial tenants occupying premises for the purposes of a business will have security of tenure – although it is possible to contract out of this. Contracting out can be effected by agreement between the parties provided the landlord has served and the tenant has signed the correct form of notice. If the notice is received within 14 days of the grant of the lease, the tenant must make a statutory declaration. Security means that the lease will not come to an end in the normal way at the end of a fixed term but will be continued under the Act on the same terms. The tenant also has a right to a new lease unless the landlord can establish one of seven grounds. To claim possession or the grant of a new lease at a higher rent, the landlord must serve notice in the prescribed form under s 25, giving at least six months but not more than 12 months notice. In the case of a sub-lease, it will normally be the sub-tenant who will have security under the Act. There are complex rules for determining who will be the sub-tenant's competent landlord for the purposes of the Act.	Chapter 31

Part III
RESIDENTIAL TENANCIES

Chapter 32

Introduction to Residential Tenancies

32.1 Residential occupiers

This part of the book is concerned with both short-term and long-term lettings of residential property. It deals with the following potential problem areas:

(a) What happens at the end of a tenancy? Does the landlord have a right to possession?

(b) Who is responsible for repairs?

(c) Does the tenant have a right to compel the landlord to sell him the freehold or grant him a new lease?

Tenants with long leases (exceeding 21 years) are often given rights to compel the sale of the freehold; all residential tenants may have security of tenure, ie, the right to stay on in possession even after the end of the contractual term.

All of these matters are significant, not only from the point of view of the tenant, but also from the point of view of the landlord or a potential purchaser of the freehold, who might have plans for redevelopment which may be affected by the tenant's rights.

In dealing with or advising upon a residential landlord and tenant matter, the question of the status of the residential occupier is of paramount importance in determining the relevant law.

It is first necessary to determine whether the occupier is a tenant or a licensee. The rights and obligations of the parties and the appropriate statutory provisions will, in many cases, hinge on this distinction. If a residential occupier is merely a licensee, he has no proprietary interest in the property that he occupies so that, in general terms, when the licence terminates or expires or when the owner dies or transfers ownership of the property, the occupier's right to occupy ceases. Further, there is very little statutory protection (or 'security of tenure') for residential licensees. Most legislation is aimed at the protection of tenants. Thus, the distinction between a tenancy/lease and a licence is of fundamental importance. This distinction is considered in detail at **9.4**.

Having dealt with the question of the status of the occupier as between tenant and licensee, it is then necessary to look at the relevant law affecting the tenancy or licence. It will normally be a mixture of common law and statute.

32.2 The common law

All licences, leases and tenancies are, to some extent, governed by common law. The law of contract, land law and the law of torts each play an important part, and must be the starting point when considering any problem that concerns leases, licences or tenancies. The relevant common law is dealt with where appropriate in later sections of the book. However, it must be appreciated that the common law is frequently modified or supplemented by statute.

32.3   The statutes

The major statutory provisions are contained in the Leasehold Reform Act 1967 (LRA 1967), the Rent Act 1977 (RA 1977), the Protection from Eviction Act 1977 (PEA 1977), the Housing Act 1985 (HA 1985), the Landlord and Tenant Act 1985 (LTA 1985), the Landlord and Tenant Act 1987 (LTA 1987), the Housing Act 1988 (HA 1988), the Leasehold Reform, Housing and Urban Development Act 1993 (LRHUDA 1993) and the Housing Act 1996 (HA 1996). Most of these statutes have been further amended by the provisions of the Commonhold and Leasehold Reform Act 2002. This Act also introduces a new kind of land ownership known as commonhold. This is designed for use in the case of interdependent properties such as flats, shopping malls and the like. It is considered in **Chapter 41**.

These provisions will be looked at in detail in later chapters. It should be appreciated at the outset, however, that most of this legislation was introduced on an ad hoc basis to deal with a particular problem and does not form part of an integrated consistent whole. So the qualifying conditions for each statute need to be looked at carefully to see whether any particular tenant is or is not protected.

32.4   Public sector lettings

Most tenants of local authorities (and certain others in the public sector) enjoy protection as secure tenants under the HA 1985. They have substantial security of tenure. If the landlord wishes to regain possession, it must usually comply with the procedure and the established grounds for possession laid down in that Act. However, there is no statutory control over the amounts of rent that local authorities can charge. In relation to repairs, harassment or unlawful eviction, there is generally no difference between public sector tenants and private sector tenants. Similarly, the rights given to long leaseholders under LRHUDA 1993 also apply to local authority tenants (see **Chapter 40**). However, the rights of secure tenants are otherwise outside the scope of this book.

32.5   Private sector lettings

The rights of short-term tenants of private landlords often depend upon when the tenancy was originally entered into. As regards security of tenure and rent control in the private sector, a clear distinction must be made between tenancies granted prior to 15 January 1989 and those granted on or after that date. The former are usually governed by the RA 1977 under which tenants enjoy substantial security of tenure and significant statutory control over the amount of rent that the landlord can charge. As regards tenancies granted on or after 15 January 1989 the rules are quite different and are contained in the HA 1988. This established the concept of the 'assured tenancy', with full security of tenure, and the 'assured shorthold tenancy', under which the landlord has an absolute right to possession at the end of the letting. However, in relation to tenancies under both the RA 1977 and the HA 1988, the rules relating to repairs, harassment and unlawful eviction are the same.

32.6   The next step

Having considered the question of residential status and, where appropriate, which statutory regime applies, it is then necessary to look at the detail of the relevant law and procedures and to apply them to the facts of the case and to the client's specific instructions.

Chapter 33
Assured Tenancies

33.1 Introduction

The concept of assured tenancies and assured shorthold tenancies was introduced by the HA 1988. This came into force on 15 January 1989, and virtually all new lettings by private landlords after that date will be one or the other (but see **33.4**). Lettings entered into before that date will generally remain subject to the provisions of the RA 1977, see **33.3.1**.

An assured tenancy gives the tenant extensive security of tenure; at the end of the contractual term the tenant has a statutory right to remain in possession. If the landlord wishes to obtain possession, he must not only follow the prescribed procedure but also establish one of the prescribed grounds for possession. However, there is no statutory control over the amount of the rent which the landlord can charge; the rent is left to be decided by the ordinary operation of market forces. There is, however, some protection given to a tenant where the landlord wishes to increase the rent payable under an existing tenancy.

In the case of lettings entered into on or after 28 February 1997 (the commencement date of the HA 1996), most will be assured shorthold tenancies (see, generally, **Chapter 39**) and *not* assured tenancies. However, a shorthold is merely a type of assured tenancy and so must comply with the definition of an assured tenancy as well as the extra requirements which make it a shorthold (see **34.2.1**).

Tenancies which do *not* satisfy the definition of an assured tenancy (and so cannot be sortholds either) will not be subject to the provisions of the HA 1988 as set out in this chapter. Instead, ordinary common law rules as to termination etc will apply. They will, however, be subject to the protection from eviction protections set out in **Chapter 36**.

33.2 What is an assured tenancy?

The definition of an assured tenancy is set out in s 1 of the HA 1988. A tenancy under which a dwelling house is let as a separate dwelling will be an assured tenancy, if and so long as all of the following requirements are met:

(a) the tenant or each of joint tenants is an individual; and

(b) the tenant or at least one of joint tenants occupies the dwelling house as his only or principal home; and

(c) the tenancy is not specifically excluded by other provisions of the Act.

Each of these requirements must be looked at in detail.

33.2.1 Tenancy

There must be a 'tenancy'; licences to occupy dwelling houses are excluded from protection. See **9.4** as to the distinction between a licence and a tenancy.

33.2.2 Dwelling house

There is no statutory definition of 'dwelling house', and it will be a question of fact whether premises are a house or not, but any building designed or adapted for living in is capable of forming a dwelling house for these purposes. As well as including lettings of whole houses and self-contained flats, lettings of single rooms in a house will also be included, as will converted barns, windmills, etc.

33.2.3 Let as a separate dwelling

The premises, as well as being a dwelling house, must be let *as* a dwelling. So, if a building that would otherwise qualify as a dwelling house is let for business purposes, the tenant cannot claim that it is let on an assured tenancy merely because he decides to move in and live there.

There must be a *separate* dwelling. However, the House of Lords has held that even where the accommodation lacks one of the usual features of a dwelling, such as a kitchen, the property can still be the subject of an assured tenancy if the tenant does not actually live there. Further, s 3 of the HA 1988 makes special provision for the situation where the tenant shares some of the essential features of a dwelling with others. Such a letting is deemed to be an assured tenancy (assuming that all the other conditions are met). The tenant must, however, have the exclusive occupation of at least one room (otherwise it cannot be a tenancy), and if the other accommodation is shared with the landlord, the tenancy will be excluded from the definition of an assured tenancy for different reasons. However, the provisions of s 3 mean that arrangements whereby each tenant is given exclusive occupation of his own bedsitting room, but shares bathroom and kitchen with other tenants, will be deemed to be capable of being assured tenancies. Such an arrangement must be contrasted, however, with the situation where each member of a group of people is given a right to share the occupation of the whole of the house with the others. No one has the right to exclusive possession of any part of the house, and the arrangement can only give rise to a licence.

33.2.4 'If and so long as'

The status of the tenancy is not to be determined once and for all at the commencement of the letting. Whether a tenancy is an assured tenancy can fluctuate according to changed circumstances. For example, one requirement of the definition is that the tenant must be occupying the house as his only or principal home. This may have been the case at the start of the tenancy, and so the tenancy would be assured, but if subsequently the tenant ceases to reside, the tenancy will no longer be assured. The tenant will thus lose his security of tenure.

33.2.5 The tenant must be an individual

Lettings to companies are excluded from the definition, even though an individual (eg, a director or employee of the company) may be in occupation of the house.

33.2.6 The tenant must occupy as his 'only or principal home'

It is possible for a person to have more than one 'home'. If that is the case, then it is a question of fact as to which is the tenant's principal home. This could be a significant question, for example, for the person working in the City who has a flat nearby in which he lives during the week, and a house in the country in which he lives at weekends. Which is his principal home? Only a tenancy of the principal home can be an assured tenancy. Although the provision requires 'occupation', this does not mean continuous occupation. A mere temporary absence will not deprive a tenancy of its status as an assured tenancy.

33.3   Tenancies which cannot be assured

Various lettings which satisfy the basic definition of an assured tenancy will, in fact, not be protected if they fall within one of the following exceptions. Equally, as they cannot be assured tenancies, they cannot be assured shorthold tenancies either. The exceptions are as follows.

33.3.1   Tenancies entered into before the commencement of the HA 1988

The HA 1988 came into force on 15 January 1989; it is not retrospective. Only lettings entered into on or after that date can be assured tenancies. Any pre-existing tenancy will, if it has any protection at all, still remain subject to the provisions of the RA 1977 (see **Chapter 35**).

33.3.2   High value properties

Because of the abolition of domestic rates, a distinction has to be drawn between those tenancies granted before 1 April 1990 and those granted on or after that date. For tenancies granted before 1 April 1990, a tenancy of a dwelling house with a rateable value in excess of £750 (£1,500 in Greater London) cannot be an assured tenancy. If the tenancy was granted on or after 1 April 1990, it cannot be an assured tenancy if the rent payable is £25,000 or more per annum.

33.3.3   Tenancies at a low rent

This exclusion has also been affected by the abolition of domestic rates. Lettings made before 1 April 1990 cannot be assured if the annual rent is less than two-thirds of the rateable value of the property. For tenancies granted on or after 1 April 1990, the exclusion applies to tenancies in which the rent does not exceed £250 per annum (£1,000 per annum in Greater London).

33.3.4   Business tenancies

A tenancy to which Pt II of the LTA 1954 applies cannot be an assured tenancy; see **Chapter 31**. This means that mixed-user lettings, ie, lettings of property used partly for business and partly for residential purposes cannot be assured tenancies, despite being occupied by the tenant as his only or principal home, etc. Lettings contracted out, or otherwise outside the security of tenure provisions of the LTA 1954, will still not be within the definition of an assured tenancy.

33.3.5   Lettings to students

Lettings to students by specified educational bodies are outside the definition of an assured tenancy. This exception does not apply to lettings to students by landlords other than the specified universities and colleges; these are capable of being assured tenancies, subject to the normal requirements being fulfilled.

33.3.6   Holiday lettings

A letting for the purpose of a holiday cannot be an assured tenancy.

33.3.7   Lettings by resident landlords

A tenancy will have a resident landlord where the landlord lives in another part of the same building in which the accommodation let to the tenant is situated.

33.3.8   Crown, local authority and housing association lettings

Although Crown, local authority and housing association lettings are excluded from the definition of an assured tenancy, lettings by local authorities and housing associations may have other protections (see **32.4**).

33.4   Transitional provisions

Provisions were inserted in the HA 1988 to ensure that any existing RA 1977 tenants were not deprived of their existing protections under that Act by landlords granting them new tenancies after the HA 1988 came into force. Thus, a tenancy granted to a person who was a protected or statutory tenant under the RA 1977 by that person's landlord (or one of joint landlords) will still be a protected tenancy even though it is granted on or after 15 January 1989. This will still be the case even if the new letting is of a different property to that comprised in the previous tenancy. Note also that it is the identity of the landlord at the time of the new letting that is relevant, not the landlord at the time of the original grant of the tenancy. So, if L grants a Rent Act tenancy to T on or after 15 January 1989, that new letting will still be protected by the Rent Act.

33.5   Rents under assured tenancies

There is no restriction on the amount of rent which can initially be charged on the grant of an assured tenancy. This is so even if there is a subsisting registration of a fair rent for the purposes of the RA 1977 (see **Chapter 35**). However, if the landlord subsequently wishes to increase the rent, he may not be able to do so unless he follows the correct procedure. The details of this are outside the scope of this book.

33.6   Succession on death

On the death of a tenant, his tenancy does not die with him; it is a proprietary right and will pass in the same way as the deceased's other property. On the death of one of joint tenants, the tenancy will vest in the survivor(s). On the death of a sole tenant the tenancy will pass under his will or intestacy. The HA 1988, however, contains specific provisions (s 17) dealing with the succession to an assured periodic tenancy on the death of a sole tenant which will override these normal rules.

On the death of a sole periodic tenant the tenancy will vest in the tenant's spouse, notwithstanding the terms of the deceased's will, provided that immediately before the deceased tenant's death the spouse was occupying the dwelling house as his or her only or principal home. 'Spouse' is defined to include a person who was living with the tenant as his or her wife or husband as well as persons who were lawfully married. It also includes persons in an established same-sex relationship.

33.7   Sub-lettings

As between the particular landlord and tenant, it is irrelevant whether the landlord owns the freehold interest in the property or merely a leasehold interest. If the conditions are complied with for the creation of an assured tenancy, then the tenant will have the benefit of security of tenure and the other assured tenancy provisions against his landlord, whether or not that landlord owns the freehold or is himself a tenant.

The question arises as to whether an assured sub-tenant has protection against the owner of the freehold reversion. The normal rule at common law is that if a head-lease comes to an end then any sub-lease derived out of it will also determine. This, however, is varied by the provisions of s 18 of the HA 1988. This provides that in the case of a house lawfully sub-let on an assured tenancy, that on the ending of the head-lease, the sub-tenancy will still continue. The assured sub-tenant will then become the direct tenant of the head landlord with full security of tenure.

33.8 Security of tenure

33.8.1 Restriction on termination by landlord

An assured tenancy cannot be brought to an end by the landlord otherwise than by obtaining a court order for possession. Thus, in the case of a periodic assured tenancy, a notice to quit is of no effect. On the ending of a fixed-term assured tenancy (including a shorthold) otherwise than by an order of the court or by surrender, the tenant is entitled to remain in possession as a statutory periodic tenant. This statutory periodic tenancy will be on the same terms as the previous fixed-term tenancy (although there is a little used procedure for changing those terms: see s 6 of the HA 1988).

33.8.2 Obtaining a court order

The landlord will only obtain a court order for possession if he follows the correct procedure and can establish one or more of the grounds for possession set out in Sch 2 to the HA 1988. Further, although some of these grounds are mandatory grounds, ie, the court must order possession if the ground is established, many of them are discretionary grounds. With these, the court, on proof of the ground, may order possession only if it considers it reasonable to do so. The procedure for obtaining possession involves the landlord serving a notice on the tenant (a 's 8 notice'), in the prescribed form. The s 8 notice must specify the ground(s) upon which the landlord intends to rely and must give two weeks' notice of the landlord's intention to commence possession proceedings. (Sometimes two months' notice has to be given depending upon the ground used.) However, if Ground 14 is specified (whether or not with any other ground) then the proceedings can be commenced as soon as the s 8 notice has been served. The proceedings must then be commenced not earlier than the date specified and not later than 12 months from the date of service of the notice. It is possible for the court to dispense with the requirement for a s 8 notice (unless Ground 8 is being relied upon), but only if it considers it 'just and equitable' to do so.

In the case of a fixed-term assured tenancy, the landlord cannot normally obtain possession until after the end of the contractual fixed term (assuming that a ground for possession can then be established). However, as an exception to this, certain of the grounds for possession will be available to the landlord during the fixed term provided that the tenancy agreement contains a provision for it to be brought to an end on the ground in question. This provision can take any form at all, including a proviso for re-entry or a forfeiture clause. The grounds on which the landlord can obtain possession in this way during the fixed term are Grounds 2, 8 and 10 to 15.

33.8.3 The grounds for possession: mandatory grounds

The grounds are set out in Sch 2 to the HA 1988. Part I of the Schedule contains the mandatory grounds, ie, those, on proof of which, the court must make an order for possession in the landlord's favour.

Ground 1 (owner-occupier etc)

Not later than the beginning of the tenancy the landlord gave notice in writing to the tenant that possession might be recovered on this ground or the court is of the opinion that it is just and equitable to dispense with the requirement of notice and (in either case)—

(a)   at some time before the beginning of the tenancy, the landlord who is seeking possession or, in the case of joint landlords seeking possession, at least one of them occupied the dwelling house as his only or principal home; or

(b)   the landlord who is seeking possession or, in the case of joint landlords seeking possession, at least one of them requires the dwelling house as his or his spouse's only or principal home and neither the landlord (or, in the case of joint landlords, any one of them) nor any other person who, as landlord, derived title under the landlord who gave the notice mentioned above acquired the reversion on the tenancy for money or money's worth.

This is one of the grounds for which s 8 requires two months' notice of impending proceedings being given.

Ground 2 (mortgagee exercising power of sale)

The dwelling house is subject to a mortgage granted before the beginning of the tenancy; and

(a)   the mortgagee is entitled to exercise a power of sale conferred on him by the mortgage or by section 101 of the Law of Property Act 1925; and

(b)   the mortgagee requires possession of the dwelling house for the purpose of disposing of it with vacant possession in exercise of that power; and

(c)   either notice was given as mentioned in Ground 1 above or the court is satisfied that it is just and equitable to dispense with the requirement of notice.

As with Ground 1, two months' notice of proceedings must be served.

Ground 3 (out-of-season holiday accommodation)

The tenancy is a fixed-term tenancy for a term not exceeding eight months and—

(a)   not later than the beginning of the tenancy the landlord gave notice in writing to the tenant that possession might be recovered on this ground; and

(b)   at some time within the period of twelve months ending with the beginning of the tenancy, the dwelling house was occupied under a right to occupy it for a holiday.

Ground 4 (out of term student accommodation)

The tenancy is fixed-term tenancy for a term not exceeding twelve months and—

(a)   not later than the beginning of the tenancy the landlord gave notice in writing to the tenant that possession might be recovered on this ground; and

(b)   at some time within the period of twelve months ending with the beginning of the tenancy, the dwelling house was let on a tenancy falling within paragraph 8 of Schedule 1 to this Act.

Paragraph 8 of Sch 1 applies to tenancies granted to students by a specified educational institution and which are outside the definition of an assured tenancy.

Ground 5 (minister of religion's house)

The dwelling house is held for the purpose of being available for occupation by a minister of religion as a residence from which to perform the duties of his office and—

(a)   not later than the beginning of the tenancy the landlord gave notice in writing to the tenant that possession might be recovered on this ground; and

(b)   the court is satisfied that the dwelling house is required for occupation by a minister of religion as such a residence.

Two months' notice of proceedings is required for this ground.

Ground 6 (demolition etc)

This is a long and complicated ground, but is quite simple in its basic intent. It allows a landlord to obtain possession if he intends to demolish or reconstruct the house (or a substantial part of it) and cannot reasonably do so without obtaining possession. However, if the landlord has acquired his interest in the property for money or money's worth since the date of the grant of the tenancy, then this ground is not available.

Two months' notice of proceedings must be served by the landlord for this ground to be available.

If this ground is established, the landlord must pay the tenant's reasonable removal costs.

Ground 7 (death)

The tenancy is a periodic tenancy (including a statutory periodic tenancy) which has devolved under the will or intestacy of the former tenant and the proceedings for the recovery of possession are begun not later than twelve months after the death of the former tenant or, if the court so directs, after the date on which, in the opinion of the court, the landlord or, in the case of joint landlords, any one of them became aware of the former tenant's death.

Ground 8 (substantial rent arrears)

Both at the date of the service of the notice under section 8 of this Act relating to the proceedings for possession and at the date of the hearing—

(a)   if rent is payable weekly or fortnightly, at least eight weeks' rent is unpaid;

(b)   if rent is payable monthly, at least two months' rent is unpaid;

(c)   if rent is payable quarterly, at least one quarter's rent is more than three months in arrears; and

(d)   if rent is payable yearly, at least three months' rent is more than three months in arrears;

and for the purpose of this ground 'rent' means rent lawfully due from the tenant.

Note that the rent must be 'lawfully due'. Under s 48 of the LTA 1987, no rent is lawfully due from a tenant unless and until the landlord has given to the tenant notice in writing of an address in England and Wales at which notices (including notices in proceedings) can be served upon him. In *Rogan v Woodfield Building Services Ltd* [1994] EGCS 145, the Court of Appeal decided that if the landlord's name and address in England and Wales was stated on the tenancy agreement without any qualification or limitation, then this would be sufficient to comply with s 48. Obviously, however, if the landlord's address changes during the currency of the tenancy, eg, on a change of landlord, then a separate s 48 notice will be needed. This s 48 notice need not be in any prescribed form nor need the address be the landlord's home address (or registered office, in the case of a limited company); it could be, for example, the address of a solicitor or other agent.

It is not possible for the court to dispense with the requirement for the service of a notice under s 8 of the HA 1988 if this ground is being relied upon.

33.8.4   Grounds for possession: discretionary grounds

Proof of the following grounds for possession will not inevitably result in a possession order being made against a tenant. The court can only make such an order if it considers it 'reasonable to do so'. This will be a question of fact in each case, but this proviso will enable the court to consider the prospective hardship likely to be suffered by both the landlord and the tenant, depending upon whether it makes a possession order or not. The conduct of the parties during the tenancy will also be relevant to the question of 'reasonableness'.

Ground 9 (alternative accommodation)

Suitable alternative accommodation is available for the tenant or will be available for him when the order for possession takes effect.

To make use of this ground, two months' notice of proceedings is required. As with mandatory Ground 6, the landlord must pay the tenant's reasonable removal expenses if possession is ordered on this ground.

Ground 10 (rent arrears)

Some rent lawfully due from the tenant—

(a)   is unpaid on the date on which the proceedings for possession are begun; and

(b)   … was in arrears at the date of the service of the notice under that section relating to those proceedings.

Ground 11 (persistent delay)

Whether or not any rent is in arrears on the date on which proceedings for possession are begun, the tenant has persistently delayed paying rent which has become lawfully due.

Ground 12 (breach of covenant etc)

Any obligation of the tenancy (other than one related to the payment of rent) has been broken or not performed.

Ground 13 (waste or neglect etc)

The condition of the dwelling house or any of the common parts has deteriorated owing to acts of waste by, or the neglect or default of, the tenant or any other person residing in the dwelling house and, in the case of an act of waste by, or the neglect or default of, a person lodging with the tenant or a sub-tenant of his, the tenant has not taken such steps as he ought reasonably to have taken for the removal of the lodger or sub-tenant.

Ground 14 (nuisance etc)

The tenant or a person residing in or visiting the dwelling house—

(a)   has been guilty of conduct causing or likely to cause a nuisance or annoyance to a person residing, visiting or otherwise engaging in a lawful activity in the locality, or

(b)   has been convicted of—

   (i)   using the dwelling house or allowing it to be used for immoral or illegal purposes, or

   (ii)   an arrestable offence committed in, or in the locality of, the dwelling house.

Normally, under s 8 of the HA 1988, two weeks' (or sometimes even two months') notice of the commencement of proceedings has to be given to a tenant; in the case of this ground, whether pleaded alone or with other grounds, proceedings can be commenced as soon as the s 8 notice has been served (see **33.8.2**).

Ground 14A (domestic violence)

The dwelling house was occupied (whether alone or with others) by a married couple or a couple living together as husband and wife and—

(a)   one of the partners is a tenant of the dwelling house,

(b)   the landlord who is seeking possession is a registered social landlord or a charitable housing trust,

(c)   one partner has left the dwelling house because of violence or threats of violence by the other towards —

   (i)   that partner, or

   (ii)   a member of the family of that partner who was residing with that partner immediately before the partner left, and

(d)   the court is satisfied that the partner who has left is unlikely to return.

Ground 15 (damage to furniture etc)

The condition of any furniture provided for use under the tenancy has, in the opinion of the court, deteriorated owing to ill-treatment by the tenant or any other person residing in the dwelling house and, in the case of ill-treatment by a person lodging with the tenant or by a sub-tenant of his, the tenant has not taken such steps as he ought reasonably to have taken for the removal of the lodger or sub-tenant.

Ground 16 (former employee)

The dwelling house was let to the tenant in consequence of his employment by the landlord seeking possession or a previous landlord under the tenancy and the tenant has ceased to be in that employment.

Ground 17 (false statement by tenant)

The tenant is the person, or one of the persons, to whom the tenancy was granted and the landlord was induced to grant the tenancy by a false statement made knowingly or recklessly by—

(a)   the tenant, or

(b)   a person acting at the tenant's instigation.

Chapter 34

Assured Shorthold Tenancies

34.1 Introduction

A distinction must first of all be drawn between 'old' shortholds, ie, those entered into before 28 February 1997, the commencement date of the HA 1996, and 'new' shortholds, ie, those entered into on or after that date.

An old shorthold is a fixed-term tenancy of at least six months' duration with no security of tenure. Thus, once the fixed term has expired the landlord has an absolute right to recover possession, provided that he complies with the correct procedure. Prior to the grant of the tenancy, however, the landlord must have served a notice on the tenant, in the prescribed form, warning him of the lack of security of tenure. This notice cannot be dispensed with.

Because of the lack of security, shortholds became very popular with landlords and most lettings purported to be shortholds. However, sometimes a purported shorthold would fail due to non-compliance with the conditions, leading to an assured tenancy with full security of tenure (see **Chapter 33**). From 28 February 1997, however, all new lettings (with certain exceptions, see **34.3.2**) are deemed to be shortholds. The old conditions need no longer be complied with; the letting need not be for a fixed term, there is no need for a warning notice etc. However, the landlord still has the same absolute right to possession as in an old shorthold.

Note that 'old' shortholds continue as before and if one fails due to the conditions not have being complied with, for example, no warning notice was served, the tenancy will still become a fully protected assured tenancy. This means that the conditions for the grant of an old shorthold are still of considerable practical importance even after the introduction of new shortholds.

The only disadvantage of a shorthold (whether new or old) from a landlord's point of view is the right given to the tenant to refer the rent initially payable to the Rent Assessment Committee. However, the Committee can reduce the rent only if it is 'significantly higher' than the rents under other comparable assured tenancies.

34.2 Old shortholds

34.2.1 Definition

Section 20 of the HA 1988 sets out the qualifying conditions for shortholds entered into before 28 February 1997. It provides that an assured shorthold tenancy is an assured tenancy which:

(a)   is a fixed-term tenancy granted for a term of not less than six months; and

(b)   contains no power for the landlord to terminate it during the first six months; and

(c)   was preceded by the giving to the tenant of the prescribed shorthold notice.

34.2.1.1 An assured tenancy

An assured shorthold tenancy is merely a type of assured tenancy. It must, therefore, comply with all the requirements of an assured tenancy (see **Chapter 33**).

A shorthold cannot be granted to an existing tenant under an ordinary assured tenancy (or to one of joint tenants), if it is granted by the landlord under that existing tenancy. This is so even if the lettings are not of the same premises. This is an anti-avoidance device to prevent landlords from depriving their existing tenants of security of tenure by purportedly granting them a shorthold. Similarly, as with all assured tenancies, a shorthold cannot be granted to an existing RA 1977 protected or statutory tenant (see **33.4**).

34.2.1.2 Minimum six-month fixed term

The initial grant of a shorthold could not be for a periodic term. It had to be for a fixed term and for a minimum duration of six months.

34.2.1.3 No power for landlord to terminate during first six months

Even if a minimum period of six months is granted, any power, however expressed, which would or might allow the landlord to terminate the tenancy within the first six months of the tenancy will prevent the tenancy from amounting to a shorthold. Note, however, that a forfeiture clause or a clause allowing termination on assured tenancy Grounds 2, 8 and 10 to 15 will not breach this requirement even though it is exercisable during the first six months of the term.

34.2.1.4 Preceded by the giving of the prescribed shorthold notice

As the tenant under an assured shorthold has no security of tenure, he had to be served with a notice prior to the grant of the tenancy warning him of this fact. This notice must be in the prescribed form. The content of the necessary form changed twice since the introduction of assured shortholds on 15 January 1989 and care must be taken to ensure that the shorthold notice served was the correct one as at the date of service.

The notice must have been served before the tenancy agreement was entered into and not at the same time. Thus, it could not be included in the tenancy agreement itself.

34.2.1.5 Relevance of old shorthold rules

Although an old shorthold can no longer be created after 28 February 1997, it is still relevant to consider the application of these old shorthold rules in the case of shortholds granted before that date which are still subsisting or have been subsequently renewed. In the case, for example, of a purported old shorthold granted on 1 January 1997, if the old shorthold rules were not fully complied with, that tenancy would be a fully protected assured tenancy, as would any further letting on or after 28 February 1997 by the same landlord to the same tenant.

34.3 New shortholds

34.3.1 Definition

Shortholds entered into on or after 28 February 1997 (otherwise than pursuant to a contract made before that date) are governed by s 19A of the HA 1988 (as inserted by the HA 1996). This provides that *any* assured tenancy entered into on or after the commencement date will be a shorthold *unless* it falls within one of the specified exceptions.

So there is no longer any need for a shorthold to be preceded by a prescribed form of notice. There is no need for a shorthold to be for a fixed term, it can be periodic; there is no need for a minimum period of six months; it can be for any period, no matter how short. However, although there is no prohibition on the landlord being able to terminate during the first six months, no order for possession using the shorthold ground can be made earlier than six months from the start of the tenancy, whether the tenancy is for a fixed term or it is a periodic tenancy (see **34.7**). However, this does not stop possession being obtained during the first six months using an assured tenancy ground, eg, Ground 14; a new shorthold, like an old shorthold, is merely a type of assured tenancy, see **34.2.1.1**.

As a new shorthold is a type of assured tenancy, it must still comply with all the requirements of an assured tenancy (see **Chapter 33**). A tenancy which falls outside of the definition of an assured tenancy (eg due to the resident landlord rule) cannot be a shorthold either. Such a tenancy will be subject to ordinary common law rules as to termination.

34.3.2   Which lettings will not be new shortholds?

As previously stated (see **34.3.1**), all new assured tenancies granted on or after 28 February 1997 (other than those granted pursuant to a contract made before that date) will be shortholds subject to certain exceptions. These exceptions are set out in Sch 2A to the HA 1988 as inserted by the HA 1996. The following lettings will be excluded and will thus take effect as ordinary assured tenancies.

34.3.2.1   Tenancies excluded by notice

The Schedule allows the landlord to serve a notice on the tenant either before or after the grant of the tenancy stating that the letting is not to be a shorthold. There is no prescribed form for this notice.

It is rather strange that a landlord can change the status of a tenancy *after* it has been entered into. In most cases this will be to the advantage of the tenant in that it will give him greater security of tenure than before; it will, however, take away from the tenant his right to refer the rent to the Rent Asessment Committee if he considers it excessive (see **34.4**).

34.3.2.2   Tenancies containing a provision stating that the tenancy is not to be a shorthold

Similarly, if the tenancy agreement itself states that it is not to be a shorthold, it will then take effect as an ordinary assured tenancy.

34.3.2.3   Lettings to existing assured tenants

A letting to an existing assured (ie, not shorthold) tenant (whether alone or with others) by a person who is the landlord (or one of the landlords) under the existing tenancy will *not* be a shorthold *unless* the tenant serves notice on the landlord, in the prescribed form, before the new tenancy is entered into that he wants it to be a shorthold.

The requirements that this notice must be served *before* the new tenancy is entered into will give rise to similar considerations as already exist with regard to the service of s 20 notices for old shortholds; see **34.2.1**.

Of course, this provision begs the question as to *why* should a tenant want to serve such a notice when it will result in him losing the security of tenure he had before? One possible advantage would be for a tenant who had no security as an assured tenant (eg, because of Ground 1) and was unhappy about the rent under the new letting. By serving a notice stating that the tenancy was to be a shorthold, he would then have the right to refer the rent to the Rent Assessment Committee as being excessive (see **34.4**).

The existence of this procedure, allowing a tenant to elect to have a shorthold, does give rise to worries as to whether there is a danger of undue pressure being placed on tenants by landlords anxious to take advantage of the provisions of the HA 1996.

34.4 Rent control

The protection given differs slightly depending upon whether the tenant has a new shorthold or an old shorthold, but the general principles are the same for both.

On the granting of the tenancy, the landlord can charge such rent for the premises as the market will bear. There is no statutory restriction on the amount of rent chargeable. Any existing registration of a 'fair rent' under the provisions of the RA 1977 (see **Chapter 35**) can be ignored, as can any rental figure previously determined by the Rent Assessment Committee under these provisions. However, an assured shorthold tenant can apply to the local Rent Assessment Committee for the determination of the rent which, in the Committee's opinion, the landlord might reasonably be expected to obtain under the shorthold tenancy.

If the tenant has an old shorthold, he can apply at any time during the first tenancy entered into between the parties; no application can be made during any subsequent letting.

If the tenant has a new shorthold, whether for a fixed term or a periodic letting, he cannot apply if more than six months have elapsed since the beginning of the tenancy.

In the case of old shortholds and fixed-term new shortholds, the rent as assessed will become the maximum rent chargeable for the property throughout the remainder of the fixed term.

In the case of a new shorthold which is a periodic tenancy, again the rent once fixed will, in theory, remain fixed throughout the tenancy. However, in practice, once 12 months have expired, the landlord will then be able to make an application under ss 13 and 14 of the HA 1988 to increase the rent. These provisions are, however, outside the scope of this book.

With both old and new shortholds, once the rent has been determined by the Committee no further application for the fixing of a different figure can be made by either landlord or tenant. However, the rent determined by the Committee only has relevance to the particular tenancy in question. It will not limit the amount of rent chargeable under any subsequent letting, even if this is between the same parties.

34.5 What happens when a shorthold expires?

On the ending of a fixed term, the tenant is allowed to remain in possession as a statutory periodic tenant. However, the tenant still has no security of tenure. Under s 21(1) of the HA 1988 the court must still make an order for possession if the landlord follows the correct procedure. This involves the service on the tenant of not less than two months' notice stating that the landlord requires possession (see **34.6**).

34.6 How does the landlord obtain possession?

Unless the tenant leaves voluntarily, the landlord must apply to the court and obtain an order for possession. The court must order possession provided that the landlord follows the correct procedure. This involves the landlord serving a notice on the tenant (the 's 21 notice') giving the tenant at least two months' notice that he requires possession. Note, however, that possession cannot be obtained using this shorthold procedure during the continuance of a fixed term; possession is available only after its expiry (although the procedure can be set in motion during the fixed term so that possession can be obtained as soon as it has ended). Note also, that in the case of a new shorthold, possession cannot be obtained within six months of the commencement of the term using the shorthold procedure. This is so whether the tenancy is for a fixed term or is periodic.

34.7 Are there any other grounds for possession?

A shorthold is a type of assured tenancy and so, during the term, the mandatory and discretionary grounds which apply to ordinary assured tenancies can also apply. For full details of these see **33.8.3** and **33.8.4**, but it does mean, for example, that mandatory Ground 8 and discretionary Grounds 10 and 11 (all of which relate to rent arrears) can be used during the subsistence of the shorthold should the landlord be faced with a defaulting tenant. However, in the case of a fixed-term letting, as with other assured tenancies, these grounds can be used during the fixed term only if the tenancy agreement so provides. In the case of a shorthold which is a periodic tenancy, these ordinary assured tenancy grounds will be available to a landlord without the need for any such provision in the tenancy agreement.

In the case of a fixed-term shorthold, however, it is always sensible to insert a provision allowing the landlord to terminate the tenancy on the specified grounds. In the case of an old shorthold, this is permissible despite the usual rule that there must be no power for the landlord to terminate within the first six months of the tenancy. This rule does not apply to termination because of a breach of the terms of the tenancy, for example non-payment of rent. Similarly, in the case of new shortholds, although possession cannot be obtained using the shorthold procedure within six months of the commencement (see **34.6**), possession can be obtained during that period using the ordinary assured grounds should they be satisfied.

When the landlord is seeking to obtain possession on one of the ordinary assured grounds, then the procedure relevant to an ordinary assured tenancy should be followed, and *not* the shorthold procedure. In particular, this will mean that a s 8 notice will have to be served on the tenant before proceedings can be commenced, and *not* a s 21 notice.

Chapter 35
The Rent Act 1977

35.1 Introduction

The RA 1977 applies to lettings entered into prior to 15 January 1989. There are still many thousands of such tenancies in existence today, although their numbers are likely to decline as the years go by and tenants leave. Further, it is also still possible for new RA 1977 tenancies to be created today, albeit in very limited circumstances (see **33.4**). Tenancies within the RA 1977 are given wide-ranging security of tenure, in many ways similar to that given to assured tenancies. The main difference from assured tenancies, though, is that they are also subject to rent control, the 'fair rent' system which tends to keep rents below those which would prevail in the open market. On the death of a tenant there are succession rights which tend to be more generous than those applying to assured tenancies.

35.2 Protected tenancies

There will be a protected tenancy within the RA 1977 where a dwelling house is 'let as a separate dwelling' (RA 1977, s 1). See the discussion of the similarly worded requirement for an assured tenancy under the HA 1988 (at **33.2.3**). Unlike the HA 1988, there is no need for the letting to be to an individual, nor does the house need to be the tenant's only or principal home. There are various exceptions which are generally very similar to those for assured tenancies, for example, lettings by resident landlords, holiday lettings, tenancies at a low rent (see **33.3**). Protected tenancies will have rent control and succession rights, but not necessarily security of tenure.

35.3 Statutory tenancies

The statutory tenancy is the device by which security of tenure is given. At the end of the contractual protected tenancy, the tenant is given security of tenure and is allowed to remain in possession only 'if and so long as he occupies the dwelling house as his residence'. Only an individual can occupy as a residence, so a company tenant can be a protected tenant but not a statutory tenant. There is no requirement that the dwelling house should be occupied as the tenant's only or main residence; for RA 1977 purposes, it is accepted that a person can have two homes and that there can be a statutory tenancy of either or both of them. In order to obtain possession against a protected tenant, therefore, a landlord must first of all terminate that protected tenancy, for example, by serving notice to quit. If the tenant does not qualify as a statutory tenant, the landlord will be immediately entitled to a court order for possession. If a statutory tenancy does arise, the landlord will have to establish one (or more) of the grounds for possession laid down in the Act. As with assured tenancies, some of these grounds are mandatory and so the court must order possession on proof of the ground, but many are discretionary where the court can only order possession if it considers it reasonable to do so. The RA 1977 grounds are called 'cases' and are set out in Sch 15 to the RA 1977. Many are assured tenancy grounds.

35.4   The fair rent system

35.4.1   The system

Both protected and statutory tenancies are subject to control as to the amount of the rent the landlord can charge for the property. The RA 1977 set up a register of 'fair rents' for dwelling houses. Once a rent has been registered in relation to a property then that becomes the maximum chargeable under any protected or statutory tenancy of that property. The rent is assessed by the rent officer, a local authority official, in accordance with criteria laid down by the Act. By requiring the rent officer to assume that there is no shortage of accommodation to let (even though there might be), the rent assessed is often considerably lower than it otherwise would be in the open market.

35.4.2   Applying for a fair rent

Assuming that no fair rent is registered in respect of the property, on the grant of a tenancy the landlord can charge whatever rent the market will bear. However, at any time during the continuance of the tenancy the tenant can apply for a fair rent to be assessed. Once assessed, this then becomes the maximum payable, despite the existence of a higher agreed figure in the tenancy agreement. The only way in which the landlord can increase the rent is by applying himself to the rent officer for the assessment of a higher fair rent. However, he normally cannot make such an application within two years of an earlier fair rent having been assessed.

35.5   Succession to Rent Act tenancies

On the death of a statutory or a protected tenant, that person's spouse (or a person living with the tenant as husband or wife) will become the statutory tenant of the property and thus entitled to the benefits of security of tenure and rent control. If there is no surviving spouse (or person who had lived with the tenant as husband or wife), then the succession rules differ depending upon the date of death of the tenant.

35.5.1   Deaths prior to 15 January 1989

In this case any member of the tenant's family who was living with him at the time of death and had lived with him for at least six months prior to the death would succeed as a statutory tenant.

35.5.2   Deaths on or after 15 January 1989

Now, for a family member to succeed, he needs to have resided for two years prior to the death. Further, in such cases the family member will only become entitled to an assured tenancy on the succession and *not* a statutory tenancy.

35.5.3   Second transmissions

On the death of the 'first successor', it is sometimes possible for a second 'transmission' to a 'second successor' to occur. In the situation where the first successor died before 15 January 1989, a second transmission was always possible in favour of the first successor's spouse or family member, using the same succession rules as applicable to the first succession. However, in the case of the death of a first successor after 15 January 1989, a second transmission is only possible in very limited circumstances.

Chapter 36
Protection from Eviction

36.1 Introduction

The most traumatic experience that residential tenants or licensees may have to face is the peremptory eviction from, or harassment in, their homes by their landlords. Landlords sometimes resort to threats and violence because they think it is a cheaper and quicker method of eviction than taking court proceedings for possession, which may not in any event be successful due to the security of tenure legislation. Tenants suffering such unacceptable actions on the part of their landlords may have civil remedies against them. There may also be criminal sanctions. The tenant's basic remedy will be damages, although an injunction will often be available to restrain future actions and to restore a dispossessed tenant to the property. The statutory protections apply not only to tenants but also to licensees.

36.2 Criminal sanctions: The Protection from Eviction Act 1977

36.2.1 Protection from eviction

36.2.1.1 The offence

It is an offence unlawfully to evict a residential occupier unless it is reasonably believed that he no longer lives in the premises (PEA 1977, s 1).

Except in the case of an excluded licence or tenancy, eviction will be unlawful if a residential occupier is evicted otherwise than by means of a court order.

36.2.1.2 Residential occupier

Protection is given to residential occupiers as defined in s 1(1) of the PEA 1977. These are persons occupying the premises as a residence 'whether under a contract or by virtue of any enactment or rule of law giving him the right to remain in occupation or restricting the right of any other person to recover possession of the premises'. The definition thus includes all tenants, whether they are protected tenants under the RA 1977, assured or assured shorthold tenants under the HA 1988, secure tenants under HA 1985 or whether they have no statutory protection at all. The use of the term 'contract' will also include contractual licensees within these protections.

36.2.2 Protection from harassment

36.2.2.1 The offences

There are two offences of harassment laid down by PEA 1977: one requires intent on the part of the offender and is set out in s 1(3); the other is contained in s 1(3A) and requires only knowledge or belief. In both cases, protection is given to residential occupiers as defined in s 1(1) of the PEA 1977 (see **36.2.1.2**). The actions amounting to harassment would include, for example, removing doors and windows, disconnecting services, and acts and threats of violence.

36.2.2.2   Section 1(3) harassment

It is an offence to do acts likely to interfere with the peace or comfort of a residential occupier or to withhold services reasonably required for the occupation of the premises with intent to cause the residential occupier to give up the occupation of the premises. Problems are caused by the need to prove intent although it might be possible to infer intent if the particular result could be foreseen as the natural consequence of the actions in question.

36.2.2.3   Section 1(3A) harassment

It is an offence for a landlord to do acts likely to interfere with the peace and comfort of a residential occupier, or withhold services reasonably required for the occupation of the premises, if he knows or has reasonable cause to believe that the conduct is likely to cause the residential occupier to give up the occupation of the premises. As no specific intent is required for this offence, it may be easier to establish than s 1(3) harassment; this was certainly the intention of the legislature. It is a defence to the withholding of services if this can be justified on 'reasonable grounds'.

36.3   Criminal sanctions: The Criminal Law Act 1977

Under s 6(1) of the Criminal Law Act 1977, any person who 'without lawful authority' uses, or threatens to use, violence to secure entry to premises commits an offence if there is someone present on those premises at the time who is opposed to the entry.

36.4   Civil proceedings

36.4.1   Why take civil proceedings?

Criminal sanctions will often not be an adequate remedy for a dispossessed or threatened occupier. The occupier may want an injunction to restrain future actions on the part of the landlord or to restore the tenant to possession of the property; compensation awarded in criminal proceedings is often not as much as would be ordered in civil proceedings. Damages and injunctions are available in civil proceedings in the county court and often provide a more effective and speedy remedy; if need be, emergency procedures can be followed in order to obtain immediate relief.

36.4.2   Causes of action

36.4.2.1   Alternative causes of action

Various causes of action are available to dispossessed or harassed tenants, some statutory, and some based upon the common law, depending upon the precise facts of the case in question. It is sensible to plead as many alternative causes of action as reasonably present themselves in the circumstances. Claims in both contract and tort may be possible.

36.4.2.2   Claims for breach of contract

Breach of the covenant for quiet enjoyment

It is an implied term of every tenancy that the landlord will allow his tenant 'quiet enjoyment' of the premises. The obligation is for the landlord to allow the tenant peaceable, uninterrupted enjoyment of the property. Unlawful eviction and most actions of harassment will be a breach of this covenant. Thus, knocking on the tenant's door and shouting threats would be a breach of this implied term.

Breach of contract in general

Any other breach of a term of the tenancy or licence agreement will be actionable by the occupier. So if a landlord evicts a tenant before the ending of the tenancy, he is in breach of contract. Similarly, if the landlord agrees to provide gas and electricity to a house and then withdraws these facilities, he is again liable for a breach of contract.

36.4.2.3 Claims in tort

Trespass to land

A tenant has the right to the exclusive possession of the demised premises. If the landlord enters onto those premises without permission, he is liable as a trespasser. Licensees who do not have the right to exclusive possession probably cannot sue in trespass.

Trespass to the person

Harassment and unlawful eviction are frequently accompanied by violence or threats of violence. These may well amount to the torts of assault and battery. A battery is the infliction of physical violence on another without lawful excuse; assault is any act which puts a person in immediate and reasonable fear of a battery. This cause of action will be available both to tenants and to licensees.

Trespass to goods

In the process of harassing or evicting an occupier, a landlord frequently damages the occupier's furniture or other personal belongings. This would amount to trespass to goods. If the landlord detains or otherwise deprives the occupier of the use of the goods, this might amount to the tort of conversion. Both tenants and licensees can use this cause of action.

36.4.2.4 The Protection from Eviction Act 1977, s 3

Section 3 of the PEA 1977 provides that when a tenancy or licence which is not 'statutorily protected' comes to an end, but the former tenant continues to reside in the premises, he cannot be evicted without a court order. Any eviction of such a tenant will give rise to a claim in tort for breach of statutory duty. The definition of 'statutorily protected tenancy' excludes from the protection of this section assured and assured shorthold tenancies under the HA 1988 and protected tenancies under the RA 1977.

36.4.2.5 Breach of the Housing Act 1988, s 27

Section 27 of the HA 1988 creates a statutory tort if a landlord:

(a)   attempts unlawfully to deprive a residential occupier of his occupation; or

(b)   knowing or having reasonable cause to believe that the conduct is likely to cause a residential occupier to give up his occupation, does acts likely to interfere with the peace or comfort of the residential occupier or members of his household

and (in either case) as a result the residential occupier gives up his occupation.

For definition of 'residential occupier', see **36.2.1.2**. Note, in particular, that it will include licensees. This tort is satisfied only if the residential occupier actually gives up occupation; this cause of action cannot be used for harassment that does not cause the occupier to leave. Further, there will be no liability under s 27 if the occupier is reinstated in the property either by the landlord or on an order of the court. It is a defence to this claim if the landlord can prove that he believed and had reasonable cause to believe that the occupier had ceased to reside in the premises, or that he had reasonable grounds for doing the acts complained of.

Chapter 37

Repairs to Residential Properties

37.1 Introduction

The issue of repairs may arise in various contexts. The most common is where the tenant complains that work needs doing to the house or flat, for example, that a leaking roof or defective gutter is causing dampness. The question may also arise in a rent arrears case where the tenant has refused to pay rent because of an alleged disrepair; or in a personal injury case where the tenant (or a visitor) has been injured by reason of defective premises.

The first question to be considered is the meaning of the word 'repair'. The basic definition of 'repair' is not affected by the nature of the property involved and so reference should be made to the chapter on repairs in Part II, Commercial Leases (**Chapter 17**).

37.2 Who is liable for repair?

37.2.1 Position at common law

In the absence of any express provisions in the lease or tenancy agreement, the landlord gives no warranty that the premises will be fit for habitation or that he will repair them.

There are two exceptions.

(a) *Furnished lettings*. Where there is a furnished letting, the landlord impliedly warrants that the premises are fit for habitation at the commencement of the term. This is a very limited exception based on the case of *Smith v Marrable* [1843] 11 M&W 5, where a furnished house was infested with bugs. It was held that the tenant could repudiate the tenancy and recover damages for loss suffered. However, there is no continuing obligation on the part of the landlord to keep the premises fit for habitation during the term.

(b) *Common parts*. In certain cases, the courts may imply a covenant to give business efficacy to a lease or tenancy. For example, if the premises consist of a tower block containing lifts, staircases, rubbish chutes and other common parts and the tenancy agreements of the individual flats do not impose obligations on either the tenant or landlord to maintain the common parts, the court may hold that, since the terms of the tenancy agreement are obviously incomplete, and that the premises cannot function without such common parts being maintained, the landlord must have impliedly taken responsibility to keep them in reasonable condition: see *Liverpool City Council v Irwin* [1977] AC 239. However, such implied term is not automatic and depends on the facts of each particular case and is based on the contractual principle that the courts may imply a term to make a contract function. If the lease or tenancy agreement expressly deals with these matters, there is clearly no room for an implied term.

As regards the tenant, there are no implied repairing obligations on his part at common law so that, in the absence of an express agreement, the tenant is not responsible for repair as such. However, a tenant must not commit waste. A tenant under a fixed-term lease is liable for both voluntary and permissive waste. This means that he must not carry out alterations or allow the property to fall into serious disrepair. A yearly periodic tenant is, however, only liable to keep the premises 'wind and water tight'. A weekly tenant on the other hand is not liable for permissive waste but must use the premises in 'a tenant-like manner'. This means that he must take proper care of them, for example, by unblocking drains, cleaning chimneys, mending fuses and doing the little jobs around the property that a reasonable tenant would do. The position at common law is not satisfactory from either the landlord's or the tenant's point of view. The question of repairing liability is, therefore, usually either dealt with expressly by the terms of the tenancy agreement or covered by some statutory provision. If a matter is covered both by an express obligation and also by a statutory provision, and the express obligation is in conflict with the statutory obligation, the statutory obligation prevails.

37.2.2 Express covenants

In many cases the lease or tenancy agreement will expressly set out the repairing obligations of the parties. Subject to the statutory provisions mentioned below, the parties are free to agree who should be liable for which repairs. For example, it may have been agreed that the landlord will be liable for exterior repairs and that the tenant will be liable for interior repairs and decoration. If the lease or tenancy agreement sets out these obligations expressly, those provisions will override the common law and will be enforceable, subject only to statutory intervention.

37.2.3 Modification by statute

Despite the presence or absence of express repairing obligations, the LTA 1985 implies certain repairing obligations on the part of the landlord which cannot be excluded except with leave of the court. These statutory implied terms are important and must now be considered.

37.3 The Landlord and Tenant Act 1985, s 11

37.3.1 Leases to which s 11 applies

Section 11 of the LTA 1985 applies to any lease or agreement for lease of a dwelling house, granted on or after 24 October 1961, if the term is less than seven years. This includes periodic tenancies even if the tenant has been in occupation for more than seven years. It also applies to a fixed-term lease granted for more than seven years if the landlord can determine the term within the first seven years, ie, there is a break clause in the landlord's favour. However, s 11 does not apply to a lease for less than seven years if it contains an option for renewal by the tenant where the term can be extended to more than seven years. No contracting out is allowed unless sanctioned by the county court. This includes indirect contracting out, for example, by placing an obligation on the tenant to pay money in lieu of repairs.

37.3.2 The implied terms

There is an implied covenant by the landlord:

(a) to keep in repair the structure and exterior of the dwelling house (including drains, gutters and external pipes); and

(b) to keep in repair and proper working order the installations in the dwelling house for the supply of water, gas and electricity and for sanitation (including basins, sinks, baths and sanitary conveniences but not other fixtures, fittings and appliances for making use of the supply of water, gas or electricity); and

(c) to keep in repair and proper working order the installations in the dwelling house for space heating and heating water.

37.3.3 'Structure and exterior'

The word 'structure' is not defined by the Act but would clearly include the main fabric of the building such as the main walls, roof, timbers and foundations as distinguished from decorations or fittings. The word 'exterior' is not defined either, but has been held to include paths or steps which form an essential means of access (*Brown v Liverpool Corporation* [1969] 3 All ER 1345) but not paving in the back yard (*Hopwood v Cannock Chase District Council* [1975] 1 WLR 373) nor a footpath at the rear of the house (*King v South Northamptonshire District Council* [1992] 06 EG 152). The words 'structure and exterior' can cause particular problems where a tenant in a block of flats is seeking to force the landlord to do repairs in respect of common parts or to the entire block rather than just the particular flat occupied by the complaining tenant.

It was held in *Campden Hill Towers v Gardner* [1977] QB 823 that the landlord's implied covenant extends only to the flat in question and not to the entire block; it extends to the outside of the inner party wall of the flat, the outer side of the horizontal division between the flat and the flats below and above but does not extend to the entire building. This problem has now been resolved by an amendment made by the HA 1988 but only in respect of leases or tenancies granted on or after 15 January 1989. The position now is that reference to 'dwelling house' in s 11 is extended to include any part of the building in which the landlord has an estate or interest and that any references to 'installations' in the dwelling house include installations directly or indirectly serving the house forming part of the same building or which are owned or under the control of the landlord. Thus, for leases granted on or after 15 January 1989 where the landlord owns the entire block, the landlord will be under an obligation to maintain the structure and exterior of the entire block including common parts and the stipulated facilities. However, it is expressly provided that the landlord is not liable unless the disrepair is such as to affect the tenant's enjoyment of the flat or common parts in question. As to the position with regard to common parts in the case of tenancies granted before 15 January 1989, see **37.2.1**.

37.3.4 'Installations in the dwelling house'

The landlord is also obliged to repair and keep in working order the installations for the supply of water, gas, electricity, sanitation, space heating and water heating. The section does not oblige the landlord to provide these facilities but simply to maintain such as exist at the commencement of the tenancy. Thus, if the house does not have these facilities to begin with there is no obligation on the part of the landlord to provide the necessary installations. Further, it applies only to installations that are actually within the house. If a fault occurs in a supply installation outside the house this is not within the section. However, in the case of flats, where the tenancy was granted on or after 15 January 1989, the obligation extends to installations within the entire building which the landlord owns or to installations within the building over which the landlord has control. Thus, if a flat is centrally heated by a communal boiler in the basement and the boiler breaks down, liability under the section will depend on when the tenancy commenced. If the tenancy commenced prior to 15 January 1989, the landlord will not be liable (under s 11) whereas if the tenancy was granted on or after that date the landlord will be liable.

37.3.5 Standards of repair

Section 11 provides that in determining the standards of repair regard must be had to the age, character and prospective life of the dwelling and the locality in which it is situated (LTA 1985, s 11(3)). Thus, a house in a poor condition at the commencement of the tenancy, in an area of poor quality housing, does not need to be comprehensively repaired under s 11. 'Patching' repairs may satisfy the section depending on the circumstances of each particular case.

37.3.6 Exceptions

There are some specific exceptions to liability under s 11.

Under s 11(2) the covenant does not extend to:

(a)   repairs for which the tenant is liable by virtue of his duty to use the premises in a tenant-like manner;

(b)   rebuilding or reinstating the premises in the case of destruction or damage by fire or by tempest or other accident;

(c)   keeping in repair or maintaining anything that the tenant is entitled to remove from the dwelling house (tenant's fixtures).

Further, the landlord is not liable unless he has notice of the need for repair. Thus, in *O'Brien v Robinson* [1973] AC 912 the claimants were injured when the ceiling of their flat fell on them. This was found to be the result of a latent defect. The landlords were not liable for the personal injuries caused to the claimants since there had been no breach of the duty of repair under s 11 in that the landlord did not know of this latent defect at the material time. However, this requirement for notice applies only to those premises or parts of premises actually demised to the tenant. There is no need for notice in respect of those parts of the premises which remain in the possession or control of the landlord. This will be particularly relevant in relation to the extension of the landlord's liability to the whole of a building made by the HA 1988 (see **37.3.3**).

Chapter 38

Enfranchisement: Long Leases of Houses

38.1 Introduction

The LRA 1967 confers on certain tenants holding long leases of houses the right to acquire the freehold (and superior leasehold reversions) on their properties. Alternatively, they can acquire an extended lease. For these rights to apply, various conditions must be fulfilled. The qualifying conditions in the 1967 Act were amended by the Commonhold and Leasehold Reform Act 2002 in respect of applications received on or after 26 July 2002. This book sets out the conditions applicable as from that date. In particular, the former requirements that the lease must be at a low rent and that the tenant must have resided in the house for at least three years have been removed.

38.2 The qualifying conditions in outline

There are three major requirements:

(a)   there must be a 'house';

(b)   let on a 'long lease';

(c)   tenanted by a 'qualifying tenant'.

38.2.1 'A house'

The LRA 1967 applies only to houses and not to flats.

Section 2(1) of the LRA 1967 defines a house as:

> For the purposes of this Part of this Act, 'house' includes any building designed or adapted for living in and reasonably so called, notwithstanding that the building is not structurally detached, or was not or is not solely designed or adapted for living in, or is divided horizontally into flats or maisonettes.

This definition includes ordinary purpose-built houses, and it can include buildings which were not originally houses (eg, barns, warehouses, stables, etc) later converted or adapted as houses.

The main problem area is deciding what is a house 'reasonably so called'. This definition can cause problems in relation to shops with living accommodation above and also with properties which have been converted into flats.

As regards shops with living accommodation, the leading authority is the House of Lords' decision in the case of *Tandon v Trustees of Spurgeons Homes* [1982] AC 755, which concerned a purpose-built shop with a flat above. Approximately 75% of the property was attributed to the shop and 25% to the living accommodation. By a majority decision, it was held that the premises were a house reasonably so called even though it was also reasonable to call them something else, ie, a shop! It is a question of law whether it is reasonable to call a building a house, but if the building is designed or adapted for living in, in exceptional circumstances only will a judge be justified in holding that it is not reasonable to call it a house.

Another problem concerns buildings which are converted into flats. Many properties which were originally houses have been converted into flats. An individual flat cannot be a house but, nevertheless, the whole building may retain its characteristics as a house. For example, if a house is converted into two self-contained flats by the owner of a long lease who continues to occupy one of the flats, sub-letting the other, the long leaseholder may be in a position to enfranchise. The building looked at as a whole may still reasonably be called a house notwithstanding the internal sub-division.

38.2.2   'Long lease'

Section 3 of the LRA 1967 defines a long lease as a 'tenancy granted for a term of years certain exceeding 21 years'. It is the length of the original term that matters. The fact that less than 21 years remains unexpired when the rights are exercised is not relevant to this particular issue. Further, the fact that the lease may be terminated before it runs 21 years (eg, by forfeiture, break clause, etc) is to be ignored. If the long lease has expired but the tenant holds over under another tenancy of the property, the new tenancy is deemed to be a long lease (subject to exceptions).

38.2.3   'Qualifying tenant'

The LRA 1967 does not use the expression 'qualifying tenant' but it does impose certain minimum requirements which must be satisfied before the tenant 'qualifies' for enfranchisement or an extended lease. The tenant must, at the date when he serves the appropriate notice (see **38.3.1**) exercising his rights, have had the lease vested in him for at least two years.

38.3   Enfranchisement or extended lease

The tenant who satisfies the above conditions will normally wish to enfranchise. This means that the landlord must convey the fee simple to the tenant at a price, and on the terms, referred to in the LRA 1967. Alternatively, the tenant may elect to take an extended lease. Here, the landlord must grant the tenant a new lease for the unexpired residue of the term of the existing lease plus a further 50 years. The new lease will be, broadly, on the same terms as the existing lease and the rent will be the same until the expiry date of the existing lease, but thereafter, the rent will be replaced by a modern ground rent (reviewed after 25 years of the extra 50 years).

38.3.1   Desire notice

The tenant must serve written notice of his desire ('the desire notice') in the prescribed form to have either the freehold or an extended lease. This desire notice is normally the first step in the procedure to obtain the rights granted by the Act. The desire notice is deemed to be an estate contract and it should, therefore, be protected by an appropriate registration under the Land Charges Act 1972 or the LRA 2002 as the case may be. The landlord must, within two months, serve a Notice in Reply admitting or objecting to the tenant's claim. For the detailed procedure, reference should be made to the Act and the regulations made under it.

Although the desire notice is deemed to create an estate contract, it is generally personal to the tenant and is not assignable to third parties. However, if the tenant assigns the lease, he can assign the benefit of the desire notice at the same time to the assignee of the lease. The assignee could then proceed with the acquisition of the freehold or an extended lease even though the assignee does not qualify under the Act (LRA 1967, s 5).

38.4   Terms of the conveyance of the freehold

The conveyance (or transfer if the landlord's title is registered) will be subject to:

(a)   the tenancy; and

(b)   tenant's incumbrances but free from other incumbrances.

The broad effect of this is that the tenant will be bound by any mortgages or charges which have been created in respect of the leasehold interest, but will take free from mortgages or charges created by the landlord over the freehold interest.

The conveyance will grant and reserve, broadly, the same easements as existed under the lease.

Disputes about the terms of the conveyance (other than as to price) are resolved by the court.

38.5   The price of the freehold

The LRA 1967 lays down the principles and formulae for ascertaining the price and the appeals machinery if it cannot be agreed between the parties.

There are two methods of ascertaining the price depending on the value of the house and premises. They are dealt with by s 9(1) and s 9(1A) of the LRA 1967 respectively.

The valuation under s 9(1) is very favourable to the tenant. It must be assumed for valuation purposes that the landlord is selling the freehold subject to the lease and on the assumption that this had been extended for a further 50 years under the Act and assuming the tenant is not the buyer. It is thus looked at as if the freehold is being bought largely for its investment income (which, by definition, is likely to be fairly small). The fact that the tenant can, on acquisition, merge the freehold and leasehold interests is ignored. This 'marriage value', as it is sometimes called, is not taken into account under s 9(1).

The valuation under s 9(1) only applies to lower value properties. For higher value properties, a much less favourable formula has to be used. This not only requires marriage value to be taken into account, but also requires an assumption that the tenant has no right to extend the lease under LRA 1967. Both these assumptions will result in a considerably higher price being paid than if the lower value formula were to be used. The method of deciding whether a house falls into the lower or higher value bands depends upon whether the house had a rateable value on 31 March 1990. If it did (and most houses in existence at that date would have had a rateable value), then the rule is that houses with rateable values of £500 or less (£1,000 or less if the house is in Greater London) will be classed as lower value. Any other houses will be classed as higher value. Owing to the abolition of domestic rates, it is not possible to use rateable value as a deciding factor for houses not rated on 31 March 1990, ie, basically houses built since that date. For these houses, a complex formula is applied based on the premium originally paid on the grant and the length of the term, for which, see s 1(1)(a)(i) of the LRA 1967 (as amended).

In addition to the purchase price, the tenant must pay all reasonable legal and valuation fees incurred by the landlord. Disputes as to price are dealt with by the Leasehold Valuation Tribunal.

Chapter 39
The Landlord and Tenant Act 1987

39.1 Introduction

Under the LTA 1987, if a landlord of a building composed of flats wishes to dispose of his freehold reversion he is obliged, subject to the conditions specified in the Act, to offer it first to the relevant tenants.

Further, in the case of 'bad management' by the landlord the court can, in certain circumstances, compel the landlord to transfer his interest to the tenants.

However, the main impact of the Act is the so-called 'tenant's right of first refusal'. The relevant law is contained in Pt I of the Act. This has been almost entirely substituted by the HA 1996, with the object of making it easier for tenants to enforce their rights. Criminal sanctions have also been imposed for landlords who evade the Act.

39.2 The tenant's right of first refusal

There are four major conditions before tenants can claim the pre-emption rights conferred by Pt I of the Act:

(a)   the premises must come within the Act;

(b)   the landlord must not be an exempt landlord;

(c)   the tenant must be a qualifying tenant; and

(d)   there must be a proposed 'relevant disposal'.

39.2.1 The premises

The premises must consist of a building divided into at least two flats occupied by 'qualifying tenants' where not more than 50% of the floor area is used for non-residential purposes. Thus, if there are shops on the ground floor with flats above, the Act will not apply if the floor area of the shops exceeds the floor area of the flats.

39.2.2 The landlord

Certain landlords are excluded from the Act. These are mainly public sector landlords, for example, local authorities, the Housing Corporation and certain housing associations. In the private sector, resident landlords are excluded. A resident landlord is a landlord who lives in part of the building (not being a purpose-built block of flats) and who occupies a flat in the premises as his only or principal home and who has occupied it for at least 12 months.

Subject to the above, the landlord is the tenant's immediate landlord but if that landlord does not own the freehold or a reversion of at least seven years then the superior landlord is also regarded as a landlord for the purposes of the Act.

39.2.3 Qualifying tenants

A tenant is a qualifying tenant unless his tenancy falls into one of the following categories:

(a)   a protected shorthold tenancy;

(b)   a business tenancy under Pt II of the LTA 1954;

(c)   a tenancy terminable on cessation of employment;

(d)   an assured tenancy under the HA 1988.

So which tenancies will be qualifying? Although there is no requirement for a qualifying tenant to have a long lease, the exclusion of assured tenancies in practical terms dictates that most qualifying tenants will be long leaseholders at low rents. However, any surviving RA 1977 tenants will also qualify, as these are not excluded from the definition.

39.2.4   Relevant disposal

A relevant disposal is the disposal of any estate or interest in the premises which is not excluded from the Act. The exclusions consist of the following:

(a)   the grant of a tenancy of a single flat;

(b)   the grant of a mortgage, although a sale by a lender in exercise of his power of sale would be a relevant disposal;

(c)   a disposal to a trustee in bankruptcy or liquidator;

(d)   transfers ordered by the court in connection with matrimonial or succession proceedings;

(e)   a disposal following a compulsory purchase order;

(f)   a gift to a member of the landlord's family or to a charity;

(g)   the surrender of a lease in pursuance of a provision in the lease to that effect;

(h)   a disposal to the Crown;

(i)   a disposal within a group of companies which have been associated for at least two years.

If the landlord proposes to make a relevant disposal (as defined above), he must serve notice on the qualifying tenants detailing the proposed terms, including the price, and stating that the notice constitutes an offer to dispose of the property to them on these terms and certain other particulars. If more than 50% of the qualifying tenants decide to accept the offer, they must do so within the period stated by the notice which must be not less than two months. The purchasing tenants are then given a further two months in which to nominate a person who will purchase the landlord's interest on the tenants' behalf, for example, a limited company formed for that purpose. If the tenants do not elect to purchase within the first two months or do not make a nomination within the second two months or if the tenants fail to complete within three months, the landlord is free to proceed with the disposal elsewhere.

If the landlord makes a disposal without complying with the Act, the tenants have a right of acquisition against the buyer. Thus, a buyer from a landlord falling within the Act should always ensure the requisite notices have been served and the time limits complied with before the relevant disposal proceeds.

39.2.5   Anti-avoidance measures – HA 1996

As originally drafted, the LTA 1987 did not impose any real sanctions for landlords who failed to comply with its provisions and some freeholders sought to exploit ways round the legislation. The HA 1996 attempts to solve these omissions.

A new s 10A is inserted into the LTA 1987 which makes it a criminal offence not to notify the tenants of a proposal to make a relevant disposal. New provisions are also inserted making it clear that a contract to make a relevant disposal is itself a relevant disposal and making it easier for tenants to enforce their rights both against a disposing landlord and against a person who takes the property under a disposal not complying with the Act.

39.3 Compulsory acquisition of the reversion

Part I of the Act applies where the landlord wishes to dispose of his reversion, but under Pt III of the Act the landlord can, in certain circumstances, be forced to sell his interest to the tenants against his wishes. Part III applies where there has been a history of bad management by the landlord. The detailed rules are complex and are beyond the scope of this book.

Chapter 40

The Leasehold Reform, Housing and Urban Development Act 1993

40.1 Introduction

Tenants of flats have traditionally been excluded from the benefits of enfranchisement afforded to other long leaseholders (see **Chapter 38**). One major problem has always been the need to ensure the proper management and repair of a block of flats. This might prove difficult between freehold flat-owners. There is also the question as to who would own the common parts of the block. The LRHUDA 1993 has now given to flat-owners a collective right to enfranchise, the freehold in the whole block being acquired by a nominee on behalf of the individual tenants. It also contains an alternative right for individual tenants to purchase a new lease running until 90 years after the term date of their original lease. Tenants under long leases of flats (and houses) do, in any event, have a right under the LTA 1954, Pt I (as amended) to remain in possession following the ending of their leases, basically as assured tenants under the HA 1988. Although flat tenants do thus have security of tenure at the end of their long leases, this is only at a price. As an assured tenant, they will be required to pay the full open market rent for their flat. This will be fixed, without taking into account any premium which was paid on the acquisition of the lease.

The qualifying conditions under the 1993 Act were amended by the Commonhold and Leasehold Reform Act 2002 in respect of applications received on or after 26 July 2002. This book sets out the conditions applicable as from that date. When further provisions of the 2002 Act are brought into force, it will then be mandatory for the enfranchisement to be effected by a 'right to enfranchise' (RTE) company. This will be a private company, limited by guarantee, with articles and memorandum in a form prescribed by the Secretary of State.

40.2 Collective enfranchisement

40.2.1 The right

Collective enfranchisement consists of the tenants in a block of flats acquiring the freehold in the block, the freehold being conveyed into the name of a nominee on their behalf. This conveyance can take place without the landlord's consent, although there are limited grounds on which the landlord can resist a claim (see **40.2.4**). For the right to exist, various conditions must also be fulfilled. In particular, the tenants must be 'qualifying tenants' of 'flats' which are themselves in 'premises', all as defined by the Act.

For the right to be available, 'qualifying tenants' must hold at least two-thirds of the total number of flats in the premises. The premises in question, therefore, need not be let exclusively to tenants on long leases; some of the flats might be let to HA 1988 tenants, for example. Equally, the premises need not be let exclusively for residential purposes, but see **40.2.8**.

40.2.2 Nature of the collective right

The right to collective enfranchisement is the right to have the freehold in the premises acquired on behalf of the participating qualifying tenants by a person or persons appointed by them at a price to be determined in accordance with the Act.

40.2.3 Exercise of the collective right

As stated in **40.2.1**, at least two-thirds of the flats in a block must be held by 'qualifying tenants' before the collective right arises. However, it is not necessary for all of the qualifying tenants in the block to be involved in the enfranchisement. The right to enfranchise is exercised by the service of the appropriate notice on the reversioner and to be valid, the tenants serving the notice must occupy at least one-half of the flats in the block. When further provisions of the Commonhold and Leasehold Reform Act 2002 are brought into force, the right to enfranchise will only be exercisable by a 'right to enfranchise' company. This will be a company limited by guarantee with articles and memorandum in a prescribed form. Membership of the company is limited to the qualifying tenants, and at least half of the qualifying tenants in the block must be members of the company.

40.2.4 Landlord's grounds for opposition

A landlord can dispute the right to enfranchise if he can establish that one or more of the qualifying conditions have not been complied with by the applicants, for example, if two-thirds of the flats in the block are not held by qualifying tenants. Apart from this, his only ground of opposition will be if he can establish that he intends to redevelop the whole or a substantial part of the premises. Such a ground for opposition will only be possible, however, where not less than two-thirds of the long leases in the block are due to terminate within five years and the landlord cannot reasonably carry out his redevelopment without obtaining possession.

40.2.5 Qualifying tenants

A person will be a 'qualifying tenant' for collective enfranchisement if he is a 'tenant' of a 'flat' under a 'long lease'.

'Tenant' is defined to include a person holding a lease or tenancy or an agreement for a lease or tenancy; and lease and tenancy includes a sub-lease and a sub-tenancy. Joint leaseholders are treated together as a single tenant.

'Flat' means a separate set of premises, whether or not on the same floor, which forms part of a building, and is constructed or adapted for use as a dwelling, and either the whole or some material part lies above or below some other part of the building. The emphasis in the definition is to at least part of the flat being above or below some other part of the building. Thus, flats above shops etc will be included in this definition, but 'granny flats', or similar premises, which consist of an extension to an existing building, but are not above or below part of that building, will not be within the definition. This part of the definition ties in with the definition of a house for the purposes of the LRA 1967 (see **38.2.1**).

'Long lease' is defined to mean, inter alia:

(a)   a lease granted for a term of years certain exceeding 21 years. Any provisions for determination within that period, whether by landlord or by tenant, and whether by forfeiture or otherwise, will not prevent the lease from being a long lease;

(b)   a new tenancy granted expressly or impliedly to a tenant on the expiry of a long lease at a low rent will itself be deemed to be a long lease irrespective of its length. Similarly, where a lease is being continued under the terms of Pt I of the LTA 1954, it will be included in the definition of a long lease.

40.2.6 Qualifying tenants: exclusions

A person will not be a qualifying tenant if:

(a)   his lease is within Pt II of the LTA 1954 (business tenancies);

(b)   his immediate landlord is a charitable housing trust and the flat forms part of the accommodation provided by it for its charitable purposes;

(c)   the lease is an unlawful sub-lease out of a superior lease which is not itself a long lease at a low rent.

40.2.7 Premises: definition

The flats must be in premises, as defined. Premises are defined as a self-contained building or as a self-contained part of a building.

A building is a self-contained building if it is structurally detached; part of a building is a self-contained part if it consists of a vertical division of the building and its structure is such that that part could be redeveloped independently of the remainder. In addition, the services provided for the occupiers (by pipes, cables, etc) are or could be provided independently of the services provided for the rest of the building.

40.2.8 Premises: exclusions

The 'premises' need not be used exclusively for residential purposes, provided that any parts occupied or intended to be occupied for non-residential purposes do not exceed 25% of the internal floor area of the premises as a whole. In making this calculation, any common parts of the building are to be ignored.

Premises will not be included within the definition if they have a resident landlord. There will be a resident landlord if, at any time, the freeholder or an adult member of his family occupies a flat in the premises as his only or principal home and has done so for at least the previous 12 months. However, this exclusion does not apply if the premises contain more than four units or are a purpose-built block of flats. Nor, as from 26 July 2002, does it apply unless the same person has owned the freehold since before the conversion. In these cases, the Act will still apply even though there is a resident landlord.

40.2.9 Interests included in the collective right

The acquisition will cover not only the freehold of the premises in which the flats are situated, but also any garages, etc let with the flats and any surrounding grounds over which the flat-owners have easements, for example, for access or for parking.

40.2.10 Interests excluded from the collective right

The freeholder can retain the title to any underlying minerals, provided that proper provision is made for the support of the premises.

40.2.11 Interests to be leased back

The freeholder can also retain, by means of a lease-back arrangement, certain parts of the acquired premises. The following must be leased back:

(a)   flats let by the freeholder on secure tenancies;

(b)   flats let by housing associations on tenancies other than secure tenancies.

The following are to be leased back if the freeholder so requires:

(a)   units which are not flats let to qualifying tenants. This could include any part of the premises which are let on a business tenancy, or on tenancies which are not long leases at a low rent; it will also include unlet flats;

(b)   a flat occupied by a resident landlord.

40.2.12 Terms of the lease back

There are detailed provisions dealing with the terms of any lease to be granted back to the freeholder (see Sch 8 to the Act). Basically, unless the parties agree otherwise, or the Residential Property Tribunal otherwise directs, they are to be 999-year leases at a peppercorn rent with appropriate appurtenant rights, landlord's covenant for repair, rebuilding and insurance and service charge provisions.

40.2.13 Enfranchisement price (Sch 5)

The price to be paid for the freehold will be the total of three separate elements:

(a)   market value;

(b)   half of the marriage value;

(c)   compensation.

Where the freehold and intermediate leases are being acquired, each interest is to be valued and paid for separately, so the market value, marriage value and any compensation for each individual interest being acquired will need to be calculated and paid over to the respective owner. In addition, the reasonable costs of each respective owner will be payable.

40.2.14 Market value

Market value is the price which might be expected to be realised if the property was sold on the open market by a willing seller, with neither the nominee buyer nor any participating tenant seeking to buy. Any defects in the landlord's title will thus serve to reduce the value of his interest as they would on any other sale. The following assumptions (inter alia) are also to be made in arriving at the market value of the interest:

(a)   On the assumption that the seller is selling the fee simple:
  (i)   subject to any leases subject to which the freeholder's interest is to be acquired by the buyer; but
  (ii)   subject also to any intermediate or other leasehold interests in the premises which are to be acquired by the buyer.

(b)   On the assumption that the Act confers no rights to acquire the premises or to acquire a new lease.

(c)   On the assumption that any increase in value caused by improvements carried out by any participating tenant is to be disregarded.

40.2.15 Marriage value

Marriage value is a complex valuation principle and follows from the fact that when both leasehold and freehold interests in a property become vested in the same person then the value of those interests to that person will be more than the combined value of the interests when held by different persons. It is, of course, generally the case that a freehold subject to a tenancy will be worth a lot less than the same freehold when vacant possession is available. So, to give an example, if the freehold when held by X is worth £30,000 and the leasehold interest when held by Y £40,000, it may well be that when Y also acquires the freehold the value of the property may now be £110,000, ie, £40,000 more than the sum total of freehold and leasehold interests when owned by different people. This £40,000 is the marriage value and the landlord is entitled to one half of it. However, the landlord is not entitled to any share of the marriage value in the case of leases having more than 80 years unexpired.

40.2.16 Compensation

The third element in assessing the price is compensation to the freeholder for any loss or damage he may suffer by result of the enfranchisement. This will include any diminution in the value of any other property owned by the landlord, including loss of development value. This is to cover the situation, for example, where the landlord is now unable to redevelop his adjoining property due to the fact that he no longer is the owner of the enfranchised premises.

40.3 Individual acquisition of a long lease

40.3.1 Nature of the right

The right given is the right to be granted a new lease to expire 90 years after the expiry date of the tenant's existing lease. This new lease is to be at a peppercorn rent, but the tenant must pay a premium to be calculated as laid down by the Act. The new lease is to take effect immediately in substitution for the tenant's existing lease. This right is available whether or not the right to collective enfranchisement is also available. The new lease will be binding upon the landlord's lenders even if the existing lease was granted in breach of the terms of the mortgage.

40.3.2 Entitlement to a new lease

Entitlement to a new lease is given to a tenant if:

(a)   he is a qualifying tenant; and

(b)   the lease has been vested in him for at least the previous two years.

The definition of qualifying tenant is the same as for the purposes of enfranchisement (see **40.2.5**).

40.3.3 Refusal of new lease

The landlord can obtain a court order declaring that the tenant's right to a new lease is not exercisable, where the court is satisfied that:

(a)   the tenant's existing lease is due to terminate within five years from the date of the tenant requesting a new lease; and

(b)   the landlord intends, once the existing lease has expired, to demolish or reconstruct the whole or a substantial part of the premises and he could not reasonably do so without obtaining possession of the flat.

40.3.4 Terms of the new lease

The new lease is to be on the same terms as the existing lease except with regard to the following:

(a)   the rent, which will be a peppercorn;

(b)   the term, which will be for a period to end 90 years after the term date of the existing lease;

(c)   the omission of property comprised in the existing lease but not comprised in the flat. However, for these purposes, 'flat' includes any garage, outhouse, garden or yard let to the tenant with the flat;

(d)   the inclusion, where the existing lease is inadequate, of provisions for variable service charges in respect of repairs, services, maintenance and insurance;

(e)   the inclusion of a statement that the lease has been granted under these provisions;

(f)   the omission of any options or pre-emptions contained in the existing lease;

(g)   limitation of the landlord's liability under his covenants to breaches for which he is personally responsible;

(h)   modifications to reflect defects in the existing lease or other provisions which it would be unreasonable to include without modification;

(i)   the reservation of a right for the landlord to apply to the court for possession for redevelopment purposes during the last 12 months of the term of the original lease or during the last five years of the new lease, subject to compensation being payable.

40.3.5   The amount of the premium

Complex provisions are laid down for the calculation of the premium. Briefly, the premium is to be the aggregate of:

(a)   the diminution in the market value of the landlord's interest, comparing the value before and after the grant of the new lease, and ignoring the tenants' rights under this Act; and

(b)   50% of the marriage value. However, the landlord has no entitlement to any share if the marriage value has more than 80 years left unexpired; and

(c)   reasonable compensation to the landlord for loss or damage resulting from the grant of the new lease in respect of other property, including loss of development value.

In addition, the tenant will be responsible for the landlord's costs in granting the new lease.

40.3.6   The effect of the grant of a new lease

Once a new lease has been granted, this will not preclude a subsequent exercise of the right to collective enfranchisement. Equally, a further claim to another new lease under these provisions can be brought in relation to any new lease granted. However, that is the only security of tenure applicable to such lease; no other security of tenure provisions are to apply to the lease nor to any sub-tenancies granted out of it once the term date has passed. This means that neither the tenant nor any sub-tenant (whether lawful or otherwise) can claim protection after the end of the 90-year extended term, whether under the LTA 1954 (Pts I or II), RA 1977, HA 1988 or any similar legislation.

40.4   Enfranchisement, extended lease or right to manage?

So, most flat tenants will have a choice – individual lease extension or collective enfranchisement. Which should they choose? The convenience of an individual extension – rather than having to try to obtain a required number of other flat owners to agree to join in enfranchisement – will often be persuasive.

But the first question has to be *why* one or other option is on the agenda. Flat owners have two major problems: the rapidly diminishing value of their flat when the term starts to run out; and problems with landlords overcharging for services, or maybe just not carrying out the services to a satisfactory standard. Enfranchisement will solve both of those problems; lease extension will not solve problems with the services.

Under s 71 of the Commonhold and Leasehold Reform Act 2002, flat owners are given a 'right to manage'. It is available in the same circumstances as enfranchisement and enables the tenants compulsorily to take over the running of the block, provision of services, etc from the landlord. There is no need to prove any fault on the landlord's part and no monetary payment is required (other than the landlord's costs). For flat owners whose main concern is the services, this is another alternative.

Chapter 41

Commonhold

41.1 What is it?

Commonhold is a new system of freehold ownership designed for use in the case of interdependent properties (eg, blocks of flats or offices, shopping malls and business parks, etc). Technically, it is not a new estate in land; it is the ordinary fee simple (or freehold) estate with special attributes to make it suitable for use in the case of such properties by ensuring that positive covenants can be enforced against successors in title.

41.2 Why is it needed?

Previously, such properties were usually disposed of as leaseholds. In the case of blocks of flats and the like, the stability of the whole building depends upon satisfactory arrangements for the proper maintenance and repair of the structure of the building. Positive obligations (eg, repair, payment of service charges) could only be enforced satisfactorily by the grant of leases; the burden of a positive covenant does not pass on a sale of freehold land. But leases, by their very nature, are a depreciating asset. As the unexpired residue reduces, they become less saleable (or mortgageable — see the *CML Lenders' Handbook* as to mortgage lenders often requiring a minimum unexpired residue of 50 years before they will accept a leasehold flat for mortgage purposes.)

41.3 History

Other jurisdictions (including Scotland!) have had similar schemes for many years. We have been thinking about it since the report of the Wilberforce Committee on positive covenants recommended the introduction of a similar scheme in 1965!

The Commonhold and Leasehold Reform Act 2002 received the Royal Assent on 1 May 2002. The commonhold provisions were brought into force on 27 September 2004.

41.4 How does it work?

Commonhold can only be created out of registered land. Each separate property in the development (eg, each flat) is called a 'unit'. This is to emphasise that commonhold is not just designed for use in the context of residential flats; it is also be available for use in commercial developments.

Each 'unit-holder' owns the freehold in his respective unit; the unit-holder is registered at Land Registry as 'the proprietor of the fee simple in a Commonhold unit'. So it will be clear to any buyer that the land is commonhold.

The freehold in the common parts is then vested in a 'Commonhold Association' (CA) of which all the unit-holders are members. There is also a 'Commonhold Community Statement' (CCS) which sets out the rights and liabilities of the unit-holders and the CA.

It is possible for a unit to consist of two or more physically separate areas of land (eg, a flat and a garage in a separate block).

Units may be divided from one another vertically (eg, terraced houses), horizontally (eg, flats) or may be free-standing (eg, detached houses).

Where the divisions are horizontal, no part of the commonhold may be over or under any part of the building which is not part of the commonhold development. So the whole of a building must be developed as commonhold; part cannot be sold off as commonhold and the remainder let leasehold.

41.5   The Commonhold Association (CA) (ss 34–36)

41.5.1   What is it?

This is a private company limited by guarantee and registered at Companies House in the usual way.

Membership, however, is limited to the unit-holders within the development.

The CA has a standard set of memorandum and articles prescribed by the Lord Chancellor from time to time.

41.5.2   Rights and duties

The CA is under a duty to manage the development in such a way as to allow the unit-holders to exercise their rights and enjoy their occupation of their units. It is also charged with ensuring that the unit-holders comply with their obligations. However, the CA is given discretion not to enforce unit-holders' obligations if that would be more conducive to maintaining harmonious relationships between all the unit-holders, provided that this will not cause any unit-holder significant loss or significant disadvantage.

The CA is obliged to consider the use of conciliation, mediation and arbitration before legal proceedings are commenced.

41.6   The Commonhold Community Statement (CCS) (ss 31–33)

41.6.1   What is it?

The CCS contains the rules and regulations of the development. It sets out the rights and duties of the CA and of the individual unit-holders. In many respects it takes the place of the lease in a leasehold development and contains many of the same provisions.

41.6.2   What does it contain?

It contains many of the usual provisions found in a lease, for example:

(a)   rights over the common parts (these can be granted in the CCS without any further formality, eg, a deed which is usually required to grant an easement);

(b)   obligation to pay the service charge;

(c)   obligation to repair and maintain;

(d)   the permitted use for the development;

(e)   obligation to insure;

(f)   obligation to repair and maintain the common parts.

41.6.3   Effect of CCS (s 16)

The terms of the CCS are binding on the CA and all present and future unit-holders. However, former unit-holders will not be liable in relation to matters arising after they have ceased to be unit-holders; any existing liability will continue.

41.7   How is a commonhold created? (ss 1–10)

41.7.1   New developments

Creation is voluntary, both for new and existing developments. A developer can choose to develop a new block of flats etc leasehold, should he wish to do so.

There need only be a minimum of two units in the development.

In the case of a new development, the freeholder applies to Land Registry for the registration of a commonhold in relation to the land in question. The application must be accompanied by the prescribed documentation. This includes detailed plans of the development, the CCS and the articles and memorandum of the CA.

41.7.2   Conversions of existing developments

In the case of an existing leasehold development (eg, a block of flats), it is again only the freeholder who can convert it into a commonhold. However, he will need the consent of *all* existing tenants with leases for terms of more than 21 years and their mortgagees. Because of the requirement for unanimity, it is thought likely that only a few existing blocks of flats will convert in the short term.

The application must again be accompanied by the prescribed documentation.

There is provision for consent to be deemed or dispensed with in certain circumstances. However, due to the emphasis on the need for unanimous consent, this only applies in cases where a person whose consent is needed cannot be traced or fails to reply to correspondence.

It is not possible for long leaseholders to convert directly to commonhold; first they must enfranchise under the existing leasehold reform legislation (as amended) and then the company owning the freehold must apply to convert as above. Consent of all the leaseholders (etc) is still required, as above.

41.8   Ombudsman scheme (s 42)

The Act provides for an Ombudsman scheme to be set up and for a CA to be a member of it. The Ombudsman deals with disputes between the CA and a unit-holder. The CA is required to comply with any decision of the Ombudsman and, if it does not, the matter may be referred to the High Court which may order the directors of the CA to ensure that it complies with the decision.

41.9   Termination of commonhold (ss 43–56)

There are detailed provisions dealing with the termination of a CA (eg, if the block becomes life-expired). There are two basic methods:

(a)   where a winding-up resolution has been passed with 100% of the members voting in favour, by application to Land Registry; *or*

(b)   where 80% of the members have voted in favour, by application to the court.

41.10 Commonhold in practice

Despite its availability for both residential and commercial developments, it is thought that, initially at least, the main use of commonhold will be for blocks of flats and other residential developments. There may well be a commercial advantage in this as many lay clients regard leases with suspicion as being something inferior to freehold land and may, therefore, be prepared to pay a premium to obtain a freehold flat. It is likely, therefore, that most new flat developments will be as commonholds.

The position with regard to commercial developments is less clear. Currently, office blocks, shopping centres, business parks are generally developed as leasehold. This, however, is perhaps less driven by the legal need to make covenants enforceable than by commercial realities. Many occupiers of commercial premises do not want to buy the freehold in their unit; they prefer the flexibility of a lease. Of course, it would be possible for a property company to purchase the freehold in a particular unit from a commonhold developer and then let it on a commercial lease, but it is thought that most commercial developments will remain as leasehold. In Sydney, it is estimated that about 17% of commercial units are held under the New South Wales equivalent of commonhold – some 40 years after its introduction.

So far, commonhold has only been adopted in a handful of developments. In February 2006, however, Crest Nicholson plc announced that it would adopt commonhold for its Oakgrove scheme in Milton Keynes. This will provide up to 2,300 new homes, a landscaped wildlife corridor, shops and a commercial centre. No doubt other developers will watch this scheme with interest.

Part III Summary – Residential Tenancies

Topic	Summary	Reference
Introduction to residential tenancies	Residential tenancies have different statutory protections depending upon whether they are granted for a short term at a full rent or for a long term in return for a premium.	Chapter 32
Assured tenancies	Assured tenancies were introduced by the Housing Act 1988. They have extensive security of tenure but no rent control. Lettings on or after 28 February 1997 will only be assured if written notice to that effect is given.	Chapter 33
Assured shorthold tenancies	All lettings on or after 28 February 1997 will be shortholds. These confer no security of tenure – although two months notice to terminate must be given.	Chapter 34
Rent Act 1977	This Act gives wide ranging security of tenure and control over the amount of rent which can be charged to tenants whose letting commenced prior to 15 January 1989.	Chapter 35
Protection from eviction	There are criminal sanctions preventing the obtaining of possession of residential properties without a court order or for attempting to harass residential tenants in order to make them give up possession.	Chapter 36
Repairs to residential properties	A landlord of a residential property let under a lease not exceeding seven years in length is statutorily liable to repair the structure and exterior of the property as well as certain installations inside the property.	Chapter 37
Enfranchisement – long leases of houses	The Leasehold Reform Act 1967 enables tenants of long leasehold houses to compulsorily acquire the freehold reversion or to acquire an extended lease.	Chapter 38
Landlord and Tenant Act 1987	This Act gives owners of most leasehold flats a right of first refusal should the landlord, amongst other things, wish to dispose of the freehold reversion in the block.	Chapter 39
Leasehold Reform, Housing and Urban Development Act 1993	This Act gives most owners of leasehold flats three rights: to acquire an extended lease; collectively to compulsorily acquire the freehold reversion; and collectively to take over the management of the block.	Chapter 40

Topic	Summary	Reference
Commonhold	The Government introduced this new system of land ownership in 2004 to facilitate the freehold ownership of flats and other interdependent properties. It has not been used much in practice.	Chapter 41

Appendix 1
Prescribed forms of notice under the Landlord and Tenant Act 1954

Form 1

LANDLORD'S NOTICE ENDING A BUSINESS TENANCY WITH PROPOSALS FOR A NEW ONE

Section 25 of the Landlord and Tenant Act 1954

IMPORTANT NOTE FOR THE LANDLORD: If you are willing to grant a new tenancy, complete this form and send it to the tenant. If you wish to oppose the grant of a new tenancy, use form 2 in Schedule 2 to the Landlord and Tenant Act 1954, Part 2 (Notices) Regulations 2004 or, where the tenant may be entitled to acquire the freehold or an extended lease, form 7 in that Schedule, instead of this form.

To: (*insert name and address of tenant*)

From: (*insert name and address of landlord*)

1. This notice applies to the following property: (*insert address or description of property*).

2. I am giving you notice under section 25 of the Landlord and Tenant Act 1954 to end your tenancy on (*insert date*).

3. I am not opposed to granting you a new tenancy. You will find my proposals for the new tenancy, which we can discuss, in the Schedule to this notice.

4. If we cannot agree on all the terms of a new tenancy, either you or I may ask the court to order the grant of a new tenancy and settle the terms on which we cannot agree.

5. If you wish to ask the court for a new tenancy you must do so by the date in paragraph 2, unless we agree in writing to a later date and do so before the date in paragraph 2.

6. Please send all correspondence about this notice to:

Name:

Address:

Signed: Date:

*[Landlord] *[On behalf of the landlord] *[Mortgagee] *[On behalf of the mortgagee]

*(*delete if inapplicable*)

SCHEDULE

LANDLORD'S PROPOSALS FOR A NEW TENANCY

(*attach or insert proposed terms of the new tenancy*)

IMPORTANT NOTE FOR THE TENANT

This Notice is intended to bring your tenancy to an end. If you want to continue to occupy your property after the date specified in paragraph 2 you must act quickly. If you are in any doubt about the action that you should take, get advice immediately from a solicitor or a surveyor.

The landlord is prepared to offer you a new tenancy and has set out proposed terms in the Schedule to this notice. You are not bound to accept these terms. They are merely

suggestions as a basis for negotiation. **In the event of disagreement, ultimately the court would settle the terms of the new tenancy.**

It would be wise to seek professional advice before agreeing to accept the landlord's terms or putting forward your own proposals.

NOTES

The sections mentioned below are sections of the Landlord and Tenant Act 1954, as amended, (most recently by the **Regulatory Reform** (Business Tenancies) (England and Wales) Order 2003).

Ending of tenancy and grant of new tenancy

This notice is intended to bring your tenancy to an end on the date given in paragraph 2. Section 25 contains rules about the date that the landlord can put in that paragraph.

However, your landlord is prepared to offer you a new tenancy and has set out proposals for it in the Schedule to this notice (section 25(8)). You are not obliged to accept these proposals and may put forward your own.

If you and your landlord are unable to agree terms either one of you may apply to the court. You may not apply to the court if your landlord has already done so (section 24(2A)). If you wish to apply to the court you must do so by the date given in paragraph 2 of this notice, unless you and your landlord have agreed in writing to extend the deadline (sections 29A and 29B).

The court will settle the rent and other terms of the new tenancy or those on which you and your landlord cannot agree (sections 34 and 35). If you apply to the court your tenancy will continue after the date shown in paragraph 2 of this notice while your application is being considered (section 24).

If you are in any doubt about what action you should take, get advice immediately from a solicitor or a surveyor.

Negotiating a new tenancy

Most tenancies are renewed by negotiation. You and your landlord may agree in writing to extend the deadline for making an application to the court while negotiations continue. Either you or your landlord can ask the court to fix the rent that you will have to pay while the tenancy continues (sections 24A to 24D).

You may only stay in the property after the date in paragraph 2 (or if we have agreed in writing to a later date, that date), if by then you or the landlord has asked the court to order the grant of a new tenancy.

If you do try to agree a new tenancy with your landlord remember:

- that your present tenancy will not continue after the date in paragraph 2 of this notice without the agreement in writing mentioned above, unless you have applied to the court or your landlord has done so, and
- that you will lose your right to apply to the court once the deadline in paragraph 2 of this notice has passed, unless there is a written agreement extending the deadline.

Validity of this notice

The landlord who has given you this notice may not be the landlord to whom you pay your rent (sections 44 and 67). This does not necessarily mean that the notice is invalid.

If you have any doubts about whether this notice is valid, get advice immediately from a solicitor or a surveyor.

Form 2

LANDLORD'S NOTICE ENDING A BUSINESS TENANCY AND REASONS FOR REFUSING A NEW ONE

Section 25 of the Landlord and Tenant Act 1954

IMPORTANT NOTE FOR THE LANDLORD: If you wish to oppose the grant of a new tenancy on any of the grounds in section 30(1) of the Landlord and Tenant Act 1954, complete this form and send it to the tenant. If the tenant may be entitled to acquire the freehold or an extended lease, use form 7 in Schedule 2 to the Landlord and Tenant Act 1954, Part 2 (Notices) Regulations 2004 instead of this form.

To: (*insert name and address of tenant*)

From: (*insert name and address of landlord*)

1. This notice relates to the following property: (*insert address or description of property*)

2. I am giving you notice under section 25 of the Landlord and Tenant Act 1954 to end your tenancy on (*insert date*).

3. I am opposed to the grant of a new tenancy.

4. You may ask the court to order the grant of a new tenancy. If you do, I will oppose your application on the ground(s) mentioned in paragraph(s)* of section 30(1) of that Act. I draw your attention to the Table in the Notes below, which sets out all the grounds of opposition.

*(*insert letter(s) of the paragraph(s) relied on*)

5. If you wish to ask the court for a new tenancy you must do so before the date in paragraph 2 unless, before that date, we agree in writing to a later date.

6. I can ask the court to order the ending of your tenancy without granting you a new tenancy. I may have to pay you compensation if I have relied only on one or more of the grounds mentioned in paragraphs (e), (f) and (g) of section 30(1). If I ask the court to end your tenancy, you can challenge my application.

7. Please send all correspondence about this notice to:

Name:

Address:

Signed: Date:

*[Landlord] *[On behalf of the landlord] *[Mortgagee] *[On behalf of the mortgagee]

(*delete if inapplicable*)

IMPORTANT NOTE FOR THE TENANT

This notice is intended to bring your tenancy to an end on the date specified in paragraph 2.

Your landlord is not prepared to offer you a new tenancy. You will not get a new tenancy unless you successfully challenge in court the grounds on which your landlord opposes the grant of a new tenancy.

If you want to continue to occupy your property you must act quickly. The notes below should help you to decide what action you now need to take. If you want to challenge your landlord's refusal to renew your tenancy, get advice immediately from a solicitor or a surveyor.

NOTES

The sections mentioned below are sections of the Landlord and Tenant Act 1954, as amended, (most recently by the **Regulatory Reform** (Business Tenancies) (England and Wales) Order 2003).

Ending of your tenancy

This notice is intended to bring your tenancy to an end on the date given in paragraph 2. Section 25 contains rules about the date that the landlord can put in that paragraph.

Your landlord is not prepared to offer you a new tenancy. If you want a new tenancy you will need to apply to the court for a new tenancy and successfully challenge the landlord's grounds for opposition (see the section below headed '*Landlord's opposition to new tenancy*'). If you wish to apply to the court you must do so before the date given in paragraph 2 of this notice, unless you and your landlord have agreed in writing, before that date, to extend the deadline (sections 29A and 29B).

If you apply to the court your tenancy will continue after the date given in paragraph 2 of this notice while your application is being considered (section 24). You may not apply to the court if your landlord has already done so (section 24(2A) and (2B)).

You may only stay in the property after the date given in paragraph 2 (or such later date as you and the landlord may have agreed in writing) if before that date you have asked the court to order the grant of a new tenancy or the landlord has asked the court to order the ending of your tenancy without granting you a new one.

If you are in any doubt about what action you should take, get advice immediately from a solicitor or a surveyor.

Landlord's opposition to new tenancy

If you apply to the court for a new tenancy, the landlord can only oppose your application on one or more of the grounds set out in section 30(1). If you match the letter(s) specified in paragraph 4 of this notice with those in the first column in the Table below, you can see from the second column the ground(s) on which the landlord relies.

Paragraph of section 30(1)	Grounds
(a)	Where under the current tenancy the tenant has any obligations as respects the repair and maintenance of the holding, that the tenant ought not to be granted a new tenancy in view of the state of repair of the holding, being a state resulting from the tenant's failure to comply with the said obligations.
(b)	That the tenant ought not to be granted a new tenancy in view of his persistent delay in paying rent which has become due.
(c)	That the tenant ought not to be granted a new tenancy in view of other substantial breaches by him of his obligations under the current tenancy, or for any other reason connected with the tenant's use or management of the holding.

Paragraph of section 30(1)	Grounds
(d)	That the landlord has offered and is willing to provide or secure the provision of alternative accommodation for the tenant, that the terms on which the alternative accommodation is available are reasonable having regard to the terms of the current tenancy and to all other relevant circumstances, and that the accommodation and the time at which it will be available are suitable for the tenant's requirements (including the requirement to preserve goodwill) having regard to the nature and class of his business and to the situation and extent of, and facilities afforded by, the holding.
(e)	Where the current tenancy was created by the sub-letting of part only of the property comprised in a superior tenancy and the landlord is the owner of an interest in reversion expectant on the termination of that superior tenancy, that the aggregate of the rents reasonably obtainable on separate lettings of the holding and the remainder of that property would be substantially less than the rent reasonably obtainable on a letting of that property as a whole, that on the termination of the current tenancy the landlord requires possession of the holding for the purposes of letting or otherwise disposing of the said property as a whole, and that in view thereof the tenant ought not to be granted a new tenancy.
(f)	That on the termination of the current tenancy the landlord intends to demolish or reconstruct the premises comprised in the holding or a substantial part of those premises or to carry out substantial work of construction on the holding or part thereof and that he could not reasonably do so without obtaining possession of the holding.
(g)	On the termination of the current tenancy the landlord intends to occupy the holding for the purposes, or partly for the purposes, of a business to be carried on by him therein, or as his residence.

In this Table 'the holding' means the property that is the subject of the tenancy.

In ground (e), 'the landlord is the owner an interest in reversion expectant on the termination of that superior tenancy' means that the landlord has an interest in the property that will entitle him or her, when your immediate landlord's tenancy comes to an end, to exercise certain rights and obligations in relation to the property that are currently exercisable by your immediate landlord.

If the landlord relies on ground (f), the court can sometimes still grant a new tenancy if certain conditions set out in section 31A are met.

If the landlord relies on ground (g), please note that 'the landlord' may have an extended meaning. Where a landlord has a controlling interest in a company then either the landlord or the company can rely on ground (g). Where the landlord is a company and a person has a controlling interest in that company then either of them can rely on ground (g) (section 30(1A) and (1B)). A person has a 'controlling interest' in a company if, had he been a company, the other company would have been its subsidiary (section 46(2)).

The landlord must normally have been the landlord for at least five years before he or she can rely on ground (g).

Compensation

If you cannot get a new tenancy solely because one or more of grounds (e), (f) and (g) applies, you may be entitled to compensation under section 37. If your landlord has opposed your application on any of the other grounds as well as (e), (f) or (g) you can only get compensation if the court's refusal to grant a new tenancy is based solely on one or more of grounds (e), (f) and (g). In other words, you cannot get compensation under section 37 if the court has refused your tenancy on *other* grounds, even if one or more of grounds (e), (f) and (g) also applies.

If your landlord is an authority possessing compulsory purchase powers (such as a local authority) you may be entitled to a disturbance payment under Part 3 of the Land Compensation Act 1973.

Validity of this notice

The landlord who has given you this notice may not be the landlord to whom you pay your rent (sections 44 and 67). This does not necessarily mean that the notice is invalid.

If you have any doubts about whether this notice is valid, get advice immediately from a solicitor or a surveyor.

Form 3

TENANT'S REQUEST FOR A NEW BUSINESS TENANCY

Section 26 of the Landlord and Tenant Act 1954

To (*insert name and address of landlord*):

From (*insert name and address of tenant*):

   1. This notice relates to the following property: (*insert address or description of property*).

   2. I am giving you notice under section 26 of the Landlord and Tenant Act 1954 that I request a new tenancy beginning on (*insert date*).

   3. You will find my proposals for the new tenancy, which we can discuss, in the Schedule to this notice.

   4. If we cannot agree on all the terms of a new tenancy, either you or I may ask the court to order the grant of a new tenancy and settle the terms on which we cannot agree.

   5. If you wish to ask the court to order the grant of a new tenancy you must do so by the date in paragraph 2, unless we agree in writing to a later date and do so before the date in paragraph 2.

   6. You may oppose my request for a new tenancy only on one or more of the grounds set out in section 30(1) of the Landlord and Tenant Act 1954. You must tell me what your grounds are within two months of receiving this notice. If you miss this deadline you will not be able to oppose renewal of my tenancy and you will have to grant me a new tenancy.

   7. Please send all correspondence about this notice to:

Name:

Address:

Signed: Date:

*[Tenant] *[On behalf of the tenant] (*delete whichever is inapplicable*)

SCHEDULE

TENANT'S PROPOSALS FOR A NEW TENANCY

(*attach or insert proposed terms of the new tenancy*)

IMPORTANT NOTE FOR THE LANDLORD

This notice requests a new tenancy of your property or part of it. If you want to oppose this request you must act quickly.

Read the notice and all the Notes carefully. It would be wise to seek professional advice.

NOTES

The sections mentioned below are sections of the Landlord and Tenant Act 1954, as amended, (most recently by the **Regulatory Reform** (Business Tenancies) (England and Wales) Order 2003).

Tenant's request for a new tenancy

This request by your tenant for a new tenancy brings his or her current tenancy to an end on the day before the date mentioned in paragraph 2 of this notice. Section 26 contains rules about the date that the tenant can put in paragraph 2 of this notice.

Your tenant can apply to the court under section 24 for a new tenancy. You may apply for a new tenancy yourself, under the same section, but not if your tenant has already served an application. Once an application has been made to the court, your tenant's current tenancy will continue after the date mentioned in paragraph 2 while the application is being considered by the court. Either you or your tenant can ask the court to fix the rent which your tenant will have to pay whilst the tenancy continues (sections 24A to 24D). The court will settle any terms of a new tenancy on which you and your tenant disagree (sections 34 and 35).

Time limit for opposing your tenant's request

If you do not want to grant a new tenancy, you have two months from the making of your tenant's request in which to notify him or her that you will oppose any application made to the court for a new tenancy. You do not need a special form to do this, but the notice must be in writing and it must state on which of the grounds set out in section 30(1) you will oppose the application. If you do not use the same wording of the ground (or grounds), as set out below, your notice may be ineffective.

If there has been any delay in your seeing this notice, you may need to act very quickly. If you are in any doubt about what action you should take, get advice immediately from a solicitor or a surveyor.

Grounds for opposing tenant's application

If you wish to oppose the renewal of the tenancy, you can do so by opposing your tenant's application to the court, or by making your own application to the court for termination without renewal. However, you can only oppose your tenant's application, or apply for termination without renewal, on one or more of the grounds set out in section 30(1). These grounds are set out below. You will only be able to rely on the ground(s) of opposition that you have mentioned in your written notice to your tenant.

In this Table 'the holding' means the property that is the subject of the tenancy.

Paragraph of section 30(1)	Grounds
(a)	Where under the current tenancy the tenant has any obligations as respects the repair and maintenance of the holding, that the tenant ought not to be granted a new tenancy in view of the state of repair of the holding, being a state resulting from the tenant's failure to comply with the said obligations.
(b)	That the tenant ought not to be granted a new tenancy in view of his persistent delay in paying rent which has become due.
(c)	That the tenant ought not to be granted a new tenancy in view of other substantial breaches by him of his obligations under the current tenancy, or for any other reason connected with the tenant's use or management of the holding.
(d)	That the landlord has offered and is willing to provide or secure the provision of alternative accommodation for the tenant, that the terms on which the alternative accommodation is available are reasonable having regard to the terms of the current tenancy and to all other relevant circumstances, and that the accommodation and the time at which it will be available are suitable for the tenant's requirements (including the requirement to preserve goodwill) having regard to the nature and class of his business and to the situation and extent of, and facilities afforded by, the holding.
(e)	Where the current tenancy was created by the sub-letting of part only of the property comprised in a superior tenancy and the landlord is the owner of an interest in reversion expectant on the termination of that superior tenancy, that the aggregate of the rents reasonably obtainable on separate lettings of the holding and the remainder of that property would be substantially less than the rent reasonably obtainable on a letting of that property as a whole, that on the termination of the current tenancy the landlord requires possession of the holding for the purposes of letting or otherwise disposing of the said property as a whole, and that in view thereof the tenant ought not to be granted a new tenancy.
(f)	That on the termination of the current tenancy the landlord intends to demolish or reconstruct the premises comprised in the holding or a substantial part of those premises or to carry out substantial work of construction on the holding or part thereof and that he could not reasonably do so without obtaining possession of the holding.
(g)	On the termination of the current tenancy the landlord intends to occupy the holding for the purposes, or partly for the purposes, of a business to be carried on by him therein, or as his residence.

Compensation

If your tenant cannot get a new tenancy solely because one or more of grounds (e), (f) and (g) applies, he or she is entitled to compensation under section 37. If you have opposed your tenant's application on any of the other grounds mentioned in section 30(1), as well as on one or more of grounds (e), (f) and (g), your tenant can only get compensation if the court's refusal to grant a new tenancy is based solely on ground (e), (f) or (g). In other words, your tenant cannot get compensation under section 37 if the court has refused the tenancy on *other* grounds, even if one or more of grounds (e), (f) and (g) also applies.

If you are an authority possessing compulsory purchase powers (such as a local authority), your tenant may be entitled to a disturbance payment under Part 3 of the Land Compensation Act 1973.

Negotiating a new tenancy

Most tenancies are renewed by negotiation and your tenant has set out proposals for the new tenancy in paragraph 3 of this notice. You are not obliged to accept these proposals and may put forward your own. You and your tenant may agree in writing to extend the deadline for making an application to the court while negotiations continue. Your tenant may not apply to the court for a new tenancy until two months have passed from the date of the making of the request contained in this notice, unless you have already given notice opposing your tenant's request as mentioned in paragraph 6 of this notice (section 29A(3)).

If you try to agree a new tenancy with your tenant, remember:

- that one of you will need to apply to the court before the date in paragraph 2 of this notice, unless you both agree to extend the period for making an application.
- that any such agreement must be in writing and must be made before the date in paragraph 2 (sections 29A and 29B).

Validity of this notice

The tenant who has given you this notice may not be the person from whom you receive rent (sections 44 and 67). This does not necessarily mean that the notice is invalid.

If you have any doubts about whether this notice is valid, get advice immediately from a solicitor or a surveyor.

Form 4

LANDLORD'S REQUEST FOR INFORMATION ABOUT OCCUPATION AND SUB-TENANCIES

Section 40(1) of the Landlord and Tenant Act 1954

To: (*insert name and address of tenant*)

From: (*insert name and address of landlord*)

1. This notice relates to the following premises: (*insert address or description of premises*)

2. I give you notice under section 40(1) of the Landlord and Tenant Act 1954 that I require you to provide information—

- (a) by answering questions (1) to (3) in the Table below;
- (b) if you answer 'yes' to question (2), by giving me the name and address of the person or persons concerned;
- (c) if you answer 'yes' to question (3), by also answering questions (4) to (10) in the Table below;
- (d) if you answer 'no' to question (8), by giving me the name and address of the sub-tenant; and
- (e) if you answer 'yes' to question (10), by giving me details of the notice or request.

TABLE

(1)	Do you occupy the premises or any part of them wholly or partly for the purposes of a business that is carried on by you?
(2)	To the best of your knowledge and belief, does any other person own an interest in reversion in any part of the premises?
(3)	Does your tenancy have effect subject to any sub-tenancy on which your tenancy is immediately expectant?
(4)	What premises are comprised in the sub-tenancy?
(5)	For what term does it have effect or, if it is terminable by notice, by what notice can it be terminated?
(6)	What is the rent payable under it?
(7)	Who is the sub-tenant?
(8)	To the best of your knowledge and belief, is the sub-tenant in occupation of the premises or of part of the premises comprised in the sub-tenancy?
(9)	Is an agreement in force excluding, in relation to the sub-tenancy, the provisions of sections 24 to 28 of the Landlord and Tenant Act 1954?
(10)	Has a notice been given under section 25 or 26(6) of that Act, or has a request been made under section 26 of that Act, in relation to the sub-tenancy?

3. You must give the information concerned in writing and within the period of one month beginning with the date of service of this notice.

4. Please send all correspondence about this notice to:

Name:

Address:

Signed: Date:

*[Landlord] *[on behalf of the landlord] *delete whichever is inapplicable

IMPORTANT NOTE FOR THE TENANT

This notice contains some words and phrases that you may not understand. The Notes below should help you, but it would be wise to seek professional advice, for example, from a solicitor or surveyor, before responding to this notice.

Once you have provided the information required by this notice, you must correct it if you realise that it is not, or is no longer, correct. This obligation lasts for six months from the date of service of this notice, but an exception is explained in the next paragraph. If you need to correct information already given, you must do so within one month of becoming aware that the information is incorrect.

The obligation will cease if, after transferring your tenancy, you notify the landlord of the transfer and of the name and address of the person to whom your tenancy has been transferred.

If you fail to comply with the requirements of this notice, or the obligation mentioned above, you may face civil proceedings for breach of the statutory duty that arises under

section 40 of the Landlord and Tenant Act 1954. In any such proceedings a court may order you to comply with that duty and may make an award of damages.

NOTES

The sections mentioned below are sections of the Landlord and Tenant Act 1954, as amended, (most recently by the **Regulatory Reform** (Business Tenancies) (England and Wales) Order 2003).

Purpose of this notice

Your landlord (or, if he or she is a tenant, possibly your landlord's landlord) has sent you this notice in order to obtain information about your occupation and that of any sub-tenants. This information may be relevant to the taking of steps to end or renew your business tenancy.

Time limit for replying

You must provide the relevant information within one month of the date of service of this notice (section 40(1), (2) and (5)).

Information required

You do not have to give your answers on this form; you may use a separate sheet for this purpose. The notice requires you to provide, in writing, information in the form of answers to questions (1) to (3) in the Table above and, if you answer 'yes' to question (3), also to provide information in the form of answers to questions (4) to (10) in that Table. Depending on your answer to question (2) and, if applicable in your case, questions (8) and (10), you must also provide the information referred to in paragraph 2(b), (d) and (e) of this notice. Question (2) refers to a person who owns an interest in reversion. You should answer 'yes' to this question if you know or believe that there is a person who receives, or is entitled to receive, rent in respect of any part of the premises (other than the landlord who served this notice).

When you answer questions about sub-tenants, please bear in mind that, for these purposes, a sub-tenant includes a person retaining possession of premises by virtue of the Rent (Agriculture) Act 1976 or the Rent Act 1977 after the coming to an end of a sub-tenancy, and 'sub-tenancy' includes a right so to retain possession (section 40(8)).

You should keep a copy of your answers and of any other information provided in response to questions (2), (8) or (10) above.

If, once you have given this information, you realise that it is not, or is no longer, correct, you must give the correct information within one month of becoming aware that the previous information is incorrect. Subject to the next paragraph, your duty to correct any information that you have already given continues for six months after you receive this notice (section 40(5)). You should give the correct information to the landlord who gave you this notice unless you receive notice of the transfer of his or her interest, and of the name and address of the person to whom that interest has been transferred. In that case, the correct information must be given to that person.

If you transfer your tenancy within the period of six months referred to above, your duty to correct information already given will cease if you notify the landlord of the transfer and of the name and address of the person to whom your tenancy has been transferred.

If you do not provide the information requested, or fail to correct information that you have provided earlier, after realising that it is not, or is no longer, correct, proceedings may be taken against you and you may have to pay damages (section 40B).

If you are in any doubt about the information that you should give, get immediate advice from a solicitor or a surveyor.

Validity of this notice

The landlord who has given you this notice may not be the landlord to whom you pay your rent (sections 44 and 67). This does not necessarily mean that the notice is invalid.

If you have any doubts about whether this notice is valid, get advice immediately

Form 5

TENANT'S REQUEST FOR INFORMATION FROM LANDLORD OR LANDLORD'S MORTGAGEE ABOUT LANDLORD'S INTEREST

Section 40(3) of the Landlord and Tenant Act 1954

To: (*insert name and address of reversioner or reversioner's mortgagee in possession [see the first note below]*)

From: (*insert name and address of tenant*)

1. This notice relates to the following premises: (*insert address or description of premises*)

2. In accordance with section 40(3) of the Landlord and Tenant Act 1954 I require you—

    (a)   to state in writing whether you are the owner of the fee simple in respect of the premises or any part of them or the mortgagee in possession of such an owner,

    (b)   if you answer 'no' to (a), to state in writing, to the best of your knowledge and belief—

        (i)   the name and address of the person who is your or, as the case may be, your mortgagor's immediate landlord in respect of the premises or of the part in respect of which you are not, or your mortgagor is not, the owner in fee simple;

        (ii)   for what term your or your mortgagor's tenancy has effect and what is the earliest date (if any) at which that tenancy is terminable by notice to quit given by the landlord; and

        (iii)   whether a notice has been given under section 25 or 26(6) of the Landlord and Tenant Act 1954, or a request has been made under section 26 of that Act, in relation to the tenancy and, if so, details of the notice or request;

    (c)   to state in writing, to the best of your knowledge and belief, the name and address of any other person who owns an interest in reversion in any part of the premises;

    (d)   if you are a reversioner, to state in writing whether there is a mortgagee in possession of your interest in the premises; and

    (e)   if you answer 'yes' to (d), to state in writing, to the best of your knowledge and belief, the name and address of the mortgagee in possession.

3. You must give the information concerned within the period of one month beginning with the date of service of this notice.

4. Please send all correspondence about this notice to:

Name:

Address:

Signed: Date:

*[Tenant] *[on behalf of the tenant] (*delete whichever is inapplicable*)

IMPORTANT NOTE FOR LANDLORD OR LANDLORD'S MORTGAGEE

This notice contains some words and phrases that you may not understand. The Notes below should help you, but it would be wise to seek professional advice, for example, from a solicitor or surveyor, before responding to this notice.

Once you have provided the information required by this notice, you must correct it if you realise that it is not, or is no longer, correct. This obligation lasts for six months from the

date of service of this notice, but an exception is explained in the next paragraph. If you need to correct information already given, you must do so within one month of becoming aware that the information is incorrect.

The obligation will cease if, after transferring your interest, you notify the tenant of the transfer and of the name and address of the person to whom your interest has been transferred.

If you fail to comply with the requirements of this notice, or the obligation mentioned above, you may face civil proceedings for breach of the statutory duty that arises under section 40 of the Landlord and Tenant Act 1954. In any such proceedings a court may order you to comply with that duty and may make an award of damages.

NOTES

The sections mentioned below are sections of the Landlord and Tenant Act 1954, as amended, (most recently by the **Regulatory Reform** (Business Tenancies) (England and Wales) Order 2003).

Terms used in this notice

The following terms, which are used in paragraph 2 of this notice, are defined in section 40(8):

> 'mortgagee in possession' includes a receiver appointed by the mortgagee or by the court who is in receipt of the rents and profits;
>
> 'reversioner' means any person having an interest in the premises, being an interest in reversion expectant (whether immediately or not) on the tenancy; and
>
> 'reversioner's mortgagee in possession' means any person being a mortgagee in possession in respect of such an interest.

Section 40(8) requires the reference in paragraph 2(b) of this notice to your mortgagor to be read in the light of the definition of 'mortgagee in possession'.

A mortgagee (mortgage lender) will be 'in possession' if the mortgagor (the person who owes money to the mortgage lender) has failed to comply with the terms of the mortgage. The mortgagee may then be entitled to receive rent that would normally have been paid to the mortgagor.

The term 'the owner of the fee simple' means the freehold owner.

The term 'reversioner' includes the freehold owner and any intermediate landlord as well as the immediate landlord of the tenant who served this notice.

Purpose of this notice and information required

This notice requires you to provide, in writing, the information requested in paragraph 2(a) and (c) of the notice and, if applicable in your case, in paragraph 2(b), (d) and (e). You do not need to use a special form for this purpose.

If, once you have given this information, you realise that it is not, or is no longer, correct, you must give the correct information within one month of becoming aware that the previous information is incorrect. Subject to the last paragraph in this section of these Notes, your duty to correct any information that you have already given continues for six months after you receive this notice (section 40(5)).

You should give the correct information to the tenant who gave you this notice unless you receive notice of the transfer of his or her interest, and of the name and address of the person to whom that interest has been transferred. In that case, the correct information must be given to that person.

If you do not provide the information requested, or fail to correct information that you have provided earlier, after realising that it is not, or is no longer, correct, proceedings may be taken against you and you may have to pay damages (section 40B).

If you are in any doubt as to the information that you should give, get advice immediately from a solicitor or a surveyor.

If you transfer your interest within the period of six months referred to above, your duty to correct information already given will cease if you notify the tenant of that transfer and of the name and address of the person to whom your interest has been transferred.

Time limit for replying

You must provide the relevant information within one month of the date of service of this notice (section 40(3), (4) and (5)).

Validity of this notice

The tenant who has given you this notice may not be the person from whom you receive rent (sections 44 and 67). This does not necessarily mean that the notice is invalid.

If you have any doubts about the validity of the notice, get advice immediately from a solicitor or a surveyor.

Appendix 2
The Code for Leasing Business Premises in England and Wales 2007

Leasing Business Premises: Landlord Code

Introduction

This revised lease code is the result of pan-industry discussion between representatives of landlords, tenants and government. The objective is to create a document which is clear, concise and authoritative.

However, our aims are wider. We want the lease code to be used as a checklist for negotiations before the grant of a lease and lease renewals. Landlords should be transparent about any departures from the code in a particular case and the reasons for them.

We have provided model heads of terms and whilst we recognise the code will apply to leases in England and Wales, we believe its intent should apply to the whole of the UK.

Most importantly, we are launching the code with an objective to ensure that parties to a lease have easy access to information explaining the commitments they are making in clear English. We will encourage trade and professional bodies, lenders and government (at all levels) to ensure small businesses are made aware of the code and the advisory pages which accompany it.

Although the code applies to new leases, please also see the British Property Federation declaration, which applies to existing leases, in relation to applications for consent to sublet where there is an existing lease covenant requiring subleases to be at the higher of the passing rent and the market rent.

We hope the code will help the industry in its quest to promote efficiency and fairness in landlord and tenant relationships.

1 Lease Negotiations

Landlords must make offers in writing which clearly state: the rent; the length of the term and any break rights; whether or not tenants will have security of tenure; the rent review arrangements; rights to assign, sublet and share the premises; repairing obligations; and the VAT status of the premises.

Landlords must promote flexibility, stating whether alternative lease terms are available and must propose rents for different lease terms if requested by prospective tenants.

2 Rent Deposits and Guarantees

The lease terms should state clearly any rent deposit proposals, including the amount, for how long and the arrangements for paying or accruing interest at a proper rate. Tenants should be protected against the default or insolvency of the landlord.

State clearly the conditions for releasing rent deposits and guarantees.

3 Length of Term, Break Clauses and Renewal Rights

The length of term must be clear.

The only pre-conditions to tenants exercising any break clauses should be that they are up to date with the main rent, give up occupation and leave behind no continuing subleases. Disputes about the state of the premises, or what has been left behind or removed, should be settled later (like with normal lease expiry).

The fallback position under the Landlord and Tenant Act 1954 is that business tenants have rights to renew their lease. It is accepted that there are a number of circumstances in which that is not appropriate. In such cases landlords should state at the start of negotiations that the protection of the 1954 Act is to be excluded and encourage tenants to seek early advice as to the implications.

4 Rent Review

Rent reviews should be clear and headline rent review clauses should not be used. Landlords should on request offer alternatives to their proposed option for rent review priced on a risk-adjusted basis.

For example, alternatives to upward only rent review might include up/down reviews to market rent with a minimum of the initial rent, or reference to another measure such as annual indexation.

Where landlords are unable to offer alternatives, they should give reasons.

Leases should allow both landlords and tenants to start the rent review process.

The Code for Leasing Business Premises
in England and Wales 2007
www.leasingbusinesspremises.co.uk

5   Assignment and Subletting

Leases should:

- allow tenants to assign the whole of the premises with the landlord's consent not to be unreasonably withheld or delayed; and

- not refer to any specific circumstances for refusal, although a lease would still be Code compliant if it requires that any group company taking an assignment, when assessed together with any proposed guarantor, must be of at least equivalent financial standing to the assignor (together with any guarantor of the assignor).

Authorised Guarantee Agreements should not be required as a condition of the assignment, unless at the date of the assignment the proposed assignee, when assessed together with any proposed guarantor:

- is of lower financial standing than the assignor (and its guarantor); or

- is resident or registered overseas.

For smaller tenants a rent deposit should be acceptable as an alternative.

If subletting is allowed, the sublease rent should be the market rent at the time of subletting.

Subleases to be excluded from the 1954 Act should not have to be on the same terms as the tenant's lease.

6   Service Charges

Landlords must, during negotiations, provide best estimates of service charges, insurance payments and any other outgoings that tenants will incur under their leases.

Landlords must disclose known irregular events that would have a significant impact on the amount of future service charges.

Landlords should be aware of the RICS 2006 Code of Practice on Service Charges in Commercial Property and seek to observe its guidance in drafting new leases and on renewals (even if granted before that Code is effective).

7   Repairs

Tenants' repairing obligations should be appropriate to the length of term and the condition of the premises.

Unless expressly stated in the heads of terms, tenants should only be obliged to give the premises back at the end of their lease in the same condition as they were in at its grant.

8   Alterations and Changes of Use

Landlords' control over alterations and changes of use should not be more restrictive than is necessary to protect the value, at the time of the application, of the premises and any adjoining or neighbouring premises of the landlord.

Internal non-structural alterations should be notified to landlords but should not need landlords' consent unless they could affect the services or systems in the building.

Landlords should not require tenants to remove permitted alterations and make good at the end of the lease, unless reasonable to do so. Landlords should notify tenants of their requirements at least six months before the termination date.

9   Insurance

Where landlords are insuring the landlord's property, the insurance policy terms should be fair and reasonable and represent value for money, and be placed with reputable insurers.

Landlords must always disclose any commission they are receiving and must provide full insurance details on request.

Rent suspension should apply if the premises are damaged by an insured risk or uninsured risk, other than where caused by a deliberate act of the tenant. If rent suspension is limited to the period for which loss of rent is insured, leases should allow landlords or tenants to terminate their leases if reinstatement is not completed within that period.

Landlords should provide appropriate terrorism cover if practicable to do so.

If the whole of the premises are damaged by an uninsured risk as to prevent occupation, tenants should be allowed to terminate their leases unless landlords agree to rebuild at their own cost.

10 Ongoing Management

Landlords should handle all defaults promptly and deal with tenants and any guarantors in an open and constructive way.

At least six months before the termination date, landlords should provide a schedule of dilapidations to enable tenants to carry out any works and should notify any dilapidations that occur after that date as soon as practicable.

When receiving applications for consents, landlords should where practicable give tenants an estimate of the costs involved.

Landlords should normally request any additional information they require from tenants within five working days of receiving the application. Landlords should consider at an early stage what other consents they will require (for example, from superior landlord or mortgagees) and then seek these. Landlords should make decisions on consents for alterations within 15 working days of receiving full information.

Leasing Business Premises: Occupier Guide

Introduction

A business lease is a legally binding contract between the legal owner (Landlord) and the occupier (Tenant). Failure by either party to comply with the terms of the agreement could result in court action.

The 2007 Code for Leasing Business Premises ('the Lease Code') provides a framework within which a prospective tenant can reasonably expect a landlord to operate. As a prospective tenant, you should not assume that a landlord complies with the Lease Code. The Lease Code does not provide all of the protection you need for your business in leasing premises.

Sometimes the Landlord is also the tenant of another owner. This may restrict the flexibility of terms the Landlord can offer. The Landlord should always state in advance if this is so and provide a copy of the current lease.

If it is proposed to buy an existing lease (assignment) from someone else, be aware that, though parts of this Occupier Guide may help in interpreting some of the terms of the lease, there may be many additional liabilities. Professional advice from a qualified surveyor and a lawyer should be sought.

In this document the following terms have been used:

Landlord   This is the owner of the property or the person owning an existing lease of the property

Tenant   This is the occupier of the property or the person paying rent to a landlord (this Occupier Guide assumes the tenant will be you)

Heads of Terms This is a summary of the agreement between the parties and is used to instruct lawyers to produce the formal lease. Both the lease and the Heads of Terms should comply with the recommendations of the Lease Code but the Heads of Terms will be superseded once the lease has been granted.

For more information on the Lease Code see Useful Links.

1   Lease negotiations

You should expect the Landlord to make very clear exactly what you are being asked to agree.

You should be able to understand the total extent and duration of the cost and liability you will be taking on if you sign a lease based on the terms being offered by the Landlord.

> **Tip 1**
>
> Make sure you understand every term and condition in the offer including the total cost until the lease ends and ask the Landlord or the Landlord's representative to confirm in writing that the offer meets the Lease Code.

You should know from the offer exactly what the property is.

> **Tip 2**
>
> Make sure the offer clearly shows the extent of the property, with the boundaries clearly marked on plan and the floor area noted, together with all means of access, any access or areas you must share with other occupiers, any limitation of hours of use, any restrictions in the type of use, any legal or planning limitations or obligations that come with the property.

You should also remember that, however good your relationship is or seems to be with the Landlord, the Landlord may sell to another party; the terms you agree and the lease you take on must reflect everything you rely on to conduct and safeguard your business.

The Code for Leasing Business Premises
in England and Wales 2007
www.leasingbusinesspremises.co.uk

Tip 3

Make sure the offer sets out clearly who the Landlord is,
together with any superior landlords, and assume that any
Landlord will sell his interest to someone else and that you will
have to deal with the new owner.

You should request alternative terms if you are not happy with the
initial terms of the Landlord's offer, always bearing in mind that
any variation (such as lease length, rent review terms – including
frequency and basis – break options, etc) may change the level
of rent or other terms.

Tip 4

Request written responses from the Landlord, where you expect
to need to rely on them. Check that all the things which are
important to you and your business have been accurately
written down in the Heads of Terms and documented in the
lease.

2   Financial matters, rent deposits and guarantees

The Landlord should provide full details of your expected costs
involved in leasing the property. This should include all personal
or company guarantees, security deposits or other bank guarantees.

Not all costs will be fixed at the time of agreeing the lease. You should
expect the Landlord to explain how any costs are calculated so that
you can understand the risks and make sure you can afford all of the
costs of leasing the property.

Tip 5

It may be helpful to use a checklist (such as that set out below)
so that you can ask the Landlord to be explicit about costs and
obligations in the lease.

If the Landlord demands a deposit, you should make sure you
understand the conditions under which it is held and the basis
on which it will be returned to you. You should remember that this
is YOUR money that the Landlord is holding as a protection against
any failure on your part.

Tip 6

Keep thinking of the deposit as your money and demand that
interest on it is accrued at a fair rate. Ask the Landlord to
make sure it is held in an account that belongs to you (escrow
or stakeholder account) in case the Landlord becomes
insolvent. Throughout the term of the lease, make sure you
obtain statements from the Landlord to confirm that the money
is still in the account and that all interest earned has been paid
to you or, if required by the lease, has been held on your
behalf within the account. Check that your deposit will be
transferred to the new Landlord if the Landlord sells the
property to another owner.

Tip 7

Make sure you know when and how you can get your deposit
back, such as when you no longer have an interest or have
satisfied agreed conditions.

If you are asked to give a personal guarantee, you should avoid using
your home as security. You should be able to understand both when
and how the Landlord may call on your guarantee, and also what the
guarantee would actually cover.

Tip 8

Think of any guarantee as if it WILL be called on the first day of
the lease; what would be the personal consequences for you?
Can you afford it?

Cost Item	Who pays?	How much? How often?	What is the occupier's cost each year?	If this cost is not fixed, what does it depend on?
Rent	e.g. Tenant			
VAT				
Rates				
Service charges				
Insurance				
Utilities				
Repairs/Dilapidations				
Fitting out/Alterations				
Total each year				
Total lease cost				

3   Rent review

Your lease may contain provisions allowing the Landlord to change the rent. The rules by which the rent can be changed should be clear and understandable. It should be arranged that the Landlord cannot simply impose a rental increase. The basis of rent review should be to the market rent unless clearly stated otherwise. If you agreed increases fixed to an index, the basis should be a published, independent, authoritative source.

If there is an open market rental value provision, it should specifically exclude (or disregard) any improvements you make, other than as part of an explicit obligation, or any value arising from your business. You should also make sure there are controls in the event of disagreement that will be referred to an independent expert or arbitrator to settle.

> **Tip 9**
>
> Check that you understand the basis on which the rent can be changed. Can the rent go down as well as up? You should see if the Landlord is prepared to allow upward or downward rent reviews and if not, you should consider asking for a break option exercisable only by the tenant.

Your lease should include a provision allowing you to serve a rent review notice on the Landlord. If the Landlord does not initiate the rent review, think very carefully before deciding not to serve notice on the Landlord as you may be responsible for paying interest on any increase in rent above the original rent from the appropriate rent review date until the review has been agreed.

> **Tip 10**
>
> Make sure that the interest rate on the difference is no higher than bank base rate. Try to introduce a provision whereby the Landlord forfeits interest on the difference if he/she does not initiate the rent review process prior to the review date.

> **Tip 11**
>
> Avoid strict time limits in the rent review clause (other than referred to in Tip 10) – these could result in you losing the ability to negotiate.

4   Subletting and assignment

Subletting (creating a new lease of all or part of the property)

If your lease allows subletting, you should understand any limitations (in terms of the amount of space, the use and the rent you can charge and the nature of the subtenant you can sublet to).

It is usual for Landlords to insist that subleases are granted outside the protection of the Landlord and Tenant Act 1954 and on similar terms to your lease.

> **Tip 12**
>
> Try to make sure you are NOT required to sublet at the same or higher rent than you pay. You should not be limited other than by reference to the market rent at the time of the subletting.

Be careful that restrictive subletting provisions do not prevent you from, say, sharing your space with a supplier or service provider (for example, an outside cleaning company which you provide with its own cleaner's cupboard)

> **Tip 13**
>
> Ask your Landlord to reflect the flexibility you require in the sharing provisions of the lease. This probably means you must not create a tenancy for your supplier.

Landlord's written consent is likely to be required for subleases.

> **Tip 14**
>
> Make sure your Landlord, including any superior landlords, is required to give consent within a defined (and short) period of time and that he is not allowed to refuse without good reason.

Assignment (disposing of your existing legal interest in the whole premises)

It is common for Landlords to require you to guarantee the lease once you have assigned it to a third party. The form of guarantee (an Authorised Guarantee Agreement or AGA) usually makes you responsible, as a guarantor, for the lease obligations until your assignee (the person to whom you sold your lease) assigns the lease to another party.

> **Tip 15**
>
> Ask the Landlord to limit his requirement for an Authorised Guarantee Agreement to those cases where your proposed buyer (assignee) is financially weaker than you are at the date of assignment. Ask the Landlord to include provisions that will allow you to cancel the Guarantee if defined conditions are met and/or after an agreed period.

> **Tip 16**
>
> Try to agree alternative conditions to avoid you having to enter into an Authorised Guarantee Agreement (for example, by having the new tenant pay a rent deposit).

The Landlord should not impose any condition which requires you to be in compliance with the lease at the time of assignment.

> **Tip 17**
>
> Try to make sure the only precondition for assignment is obtaining the Landlord's consent in writing and that the Landlord may not unreasonably withhold or delay giving his consent.

The Code for Leasing Business Premises
in England and Wales 2007
www.leasingbusinesspremises.co.uk

5   Lease length, break clauses and renewals

The Landlord should make clear the length of the lease, whether there are any rights to break the lease and whether you will be entitled to an extension of the lease on expiry (see section 11 below).

Make sure that the length of the lease is appropriate for your business needs; ask the Landlord to offer you a break option exercisable only by the tenant (this will be you unless you have assigned your lease) to give you the opportunity to cancel the lease at a time that suits your business.

A right to break should allow you to walk away from the lease at a given time after informing the Landlord in writing. This should be conditional only upon having paid the rent due under the lease and giving up occupation of the property, leaving behind no continuing subleases. You may have other liabilities to fulfil, but these should not be used to invalidate the right to break.

Tip 18

Be careful that it is only the principal rent and not any other sums (such as service charges) that must be paid in cleared funds before the break date.

When your lease ends, whether by expiry or by exercise of a break option, you will be liable to the Landlord for any sums due and for any repairs you should have carried out during the lease (dilapidations).

Tip 19

When granting any subleases or in sharing possession with any suppliers or business partners, always make sure your agreement with them expires on a date before your right to break, AND that you have not given them any rights to stay in the property beyond the term of your agreement with them.

Be sure that you understand what notices you would be required to serve on the Landlord to end the lease, and how and when these should be served.

The Landlord and Tenant Act 1954 gives you the right to extend your tenancy when your lease runs out.

Unless both you and the Landlord have agreed (in the correct procedure) that the lease is to be excluded from the relevant sections of the Landlord and Tenant Act 1954, you will be entitled to renew your lease unless your Landlord can prove certain specific circumstances, which include redeveloping the property or occupying the space himself.

You should make sure you understand the options available to you when your lease expires. Take professional advice to make sure all notices are properly served and that your interests are protected.

Tip 20

Take professional advice at least six months before the end of the lease and on receipt of any notice from the Landlord under the Act.

6   Service charges

You should expect the Landlord to be explicit in his offer about any service charges, including how these costs are calculated, what they cover (and don't include) and the extent to which you will be obliged to pay towards any capital improvements and long-term repairs or replacements of structure, fabric or machinery and equipment.

Tip 21

Ask the Landlord whether he complies with the Service Charge Code 2006, and ask for a clear estimate in writing of the likely service charge costs for each year of the lease term (to include any known or planned capital costs).

Tip 22

As you are likely to be responsible for the repairs to a proportionate part or the whole of the building you should satisfy yourself that there are no major repairs required at the beginning of your lease or that are likely shortly afterwards.

Tip 23

Make sure the Landlord cannot charge you a greater proportion of cost when he has other space vacant in the estate or building.

7   Repairs

UNLESS you specifically agree at the time of taking the lease to carry out works or to reinstate the property to its original state, check that the lease does not require you to put the property into a better condition than when you take the lease.

Tip 24

It is worthwhile either getting a formal photographic schedule of condition carried out by a firm of surveyors or taking plenty of photographs on or before taking the lease to record the condition at the beginning of the lease.

Tip 25

If you take the photographs yourself, make sure you get the photographs dated and witnessed and keep a set with your lease documents. If you produce your own video schedule of condition, send the Landlord a copy by Recorded Delivery Post.

You should bear in mind if you buy an existing lease (take an assignment of someone else's lease), that the condition of the property when you take it may be poorer than it was at the beginning of the lease. You may be required to put the property back into its original condition so it is worth taking professional advice.

The Code for Leasing Business Premises
in England and Wales 2007
www.leasingbusinesspremises.co.uk

8   Alterations and changes of use

Your lease will limit the use of the property to a specified purpose (for example, B1 (Offices). The lease will usually put the responsibility on you to check that your proposed use complies with any planning consent.

> **Tip 26**
>
> Make sure the Landlord provides you with all relevant information and, if possible, confirms to you that your use complies with his planning consent.

The lease may be quite restrictive in terms of any signage and any alterations you are permitted to make. Before you enter into the lease, you should make sure you are permitted to carry out any works your business needs.

> **Tip 27**
>
> Check what you need to do to the property in order to trade. Make sure the Landlord agrees in writing any changes you intend to make at the beginning of the lease period. Check whether you will be required to remove your alterations at the end of the lease.

The Landlord should be required to give his consent within a reasonable time period (say 21 days) and should not be able to refuse your proposed alterations without good reason.

> **Tip 28**
>
> Make sure your lease allows you to make non-structural alterations except where the Landlord can demonstrate it would affect the operation of the building. You should remember that you should notify the Landlord of any non-structural alterations you do make.

You should be aware of statutory requirements (such as Construction (Design and Management) Regulations 2007 (CDM) that you must comply with when carrying out any works or alterations to the Property. The CDM regulations require you to keep full and detailed formal records and your Landlord will require you to maintain these records throughout the lease.

9   Insurance

You may be required to reimburse the Landlord for his insurance premiums, and the Landlord should tell you what commission payments (if any) he receives.

> **Tip 29**
>
> Ask for a copy of the Landlord's insurance policy and before signing the lease, check with alternative insurers that you are getting value for money for the given level of premium and that the insurance company is reputable. Ask him to confirm to you that he has no intention of changing the scope (and, therefore, the cost and nature) of the insurance cover.

The lease should provide for the Landlord's policy to be used to repair or rebuild the property unless the insurance is invalidated by anything you do, in which case you may be liable for the reinstatement.

> **Tip 30**
>
> Remember to inform the Landlord and his insurer if you intend to change the way you use the property; let them know if you are storing any hazardous chemicals in the context of your business or if you propose to leave the property vacant and unattended at any time. Ask the Landlord to ensure inclusion of such activities in the insurance policy and to consult you over any changes in the insurance policy terms.

> **Tip 31**
>
> Check whether your alterations or improvements would be covered under the Landlord's policy.

10   Tenant's defaults and applications for consent

Tenant default

The lease forms a legal contract between you and your Landlord. Any breach of contract may have serious consequences and you should take care to understand your obligations and steps the Landlord may take against you and, if applicable, your guarantors, including Court action.

The laws relating to Landlord and Tenant relationships are complex and you should seek professional advice so you are clear on your obligations and rights.

A fair lease is one which allows you enough opportunity to fix any problems (without loss to the Landlord) before any legal action is taken.

> **Tip 32**
>
> Check that the Landlord must let you know you are in breach and give you a reasonable opportunity to remedy the breach before taking legal action against you.

You may find that you have failed or forgotten to carry out some obligations under your lease. It is usually best if you are able to carry out these obligations yourself. It may be better sometimes to approach the Landlord and negotiate a reasonable payment to have the Landlord carry out the obligations after your lease has expired.

> **Tip 33**
>
> Try to stay on good terms with the Landlord. This should help make any situation easier to handle and should allow you to run your business without unnecessary outside interruptions.

The remedy for a breach of your agreement may range from the Landlord sending in bailiffs, who may seize goods to the value of the breach, to the Landlord taking back the property from you ('Forfeiture'). You should note that this would not take away your liability to pay arrears of rent.

The Code for Leasing Business Premises in England and Wales 2007
www.leasingbusinesspremises.co.uk

Tip 34

Make sure the 'Forfeiture' provisions in the lease are clear; they should allow you enough time to pay, and should allow you to restructure your business without necessarily making your lease vulnerable to forfeiture.

The Landlord may try to forfeit your lease by locking you out of the Property or by obtaining a court order. In either case you can apply to the Court to give you time to put matters right or to pay what you owe. Seek urgent professional advice in that situation.

New legislation often brings new obligations for owners and occupiers of property. Leases often require tenants to comply with statute at their own cost. You should ensure your obligations under the lease are proportionate to the length and terms of your lease and you should take professional advice and make your own estimate of any expected costs. You should research possible new Regulations that could affect your occupation and your business.

This provision should not be taken lightly and you should ensure that the Property is in compliance with existing regulations (for example, with Disability Discrimination Acts, Town and Country Planning Acts, Health & Safety Acts or Environmental Protection Acts) when you take the lease.

Tip 35

Ask the Landlord to confirm to you in writing that the Property complies with all regulations (some of which are "Statutory Instruments") before entering into the lease.

Tip 36

Stay aware of potential new legislation and Regulations that will affect occupiers of business premises (many trade bodies and professional firms send out newsletters which can help to identify significant changes). Identify the costs and take professional advice to ensure you comply where you are obliged to by your lease.

Applications for consent

You will need to make applications to the Landlord during the lease, for example, if you intend to carry out alterations (see Section 8) or if you propose to sublease or assign your lease (see Section 4). The lease should specify that the Landlord may not unreasonably withhold or delay his consent.

The Landlord's duty to respond only applies from when he has received from you adequate information about the proposed alterations or about the proposed assignee or subtenant and full details of the proposed transaction.

Tip 37

Check what information will be required before making an application and make sure you are able to give the Landlord full details. Ask the Landlord in advance what other consents he may have to get and ask for assurances that this will not add any further delay to the approval process.

Useful Links

The Code for Leasing Business Premises in England and Wales 2007
www.leasingbusinesspremises.co.uk

Bills before Parliament
www.publications.parliament.uk/pa/pabills.htm

Building Regulations
www.communities.gov.uk/index.asp?id=1130474

Health and Safety Executive
www.hse.gov.uk

Service Charge Code
www.servicechargecode.co.uk

Town Planning (Link Site)
www.ukplanning.com/ukp/index.htm

Uniform Business Rates
www.voa.gov.uk

Organisations Endorsing the Code

Association of British Insurers
www.abi.org.uk/

British Council for Offices
www.bco.org.uk

British Property Federation
www.bpf.org.uk

British Retail Consortium
www.brc.org.uk

Communities and Local Government
www.communities.gov.uk

Confederation of British Industry
www.cbi.org.uk

CoreNet Global
www.corenetglobal.org.uk

The Forum of Private Business
www.fpb.org.uk

Federation of Small Businesses
www.fsb.org.uk

Investment Property Forum
www.ipf.org.uk/

The Law Society of England and Wales
www.lawsociety.org.uk

The Royal Institution of Chartered Surveyors
www.rics.org

Welsh Assembly Government
www.wales.gov.uk/index.htm

The Code for Leasing Business Premises
in England and Wales 2007
www.leasingbusinesspremises.co.uk

Leasing Business Premises: Model Heads of Terms

Note: These Model Heads of Terms follow a similar format to the Code for Leasing Business Premises: Landlord Code.

1.0	**Initial information**	Lease to be Code compliant: Yes / No.
1.1	**Property address**	Detailed description (and Land Registry compliant plan if available) and measured area if relevant, e.g. for rent, service charge and rent reviews.
1.2	**Landlord**	[ ] (Registered no. [ ]) Registered office: Correspondence address: Contact name: E-mail: Telephone: (Fax:) Mobile:
1.3	**Tenant**	[ ] (Registered no. [ ]) Registered office: Correspondence address: Contact name: E-mail: Telephone: (Fax:) Mobile:
1.4	**Rent**	£ per annum exclusive of VAT. Payment dates monthly/quarterly. Is the property VAT elected?
1.5	**Rent free period (and other Incentives)**	
1.6	**Type of lease**	Head lease or sub lease.
1.7	**Landlord's initial works (including timing)**	Long stop date by which works must be done. Is the specification agreed/if not who is providing it?
1.8	**Tenant's initial works (including timing)**	
2.0	**Guarantor / rent deposits**	(a) Identity of guarantor (if any). (b) Rent deposit amount (if any).
3.0	**Lease length, breaks, extensions and rights**	
3.1	**Lease length and start date**	
3.2	**Break clauses or renewal rights**	(a) Notice periods for exercising? To be at least [ ]. (b) Any break clause payments?
3.3	**1954 Act protection**	Does the lease have 1954 Act protection?

The Code for Leasing Business Premises
in England and Wales 2007
www.leasingbusinesspremises.co.uk

| 3.4 | **Rights** | eg. Satellite dish, air conditioning platforms, remote storage areas, signage, etc. Any rights of access, servicing, wayleaves or other matters inc. fire escape.
For car parking – state number and attach plan if relevant. |

| 4.0 | **Rent reviews** | (a) Type (market rent, fixed increases, link to an index?).
(b) How often do reviews occur?
(c) For market rent, are there any unusual disregards or assumptions. Arbitrator/Expert. |

5.0   **Assignment and subletting**
See check box >

	Prohibited	If not prohibited is CNUW	Permitted without consent
Assignment of whole	Yes/No	Yes/No	Yes/No
Sub-Lease whole	Yes/No	Yes/No	Yes/No
Sub-Lease part	Yes/No	Yes/No	Yes/No
Sub-sub-lease	Yes/No	Yes/No	Yes/No
Concession	Yes/No	Yes/No	Yes/No
Group sharing	Yes/No	Yes/No	Yes/No

For sub lettings consider: Maximum number of occupiers, limitations
Code requires sublettings to be at market rent.
CNUW = Consent not to be unreasonably withheld.

| 6.0 | **Services and service charge** | Provide estimate or actual budgets and confirm proportion. Any special provisions, eg. exclusions special services, e.g. enhanced security? Any unusual provisions, e.g. sinking fund?

Note: Owners and Occupiers should be aware of the RICS 2006 Code of Practice on Service Charges in Commercial Property and seek to observe its guidance in drafting new leases and on renewals. |

| 7.0 | **Repairing obligations** | |

| 7.1 | **FRI and schedule of condition** | (a) is it full repairing; if so
(b) is it the Landlord who repairs and recovers the cost, or the Tenant who repairs at its own cost?;
(c) is there to be a schedule of condition? |

| 7.2 | **Collateral warranties** | Who is giving them? |

| 8.0 | **Alterations and use** | |

8.1   **Alterations**
See check box >

	Prohibited	If not prohibited is CNUW	Permitted without consent
External	Yes/No	Yes/No	Yes/No
External structural	Yes/No	Yes/No	Yes/No
Internal structural	Yes/No	Yes/No	Yes/No
Internal non structural	Yes/No	Yes/No	Yes/No

Note: Is an agreed form of licence to be attached to lease?

| 8.2 | **Permitted use** | Specify use and any ability to change use. |

| 9.0 | **Insurance** | (a) Landlord insures and recovers the premium from the Tenant.
(b) Will terrorism be an insured risk?
(c) Mutual break clause on:
• Insured damage?
• Uninsured damage? |

The Code for Leasing Business Premises
in England and Wales 2007
www.leasingbusinesspremises.co.uk

10.0	Lease management	
10.1	Dilapidations	e.g. Dilapidations to be scheduled and given to the Tenant six months before the termination date.
11.0	Other issues	
11.1	Rates and utilities	Confirm that the Tenant is responsible. Tenant must check actual amount with Local Authority and utility provider.
11.2	Legal costs	Each party to pay own including costs of approval for tenant's fit out.
11.3	Conditions	e.g. 1. Board approvals 2. Planning 3. Local authority consents. 4. References 5. Superior landlord's consent 6. Survey.
11.4	General	1. DDA 1995? 2. Asbestos register? 3. Environmental issues? 4. Health & safety file and other Issues? 5. Energy efficiency certificate?
11.5	Landlord's solicitors	[ ] Company address: Contact name: E-mail: Telephone: (Fax:) Mobile:
11.6	Tenant's solicitors	[ ] Company address: Contact name: E-mail: Telephone: (Fax:) Mobile:
11.7	Timing and other matters	e.g. Exclusivity period, target for exchange?
11.8	No contract	These Heads of Terms are subject to contract.
11.9	Landlord's agent(s)	[ ] (Registered no. [ ]) Registered office: Correspondence address: Contact name: E-mail: Telephone: (Fax:) Mobile:
11.10	Tenant's agent(s)	[ ] (Registered no. [ ]) Registered office: Correspondence address: Contact name: E-mail: Telephone: (Fax:) Mobile:

Appendix 3
Lease of floor(s) of an office block with guarantee and prescribed clauses

The College of Law would like to thank the Practical Law Company for authorising the use in this publication of the following document: Lease of floor(s) of an office block with guarantee and prescribed clauses (complies with Lease Code 2007) (http://uk.practicallaw.com/9-218-6006). For further information about the Practical Law Company, visit http://uk.practicallaw.com/ or call 020 7202 1200. © Legal & Commercial Publishing Limited 2009.

A full repairing and insuring lease of one or more floors of an office block. The landlord retains all external and structural parts of the building and insures. Comprehensive service charge provisions are included that comply with the RICS 2006 Code of Practice on Service Charges in Commercial Property (Service Charge Code).

The lease has been specifically drafted to comply with the Code for Leasing Business Premises in England and Wales 2007 (Lease Code 2007). However, some issues are open to interpretation and for a proper understanding it is important that the lease is read in conjunction with the Drafting note [not reproduced here].

Contents

Schedules

PRESCRIBED CLAUSES

LR1. Date of lease
[DATE]

LR2. Title number(s)

LR2.1 Landlord's title number(s)
[INSERT TITLE NUMBER(S) OR LEAVE BLANK IF NONE]

LR2.2 Other title numbers
[TITLE NUMBER(S)] OR [None]

LR3. Parties to this lease

Landlord
[COMPANY NAME]
[REGISTERED OFFICE ADDRESS]
[COMPANY REGISTERED NUMBER]

Tenant
[COMPANY NAME]
[REGISTERED OFFICE ADDRESS]
[COMPANY REGISTERED NUMBER]

Other parties
[[COMPANY] NAME]

[[REGISTERED OFFICE] ADDRESS]
[COMPANY REGISTERED NUMBER]

Guarantor

LR4. Property
In the case of a conflict between this clause and the remainder of this lease then, for the purposes of registration, this clause shall prevail.
See the definition of 'Property' in *Clause 1.1* of this lease.

LR5. Prescribed statements etc.
None.

LR6. Term for which the Property is leased
The term as specified in this lease at *Clause 1.1* in the definition of 'Contractual Term'.

LR7. Premium
None.

LR8. Prohibitions or restrictions on disposing of this lease
This lease contains a provision that prohibits or restricts dispositions.

LR9. Rights of acquisition etc.

LR9.1 Tenant's contractual rights to renew this lease, to acquire the reversion or another lease of the Property, or to acquire an interest in other land
None.

LR9.2 Tenant's covenant to (or offer to) surrender this lease
None.

LR9.3 Landlord's contractual rights to acquire this lease
None.

LR10. Restrictive covenants given in this lease by the Landlord in respect of land other than the Property
None.

LR11. Easements

LR11.1 Easements granted by this lease for the benefit of the Property
The easements as specified in *Clause 3* of this lease.

LR11.2 Easements granted or reserved by this lease over the Property for the benefit of other property
The easements as specified in *Clause 4* of this lease.

LR12. Estate rentcharge burdening the Property
None.

LR13. Application for standard form of restriction
The Parties to this lease apply to enter the following standard form of restriction [against the title of the Property] [against title number]
None.

LR14. Declaration of trust where there is more than one person comprising the Tenant
[OMIT ALL INAPPLICABLE STATEMENTS]
[The Tenant is more than one person. They are to hold the Property on trust for themselves as joint tenants.]
[The Tenant is more than one person. They are to hold the Property on trust for themselves as tenants in common in equal shares.]

[The Tenant is more than one person. They are to hold the Property on trust [COMPLETE AS NECESSARY]]

This lease is dated [DATE]

PARTIES

(1) [COMPANY NAME], incorporated and registered in England and Wales with company number [NUMBER] whose registered office is at [REGISTERED OFFICE ADDRESS] (**Landlord**).

(2) [COMPANY NAME], incorporated and registered in England and Wales with company number [NUMBER] whose registered office is at [REGISTERED OFFICE ADDRESS] (**Tenant**).

[(3) [COMPANY NAME], incorporated and registered in England and Wales with company number [NUMBER] whose registered office is at [REGISTERED OFFICE ADDRESS] **OR** [NAME] of [ADDRESS] and [NAME] of [ADDRESS] (**Guarantor**).]

AGREED TERMS

1. INTERPRETATION

1.1   The definitions and rules of interpretation set out in this clause apply to this lease.

Annual Rent: rent at an initial rate of £[ ] per annum and then as revised pursuant to this lease [and any interim rent determined under the 1954 Act].

[**Break Date:** a date which is at least [NUMBER] [weeks][months] after service of the Break Notice.]

[**Break Notice:** written notice to terminate this lease [in the form set out in *Schedule 2*] specifying the Break Date.]

Building: [DESCRIPTION OF THE BUILDING] shown edged blue on Plan 2.

Certificate: a certificate prepared by the Landlord or the Manager setting out the Service Charge and the Service Costs for the preceeding Service Charge Year.

Certified Accounts: service charge accounts prepared [and audited] by the Landlord's [independent accountants] [or] [managing agents].

CDM Regulations: the Construction (Design and Management) Regulations 2007.

Common Parts: the Building other than the Property and the Lettable Units.

Contractual Term: a term from and including [DATE] to and including [DATE].

Default Interest Rate: [four] percentage points above the Interest Rate.

Deliberate Damage: damage caused deliberately [with the intention of causing damage] by the Tenant [or anyone at the Property or on the Common Parts with the express or implied authority of the Tenant [other than anyone deriving title under the Tenant]].

Excluded Costs: the costs set out in *paragraph 3* of Schedule 3.

Insurance Rent: The aggregate in each year of:

(a)   a fair and reasonable proportion of:

   (i)   the cost of any premiums (including any IPT chargeable thereon) that the Landlord expends ([before][after] any discount or commission is allowed or paid to the Landlord); and

   (ii)   any fees and other expenses that the Landlord reasonably incurs, in effecting and maintaining insurance of the Building in accordance with this lease, including any professional fees for carrying out any insurance valuation of the Reinstatement [Cost][Value];

(b)   a fair and reasonable proportion of the cost of any premiums (including any IPT chargeable thereon) that the Landlord expends ([before][after] any discount or commission is allowed or paid to the Landlord) in effecting public liability insurance in relation to the Common Parts;

(c)   the cost of any additional premiums (including any IPT chargeable thereon) and loadings that may be demanded by the Landlord's insurer as a result of any act or default of the Tenant, any person deriving title under the Tenant or any person at the Property with the express or implied authority of any of them;

(d)   the cost of any premiums (including any IPT chargeable thereon) that the Landlord expends ([before][after] any discount or commission is allowed or paid to the Landlord) in effecting insurance against loss of the Annual Rent from the Property for [three] years; and

(e)   any VAT payable on any sum in (a) to (d) inclusive.

Insured Risks: fire, lightning, explosion, impact, earthquake, storm, tempest, flood, bursting or overflowing of water tanks or pipes, damage to underground water, oil or gas pipes or electricity wires or cables, subsidence, ground slip, heave, riot, civil commotion, strikes, labour or political disturbances, malicious damage, aircraft and aerial devices and articles dropped accidentally from them, and such other risk against which the Landlord may reasonably insure from time to time, and **Insured Risk** means any one of the Insured Risks.

Interest Rate: interest at the base lending rate from time to time of [NAME OF BANK], or if that base lending rate stops being used or published then at a comparable commercial rate reasonably determined by the Landlord.

IPT: Insurance Premium Tax chargeable under the Finance Act 1994 or any similar replacement or additional tax.

Landlord's Neighbouring Property: each and every part of the adjoining and neighbouring property in which the Landlord has an interest known as [DESCRIPTION/ADDRESS OF THE LANDLORD'S NEIGHBOURING PROPERTY] [registered at HM Land Registry with title number[s] [INSERT TITLE NUMBER[S] IF REGISTERED]] [shown edged green on the attached plan marked [INSERT PLAN REFERENCE].

Lettable Unit: a floor [or part of a floor] of the Building other than the Property, that is capable of being let and occupied.

Management Fee: the total of the reasonable costs, fees and disbursements of the Manager which are properly incurred by the Landlord relating to the carrying out and provision of the Management Service.

Management Service: any service provided by, or any function of, the Manager in relation to the provision of the Services and the administration of the Service Charge.

Manager: any managing agent, team, individual or in-house person or persons employed by the Landlord, or by managing agents themselves, or otherwise retained by the Landlord to act on the Landlord's behalf, to budget for, forecast, procure, manage, account for, provide and otherwise administer any of the Building, the Services or the Service Charge.

NIC: National Insurance Contributions or any similar, replacement or additional contributions.

Permitted Use: offices within Use Class B1 of the Town and Country Planning (Use Classes) Order 1987 as at the date this lease is granted.

Permitted Hours: [LIMITS OF NORMAL WEEKDAY HOURS] Mondays to Fridays and [LIMITS OF NORMAL SATURDAY HOURS] on Saturdays other than days which are bank holidays or public holidays in [England][Wales].

Plan 1: the plan attached to this lease marked 'Plan 1'.

Plan 2: the plan attached to this lease marked 'Plan 2'.

Property: the [part of the][ ] [and [ ]] floor[s] of the Building (the floor plan[s] of which [is][are] shown edged red on Plan 1) [in respect of each of those floors] bounded by and including:

(a)   [the [floorboards] [floor screed] [OTHER FLOORING BOUNDARY]];

(b)   [the [DESCRIPTION OF CEILING BOUNDARY];]

(c)   [the interior plaster finishes of exterior walls and columns;]

(d)   the plaster finishes of the interior [structural][load-bearing] walls and columns that adjoin [another Lettable Unit or] the Common Parts;]

(e)   [the doors and windows within the interior, [structural] [load-bearing] walls and columns that adjoin [another Lettable Unit or] the Common Parts and their frames and fittings;]

(f)   [one half of the thickness of the interior, [non-structural] [non-load-bearing] walls [and columns] that adjoin [another Lettable Unit or] the Common Parts;] [and]

(g)   [the doors and windows within the interior, [non-structural][non-load-bearing] walls [and columns] that adjoin the Common Parts and their frames and fittings;]

but excluding:

(h)   [the windows in the exterior walls and their frames and fittings;]

(i)   [the whole of the interior [structural] [load-bearing] walls and columns within that part of the Building other than their plaster finishes and other than the doors and windows and their frames and fittings within such walls;] and

(j)   [all Service Media within that part of the Building which do not exclusively serve that part of the Building].

Reinstatement [Cost][Value]: the full [cost of reinstatement][reinstatement value] of the Building as reasonably determined by the Landlord from time to time, taking into account inflation of building costs and including any costs of demolition, site clearance, site protection, shoring up and any other work to the Building that may be required by law and any VAT on any such costs.

[Rent Commencement Date: [SPECIFY DATE].]

Rent Payment Dates: [25 March, 24 June, 29 September and 25 December] **OR** [SPECIFY ALTERNATIVE RENT PAYMENT DATES].

Reservations: all of the rights excepted, reserved and granted to the Landlord by this lease.

Review Date: [SPECIFY EACH REVIEW DATE].

Rights: The rights granted by the Landlord to the Tenant in *clause 3.1*.

Service Charge: a fair and reasonable proportion of the Service Costs, calculated by a recognised method on a consistent basis across the Building and the occupiers of the Building, having regard to the physical size, nature of use and benefits to and use by each occupier.

Service Charge Account: any account set up and maintained by the Landlord into which the [estimated] Service Charge paid by the occupiers of the Building is paid.

Service Charge Code: the RICS Code of Practice known as 'Service Charges in Commercial Property' which came into effect on 1 April 2007.

Service Charge Year: the annual accounting period relating to the Services and the Service Costs beginning on [SPECIFY DATE] in [YEAR] and each subsequent year during the term.

Service Costs: the costs listed in *paragraph 2* of Schedule 3.

Service Media: [lifts and lift machinery and equipment and] all media for the supply or removal of heat, electricity, gas, water, sewage, [air-conditioning,] energy, telecommunications, data and all other services and utilities and all structures, machinery and equipment ancillary to those media.

Service Provider: any body, individual, contractor or sub-contractor which is responsible for providing any of the Services, excluding utility providers.

Services: the services listed in *paragraph 1* of Schedule 3.

Third Party Rights: all rights, covenants and restrictions affecting the Building including the matters referred to at the date of this lease in [the property register] [and [entry][entries] [STATE RELEVANT ENTRY NUMBER(S)] of the charges register] of title number [] **OR** [DESCRIPTION OF RELEVANT MATTERS AFFECTING AN UNREGISTERED REVERSION].

VAT: value added tax chargeable under the Value Added Tax Act 1994 or any similar replacement or additional tax.

1927 Act: Landlord and Tenant Act 1927.

1954 Act: Landlord and Tenant Act 1954.

1995 Act: Landlord and Tenant (Covenants) Act 1995.

1.2   A reference to this **lease**, except a reference to the date of this lease or to the grant of this lease, is a reference to this deed and any deed, licence, consent, approval or other instrument supplemental to it.

1.3   The Schedules form part of this agreement and shall have effect as if set out in full in the body of this agreement. Any reference to this agreement includes the Schedules.

1.4   Except where a contrary intention appears, a reference to a clause or Schedule is a reference to a clause of, or Schedule to, this lease and a reference in a Schedule to a paragraph is to a paragraph of that Schedule.

1.5   Clause, Schedule and paragraph headings shall not affect the interpretation of this lease.

1.6   A reference to the **Landlord** includes a reference to the person entitled to the immediate reversion to this lease. A reference to the **Tenant** includes a reference to its successors in title and assigns. A reference to a **guarantor** [is a reference to any guarantor] [includes a reference to the Guarantor and to any other guarantor] of the tenant covenants of this lease including a guarantor who has entered into an authorised guarantee agreement.

1.7   A **person** includes a natural person, corporate or unincorporated body (whether or not having separate legal personality).

1.8   A reference to one gender shall include a reference to the other genders.

1.9   The expressions **landlord covenant** and **tenant covenant** each has the meaning given to it by the 1995 Act.

1.10   Any obligation in this lease on the Tenant not to do something includes an obligation not to agree to or suffer that thing to be done and an obligation to use best endeavours to prevent that thing being done by another person.

1.11   References to the **consent** of the Landlord are to the consent of the Landlord given in accordance with *clause 41.5* and references to the **approval** of the Landlord are to the approval of the Landlord given in accordance with *clause 41.6*.

1.12   Unless the context otherwise requires, references to the **Building**, the **Common Parts**, a **Lettable Unit** and the **Property** are to the whole and any part of them or it.

1.13   The expression **neighbouring property** does not include the Building.

1.14   A reference to the **term** is to the Contractual Term [and any agreed or statutory continuation of this lease].

1.15   A reference to the **end of the term** is to the end of the term however it ends.

1.16   Any phrase introduced by the terms **including, include, in particular** or any similar expression shall be construed as illustrative and shall not limit the sense of the words preceding those terms.

1.17   A reference to **writing** or **written** includes faxes but does not include e-mail.

1.18   Words in the singular shall include the plural and vice versa.

1.19   References to the **perpetuity period** are to the period of 80 years from the commencement of the term and that period is the perpetuity period for the purposes of section 1 of the Perpetuities and Accumulations Act 1964.

1.20   A **working day** is a day other than a Saturday, Sunday or public holiday in [England][Wales].

1.21   A reference to a statute, statutory provision or subordinate legislation is a reference to it as it is in force [from time to time **OR** as at the date of this lease], taking account of any amendment or re-enactment [and includes any statute, statutory provision or subordinate legislation which it amends or re-enacts].

1.22   A reference to a statute or statutory provision shall include any subordinate legislation made [from time to time **OR** as at the date of this lease] under that statute or statutory provision.

2. GRANT

2.1   [At the request of the Guarantor, the] [The] Landlord lets [with full title guarantee][with limited title guarantee] the Property to the Tenant for the Contractual Term.

2.2   The grant is made together with the Rights, excepting and reserving to the Landlord the Reservations, and subject to the Third Party Rights.

2.3   The grant is made with the Tenant paying the following as rent to the Landlord:

   (a)   the Annual Rent and all VAT in respect of it;

   (b)   the Service Charge and all VAT in respect of it;

   (c)   the Insurance Rent; [and]

   (d)   all interest payable under this lease[; and

   (e)   all other sums due under this lease].

3. ANCILLARY RIGHTS

3.1   The Landlord grants the Tenant the following rights:

   (a)   the right to support and protection from the Common Parts to the extent that the Common Parts provide support and protection to the Property to the date of this lease;

(b) [the right to use external areas of the Common Parts shown hatched [ ] on Plan 2 for the purposes of vehicular and pedestrian access to and egress from the interior of the Building [and to and from the parts of the Common Parts referred to in *clause 3.1(c)* to *clause 3.1(f)*;]

(c) [the right to park [ ] private cars or motorbikes belonging to the Tenant, its employees and visitors within the area edged [ ] on Plan 2;]

(d) [the right to use the area edged [] on Plan 2 for keeping bicycles belonging to the Tenant, its employees and visitors;]

(e) [the right to use the area edged [ ] on Plan 2 for loading and unloading goods and materials;]

(f) [the right to use [ ] bins in the area edged [ ] on Plan 2;]

(g) the right to use the hallways, corridors, stairways, [lifts] and landings of the Common Parts [shown hatched [ ] on Plan 2] for the purposes of access to and egress from the Property [and the lavatories and washrooms referred to in *clause 3.1(h)*];

(h) [the right to use the lavatories [and washrooms] on the [ ] [and [ ]] floor[s] of the Building;]

(i) the right to use and to connect into any Service Media at the Building that belong to the Landlord and serve (but do not form part of) the Property which are in existence at the date of this lease or are installed during the perpetuity period;]

(j) [the right to attach any item to the Common Parts adjoining the Property so far as is reasonably necessary to carry out any works to the Property required or permitted by this lease;]

(k) [the right to display the name and logo of the Tenant (and any authorised undertenant) on a [sign or noticeboard] provided by the Landlord [in the entrance hall of] the Building [and on the Common Parts at the entrance to the Property, in each case] in a form and manner [reasonably] approved by the Landlord; [and]

(l) the right to enter the Common Parts or any other Lettable Unit so far as is reasonably necessary to carry out any works to the Property required or permitted by this lease[; and]

(m) [ANY OTHER SPECIFIC RIGHTS THAT NEED TO BE GRANTED].

3.2 The Rights are granted in common with the Landlord and any other person authorised by the Landlord.

3.3 The Rights are granted subject to the Third Party Rights insofar as the Third Party Rights affect the Common Parts and the Tenant shall not do anything that may interfere with any Third Party Right.

3.4 The Tenant shall exercise the Rights (other than the Right mentioned in *clause 3.1(a)*) only in connection with its use of the Property for the Permitted Use and only during the Permitted Hours and in accordance with any regulations made by the Landlord as mentioned in *clause 31.1*.

3.5 The Tenant shall comply with all laws relating to its use of the Common Parts pursuant to the Rights.

3.6 In relation to the Rights mentioned in *clause 3.1(b)* to *clause 3.1(h)*, the Landlord may, at its discretion, change the route of any means of access to or egress from the interior of the Building and may change the area over which any of those Rights are exercised.

3.7 In relation to the Rights mentioned in *clause 3.1(c)* and *clause 3.1(f)* the Landlord may from time to time designate the spaces or bins (as the case may be) in respect of which the Tenant may exercise that Right.

3.8   In relation to the Rights mentioned in *clause 3.1(i)*, the Landlord may, at its discretion, re-route or replace any such Service Media and that Right shall then apply in relation to the Service Media as re-routed or replaced.

3.9   [In relation to the Right mentioned in *clause 3.1(j)*, where the Tenant requires the consent of the Landlord to carry out the works to the Property, the Tenant may only exercise that Right when that consent has been granted and in accordance with the terms of that consent.]

3.10   In exercising the Right mentioned in *clause 3.1(l)*, the Tenant shall:

(a)   except in case of emergency, give reasonable notice to the Landlord and any occupiers of the relevant Lettable Unit(s) of its intention to exercise that Right;

(b)   where reasonably required by the Landlord or the occupier of the relevant Lettable Unit(s), exercise that Right only if accompanied by a representative of the Landlord and/or the tenant and/or the occupier of the relevant Lettable Unit(s);

(c)   cause as little damage as possible to the Common Parts and the other Lettable Units and to any property belonging to or used by the Landlord or the tenants or occupiers of the other Lettable Units;

(d)   cause as little inconvenience as possible to the Landlord and the tenants and occupiers of the other Lettable Units as is reasonably practicable; and

(e)   promptly make good (to the satisfaction of the Landlord) any damage caused to the Common Parts (or to any property belonging to or used by the Landlord) by reason of the Tenant exercising that Right.

3.11   Except as mentioned in this *clause 3*, neither the grant of this lease nor anything in it confers any right over the Common Parts or any Lettable Unit or any neighbouring property nor is to be taken to show that the Tenant may have any right over the Common Parts or any Lettable Unit or any neighbouring property, and section 62 of the Law of Property Act 1925 does not apply to this lease.

4.   RIGHTS EXCEPTED AND RESERVED

4.1   The following rights are excepted and reserved from this lease to the Landlord for the benefit of the Building and the Landlord's Neighbouring Property [and to the extent possible for the benefit of any neighbouring or adjoining property in which the Landlord acquires an interest during the term]:

(a)   rights of light, air, support and protection to the extent those rights are capable of being enjoyed at any time during the term;

(b)   the right to use and to connect into Service Media at, but not forming part of, the Property which are in existence at the date of this lease or which are installed or constructed during the perpetuity period; the right to install and construct Service Media at the Property to serve any part of the Building (whether or not such Service Media also serve the Property); and the right to re-route any Service Media mentioned in this clause;

(c)   at any time during the term, the full and free right to develop the Landlord's Neighbouring Property [and any neighbouring or adjoining property in which the Landlord acquires an interest during the term] as the Landlord may think fit;

(d)   the right to erect scaffolding at the Property or the Building and attach it to any part of the Property or the Building in connection with any of the Reservations;

(e)   the right to attach any structure, fixture or fitting to the boundary of the Property in connection with any of the Reservations;

(f)   the right to re-route any means of access to or egress from the Property or the Building and to change the areas over which the Rights mentioned in *clause 3.1(a)* to *clause 3.1(e)* are exercised; [and]

(g)   the right to re-route and replace any Service Media over which the Rights mentioned in *clause 3.1(i)* are exercised; [and]

(h)   [ANY OTHER SPECIFIC RIGHTS THAT NEED TO BE RESERVED].]

notwithstanding that the exercise of any of the Reservations or the works carried out pursuant to them result in a reduction in the flow of light or air to the Property or the Common Parts or loss of amenity for the Property or the Common Parts [provided that they do not materially adversely affect the use and enjoyment of the Property for the Permitted Use].

4.2   The Landlord reserves the right to enter the Property:

(a)   to repair, maintain, install, construct, re-route or replace any Service Media or structure relating to any of the Reservations;

(b)   to carry out any works to any other Lettable Unit; and

(c)   for any other purpose mentioned in or connected with:

(i)   this lease;

(ii)   the Reservations; and

(iii)   the Landlord's interest in the Property, the Building or the Landlord's Neighbouring Property.

4.3   The Reservations may be exercised by the Landlord and by anyone else who is or becomes entitled to exercise them, and by anyone authorised by the Landlord.

4.4   The Tenant shall allow all those entitled to exercise any right to enter the Property, to do so with their workers, contractors, agents and professional advisors, and to enter the Property at any reasonable time (whether or not during usual business hours) and, except in the case of an emergency, after having given reasonable notice (which need not be in writing) to the Tenant.

4.5   No party exercising any of the Reservations, nor its workers, contractors, agents and professional advisors, shall be liable to the Tenant or to any undertenant or other occupier of or person at the Property for any loss, damage, injury, nuisance or inconvenience arising by reason of its exercising any of the Reservations except for:

(a)   physical damage to the Property; or

(b)   any loss, damage, injury, nuisance or inconvenience in relation to which the law prevents the Landlord from excluding liability.

5.   THIRD PARTY RIGHTS

5.1   The Tenant shall comply with all obligations on the Landlord relating to the Third Party Rights insofar as those obligations relate to the Property and shall not do anything (even if otherwise permitted by this lease) that may interfere with any Third Party Right.

5.2   The Tenant shall allow the Landlord and any other person authorised by the terms of the Third Party Right to enter the Property in accordance with its terms.

6.   THE ANNUAL RENT

6.1   The Tenant shall pay the Annual Rent and any VAT in respect of it by four equal instalments in advance on or before the Rent Payment Dates. The payments shall be made by banker's standing order or by any other method that the Landlord requires at any time by giving notice to the Tenant.

6.2   The first instalment of the Annual Rent and any VAT in respect of it shall be made on [the date of this lease and shall be the proportion, calculated on a daily basis, in respect of the period from the date of this lease until the day before the next Rent Payment Date] **OR** [the Rent Commencement Date and shall be the proportion, calculated on a daily basis, in respect of the period from the Rent Commencement Date until the day before the next Rent Payment Date].

7.   REVIEW OF THE ANNUAL RENT

7.1   In this clause the **President** is the President for the time being of the Royal Institution of Chartered Surveyors or a person acting on his behalf, and the **Surveyor** is the independent valuer appointed pursuant to *clause 7.7*.

7.2   [The amount of Annual Rent shall be reviewed on each Review Date to the open market rent agreed or determined pursuant to this clause.]

OR

[The amount of Annual Rent shall be reviewed on each Review Date to the greater of:

(a)   [the Annual Rent payable immediately before the relevant Review Date (or which would then be payable but for any abatement or suspension of the Annual Rent or restriction on the right to collect it)] **OR** [£[] per annum]; and

(b)   the open market rent agreed or determined pursuant to this clause.]

7.3   The open market rent may be agreed between the Landlord and the Tenant at any time before it is determined by the Surveyor.

7.4   If the open market rent is determined by the Surveyor, it shall be the amount that the Surveyor determines is the best annual rent (exclusive of any VAT) at which the Property could reasonably be expected to be let:

(a)   in the open market;

(b)   at the relevant Review Date;

(c)   on the assumptions listed in *clause 7.5*; and

(d)   disregarding the matters listed in *clause 7.6*.

7.5   The assumptions are:

(a)   the Property is available to let in the open market:

(i)   by a willing lessor to a willing lessee (which may be the Tenant);

(ii)   as a whole;

(iii)   with vacant possession;

(iv)   without a fine or a premium;

(v)   for a term equal to the unexpired residue of the Contractual Term at the relevant Review Date or a term of [SPECIFY MINIMUM LENGTH OF HYPOTHETICAL TERM] years commencing on the relevant Review Date, if longer; and

(vi)   otherwise on the terms of this lease other than as to the amount of the Annual Rent but including the provisions for review of the Annual Rent [, and other than the provision in this lease for a rent-free period];

(b)   the willing lessee has had the benefit of any rent-free or other concession or contribution which would be offered in the open market at the relevant Review Date to reflect the need to fit out the Property;

(c)   the Property may lawfully be used, and is in a physical state to enable it to be lawfully used, by the willing lessee (or any potential undertenant or assignee of the willing lessee) for any purpose permitted by this lease;

(d)   the Landlord and the Tenant have fully complied with their obligations in this lease;

(e)   if the Property or any other part of the Building or any Service Media serving the Property, has been destroyed or damaged, it has been fully restored;

(f)   no work has been carried out on the Property or any other part of the Building that has diminished the rental value of the Property;

(g) any fixtures, fittings, machinery or equipment supplied to the Property by the Landlord that have been removed by or at the request of the Tenant, or any undertenant or their respective predecessors in title (otherwise than to comply with any law) remain at the Property; and

(h) the willing lessee and its potential assignees and undertenants shall not be disadvantaged by any actual or potential election to waive exemption from VAT in relation to the Property.

7.6 The matters to be disregarded are:

(a) any effect on rent of the fact that the Tenant or any authorised undertenant has been in occupation of the Property;

(b) any goodwill attached to the Property by reason of any business carried out there by the Tenant or by any authorised undertenant or by any of their predecessors in business;

(c) any effect on rent attributable to any physical improvement to the Property carried out [before or] [after the date of this lease,] by or at the expense of the Tenant or any authorised undertenant with all necessary consents, approvals and authorisations and not pursuant to an obligation to the Landlord (other than an obligation to comply with any law);

(d) any effect on rent of any obligation on the Tenant [to fit out the Property or] [to reinstate the Property to the condition or design it was in before any alterations or improvements were carried out]; and

(e) any statutory restriction on rents or the right to recover them.

7.7 The Landlord and the Tenant may appoint an independent valuer at any time before either of them applies to the President for an independent valuer to be appointed. The Landlord or the Tenant may apply to the President for an independent valuer to be appointed at any time after the date which is three months before the relevant Review Date. The independent valuer shall be an associate or fellow of the Royal Institution of Chartered Surveyors.

7.8 The Surveyor shall act as an expert and not as an arbitrator.

7.9 [The Surveyor shall give the Landlord and the Tenant an opportunity to make written representations to the Surveyor and to make written counter-representations commenting on the representations of the other party to the Surveyor.]

7.10 If the Surveyor dies, delays or becomes unwilling or incapable of acting, then either the Landlord or the Tenant may apply to the President to discharge the Surveyor and *clause 7.7* shall then apply in relation to the appointment of a replacement.

7.11 The fees and expenses of the Surveyor and the cost of the Surveyor's appointment and any counsel's fees incurred by the Surveyor shall be payable by the Landlord and the Tenant in the proportions that the Surveyor directs (or if the Surveyor makes no direction, then equally). If the Tenant does not pay its part of the Surveyor's fees and expenses within ten working days after demand by the Surveyor, the Landlord may pay that part and the amount it pays shall be a debt of the Tenant due and payable on demand to the Landlord. The Landlord and the Tenant shall otherwise each bear their own costs in connection with the rent review.

7.12 If the revised Annual Rent has not been agreed by the Landlord and the Tenant or determined by the Surveyor on or before the relevant Review Date, the Annual Rent payable from that Review Date shall continue at the rate payable immediately before that Review Date. [On the date] [No later than five working days after] the revised Annual Rent is agreed or the Surveyor's determination is notified to the Landlord and the Tenant, the Tenant shall pay:

(a) the shortfall (if any) between the amount that it has paid for the period from the Review Date until the Rent Payment Date following the date of agreement or notification of the revised Annual Rent and the amount that would have been payable had the revised Annual Rent been agreed or determined on or before that Review Date; and

(b)   interest at the Interest Rate on that shortfall calculated on a daily basis by reference to the Rent Payment Dates on which parts of the shortfall would have been payable if the revised Annual Rent had been agreed or determined on or before that Review Date and the date payment is received by the Landlord.

7.13   Time shall not be of the essence for the purposes of this clause.

7.14   No guarantor shall have any right to participate in the review of the Annual Rent.

7.15   As soon as practicable after the amount of the revised Annual Rent has been agreed or determined, a memorandum recording the amount shall be signed by or on behalf of the Landlord and the Tenant and endorsed on or attached to this lease and its counterpart. The Landlord and the Tenant shall each bear their own costs in connection with the memorandum.

8.   SERVICES AND SERVICE CHARGE

8.1   Subject to *clause 8.5* the Landlord shall provide the Services.

8.2   The Landlord shall administer the Services and the Service Charge in good faith and, except where there are sound reasons for implementing alternative procedures that can be justified and explained, the Landlord shall have regard to the provisions and recommendations of the Service Charge Code.

8.3   The Landlord shall:

(a)   ensure that the Services are provided in a commercial and professional manner and that the quality and cost of the Services are appropriate for the Building and are regularly reviewed;

(b)   require that Service Providers comply with written performance standards and regularly review, monitor and measure the performance of Service Providers against those written performance standards;

(c)   regularly review the cost of each of the Services against the market cost of similar services and, where appropriate, require contractors and suppliers to submit competitive tenders for the supply of any of the Services;

(d)   require that each Service Provider regularly reviews the methods, procedures, value and efficiency of the Services that it provides and, where possible, that it demonstrates that it is reviewing the Services where so required, that the Services are being provided to an appropriate standard and that value for money is being achieved;

(e)   provide sufficient, capable and appropriately qualified staff of the right type who are capable of administering and providing the Services efficiently and cost-effectively;

(f)   establish and maintain a written management policy which shall identify the aims of the Landlord and/or the Manager and any other members of any management team, the method of procurement, administration and management of the Services and shall [make this management policy available for inspection by the Tenant] [provide a copy of the management policy to the Tenant as soon as possible upon request];

(g)   establish and operate sound management procedures to ensure that the respective obligations of the Landlord and the Tenant which are set out in this clause are complied with and the Landlord shall record these procedures in the management policy referred to in *clause 8.3(f)*;

(h)   ensure that the Management Fee:

(i)   is transparent so that the basis on which it is charged and the way in which it is calculated is clear;

(ii)   relates only to, and is reasonable for, the Management Service;

(iii)   has due regard to the duty of the Manager to observe the principles of the Service Charge Code;

(iv)   is charged to the Tenant in accordance with the relevant provisions of the Service Charge Code;

(v)   is not linked to a percentage of expenditure on the Services; and

(vi)   shall be fixed for a reasonable period of time (subject to indexing);

(i)   at reasonable intervals review the cost and quality of the Management Service and compare it against the market cost and quality of similar services. Unless the Landlord and the majority of the occupiers in the Building are satisfied with the results of such review, the Management Service shall be put out to tender in the open market and the tenderer providing the best value for money shall be appointed as the Manager;

(j)   require the Manager and the Service Providers to, respectively, operate the Management Service and provide the Services, in accordance with all procedures which are established by the Landlord, pursuant to this clause, in order to maintain the quality of the Services to the standard required by the Service Charge Code;

(k)   establish standard procedures for the Building in order to maintain the quality of the Services and shall require that the Manager ensures that the Service Providers comply with those procedures;

(l)   deal promptly and efficiently with any reasonable enquiry made by the Tenant which relates to the Service Charge or any of the Services;

(m)   invite (and, where appropriate act upon) comment from the Tenant on the performance of the Service Providers, the standard of the Management Service and delivery of the Services;

(n)   ensure that (where appropriate) regular meetings are held between the Landlord, the Tenant, the other occupiers in the Building and the Manager;

(o)   ensure that any interest earned on the Service Charge Account (in each case, after bank charges, tax and all other appropriate deductions have been accounted for) is credited to the Service Charge Account;

(p)   allocate the whole of the Service Cost relating to any of the Services which benefits only one occupier, to that specific occupier; and

(q)   as soon as practicable but not later than four months after a disposal of the reversion immediately expectant on the determination of this lease, provide the purchaser with full details of the Service Costs, accruals, prepayments, and all other relevant information for the last [ ] Service Charge Years or any other Service Charge Year for which any part of the procedure set out in *clause 8.8* remains outstanding and up to the date of sale.

8.4   The Landlord shall provide to the Tenant:

(a)   details of any proposed works or Services which may substantially increase the Service Charge due for the relevant Service Charge Year and shall notify the Tenant promptly (and in any event within the relevant Service Charge Year) of any likely significant variation in the actual Service Costs of which the Landlord becomes aware;

(b)   at the Tenant's request, a summary of the process of any tender which is undertaken in accordance with *clause 8.3* and the results of any tender which applies to any proposed substantial works that would fall within the Service Costs together with full information on the programme of works, costs and the process for keeping the Tenant informed;

(c)   information contained in any report or other item where the cost of obtaining this information is a Service Cost;

(d)   a schedule showing the apportionment of the Service Costs for each Lettable Unit, together with a commentary on how the apportionments have been calculated;

(e)   full details of any plans for the Building where such are likely to affect the Service Costs; and

(f)   the Manager's (and where appropriate other Service Providers') contact details and details of each of their respective roles and responsibilities.

8.5   The Landlord shall not be required to:

(a)   carry out any works where the need for those works has arisen by reason of any damage or destruction by a risk against which the Landlord is not obliged to insure;

(b)   provide any of the Services outside the Permitted Hours; or

(c)   replace or renew any part of the Building or any item or system within the Building which has not become beyond economic repair.

8.6   [The Landlord shall not be liable for any interruption in, or disruption to, the provision of any of the Services for any reason that is outside the reasonable control of the Landlord.]

8.7   The Landlord shall not charge any of the Excluded Costs as part of the Service Charge.

8.8   The procedure and obligations of the parties relating to operation of the Service Charge are as follows:

(a)   at least one month before the start of each Service Charge Year, the Landlord shall prepare and send to the Tenant an estimate of the Service Costs for that Service Charge Year (in such form to enable the Tenant to compare it with the last issued Certified Accounts) together with an explanatory commentary where appropriate and a statement of the estimated Service Charge for that Service Charge Year;

(b)   the Tenant shall pay the estimated Service Charge for each Service Charge Year in four equal instalments on each of the Rent Payment Dates;

(c)   in relation to the Service Charge Year current at the date of this lease:

(i)   the Tenant's obligations to pay the estimated Service Charge and the actual Service Charge shall be limited to an apportioned part of those amounts, such apportioned part to be calculated on a daily basis for the period from the date of this lease to the end of the Service Charge Year; and

(ii)   the estimated Service Charge for which the Tenant is liable shall be paid in equal instalments on [the date of this lease and] the [remaining] Rent Payment Days during the Period from the date of this lease until the end of the Service Charge Year;

(d)   as soon as reasonably practicable and no later than four months after the end of each Service Charge Year, the Landlord shall prepare and send to the Tenant a Certificate together with Certified Accounts and the Certificate shall:

(i)   be in a form which is reasonably consistent from year to year;

(ii)   provide an appropriately detailed and comprehensive summary of Service Costs;

(iii)   provide full details of and reasons for any material variations against the estimated Service Charge;

(iv)   be accompanied by a separate report providing any other relevant information which is required by the Service Charge Code; and

(v)   specify the name and role of the person who has given the Certificate;

(e)   if any cost is omitted from the calculation of the Service Charge in any Service Charge Year, the Landlord shall be entitled to include it in the estimate of the Service Charge and the Certificate in any following Service Charge Year;

(f)   subject to *clause 8.8(e)* and except in the case of manifest error, the Certificate shall be conclusive as to all matters of fact to which it refers, subject to the Tenant's right to reasonably challenge the expenditure by [referring the matter for Alternative Dispute

Resolution (ADR)], and in the event of any such referral to ADR, each party shall bear its own costs;

(g)   the Landlord shall allow the Tenant a reasonable period in which to raise enquiries in respect of the Certified Accounts, shall respond promptly and efficiently to any reasonable enquiries of the Tenant and shall [make] [provide copies of] all relevant paperwork and copies of any supporting documentation [available for inspection by the Tenant] [to the Tenant upon request and upon payment by the Tenant of a reasonable fee];

(h)   at the Tenant's request the Landlord shall agree to an independent audit of the Service Costs which shall be undertaken at the Tenant's cost; and

(i)   if in respect of any Service Charge Year, the Landlord's estimate of the Service Charge is less than the Service Charge, the Tenant shall pay the difference immediately upon the expiry of the period specified in *clause 8.8(g)* (unless the Tenant shall challenge the Service Charge pursuant to *clause 8.8(f)* in which case the Tenant shall pay the difference immediately upon the final determination of that challenge). If in respect of any Service Charge Year, the Landlord's estimate of the Service Charge is more than the Service Charge, the Landlord shall promptly repay to the Tenant the difference.

8.9   In addition to the Tenant's obligations contained in *clause 8.8* the Tenant shall:

(a)   co-operate fully with the Landlord and the Manager in order that the Landlord and the Manager may administer the Service Charge in accordance with the provisions of this clause;

(b)   promptly advise the Landlord and the Manager of any changes within the Tenant's organisation that may affect the operation of the Service Charge;

(c)   promptly make a written record upon being advised by the Landlord or the Manager of any changes to the operation of the Service Charge;

(d)   respond promptly and efficiently to any reasonable enquiry of the Landlord or the Manager; and

(e)   be proactive in assisting the Landlord and the Manager with operating and using the Services on a value for money and quality standard basis and follow all procedures reasonably required by the Landlord or the Manager in order to maintain and promote the quality and economic effectiveness of the Services. Such procedures include, but are not be limited to, separating waste to facilitate appropriate and cost effective recycling.

8.10   Where the Landlord is required to comply with any obligation contained in this clause such obligation shall, where relevant, include, in the alternative, an obligation on the Landlord to ensure that the Manager complies with that obligation.

9.   INSURANCE

9.1   The Landlord shall effect and maintain insurance of the Building (but excluding [any plate glass and] any Tenant's and trade fixtures in the Property) in accordance with this clause:

(a)   unless the insurance is vitiated by any act or omission of either:

(i)   the Tenant, any person deriving title under the Tenant or any person at the Property with the express or implied authority of any of them; or

(ii)   any tenant of the Landlord of any part of the Building other than the Property, any person deriving title under them or any person in the Building with the express or implied authority of any of them; and

(b)   subject to:

(i)   any exclusions, limitations, conditions or excesses that may be imposed by the Landlord's insurer; and

(ii)   insurance being available on reasonable terms in the London Insurance market.

9.2   Insurance of the Building shall be with reputable insurers, on fair and reasonable terms that represent value for money, for an amount not less than the [Reinstatement Cost][Reinstatement Value] against loss or damage caused by any of the Insured Risks, and shall include additional cover, if practicable, against damage arising from an act of terrorism.

9.3   In relation to any insurance effected by the Landlord under this clause, the Landlord shall:

(a)   at the request of the Tenant supply the Tenant with:

(i)   full details of the insurance policy;

(ii)   evidence of payment of the current year's premiums; and

(iii) details of any commission paid to the Landlord by the Landlord's insurer;

(b)   procure that the Tenant is informed of any change in the scope, level or terms of cover [as soon as reasonably practicable after][within five working days after] the Landlord or its agents have become aware of the change;

(c)   use all reasonable endeavours to procure that the Landlord's insurer waives its rights of subrogation against the Tenant and any lawful sub-tenants or occupiers of the Property and that the insurance policy contains a non-invalidation provision in favour of the Landlord in respect of any act or default of the Tenant; and

(d)   procure that the interest of the Tenant is noted on the policy of insurance either specifically or by way of a general noting of tenants' interests under the conditions of the insurance policy.

9.4   The Tenant shall pay each of the following to the Landlord on demand:

(a)   the Insurance Rent; and

(b)   a reasonable proportion of any amount that is deducted or disallowed by the Landlord's insurer pursuant to any excess provision in the insurance policy.

9.5   The Tenant shall:

(a)   comply at all times with any requirements or recommendations of the Landlord's insurer that relate to the Property or the use by the Tenant of the Common Parts, where written details of those requirements or recommendations have first been given to the Tenant;

(b)   give the Landlord notice immediately that any matter occurs in relation to the Tenant or the Property that any insurer or underwriter may treat as material in deciding whether or on what terms, to insure or continue insuring the Building; and

(c)   give the Landlord notice immediately that any damage or loss occurs that relates to the Property.

9.6   If the Tenant makes any alteration or addition to the Property, the Tenant shall arrange at its own cost, for a current, independent, VAT inclusive valuation of the [Reinstatement Cost][Reinstatement Value] of the Property, taking into account the alteration or addition, such valuation to be prepared in writing and given to the Landlord within [four weeks] of the alteration or addition being completed.

9.7   In relation to any insurance arranged by the Landlord under this clause, the Tenant shall not do or omit to do anything and shall not permit or suffer anything to be done that may:

(a)   vitiate the insurance contract; or

(b)   cause any money claimed under the insurance to be withheld; or

(c)   cause any premium paid for the insurance to be increased or cause any additional premium to be payable[, unless previously agreed in writing with the Landlord].

9.8   Other than [plate glass and] Tenant's and trade fixtures, the Tenant shall not insure the Property against any of the Insured Risks in such a manner as would permit the Landlord's insurer to cancel the Landlord's insurance or to reduce the amount of any money payable to the Landlord in respect of any insurance claim.

9.9 Notwithstanding the obligation on the Tenant in *clause 9.8*, if the Tenant [or any person deriving title under or through the Tenant] shall at any time be entitled to the benefit of any insurance of the Property, the Tenant shall immediately cause any money paid to the Tenant under that insurance to be applied in making good the loss or damage in respect of which it was paid.

9.10 If the Building or any part of it is damaged or destroyed by an Insured Risk, the Landlord shall:

(a) make a claim under the insurance policy effected in accordance with this clause;

(b) notify the Tenant immediately if the Landlord's insurer indicates that the [Reinstatement Cost][Reinstatement Value] will not be recoverable in full under the insurance policy; and

(c) subject to *clause 9.11*, use any insurance money received (other than for loss of rent) and any money received from the Tenant under *clause 9.4(b)* to repair the damage in respect of which the money was received or (as the case may be) to rebuild the Building.

9.11 The Landlord shall not be obliged under *clause 9.10* to repair or reinstate the Building or any part of it:

(a) unless and until the Landlord has obtained any necessary planning and other consents for the repairs and reinstatement work; or

(b) so as to provide premises or facilities identical in size, quality and layout to those previously at the Building so long as the premises and facilities provided are reasonably equivalent; or

(c) after a notice has been served pursuant to *clause 9.13* or *clause 9.14*.

9.12 If the Building is damaged or destroyed (other than by Deliberate Damage [that causes either the insurance policy to be vitiated or any money claimed under the insurance to be withheld]) so that the Property is wholly or partly unfit for occupation and use, or the Common Parts are damaged or destroyed so as to make the Property inaccessible or unusable, then payment of the Annual Rent or a fair proportion of it according to the nature and extent of the damage, shall be suspended until the earlier of the following:

(a) the date the Tenant can occupy and use the Property in the manner contemplated by this lease prior to the date of the damage or destruction; and

(b) the end of [three] years from the date of damage or destruction.

9.13 Subject to *clause 9.15*, the Landlord may give the Tenant notice terminating the lease with immediate effect if:

(a) the Property is damaged or destroyed or the Common Parts are damaged or destroyed so as to make the Property inaccessible or unusable; and

(b) the Landlord reasonably decides that it is either impracticable or impossible to reinstate the Property and the Common Parts within [three] years from the date of the damage or destruction.

9.14 The Tenant may give the Landlord notice terminating this lease with immediate effect (subject to *clause 9.15*) in either of the following situations:

(a) where the Property is:

(i) damaged or destroyed in whole [or in part] [other than by Deliberate Damage] so that it is unfit for occupation or use, or the Common Parts are damaged or destroyed so as to make the Property inaccessible or unusable; and

        (ii)   is not accessible and/or not fit for occupation and use by the end of [three] years from the date of damage or destruction; or

    (b)   where:

        (i)   the Property is damaged or destroyed in whole [or in part] [other than by Deliberate Damage and] other than by an Insured Risk[or is not covered by the Landlord's insurance by reason of a limitation in the insurance policy] so that it is unfit for occupation or use, or the Common Parts are damaged or destroyed so as to make the Property inaccessible or unusable; and

        (ii)   the loss or damage was caused other than by an Insured Risk [or is not covered by the Landlord's insurance by reason of a limitation in the insurance policy] and the Landlord has not given notice to the Tenant within [six months] of the date of damage or destruction that the Landlord will reinstate the Property at the Landlord's own cost.

9.15   Any notice to terminate this lease by either the Landlord or the Tenant under this clause shall be without prejudice to the rights of either party for breach of any of the covenants in the lease.

9.16   If this lease is terminated by either the Landlord or the Tenant under this clause, then any proceeds of the insurance effected by the Landlord shall belong to the Landlord.

10. RATES AND TAXES

10.1   The Tenant shall pay all present and future rates, taxes and other impositions payable in respect of the Property, its use and any works carried out there, other than:

    (a)   any taxes payable by the Landlord in connection with any dealing with or disposition of the reversion to this lease; or

    (b)   any taxes, other than VAT and insurance premium tax, payable by the Landlord by reason of the receipt of any of the rents due under this lease.

10.2   If any such rates, taxes or other impositions are payable in respect of the Property together with other land (including any other part of the Building) the Tenant shall pay a fair proportion of the total.

10.3   The Tenant shall not make any proposal to alter the rateable value of the Property or that value as it appears on any draft rating list, without the approval of the Landlord.

10.4   If, after the end of the term, the Landlord loses rating relief (or any similar relief or exemption) because it has been allowed to the Tenant, then the Tenant shall pay the Landlord an amount equal to the relief or exemption that the Landlord has lost.

11. UTILITIES

11.1   The Tenant shall pay all costs in connection with the supply [and removal] of [electricity, gas, water, sewage,] telecommunications [and] data [and other services and utilities] to [or from] the Property.]

11.2   The Tenant shall comply with all laws and with any recommendations of the relevant suppliers relating to [the use of those services and utilities] [the supply and removal of electricity, gas, water, sewage, telecommunications, data and other services and utilities to or from the Property].

12. COMMON ITEMS

12.1   The Tenant shall pay the Landlord on demand a fair proportion of all costs payable by the Landlord for the maintenance, repair, lighting, cleaning and renewal of all Service Media, structures and other items not on the Building but used or capable of being used by the Building in common with other land.

12.2   The Tenant shall comply with all reasonable regulations the Landlord may make from time to time in connection with the use of any of those Service Media, structures or other items.

13. VAT

13.1   All sums payable by the Tenant are exclusive of any VAT that may be chargeable. The Tenant shall pay VAT in respect of all taxable supplies made to it in connection with this lease on the due date for making any payment or, if earlier, the date on which that supply is made for VAT purposes.

13.2   Every obligation on the Tenant, under or in connection with this lease, to pay the Landlord or any other person any sum by way of a refund or indemnity, shall include an obligation to pay an amount equal to any VAT incurred on that sum by the Landlord or other person, except to the extent that the Landlord or other person obtains credit for such VAT under the Value Added Tax Act 1994.

14. DEFAULT INTEREST AND INTEREST

14.1   If any Annual Rent or any other money payable under this lease has not been paid by the date it is due, whether it has been formally demanded or not, the Tenant shall pay the Landlord interest at the Default Interest Rate (both before and after any judgment) on that amount for the period from the due date to and including the date of payment.

14.2   If the Landlord does not demand or accept any Annual Rent or other money due or tendered under this lease because the Landlord reasonably believes that the Tenant is in breach of any of the tenant covenants of this lease, then the Tenant shall, when that amount is accepted by the Landlord, also pay interest at the Interest Rate on that amount for the period from the date the amount (or each part of it) became due until the date it is accepted by the Landlord.

15. COSTS

15.1   The Tenant shall pay the costs and expenses of the Landlord including any solicitors' or other professionals' costs and expenses (incurred both during and after the end of the term) in connection with or in contemplation of:

(a)   the enforcement of the tenant covenants of this lease;

(b)   serving any notice in connection with this lease under section 146 or 147 of the Law of Property Act 1925 or taking any proceedings under either of those sections, notwithstanding that forfeiture is avoided otherwise than by relief granted by the court;

(c)   serving any notice in connection with this lease under section 17 of the 1995 Act;

(d)   the preparation and service of a schedule of dilapidations in connection with this lease; and

(e)   any consent or approval applied for under this lease, whether or not it is granted [(unless the consent or approval is unreasonably withheld by the Landlord in circumstances where the Landlord is not unreasonably to withhold it)].

15.2   Where the Tenant is obliged to pay or indemnify the Landlord against any solicitors' or other professionals' costs and expenses (whether under this or any other clause of this lease) that obligation extends to those costs and expenses assessed on a full indemnity basis.

16. [COMPENSATION ON VACATING]

Any right of the Tenant or anyone deriving title under the Tenant to claim compensation from the Landlord on leaving the Property under the 1927 Act or the 1954 Act is excluded, except to the extent that the legislation prevents that right being excluded.

17. NO DEDUCTION, COUNTERCLAIM OR SET-OFF

The Annual Rent and all other money due under this lease are to be paid by the Tenant or any guarantor (as the case may be) without deduction, counterclaim or set-off.

18. REGISTRATION OF THIS LEASE

Promptly following the grant of this lease, the Tenant shall apply to register this lease at HM Land Registry. The Tenant shall ensure that any requisitions raised by HM Land Registry in connection with that application are dealt with promptly and properly. Within one month after completion of the registration, the Tenant shall send the Landlord official copies of its title.

19. PROHIBITION OF DEALINGS

Except as expressly permitted by this lease, the Tenant shall not assign, underlet, charge, part with or share possession or share occupation of this lease or the Property or hold the lease on trust for any person (except pending registration of a dealing permitted by this lease at HM Land Registry or by reason only of joint legal ownership).

20. ASSIGNMENTS

20.1   The Tenant shall not assign the whole of this lease without the consent of the Landlord, such consent not to be unreasonably withheld.

20.2   The Tenant shall not assign part only of this lease.

20.3   For the purposes of section 19(1A) of the 1927 Act, where at the date of assignment, either :

(a)   the assignee is an individual resident overseas or is a company not incorporated in the United Kingdom; or

(b)   in the reasonable opinion of the Landlord, the proposed assignee, when assessed together with any proposed guarantor, is of a lower financial standing than the tenant and its guarantor (if any),

the Landlord and the Tenant agree that the Landlord may impose the condition in *clause 20.4* upon assignment.

20.4   A condition that the assignor [(and any former tenant who because of section 11 of the 1995 Act has not been released from the tenant covenants of this lease)] enters into an authorised guarantee agreement which:

(a)   is in respect of all the tenant covenants of this lease;

(b)   is in respect of the period beginning with the date the assignee becomes bound by those covenants and ending on the date when the assignee is released from those covenants by virtue of section 5 of the 1995 Act;

(c)   imposes principal debtor liability on the assignor (and any former tenant);

(d)   requires (in the event of a disclaimer of liability of this lease) the assignor (or former tenant as the case may be) to enter into a new tenancy for a term equal to the unexpired residue of the Contractual Term; and

(e)   is otherwise in a form reasonably required by the Landlord.

20.5   The Landlord and the Tenant agree that [if reasonable] the Landlord may give its consent to any assignment subject to a condition that a person of standing acceptable to the Landlord enters into a guarantee and indemnity of the tenant covenants of this lease in the form set out in *Schedule 1* (but with such amendments and additions as the Landlord may reasonably require).

20.6   For the purposes of section 19(1A) of the 1927 Act, if the Tenant wishes to assign this lease to any company that, at the date of assignment is a member of the same group (within the meaning of section 42 of the 1954 Act), the Landlord and the Tenant agree that the Landlord shall not be unreasonable in refusing its consent if in the reasonable opinion of the Landlord, the proposed assignee, when assessed together with any proposed guarantor, is of a lower financial standing than the tenant and its guarantor (if any).

20.7   Nothing in this clause shall prevent the Landlord from giving consent subject to any other reasonable condition, nor from refusing consent to an assignment in any other circumstance where it is reasonable to do so.

21.   UNDERLETTINGS

21.1   The Tenant shall not underlet the whole of the Property except in accordance with this clause nor without the consent of the Landlord, such consent not to be unreasonably withheld.

21.2   The Tenant shall not underlet part only of the Property.

21.3   The Tenant shall not underlet the Property:

(a)   together with any property or any right over property that is not included within this lease; nor

(b)   at a fine or premium or reverse premium; nor

(c)   allowing any rent free period to the undertenant that exceeds the period as is then usual in the open market in respect of such a letting.

21.4   The Tenant shall not underlet the Property unless, before the underlease is granted, the Tenant has given the Landlord:

(a)   a certified copy of the notice served on the undertenant, as required by section 38A(3)(a) of the 1954 Act, applying to the tenancy to be created by the underlease; and

(b)   a certified copy of the declaration or statutory declaration made by the undertenant in accordance with the requirements of section 38A(3)(b) of the 1954 Act.

21.5   Any underletting by the Tenant shall be by deed and shall include:

(a)   an agreement between the Tenant and the undertenant that the provisions of sections 24 to 28 of the 1954 Act are excluded from applying to the tenancy created by the underlease;

(b)   the reservation of a rent which is not less than the open market rental value of the Property at the date the Property is underlet and which is payable at the same times as the Annual Rent under this lease [(but this shall not prevent an underlease providing for a rent-free period of a length permitted by *clause 21.3(c)*];

(c)   provisions for the review of rent at the same dates and on the same basis as the review of rent in this lease, unless the term of the underlease does not extend beyond the next Review Date;

(d)   a covenant by the undertenant, enforceable by and expressed to be enforceable by the Landlord (as superior landlord at the date of grant) and its successors in title in their own right, to observe and perform the tenant covenants in the underlease and any document that is supplemental or collateral to it; and

(e)   provisions requiring the consent of the Landlord to be obtained in respect of any matter for which the consent of the Landlord is required under this lease,

and shall otherwise not conflict with the terms of this lease and shall be in a form approved by the Landlord [such approval to be given, or refused with reasons, in writing within [ ] days of receipt by the Landlord of the final draft of the underlease and] such approval not to be unreasonably withheld.

21.6 In relation to any underlease granted by the Tenant, the Tenant shall:

(a) not vary the terms of the underlease nor accept a surrender of the underlease without the consent of the Landlord, such consent not to be unreasonably withheld;

(b) enforce the tenant covenants in the underlease and not waive any of them; and

(c) ensure that in relation to any rent review the revised rent is not agreed without the approval of the Landlord, such approval not to be unreasonably withheld.

22. SHARING OCCUPATION

The Tenant may share occupation of the Property with any company that is a member of the same group (within the meaning of section 42 of the 1954 Act) as the Tenant for as long as that company remains within that group and provided that no relationship of landlord and tenant is established by that arrangement.

23. CHARGING

23.1 The Tenant shall not charge the whole of this lease without the consent of the Landlord, such consent not to be unreasonably withheld.

23.2 The Tenant shall not charge part only of this lease.

24. REGISTRATION AND NOTIFICATION OF DEALINGS AND OCCUPATION

24.1 In this clause a **Transaction** is:

(a) any dealing with this lease or the devolution or transmission of, or parting with possession of any interest in it; or

(b) the creation of any underlease or other interest out of this lease, or out of any interest, underlease derived from it, and any dealing, devolution or transmission of, or parting with possession of any such interest or underlease; or

(c) the making of any other arrangement for the occupation of the Property.

24.2 In respect of every Transaction that is registrable at HM Land Registry, the Tenant shall promptly following completion of the Transaction apply to register it (or procure that the relevant person so applies). The Tenant shall (or shall procure that) any requisitions raised by HM Land Registry in connection with an application to register a Transaction are dealt with promptly and properly. Within [one month] of completion of the registration, the Tenant shall send the Landlord official copies of its title (and where applicable of the undertenant's title).

24.3 No later than one month after a Transaction the Tenant shall:

(a) give the Landlord's solicitors notice of the Transaction; [and]

(b) deliver two certified copies of any document effecting the Transaction to the Landlord's solicitors[; and

(c) pay the Landlord's solicitors a registration fee of £30 (plus VAT)].

24.4 If the Landlord so requests, the Tenant shall promptly supply the Landlord with full details of the occupiers of the Property and the terms upon which they occupy it.

25. CLOSURE OF THE REGISTERED TITLE OF THIS LEASE

[Within one month] [Immediately] after the end of the term (and notwithstanding that the term has ended), the Tenant shall make an application to close the registered title of this lease and shall ensure that any requisitions raised by HM Land Registry in connection with that application are dealt with promptly and properly; the Tenant shall keep the Landlord informed of the progress and completion of its application.

26. REPAIRS

26.1   The Tenant shall keep the Property clean and tidy and in good repair [and condition] [except that the Tenant shall not be required to put the Property into any better state of repair or condition than it was in at the date of this lease as evidenced by the schedule of condition initialled by the parties to this lease and annexed to this lease].

26.2   The Tenant shall not be liable to repair the Property to the extent that any disrepair has been caused by an Insured Risk, unless and to the extent that:

(a)   the Landlord's insurance has been vitiated or any insurance proceeds withheld in consequence of any act or omission of the Tenant, any person deriving title under the Tenant or any person at the Property or on the Common Parts with the actual or implied authority of the Tenant or any person deriving title under the Tenant; or

(b)   the insurance cover in relation to that disrepair is excluded, limited or unavailable.

27. DECORATION

27.1   The Tenant shall decorate the Property as often as is reasonably necessary and also in the last three months before the end of the term.

27.2   All decoration shall be carried out in a good and proper manner using good quality materials that are appropriate to the Property and the Permitted Use and shall include all appropriate preparatory work.

27.3   All decoration carried out in the last three months of the term shall also be carried out to the satisfaction of the Landlord and using materials, designs and colours approved by the Landlord.

27.4   [The Tenant shall replace the floor coverings at the Property within the three months before the end of the term with new ones of good quality and appropriate to the Property and the Permitted Use.]

28. ALTERATIONS AND SIGNS

28.1   The Tenant shall not make any alteration to the Property without the consent of the Landlord, such consent not to be unreasonably withheld, other than as mentioned in *clause 28.2*.

28.2   Subject to *clause 28.3*, the Tenant may make non-structural alterations without the consent of the Landlord provided that the Tenant shall:

(a)   make good any damage to the Property and to any part of the Common Parts; and

(b)   immediately after completion of such alterations give to the Landlord copies of the plans and specifications for the alterations.

28.3   The Tenant shall not install nor alter the route of any Service Media at the Property, nor do anything that may affect the Service Media, without the consent of the Landlord, such consent not to be unreasonably withheld.

28.4   The Tenant shall not attach any sign, fascia, placard, board, poster or advertisement to the Property so as to be seen from the outside of the Building.

28.5   Where the consent of the Landlord is required under this clause, the Landlord shall determine the Tenant's application for consent within [15] working days of receiving all the information that the Landlord [reasonably] considers necessary to allow the Landlord to determine the application.

29. RETURNING THE PROPERTY TO THE LANDLORD

29.1   At the end of the term the Tenant shall return the Property to the Landlord in the repair and condition required by this lease.

29.2   If the Landlord reasonably so requires and gives the Tenant notice no later than six months before the end of the term, the Tenant shall remove items it has fixed to the Property, remove any alterations it has made to the Property and make good any damage caused to the Property by that removal.

29.3   At the end of the term, the Tenant shall remove from the Property all chattels belonging to or used by it.

29.4   The Tenant irrevocably appoints the Landlord to be the Tenant's agent to store or dispose of any chattels or items it has fixed to the Property and which have been left by the Tenant on the Property for more than ten working days after the end of the term. The Landlord shall not be liable to the Tenant by reason of that storage or disposal. The Tenant shall indemnify the Landlord in respect of any claim made by a third party in relation to that storage or disposal.

29.5   If the Tenant does not comply with its obligations in this clause, then, without prejudice to any other right or remedy of the Landlord, the Tenant shall pay the Landlord an amount equal to the Annual Rent at the rate reserved immediately before the end of the term for the period that it would reasonably take to put the Property into the condition it would have been in had the Tenant performed its obligations under this clause. The amount shall be a debt due on demand from the Tenant to the Landlord.

30.   USE

30.1   The Tenant shall not use the Property for any purpose other than the Permitted Use.

30.2   [The Tenant shall not use the Property outside the Permitted Hours [without the approval of the Landlord].]

30.3   [If the Landlord gives its approval to the Tenant using the Property outside the Permitted Hours, the Tenant shall observe all [reasonable and proper] regulations that the Landlord makes relating to that use and shall pay the Landlord all costs incurred by the Landlord in connection with that use, including the whole of the cost of any Services provided by the Landlord attributable to the use by the Tenant of the Property outside the Permitted Hours.]

30.4   The Tenant shall not use the Property for any illegal purpose nor for any purpose or in a manner that would cause loss, damage, injury, nuisance or inconvenience to the Landlord, the other tenants or occupiers of the Lettable Units or any owner or occupier of neighbouring property.

30.5   The Tenant shall not overload any structural part of the Building nor any Service Media at or serving the Property.

31.   MANAGEMENT OF THE BUILDING

31.1   The Tenant shall observe all [reasonable and proper] regulations made by the Landlord from time to time in accordance with the principles of good estate management and notified to the Tenant relating to:

(a)   the use of the Common Parts;

(b)   the management of the Building; and

(c)   the use of any Service Media, structures or other items outside the Building which are used or capable of being used by the Building in common with other land.

31.2   Nothing in this lease shall impose or be deemed to impose any restriction on the use of any other Lettable Unit or any neighbouring property.

32.   COMPLIANCE WITH LAWS

32.1   The Tenant shall comply with all laws relating to:

(a)   the Property and the occupation and use of the Property by the Tenant;

(b)   the use of all Service Media and machinery and equipment at or serving the Property;

(c)   any works carried out at the Property; and

(d)   all materials kept at or disposed from the Property.

32.2   Without prejudice to any obligation on the Tenant to obtain any consent or approval under this lease, the Tenant shall carry out all works that are required under any law to be carried out at the Property whether by the owner or the occupier.

32.3   Within five working days after receipt of any notice or other communication affecting the Property or the Building (and whether or not served pursuant to any law) the Tenant shall:

(a)   send a copy of the relevant document to the Landlord; and

(b)   in so far as it relates to the Property, take all steps necessary to comply with the notice or other communication and take any other action in connection with it as the Landlord may require.

32.4   The Tenant shall not apply for any planning permission for the Property.

32.5   The Tenant shall comply with its obligations under the CDM Regulations including all requirements in relation to the provision and maintenance of a health and safety file.

32.6   The Tenant shall supply all information to the Landlord that the Landlord reasonably requires from time to time to comply with the Landlord's obligations under the CDM Regulations.

32.7   As soon as the Tenant becomes aware of any defect in the Property, it shall give the Landlord notice of it. The Tenant shall indemnify the Landlord against any liability under the Defective Premises Act 1972 in relation to the Property by reason of any failure of the Tenant to comply with any of the tenant covenants in this lease.

32.8   The Tenant shall keep the Property equipped with all fire prevention, detection and fighting machinery and equipment and fire alarms which are required under all relevant laws or required by the insurers of the Property or reasonably recommended by them or reasonably required by the Landlord and shall keep that machinery, equipment and alarms properly maintained and available for inspection.

33.   ENCROACHMENTS, OBSTRUCTIONS AND ACQUISITION OF RIGHTS

33.1   The Tenant shall not grant any right or licence over the Property to any person nor permit any person to make any encroachment over the Property.

33.2   The Tenant shall not obstruct the flow of light or air to the Property.

33.3   The Tenant shall not make any acknowledgement that the flow of light or air to the Property or any other part of the Building or that the means of access to the Building is enjoyed with the consent of any third party.

33.4   The Tenant shall immediately notify the Landlord if any person takes or threatens to take any action to obstruct the flow of light or air to the Property.

34.   REMEDY BREACHES

34.1   The Landlord may enter the Property to inspect its condition and state of repair and may give the Tenant notice of any breach of any of the tenant covenants in this lease relating to the condition or repair of the Property.

34.2   If the Tenant has not begun any works needed to remedy that breach within two months following that notice (or if works are required as a matter of emergency, then immediately) or if the Tenant is not carrying out the works with all due speed, then the Landlord may enter the Property and carry out the works needed.

34.3   The costs incurred by the Landlord in carrying out any works pursuant to this clause (and any professional fees and any VAT in respect of those costs) shall be a debt due from the Tenant to the Landlord and payable on demand.

34.4   Any action taken by the Landlord pursuant to this clause shall be without prejudice to the Landlord's other rights.

34.5   Not less than six months before the end of the term, the Landlord shall serve a schedule of dilapidations on the Tenant and shall notify the Tenant of any other dilapidations that occur after the schedule of dilapidations has been served as soon as possible.

35.   [INDEMNITY]

The Tenant shall keep the Landlord indemnified against all expenses, costs, claims, damage and loss (including any diminution in the value of the Landlord's interest in the Building and loss of amenity of the Building) arising from any breach of any tenant covenants in this lease, or any act or omission of the Tenant, any undertenant or their respective workers, contractors or agents or any other person on the Property or the Common Parts with the actual or implied authority of any of them.

36.   LANDLORD'S COVENANT FOR QUIET ENJOYMENT

The Landlord covenants with the Tenant, that, so long as the Tenant pays the rents reserved by and complies with its obligations in this lease, the Tenant shall have quiet enjoyment of the Property without any lawful interruption by the Landlord or any person claiming under the Landlord.

37.   GUARANTEE AND INDEMNITY

37.1   [The provisions of *Schedule 1* apply.]

37.2   [If any of the events mentioned in *clause 38.1(c)* occur in relation to a guarantor that is a corporation, or if any of the events mentioned in *clause 38.1(d)* occur in relation to one or more individuals that is a guarantor or if one or more of those individuals dies or becomes incapable of managing its affairs the Tenant shall, if the Landlord requests, procure that a person of standing acceptable to the Landlord, within [ ] days of that request, enters into a replacement or additional guarantee and indemnity of the tenant covenants of this lease in the same form as that entered into by the former guarantor.]

37.3   [*Clause 37.2* shall not apply in the case of a person who is guarantor by reason of having entered into an authorised guarantee agreement.]

37.4   For so long as any guarantor remains liable to the Landlord, the Tenant shall, if the Landlord requests, procure that the guarantor joins in any consent or approval required under this lease and consents to any variation of the tenant covenants of this lease.

38.   CONDITION FOR RE-ENTRY

38.1   The Landlord may re-enter the Property (or any part of the Property in the name of the whole) at any time after any of the following occurs:

(a)   any rent is unpaid 21 days after becoming payable whether it has been formally demanded or not; or

(b)   any breach of any condition of, or tenant covenant, in this lease; or

(c)   where the Tenant [or any guarantor] is a corporation:

(i)   the taking of any step in connection with any voluntary arrangement or any other compromise or arrangement for the benefit of any creditors of the Tenant [or guarantor]; or

(ii)   the making of an application for an administration order or the making of an administration order in relation to the Tenant [or guarantor]; or

(iii)   the giving of any notice of intention to appoint an administrator, or the filing at court of the prescribed documents in connection with the appointment of an administrator, or the appointment of an administrator, in any case in relation to the tenant [or the guarantor]; or

(iv)   the appointment of a receiver or manager or an administrative receiver in relation to any property or income of the Tenant [or guarantor]; or

(v)   the commencement of a voluntary winding-up in respect of the Tenant [or guarantor], except a winding-up for the purpose of amalgamation or reconstruction of a solvent company in respect of which a statutory declaration of solvency has been filed with the Registrar of Companies; or

(vi)   the making of a petition for a winding-up order or a winding-up order in respect of the Tenant [or guarantor]; or

(vii)   the striking-off of the Tenant [or guarantor] from the Register of Companies or the making of an application for the Tenant [or the guarantor] to be struck-off; or

(viii)   the Tenant [or guarantor] otherwise ceasing to exist; or

(d)   where the Tenant [or any guarantor] is an individual:

(i)   the taking of any step in connection with any voluntary arrangement or any other compromise or arrangement for the benefit of any creditors of the Tenant [or guarantor]; or

(ii)   the presentation of a petition for a bankruptcy order or the making of a bankruptcy order against the Tenant [or guarantor].

38.2   If the Landlord re-enters the Property (or any part of the Property in the name of the whole) pursuant to this clause, this lease shall immediately end, but without prejudice to any right or remedy of the Landlord in respect of any breach of covenant by the Tenant [or any guarantor].

39. LIABILITY

39.1   At any time when the Landlord, the Tenant or a guarantor is more than one person, then in each case those persons shall be jointly and severally liable for their respective obligations arising under this lease. The Landlord may take action against, or release or compromise the liability of, any one of those persons or grant time or other indulgence to any one of them without affecting the liability of any other of them.

39.2   The obligations of the Tenant and any guarantor arising by virtue of this lease are owed to the Landlord and the obligations of the Landlord are owed to the Tenant.

39.3   In any case where the facts are or should reasonably be known to the Tenant, the Landlord shall not be liable to the Tenant for any failure of the Landlord to perform any landlord covenant in this lease unless and until the Tenant has given the Landlord notice of the facts that give rise to the failure and the Landlord has not remedied the failure within a reasonable time.

40. ENTIRE AGREEMENT AND EXCLUSION OF REPRESENTATIONS

40.1   This lease constitutes the whole agreement between the parties relating to the transaction contemplated by the grant of this lease and supersedes all previous agreements between the parties relating to the transaction.

40.2   [The Tenant acknowledges that in entering into this lease it has not relied on] [The Tenant and the Guarantor acknowledge that in entering into this lease neither has relied on], and shall have no right or remedy in respect of, any statement or representation made by or on behalf of the Landlord.

40.3   Nothing in this lease constitutes or shall constitute a representation or warranty that the Property or the Common Parts may lawfully be used for any purpose allowed by this lease.

40.4   Nothing in this clause shall limit or exclude any liability for fraud.

41.   NOTICES, CONSENTS AND APPROVALS

41.1   Except where this lease specifically states that a notice need not be in writing, or where notice is given in an emergency, any notice given pursuant to this lease shall:

(a)   be in writing in the English language; and

(b)   be:

(i)   delivered personally; or

(ii)   delivered by commercial courier; or

(iii)   sent by fax; or

(iv)   sent by pre-paid first-class post or recorded delivery; or

(v)   (if the notice is to be served by post outside the country from which it is sent) sent by airmail requiring signature on delivery.

41.2   A notice is deemed to have been received:

(a)   if delivered personally, at the time of delivery; or

(b)   if delivered by commercial courier, at the time of signature of the courier's receipt; or

(c)   if sent by fax, at the time of transmission; or

(d)   if sent by pre-paid first-class post or recorded delivery, 48 hours from the date of posting; or

(e)   if sent by airmail, five days from the date of posting;

(f)   if deemed receipt under the previous paragraphs of this clause is not within business hours (meaning 9.00 am to 5.30 pm on a working day in the place of receipt), when business next starts in the place of receipt.

41.3   To prove service, it is sufficient to prove that the notice:

(a)   if sent by fax, was transmitted by fax to the fax number of the party; or

(b)   if sent by post, that the envelope containing the notice was properly addressed and posted.

41.4   Section 196 of the Law of Property Act 1925 shall otherwise apply to notices given under this lease.

41.5   Where the consent of the Landlord is required under this lease, a consent shall only be valid if it is given by deed, unless:

(a)   it is given in writing and signed by a person duly authorised on behalf or the Landlord; and

(b)   it expressly states that the Landlord waives the requirement for a deed in that particular case.

If a waiver is given, it shall not affect the requirement for a deed for any other consent.

41.6   Where the approval of the Landlord is required under this lease, an approval shall only be valid if it is in writing and signed by or on behalf of the Landlord, unless:

(a)   the approval is being given in a case of emergency; or

(b)   this lease expressly states that the approval need not be in writing.

41.7   If the Landlord gives a consent or approval under this lease, the giving of that consent or approval shall not imply that any consent or approval required from a third party has been obtained, nor shall it obviate the need to obtain any consent or approval from a third party.

42.   GOVERNING LAW AND JURISDICTION

42.1   This lease and any dispute or claim arising out of or in connection with it or its subject matter shall be governed by and construed in accordance with the law of England and Wales.

42.2   The Landlord, the Tenant, [the Guarantor] and any [other] guarantor irrevocably agree that the courts of England and Wales shall have exclusive jurisdiction to settle any dispute or claim or matter arising under or in connection with this lease or its subject matter or the legal relationships established by it.

43.   EXCLUSION OF 1954 ACT PROTECTION

43.1   The parties confirm that:

(a)   the Landlord served a notice on the Tenant, as required by section 38A(3)(a) of the 1954 Act, applying to the tenancy created by this lease, [not less than 14 days] before [this lease] [DETAILS OF AGREEMENT FOR LEASE] was entered into [a certified copy of which notice is annexed to this lease];

(b)   [the Tenant] [[NAME OF DECLARANT] who was duly authorised by the Tenant to do so] made a [statutory] declaration dated [DATE] in accordance with the requirements of section 38A(3)(b) of the 1954 Act [a certified copy of which [statutory] declaration is annexed to this lease]; and

(c)   [there is no agreement for lease to which this lease gives effect.]

43.2   The parties agree that the provisions of sections 24 to 28 of the 1954 Act are excluded in relation to the tenancy created by this lease.

43.3   The parties confirm that:

(a)   the Landlord served a notice on the Guarantor, as required by section 38A(3)(a) of the 1954 Act, applying to the tenancy to be entered into by the Guarantor pursuant to paragraph 4 of the Schedule, [not less than 14 days] before [this lease] [DETAILS OF AGREEMENT FOR LEASE] was entered into (a certified copy of which notice is annexed to this lease); and

(b)   [the Guarantor] [[NAME OF DECLARANT], who was duly authorised by the Guarantor to do so], made a [statutory] declaration dated [DATE] in accordance with the requirements of section 38A(3)(b) of the 1954 Act (a certified copy of which [statutory] declaration is annexed to this lease).

44.   [TENANT'S BREAK CLAUSE]

44.1   The Tenant may terminate this lease by serving a Break Notice [at any time on or after [EARLIEST DATE]] on the Landlord.

44.2   A Break Notice served by the Tenant shall be of no effect if, at the Break Date:

(a)   the Tenant has not paid [in cleared funds] any part of the Annual Rent, or any VAT in respect of it, which was due to have been paid; or

(b)   the Tenant remains in occupation of any part of the Property; or

(c)   there are any continuing subleases of the Property.

44.3   Subject to *clause 44.2*, following service of a Break Notice this lease shall terminate on the Break Date.

44.4   Termination of this lease on the Break Date shall not affect any other right or remedy that either party may have in relation to any earlier breach of this lease.

44.5   On the Break Date, the Landlord shall refund to the Tenant the proportion of the Annual Rent and any VAT paid in respect of it for the period from and including the Break Date, to but excluding the next Rent Payment Date, calculated on a daily basis.

45.   CONTRACTS (RIGHTS OF THIRD PARTIES) ACT 1999

A person who is not a party to this lease shall not have any rights under or in connection with it by virtue of the Contracts (Rights of Third Parties) Act 1999.

46.   NEW TENANCY UNDER 1995 ACT

This lease creates a new tenancy for the purposes of the 1995 Act.

This document has been executed as a deed and is delivered and takes effect on the date stated at the beginning of it.

SCHEDULE 1
GUARANTEE AND INDEMNITY

1.   GUARANTEE AND INDEMNITY

1.1   The Guarantor guarantees to the Landlord that the Tenant shall:

(a)   pay the rents reserved by this lease and observe and perform the tenant covenants of this lease and that if the Tenant fails to pay any of those rents or to observe or perform any of those tenant covenants, the Guarantor shall pay or observe and perform them; and

(b)   observe and perform any obligations the Tenant enters into in an authorised guarantee agreement made in respect of this lease (the **Authorised Guarantee Agreement**) and that if the Tenant fails to do so, the Guarantor shall observe and perform those obligations.

1.2   The Guarantor covenants with the Landlord as a separate and independent primary obligation to indemnify the Landlord against any failure by the Tenant:

(a)   to pay any of the rents reserved by this lease or any failure to observe or perform any of the tenant covenants of this lease; and

(b)   to observe or perform any of the obligations the Tenant enters into in the Authorised Guarantee Agreement.

2.   GUARANTOR'S LIABILITY

2.1   The liability of the Guarantor under *paragraph 1.1(a)* and *paragraph 1.2(a)* shall continue until the end of the term, or until the Tenant is released from the tenant covenants of this lease by virtue of the 1995 Act, if earlier.

2.2   The liability of the Guarantor shall not be affected by:

(a)   any time or indulgence granted by the Landlord to the Tenant; or

(b)   any delay or forbearance by the Landlord in enforcing the payment of any of the rents or the observance or performance of any of the tenant covenants of this lease (or the Tenant's obligations under the Authorised Guarantee Agreement) or in making any demand in respect of any of them; or

(c)   any refusal by the Landlord to accept any rent or other payment due under this lease where the Landlord believes that the acceptance of such rent or payment may prejudice its ability to re-enter the Property; or

(d)   the Landlord exercising any right or remedy against the Tenant for any failure to pay the rents reserved by this lease or to observe or perform the tenant covenants of this lease (or the Tenant's obligations under the Authorised Guarantee Agreement); or

(e)   the Landlord taking any action or refraining from taking any action in connection with any other security held by the Landlord in respect of the Tenant's liability to pay the rents reserved by this lease or observe and perform the tenant covenants of the lease (or the Tenant's obligations under the Authorised Guarantee Agreement) including the release of any such security; or

(f)   [a release or compromise of the liability of any one of the persons who is the Guarantor, or the grant of any time or concession to any one of them; or]

(g)   any legal limitation or disability on the Tenant or any invalidity or irregularity of any of the tenant covenants of the lease (or the Tenant's obligations under the Authorised Guarantee Agreement) or any unenforceability of any of them against the Tenant; or

(h)   the Tenant being dissolved, or being struck off the register of companies or otherwise ceasing to exist, or, if the Tenant is an individual, by the Tenant dying or becoming incapable of managing its affairs; or

(i)   without prejudice to *paragraph 4*, the disclaimer of the Tenant's liability under this lease or the forfeiture of this lease; or

(j)   the surrender of part of the Property, except that the Guarantor shall not be under any liability in relation to the surrendered part in respect of any period after the surrender; or

(k)   by any other act or omission except an express [written] release [under seal] of the Guarantor by the Landlord

2.3   [The liability of each of the persons making up the Guarantor is joint and several.]

2.4   Any sum payable by the Guarantor shall be paid without any deduction, set-off or counter-claim against the Landlord or the Tenant.

3.   VARIATIONS AND SUPPLEMENTAL DOCUMENTS

3.1   The Guarantor shall, at the request of the Landlord, join in and give its consent to the terms of any consent, approval, variation or other document that may be entered into by the Tenant in connection with this lease (or the Authorised Guarantee Agreement).

3.2   The Guarantor shall not be released by any variation of the rents reserved by, or the tenant covenants in, this Lease (or the Tenant's obligations under the Authorised Guarantee Agreement) whether or not:

(a)   the variation is material or prejudicial to the Guarantor; or

(b)   the variation is made in any document; or

(c)   the Guarantor has consented, in writing or otherwise, to the variation.

3.3   The liability of the Guarantor shall apply to the rents reserved by and the tenant covenants in this lease (and the Tenant's obligations under the Authorised Guarantee Agreement) as varied except to the extent that the liability of the Guarantor is affected by section 18 of the 1995 Act.

4.   GUARANTOR TO TAKE A NEW LEASE OR MAKE PAYMENT

4.1   If this lease is forfeited or the liability of the Tenant under this lease is disclaimed and the Landlord gives the Guarantor notice not later than [six] months after the forfeiture or the Landlord having received notice of the disclaimer, the Guarantor shall enter into a new lease of the Property on the terms set out in *paragraph 4.2*.

4.2   The rights and obligations under the new lease shall take effect from the date of the forfeiture or disclaimer and the new lease shall:

(a)   be granted subject to the right of any person to have this lease vested in them by the court and to the terms on which any such order may be made and subject to the rights of any third party existing at the date of the grant;

(b)   be for a term that expires at the same date as the end of the Contractual Term of this lease had there been no forfeiture or disclaimer;

(c)   reserve as an initial annual rent an amount equal to the Annual Rent payable under this lease at the date of the forfeiture or disclaimer or which would be payable but for any abatement or suspension of the Annual Rent or restriction on the right to collect it and which is subject to review on the same terms and dates provided by this lease (subject to *paragraph 5*); [and]

(d)   be excluded from sections 24 to 28 of the 1954 Act; and

(e)   otherwise be on the same terms as this lease (as varied if there has been any variation).

4.3   The Guarantor shall pay the Landlord's solicitors' costs and disbursements (on a full indemnity basis) and any VAT in respect of them in relation to the new lease and shall execute and deliver to the Landlord a counterpart of the new lease within one month after service of the Landlord's notice.

4.4   The grant of a new lease and its acceptance by the Guarantor shall be without prejudice to any other rights which the Landlord may have against the Guarantor or against any other person or in respect of any other security that the Landlord may have in connection with this lease.

4.5   The Landlord may, instead of giving the Guarantor notice pursuant to *paragraph 4.1* but in the same circumstances and within the same time limit, require the Guarantor to pay an amount equal to [six] months Annual Rent and the Guarantor shall pay that amount on demand.

5.   RENT AT THE DATE OF FORFEITURE OR DISCLAIMER

5.1   If at the date of the forfeiture or disclaimer there is a rent review pending under this lease, then the initial annual rent to be reserved by the new lease shall be subject to review on the date on which the term of the new lease commences on the same terms as those that apply to a review of the Annual Rent under this lease, such review date to be included in the new lease.

5.2   If *paragraph 5.1* applies, then the review for which it provides shall be in addition to any rent reviews that are required under *paragraph 4.2(c)*.

6.   PAYMENTS IN GROSS AND RESTRICTIONS ON THE GUARANTOR

6.1   Any payment or dividend that the Landlord receives from the Tenant (or its estate) or any other person in connection with any insolvency proceedings or arrangement involving the Tenant shall be taken and applied as a payment in gross and shall not prejudice the right of the Landlord to recover from the Guarantor to the full extent of the obligations that are the subject of this guarantee and indemnity.

6.2   The Guarantor shall not claim in competition with the Landlord in any insolvency proceedings or arrangement of the Tenant in respect of any payment made by the Guarantor pursuant to this guarantee and indemnity. If it otherwise receives any money in such proceedings or arrangement, it shall hold that money on trust for the Landlord to the extent of its liability to the Landlord.

6.3   The Guarantor shall not, without the consent of the Landlord, exercise any right or remedy that it may have (whether against the Tenant or any other person) in respect of any amount paid or other obligation performed by the Guarantor under this guarantee and indemnity unless and until all the obligations of the Guarantor under this guarantee and indemnity have been fully performed.

7. OTHER SECURITIES

7.1 The Guarantor warrants that it has not taken and covenants that it shall not take any security from or over the assets of the Tenant in respect of any liability of the Tenant to the Guarantor. If it does take or hold any such security it shall hold it for the benefit of the Landlord.

7.2 This guarantee and indemnity is in addition to any other security that the Landlord may at any time hold from the Guarantor or the Tenant or any other person in respect of the liability of the Tenant to pay the rents reserved by this lease and to observe and perform the tenant covenants of this lease. It shall not merge in or be affected by any other security.

7.3 The Guarantor shall not be entitled to claim or participate in any other security held by the Landlord in respect of the liability of the Tenant to pay the rents reserved by this lease or to observe and perform the tenant covenants of this lease.

SCHEDULE 2
BREAK NOTICE

[INSERT FORM OF BREAK NOTICE]

SCHEDULE 3
SERVICES, SERVICE COSTS AND EXCLUDED COSTS

1. SERVICES

The **Services** are:

(a) cleaning, maintaining, decorating and repairing the Common Parts, including the structural parts, the outsides of the windows and all Service Media forming part of the Common Parts, and remedying any inherent defect;

(b) providing heating to the internal areas of the Common Parts [and the Lettable Units] during such periods of the year as the Landlord reasonably considers appropriate, and cleaning, maintaining, repairing and replacing the heating machinery and equipment;

(c) lighting the Common Parts and cleaning, maintaining, repairing and replacing lighting machinery and equipment on the Common Parts;

(d) supplying hot and cold water, soap, paper, towels and other supplies for any lavatories, washrooms, kitchens and utility areas on the Common Parts, and cleaning, maintaining, repairing and replacing the furniture, fittings and equipment in those areas;

(e) keeping the lifts on the Common Parts in reasonable working order and cleaning, maintaining, repairing and replacing the lifts and lift machinery and equipment;

(f) cleaning, maintaining, repairing and replacing refuse bins on the Common Parts;

(g) cleaning, maintaining, repairing and replacing signage for the Common Parts;

(h) cleaning, maintaining, repairing, operating and replacing security machinery and equipment (including closed circuit television) on the Common Parts;

(i) cleaning, maintaining, repairing, operating and replacing fire prevention, detection and fighting machinery and equipment and fire alarms on the Common Parts;

(j) cleaning, maintaining, repairing and replacing a signboard showing the names and logos of the tenants and other occupiers [in the entrance hall of the Building];

(k) maintaining the landscaped and grassed areas of the Common Parts;

(l) cleaning, maintaining, repairing and replacing the floor coverings on the internal areas of the Common Parts;

(m) cleaning, maintaining, repairing and replacing the furniture and fittings on the Common Parts;

(n)   [providing air conditioning for the internal areas of the [Common Parts] [Building] and cleaning, maintaining, repairing and replacing air conditioning equipment serving the [Common Parts][Building];

(o)   [providing [security] [reception] [cleaning and maintenance] staff for the Building;]

(p)   [ANY OTHER SPECIFIC SERVICES REQUIRED]; and

(q)   any other service or amenity that the Landlord may in its reasonable discretion (acting in accordance with the principles of good estate management) provide for the benefit of the tenants and occupiers of the Building.

2. SERVICE COSTS

The **Service Costs** (excepting the Excluded Costs) are the total of:

(a)   all of the reasonable and properly incurred costs of:

(i)   providing the Services;

(ii)   the supply and removal of electricity, gas, water, sewage and other utilities to and from the [Common Parts][Building];

(iii)   complying with the recommendations and requirements of the insurers of the Building (insofar as those recommendations and requirements relate to the Common Parts);

(iv)   complying with all laws relating to the Common Parts, their use and any works carried out to them, relating to the use of all Service Media, machinery and equipment at or serving the Common Parts and relating to any materials kept at or disposed of from the Common Parts;

(v)   complying with the Third Party Rights insofar as they relate to the Common Parts;

(vi)   taking any steps (including proceedings) that the Landlord considers necessary to prevent or remove any encroachment over the Common Parts or to prevent the acquisition of any right over the Common Parts (or Building as a whole) or to remove any obstruction to the flow of light or air to the Common Parts (or the Building as a whole); and

(vii)   borrowing to fund major expenditure on any Service which is infrequent or of an unusual nature.

(b)   the Management Fee and all of the reasonable and properly incurred costs, fees and disbursements of:

(i)   the accountants employed by the Landlord to prepare, audit and certify the service charge accounts; and

(ii)   a procurement specialist who is employed or retained to achieve greater value for money and cost effectiveness in relation to the Service Costs.

(c)   all costs incurred in relation to [security][reception][cleaning and maintenance] staff for the Building as follows:

(i)   salaries (and all appropriate benefits);

(ii)   employers' costs (including NIC and tax, costs of compliance with statutory requirements, pension, welfare, training and insurance contributions);

(iii)   uniforms; and

(iv)   all equipment and supplies needed for the proper performance of their duties.

(d)   all rates, taxes and impositions payable in respect of the Common Parts, their use and any works carried out on them (other than any taxes payable by the Landlord in connection with any dealing with or disposition of its reversionary interest in the Building);

(e)   the reasonable and proper cost of complying with any of the Landlord's obligations contained in *clause 8*;

(f)   any VAT payable in respect of any of the items mentioned above except to the extent that the Landlord is able to recover such VAT.

3.   EXCLUDED COSTS

The **Excluded Costs** are any costs which relate to or arise from:

(a)   matters between the Landlord and an occupier in the Building, including, but not limited to, costs relating to or arising from:

(i)   enforcement of covenants to pay rent and other monies payable under the occupier's lease;

(ii)   the letting of any Lettable Unit;

(iii)   any consents required under the relevant lease, including but not limited to consents to assign, sublet, alterations and extended opening hours; and

(iv)   rent reviews;

(b)   failure or negligence of the Landlord or Manager;

(c)   any Lettable Unit which is unlet;

(d)   any shortfall in the costs of providing any of the Services to a Lettable Unit for which the Landlord has agreed a special concession (not being a properly constituted weighting formula);

(e)   the maintenance or operation of:

(i)   any premises within the Building used by the Landlord for its own purposes (except where such use is wholly or partly in connection with the management of the Building itself, in which case the whole or a reasonable part, as the case may be, of such costs shall be a Service Cost);

(ii)   any cost centre within the Building that generates income for the Landlord (except where such income is credited to the Service Charge Account, in which case the whole of such costs shall be a Service Cost);

(iii)   the initial provision of any items that are reasonably to be considered part of the original design and construction of the fabric, plan or equipment of the Building together with the initial setting up that is reasonably to be considered part of the original development of the Building;

(iv)   any future development of the Building;

(v)   the replacement of any item of the fabric, plant, equipment or materials necessary for the operation of the Building, except where it is beyond economic repair at the time of such replacement or except where the expenditure is necessary for the purposes of good estate management and following the analysis of reasonable options and alternatives (in which case the Landlord shall upon request provide to the Tenant evidence justifying such cost);

(vi)   the improvement of any item (where the cost exceeds the costs of normal maintenance, repair or replacement) except where the expenditure can be justified for the purposes of good estate management and following the analysis of reasonable options and alternatives (in which case the Landlord shall upon request provide to the Tenant evidence justifying such cost); and

(vii)   any service provided by reason of damage to or destruction of the Common Parts by a risk against which the Landlord is obliged to insure.

Signed as a deed by [NAME OF LANDLORD] acting by [NAME OF FIRST DIRECTOR] and [NAME OF SECOND DIRECTOR/SECRETARY]

....
Director

....
Director/
Secretary

Signed as a deed by [NAME OF TENANT] acting by [NAME OF FIRST DIRECTOR] and [NAME OF SECOND DIRECTOR/SECRETARY]

....
Director

....
Director/
Secretary

Signed as a deed by [NAME OF GUARANTOR] acting by [NAME OF FIRST DIRECTOR] and [NAME OF SECOND DIRECTOR/SECRETARY]

....
Director

....
Director/
Secretary

OR

Signed as a deed by [NAME OF GUARANTOR] in the presence of [NAME OF WITNESS]

....
[SIGNATURE OF GUARANTOR]

....
[SIGNATURE OF WITNESS]

....
[NAME OF WITNESS]

....

....
[ADDRESS OF WITNESS]

Signed as a deed by [NAME OF GUARANTOR] in the
presence of [NAME OF WITNESS]

....
[SIGNATURE
OF
GUARANTOR
]

....
[SIGNATURE
OF WITNESS]

....
[NAME OF
WITNESS]

....

....
[ADDRESS OF
WITNESS]

Appendix 4
Specimen Authorised Guarantee Agreement

THIS DEED IS DATED . . . .

Parties

- [*FULL COMPANY NAME*] incorporated and registered in England and Wales with company number [*NUMBER*] whose registered office is at [*REGISTERED OFFICE ADDRESS*](Landlord).
- [*FULL COMPANY NAME*] incorporated and registered in England and Wales with company number [*NUMBER*] whose registered office is at [*REGISTERED OFFICE ADDRESS*](Tenant).

Background

1   This agreement is supplemental and collateral to the Lease and to the Licence to Assign.

2   The Landlord is entitled to the immediate reversion to the Lease.

3   The residue of the term granted by the Lease is vested in the Tenant.

4   The Tenant intends to assign the Lease and has agreed to enter into an authorised guarantee agreement with the Landlord.

1. Agreed terms

1.1   The definitions and rules of interpretation set out in this clause apply to this agreement.

Assignee: the person or persons defined as assignee in the Licence to Assign.

Lease: a lease of [*ADDRESS/DESCRIPTION OF THE PROPERTY*] dated [*DATE*] and made between [*PARTIES*], and all documents supplemental or collateral to that lease.

Licence to Assign: a licence to assign the Lease dated [*DATE*] and made between [*PARTIES*].

Property: [*ADDRESS/DESCRIPTION OF THE PROPERTY*] as [more particularly described in and] demised by the Lease.

[1954 Act: Landlord and Tenant Act 1954.]

1.2   References to the Landlord include a reference to the person entitled for the time being to the immediate reversion to the Lease.

1.3   The expression Tenant Covenants has the meaning given to it by the Landlord and Tenant (Covenants) Act 1995.

1.4   References to the Completion of the Assignment are to the date on which the deed of assignment to the Assignee is dated and not to the registration of that deed at Land Registry.

1.5   Unless otherwise specified a reference to a particular law is a reference to it as it is in force for the time being taking account of any amendment, extension, application or re-enactment and includes any subordinate laws for the time being in force made under it.

1.6   A Person includes a corporate or unincorporated body.

1.7   Except where a contrary intention appears, a reference to a clause or schedule is a reference to a clause of, or schedule to this agreement, and a reference in a schedule to a paragraph is to a paragraph of that schedule.

1.8   Clause, schedule and paragraph headings are not to affect the interpretation of this agreement.

2. Consideration and effect

2.1   The obligations on the Tenant in this agreement are owed to the Landlord and are made in consideration of the Landlord's consent granted in the Licence to Assign.

2.2   The provisions of this agreement shall take effect on the date the Assignee becomes bound by the Tenant Covenants of the Lease, and are to continue until the end of the term of the Lease (however it may end) and during any agreed or statutory continuation of it, or until the Assignee is released from the tenant covenants of the Lease by virtue of the Landlord and Tenant (Covenants) Act 1995, whichever is earlier.

2.3   If the Tenant is more than one person, then each of those persons shall be jointly and individually liable for their respective obligations arising by virtue of this agreement or the assignment. The Landlord may release or compromise the liability of any one of those persons or grant any time or concession to any one of them without affecting the liability of any other of them.

3. Guarantee and indemnity

3.1   The Tenant guarantees to the Landlord that the Assignee will pay the rents reserved by the Lease and observe and perform the Tenant Covenants of the Lease and that if the Assignee fails to pay any of those rents or to observe or perform any of those Tenant Covenants, the Tenant will pay or observe and perform them.

3.2   The Tenant covenants with the Landlord as a separate and independent primary obligation to indemnify the Landlord against any failure to pay any of the rents reserved by the Lease or any failure to observe or perform any of the Tenant Covenants of the Lease.

4. Tenant's liability

4.1   The liability of the Tenant shall not be affected by:

4.1.1   Any time or indulgence granted by the Landlord to the Assignee (or to any person to whom the Assignee has assigned the Lease pursuant to an assignment that is an excluded assignment under section 11 of the Landlord and Tenant (Covenants) Act 1995); or

4.1.2   Any delay or forbearance by the Landlord in enforcing the payment of any of the rents or the observance or performance of any of the tenant covenants of the Lease or in making any demand in respect of any of them; or

4.1.3   Any refusal by the Landlord to accept any rent or other payment due under the Lease where the Landlord believes that the acceptance of such rent or payment may prejudice its ability to re-enter the Property; or

4.1.4   The Landlord exercising any right or remedy against the Assignee for any failure to pay the rents reserved by the Lease or to observe or perform the tenant covenants of the Lease; or

4.1.5   The Landlord taking any action or refraining from taking any action in connection with any other security held by the Landlord in respect of the Assignee's liability to pay the rents reserved by the Lease and observe and perform the tenant covenants of the Lease (including the release of any such security); or

4.1.6   A release or compromise of the liability of any one of the persons who is the Tenant, or the grant of any time or concession to any one of them; or

4.1.7   Any legal limitation or disability on the Assignee or any invalidity or irregularity of any of the tenant covenants of the Lease or any unenforceability of any of them against the Assignee; or

4.1.8   The Assignee being dissolved or being struck off the register of companies or otherwise ceasing to exist; or

4.1.9   Without prejudice to clause 6, the disclaimer of the liability of the Assignee under the Lease; or

4.1.10   The surrender of part of the Property, except that the Tenant shall not be under any liability in relation to the surrendered part in respect of any period after the surrender; or

4.1.11   Any other act or omission except an express release of the Tenant made by the Landlord under seal.

4.2   Any sum payable by the Tenant under this agreement is to be paid without any deduction, set-off or counter-claim against the Landlord or the Assignee.

5. Variations and supplemental documents

5.1   The Tenant shall, at the request of the Landlord, join in and give its consent to the terms of any licence, consent, variation or other document that may be entered into by the Assignee in connection with the Lease.

5.2   The Tenant is not be released from liability under this agreement by any variation of the rents reserved by, or the Tenant Covenants in, the Lease, whether or not:

5.2.1   The variation is material or prejudicial to the Tenant; or

5.2.2   The Tenant has consented to the variation.

5.3   The liability of the Tenant under this agreement shall apply to the rents reserved by and the Tenant Covenants of the Lease as varied except to the extent that the liability of the Tenant is affected by section 18 of the Landlord and Tenant (Covenants) Act 1995.

6. Tenant to take a new lease

6.1   If the liability of the Assignee under the Lease is disclaimed and the Landlord gives the Tenant written notice within six months after the Landlord receives notice of that disclaimer, the Tenant shall enter into a new lease of the Property on the terms set out in clause 6.2.

6.2   The rights and obligations under the new lease are to take effect from the date of the disclaimer and the new lease shall:

6.2.1   Be granted subject to the right of any person to have the Lease vested in them by the court and to the terms on which any such order may be made and subject to the rights of any third party existing at the date of the grant;

6.2.2   Be for a term that expires at the same date as the end of the contractual term granted by the Lease had there been no disclaimer;

6.2.3   Reserve as an initial annual rent an amount equal to the rent which is payable under the Lease on the date of the disclaimer (subject to clause 7) and which is subject to review on the same terms and dates provided by the Lease; [and]

6.2.4   [Be excluded from sections 24 to 28 of the 1954 Act; and]

6.2.5   Otherwise be on the same terms as the Lease (as varied if there has been any variation other than a variation in respect of which and to the extent that the Tenant is not liable by virtue of section 18 of the Landlord and Tenant (Covenants) Act 1995).

6.3   [The parties confirm that:

6.3.1   the Landlord served a notice on the Tenant, as required by section 38A(3)(a) of the 1954 Act, applying to the tenancy to be entered into by the Tenant pursuant to clause 6.1 [not less than

14 days] before the authorised guarantee agreement was entered into (a certified copy of which notice is annexed to this agreement); and

6.3.2 [the Tenant] [[*NAME OF DECLARANT*], who was duly authorised by the Tenant to do so], made a [statutory] declaration dated [*DATE*] in accordance with the requirements of section 38A(3)(b) of the 1954 Act (a certified copy of which [statutory] declaration is annexed to this agreement).]

6.4 The Tenant shall pay the Landlord's solicitor's costs and disbursements (on a full indemnity basis) and any VAT on them in relation to the new lease and shall execute and deliver to the Landlord a counterpart of the new lease within one month after service of the Landlord's notice.

6.5 The grant of a new lease and its acceptance by the Tenant shall be without prejudice to any other rights which the Landlord may have against the Tenant or against any other person or in respect of any other security that the Landlord may have in connection with the Lease.

7. Rent at the date of disclaimer

7.1 If at the date of the disclaimer there is a rent review pending under the Lease, then:

7.1.1 the relevant review date in the Lease shall also be a rent review date in the new lease;

7.1.2 the rent to be first reserved by the new lease shall be the open market rent of the Property at the relevant review date as agreed or determined in accordance with the new lease;

7.1.3 until the rent is agreed or determined the rent under the new lease shall be payable at the rate that was payable under the Lease immediately before the disclaimer; and

7.1.4 the provisions in the new lease relating to the payment of any shortfall and interest following agreement or determination of a rent review shall apply in relation to any shortfall between the rent payable and the rent first reserved, in respect of the period after the date of the disclaimer.

7.2 If at the date of the disclaimer there is any abatement or suspension of the rent reserved by the Lease, then, for the purposes for this agreement, that rent shall be deemed to be the amount which would be payable under the Lease but for the abatement or suspension, but without prejudice to the provisions relating to abatement or suspension to be contained in the new lease.

8. Payments in gross and restrictions on the Tenant

8.1 Any payment or dividend that the Landlord receives from the Assignee (or its estate) or any other person in connection with any insolvency proceedings or arrangement involving the Assignee shall be taken and applied as a payment in gross and shall not prejudice the right of the Landlord to recover from the Tenant to the full extent of the obligations that are the subject of the guarantee and indemnity in this agreement.

8.2 The Tenant shall not claim in competition with the Landlord in any insolvency proceedings or arrangement of the Assignee in respect of any payment made by the Tenant pursuant to the guarantee and indemnity in this agreement. If it otherwise receives any money in such proceedings or arrangement, it shall hold that money on trust for the Landlord to the extent of its liability to the Landlord.

8.3 The Tenant shall not, without the consent of the Landlord, exercise any right or remedy that it may have (whether against the Assignee or any other person) in respect of any amount paid or other obligation performed by the Tenant under the guarantee and indemnity in this agreement unless and until all the obligations of the Tenant under the guarantee and indemnity in this agreement have been fully performed.

9 Other securities

9.1 The Tenant warrants that it has not taken and covenants that it will not take any security from or over the assets of the Assignee in respect of any liability of the Assignee to the Tenant. If it does take or hold any such security it shall hold it for the benefit of the Landlord.

9.2 This agreement is in addition to any other security that the Landlord may at any time hold from the Tenant or the Assignee or any other person in respect of the liability of the Assignee to pay the rents reserved by the Lease and to observe and perform the tenant covenants of the Lease. It shall not merge in or be affected by any other security.

9.3 The Tenant shall not be entitled to claim or participate in any other security held by the Landlord in respect of the liability of the Assignee to pay the rents reserved by the Lease or to observe and perform the tenant covenants of the Lease.

10. Costs

On completion of this agreement the Tenant is to pay the reasonable costs and disbursements of the Landlord's solicitors and its managing agents in connection with this agreement. This obligation extends to costs and disbursements assessed on a full indemnity basis and to any value added tax in respect of those costs and disbursements except to the extent that the Landlord is able to recover that value added tax.

11. Indemnity

The Tenant will indemnify the Landlord against all costs and claims arising from any breach of the terms of this agreement.

12. Notices

Any notice given pursuant to this agreement shall be in writing and shall be delivered by hand or sent by pre-paid first class post or recorded delivery or by any other means permitted by the Lease. A correctly addressed notice sent by pre-paid first class post shall be deemed to have been delivered at the time at which it would have been delivered in the normal course of the post.

13. Contracts (Rights of Third Parties) Act 1999

No term of this agreement shall be enforceable under the Contracts (Rights of Third Parties) Act 1999 by any third party.

Appendix 5
Extracts from the Landlord and Tenant Act 1954, Part II

SECURITY OF TENURE FOR BUSINESS, PROFESSIONAL AND
OTHER TENANTS

TENANCIES TO WHICH PART II APPLIES

23. Tenancies to which Part II applies

(1) Subject to the provisions of this Act, this Part of this Act applies to any tenancy where the property comprised in the tenancy is or includes premises which are occupied by the tenant and are so occupied for the purposes of a business carried on by him or for those and other purposes.

(1A) Occupation or the carrying on of a business—

    (a) by a company in which the tenant has a controlling interest; or

    (b) where the tenant is a company, by a person with a controlling interest in the company,

shall be treated for the purposes of this section as equivalent to occupation or, as the case may be, the carrying on of a business by the tenant.

(1B) Accordingly references (however expressed) in this Part of this Act to the business of, or to use, occupation or enjoyment by, the tenant shall be construed as including references to the business of, or to use, occupation or enjoyment by, a company falling within subsection (1A)(a) above or a person falling within subsection (1A)(b) above.

(2) In this Part of this Act the expression 'business' includes a trade, profession or employment and includes any activity carried on by a body of persons, whether corporate or unincorporate.

(3) In the following provisions of this Part of this Act the expression 'the holding', in relation to a tenancy to which this Part of this Act applies, means the property comprised in the tenancy, there being excluded any part thereof which is occupied neither by the tenant nor by a person employed by the tenant and so employed for the purposes of a business by reason of which the tenancy is one to which this Part of this Act applies.

(4) Where the tenant is carrying on a business, in all or any part of the property comprised in a tenancy, in breach of a prohibition (however expressed) of use for business purposes which subsists under the terms of the tenancy and extends to the whole of that property, this Part of this Act shall not apply to the tenancy unless the immediate landlord or his predecessor in title has consented to the breach or the immediate landlord has acquiesced therein.

In this subsection the reference to a prohibition of use for business purposes does not include a prohibition of use for the purposes of a specified business, or of use for purposes of any but a specified business, but save as aforesaid includes a prohibition of use for the purposes of some one or more only of the classes of business specified in the definition of that expression in subsection (2) of this section.

Continuation and Renewal of Tenancies

24. Continuation of tenancies to which Part II applies and grant of new tenancies

(1) A tenancy to which this Part of this Act applies shall not come to an end unless terminated in accordance with the provisions of this Part of this Act; and, subject to the following provisions of this Act either the tenant or the landlord under such a tenancy may apply to the court for an order for the grant of a new tenancy—

     (a)   if the landlord has given notice under section 25 of this Act to terminate the tenancy, or

     (b)   if the tenant has made a request for a new tenancy in accordance with section twenty-six of this Act.

(2)   The last foregoing subsection shall not prevent the coming to an end of a tenancy by notice to quit given by the tenant, by surrender or forfeiture, or by the forfeiture of a superior tenancy unless—

     (a)   in the case of a notice to quit, the notice was given before the tenant had been in occupation in right of the tenancy for one month; . . .

     (b)   . . ..

(2A) Neither the tenant nor the landlord may make an application under subsection (1) above if the other has made such an application and the application has been served.

(2B) Neither the tenant nor the landlord may make such an application if the landlord has made an application under section 29(2) of this Act and the application has been served.

(2C) The landlord may not withdraw an application under subsection (1) above unless the tenant consents to its withdrawal.

(3)   Notwithstanding anything in subsection (1) of this section,—

     (a)   where a tenancy to which this Part of this Act applies ceases to be such a tenancy, it shall not come to an end by reason only of the cesser, but if it was granted for a term of years certain and has been continued by subsection (1) of this section then (without prejudice to the termination thereof in accordance with any terms of the tenancy) it may be terminated by not less than three nor more than six months' notice in writing given by the landlord to the tenant;

     (b)   where, at a time when a tenancy is not one to which this Part of this Act applies, the landlord gives notice to quit, the operation of the notice shall not be affected by reason that the tenancy becomes one to which this Part of this Act applies after the giving of the notice.

24A. Applications for determination of interim rent while tenancy continues

(1)   Subject to subsection (2) below, if—

     (a)   the landlord of a tenancy to which this Part of this Act applies has given notice under section 25 of this Act to terminate the tenancy; or

     (b)   the tenant of such a tenancy has made a request for a new tenancy in accordance with section 26 of this Act,

either of them may make an application to the court to determine a rent (an 'interim rent') which the tenant is to pay while the tenancy ('the relevant tenancy') continues by virtue of section 24 of this Act and the court may order payment of an interim rent in accordance with section 24C or 24D of this Act.

(2)   Neither the tenant nor the landlord may make an application under subsection (1) above if the other has made such an application and has not withdrawn it.

(3)   No application shall be entertained under subsection (1) above if it is made more than six months after the termination of the relevant tenancy.

24B. Date from which interim rent is payable

(1)   The interim rent determined on an application under section 24A(1) of this Act shall be payable from the appropriate date.

(2)   If an application under section 24A(1) of this Act is made in a case where the landlord has given a notice under section 25 of this Act, the appropriate date is the earliest date of termination that could have been specified in the landlord's notice.

(3)   If an application under section 24A(1) of this Act is made in a case where the tenant has made a request for a new tenancy under section 26 of this Act, the appropriate date is

the earliest date that could have been specified in the tenant's request as the date from which the new tenancy is to begin.

24C. Amount of interim rent where new tenancy of whole premises granted and landlord not opposed

(1)   This section applies where—

    (a)   the landlord gave a notice under section 25 of this Act at a time when the tenant was in occupation of the whole of the property comprised in the relevant tenancy for purposes such as are mentioned in section 23(1) of this Act and stated in the notice that he was not opposed to the grant of a new tenancy; or

    (b)   the tenant made a request for a new tenancy under section 26 of this Act at a time when he was in occupation of the whole of that property for such purposes and the landlord did not give notice under subsection (6) of that section,

    and the landlord grants a new tenancy of the whole of the property comprised in the relevant tenancy to the tenant (whether as a result of an order for the grant of a new tenancy or otherwise).

(2)   Subject to the following provisions of this section, the rent payable under and at the commencement of the new tenancy shall also be the interim rent.

(3)   Subsection (2) above does not apply where—

    (a)   the landlord or the tenant shows to the satisfaction of the court that the interim rent under that subsection differs substantially from the relevant rent; or

    (b)   the landlord or the tenant shows to the satisfaction of the court that the terms of the new tenancy differ from the terms of the relevant tenancy to such an extent that the interim rent under that subsection is substantially different from the rent which (in default of such agreement) the court would have determined under section 34 of this Act to be payable under a tenancy which commenced on the same day as the new tenancy and whose other terms were the same as the relevant tenancy.

(4)   In this section 'the relevant rent' means the rent which (in default of agreement between the landlord and the tenant) the court would have determined under section 34 of this Act to be payable under the new tenancy if the new tenancy had commenced on the appropriate date (within the meaning of section 24B of this Act).

(5)   The interim rent in a case where subsection (2) above does not apply by virtue only of subsection (3)(a) above is the relevant rent.

(6)   The interim rent in a case where subsection (2) above does not apply by virtue only of subsection (3)(b) above, or by virtue of subsection (3)(a) and (b) above, is the rent which it is reasonable for the tenant to pay while the relevant tenancy continues by virtue of section 24 of this Act.

(7)   In determining the interim rent under subsection (6) above the court shall have regard—

    (a)   to the rent payable under the terms of the relevant tenancy; and

    (b)   to the rent payable under any sub-tenancy of part of the property comprised in the relevant tenancy,

    but otherwise subsections (1) and (2) of section 34 of this Act shall apply to the determination as they would apply to the determination of a rent under that section if a new tenancy of the whole of the property comprised in the relevant tenancy were granted to the tenant by order of the court and the duration of that new tenancy were the same as the duration of the new tenancy which is actually granted to the tenant.

(8)   In this section and section 24D of this Act 'the relevant tenancy' has the same meaning as in section 24A of this Act.

24D. Amount of interim rent in any other case

(1)   The interim rent in a case where section 24C of this Act does not apply is the rent which it is reasonable for the tenant to pay while the relevant tenancy continues by virtue of section 24 of this Act.

(2)   In determining the interim rent under subsection (1) above the court shall have regard—

(a)   to the rent payable under the terms of the relevant tenancy; and

(b)   to the rent payable under any sub-tenancy of part of the property comprised in the relevant tenancy,

but otherwise subsections (1) and (2) of section 34 of this Act shall apply to the determination as they would apply to the determination of a rent under that section if a new tenancy from year to year of the whole of the property comprised in the relevant tenancy were granted to the tenant by order of the court.

(3)   If the court—

(a)   has made an order for the grant of a new tenancy and has ordered payment of interim rent in accordance with section 24C of this Act, but

(b)   either—

(i)   it subsequently revokes under section 36(2) of this Act the order for the grant of a new tenancy; or

(ii)   the landlord and tenant agree not to act on the order,

the court on the application of the landlord or the tenant shall determine a new interim rent in accordance with subsections (1) and (2) above without a further application under section 24A(1) of this Act.

25. Termination of tenancy by the landlord

(1)   The landlord may terminate a tenancy to which this Part of this Act applies by a notice given to the tenant in the prescribed form specifying the date at which the tenancy is to come to an end (hereinafter referred to as 'the date of termination'):

Provided that this subsection has effect subject to the provisions of section 29B(4) of this Act and the provisions of Part IV of this Act as to the interim continuation of tenancies pending the disposal of applications to the court.

(2)   Subject to the provisions of the next following subsection, a notice under this section shall not have effect unless it is given not more than twelve nor less than six months before the date of termination specified therein.

(3)   In the case of a tenancy which apart from this Act could have been brought to an end by notice to quit given by the landlord—

(a)   the date of termination specified in a notice under this section shall not be earlier than the earliest date on which apart from this Part of this Act the tenancy could have been brought to an end by notice to quit given by the landlord on the date of the giving of the notice under this section; and

(b)   where apart from this Part of this Act more than six months' notice to quit would have been required to bring the tenancy to an end, the last foregoing subsection shall have effect with the substitution for twelve months of a period six months longer than the length of notice to quit which would have been required as aforesaid.

(4)   In the case of any other tenancy, a notice under this section shall not specify a date of termination earlier than the date on which apart from this Part of this Act the tenancy would have come to an end by effluxion of time.

(5)   . . .

(6)   A notice under this section shall not have effect unless it states whether the landlord is opposed to the grant of a new tenancy to the tenant.

(7)   A notice under this section which states that the landlord is opposed to the grant of a new tenancy to the tenant shall not have effect unless it also specifies one or more of the grounds specified in section 30(1) of this Act as the ground or grounds for his opposition.

(8)   A notice under this section which states that the landlord is not opposed to the grant of a new tenancy to the tenant shall not have effect unless it sets out the landlord's proposals as to—

    (a)   the property to be comprised in the new tenancy (being either the whole or part of the property comprised in the current tenancy);

    (b)   the rent to be payable under the new tenancy; and

    (c)   the other terms of the new tenancy.

26. Tenant's request for a new tenancy

(1)   A tenant's request for a new tenancy may be made where the current tenancy is a tenancy granted for a term of years certain exceeding one year, whether or not continued by section twenty-four of this Act, or granted for a term of years certain and thereafter from year to year.

(2)   A tenant's request for a new tenancy shall be for a tenancy beginning with such date, not more than twelve nor less than six months after the making of the request, as may be specified therein:

    Provided that the said date shall not be earlier than the date on which apart from this Act the current tenancy would come to an end by effluxion of time or could be brought to an end by notice to quit given by the tenant.

(3)   A tenant's request for a new tenancy shall not have effect unless it is made by notice in the prescribed form given to the landlord and sets out the tenant's proposals as to the property to be comprised in the new tenancy (being either the whole or part of the property comprised in the current tenancy), as to the rent to be payable under the new tenancy and as to the other terms of the new tenancy.

(4)   A tenant's request for a new tenancy shall not be made if the landlord has already given notice under the last foregoing section to terminate the current tenancy, or if the tenant has already given notice to quit or notice under the next following section; and no such notice shall be given by the landlord or the tenant after the making by the tenant of a request for a new tenancy.

(5)   Where the tenant makes a request for a new tenancy in accordance with the foregoing provisions of this section, the current tenancy shall, subject to the provisions of sections 29B(4) and 36(2) of this Act and the provisions of Part IV of this Act as to the interim continuation of tenancies, terminate immediately before the date specified in the request for the beginning of the new tenancy.

(6)   Within two months of the making of a tenant's request for a new tenancy the landlord may give notice to the tenant that he will oppose an application to the court for the grant of a new tenancy, and any such notice shall state on which of the grounds mentioned in section thirty of this Act the landlord will oppose the application.

27. Termination by tenant of tenancy for fixed term

(1)   Where the tenant under a tenancy to which this Part of this Act applies, being a tenancy granted for a term of years certain, gives to the immediate landlord, not later than three months before the date on which apart from this Act the tenancy would come to an end by effluxion of time, a notice in writing that the tenant does not desire the tenancy to be continued, section twenty-four of this Act shall not have effect in relation to the tenancy

unless the notice is given before the tenant has been in occupation in right of the tenancy for one month.

(1A)   Section 24 of this Act shall not have effect in relation to a tenancy for a term of years certain where the tenant is not in occupation of the property comprised in the tenancy at the time when, apart from this Act, the tenancy would come to an end by effluxion of time.

(2)   A tenancy granted for a term of years certain which is continuing by virtue of section twenty-four of this Act shall not come to an end by reason only of the tenant ceasing to occupy the property comprised in the tenancy but may be brought to an end on any day by not less than three months' notice in writing given by the tenant to the immediate landlord, whether the notice is given after the date on which apart from this Act the tenancy would have come to an end or before that date, but not before the tenant has been in occupation in right of the tenancy for one month.

(3)   Where a tenancy is terminated under subsection (2) above, any rent payable in respect of a period which begins before, and ends after, the tenancy is terminated shall be apportioned, and any rent paid by the tenant in excess of the amount apportioned to the period before termination shall be recoverable by him.

28.   Renewal of tenancies by agreement

Where the landlord and tenant agree for the grant to the tenant of a future tenancy of the holding, or of the holding with other land, on terms and from a date specified in the agreement, the current tenancy shall continue until that date but no longer, and shall not be a tenancy to which this Part of this Act applies.

29.   Order by court for grant of new tenancy or termination of current tenancy

(1)   Subject to the provisions of this Act, on an application under section 24(1) of this Act, the court shall make an order for the grant of a new tenancy and accordingly for the termination of the current tenancy immediately before the commencement of the new tenancy.

(2)   Subject to the following provisions of this Act, a landlord may apply to the court for an order for the termination of a tenancy to which this Part of this Act applies without the grant of a new tenancy—

(a)   if he has given notice under section 25 of this Act that he is opposed to the grant of a new tenancy to the tenant; or

(b)   if the tenant has made a request for a new tenancy in accordance with section 26 of this Act and the landlord has given notice under subsection (6) of that section.

(3)   The landlord may not make an application under subsection (2) above if either the tenant or the landlord has made an application under section 24(1) of this Act.

(4)   Subject to the provisions of this Act, where the landlord makes an application under subsection (2) above—

(a)   if he establishes, to the satisfaction of the court, any of the grounds on which he is entitled to make the application in accordance with section 30 of this Act, the court shall make an order for the termination of the current tenancy in accordance with section 64 of this Act without the grant of a new tenancy; and

(b)   if not, it shall make an order for the grant of a new tenancy and accordingly for the termination of the current tenancy immediately before the commencement of the new tenancy.

(5)   The court shall dismiss an application by the landlord under section 24(1) of this Act if the tenant informs the court that he does not want a new tenancy.

(6)   The landlord may not withdraw an application under subsection (2) above unless the tenant consents to its withdrawal.

29A. Time limits for applications to court

    (1)   Subject to section 29B of this Act, the court shall not entertain an application—

        (a)   by the tenant or the landlord under section 24(1) of this Act; or

        (b)   by the landlord under section 29(2) of this Act,

        if it is made after the end of the statutory period.

    (2)   In this section and section 29B of this Act 'the statutory period' means a period ending—

        (a)   where the landlord gave a notice under section 25 of this Act, on the date specified in his notice; and

        (b)   where the tenant made a request for a new tenancy under section 26 of this Act, immediately before the date specified in his request.

    (3)   Where the tenant has made a request for a new tenancy under section 26 of this Act, the court shall not entertain an application under section 24(1) of this Act which is made before the end of the period of two months beginning with the date of the making of the request, unless the application is made after the landlord has given a notice under section 26(6) of this Act.

29B. Agreements extending time limits

    (1)   After the landlord has given a notice under section 25 of this Act, or the tenant has made a request under section 26 of this Act, but before the end of the statutory period, the landlord and tenant may agree that an application such as is mentioned in section 29A(1) of this Act, may be made before the end of a period specified in the agreement which will expire after the end of the statutory period.

    (2)   The landlord and tenant may from time to time by agreement further extend the period for making such an application, but any such agreement must be made before the end of the period specified in the current agreement.

    (3)   Where an agreement is made under this section, the court may entertain an application such as is mentioned in section 29A(1) of this Act if it is made before the end of the period specified in the agreement.

    (4)   Where an agreement is made under this section, or two or more agreements are made under this section, the landlord's notice under section 25 of this Act or tenant's request under section 26 of this Act shall be treated as terminating the tenancy at the end of the period specified in the agreement or, as the case may be, at the end of the period specified in the last of those agreements.

30. Opposition by landlord to application for a new tenancy

    (1)   The grounds on which a landlord may oppose an application under section 24(1) of this Act, or make an application under section 29(2) of this Act, are such of the following grounds as may be stated in the landlord's notice under section twenty-five of this Act or, as the case may be, under subsection (6) of section twenty-six thereof, that is to say:—

        (a)   where under the current tenancy the tenant has any obligations as respects the repair and maintenance of the holding, that the tenant ought not to be granted a new tenancy in view of the state of repair of the holding, being a state resulting from the tenant's failure to comply with the said obligations;

        (b)   that the tenant ought not to be granted a new tenancy in view of his persistent delay in paying rent which has become due;

        (c)   that the tenant ought not to be granted a new tenancy in view of other substantial breaches by him of his obligations under the current tenancy, or for any other reason connected with the tenant's use or management of the holding;

(d)   that the landlord has offered and is willing to provide or secure the provision of alternative accommodation for the tenant, that the terms on which the alternative accommodation is available are reasonable having regard to the terms of the current tenancy and to all other relevant circumstances, and that the accommodation and the time at which it will be available are suitable for the tenant's requirements (including the requirement to preserve goodwill) having regard to the nature and class of his business and to the situation and extent of, and facilities afforded by, the holding;

(e)   where the current tenancy was created by the sub-letting of part only of the property comprised in a superior tenancy and the landlord is the owner of an interest in reversion expectant on the termination of that superior tenancy, that the aggregate of the rents reasonably obtainable on separate lettings of the holding and the remainder of that property would be substantially less than the rent reasonably obtainable on a letting of that property as a whole, that on the termination of the current tenancy the landlord requires possession of the holding for the purpose of letting or otherwise disposing of the said property as a whole, and that in view thereof the tenant ought not to be granted a new tenancy;

(f)   that on the termination of the current tenancy the landlord intends to demolish or reconstruct the premises comprised in the holding or a substantial part of those premises or to carry out substantial work of construction on the holding or part thereof and that he could not reasonably do so without obtaining possession of the holding;

(g)   subject as hereinafter provided, that on the termination of the current tenancy the landlord intends to occupy the holding for the purposes, or partly for the purposes, of a business to be carried on by him therein, or as his residence.

(1A)   Where the landlord has a controlling interest in a company, the reference in subsection (1)(g) above to the landlord shall be construed as a reference to the landlord or that company.

(1B)   Subject to subsection (2A) below, where the landlord is a company and a person has a controlling interest in the company, the reference in subsection (1)(g) above to the landlord shall be construed as a reference to the landlord or that person.

(2)   The landlord shall not be entitled to oppose an application under section 24(1) of this Act, or make an application under section 29(2) of this Act, on the ground specified in paragraph (g) of the last foregoing subsection if the interest of the landlord, or an interest which has merged in that interest and but for the merger would be the interest of the landlord, was purchased or created after the beginning of the period of five years which ends with the termination of the current tenancy, and at all times since the purchase or creation thereof the holding has been comprised in a tenancy or successive tenancies of the description specified in subsection (1) of section twenty-three of this Act.

(2A)   Subsection (1B) above shall not apply if the controlling interest was acquired after the beginning of the period of five years which ends with the termination of the current tenancy, and at all times since the acquisition of the controlling interest the holding has been comprised in a tenancy or successive tenancies of the description specified in section 23(1) of this Act.

(3)   . . .

31.   Dismissal of application for new tenancy where landlord successfully opposes

(1)   If the landlord opposes an application under subsection (1) of section twenty-four of this Act on grounds on which he is entitled to oppose it in accordance with the last foregoing section and establishes any of those grounds to the satisfaction of the court, the court shall not make an order for the grant of a new tenancy.

(2)   Where the landlord opposes an application under section 24(1) of this Act, or makes an application under section 29(2) of this Act, on one or more of the grounds specified in section 30(1)(d) to (f) of this Act but establishes none of those grounds, and none of the other grounds specified in section 30(1) of this Act, to the satisfaction of the court, then if the court would have been satisfied on any of the grounds specified in section 30(1)(d) to (f) of this Act if the date of termination specified in the landlord's notice or, as the case may be, the date specified in the tenant's request for a new tenancy as the date from which the new tenancy is to begin, had been such later date as the court may determine, being a date not more than one year later than the date so specified,—

  (a)   the court shall make a declaration to that effect, stating of which of the said grounds the court would have been satisfied as aforesaid and specifying the date determined by the court as aforesaid, but shall not make an order for the grant of a new tenancy;

  (b)   if, within fourteen days after the making of the declaration, the tenant so requires the court shall make an order substituting the said date for the date specified in the said landlord's notice or tenant's request, and thereupon that notice or request shall have effect accordingly.

31A.   Grant of new tenancy in some cases where section 30(1)(f) applies

(1)   Where the landlord opposes an application under section 24(1) of this Act on the ground specified in paragraph (f) of section 30(1) of this Act, or makes an application under section 29(2) of this Act on that ground, the court shall not hold that the landlord could not reasonably carry out the demolition, reconstruction or work of construction intended without obtaining possession of the holding if—

  (a)   the tenant agrees to the inclusion in the terms of the new tenancy of terms giving the landlord access and other facilities for carrying out the work intended and, given that access and those facilities, the landlord could reasonably carry out the work without obtaining possession of the holding and without interfering to a substantial extent or for a substantial time with the use of the holding for the purposes of the business carried on by the tenant; or

  (b)   the tenant is willing to accept a tenancy of an economically separable part of the holding and either paragraph (a) of this section is satisfied with respect to that part or possession of the remainder of the holding would be reasonably sufficient to enable the landlord to carry out the intended work.

(2)   For the purposes of subsection (1)(b) of this section a part of a holding shall be deemed to be an economically separable part if, and only if, the aggregate of the rents which, after the completion of the intended work, would be reasonably obtainable on separate lettings of that part and the remainder of the premises affected by or resulting from the work would not be substantially less than the rent which would then be reasonably obtainable on a letting of those premises as a whole.

32.   Property to be comprised in new tenancy

(1)   Subject to the following provisions of this section, an order under section twenty-nine of this Act for the grant of a new tenancy shall be an order for the grant of a new tenancy of the holding; and in the absence of agreement between the landlord and the tenant as to the property which constitutes the holding the court shall in the order designate that property by reference to the circumstances existing at the date of the order.

(1A)   Where the court, by virtue of paragraph (b) of section 31A(1) of this Act, makes an order under section 29 of this Act for the grant of a new tenancy in a case where the tenant is willing to accept a tenancy of part of the holding, the order shall be an order for the grant of a new tenancy of that part only.

(2)   The foregoing provisions of this section shall not apply in a case where the property comprised in the current tenancy includes other property besides the holding and the landlord requires any new tenancy ordered to be granted under section twenty-nine of this Act to be a tenancy of the whole of the property comprised in the current tenancy; but in any such case—

    (a)   any order under the said section twenty-nine for the grant of a new tenancy shall be an order for the grant of a new tenancy of the whole of the property comprised in the current tenancy, and

    (b)   references in the following provisions of this Part of this Act to the holding shall be construed as references to the whole of that property.

(3)   Where the current tenancy includes rights enjoyed by the tenant in connection with the holding, those rights shall be included in a tenancy ordered to be granted under section twenty-nine of this Act except as otherwise agreed between the landlord and the tenant or, in default of such agreement, determined by the court.

33.   Duration of new tenancy

Where on an application under this Part of this Act the court makes an order for the grant of a new tenancy, the new tenancy shall be such tenancy as may be agreed between the landlord and the tenant, or, in default of such an agreement, shall be such a tenancy as may be determined by the court to be reasonable in all the circumstances, being, if it is a tenancy for a term of years certain, a tenancy for a term not exceeding fifteen years, and shall begin on the coming to an end of the current tenancy.

34.   Rent under new tenancy

(1)   The rent payable under a tenancy granted by order of the court under this Part of this Act shall be such as may be agreed between the landlord and the tenant or as, in default of such agreement, may be determined by the court to be that at which, having regard to the terms of the tenancy (other than those relating to rent), the holding might reasonably be expected to be let in the open market by a willing lessor, there being disregarded—

    (a)   any effect on rent of the fact that the tenant has or his predecessors in title have been in occupation of the holding,

    (b)   any goodwill attached to the holding by reason of the carrying on thereat of the business of the tenant (whether by him or by a predecessor of his in that business),

    (c)   any effect on rent of an improvement to which this paragraph applies,

    (d)   in the case of a holding comprising licensed premises, any addition to its value attributable to the licence, if it appears to the court that having regard to the terms of the current tenancy and any other relevant circumstances the benefit of the licence belongs to the tenant.

(2)   Paragraph (c) of the foregoing subsection applies to any improvement carried out by a person who at the time it was carried out was the tenant, but only if it was carried out otherwise than in pursuance of an obligation to his immediate landlord, and either it was carried out during the current tenancy or the following conditions are satisfied, that is to say,—

    (a)   that it was completed not more than twenty-one years before the application to the court was made; and

    (b)   that the holding or any part of it affected by the improvement has at all times since the completion of the improvement been comprised in tenancies of the description specified in section 23(1) of this Act; and

    (c)   that at the termination of each of those tenancies the tenant did not quit.

(2A) If this Part of this Act applies by virtue of section 23(1A) of this Act, the reference in subsection (1)(d) above to the tenant shall be construed as including—

    (a)   a company in which the tenant has a controlling interest, or

    (b)   where the tenant is a company, a person with a controlling interest in the company.

(3)   Where the rent is determined by the court the court may, if it thinks fit, further determine that the terms of the tenancy shall include such provision for varying the rent as may be specified in the determination.

(4)   It is hereby declared that the matters which are to be taken into account by the court in determining the rent include any effect on rent of the operation of the provisions of the Landlord & Tenant (Covenants) Act 1995.

35. Other terms of new tenancy

(1)   The terms of a tenancy granted by order of the court under this Part of this Act (other than terms as to the duration thereof and as to the rent payable thereunder), including, where different persons own interests which fulfil the conditions specified in section 44(1) of this Act in different parts of it, terms as to the apportionment of the rent, shall be such as may be agreed between the landlord and the tenant or as, in default of such agreement, may be determined by the court; and in determining those terms the court shall have regard to the terms of the current tenancy and to all relevant circumstances.

(2)   In subsection (1) of this section the reference to all relevant circumstances includes (without prejudice to the generality of that reference) a reference to the operation of the provisions of the Landlord and Tenant (Covenants) Act 1995.

36. Carrying out of order for new tenancy

(1)   Where under this Part of this Act the court makes an order for the grant of a new tenancy, then, unless the order is revoked under the next following subsection or the landlord and the tenant agree not to act upon the order, the landlord shall be bound to execute or make in favour of the tenant, and the tenant shall be bound to accept, a lease or agreement for a tenancy of the holding embodying the terms agreed between the landlord and the tenant or determined by the court in accordance with the foregoing provisions of this Part of this Act; and where the landlord executes or makes such a lease or agreement the tenant shall be bound, if so required by the landlord, to execute a counterpart or duplicate thereof.

(2)   If the tenant, within fourteen days after the making of an order under this Part of this Act for the grant of a new tenancy, applies to the court for the revocation of the order the court shall revoke the order; and where the order is so revoked, then, if it is so agreed between the landlord and the tenant or determined by the court, the current tenancy shall continue, beyond the date at which it would have come to an end apart from this subsection, for such period as may be so agreed or determined to be necessary to afford to the landlord a reasonable opportunity for reletting or otherwise disposing of the premises which would have been comprised in the new tenancy; and while the current tenancy continues by virtue of this subsection it shall not be a tenancy to which this Part of this Act applies.

(3)   Where an order is revoked under the last foregoing subsection any provision thereof as to payment of costs shall not cease to have effect by reason only of the revocation; but the court may, if it thinks fit, revoke or vary any such provision or, where no costs have been awarded in the proceedings for the revoked order, award such costs.

(4)   A lease executed or agreement made under this section, in a case where the interest of the lessor is subject to a mortgage, shall be deemed to be one authorised by section ninety-nine of the Law of Property Act 1925 (which confers certain powers of leasing on mortgagors in possession), and subsection (13) of that section (which allows those

powers to be restricted or excluded by agreement) shall not have effect in relation to such a lease or agreement.

37. Compensation where order for new tenancy precluded on certain grounds

(1)   Subject to the provisions of this Act, in a case specified in subsection (1A), (1B) or (1C) below (a 'compensation case') the tenant shall be entitled on quitting the holding to recover from the landlord by way of compensation an amount determined in accordance with this section.

(1A)   The first compensation case is where on the making of an application by the tenant under section 24(1) of this Act the court is precluded (whether by subsection (1) or subsection (2) of section 31 of this Act) from making an order for the grant of a new tenancy by reason of any of the grounds specified in paragraphs (e), (f) and (g) of section 30(1) of this Act (the 'compensation grounds') and not of any grounds specified in any other paragraph of section 30(1).

(1B)   The second compensation case is where on the making of an application under section 29(2) of this Act the court is precluded (whether by section 29(4)(a) or section 31(2) of this Act) from making an order for the grant of a new tenancy by reason of any of the compensation grounds and not of any other grounds specified in section 30(1) of this Act.

(1C)   The third compensation case is where—

(a)   the landlord's notice under section 25 of this Act or, as the case may be, under section 26(6) of this Act, states his opposition to the grant of a new tenancy on any of the compensation grounds and not on any other grounds specified in section 30(1) of this Act; and

(b)   either—

(i)   no application is made by the tenant under section 24(1) of this Act or by the landlord under section 29(2) of this Act; or

(ii)   such an application is made but is subsequently withdrawn.

(2)   Subject to the following provisions of this section, compensation under this section shall be as follows, that is to say,—

(a)   where the conditions specified in the next following subsection are satisfied in relation to the whole of the holding it shall be the product of the appropriate multiplier and twice the rateable value of the holding,

(b)   in any other case it shall be the product of the appropriate multiplier and the rateable value of the holding.

(3)   The said conditions are—

(a)   that, during the whole of the fourteen years immediately preceding the termination of the current tenancy, premises being or comprised in the holding have been occupied for the purposes of a business carried on by the occupier or for those and other purposes;

(b)   that, if during those fourteen years there was a change in the occupier of the premises, the person who was the occupier immediately after the change was the successor to the business carried on by the person who was the occupier immediately before the change.

. . .

(8)   In subsection (2) of this section 'the appropriate multiplier' means such multiplier as the Secretary of State may by order made by statutory instrument prescribe and different multipliers may be so prescribed in relation to different cases.

37A. Compensation for possession obtained by misrepresentation

(1)   Where the court—

    (a)   makes an order for the termination of the current tenancy but does not make an order for the grant of a new tenancy, or

    (b)   refuses an order for the grant of a new tenancy,

and it subsequently made to appear to the court that the order was obtained, or the court was induced to refuse the grant, by misrepresentation or the concealment of material facts, the court may order the landlord to pay to the tenant such sum as appears sufficient as compensation for damage or loss sustained by the tenant as the result of the order or refusal.

(2)   Where—

    (a)   the tenant has quit the holding—

        (i)   after making but withdrawing an application under section 24(1) of this Act; or

        (ii)   without making such an application; and

    (b)   it is made to appear to the court that he did so by reason of misrepresentation or the concealment of material facts,

the court may order the landlord to pay to the tenant such sum as appears sufficient as compensation for damage or loss sustained by the tenant as the result of quitting the holding.

38. Restriction on agreements excluding provisions of Part II

(1)   Any agreement relating to a tenancy to which this Part of this Act applies (whether contained in the instrument creating the tenancy or not) shall be void (except as provided by section 38A of this Act) in so far as it purports to preclude the tenant from making an application or request under this Part of this Act or provides for the termination or the surrender of the tenancy in the event of his making such an application or request or for the imposition of any penalty or disability on the tenant in that event.

(2)   Where—

    (a)   during the whole of the five years immediately preceding the date on which the tenant under a tenancy to which this Part of this Act applies is to quit the holding, premises being or comprised in the holding have been occupied for the purposes of a business carried on by the occupier or for those and other purposes, and

    (b)   if during those five years there was a change in the occupier of the premises, the person who was the occupier immediately after the change was the successor to the business carried on by the person who was the occupier immediately before the change,

any agreement (whether contained in the instrument creating the tenancy or not and whether made before or after the termination of that tenancy) which purports to exclude or reduce compensation under section 37 of this Act shall to that extent be void, so however that this subsection shall not affect any agreement as to the amount of any such compensation which is made after the right to compensation has accrued.

(3)   In a case not falling within the last foregoing subsection the right to compensation conferred by section 37 of this Act may be excluded or modified by agreement.

38A. Agreements to exclude provisions of Part 2

(1)   The persons who will be the landlord and the tenant in relation to a tenancy to be granted for a term of years certain which will be a tenancy to which this Part of this Act applies may agree that the provisions of sections 24 to 28 of this Act shall be excluded in relation to that tenancy.

(2)   The persons who are the landlord and the tenant in relation to a tenancy to which this Part of this Act applies may agree that the tenancy shall be surrendered on such date or

in such circumstances as may be specified in the agreement and on such terms (if any) as may be so specified.

(3)   An agreement under subsection (1) above shall be void unless—

(a)   the landlord has served on the tenant a notice in the form, or substantially in the form, set out in Schedule 1 to the Regulatory Reform (Business Tenancies) (England and Wales) Order 2003 ('the 2003 Order'); and

(b)   the requirements specified in Schedule 2 to that Order are met.

(4)   An agreement under subsection (2) above shall be void unless—

(a)   the landlord has served on the tenant a notice in the form, or substantially in the form, set out in Schedule 3 to the 2003 Order; and

(b)   the requirements specified in Schedule 4 to that Order are met.

40. Duties of tenants and landlords of business premises to give information to each other

(1)   Where a person who is an owner of an interest in reversion expectant (whether immediately or not) on a tenancy of any business premises has served on the tenant a notice in the prescribed form requiring him to do so, it shall be the duty of the tenant to give the appropriate person in writing the information specified in subsection (2) below.

(2)   That information is—

(a)   whether the tenant occupies the premises or any part of them wholly or partly for the purposes of a business carried on by him;

(b)   whether his tenancy has effect subject to any sub-tenancy on which his tenancy is immediately expectant and, if so—

(i)   what premises are comprised in the sub-tenancy;

(ii)   for what term it has effect (or, if it is terminable by notice, by what notice it can be terminated);

(iii)   what is the rent payable under it;

(iv)   who is the sub-tenant;

(v)   (to the best of his knowledge and belief) whether the sub-tenant is in occupation of the premises or of part of the premises comprised in the sub-tenancy and, if not, what is the sub-tenant's address;

(vi)   whether an agreement is in force excluding in relation to the sub-tenancy the provisions of sections 24 to 28 of this Act; and

(vii)   whether a notice has been given under section 25 or 26(6) of this Act, or a request has been made under section 26 of this Act, in relation to the sub-tenancy and, if so, details of the notice or request; and

(c)   (to the best of his knowledge and belief) the name and address of any other person who owns an interest in reversion in any part of the premises.

(3)   Where the tenant of any business premises who is a tenant under such a tenancy as is mentioned in section 26(1) of this Act has served on a reversioner or a reversioner's mortgagee in possession a notice in the prescribed form requiring him to do so, it shall be the duty of the person on whom the notice is served to give the appropriate person in writing the information specified in subsection (4) below.

(4)   That information is—

(a)   whether he is the owner of the fee simple in respect of the premises or any part of them or the mortgagee in possession of such an owner,

(b)   if he is not, then (to the best of his knowledge and belief)—

(i)   the name and address of the person who is his or, as the case may be, his mortgagor's immediate landlord in respect of those premises or of the part in respect of which he or his mortgagor is not the owner in fee simple;

> (ii)   for what term his or his mortgagor's tenancy has effect and what is the earliest date (if any) at which that tenancy is terminable by notice to quit given by the landlord; and
>
> (iii)   whether a notice has been given under section 25 or 26(6) of this Act, or a request has been made under section 26 of this Act, in relation to the tenancy and, if so, details of the notice or request;

(c)   (to the best of his knowledge and belief) the name and address of any other person who owns an interest in reversion in any part of the premises; and

(d)   if he is a reversioner, whether there is a mortgagee in possession of his interest in the premises and, if so, (to the best of his knowledge and belief) what is the name and address of the mortgagee.

(5)   A duty imposed on a person by this section is a duty—

(a)   to give the information concerned within the period of one month beginning with the date of service of the notice; and

(b)   if within the period of six months beginning with the date of service of the notice that person becomes aware that any information which has been given in pursuance of the notice is not, or is no longer, correct, to give the appropriate person correct information within the period of one month beginning with the date on which he becomes aware.

(6)   This section shall not apply to a notice served by or on the tenant more than two years before the date on which apart from this Act his tenancy would come to an end by effluxion of time or could be brought to an end by notice to quit given by the landlord.

(7)   Except as provided by section 40A of this Act, the appropriate person for the purposes of this section and section 40A(1) of this Act is the person who served the notice under subsection (1) or (3) above.

(8)   In this section—

'business premises' means premises used wholly or partly for the purposes of a business;

'mortgagee in possession' includes a receiver appointed by the mortgagee or by the court who is in receipt of the rents and profits, and 'his mortgagor' shall be construed accordingly;

'reversioner' means any person having an interest in the premises, being an interest in reversion expectant (whether immediately or not) on the tenancy;

'reversioner's mortgagee in possession' means any person being a mortgagee in possession in respect of such an interest; and

'sub-tenant' includes a person retaining possession of any premises by virtue of the Rent (Agriculture) Act 1976 or the Rent Act 1977 after the coming to an end of a sub-tenancy, and 'sub-tenancy' includes a right so to retain possession.

40B. Proceedings for breach of duties to give information

A claim that a person has broken any duty imposed by section 40 of this Act may be made the subject of civil proceedings for breach of statutory duty; and in any such proceedings a court may order that person to comply with that duty and may make an award of damages.

42. Groups of companies

(1)   For the purposes of this section two bodies corporate shall be taken to be members of a group if and only if one is a subsidiary of the other or both are subsidiaries of a third body corporate or the same person has a controlling interest in both.

(2)   Where a tenancy is held by a member of a group, occupation by another member of the group, and the carrying on of a business by another member of the group, shall be treated for the purposes of section twenty-three of this Act as equivalent to occupation or the carrying on of a business by the member of the group holding the tenancy; and in

relation to a tenancy to which this Part of this Act applies by virtue of the foregoing provisions of this subsection—

(a) references (however expressed) in this Part of this Act and in the Ninth Schedule to this Act to the business of or to use occupation or enjoyment by the tenant shall be construed as including references to the business of or to use occupation or enjoyment by the said other member;

(b) the reference in paragraph (d) of subsection (1) of section thirty-four of this Act to the tenant shall be construed as including the said other member; and

(c) an assignment of the tenancy from one member of the group to another shall not be treated as a change in the person of the tenant.

(3) Where the landlord's interest is held by a member of a group—

(a) the reference in paragraph (g) of subsection (1) of section 30 of this Act to intended occupation by the landlord for the purposes of a business to be carried on by him shall be construed as including intended occupation by any member of the group for the purposes of a business to be carried on by that member; and

(b) the reference in subsection (2) of that section to the purchase or creation of any interest shall be construed as a reference to a purchase from or creation by a person other than a member of the group.

43. Tenancies excluded from Part II

(1) This Part of this Act does not apply—

(a) to a tenancy of an agricultural holding which is a tenancy in relation to which the Agricultural Holdings Act 1986 applies or a tenancy which would be a tenancy of an agricultural holding in relation to which that Act applied if subsection (3) of section 2 of that Act did not have effect or, in a case where approval was given under subsection (1) of that section, if that approval had not been given;

(aa) to a farm business tenancy;

(b) to a tenancy created by a mining lease;

(2) This Part of this Act does not apply to a tenancy granted by reason that the tenant was the holder of an office, appointment or employment from the grantor thereof and continuing only so long as the tenant holds the office, appointment or employment, or terminable by the grantor on the tenant's ceasing to hold it, or coming to an end at a time fixed by reference to the time at which the tenant ceases to hold it:

Provided that this subsection shall not have effect in relation to a tenancy granted after the commencement of this Act unless the tenancy was granted by an instrument in writing which expressed the purpose for which the tenancy was granted.

(3) This Part of this Act does not apply to a tenancy granted for a term certain not exceeding six months unless—

(a) the tenancy contains provision for renewing the term or for extending it beyond six months from its beginning; or

(b) the tenant has been in occupation for a period which, together with any period during which any predecessor in the carrying on of the business carried on by the tenant was in occupation, exceeds twelve months.

44. Meaning of 'the landlord' in Part II, and provisions as to mesne landlords, etc

(1) Subject to subsections (1A) and (2) below, in this Part of this Act the expression 'the landlord', in relation to a tenancy (in this section referred to as 'the relevant tenancy'), means the person (whether or not he is the immediate landlord) who is the owner of that interest in the property comprised in the relevant tenancy which for the time being fulfils the following conditions, that is to say—

(a)   that it is an interest in reversion expectant (whether immediately or not) on the termination of the relevant tenancy, and

(b)   that it is either the fee simple or a tenancy which will not come to an end within fourteen months by effluxion of time and, if it is such a tenancy, that no notice has been given by virtue of which it will come to an end within fourteen months or any further time by which it may be continued under section 36(2) or section 64 of this Act,

and is not itself in reversion expectant (whether immediately or not) on an interest which fulfils those conditions.

(1A) The reference in subsection (1) above to a person who is the owner of an interest such as is mentioned in that subsection is to be construed, where different persons own such interests in different parts of the property, as a reference to all those persons collectively.

(2)   References in this Part of this Act to a notice to quit given by the landlord are references to a notice to quit given by the immediate landlord.

(3)   The provisions of the Sixth Schedule to this Act shall have effect for the application of this Part of this Act to cases where the immediate landlord of the tenant is not the owner of the fee simple in respect of the holding.

Index